ROUTLEDGE LIBRARY EDITIONS:
SOVIET ECONOMICS

Volume 22

WRECKING ACTIVITIES AT POWER STATIONS IN THE SOVIET UNION

WRECKING ACTIVITIES AT POWER STATIONS IN THE SOVIET UNION

The Case of
N. P. Vitvitsky, V. A. Gussev,
A. W. Gregory, Y. I. Zivert,
N. G. Zorin, M. D. Krasheninnikov,
M. L. Kotlyarevsky, A. S. Kutuzova,
J. Cushny, V. P. Lebedev,
A. T. Lobanov, W. L. MacDonald,
A. Monkhouse, C. Nordwall,
P. Y. Oleinik, L. A. Sukhoruchkin,
L. C. Thornton, V. A. Sokolov

VARIOUS AUTHORS

Routledge
Taylor & Francis Group
LONDON AND NEW YORK

First published in 1933 by George Allen & Unwin Ltd

This edition first published in 2023
by Routledge
4 Park Square, Milton Park, Abingdon, Oxon OX14 4RN

and by Routledge
605 Third Avenue, New York, NY 10158

Routledge is an imprint of the Taylor & Francis Group, an informa business

British Library Cataloguing in Publication Data
A catalogue record for this book is available from the British Library

ISBN: 978-1-032-48466-2 (Set)
ISBN: 978-1-032-49040-3 (Volume 22) (hbk)
ISBN: 978-1-032-49043-4 (Volume 22) (pbk)
ISBN: 978-1-003-39198-2 (Volume 22) (ebk)

DOI: 10.4324/9781003391982

Publisher's Note
The publisher has gone to great lengths to ensure the quality of this reprint but points out that some imperfections in the original copies may be apparent.

Disclaimer
The publisher has made every effort to trace copyright holders and would welcome correspondence from those they have been unable to trace.

WRECKING ACTIVITIES at Power Stations in the Soviet Union

THE CASE OF

N. P. Vitvitsky, V. A. Gussev, A. W. Gregory, Y. I. Zivert, N. G. Zorin, M. D. Krasheninnikov, M. L. Kotlyarevsky, A. S. Kutuzova, J. Cushny, V. P. Lebedev, A. T. Lobanov, W. L. MacDonald, A. Monkhouse, C. Nordwall, P. Y. Oleinik, L. A. Sukhoruchkin, L. C. Thornton, V. A. Sokolov

HEARD BEFORE THE

SPECIAL SESSION OF THE

SUPREME COURT OF THE U.S.S.R.

In Moscow, April 12-19, 1933

Translation of the

OFFICIAL VERBATIM REPORT

LONDON

GEORGE ALLEN & UNWIN LTD

MUSEUM STREET

Printed in the Union of Soviet Socialist Republics

CONTENTS

ILLUSTRATIONS

COMPOSITION OF THE COURT

By decision of the Presidium of the Central Executive Committee of the U.S.S.R., dated March 30, 1933, this case was ordered to be tried by a Special Session of the Supreme Court of the U.S.S.R., composed as follows:

President:

ULRICH, V. V.
Member of the Supreme Court of the U.S.S.R

Members of the Court:

MARTENS, L. K.
Director of the Diesel Institute
Professor of the Chair of Internal Combustion Engines

DMITRIEV, G. A.
Manager of the "Glavenergo" Thermo-Electrical Planning Trust
Electrical-Engineer

Member of the Court in Reserve:

ZELIKOV, A. V.
President of the Central Committee of the Trade Union of Workers, Engineers and Technicians in the Electro-Technical Industry and Electric Power Stations

Secretary:

KOSTYUSHKO, A. F.
Senior Inspector of the Supreme Court of the U.S.S.R.

FOR THE PROSECUTION:

VYSHINSKY, A. J.
Public Prosecutor of the R.S.F.S.R.

ROGINSKY, G. K.
Assistant Public Prosecutor of the R.S.F.S.R.

FOR THE DEFENCE:

BRAUDE, I. D.; SMIRNOV, A. A.; KOMMODOV, N. V.; LIDOV, P. P.;
DOLMATOVSKY, A. M.; SCHWARTZ, L. G.; PINES, I. G.;
KAZNACHEYEV, S. K.; LIBSON, I. N.
Members of the Collegium of Defence

PROCEEDINGS OF THE SPECIAL SESSION OF THE SUPREME COURT OF THE U.S.S.R.

MORNING SESSION, APRIL 12, 1933, 12 o'clock noon

Commandant: Please, rise. The Court is coming.

The President: Please, be seated. I declare the Special Session of the Supreme Court of the U.S.S.R. open. This is a case of a group of persons—Vitvitsky, Gussev, Gregory* and others—charged under Article 58, clauses 6, 7, 9, 11, of the Criminal Code of the R.S.F.S.R. with wrecking the electric power stations of the Soviet Union and with other criminal offences. Comrade Secretary, who of the accused has appeared?

The Secretary: All the accused are present except Vitvitsky, who is certified to be sick by the doctor of the Butyrskaya prison and cannot be present in Court.

The President: Does the Public Prosecutor think it possible to proceed with the case in the absence of Vitvitsky?

Vyshinsky: I suggest that the case of Vitvitsky be excluded from the present hearing and that the Court proceed with the case of the other accused. In virtue of Article 295 of the Criminal Code, I request that the parties be permitted to refer to the deposition made by Vitvitsky at the preliminary investigation concerning the other accused.

The President: What is the opinion of the Defence?

Counsel for the Defence: We do not object.

The President: The Court decides to exclude the case of Vitvitsky which is to be dealt with separately.

Who of the experts has appeared? But first announce the names of those who have been called as experts.

The Secretary: The following experts have been called and are present: Engineers Brailov, Golubtsov, Novikov, Smirnov,

---

* The names of the first three accused in the order of the Russian alpha bet as given in the indictment.—*Ed.*

Ulatov. Snedkov has so far not appeared for reasons unknown. He should be here.

The President: Has he received the subpoena?

The Secretary: Yes.

The President: Accused Gussev, what is your first name and patronymic?

Gussev: Vassily Alexeyevich.

The President: What is your age?

Gussev: 34.

The President: Last occupation?

Gussev: Chief of the Power Station.

The President: Have you received a copy of the indictment?

Gussev: Yes.

The President: Accused Gregory, your first name and patronymic?

Gregory: Albert William Gregory.

The President: Your age?

Gregory: 48.

The President: British subject?

Gregory: Yes.

The President: Last occupation in the U.S.S.R.?

Gregory: Electric engineer at Dzerzhinsky.

The President: Have you received a copy of the indictment?

Gregory: Yes.

The President: Accused Zivert, your first name, patronymic, age and occupation?

Zivert: Yuri Ivanovich, 50 years, chief engineer of the group of turbines of the "Mosenergo."

The President: Last occupation?

Zivert: Job superintendent.

The President: Have you received a copy of the indictment?

Zivert: Yes.

The President: Accused Zorin, your first name and patronymic?

Zorin: Nikolai Grigorievich.

The President: Occupation?

Zorin: Chief engineer of the rationalization sector.

The President: Have you received a copy of the indictment?

Zorin: Yes.

The President: Accused Krasheninnikov, your first name and patronymic?

Krasheninnikov: Michael Dmitrievich.

The President: Your age?

Krasheninnikov: 33.

The President: Your occupation?

Krasheninnikov: Chief of the Repairing and Assembly Shop of MOGES I.*

The President: Have you received a copy of the indictment?

Krasheninnikov: Yes.

The President: Accused Kotlyarevsky, your first name and patronymic?

Kotlyarevsky: Moisei Lvovich.

The President: Your age?

Kotlyarevsky: 29.

The President: Your occupation?

Kotlyarevsky: Chief engineer of the Turbine Sector, "Mosenergo."

The President: Have you received a copy of the indictment?

Kotlyarevsky: Yes.

The President: Accused Cushny, your first name is John?

Cushny: Yes.

The President: Your age?

Cushny: 34.

The President: You are a British subject?

Cushny: Yes.

The President: Have you received a copy of the indictment?

Cushny: Yes.

The President: Accused Lebedev, your first name and patronymic?

Lebedev: Vyacheslav Petrovich.

The President: Your age?

Lebedev: 52.

The President: Your occupation?

Lebedev: Foreman of the Electrical Department.

The President: Have you received a copy of the indictment?

Lebedev: Yes.

*MOGES I—First Moscow State Power Station

The President: Accused Lobanov, your first name and patronymic?

Lobanov: Alexander Timofeyevich.

The President: What is your age?

Lobanov: 35.

The President: Have you received a copy of the indictment?

Lobanov: Yes.

The President: Accused MacDonald, your first name is William?

MacDonald: Yes.

The President: Your age?

MacDonald: 29.

The President: You are a British subject?

MacDonald: Yes.

The President: Have you received a copy of the indictment?

MacDonald: Yes.

The President: Your occupation?

MacDonald: Installation engineer.

The President: Accused Monkhouse, your first name and patronymic?

Monkhouse: Allan.

The President: Your age?

Monkhouse: 46.

The President: British subject?

Monkhouse: Yes.

The President: You are the representative of the Vickers firm?

Monkhouse: Yes.

The President: Have you received a copy of the indictment?

Monkhouse: Yes.

The President: Accused Nordwall, your first name and patronymic?

Nordwall: Charles.

The President: Your age?

Nordwall: 31.

The President: British subject?

Nordwall: Yes.

The President: Have you received a copy of the indictment?

Nordwall: Yes.

The President: Accused Oleinik, your first name and patronymic.

Oleinik: Peter Yeremeyevich.

The President: Your age?

Oleinik: 52.

The President: Your occupation?

Oleinik: Chief electrician for the Vickers firm.

The President: You are a citizen of the U.S.S.R.?

Oleinik: Yes.

The President: Have you received a copy of the indictment?

Oleinik: Yes.

The President: Accused Sokolov, your first name and patronymic?

Sokolov: Vassily Andreyevich.

The President: Your age?

Sokolov: 33.

The President: Your occupation?

Sokolov: Assistant chief of the power station of the Zlatoust works.

The President: Have you received a copy of the indictment?

Sokolov: Yes.

The President: Accused Sukhoruchkin, your first name and patronymic?

Sukhoruchkin: Leonid Alexeyevich.

The President: Your age?

Sukhoruchkin: 39.

The President: Your occupation?

Sukhoruchkin: Chief of the Operation Department.

The President: Have you received a copy of the indictment?

Sukhoruchkin: Yes.

The President: Accused Thornton, your first name and patronymic?

Thornton: Leslie.

The President: Your age?

Thornton: 45.

The President: Your occupation?

Thornton: Chief Engineer.

The President: You are a British subject?

Thornton: Yes.

The President: Have you received a copy of the indictment?

Thornton: Yes.

The President: Accused Kutuzova, your first name and patronymic?

Kutuzova: Anna Sergeyevna.

The President: Your age?

Kutuzova: 37.

The President: What was your occupation before you were arrested?

Kutuzova: Secretary of the representative of the firm Metro-Vickers.

The President: You are a citizen of the U.S.S.R.?

Kutuzova: Yes.

The President: Have you received a copy of the indictment?

Kutuzova: Yes.

The President: The Counsel for the Defence are all present. Announce the names of the Counsel for the Defence and for whom they are appearing.

The Secretaray: The following Counsel for the Defence have been personally called at the request and choice of the accused to appear on their behalf:

I. D. Braude to act for Thornton.

A. A. Smirnov to act for MacDonald.

N. V. Kommodov to act for Monkhouse.

P. P. Lidov to act for Cushny.

A. M. Dolmatovsky to act for Gregory and Nordwall.

L. G. Schwartz to act for Zorin, Krasheninnikov and Sukhoruchkin.

I. G. Pines to act for Lobanov and Lebedev.

S. K. Kaznacheyev to act for Gussev, Sokolov and Oleinik.

I. N. Libson to act for Kutuzova and Kotlyarevsky.

The President: Are the Counsel for the Defence all present?

The Secretary: Yes.

The President: Has the Defence any changes to make concerning the defence of the accused?

Defence: No.

The President: Has the Public Prosecutor any requests to make as to the calling of witnesses?

Public Prosecutor: So far I have no requests to make.

The President: Is such a request likely to be made?

Public Prosecutor: That depends on the course of the proceedings. So far I have none.

The President: Has the Defence any requests to make?

Defence: So far none.

The President: Composition of the Court: President of the Special Session, Ulrich, V. V.; Members of the Court: Martens, L. K., Dmitriev, G. A.; Member in Reserve: Zelikov, A. V.; for the Prosecution: Vyshinsky, A. J., Public Prosecutor of the R.S.F.S.R. and his Assistant, Roginsky, G. K.

Any objections to the composition of the Court?

Defence: No.

The President: Any objections on the part of the accused? Interpreter, please translate the question and their answers.

(The interpreter asks the accused in English.)

Interpreter: No objections.

The President: We shall now proceed to the reading of the indictment.

The Secretary (reads the indictment):

INDICTMENT

Re:

Nikolai Petrovich Vitvitsky, Vassily Alexeyevich Gussev, Albert William Gregory, Yuri Ivanovich Zivert, Nikolai Grigorievich Zorin, Michael Dmitrievich Krasheninnikov, Moisei Lvovich Kotlyarevsky, Anna Sergeyevna Kutuzova, John Cushny, Vyacheslav Petrovich Lebedev, Alexander Timofeyevich Lobanov, William Lionel MacDonald, Allan Monkhouse, Charles Nordwall, Peter Yeremeyevich Oleinik, Leonid Alexeyevich Sukhoruchkin, Leslie Charles Thornton, Vassily Andreyevich Sokolov.

An official statement of the O.G.P.U. (State Political Dept.), published on March 14, 1933, in the *Izvestia of the Central Executive Committee of the U.S.S.R. and the All-Russian Central Executive Committee*, stated:

> "An investigation by the O.G.P.U. into a series of sudden and regularly recurring breakdowns which have lately occurred in big power stations (Moscow, Chelyabinsk, Zuevka, Zlatoust) has revealed that the breakdowns were the result of wrecking activity on the part of a group of criminal

elements among State employees under the People's Commissariat of Heavy Industry, who made it their object to destroy the power stations of the U.S.S.R. (acts of diversion*) and put out of commission the State factories served by these power stations."

The investigation had revealed, as this statement indicates, that:

> "In the work of this wrecking group there actively participated certain employees of the British firm, Metropolitan-Vickers, employed in the U.S.S.R. under a contract with this firm providing for technical aid to the power plants of the U.S.S.R."

A further investigation revealed that the counter-revolutionary activity of the wrecking group, which was active in a number of State power stations, consisted of:

1) Damaging equipment with the object of undermining the power of Soviet industry and weakening the Soviet State;

2) Gathering secret information of importance for the defence of the State and utilizing it to the detriment of the State;

3) Bribing and corrupting certain employees of State power stations in connection with the carrying out of counter-revolutionary wrecking activities by these employees.

A Commission of Experts consisting of: *G. P. Brailo,* heating engineer; *V. A. Golubtsov,* electrical engineer; *M. F. Novikov,* turbine engineer; *B. N. Smirnov,* technological and electrical engineer; *A. P. Snedkov,* turbine engineer; and *P. P. Ulatov,* turbine engineer, was set up by the Public Prosecutor of the R.S.F.S.R. for the purpose of verifying and technically appraising all the documents appertaining to the case, *i.e.,* official records of the breakdowns drawn up on the spot immediately after the breakdowns, official minutes of technical conferences on those breakdowns; and all other materials collected in the course of the investigation of the circumstances accompanying the breakdowns. This Commission came to the conclusion that in all the cases of breakdowns investigated there was either criminal negligence or

* In Soviet legal terminology, *diversion* means criminal acts punishable by Article 58-9 of the Criminal Code of the R.S.F.S.R. which consist in the destruction, damaging and similar acts against State property important for the defence of the country.

deliberate wrecking on the part of a number of persons in the technical personnel serving these stations.

I

WRECKING AND ESPIONAGE AT THE ZLATOUST ELECTRIC POWER STATION

For a number of years and particularly in the period 1931-33 a number of breakdowns of motors, boilers, coal conveyor and other machinery occurred at the Zlatoust Electric Power Station and Zlatoust Metallurgical Works.

Breakdowns of the 1,400 h. p. motor in the rolling shop at the Zlatoust Metallurgical Works took place on April 16, May 12 and June 3, 1932.

Analysing the causes of the first of these breakdowns (April 16) the Commission of Experts came to the following conclusion:

> 1. "The displacement of the stator iron laminations and the subsequent damage to the rotor could take place as a consequence of the presence of an extraneous metallic body in the air gap of the motor. The displacement could take place particularly easily due to the absence of control of the tightening of the bolts which fastened the iron core.
>
> 2. "The presence of an extraneous piece of iron in the air gap of the motor must lead to the breakdown of the motor, to the deformation of the iron laminations the perforation of the insulation of the motor, *i.e.*, in the last resort, to putting the motor out of action.
>
> 3. "Under normal working conditions extraneous pieces of iron cannot work their way into the motor, but can only be introduced into it deliberately."

Shortly after this breakdown, *i.e.*, on May 12 and June 3, two further breakdowns occurred with this motor which, in the opinion of the Commission of Experts, was the result of the uneliminated defects in the motor after the first breakdown.

In the winter of 1932, at the Zlatoust Electric Power Station a breakdown occurred with boiler No. 8 which was kept in cold reserve. The boiler staff failed to close the damper and to let the water out, as a consequence of which the boiler froze and a number of tubes burst.

In the opinion of the Commission of Experts the breakdown could occur only as a result of the negligence of the boiler staff towards the equipment, or as a result of malicious intent.

At the same Zlatoust Electric Power Station, in the beginning of 1932, the reserve coal conveyor was dismantled.

In reply to the question put by the investigators to the Commission of Experts as to whether such action on the part of the management of the electric power station was permissible, the Commission of Experts replied that:

> "The dismantling of the reserve coal conveyor would be permissible only in the event of this coal conveyor being unsatisfactory or inadequate, and in the event of it being possible to substitute for it a new one for the installation of which all the necessary parts were available and all the preparatory work accomplished."

In this case these conditions did not prevail and the dismantling of the coal conveyor was carried out with obviously wrecking aims.

In addition to the facts concerning the number of breakdowns that occurred at the Zlatoust Electric Power Station, the investigation revealed facts showing a discrepancy between the working capacity of the boiler and engine rooms.

The investigation established (statement by the works management of March 20, 1933) that Sterling boilers No. 1 and No. 2, each having a heating surface of 260 square metres, had been out of action since May 1928 for the purpose of converting the stokers for pulverized fuel firing which, however, has not been completed to this day, although the imported equipment, which was lacking at first, has been on the station premises since 1930. Boiler No. 11, with a heating surface of 400 square metres, has been in the course of installation for two and a half years.

This exceptional slowness in the installation of boilers No. 1, No. 2 and No. 11, in the opinion of the Commission of Experts is to be explained

> "by malicious intent or at least by criminal negligence . . ."

as a result of which

> "the delay in the installation of boilers No. 1, No. 2 and No. 11 serves as the reason why the station develops

approximately one-half of the installed power of the turbo-generators."

In connection with these systematic breakdowns, proceedings were instituted against engineer *Vassily Alexeyevich Gussev,* chief of the Zlatoust Electric Power Station. When the evidence was put before him, he admitted that he was guilty of organizing a group of wreckers at the Zlatoust Electric Power Station and stated that for causing these breakdowns he, *Gussev,* received money from other persons and stated that such a person was the English installation engineer, *William MacDonald.*

Gussev started work at the Zlatoust Electric Power Station in 1922 in the capacity of foreman of the works' electric power station and worked at the station until the day of his arrest, occupying consecutively the following positions:

> "From 1922 to 1923, assistant foreman; from 1923 to 1925, senior foreman; from 1925 to March 1929, assistant chief of the said station; from March 1929 to the day of arrest, chief of the electric power station."

Gussev's attitude towards the Soviet Government during the whole of this period was sharply hostile. *Gussev* testifies:

> "In the main I mixed in the circles of those engineers and technicians who subsequently were convicted of wrecking *(Shalayev, Bogoslovsky* and others) and generally in the circles of such people as were hostile to the Soviet Government."

Gussev gives the date on which his active counter-revolutionary work commenced as the end of 1929 when installation engineer *MacDonald,* an employee of the British firm of Metropolitan-Vickers, arrived at the Zlatoust Electric Power Station.

> "*MacDonald* arrived at Zlatoust at the end of 1929," says *Gussev* in his deposition, "and moved into the works settlement, in a flat provided for him by the works management. I became intimate with *MacDonald* gradually, over a period of approximately two months . . ."

As he became more intimate with *MacDonald, Gussev* became more and more frank with him and openly expressed to *MacDonald* his hostility towards the Soviet Government. Meeting with the obvious sympathy of *MacDonald, Gussev* told him about his service in the White army, about his participation in the campaigns of the Whites against the Red Army, etc.

Gussev entered into criminal counter-revolutionary contact with *MacDonald* under the following circumstances:

> "During one of my meetings with him *(MacDonald)* in his flat he *(MacDonald)* openly proposed to me that I engage in collecting information about the work of the Zlatoust works. It was clear to me that he was proposing that I should engage in espionage work. I did not give him my final consent on that occasion, but approximately two or three days after, when he had spoken to me on this subject a second time, I gave my consent."
>
> "The motives which so easily induced me to agree to engage in espionage," *Gussev* goes on to state, "were my anti-Soviet views and my striving to become more active in my hostility towards the Soviet Government."

At the same time, in giving his consent to carry on espionage, *Gussev* was assured by *MacDonald* that this criminal activity would be paid for, but this aspect of the work, he declares, was only a secondary matter.

> "The material side," says *Gussev,* "played a secondary role for me, the more so that materially, I was provided for."

Nor was the question as to whose interests *MacDonald* served and for whom he was working a matter of importance for *Gussev.*

> "The question as to whom *MacDonald* was collecting information for," says *Gussev,* "did not interest me very much. I tried several times to clear this question up with *MacDonald,* but as these attempts did not meet with *MacDonald's* sympathy and he avoided giving a reply to my questions, I considered it to be embarrassing and impossible to insist upon an explanation. Moreover, I understood that my special persistence might not only be unpleasant for *MacDonald,* but might arouse in him a certain mistrust towards me."

One thing was clear to *Gussev* and that was that the information that interested *MacDonald,* "could not be collected by *MacDonald* out of his eagerness to learn as an engineer, or in the interests of Metro-Vickers. It was clear to me," says *Gussev,* "that such information could be collected exclusively for political purposes hostile to the Soviet Union."

Prosecuted in this case, *MacDonald,* after the concrete facts of his crime had been presented to him, admitted in the very first examination on March 12 the correctness of *Gussev's* evidence and corroborated it at a confrontation on March 13.

> "On the very next day after my arrival in Zlatoust," says *MacDonald,* "I made the acquaintance of the manager of the Zlatoust Electric Power Station, engineer *Gussev.* In the further course of my work at Zlatoust I met *Gussev* every day as I was directly connected with him in my work, for I was installing a turbo-generator in the very station of which *Gussev* was manager . . ."
>
> ". . . At first on meeting *Gussev* I mainly discussed business affairs with him, but later on we also began to talk about abstract questions and I interested myself in the conditions of life of the engineers and the workers."
>
> "Approximately eight or nine months after my arrival at Zlatoust," states *MacDonald* further, "I began to speak frankly to *Gussev.* Conversations took place either at my flat (I already had a flat at that time) or in *Gussev's* flat—I don't remember exactly. I frankly told *Gussev* that I required information about *the production of military supplies* at the Zlatoust works, the state of power supply, etc."

In his depositions, *MacDonald* replied to the question as to who gave him instructions to obtain from *Gussev* the above-mentioned information.

MacDonald deposes:

> "In the summer of 1929 I was at *Thornton's* villa and in conversation with me he said that he was interested in information about the political and economic situation of the U.S.S.R. and he asked me to collect and to convey to him this information."

Thornton is the chief installation engineer under whom *MacDonald* worked for Metro-Vickers.

This conversation already gave *MacDonald* to understand that in addition to his, *MacDonald's,* ordinary work in the U.S.S.R. he would have also illegal tasks. And he did not have long to wait until he received more concrete instructions from *Thornton.* Immediately before *MacDonald's* departure for the Zlatoust Electric Power Station he, as he testifies, had a second conversation with *Thornton.*

> "He then asked me to collect for him information about the production of military supplies at the Zlatoust works and also about the state of the power supply at those works."

In that same conversation with *Thornton,* as *MacDonald* asserts,

> *"Thornton,* in a rather veiled form, *i.e.,* not as a direct order, gave me the task of organizing breakdowns at Zlatoust in order to interrupt the work at the plant; in doing so he did not say concretely what kind of breakdowns I was to cause as I was to determine that myself on the spot."

MacDonald says that, in giving him his task, *Thornton* said that if money was required for this purpose he could get it from him.

Of course, *Thornton* could not have given tasks of such a character, nor could *MacDonald* have agreed to carry out these tasks, had not both persons been connected by ties other than purely business ties. *MacDonald* himself testified to this.

In reply to the question as to whom the information *Thornton* was interested in was intended for, *MacDonald* stated the following:

> "Receiving this task from *Thornton,"* says *MacDonald,* "I agreed to carry it out because it was awkward for me to refuse to do so, as he was my chief and a man for whom I have great respect. I did not ask *Thornton* for which institution he was collecting this information and on whose instructions he was acting, as I considered that in this case the less I knew the better. At all events I understood that *Thornton* was acting in the interests of England . . ."

The character and scope of *Gussev's* espionage activities gradually changed in accordance with the tasks he received from *MacDonald.*

"At first *MacDonald's* tasks," says *Gussev,* "and the information which I gave him were restricted to questions of electric supply. The information which I supplied him with gave him an idea of the state of the power supply of the works. Later the scope of the question in *MacDonald's* tasks widened...."

In reply to questions put to him, *Gussev* said:

"I began to give him information of the following character: 1) On questions concerning the power supply of the Zlatoust works and the proposed reconstruction of the electric supply. This undoubtedly was secret, because it gave an idea of the volume of the production for military defence which formed part of the production carried on at the Zlatoust works; 2) On questions concerning the shell production program, which was a purely military secret; 3) On questions concerning the type of shells and the expansion of shell production, which also was a military secret; 4) On questions concerning the production of high quality steel and particularly the production of automobile spring and aviation steel and shell steel..."

The position which *Gussev* occupied as chief of the electric power station which served the Zlatoust works gave him wide opportunity of obtaining the information he required for his espionage activity.

"The Zlatoust Electric Power Station of which I have been chief since 1929," says *Gussev,* "served the Zlatoust mechanical, ceramic and metallurgical works and also the town itself and the railways... As chief of the electric power station, I was in charge of the blast air system for the blast furnaces, the water pumps of the works and from the end of 1931 of the step-down sub-station of the Chelyabinsk Electric Power Station. In virtue of my position as chief of the electric power station, in addition to the enterprises which were in my charge, I had almost unhindered access to the mechanical munition works. . . . I was well informed of the progress of work at the metallurgical works of which the electric power station was the centre; having unhindered access to all the departments of the metallurgical works, I had every opportunity of obtaining any information and facts concerning output, including also information concerning production which was secret. . . ."

However, *Gussev* did not only take advantage of his position in order to obtain information:

> "Having worked at this station for ten years," *Gussev* states further in his evidence, "it was quite easy for me to take advantage of the confidence which certain chiefs of departments, foremen, etc., placed in me. At the mechanical works, where I did not have such free access and where it was more difficult for me to find my bearings, I took advantage of my visits to these works firstly in order to collect a definite amount of information concerning the work at the plant and secondly to take advantage of my acquaintance with the engineering and technical staff of the works, some representatives of whom had confidence in me and several of whom were subsequently found to be among those who worked for *MacDonald*."

As the chief of the power station, *Gussev* had at his command official information on questions concerning the expansion of the output of all the works, including the munition works.

Concerning the manner in which he conveyed the information he collected, *Gussev* says:

> "The fact that it was necessary to observe careful secrecy naturally affected the method of my passing on to *MacDonald* the information I collected; that is why I tried to avoid putting things in writing and preferred to convey the information to *MacDonald* orally. However, in those cases when the information contained figures, I made notes of them in my

notebook and at home drew up a brief written report which I later handed to *MacDonald* when we were alone."

Gussev also indicates how *MacDonald* preserved secrecy in receiving information:

"In receiving information from me," says *Gussev*, "*MacDonald* made notes in his notebook and, as I observed, the written reports, if they were received at home, he destroyed by burning, after making some notes in his notebook."

Gussev's evidence on the character and scope of his espionage activities was corroborated by *MacDonald*, who said:

"*Gussev* had the commission from me to gather—and he really systematically secured—secret information relative to:

1) The work of military shops of the mechanical and metallurgical works, inclusive of the production of the shell shops, the quality of shells made, their types and other data;

2) The development of military shops;

3) Data about the production of special steels used by works for making military materials;

4) The energy supply to the works, and questions related to an uninterrupted work of the military shops."

The further progress of the investigation led to the discovery of other persons connected with *MacDonald* in espionage work in addition to *Gussev*. Such a person proved to be the assistant chief of the electric power station, *Vassily Andreyevich Sokolov*.

MacDonald says:

"In this I was greatly helped by engineer *Gussev* of the power station and various men employed by him—*Sokolov* and others."

In the course of examination, *Sokolov* said:

"Being the assistant chief of the power station of the Zlatoust works, I, in the summer (June or July, I do not remember exactly which month) of 1930, got into touch with the installation engineer of the firm of Metropolitan-Vickers, the English citizen, *MacDonald*, and on the instructions and

> with the help of the chief of the power station, *Gussev,* orally gave *MacDonald* secret information of a production character concerning the output at the works of high quality steel. . . ."

In April 1931 *MacDonald* left Zlatoust and after his vacation was sent to work in the capacity of installation engineer at Zuevka. *MacDonald's* departure from Zlatoust did not interrupt his connection with *Gussev.* This connection was organized through the medium of special persons.

MacDonald says:

> "When I left Zlatoust I arranged that *Ryabova* should come to me in Zuevka and also that she should bring me any information that she had from engineer *Gussev.*"

Moreover, after *MacDonald* had gone to Zuevka, he continued to receive from *Gussev* the same kind of secret information both through the medium of his acquaintance *Ryabova* and her sons, as well as through the personal contacts he maintained with *Gussev.*

Concerning this, *MacDonald* says:

> "*Ryabova* arrived at Zuevka in January 1932 and brought me a letter from *Gussev* containing information of conditions in Zlatoust: that is, about the political situation and production of war materials, shells, etc., in the mechanical and metallurgical works. In May 1932 the son of *Ryabova,* Peter, came to Zuevka and remained there for two days. He brought with him a letter from engineer *Gussev* which contained further information in the nature of war espionage, and returned to Zlatoust taking with him a letter to *Gussev* from myself asking *Gussev* to continue this espionage work. In June 1932 the second son of *Ryabova* came to Zuevka and remained there for a month. He brought with him a letter containing espionage information from *Gussev* and took back with him a letter inviting *Gussev* to come to visit me at Zuevka. In accordance with this letter *Gussev* came to me in September 1932 and stayed for several days. He brought with him information concerning the political and economic situation in Zlatoust and concerning the work of

> the metallurgical and mechanical works on the production of war materials, shells, etc."

On his return from Zuevka, *Gussev* met *Thornton* at Khartsisk Station and conveyed to him secret information of importance for the defence of the State concerning the situation at the Zlatoust works.

> "On the eve of my departure," says *Gussev,* "a telegram was received from *Thornton* informing us of his arrival in Zuevka. On arrival at the station, while a ticket was being purchased for me, the train on which *Thornton* travelled arrived . . . He was met at the station by an engineer who had motored up from Makeyevka. This engineer and *Thornton* went into a restaurant behind the station. After a little while, *MacDonald* went to the restaurant and later I too went in, on the insistence of the latter. There I had a conversation with *Thornton,* who inquired about the position at Zlatoust in regard to food, the work of the factories and the power stations, the production of shells and the work that I had done. I replied to all these questions as far as the shortness of the interview permitted."

Similar secret information of importance for the defence of the State was conveyed to *MacDonald* through the medium of this same *Gussev* by the accused *Sokolov,* who states that he

> "also conveyed to *MacDonald* in writing, through engineer *Gussev,* on the instructions of the latter in 1932, secret information concerning the output and the running of the works. Particularly, I gave *MacDonald,* through the medium of *Gussev,* the following information in writing: a) concerning the weekly output of the large shaping rolling mill; b) the days in which shell steel was rolled; c) the difficulties at the works in connection with non-ferrous metals. . . ."

The facts concerning *MacDonald's* connection with *Gussev* and the systematic receipt by *MacDonald* of letters from *Gussev* after *MacDonald's* departure from Zlatoust for Zuevka is also corroborated by the depositions of *Maria Fedorovna Ryabova* at the preliminary investigation.

However, the main content of *Gussev's* counter-revolutionary activity was the organization and the causing of breakdowns at the Zlatoust Electric Power Station and the organization of the delay of work on the extension of the electric power station for the purpose of undermining the industry and the military power of the U.S.S.R.

> "Several months after I had commenced my espionage work," says *Gussev* on this question, "in the beginning of the second half of 1930 . . . *MacDonald,* during one of my meetings with him, told me that it was necessary to proceed to cause breakdowns which could retard the work of the factories producing shells and high quality steel."
>
> "As this proposal," continues *Gussev,* "was entirely in accord with my counter-revolutionary frame of mind. . . . I, without hesitation, adopted *MacDonald's* proposal to organize and cause breakdowns at the works."
>
> "From that time on," says *Gussev* further, "approximately from the second half of 1930, I entered on the second path of counter-revolutionary work, on the path of committing acts of wrecking and diversion."

According to *Gussev's* statement, he received two tasks from *MacDonald:*

> "1) to reduce the output of shells and cold weapons at the mechanical works, 2) to reduce the output of high quality steel at the metallurgical works."

This is corroborated by the accused *Sokolov:*

> "*MacDonald* declared to me that on me and *Gussev* was imposed the task of committing acts of diversion on the principal units at the metallurgical works, of which *Gussev* already knows, and that I should come to an understanding with him concerning the concrete acts to be committed in carrying out this task. . . ."

"... Being a school chum of *Gussev's* and knowing that he was on good terms with *MacDonald,* I finally consented to join the counter-revolutionary organization and to carry out the task imposed upon me. . . ."

MacDonald admitted the correctness of this evidence.

"Already before my departure from Zlatoust," says *MacDonald,* "I said that it was necessary to damage the equipment, so as to interrupt the work at the Works and cause a stoppage there. *Gussev* agreed . . ."

". . . . At the end of 1930," says *MacDonald,* "I, in conversation with *Sokolov,* without giving him any concrete instructions to damage equipment, said that on him and *Gussev* was imposed the work of damaging equipment and that he, *Sokolov,* should arrange this directly with *Gussev.*"

Gussev in his turn also displayed corresponding initiative.

"Having given my consent to the committing and or ganization of acts of diversion," *Gussev* admits, "I, in drawing up the plan and methods of organization of these acts, saw still another possibility of disorganizing the work of the factories by wilfully delaying the extension of electric power stations that was going on at the time. I communicated this plan to *MacDonald,* who accepted it."

Concerning his own participation in the subsequent carrying out of acts of wrecking, *Gussev* gave the following evidence:

"On the instruction of the Metro-Vickers' engineer, *MacDonald,* we, at the Zlatoust Metallurgical Works, carried out the following wrecking acts: 1) put out of action five or six times the 1,400 h.p. motor which serves to drive the large shaping rolling mill. This breakdown was caused by me and *V. A. Sokolov* in May and June 1932. In addition to that, in August, the motor, as a result of this breakdown, was put to be rewound, which lasted from 20 to 25 days; 2) at the Zlatoust Electric Power Station we froze L.M.Z. boiler No. 8 which had a heating surface of 400 sq. metres. This breakdown was caused by me in December 1931 or January

> 1932—I don't remember exactly. During very severe frost, water was left in the boiler, and the register on the discharge tunnel leading to the smokestack was not closed, as a consequence of which, the whole of the heater and part of the tubes of the boiler were frozen; 3) the coal conveyor was put out of action at the end of 1931 by the incorrect setting up of the motor and by throwing small metal objects into the cylindrical gear drive, as a consequence of which the foundation and the whole of the transmission mechanism of the belt conveyor and skip hoist were broken; this breakdown was caused by me; 4) the installation and starting of U.M.T. boiler No. 11 with a heating surface of 400 sq. metres was delayed, owing to the fact that I sent to the scrap smelting furnace details of the armature of the boiler on the pretext that they were scrap. This was done by me in April 1932."

Questioned in greater detail concerning the damage to the motor of the large shaping rolling mill, *Gussev* said:

> "I received instructions from *MacDonald* to damage the motor of the large shaping rolling mill in the rolling mill shop of the metallurgical works, with the object of stopping the output of shells and of shell steel. I carried out this instruction. The motor was put out of action, and the shell shop did not work for six weeks. This was done and fulfilled by me and the chief electrician of the metallurgical works, *Vassily Andreyevich Sokolov*."

In accordance with this concrete wrecking task, *Gussev*, according to his evidence

> "during the inspection of this motor, threw a small piece of sheet metal into the ventilation duct of the stator. Subsequently, this piece of iron served as the cause of the breakdown because dropping into the air gap, it caused the displacement of a part of the laminated iron packets of the stator iron and rotor. The displaced iron damaged the wrapping containing the winding of the stator, which was the cause of the breakdown."

Having put the motor out of action in this way, *Gussev* did not stop at this damaging of the motor.

> "The displacement of the iron occurred in several places," says *Gussev,* "because this defect was not put right and it later caused five or six breakdowns during the period up to August and made it necessary to stop the motor and give it a complete overhauling."

Questioned in connection with this, *MacDonald* said:

> "It seems that it happened in my or engineer *Gussev's* house. I told *Gussev* after getting closely befriended with him that for the purpose of a struggle with the Soviet power one must use also such means as the organization of breakages in the works and especially in their most important points. I requested him, considering it to be a very important undertaking in order to stop the production, to organize a breakage of the above-mentioned motor, being aware that it will lead to most definite effective consequences. *Gussev* first hesitated but afterwards agreed to it and in such a way that the stoppage of the motor occurred in May. And later this act was repeated several times in June and August 1932 after my departure from the Urals to the Ukraine."

Concerning his part in the systematic damaging of the motor of the rolling mill shop in the metallurgical works, the assistant chief of the power station mentioned in *Gussev's* evidence, *V. A. Sokolov,* testifies as follows:

> "The 1,400 h.p. motor in the metallurgical works turned mill "800," which was the leading mill, and mill "600." These mills prepared metal for all the other mills in the rolling mill shop. . . ."
>
> "The ventilator in the 1,400 h.p. motor was put up with my help with the object of causing systematic breakdowns. The nature of this wrecking work was that the ventilator sucked into the motor impure air and thus choked the winding, the stator and the rotor with dirt."
>
> "In carrying out capital repairs," says *Sokolov* further, "the Commission sent from Moscow by the Spetz-Stahl de-

clared that the ventilation we had put in had a bad effect upon the work of the motor and he ordered it to be removed, which was done."

Sokolov's evidence is fully corroborated by the report of the Commission of the Spetz-Stahl which on March 31, 1931, inspected the motor. In this report, which is in possession of the investigating authorities, the Commission declares that:

> "The suction ventilator installation must be removed as it does not produce any positive results in the sense of cooling and distributing equable temperature expansions of the stator and, moreover, causes the motor to become greatly clogged as a consequence of suction of impure air."

The aim which the wreckers strove for was thus achieved: the motor was put out of action for a considerable period and the rolling mill shops were stopped for six weeks.

The next act of wrecking committed was to put the coal conveyor out of action. When *MacDonald* was confronted with *Gussev* on March 13, 1933, the accused *Gussev* said:

> "I received instructions from *MacDonald* to put the coal conveyor out of action."

MacDonald corroborated *Gussev's* evidence and said that he did give *Gussev* instructions to put the coal conveyor out of action. In his further depositions *Gussev* describes in detail the method by which he carried out this act of wrecking. *Gussev* said:

> "For the purpose of putting the coal conveyor out of action, I caused the cylindrical gear drive to be destroyed by dropping a piece of iron in between the pinion teeth. Moreover, during several repairs, I incorrectly set up the motor which turned the belt conveyor and the skip hoist, as a consequence of which the foundation of the motor was destroyed."

Having destroyed the foundation of the motor, *Gussev* did not confine himself to this act of wrecking, but taking advantage of his position as chief of the electric power station, he ordered the foreman *Boronikov* to dismantle the whole of the mechanism of the coal conveyor, which was done.

> "As a result," says *Gussev* further, "approximately in December 1931 or in January 1932, the coal conveyor was put out of action and has not worked until the day of my arrest. . . ."

Questioned as a witness, the technical electrician of the Zlatoust Electric Power Station, *Andrei Grigorievich Sapozhnikov* said:

> "In the beginning of 1932 *Gussev* ordered repair foreman *Boronikov* to dismantle the coal conveyor No. 1, which the latter did. This dismantling was caused by the frequent repair of the coal conveyor, but this could have been avoided by strengthening the foundation of the coal conveyor No. 1 with through bolts, as the plate on which the motor and the pulley of the conveyor were installed was badly fastened. *Gussev* paid no attention to *Boronikov's* proposal to fasten the foundation with bolts, but decided to change the type of drive from the motor to the conveyor from a cylindrical gear to a worm gear drive. Now coal conveyor No. 3 is in reserve, and this does not guarantee the work of a part of the boilers. . . ."

Thus, by dismantling the coal conveyor, this object of the wreckers was also achieved, *i.e.,* to disturb the normal operation of the station by failing to secure for its work the required amount of coal.

The same witness *Sapozhnikov,* in accordance with the circumstances of the case above outlined, corroborated the fact that in the winter of 1932 boilers No. 7 and No. 8 were frozen by being kept in reserve filled with water.

> "When the assistant foreman of the shop, *Burdin,* called upon *Gussev* to let the water out, the latter replied: 'It is not your business, nothing will happen to the boilers.' "

However, according to the evidence of the same witness *Sapozhnikov,* when boiler No. 8 was examined by repair foreman

Yakov Boronikov, he discovered that in two or three of the rear tubes of the boiler there was ice. Similarly, it was discovered that the super-heater was frozen. About 5,000 rubles was spent on the repair of this boiler and the repairs lasted two months.

In giving evidence on the question of the freezing of boiler No. 8 *Gussev* admitted that

> "the freezing of boiler No. 8 was another premeditated and deliberate act of wrecking committed by me at the Zlatoust Electric Power Station."

Boiler No. 8 was damaged by *Gussev* also in agreement with *MacDonald.*

When *Gussev* was confronted with *MacDonald* on March 13. 1933, *Gussev* said that

> "he was instructed to put boilers Nos. 1, 2, 8, and 11 out of action."

At this same confrontation *MacDonald* corroborated the statement and said that he did indeed give *Gussev* the instruction to

> "put boilers Nos. 1, 2, 8 and 11 out of action."

Finally, in fulfilling this same task of reducing the work of the boiler system of the Zlatoust Electric Power Station, the wreckers caused delay in reconstructing the Sterling boilers Nos. 1 and 2, which were being changed from hard fuel to pulverized fuel firing and caused delay in installing U.M.T. boiler No. 11.

Questioned as witness, the chief mechanic of the Zlatoust works, *Grigory Alexandrovich Shevkun,* said:

> "Sterling boilers Nos. 1 and 2 were installed in the power station of the metallurgical works approximately in 1914. Being hand-stoked boilers, these, in April 1932, were stopped in order to be equipped for pulverized fuel. Who took the initiative in changing the method of stoking for boilers Nos. 1 and 2, I do not know. My own opinion is that the changes in stoking for boilers Nos. 1 and 2, were made for the purpose of increasing the productivity of the boilers. . . . I do not know what dates were fixed for the completion of the dismantling, but I do know that the dates were frequently

changed and have long been exceeded. Approximately in May-June 1931, the repairs to the boilers were completed and they were declared ready to be transferred to the Works. When these boilers were inspected by the chief of the power station, *Gussev,* they were rejected on the ground that they lacked furnace water screens. After boilers Nos. 1 and 2 were rejected by *Gussev* the work proceeded with long interruptions and slowly. Thus, these boilers Nos. 1 and 2, have not been repaired to the present time."

On the question of the installation of U.M.T. boiler No. 11, the witness *Shevkun* says:

"U.M.T. Boiler No. 11 was also installed for the purpose of increasing productivity. I do not know what dates were fixed for its installation and starting, but I do know that all the dates have certainly been exceeded. . . . All questions concerning the installation of this boiler were settled in agreement with the chief of the power station, *Gussev.* The delay in the installation of boilers Nos. 1, 2 and 11 reduced the power of the station."

Questioned on this matter, technical electrician of the Central Zlatoust Power Station, *Andrei Grigorievich Sapozhnikov,* said:

"Boilers Nos. 1 and 10 are being modernized for pulverized fuel from 1930 to this day. The date when the installation should have been finished and the boilers started is not known, although according to the plans, they should have been started in 1931. Boiler No. 11 was ready for drying and for walling in only on March 14, this year. . . . The reduction of productivity was due to the fault of the ex-chief of the station, *Gussev,* who was responsible for the control and supervision of the reconstruction of the steam-power system. His actions led to the freezing of capital investments in the reconstruction of the system and at the same time to the gradual reduction of the operation of the boilers to a minimum. . . ."

In addition to the evidence of the witnesses *Sapozhnikov* and *Shevkun,* the delay in the installation of boilers Nos. 1, 2 and 11, is corroborated by the statement of the works management and by the report of the Commission of Experts quoted above which declares that as a consequence of the delay in the installation, the station develops approximately one-half of its capacity. This delay was in complete accord with the plans of the counter-revolutionary wrecking activities in the Zlatoust Electric Power Station drawn up by the group of wreckers consisting of *Sokolov, Gussev* and *MacDonald.*

> "Discussing with *Gussev* the plan of our future work," says the accused *Sokolov,* "we decided on the boiler room as the latter determined the work of the power station. It was decided to delay the starting of Sterling boilers Nos. 1 and 2 which were being changed from hard fuel to pulverized fuel firing. Officially, the delay was explained by various defects, the newness of the work and other causes. The boilers were not started right up to the time of my arrest. In addition, the installation of U.M.T. boiler No. 11 was delayed for about two years."

Questioned in regard to the delay in the reconstruction of boilers Nos. 1 and 2, and the installation of boiler No. 11, *Gussev* gave the following evidence:

> "I received from *MacDonald* . . . instructions to put boilers Nos. 1, 2, 8 and 11 out of action. All these instructions," says *Gussev* further, "were carried out by me."

MacDonald deposes:

> "I have undertaken to disorganize the energy supply equipment of these two works (The Zlatoust Metallurgical and Mechanical Works) in order to render the work of these military plants less effective. As means for it I chose the reducing of the power output of the power station from 12,000 kw. to 6,000 kw., that means to cut it by a half. In such a state the smallest breakage on the station would fully paralyse and stop the work of the plant. Taking this into consideration I gave to *Mr. Gussev* the commission to organize the stoppage of boilers Nos. 1, 2, 8 and 11 and also of the coal conveyor."

As can be seen from the report of the Commission of Experts the task of reducing the capacity of the station by approximately one-half, which the group of wreckers working at the Zlatoust works had set themselves, was also actually fulfilled.

But the criminal activities of the group of wreckers at the Zlatoust Electric Power Station was not only restricted to putting certain machines out of action for the purpose of undermining the power of Soviet industry and of weakening the Soviet State, but was also directed towards preparing for acts of diversion in the event of war.

The accused *Gussev,* being confronted with *MacDonald* on March 13, 1933, stated in regard to this matter:

> "*MacDonald* discussed with me the measures to be taken to put the equipment of the station out of order in the event of war. He told me and gave me direct instructions to cause breakdowns on the declaration of war in the most important sections of the station, namely, in the boiler house and the coal conveyor. By this means I was to strive to keep the station constantly at a level considerably below that which was provided for in the mobilization plan. In this way, had I succeeded in maintaining the level at about 6,000 kw. instead of 12,000 nominal kw. provided for in the mobilization plan, that would have meant the disruption of the work of munitions supply in wartime."

Questioned on this matter at this confrontation, the accused *MacDonald* said:

> "The respective declaration of Mr. *Gussev* coincides with my instrucions. When I aimed to disorganize the military production in time of war I was perfectly aware that through me *Gussev* and persons connected with him I would cause great harm to military production. This is why together with Mr. *Gussev* we developed a program of organizing breakages in time of war on these electro-stations. The developed scheme contained the full disorganization plan of the boiler plant and of the coal conveyor."

The accused *Sokolov* also corroborated the existence of a plan of action on the part of the group of wreckers in the event of war when he spoke about the

> "preparation, by systematic wrecking, for a number of important diversions, the sum total of which was to put the electric power station out of action and deprive the consumers of power at a moment when the Union was faced with external difficulties (foreign intervention)."
>
> "In this connection," said the accused *Sokolov* further, "we had to draw up a plan of action for ourselves. Discussing this question in detail we *(Gussev* and *Sokolov)* decided that our acts of diversion should be concentrated on the power station with its auxiliary plant, namely: first of all to put the pumps out of order; secondly, the boiler installations; thirdly, the air blast installations for the blast furnaces; fourthly, the turbo-generators and fifthly, the switchgear of the sub-stations. . . ."

The counter-revolutionary wrecking and espionage activities of *Gussev* and *Sokolov* at the Zlatoust Electric Power Station did not remain unrewarded. According to the statements he made at the confrontation with *MacDonald* on March 13, 1933, *Gussev* received sums from *MacDonald* at various times amounting to from 2,000 to 3,000 rubles.

This was corroborated by *MacDonald* who at the confrontation said:

> "Yes, I gave money to *Gussev* for his spying work carried out in accordance with my commissions the same as for his work consisting in the organization of breakages. The total amount of money which I handed over to him was about 2,000 or 2,500 rubles."

Nor was *Sokolov* forgotten. He too received money for his acts of wrecking.

> "In June 1932," says *Sokolov, "Gussev* in his office gave me money to the amount of 1,000 rubles and in handing it to me said: 'Here is a bonus from Vassily Vassilievich.'" "I consider," continues *Sokolov,* "that I received this sum principally for putting the 1,400 h.p. motor out of order."

The depositions of *Gussev* and *MacDonald* concerning the complicity of *Leslie Charles Thornton,* chief installation engineer of the Moscow office of Metro-Vickers, in the activities of the counter-revolutionary group at the Zlatoust Electric Power Station and their references to *Thornton* as the source of the payments for the counter-revolutionary acts that were committed at the Zlatoust Electric Power Station, caused proceedings to be taken against *Thornton* in the present case.

Arrested and examined, particularly when confronted with *Gussev* and *MacDonald, Thornton* testified to the effect that:

1) In those places where *MacDonald* was engaged in installation work "*MacDonald* did indeed engage in collecting information for *Thornton* and on his instructions."

2) *Thornton* first enlisted *MacDonald* for espionage activity in May-June 1930, in Losino-Ostrovskaya.

3) *Thornton* did indeed receive information from *MacDonald* concerning the Zlatoust and Zuevka districts.

> "Regarding Zlatoust and Zuevka," *Thornton* says, "I received detailed information. . . ."

4) *Thornton* admitted also that he knew that *Gussev*

> "was the person whom *MacDonald* had brought in to collect information about the work of the Zlatoust Electric Power Station on his *(Thornton's)* instructions."

5) The evidence of *MacDonald* and *Gussev* about the two journeys *Thornton* made to Zlatoust and his meeting with *Gussev* in Zlatoust is also corroborated by *Thornton.*

> "I know the engineer of the Zlatoust Electric Power Station, *Gussev,*" says *Thornton,* "and met him personally on my two visits to Zlatoust in 1930."

6) *Thornton* admitted the correctness of the evidence of *Gussev* and *MacDonald* concerning his *(Thornton's)* meetings with *Gussev* at Khartsisk Station after *Gussev* had visited *MacDonald* in Zuevka at his special request in order to report to him on the acts of wrecking he had committed and on the information he had collected on the Zlatoust Electric Power Station.

Thornton also corroborated *MacDonald's* evidence that the latter had received from *Thornton* a sum of money to pay "the people" who had given espionage information (*MacDonald's* deposition).

In defining more concretely these acts, *Thornton* disagrees with *MacDonald* only on the question as to the amount of money he had given *MacDonald*. At the confrontation with *MacDonald* of March 19, *Thornton* said that he had handed *MacDonald* "1,500 rubles" (*Thornton's* deposition).

MacDonald, however, declared during this confrontation that he had received 4,500 rubles, but *Thornton* denies 1) that he had received from *MacDonald* and *Gussev* secret information representing military State secrets and 2) that he took part in the organization and the committing of wrecking acts to put out of action and damage equipment as committed by the group of wreckers at the Zlatoust Electric Power Station.

However, *Thornton's* denial is easily refuted by the analysis of the following of his own admissions:

a) As *Thornton* himself states, he received information about the Zlatoust district and particularly about the work of the Zlatoust Electric Power Station from *MacDonald,* and, again according to Thornton's own depositions, the principal source of his information about the Zlatoust district was *Gussev. Thornton* mentions no other source of his information about the Zlatoust district.

Thornton's statement that he received information about the Zlatoust district of an exclusively innocent nature "which might be useful to his firm" is also in direct contradiction to *Thornton's* own depositions.

In his depositions made on March 28, 1933, *Thornton* says:

> "I was not much interested in receiving information from Zlatoust in the interests of our firm."

Indeed, if "the information that might be useful to the firm" is, as *Thornton* says, information "as to whether there will be any new orders for equipment" then, according to *Thornton's* own evidence, "no such orders were expected" from Zlatoust.

If the firm was interested in "how our machines are treated" then as *Thornton* himself was compelled to admit, "there was only a small turbine at Zlatoust."

b) In the same depositions of March 28, *Thornton,* being made to give a satisfactory explanation of his denial of the facts contained in the depositions of *MacDonald* and *Gussev,* himself corroborated the receipt of information that bore an undoubtedly secret character. *Thornton* admitted that he had received from *MacDonald* information

> "concerning the load of the electric power station and hence on the state of the electric supply at the Zlatoust works, which gave an idea of the work being done at these works."
>
> "concerning the general condition of the Zlatoust Electric Power Station especially its parts most exposed to damage."

Finally, if according to *Thornton,* Zlatoust did not represent any interest to his "firm" then for what services did *Thornton* pay *MacDonald?* On this matter *Thornton* was obliged to restrict himself to the following reply:

> "I gave *MacDonald* 1,500 rubles," says *Thornton*, "on his request. As the representative of the firm, I was little interested in Zlatoust I cannot explain why *MacDonald* required so much money and what he spent it on. I did not," continues *Thornton,* "ask *MacDonald* for an account of the money."

At the same time during the confrontation with *Thornton* on March 15, 1933, in reply to the question as to whether *Thornton* knew of the plan to deliberately damage equipment and whether he took a direct part in drawing up these plans, *Gussev* openly said:

> "When I received such an instruction (to damage equipment) from *MacDonald* I outlined the methods by which this task could be carried out and communicated them to *MacDonald*. Later, when *Thornton* arrived at Zlatoust, *MacDonald* communicated this plan to *Thornton* during our conversation in my office. We endorsed this plan and I received instructions from *Thornton* to proceed with it."

MacDonald also stated that when he reported this to *Thornton*, "*Thornton* was pleased with it."

At the confrontation with *Thornton, MacDonald* stated that

> "In Zuevka last year, in September, I told *Thornton* that the motors were damaged."

In formulating more precisely his evidence concerning the instructions to carry out acts of wrecking at the Zlatoust Electric Power Station which, according to *Gussev*, were drawn up jointly and directly with *Thornton, Gussev*, at the confrontation with *Thornton* of March 16, 1933, said:

> "My plan provided for the reduction of the capacity of the power station. According to the mobilization plan the working capacity was laid down at 12,000 kw. and we planned to reduce it by half so that the Works would not be able to operate and I planned that part of the boilers and the coal conveyor be put out of action. *Thornton* agreed to this plan and said that it must be carried out. He said that our anxiety that this plan will not be effective because the Chelyabinsk State District Power Station would provide an uninterrupted supply of power was unfounded, and this should not disturb us because the Chelyabinsk State Power Station was under their influence."

The statement made by *Thornton* to *Gussev* that the Chelyabinsk State District Electric Power Station "was under their influence," was fully corroborated by the facts obtained by the investigation concerning the activities of the counter-revolutionary group at the Chelyabinsk State District Power Station which was acting under the leadership of the accused *Vitvitsky,* but which was connected with *MacDonald, Gussev* and *Thornton.*

II

WRECKING ACTIVITIES AT THE CHELYABINSK STATE DISTRICT ELECTRIC POWER STATION

As was stated by *Gussev,* according to the words of *Thornton,* his, *Thornton's,* "influence" was secure at the Chelyabinsk State District Electric Power Station. *Gussev* took this to mean that there was a counter-revolutionary group of wreckers at the Chelyabinsk Power Station. And indeed, in the course of the whole of 1931-32, a number of deliberately caused breakdowns occurred there.

On the night of March 12, 1932, when the stop valve of turbine No. 2 was opened, a piece of iron was found under the valve. The piece of iron was caught between the seat and the valve as a result of which steam passed through the closed valve. Moreover, several small parts (a nut, a pin, etc.) were found at the net.

The Commission of Experts reported as follows on this matter:

> "1) The dropping of a piece of iron 1150 x 60 x 0.7 in the steam chamber under the stop valve could not have been accidental.
>
> "2) The presence of this piece of iron might have caused a serious breakdown of the turbine. . . ."

In addition to that, in a number of cases the valve stems were broken, which is to be explained by the fact that of the two overload valves one, on examination, was not of the proper size, it was loose and all the time allowed the steam to penetrate into the overload chamber of the turbine.

The Commission of Experts declares:

> "The installation staff who installed the machine could not have failed to note that the valve was not of the proper size. Such a fact indicates either obvious lack of conscientiousness or malicious intent."

At the end of October 1931, according to the depositions of the accused in this case, the chief engineer of the Chelyabinsk State District Power Station, *Vitvitsky,* a serious breakdown occurred as a result of a short circuit at the Stroitel Works, which obtains its power from this station, when the whole load of the station was disconnected.

In the spring of 1932 a breakdown occurred of the chain grate motor of the boiler as a consequence of a short circuit on a 220 volt cable which fed the motors.

In connection with a number of accidents on unit No. 1 and in particular the overheating of the generator and the dripping off of the varnish insulation on the end windings as a consequence of that, the station reported to Electro-Import that it was necessary to rewind the end windings of the generator.

In June 1931, *Thornton* arrived at the Chelyabinsk Station to investigate these accidents. After examining the generator *Thornton* calmed all fears concerning its overheating and promised to report the dripping off of the varnish to his firm. *Vitvitsky* personally thought that these accidents to the machines were premeditated and also due to defects in the equipment supplied by the firm and to improper installation. His conversation with *Thornton* confirmed *Vitvitsky* in his opinion.

During a conversation which took place in the machine room *Thornton,* according to *Vitvitsky,* remarked

> "that the firm would suffer great loss if it had to rectify the defects that have been revealed, because it would mean sending new parts, installation engineers, etc., and he gave me to understand that the firm he represented would be very glad if I closed my eyes to these defects."

Being informed of *Vitvitsky's* political views by *Oleinik,* senior installation engineer in Metro-Vickers' office, *Thornton* was able immediately to take steps to establish contact with *Vitvitsky* in regard to counter-revolutionary wrecking activity.

In further conversation *Thornton* openly stated that the firm required constant and systematic information concerning the state of affairs at the station in regard to the progress of construction, special features connected with operating the station, etc. At the same time *Thornton* stated that the firm had detailed information concerning a number of stations in the Soviet Union, including the Zlatoust, and that it would like to have information about the Chelyabinsk station.

> "Of course, I understood perfectly well," says *Vitvitsky*, "the kind of information *Thornton* referred to and for what purpose the firm of Metropolitan-Vickers required it; I understood that *Thornton* was merely a connecting link with other persons and organizations who are engaged in collecting such information."

Thornton promised that the information would be well paid for and added that *Vitvitsky* could convey his information to the firms' installation engineer at Zlatoust, *MacDonald,* through the manager of the Zlatoust Power Station, engineer *Gussev,* when the latter came to Chelyabinsk. *Thornton* also stated that *Gussev* was already giving information about the Zlatoust station.

Vitvitsky states that he had only three conversations with *Thornton*. The first in July 1931, the second in April 1932, also at the Chelyabinsk State District Power Station when *Thornton* proposed that *Vitvitsky* run the machines in such a way as to increase their wear and tear, and the third, in Moscow, at the offices of Electro-Import, in August 1932, when *Vitvitsky* informed *Thornton* of the state of affairs at the Chelyabinsk State District Power Station and also that his instructions to cease the efforts to prevent the excessive temperature of the super-heated steam had been carried out.

As a reward for his wrecking acts, *Vitvitsky* repeatedly received bribes amounting altogether to 6,900 rubles.

The facts stated by *Vitvitsky* concerning his receipt of sums of money coincide with *Gussev's* evidence which corroborate the fact that on the first occasion, *i.e.,* in September, he, on the instructions of *MacDonald,* paid *Vitvitsky* "2,000 rubles in money."

Further, according to the evidence of this same *Gussev,* on the receipt of two other letters, he handed to *Vitvitsky* the remaining sum of money he had received from *MacDonald* so that altogether, as *Gussev* said,

> "On these three occasions I handed *Vitvitsky* about 4,500 rubles."

The letters *Vitvitsky* handed to *MacDonald* contained the following information:

a) In the report of November 1931, *Vitvitsky* reported that the counter-revolutionary group at the Chelyabinsk State District Electric Power Station were considering the drawing up of a wrecking plan.

b) In the report of January 1932, *Vitvitsky* reported on the plan, already decided upon by the counter-revolutionary group, of acts of diversion which were to put the main turbines out of order by introducing water and raw steam into the turbines.

c) The reports handed over by *Vitvitsky* in February and March 1932, were similar to the January report handed over through *Gussev,* but in these reports *Vitvitsky,* in addition, reported on the measures he had undertaken to prepare for the acts of diversion indicated in the January report, namely, to place workers with little experience in charge of responsible sections feeding the boilers.

d) The report of July 1932 contained information about the wrecking work carried on by the counter-revolutionary group on the instructions of *Thornton, viz.,* to cease the regulation of the high temperature of the super-heated steam which would have a bad effect upon the blades of the turbines.

According to *Vitvitsky's* evidence, the main task of the group of wreckers at the Chelyabinsk Electric Power Station was to exert every effort to retard the further development of the station in regard to construction and to organize and operate the station in such a manner that it would not be able to give a regular supply of power to its customers, that there should be breakdowns, and that this had been carried out.

This was achieved in the following manner:

a) Materials were not ordered in sets.

b) Information to the designing departments was delayed.

c) Procrastination in the designing of certain parts of the equipment.

d) Concentration of attention on objects that had no connection with the station.

e) The passing of equipment which was incomplete in many details, which greatly hindered its normal operation and which gave rise to a large number of breakdowns.

f) Failure to take adequate measures when conditions arose

in any part of the station which threatened to interrupt the work of the station.

The above-mentioned tasks of the counter-revolutionary group at the Chelyabinsk State District Electric Power Station were achieved by still another method of deliberately distributing the workers in an irrational manner so that the less experienced workers were placed in charge of the more responsible sections, and vice versa.

Regarding this method of wrecking, *Vitvitsky* states the following:

> "This was carried out in the following manner: usually the staff that was to supervise the feeding of the boilers was selected from among the old and tried stokers who had completely mastered the technique of this job and who would not lose their heads for a moment in the event of a breakdown. This is particularly important on boilers of large capacity like those at the Chelyabinsk State District Electric Power Station, when in the event of a stoppage in the feeding while the boilers are working at full power, the supply of water in the boiler is sufficient to last for six minutes at the utmost.
>
> "At the Chelyabinsk Station the function of water condition supervisers was allocated to men with little experience while allocations to posts, the duties of which were to watch the process of burning, were regarded as promotion, whereas on the contrary, conditions should have been created in which the more experienced stokers would strive to become water condition supervisers."

Like the group at the Zlatoust Electric Power Station the group of wreckers operating at the Chelyabinsk Power Station also had a program of action drawn up for the event of war.

While preparing major acts of diversion to put the whole power station out of order at a moment when the Union had difficulties abroad, the counter-revolutionary organization at the Chelyabinsk Station carried out separate acts of diversion with the object of laying down the necessary basis for putting the whole power station out of order in the event of war.

III

WRECKING AT THE ZUEVKA DISTRICT ELECTRIC POWER STATION

The commission of experts, having examined and given a technical appraisal of the documents concerning the breakdowns at the Zuevka Power Station, established that the breakdown on generator No. 3 in June-July 1932 took place owing to the presence of extraneous objects—bolts, pieces of board, stones, etc. and arrived at the following conclusion:

> "Cases in which various extraneous objects (bolts, pieces of board, stone, etc.) were found in generator No. 3 cannot be regarded otherwise than as the result of criminal negligence on the part of the staff installing the machine or of deliberate malice on the part of some person."

The Commission of Experts further points out that:

> "No technician could help understanding that if extraneous objects, especially a bolt, were to get into the air gap of the generator, it might lead to serious damage to the stator and the putting of the whole unit out of action."

With regard to the accidents which took place on turbines No. 1 and No. 3 on the oil pumps, the same Commission of Experts came to the conclusion that:

> "In addition to the regulation failing to work, the automatic valve of the oil turbine pump does not work, owing to which the pump fails to start automatically when the machine stops and there were also breakdowns of the main oil pump owing to incorrect assembly.
>
> "Such a condition of the oil pumps," states the Commission of Experts, "threatens the reliability of the turbine, and could only take place as a result of the lack of conscientiousness on the part of the persons installing the unit towards their work."

The number of other breakdowns which took place at the Zuevka Power Station and which were also technically appraised by the Commission of Experts, likewise testified to the unsound condition of the machines at the Zuevka Power Station.

This state of affairs was brought about by the same installation engineer of Metro-Vickers, *MacDonald,* who had been transferred to work at the Zuevka Power Station from Zlatoust in September 1931, and who himself admitted in his testimony that he:

> "set himself the aim of putting the machinery at the Zuevka Electric Power Station into a defective condition for as long a time as possible."

According to his own statement, he was to a considerable extent successful in achieving this aim.

The chief wrecker at the Zuevka Electric Power Station was the manager of the turbine department, engineer *Kotlyarevsky.* On being charged, *Kotlyarevsky* admitted his work and stated that he carried it out in conjunction with *MacDonald.* Having made the acquaintance of *MacDonald,* who had come to the Zuevka District Electric Power Station, he quickly established with him

> "close relations, even of a friendly nature, which *MacDonald* tried to maintain all the time."

The friendly relations which were established, as *Kotlyarevsky* testified, served as a basis for acts of wrecking committed jointly.

While admitting his participation in the wrecking activities, *Kotlyarevsky,* however, limits these activities merely to the deliberate concealment of defects in the equipment. These attempts of *Kotlyarevsky* to belittle his wrecking work are completely refuted by the testimony of *MacDonald* and by documents submitted in the case which represent *Kotlyarevsky's* part as having been much more active.

When questioned on April 3, 1933, *MacDonald* testified:

> "In June or July 1932 there was organized a breakdown of the third generator. This breakdown took place as a result of leaving a bolt in the air gap of the generator. This was done under my instructions by *Fomichev* or *Kotlyarevsky.*"

As has been pointed out above, this testimony is confirmed in the report of the Commission of Experts.

As for the breakdown of the oil pumps of turbines No. 1 and No. 3, *Kotlyarevsky* himself admitted that he was warned by

MacDonald that they would be put out of action for a period of several days to two weeks, as actually took place. In the same deposition, *MacDonald* admitted that on turbines No. 1 and No. 3 there were breakdowns of the oil pumps which were stopped up, and that this act of wrecking was carried out by *Vassiliev** at his instructions.

The report of the Commission of Experts on the breakdowns which took place on turbines No. 1 and No. 3 connected with the improper work of the oil pumps confirms the deposition of *MacDonald.*

Kotlyarevsky's deposition that his wrecking counter-revolutionary work was paid for was also confirmed by *MacDonald,* who admitted that he paid about 1,000 rubles to *Kotlyarevsky.*

Kotlyarevsky stated:

> "I had not sufficient firmness to refuse the money and inform the proper authorities, because I decided that this would have extremely unpleasant results for me. All this led to my taking the money and thus cutting off all prospects of being able ever to abandon the role of *MacDonald's* agent."

IV

WRECKING AT THE IVANOVO DISTRICT ELECTRIC POWER STATION

Ever since January 1932, *i.e.,* from the moment when the plant started work, up to the time when investigations were started on the present case, there were a number of breakdowns of various kinds at the Ivanovo District Electric Power Station, putting machine groups out of operation and causing great losses to the State. An analysis of the reports drawn up after each accident, caused the Commission of Experts to come to the conclusion that the causes of breakdown were as follows:

1) Unreliable regulation of the turbines, which from the time they were put into operation did not attain the required efficiency, and did not ensure normal operation.

> "The work of the unit when the regulation was not in

---

* Vassiliev died before the case started.

order," concludes the Commission of Experts, "could either lead to serious breakdowns or increase their number."

In these conditions, according to the conclusions of the Commission of Experts:

> "The operation of the unit could have been permitted only owing to the negligence or malicious intent of the station staff and the representatives of the firm."

Further, the Commission of Experts points out that:

> "Had the station staff and the representatives of the firm been conscientious towards their duties, the chronic dislocation of the regulation of all the turbines for a period of one and a half years would have attracted greater attention on their part, with a view to removing the deficiencies."

2) The second serious circumstance which put the units out of action for lengthy periods, in the opinion of the Commission of Experts, was the obviously unreliable blading. The employees of the firm well knew of accidents at Baku and other stations owing to unreliable blading. However, they did not deem it necessary to inform the station about this or to take steps to remove these defects.

The operating staff in their turn took no steps:

a) either to remedy these defects,

b) or to insist firmly that the representatives of the firm put the turbines in order.

3) The reports presented on the work of the machines at the Ivanovo Power Station speak of defects in the controlling and measuring apparatus attached to the units.

The Commission of Experts, after analysing these reports came to the conclusion that:

> "The apparatus for measuring and controlling the units had partly become useless and partly gave incorrect readings as the result of negligent assembly and careless operation."

The Commission of Experts gave the following reply to the question as to how serious these defects were:

> "The fact that measuring apparatus which was in working order practically did not exist at the station, made it impossible to maintain proper control over the work of the units; this might lead to various breakdowns and might put the units out of operation."

Such a condition was the result of the criminal attitude toward their duties, of the employees of the firm and of the station staff, who failed to secure the proper adjustment of all the apparatus.

4) The Commission of Experts also attributes the following to the obviously dishonest attitude of the employees of the firm to their duties when installing turbines at the Ivanovo Electric Power Station:

> "During the installation of the turbine, fissures were discovered in the low pressure cylinder; this cylinder had been patched up at the factory with special plates, which made the cylinder casting defective."

In the opinion of the Commission of Experts, even if the staff of the firm considered these fissures not to be harmful for the prolonged operation of the machine, it was necessary

> "to draw up a report showing the existence of the defects, to inform the purchaser of them and especially to guarantee the work of the cylinder."

The representatives of the firm who installed the machine did not do anything of the kind, and thus the defects in the equipment were concealed and it was made impossible for the power station to keep check of the effect these fissures had on the further work of the turbine, or to take any serious steps to prevent a breakdown.

5) The next weak spot at the Ivanovo Power Station was the high pressure regenerative water heater No. 3, in which the safety arrangement was plainly unreliable in case of pipes bursting. However, as can be seen from the report of the Commission of Experts, the employees of the firm prohibited the staff of the station from making the necessary alterations and they were carried out by the staff of the station only after their departure. The Commission of Experts comes to the following conclusion on this matter:

> "This justifies us in saying that the representatives of the firm put the turbine into operation while defects existed which, in view of the plainly unreliable safety apparatus, might have led to a serious accident to the turbine owing to water getting into it after the bursting of the pipes of the heater."

The firm's installation staff, in the opinion of the experts, when installing the units at the Ivanovo Power Station,

> "grossly violated technical rules, which would not have occurred if the exciter circuit were properly assembled."

The result of this gross violation of technical rules, as the Commission of Experts established, led to the fact that:

> "The rotor was grounded and stray currents set up, which caused corrosion of the face of the shaft and the babbit bushing and the corrosion of the worm drive, which operates the regulators and the oil pump."

In addition to the accidents mentioned above, a number of cases of direct damage to equipment occurred at this station in the period from 1930-32 inclusive, which are set out in detail below.

The facts revealed by the preliminary investigation into the causes of the breakdowns and the spoiling of equipment show that these did not occur as the result of inexperience or carelessness on the part of the staff, but as the result of deliberate and intentional wrecking.

As the investigation showed, all these wrecking acts at the Ivanovo Power Station were committed by a counter-revolutionary group of wreckers consisting of certain representatives of the engineering and technical staff, organized by the chief of the operating department of the Ivanovo Power Station, engineer *Lobanov,* in league with an employee of the firm Metro-Vickers, the engineer *Nordwall.*

The engineer *Lobanov,* son of a factory owner, completed his studies at the Ivanovo Institute in 1929 and took his engineer's degree. He came to work at the Ivanovo Power Station with definitely formed anti-Soviet sentiments and views.

In 1930, having made the acquaintance of engineer *Nordwall* who had come to the Ivanovo Power Station in that year to install the equipment sent to the Ivanovo Power Station by Metro-Vickers, *Lobanov* repeatedly spoke to *Nordwall* during conversations with him regarding his discontent with the existing Soviet system and spoke of the difficulties that were being experienced, particularly stating that the Five-Year Plan would not be carried out. He complained that his material conditions were not good, pointing out at the same time that before the revolution his father was a factory owner who engaged in trade, and that he, *Lobanov,* could not live as his father lived.

According to *Lobanov's* deposition, he met *Nordwall* more frequently later on, and their conversations became more frank; owing to this, *Nordwall* realized that it would be possible to make use of *Lobanov* for active anti-Soviet work, and indeed, approximately in February 1932, after one of the usual conversations with *Lobanov,* he actually made a direct proposal to him to "proceed to business"—on the work of deliberately organizing the disabling of the equipment. *Nordwall* added that he, *Lobanov,* like others who took part in this work, "would not have cause to regret it."

According to *Lobanov, Nordwall* urged that the damage to the equipment be carried out systematically, so as to cause interruptions in the supply of electric current to industry, and that

> "in this connection, attention should be paid to the damaging of equipment not supplied by Metro-Vickers and that if equipment from the Metro-Vickers Company, on which the period of guarantee had not expired, were damaged, then the damage must be carried out in such a way that the responsibility for it could not be thrown on the Metro-Vickers Company."

In accordance with these instructions, practical measures were outlined regarding the damage to be done to the turbines.

To carry out these acts of wrecking, *Lobanov* drew into the conspiracy *Lebedev,* a foreman at the power station, senior technician *Ugrumov,* and a fitter, *Kitayev,* all of whom had been employed by *Lobanov's* father before the revolution.

Lobanov made a detailed deposition on the acts of wrecking he committed, in which he indicated the following as the main points:

1) Systematically putting out of action motors, driving chain grates of boilers, by breaking the cables feeding these motors; this was carried out by *Lebedev,* foreman of the electric department;

2) Deliberately putting sand into the bearings of the motor of the boiler feed pumps, owing to which the bearings became overheated and the motor was put out of action and had to be repaired; this was also carried out by the aforesaid *Lebedev;*

3) Repeatedly disconnecting by hand house feeders from the switch room of the Ivanovo Power Station, on the pretext of their coming into action due to the effect of the overload relay;

4) Deliberately putting out of operation the motor of the forced draft fan of boiler No. 5 by deliberately closing up the ventilation ducts of the motor, as a result of which the winding of the motor burned and boiler No. 5 was put out of action;

5) Deliberately faulty insulation of the windings of the transformers and the mercury arc rectifiers with the object of putting out of action the electric locomotives which served to haul peat;

6) Leaving the lid of the contact box unrepaired on the motor of the fire-pump so that extraneous metallic bodies could fall in and cause a short circuit in the coupling;

7) Systematically putting telephone communications out of action.

In the same deposition, *Lobanov* enumerates in detail the wrecking measures planned by him after he was transferred to the rationalization department, the object of which was to cause a breakdown in the Hanneman automatics, the house generators and the coal shakers on boilers No. 3 and No. 4 and in a number of other cases.

The foreman of the electric department, *Lebedev,* under examination confirmed the above testimony of *Lobanov,* and explained that

> "the immediate aim of the counter-revolutionary group was to disorganize the work of the Ivanovo Power Station by

deliberately damaging equipment so as to cause breakdowns in the units and equipment, stoppages in the work of the station, the reduction of power transmission and the complete stoppage of the supply of power to the factories which receive their current from the Ivanovo Station."

Passing on to the concrete acts of wrecking committed by him in accordance with instructions from *Lobanov, Lebedev* stated that he was responsible for a series of breakdowns on the speed-reducing gear of the chain grates, owing to bad installation and careless treatment of the cable; he deliberately permitted this with the aim of causing these accidents to the circulation pump of the house turbine; it was also with the aim of causing an accident that he did not repair the cracked lid on the contact box of the motor of the fire-pump. As a result, water got on to the contacts and short-circuited them, and an explosion took place which blew off the box. The explosion damaged the motor oil circuit breakers in which the trip coils burned and the connecting rods were bent.

As a result of these activities, a series of breakdowns of the machines actually occurred at the Ivanovo Power Station, causing dislocations in the work of the station and reducing the supply of power to the works and factories using electricity from the Ivanovo Power Station.

The criminal wrecking group at work at the Ivanovo Power Station had also worked out a plan of action in case of war.

According to *Lebedev, Lobanov* had stated that *Nordwall* had set himself the aim of preparing to put out of action all the turbines of the Ivanovo Power Station so as to stop the supply of electricity to industry in case war was declared.

All these counter-revolutionary acts of wrecking were accompanied by bribery and corruption. Thus, according to the testimony of *Lobanov,* he received 5,000 rubles.

> "After I had informed *Nordwall* of the wrecking and diversion work performed by the group which I had organized," testifies *Lobanov,* "he, in May or June 1931, at the power station, after a conversation at the switchboard, gave me 3,000 rubles wrapped in a newspaper as we were passing through the turbine house. At the same time he said

> that if the work was carried on more energetically, the reward would be bigger. I divided the money as follows: *Lebedev* got 1,000 rubles, *Ugrumov*—800 rubles, and the rest of the money I kept myself."

Later, after the feeders had been disconnected on many occasions and the motor of the feed pump had been put out of action, *Lobanov* received a further 2,000 rubles from *Nordwall.*

Lebedev also admitted receiving money for acts of wrecking committed by him.

Charles Nordwall, engineer of Metro-Vickers, on being charged in the present case, testified that he never gave any instructions to *Lobanov* to carry out acts of wrecking and never gave any money to *Lobanov.*

When confronted with *Lobanov, Nordwall* did not deny his repeated meetings with *Lobanov* and his anti-Soviet conversations with him, but continued to deny giving any money to *Lobanov,* or any instructions connected with the commission of wrecking acts.

Thornton was also involved in the wrecking work at the Ivanovo Power Station.

Sabotage in the installation of the turbines supplied by Metro-Vickers was committed at the Ivanovo Power Station by *Yuri Ivanovich Zivert,* foreman of the transformer and oil system, who was employed in this capacity at the Ivanovo Power Station from June 1930 to July 1931.

According to the deposition of *Zivert,* he was drawn into wrecking work by *Thornton,* chief installation engineer of the Metropolitan-Vickers Company.

Zivert made the acquaintance of *Thornton* for the first time in 1925 at the Gorky Electric Power Station (at that time called Nigres), where *Zivert* was working as senior foreman on the installation of Metro-Vickers' transformers.

Zivert received his first wrecking assignment from *Thornton* in June 1930, and at that time also he received 500 rubles from *Thornton,* together with the instruction:

> "to hinder the installation of the following bank of transformers, but chiefly the transformers of the first bank which

supplied current for the peat bogs, and also not to watch the quality of the installation work, as I did at Nigres."

". . . . Won over by *Thornton's* promise to reward me, I agreed to his proposal to hinder the installation of the units which were in my charge and not to take notice of the quality of the installation work, well knowing that these proposals were wrecking proposals and dictated by the counter-revolutionary aims of hindering and deteriorating the construction of the electric power stations."

Zivert agreed to *Thornton's* proposal that he should hinder the installation of the machine groups and that he should deliberately do careless work in the installation of electric equipment in the transformer bank assemblies and of the oil system. As is plain from his further testimony, he carried out *Thornton's* instruction:

1) Deliberately did not take steps to eliminate copper dust when turning the commutator, which resulted in the breakdown of the commutator segments and risers and the putting out of action of the converter, which hindered the operation of the electric locomotives used for hauling peat.

2) Deliberately assembled the oil circuit-breakers and transformers carelessly and incorrectly.

As a result of *Zivert's* activity a series of breakdowns occurred in the electric equipment of the Ivanovo Power Station in 1931 and 1932.

In the course of ten months there were fifteen accidents to the oil pipes. After being assembled, there were five cases in two months when the oil circuit-breakers failed to act properly.

For carrying out this wrecking work, *Zivert* received a further sum of 300 rubles in addition to the 500 rubles he had received before.

V

WRECKING AT THE ELECTRIC POWER STATION OF THE "MOSENERGO" SYSTEM

During 1927 to 1932, a number of accidents occurred in the electric power stations included in the "Mosenergo" system which led to the stoppage of a number of turbines for a lengthy period, the lowering of their productive capacity and an increase in the cost of operation of the electrical equipment.

1) The Commission of Experts inquired into the accidents at the First Moscow Power Station on turbines No. 27 and No. 28 which occurred on March 9, May 10, June 16 and November 28, 1931, and which caused stoppages of the circulation pumps of the turbines. In dealing with the fact that in all these accidents the staff of the power station did not discover the causes of the accidents and that "the causes of the accidents might be defects in the construction of the Metro-Vickers oil circuit-breakers, which might from time to time open the circuit independently of outside causes," and in view of the fact that:

> "in spite of the repeated accidents, the station staff did not make the proper claims on the firm,"

and that:

> "no special tests were made on the oil circuit-breakers."

the Commission of Experts came to the conclusion that

> "this does not preclude the possibility that the opening of the oil circuit-breakers was done deliberately."

2) On October 1, 1932, transformer bank No. 2, 105,000 volts, 45,000 kw. amp. was tested after its installation. It was particularly important for "Mosenergo" to put this bank into operation in good time as the existing transformers were overloaded and could not transmit the power required for the "Mosenergo." The installation was carried out at first under the direction of a representative of Metro-Vickers, the fitter *Raizin.* The latter, however, did not complete the installation; he was recalled by the firm and sent to other work, and the firm put the installation in charge of *Marin,* a fitter of the First Moscow Power Station. A test was carried out in the presence of the engineer of the firm, *Monkhouse,* and ended in a breakdown. This is what the Commission of Experts reports on this breakdown:

> "When shifting the switch regulating the tension from one position to another on the board, a rush of current was registered after which the generator was immediately connected up by hand.... After opening the tanks, it was

found that the contacts and bushings had burned up. Both tanks on the switch were found not to have been filled with oil, which was the cause of the breakdown."

The Commission of Experts adds:

"It is absolutely incomprehensible how an experienced staff, in assembling the transformer, could forget to fill the regulator tanks with oil and apply tension without examining whether oil was present."

And notwithstanding:

"The representative of the firm, *Monkhouse,*" continues the Commission of Experts, "allowed the transformer to be tested without previously checking up to see whether it was in order and examining the quality of the installation work and the degree to which it was complete."

It should be emphasized that:

"A transformer with a capacity of 45,000 kw. amp. is a very large unit, and on testing it, all customary precautions should be observed such as are prescribed in such cases."

The Commission of Experts comes to the conclusion that:

"Such a careless and extremely frivolous attitude on the part of both the representatives of the firm and the station staff, who carried out the installation, towards such a big piece of equipment, so important for the electric supply of the Moscow Region, must, to say the least, be described as criminal negligence."

3) References to similar cases of a criminal attitude on the part of the power station staff towards the operation of the machines are found in the conclusions of the Commission of Experts on the breakdown at the Shatura Electric Power Station in 1931, where,

"When changing over from one oil cooler to another, the staff permitted an incorrect switching over of the valves owing to which lubricating oil ceased to be transmitted to the bearings of the turbo-generator. The improper action of the staff caused various degrees of fusing in all the bearings, an excessive wearing of the stuffing box covering of the generator, the tearing off of the balance weights from the working wheel on the generator side, etc."

In analysing this breakdown, the Commission of Experts came to the conclusion that:

> "The cause of the accident could be either the complete inexperience and perplexity of the staff in view of the absence of proper organization in the turbo-generator house, or the deliberate action of the staff with the object of putting the units out of commission."

4) On the breakdowns at the Orekhovo Thermo-Power Station, on May 22, 1931, November 18, 1931, and May 19, 1932, the Commission of Experts established the following:

> "*Re* the breakdown of May 22, 1931. Owing to the closing of the water outlet pipe in the circulation channel, the level in the channel rose and the water got into the switch gear; owing to this, generator No. 1 had to be disconnected and the capacity dropped by 3,000 kw. After the water level had been lowered, the generator was again connected to the circuit. The cause of the breakdown was that after the channel had been cemented by the builders, the wooden forms were left and the operating staff of the station led in the water without taking away the forms, which were washed away by the water and closed the outlet. In this case, there was either malicious intent or carelessness on the part of the building organization and the operating staff bordering on crime."

The investigation showed that in addition to the breakdowns mentioned above, there were a number of other breakdowns at the First Moscow Power Station and other stations of "Mosenergo."

It was impossible to make a full technical investigation into these breakdowns, owing to the absence of certain of the necessary documents. Their technical causes were established, however, by the direct testimony of the accused.

Among these breakdowns are the following:

1) Breakdown of turbines No. 26 and No. 27 at the First Moscow Power Station, as the result of organic defects in the turbine blades which caused the stoppage of the turbines for seven days and more and the reduction of their output after repair by 20-25 per cent. These breakdowns occurred systematically up to March 1933.

2) An organic defect in the rod of the second regulating valve of turbine No. 26 at the First Moscow Power Station, *viz.*, the rod was too deeply grooved. This led, on April 29, 1932, to the breaking of the rod, as a result of which the load on turbine No. 26 had to be reduced by 5,000 kw. On December 9, 1931, the oil supply pipe at the First Moscow Power Station burst, owing to defective brazing which led to the stoppage of the turbines and might have caused a fire at the station.

3) During the same period, the turbines were systematically stopped because oil got past the oil baffle plates in the front bearings of the generator and along the shaft into the exciter.

4) The bad insulation on the rotor leads systematically led to the stoppage of the generators.

5) On November 22, 1932, there was a breakdown which led to the stoppage of some of the machines at the First Moscow Power Station owing to the breakdown of the house turbine and insufficient chemical control.

6) At the end of 1931, on one of the generators of the First Moscow Power Station, the lead cover of the single phase cables of No. 26 and No. 27 generators were short circuited by an iron rod, which might have led to one of the generators being completely put out of action; this was avoided only thanks to the vigilance of the workers.

7) On December 11, 1932, a breakdown occurred on turbine No. 2 at the Orekhovo Thermo-Power Station owing to hydraulic knocking effect in the turbine itself. On August 31, 1932, a breakdown occurred on turbine No. 1 at the Orekhovo Thermo-Power Station, owing to sharp variations in the load, the insufficient capacity of the end bearing and the absence of relief apertures. As a result of this, the turbine was put out of action

for eight or nine months. A similar breakdown occurred on turbine No. 2 at the beginning of February 1933.

As shown by the investigation, these breakdowns were caused by the wrecking work of the engineers *Sukhoruchkin, Krasheninnikov* and *Zorin* at the power station, acting in collusion with the employees of the Metropolitan-Vickers Company.

Sukhoruchkin, the son of a merchant, began work in the First Moscow Power Station in 1925 as engineer in the electric department, then as chief of the electro-technical department, and chief of the operation department.

On his own admission, he established connections with *Thornton* as early as 1927, systematically supplying him with information of an economic nature. In 1929, *Sukhoruchkin* began wrecking activities. *Sukhoruchkin* gave the following testimony on his counter-revolutionary work:

> "From the middle of 1929 in addition to giving various pieces of information... I kept quiet about a number of defects in the equipment supplied by the firm.... In 1931 I passed on to direct acts of diversion in accordance with the instructions given me by *Thornton* personally."

With the object of wrecking, *Sukhoruchkin* carefully hushed up all the organic defects discovered by him in the course of his work in the equipment supplied by the Metro-Vickers Company, and deliberately kept this equipment in a chronic state of inefficiency. Thus, he concealed the defects in the oil baffle plates in the front bearings of the generator, defects in the rotor leads of the generators, defects in the regulators, the transformers, etc.

Besides this, *Sukhoruchkin* engaged in direct diversion activities. At the end of 1931, as manager of the electric department, he, according to his own testimony:

> "At the direct instructions of *Thornton,* personally short-circuited the lead cover of the single-phase cables of generators No. 26 and No. 27 with an iron rod with the object of causing a breakdown on one of the generators of the First Moscow Power Station. This might have led to one of the generators being completely put out of action, and did not

bring about this result only because of the vigilance of the workers."

At the same time *Sukhoruchkin* and *Thornton* discussed a number of acts of diversion which they intended to carry out on a larger scale in case of war.

> "I had four such talks with *Thornton:* 1) in February 1930, when we examined the switch gear together; he showed me how easy it is to commit an act of diversion both in the bus department of the fifth switch house and in the cable tunnel of the station; 2) in October and December 1930, at the central sub-station, he showed me how it was possible to wreak havoc in the third storey of the fourth switch-board house, which could disrupt the supply of current to the centre of Moscow, and how it was possible to destroy various transformer banks of the central sub-station; 3) in October 1931, at the central sub-station, *Thornton* explained to me in detail the method of destroying the fifth switchboard either by causing a fire on the sixth and seventh floors above the switchboard, or by blowing up the bus department."

For carrying on wrecking and diversion work, *Sukhoruchkin* received about 2,000 rubles from *Thornton* in sums of two or three hundred rubles at various times, and in addition, 350 rubles in Torgsin checks.

Simultaneously with *Sukhoruchkin,* wrecking was also committed at the First Moscow Power Station by *Krasheninnikov,* chief of the installation and repair department of the station.

Krasheninnikov also commenced by concealing defects in the equipment, which in a number of cases led to breakdowns, to damage of machines and their stoppage. At the end of 1929 and the beginning of 1930 he came in contact with *Oleinik,* chief installation mechanic of the Metro-Vickers Company, who arrived at the First Moscow Power Station to install turbine No. 28 and who gave him 500 rubles on behalf of *Thornton* for his work, stating that *Thornton* expected him to continue his activities.

This sabotaging attitude towards his duties on the part of *Krasheninnikov* resulted in the concealment of defects in the turbine working wheel blades on turbines No. 26 and No. 27, which led to frequent stoppages of these turbines and a reduction of their working capacity by 20-25 per cent, as testified by the defendants themselves. It was precisely owing to this attitude to his duties on the part of Krasheninnikov that the blades which arrived from England were not tested. In February and in March 1933 these blades began to break, and this again caused a stoppage of the turbine for a long period. *Krasheninnikov* also concealed the defect in the regulating valves of the turbine owing to their not being thermically treated, which also led to a stoppage of the turbine and the necessity of putting the old turbines into operation. This, in its turn, led to an increased expenditure of oil fuel. He also concealed the defects in the construction in the packing of the circulation pump of turbine No. 27, which on May 10, 1931, led to the stoppage of this turbine; he concealed defects in the groove of the stem of the second regulating valve, which on April 29, 1932, led to this stem breaking away and to a reduction of the load of turbine No. 26 by 5,000 kw.; and he concealed the defective brazing of the oil pipe, which on December 9 led to the bursting of the pipe and the stoppage of the turbine.

Zorin, chief engineer of the steam turbine group, whose special duty it was to investigate the causes of breakdowns of the turbines and to protect the interests of "Mosenergo" in Electro-Import in the matter of making claims on foreign firms which have supplied turbines, under the influence of his anti-Soviet convictions, energetically carried on counter-revolutionary wrecking work.

Starting in 1931 by giving information to *Thornton* on the regulation of the turbines of other foreign firms competing with Metro-Vickers in the U.S.S.R. and the breakdowns that occurred on these turbines, he gradually passed on to giving information on the plan for the further development of the "Mosenergo" station and later pledged himself to conceal the defects in the equipment supplied to the U.S.S.R. by this firm.

Thornton prudently warned *Zorin* of the criminal work of

Sukhoruchkin and *Krasheninnikov* so that he would not expose their wrecking.

Like *Krasheninnikov, Zorin* also knew of the defects in the working blades on the rotors of turbines No. 26 and No. 27, and like him he concealed these defects, which led to a number of breakdowns.

Zorin carried on the same kind of work with regard to the Orekhovo Thermo-Power Station. In his testimony of March 26, 1933, *Zorin* states the following:

> "On December 11, 1931, a breakdown occurred on turbine No. 2 at the Orekhovo Thermo-Power Station owing to hydraulic knocking effect in the turbine itself. The rotor was damaged; as the rotor was taken out I examined it and assured myself that the end thrust bearing of the rotor was not strong enough for the rotor, which had no relief apertures; this could later cause an accident to the bearing without hydraulic knocking if there were sharp changes of load, which is always possible in operation owing to rushes of current. This inherent defect in the bearings was deliberately concealed by me, and on August 31, 1932, there was a breakdown on turbine No. 1 of the Orekhovo Thermo-Power Station, which had an end bearing similar to turbine No. 2, owing to sharp load variations, and the insufficient strength of the end thrust bearing together with the absence of relief apertures. As a result of this, the turbine was out of operation for eight or ten months. A similar breakdown occurred on turbine No. 2 at the beginning of February 1933, but with much smaller results, as only the segments of the bearing were fused and the turbine was only stopped for one day."

According to *Zorin,* he received a sum of 1,000 rubles from *Thornton* for the wrecking acts committed by him.

In this counter-revolutionary group of wreckers, a special role was played by *Oleinik,* chief installation mechanic of Metro-Vickers Company. According to his own words, he had worked with the Metro-Vickers firm for almost twenty years, with brief intervals, and had lived for a number of years in America and England.

> "My whole well-being was always connected with the British firm, Metro-Vickers," says *Oleinik* in his testimony. "I always counted on this firm for my future well-being."

Oleinik carried out wrecking work, but also undertook to organize agents for wrecking work, simultaneously serving as a connecting link between some of the employees of the Metro-Vickers Company and their agents on the spot.

Having set himself the aim of causing repeated breakdowns, so as to put out of operation the existing machines and groups, *Oleinik,* who worked on the installation and repair of equipment in many power stations in the Soviet Union, systematically concealed the defects in this equipment, thus making it impossible to take steps to avoid breakdowns.

At the same time, *Oleinik,* acting on instructions, deliberately delivered defective equipment to the power stations of the U.S.S.R., delaying by all possible means the process of testing the equipment supplied.

Information on the espionage work of *Oleinik,* carried out at the instructions of the defendant *Monkhouse,* will be given below.

VI

WRECKING AT THE BAKU ELECTRIC POWER STATION

There was also a number of cases of breakdown of turbo-generators supplied by Metro-Vickers at the Baku Electric Power Station.

An analysis of the reports on the breakdowns which took place at the Baku Electric Power Station on turbo-generators No. 11 and No. 12 supplied by Metro-Vickers made it necessary for the Commission of Experts to point out first of all the similarity that all the breakdowns occurred in the blades of the driving wheel, adapted to definite stages of the turbines.

> "The nature of the breakdowns," says the report of the Commission of Experts, "makes it possible to state that there

were inherent defects in the construction of the blades in a number of defective stages of both turbines. The blades deteriorated because of the premature fatigue of the metal of the blades, caused by resonant vibrations."

The Commission of Experts claims that:

> "The fact that the breakdowns were all of one type ought to have attracted the attention of the station staff and the representatives of the firm to the necessity of radically changing the construction of the parts of the turbine which were subject to defective stages. The insufficiently complete technical appraisal of the breakdowns set out in the first documents dealing with the breakdowns at the Baku Electric Power Station did not reveal their fundamental causes at the time of the investigation, and thus did not ensure that they would be promptly and properly eliminated. As a result of this, the breakdowns were resumed three days after the machines had been repaired."

To judge the conduct of the station staff and the representative of Metro-Vickers, the following conclusion of the Commission of Experts deserves special attention:

> "The first breakdowns registered on March 11, 1930, February 15, 1931, February 21, 1931, and March 22, 1931, were discovered only when turbine No. 11 was opened up for inspection before the machines were tested according to the contract, although, in view of the extent of the breakdowns which had occurred, it must be admitted that these breakdowns should have been accompanied by external signs—knocking in the cylinder of the machine, increased vibration, the loss of smoothness of rotation, which would have imposed the duty on the staff of the firm and the station staff who were working at the turbine to stop the machine immediately."

Regarding the breakdowns at the Baku Electric Power Station, *Oleinik* testified that:

> "At the end of 1928 a breakdown occurred on a turbine owing to a jet of water having got into the turbine."

When *Thornton* spoke to *Oleinik* in 1932, about diversion activities, according to *Oleinik,* he cited precisely this case of Baku as an example, pointing out that this breakdown was organized by the engineer *Cushny.* When confronted with *Cushny,* on March 13, 1933, *Oleinik* corroborated this.

In his turn, while corroborating the fact of the breakdown, *Cushny* denied that he gave any instructions to the installation mechanics to cause this breakdown, or that it happened deliberately under his direction.

However, it should be emphasized that the cause of the breakdown which occurred at Baku in 1927 was admitted by *Cushny* to be the injection of water into the turbine, which, according to the data of the Commission of Experts, could have taken place only as a result of malicious intent.

With regard to a number of such breakdowns and particularly the breakdown on March 11, 1930, the Commission of Experts called attention to the fact that this breakdown was not discovered until later on when turbine No. 1 was opened up for inspection before the machine was tested, and was not noticed in time, in spite of the fact that the extent of the damage was such that it must have been accompanied by such outward signs that should have compelled the staff to stop the machine immediately and make an inspection.

From the testimony of the witness, *I. S. Yemelyanov,* it is clear that *Cushny* spoke of the necessity of damaging the equipment and in particular the Red Star Power Station, so as to stop the work of the station and the development of the oil fields.

To describe the situation at the Baku Electric Power Station in 1930, reference may be made to report No. 006110, concerning the damage to the rotor and its defects, in which, among other things, it was pointed out that:

> "The very nature of the damage gives grounds for suspecting not only carelessness in carrying out the work, but also malicious intent."

* * *

But the role of *Cushny* was not restricted to wrecking work at the Baku Electric Power Station, because *Cushny* and the other engineers of Metro-Vickers who are charged in the present case systematically engaged in espionage.

On this question, *MacDonald* stated in his deposition on March 12:

> "The leader of the reconnaissance work in the U.S.S.R. disguised under the shield of Metropolitan-Vickers was *Mr. Thornton,* who worked in Moscow in the representation of the firm as chief erecting engineer. The head of the representation was *Mr. Monkhouse* who also took part in this illegal work of *Mr. Thornton.* The assistant of *M. Thornton* for travelling purposes and his associate in the espionage work was engineer *Cushny,* officer of the British army, now an engineer of the firm Metropolitan-Vickers. This is the main grup of reconnaissance workers which did the espionage work in the U.S.S.R."

When *Thornton* was confronted with *Cushny* on March 22, they both admitted that *Cushny* had collected and transmitted to a certain place not only information which might interest the firm from a strictly business point of view, but also such as could be utilized for certain political purposes. The character of the information gathered on the instructions of *Thornton* has been sufficiently explained above, in connection with the Zlatoust Electric Power Station.

In addition to the above-mentioned, it should be added that, as was discovered when *Cushny* was confronted with *Emelyanov* on March 23, 1933, *Cushny* had given small sums of money to Baku workers in return for information, and had also treated them to drinks at his own expense.

When *Cushny* was informed of the facts accusing him of espionage, he refused to reply to questions which were put to him, refused also to give the reasons for his refusal, and refused to give the names of the citizens of the U.S.S.R. who had collected espionage intelligence for him.

Anna Sergeyeva Kutuzova was secretary of the Metro-Vickers office in Moscow from 1927 on. As established by the circumstances of the case and by the depositions of *Kutuzova* herself, she was there treated on a confidential footing and was conversant with all the counter-revolutionary work of the engineers of this firm. According to *Kutuzova's* testimony, she was invited to work in the Metro-Vickers office by the firm's representative, *Monkhouse,* whose acquaintance she had made at the beginning of 1927 at Volkhovstroy, where she was working at the time. In April 1927 she was put on the firm's office staff.

In 1929 the office of Metro-Vickers, which had previously been in Leningrad, was transferred to Moscow to the premises of Electro-Import. *Kutuzova* also came from Leningrad to Moscow and took up her residence in a villa at Perlovka, where all the Englishmen working for the Metro-Vickers firm lived. Later they ceased to conceal their spying and diversion work from her.

The accused *Kutuzova* testifies as follows:

> "As early as 1930 I began to notice that in addition to business connected with the interests and tasks of the firm. *Thornton, Cushny, MacDonald, Monkhouse* and other employees in the firm's office were engaged in some kind of illegal work. They had secret conversations with some Soviet citizens, often locked themselves up in their private office, made secret notes, etc."

As a result of several years of work in the Metro-Vickers office, *Kutuzova,* according to her own depositions, came, as early as 1930,

> "to the conclusion that all these people were engaged in economic and political espionage and sent the information collected by them to England."

Taking advantage of her position, *Kutuzova* decided to find out from *Thornton* the nature and objects of this illegal work.

> "I began to ask *Thornton,*" *Kutuzova* states, "and at first he told me in general terms that in addition to his work with Metro-Vickers, he also had other tasks of a secret nature. After this I continued to question him. At length *Thornton* told me that he and the other English engineers were collecting secret information of a political and economic nature through the medium of Russian engineers and technicians recruited by them, to whom they paid money for this.

As was established by the circumstances of the case, *Kutuzova* also participated directly in paying the engineers and technicians who were engaged in espionage and acts of diversion. For example, on the instructions of *MacDonald,* she sent a parcel to *Gussev* at Zlatoust, putting a fictitious sender's address with the fictitious name, *Ivanova.*

When confronted with *Thornton, Kutuzova* confirmed that she was aware of a whole series of acts of espionage and diversion by the British and Russian engineers and stated that the expenses for the remuneration of the Russian engineers and technicians who supplied secret information had been recorded by *Thornton* not in the office books, but in his notebooks which he took to England in December 1932.

> "Only one payment to the amount of 3,000 rubles was entered in the office books," *Kutuzova* stated. "*Thornton* gave this sum to *Dolgov.* It was entered under the heading 'suspense account.' "

Kutuzova's testimony was fully corroborated by an inspection of the suspense account in the books of the Moscow office of Metro-Vickers and also by the interrogation of *Monkhouse,* who confirmed that bribes were entered in the books in this manner.

A. N. Dolgov, office manager of Electro-Import, called as a witness, confirmed the fact that he had received the money, which he immediately handed over to the O.G.P.U.

In her further testimony, *Kutuzova* mentioned the names of a number of people working under the instructions of *Thornton,* and particularly mentioned *Vitvitsky, Gussev, Zorin, Sukhoruchkin* and others of the accused in the present case.

When questioned about the participation of the British engineers in acts of diversion, *Kutuzova* stated:

> "Several times I heard *Thornton* and *Monkhouse* planning to damage the turbines at the Nizhni, Zuevka, Leningrad and Baku power stations and saying that the turbines should be damaged through hired persons, by dropping various extraneous objects into the parts of the turbines."

Passing on to the question of who directed the espionage and acts of diversion committed by *Thornton* and the other employees of the firm, *Kutuzova* testified:

> "I suppose that *Thornton* and the other workers in the firm's office gave their information to *Richards* and carried on their espionage under him. I drew this conclusion from the fact that when *Richards* came over, secret talks were held with him, and besides this, *Thornton* and *Monkhouse* mentioned the name *Richards* in their secret conversations."

As established by the investigation, the man *Richards* mentioned by *Kutuzova* is the managing director of the export department of Metro-Vickers in England.

According to *Kutuzova's* testimony the directors of espionage and acts of diversion in the U.S.S.R. were *Thornton,* whose criminal activity has been characterized above, and *Monkhouse.*

In investigating the latter circumstances by interrogating *Monkhouse* and others, it was established—and *Monkhouse,* when questioned in the office of the Public Prosecutor of the Republic on March 25, 1933, confirmed this—that he had:

> "received information relating to the work of our firm as well as to the general conditions in the Soviet Union and the state of big constructions which are carried out in the U.S.S.R.

As *Monkhouse* pointed out, *Richards* expected this information from him. As a motive for gathering this information, *Monkhouse* points out that

> "this information might be interesting to the firm."

Monkhouse confirmed that he:

> "considered it possible to receive this information from employees of the Metropolitan-Vickers Co. as well as from conversations with Russian engineers."

Monkhouse admitted that:

> "Among the members of our Soviet office such information was chiefly supplied by *Messrs. Thornton* and *Cushny* who often travelled and visited the sites."

Monkhouse confirmed that he was *Thornton's* accomplice in bribing *Dolgov,* head of the control department of Electro-Import:

> "I took part in writing off the sum of 3,000 rubles given as a bribe to *Dolgov* by *Thornton,*" *Monkhouse* stated.

The 3,000 rubles given as a bribe to *Dolgov* by *Thornton,* according to *Monkhouse,* were later entered in the books as business expenses, in accordance with the instructions of the above-mentioned *Richards,* who came to Moscow and was informed of this bribe.

5) *Monkhouse* admitted that there were grave defects which caused serious breakdowns in the machines installed by the staff of Metro-Vickers in a number of power station in the U.S.S.R.—Moscow, Ivanovo, Chelyabinsk, Zuevka, Baku, *i.e.,* in the very electric power stations where the wrecking and spy groups connected with various employees of the Metro-Vickers office *(Thornton, Cushny, Nordwall, Oleinik* and *MacDonald)* were at work.

Monkhouse only denies:

1) His participation in gathering information bearing the character of State or military secrets;

2) Complicity in giving bribes for hushing up defects in the equipment installed by the employees of the Metro-Vickers office in Moscow; and

3) Complicity in the organization of damage to equipment and the organization of breakdowns in the electric power stations of the U.S.S.R.

However apart from bare denials, *Monkhouse* could not rebut the facts disclosed by the investigation.

The accused *Thornton* gives an adequate idea of the nature of the information collected and its purpose when he deposes:

> "By *Mr. Richard's* request information regarding political condition inside the country is obtained through the Metropolitan-Vickers personnel resident in different parts of the country and passed to him orally by *Monkhouse* or myself. Usually *Mr. Richards* asked for information on the political state of certain districts and suggested that this information might be obtained through the staff. We in turn," continues

Thornton, "requested our staff to obtain as much information as possible. . .

"Spying operations on U.S.S.R. territory were directed by myself and *Monkhouse* . . ."

Monkhouse's denial that he had taken part in bribing the Russian engineers and technicians to conceal defects in the equipment is contradicted by *Monkhouse's* own admission of his complicity in giving a bribe to *Dolgov* as a person who could act in the interest of the firm when placing orders for equipment and when making claims on the firm connected with defects discovered in the equipment.

Among the other employees of Metro-Vickers, who gave bribes, according to the statement of *Thornton,* there was also the engineer *Albert William Gregory.*

In connection with facts of this nature discovered by the investigation, the investigating authorities proceeded to examine more closely the pasts of *Monkhouse* and *Thornton* and established that:

1) Before the revolution, *Monkhouse* had lived a long time in tsarist Russia, having arrived in 1911 as installation engineer for the firm of Dick Kerr and Company.

After the October Revolution, *Monkhouse* went to Vladivostok and thence to London.

In the summer of 1918, during the first intervention, he was sent with the second British Expeditionary Force that was dispatched to Archangel to fight against the Bolsheviks, serving in the interventionist army as captain of engineers.

Richards served in the same Expeditionary Force with the rank of captain in the Intelligence Service.

Monkhouse left Archangel for London, together with the British troops.

Regarding his relations with *Richards,* he deposed:

> "With him I am acquainted and I am on friendly terms with him since 1913; we often met each other and he often visited me. *Mr. Richards* I met in 1917 in Moscow and later on in Archangel, where he, as I confirm, occupied the position of captain of the Intelligence Service. It is known to

me that *Mr. Richards* was in Moscow in April or May 1918. I do not know what for he came to Moscow but I know from what he told me that he secretly crossed the frontier to Finland at that time.

In 1923 he was appointed a director of the Metropolitan-Vickers Electrical Export Co. In the same year he went to Moscow for negotiations about supplying of equipment."

Monkhouse has worked with Metro-Vickers since 1919. In the autumn of 1924, as an employee of Metro-Vickers, he came to the U.S.S.R. again as representative of the firm, directly under the control of the afore-mentioned *Richards.*

2) *Thornton* is the son of the owner of a big woollen mill and big textile mills; he was born in Russia and educated abroad.

In 1911 *Thornton* returned to Moscow, where he worked with the same firm as *Monkhouse, viz.,* Dick Kerr and Co.

In 1918, he left for England via Vladivostok together with *Monkhouse.*

In 1924 he was engaged by *Richards* on behalf of Metro-Vickers specially for work in the U.S.S.R., where he arrived in 1924.

*

* *

In the course of the preliminary investigation, the Public Prosecutor of the R.S.F.S.R. instituted proceedings under articles 58-6, 58-7, 58-9 and 58-11 of the Criminal Code of the R.S.F.S.R. against the following persons:

1. *Vitvitsky, Nikolai Petrovich*
2. *Gussev, Vassily Alexeyevich*
3. *Gregory, Albert William*
4. *Zivert, Yuri Ivanovich*
5. *Zorin, Nikolai Grigoriovich*
6. *Krasheninnikov, Michael Dmitrievich*
7. *Kotlyarevsky, Moisei Lvovich*
8. *Kutuzova, Anna Sergeyevna*
9. *Cushny, John*
10. *Lebedev, Vyacheslav Petrovich*
11. *Lobanov, Alexander Timofeyevich*

12. *MacDonald, William Lionel*
13. *Monkhouse, Allan*
14. *Nordwall, Charles*
15. *Oleinik, Peter Yeremeyevich*
16. *Sukhoruchkin, Leonid Alexeyevich*
17. *Thornton, Leslie Charles*
18. *Sokolov, Vassily Andreyevich*

As regards the other members of the counter-revolutionary group of wreckers, mentioned in the indictment and prosecuted in this case under article 221, point B, of the Criminal Code of the R.S.F.S.R., further investigation is being made.

On the basis of the foregoing and by virtue of a decision of the Presidium of the Central Executive Committee of the U.S.S.R. the following are committed for trial before the Special Session of the Supreme Court of the U.S.S.R., on the following charges, respectively:

I. *Vitvitsky, Nikolai Petrovich;* 35 years of age; born in Odessa; mechanical engineer; graduated from the Kronstadt Engineering School; married; sentenced in 1921 to five years' imprisonment for participation in the whiteguard Kronstadt mutiny; released on amnesty, State employee, is charged as follows: that he, *Vitvitsky,* having joined a counter-revolutionary wrecking group in 1927, in Zlatoust, which operated at the Zlatoust works, and having later in 1931 in Chelyabinsk become the head of a counter-revolutionary group operating in the Chelyabinsk Power Station which group set itself the aim of undermining the power of Soviet industry and weakening the Soviet Government by disorganizing electric power production, by committing acts of wrecking and diversion and preparing for wide-spread acts of diversion in the event of war, committed the following acts in pursuance of the aims of this group:

1) Between September 1931 and July 1932 in Chelyabinsk, while acting as chief engineer at the Chelyabinsk Power Station, he entered into contact in July 1932 with the British citizen *Thornton,* the representative of the British firm, Metropolitan-Vickers, and under his instructions personally participated and procured the participation of other engineers in the preparation of plans for acts

of diversion and particularly the plan to effect a major act of diversion at the Chelyabinsk Power Station, having the aim of putting the chief turbines out of action at the moment of the expected war against the U.S.S.R.;

2) At the same time and place he took part in carrying out acts of diversion consisting in deliberately causing breakdowns which had the result of disorganizing the normal work of the station and interrupting the supply of current to factories; in particular he took part in carrying out the following acts of diversion:

a) A serious breakdown at the end of 1931 owing to a short circuit at the Stroitel Works, which is connected with the power station; this affected the switch gear of the station, as a result of which the feeder current transformer burned out, the arc extended to the switch gear of the house installation and the whole load of the station was disconnected;

b) A breakdown of the chain grate motors in the spring of 1932 owing to a short circuit of the 220 volt cable feeding the motors, as a result of which the whole load of the station was temporarily disconnected;

c) At the same time and place he directed the wrecking activities at the Chelyabinsk Power Station with the object of delaying the construction of the station and the work of organizing its operation so that the work should proceed amidst difficulties and interruptions in the supply of current to the factories, and received bribes for these acts amounting to the sum of 6,900 rubles, including 4,900 rubles received from *Thornton* through *Gussev*, *i.e.,* crimes coming under articles 58-7, 58-9 and 58-11 of the Criminal Code of the R.S.F.S.R.

II. *Gussev, Vassily Alexeyevich;* 35 years of age; born in Penza; single; higher technical education; not previously convicted; State employee, is charged as follows: that in 1930-32, while serving as chief of the Zlatoust Electric Power Station and being a member of a counter-revolutionary group which pursued the aim of undermining the power of Soviet industry and weakening the Soviet Government:

1) He, on the instructions of *MacDonald,* an engineer of the

British firm Metro-Vickers, organized and directed a counter-revolutionary group of wreckers in Zlatoust, pursuing the aim of disorganizing the work of the Zlatoust Power Station and disrupting the supply of current to the local factories by wrecking;

2) He systematically gathered secret information of State and military importance and transmitted it to *MacDonald;*

3) Both personally and through the agency of members of the counter-revolutionary group organized by him—*Sokolov* and others—he committed a number of acts of diversion and wrecking, damaging the equipment and causing breakdowns at the Zlatoust Power Station;

4) In return for his spying, wrecking and acts of diversion, he systematically received bribes from MacDonald, part of which he handed over to the members of the counter-revolutionary group headed by him;

5) On the instructions of the aforesaid *MacDonald,* he, at various times handed over to *Vitvitsky,* engineer of the Chelyabinsk Power Station, sums of money for wrecking work and acts of diversion committed by the latter at the Chelyabinsk Power Station, *i.e.,* crimes coming under articles 58-7, 58-9 and 58-11 of the Criminal Code of the R.S.F.S.R.

III. *Gregory, Albert William,* 52 years of age; married; born in England; graduated from a technical university; British subject, is charged with being a member of a counter-revolutionary group of wreckers while working in the U.S.S.R. since 1932 as installation engineer of the British firm Metro-Vickers, and with systematically collecting secret information of State and military importance and transmitting it to *Thornton, i.e.,* crimes coming under articles 58-6 and 58-11 of the Criminal Code of the R.S.F.S.R.

IV. *Zivert, Yuri Ivanovich,* 50 years of age; born in the former Courland Gubernia; fitter; elementary education; no previous convictions; a State employee, is charged as follows: that, in the period from June 1930 to July 1931, while working at the Ivanovo Power Station as a foreman for the installation of transformers and oil circuit-breakers, he systematically conveyed to *Thornton,* a British engineer, certain secret information appertaining to new orders for electric equipment and the condition of the Ivanovo

Power Station, and in addition, on the instructions of the aforesaid *Thornton,* deliberately carried out installation work in a manner calculated to wreck the same, which later caused a series of breakdowns at the Ivanovo Power Station; at the same time with the object of causing acts of diversion, he permitted copper dust to penetrate into the commutator while it was being turned, as a result of which the segments became short-circuited, windings broke down and the converter was put out of action; further, for his acts of wrecking and diversion he received 500 rubles from *Thornton* as a bribe, *i.e.,* crimes coming under aticle 58-6, 58-7, 58-9 and 58-11 of the Criminal Code of the R.S.F.S.R.

V. *Zorin, Nikolai Grigorievich;* 59 years of age; higher education; mechanical engineer; married; not previously convicted; State employee; charged as follows: that, while serving as chief engineer of the thermo units in the turbine department of "Mosenergo," and carrying out, parallel with this, various assignments on matters connected with the repair of turbines, the investigation of causes for, and the protection of the interests of "Mosenergo" in, making claims on foreign firms, and being a participant in a counter-revolutionary group working at the orders of *Thornton,* an engineer in the Metro-Vickers office in Moscow, with the object of undermining the normal work of the power stations of the Moscow Region throughout 1931-32,

1) He, at the First Moscow Power Station and the Orekhovo Thermo-Power Station, carried out a series of measures of wrecking, concealing inherent defects in the equipment supplied by Metro-Vickers, which led to systematic breakdowns at these stations, reduced the efficiency of the equipment, increased operating costs and led to the loss of compensation claims;

2) He received, in the beginning of November 1932, 1,000 rubles from *Thornton* for his wrecking work, *i.e.,* crimes coming under articles 58-7 and 58-11 of the Criminal Code of the R.S.F.S.R.

VI. *Krasheninnikov, Michael Dmitrievich;* 35 years of age; born in the village of Novoye in the former Vladimir Gubernia; electrical engineer; married; not previously convicted; State employee, charged as follows: that while successively occupying the posts of foreman of machine shop, chief of the machine department and head of the installation and repair department of the

First Moscow Power Station and being a participant in a counter-revolutionary group acting under the instructions of *Oleinik* and *Thornton;* he, during 1928-32, committed a number of wrecking acts at the First Moscow Power Station, concealing inherent defects in the equipment supplied by the Metro-Vickers firm, and also deficiencies in the installation of this equipment, which led to systematic breakdowns at the station, reduced the efficiency of the equipment, increased operating costs and led to the loss of compensation claims, for which he received 500 rubles from *Thornton* through *Oleinik* at the beginning of 1930, *i.e.,* crimes coming under articles 58-7 and 58-11 of the Criminal Code of the R.S.F.S.R.

VII. *Kotlyarevsky, Moisei Lvovich;* 29 years of age; of middle class origin; from Odessa District; mechanical engineer; married; not previously convicted; State employee, is charged as follows: that, while acting as head of the turbine department of the Zuevka Power Station and participating in a counter-revolutionary group acting at the orders of *MacDonald* throughout 1931-32:

1) He deliberately concealed inherent defects in the electrical equipment supplied by the Metro-Vickers firm for the Zuevka Power Station, which led to systematic breakdowns, reduced the efficiency of the equipment at the station, increased operating costs and caused the loss of compensation claims;

2) At various times he received bribes to the amount of 1,000 rubles from *MacDonald* for his wrecking work, *i.e.,* crimes coming under articles 58-7 and 58-11 of the Criminal Code of the R.S.F.S.R.

VIII. *Kutuzova, Anna Sergeyevna;* 37 years of age; daughter of an artisan; secondary education; not previously convicted; is charged with having, in the period from 1927-33, while employed in the office of Metro-Vickers as secretary, been a member of a counter-revolutionary group carrying on wrecking, spying and acts of diversion in the electric power stations of the U.S.S.R., in addition to which, acting on the instructions of *Thornton* and other British engineers, she systematically made money payments to *Gussev* and other Russian engineers and technicians for their work of espionage and wrecking, *i.e.,* crimes coming under articles 58-6 58-7, 58-9 and 58-11 of the Criminal Code of the R.S.F.S.R.

IX. *Cushny, John;* 35 years of age; born in Johannesburg. South Africa; shareholder in the British firm, Metro-Vickers; British subject; graduate of a technical university; ex-officer of the British Army; is charged with having ,in the period 1929-33, while working in a number of power stations in the U.S.S.R. as installation engineer, and having been a member of a counter-revolutionary group committed the following acts:

1) He systematically undertook economic and military espionage, gathered secret information of State and military importance through the agency of a group of Soviet engineers and technicians;

2) At the Baku Power Station he organized acts of wrecking and diversion intended to damage the equipment and cause breakdowns, giving corresponding instructions to various Russian engineers and technicians;

3) He deliberately installed improperly and dishonestly electrical equipment supplied by Metro-Vickers, which later caused a series of breakdowns at the aforementioned station;

4) He systematically paid various sums of money to various Russian engineers and technicians for spying and acts of wrecking and diversion, *i.e.*, crimes coming under articles 58-6, 58-7, 58-9 and 58-11 of the Criminal Code of the R.S.F.S.R.

X. *Lebedev, Vyacheslav Petrovich;* 52 years of age; born in Ivanovo-Voznesensk; secondary education; ex-sergeant-major; married; State employee; is charged as follows: that, in the period from March till October 1931, being a foreman of the Ivanovo Power Station, he committed the following acts:

1) He was a member of a counter-revolutionary group at the Ivanovo Power Station, which, acting under the direction of engineer *Lobanov,* pursued the counter-revolutionary aims set out above;

2) He systematically caused deliberate damage to equipment, thus causing breakdowns in a number of units of the Ivanovo Power Station;

3) For his wrecking activities and acts of diversion, he received a bribe of about 900 rubles from *MacDonald* through *Lobanov, i.e.,* crimes coming under articles 58-7, 58-9 and 58-11 of the Criminal Code of the R.S.F.S.R.

XI. *Lobanov, Alexander Timofeyevich;* 35 years of age; born in the former Vladimir Gubernia; son of a factory owner; graduated from a technical university; married; not previously convicted; State employee, is charged as follows: that, in 1931-32, while being head of the operation department of the Ivanovo Power Station, and acting on the instructions of *Nordwall,* an English engineer;

1) He organized and headed a counter-revolutionary wrecking group in the Ivanovo Power Station consisting of *Lebedev, Ugrumov* and others, and together with them systematically committed a number of acts of wrecking and diversion intended to damage the electrical equipment of the station and cause breakdowns, reducing the efficiency of the station;

2) At various times he received bribes amounting in all to 5,000 rubles and a fur coat from *Nordwall* for his acts of wrecking and diversion, *i.e.,* crimes coming under articles 58-7, 58-9 and 58-11 of the Criminal Code of the R.S.F.S.R.

XII. *MacDonald, William Lionel,* 29 years of age; born in London; son of an engineer; graduate of a technical university; British subject, is charged as follows: that, in 1930-32-33, while working as installation engineer for the British firm, Metro-Vickers, at the electric power station in Zlatoust and at the Zuevka Power Station, he participated in a counter-revolutionary group:

1) Acting on the instructions of *Thornton,* the chief installation engineer of the said firm, he gathered secret information of State and military importance at Zlatoust, the Zuevka Power Station and the Chelyabinsk Power Station and also information concerning the production of munitions at the above-mentioned places, through the agency of a group of Soviet engineers and technicians—*Gussev, Sokolov, Vassiliev* and others;

2) He gave direct instructions to various Soviet engineers and technicians—*Gussev, Sokolov, Vassiliev* and others, to commit acts of diversion and wrecking with the object of damaging equipment and causing breakdowns, which instructions were later carried out and led to a number of breakdowns at Zlatoust, the Chelyabinsk Power Station and the Zuevka Power Station;

3) He systematically gave bribes of various sums amounting

in all to about 10,000 rubles to certain Soviet engineers and technicians for carrying on espionage, acts of diversion and wrecking and also for concealing the defects in the equipment supplied by Metro-Vickers, *i.e.,* crimes coming under articles 58-6, 58-7, 58-9 and 58-11 of the Criminal Code of the R.S.F.S.R.

XIII. *Monkhouse, Allan,* 46 years of age; born in Stratford, New Zealand; son of a farmer; ex-captain of engineers in the British Army; graduate of a technical university; married; British subject, is charged as follows: that, in the period from 1927 to 1932, while working in the U.S.S.R. as representative of the British firm, Metro-Vickers, and being a member of a counter-revolutionary group pursuing the above-mentioned counter-revolutionary aims:

1) He gathered secret information of State and military importance through the agency of a number of British engineers subordinate to him and also through a number of Russian engineers and technicians;

2) He participated in acts of wrecking and diversion of the aforementioned counter-revolutionary group;

3) He systematically paid various sums of money to Soviet engineers and technicians for espionage and committing acts of diversion and wrecking;

4) He systematically gave bribes to Russian engineers for concealing defects in the equipment supplied by Metro-Vickers; *i.e.,* crimes coming under articles 58-6, 58-7, 58-9 and 58-11 of the Criminal Code of the R.S.F.S.R.

XIV. *Nordwall, Charles;* born in Berlin; son of an engineer; higher technical education; married; British subject, is charged as follows:—that, in 1931-32, while working at the Ivanovo Power Station as installation engineer for the British firm, Metro-Vickers, he belonged to a counter-revolutionary group of wreckers;

1) He gave instructions to a group of engineers and technicians of the Ivanovo Power Station—*Lobanov* and others—to carry out acts of wrecking and diversion at the Ivanovo Power Station for the purpose of damaging equipment and causing breakdowns, which instructions were carried out:

2) He systematically gave to *Lobanov, Lebedev* and others working at the Ivanovo Power Station bribes through the agency

of *Lobanov* amounting to 5,000 rubles for acts of diversion and wrecking and also for concealing defects in the electrical equipment supplied by Metro-Vickers, *i.e.,* crimes coming under articles 58-7, 58-9 and 58-11 of the Criminal Code of the R.S.F.S.R.

XV. *Oleinik, Peter Yeremeyevich;* 52 years of age; born on the Perekrestovschitsa farm, former Poltava Gubernia; secondary education; installation mechanic on turbines; married; not previously convicted; charged as follows: that while working as chief installation mechanic of Metro-Vickers in Moscow, at the same time belonging to a counter-revolutionary group and acting under the instructions of *Thornton* and *Monkhouse,* engineers of this firm, with the intent of undermining the normal work of the power stations of the U.S.S.R. from 1928 to 1932:

1) He systematically collected secret information of State and military importance and transmitted it to the accused *Thornton;*

2) In a number of electric power stations in the U.S.S.R. he committed acts of wrecking, concealed inherent defects in the equipment supplied by the Metro-Vickers firm and also the defective installation of this equipment, which led to systematic breakdowns at the power stations, reduced the efficiency of the equipment, increased operation costs and led to the loss of compensation claims;

3) He promoted organizational work in recruiting wrecking agents for the aforementioned counter-revolutionary organizations;

4) In return for his spying and wrecking work, he was enabled to open a current account in a British bank in London to which he secretly transferred 2,000 rubles and into which account 10 pounds per month were paid for his work, *i.e.,* crimes coming under articles 58-6, 58-7 and 58-11 of the Criminal Code of the R.S.F.S.R.

XVI. *Sukhoruchkin, Leonid Alexeyevich;* 39 years of age; born in the village of Novo Pavlovsk, North Caucasus; son of a merchant; electrical engineer; married; State employee, charged as follows: that while successively occupying the positions of chief of the electro-technical department and chief of the operation department of the First Moscow Power Station, participating in a counter-revolutionary group and acting on the instructions of

Thornton, engineer of the Metro-Vickers office in Moscow, with the object of undermining the normal work of the electric power stations of the Moscow Region in the period 1928-32:

1) He, at the First Moscow Power Station, carried out a number of wrecking measures, concealing defects in the equipment supplied by Metro-Vickers and also the defective installation of this equipment, which led to systematic breakdowns at the station and reduced the efficiency of the equipment, increased operation costs and led to the loss of compensation claims;

2) At the end of 1931, with the object of causing a breakdown on one of the generators of the First Moscow Power Station, he committed an act of diversion, deliberately short circuiting the lead sheath of the single-phase cables of generators No. 26 and No. 27 with an iron rod, the result of which would have been the putting of one of the generators out of action, this being avoided only by the vigilance of the workers;

3) At various times he received bribes from *Thornton* to the amount of 2,500 rubles in Soviet currency and 350 rubles in Torgsin checks for his wrecking activities and acts of diversion, *i.e.*, crimes coming under articles 58-7, 58-9 and 58-11 of the Criminal Code of the R.S.F.S.R.

XVII. *Thornton, Leslie Charles;* born in 1887 in Leningrad; son of a big manufacturer; married; British subject, is charged as follows: that in the period from 1928-33, while working in the U.S.S.R., as chief installation engineer of the British firm, Metro-Vickers, and belonging to a counter-revolutionary group which pursued the above-mentioned counter-revolutionay aims:

1) He collected secret, technical information of State and military importance through the agency of a number of Russian engineers and technicians;

2) Both personally and through the British engineers, *MacDonald, Cushny* and others subordinate to him, he systematically gave instructions to a number of Soviet engineers and technicians to carry out wrecking activities and acts of diversion with the object of damaging equipment and causing breakdowns, which wrecking and acts of diversion were later carried out in a number of electric power stations in the U.S.S.R.;

3) He systematically bribed a number of engineers and tech-

nicians—*Gussev, Zorin, Sokolov* and others—paying them for spying, wrecking and acts of diversion and also for concealing defects in the equipment supplied by the Metro-Vickers firm, *i.e.*, crimes coming under articles 58-6, 58-7, 58-9 and 58-11 of the Criminal Code of the R.S.F.S.R.

XVIII. *Sokolov, Vassily Andreyevich;* 33 years of age; born in the village of Aksino, Birsk district, Bashkir Autonomous Soviet Socialist Republic; son of a handicraftsman; graduated from the Zlatoust Technical School and the class of electro-mechanics of the Military School, electro-mechanic; married; State employee, is charged as follows: that having joined in the summer of 1930 in Zlatoust a counter-revolutionary group operating at the Zlatoust works under the direction of the chief of the power station, engineer *Gussev,* which pursued the above-mentioned counter-revolutionary aims by means of disorganizing the electric power station through methods of wrecking, espionage, acts of diversion and the preparation of extensive acts of diversion in case of war against the U.S.S.R. in pursuance of these aims:

1) He, as assistant chief of the power station at the Zlatoust works, having got in touch with *MacDonald,* the installation engineer of the British firm, Metropolitan-Vickers, on the instructions and with the assistance of the engineer *Gussev,* conveyed to *MacDonald* secret information of State and military importance in the summer of 1930;

2) In the same place, in Zlatoust, in the period from summer 1930 to autumn 1932, on the instructions and under the direct guidance of *Gussev,* he participated in, and personally committed acts of diversion, causing a number of breakdowns at the factory, in particular:

a) from May to August 1932, he caused five breakdowns on the biggest motor in the plant (1,400 h.p.) by incorrectly fixing the ventilation of the motor;

b) together with engineer *Gussev* he helped to cause breakdowns of the oil circuit breakers and connecting links at the power station;

3) By systematic wrecking, in accordance with the instructions of *Gussev* and jointly with him, he prepared a number of acts of diversion with the object of putting the power station out of action

and depriving the works of electric current at the moment of external political difficulties for the Soviet Union anticipated by the counter-revolutionary group, in particular the following acts of diversion:

a) damaging electric fittings—the main leads, transformers, oil circuit breakers;

b) damaging and putting out of action turbo-generators in the turbine room;

c) putting the feed units and boilers out of action and delaying the stoking in the boiler house;

4) In the same place, in Zlatoust, from the summer 1930 up to the moment of his arrest, on the instructions of *Gussev* and jointly with him, he carried out systematic wrecking in the electrical equipment of the plant for which he received a bribe of 1,000 rubles, *i.e.*, crimes coming under articles 58-6, 58-7, 58-9 and 58-11 of the Criminal Code of the R.S.F.S.R.

The present indictment is confirmed by:

April 8, 1933.

[Signed] A. J. VYSHINSKY
Public Prosecutor of the
Russian Socialist Federative Soviet Republic

Approved: KRASIKOV
Public Prosecutor of the
Supreme Court, U.S.S.R.

*
* *

The President: Accused Gussev, do you plead guilty to the formulated accusations?

Gussev: Yes, I plead guilty.

The President: Sit down, please. Accused Sokolov, do you plead guilty?

Sokolov: Yes, I do.

The President: Accused MacDonald, do you plead guilty?

MacDonald: Yes, I do.

The President: Accused Kotlyarevsky, do you plead guilty?

Kotlyarevsky: Yes, I do.

The President: Accused Lobanov, do you plead guilty on all counts?

Lobanov: I do, on all counts.

The President: Accused Gregory, do you plead guilty?

Gregory: Not guilty.

The President: Accused Zivert, do you plead guilty?

Zivert: I plead fully guilty.

The President: Accused Krasheninnikov, do you plead guilty?

Krasheninnikov: I plead fully guilty.

The President: Accused Thornton, do you plead guilty?

Thornton: Not guilty.

The President: Not on any count?

Thornton: No.

The President: Accused Sukhoruchkin, do you plead guilty?

Sukhoruchkin: Yes, I do.

The President: Accused Zorin, do you plead guilty?

Zorin: Yes, I do.

The President: Accused Monkhouse, do you plead guilty?

Monkhouse: Not guilty on any count.

The President: Accused Oleinik, do you plead guilty?

Oleinik: Yes, I do.

The President: Accused Nordwall, do you plead guilty?

Nordwall: Not guilty.

The President: Accused Kutuzova, do you plead guilty?

Kutuzova: Yes, I do.

The President: Accused Cushny, do you plead guilty?

Cushny: Emphatically not guilty on any count.

The President: Accused Lebedev, do you plead guilty?

Lebedev: Yes, I do.

The President: I have a question to ask the Public Prosecutor as to the mode of procedure. Have you any concrete proposals to make?

Vyshinsky: I suggest the following procedure. First, to examine the facts set forth in the indictment in connection with the Zlatoust Power Station, then the Chelyabinsk Power Station, then the Zuevka Power Station, then the Ivanovo Power Station, then "Mosenergo," the Baku Power Station and finally, the examination of the activity of the Moscow office of Metro-Vickers as represented by those of the accused who are charged in this case: Kutuzova, Monkhouse and Thornton. I propose to examine the accused in the following order: in connection with the Zlatoust Station: Gussev, Sokolov, MacDonald, Thornton; in connection with the Chelyabinsk Station: Gussev, Vitvitsky, Oleinik and Thornton; in connection with the Zuevka Power Station: Kotlyarevsky and MacDonald; in connection with the Ivanovo Power Station: Lobanov, Nordwall, Lebedev, Zivert; in connection with the "Mosenergo": Sukhoruchkin, Krasheninnikov, Zorin and Thornton; in connection with the Baku Power Station: Oleinik, MacDonald and Cushny. Thereupon I propose the following order: Kutuzova, Monkhouse and Thornton.

The President: Has the Defence any objection to this?

The Defence: No objection.

The President: The Court approves this procedure proposed by the Public Prosecutor.

(At 3:30 p.m. the Court adjourns till 6 p.m.)

[Signed] V. V. ULRICH
President of the Special Session of the Supreme Court of the U.S.S.R.

A. F. KOSTYUSHKO
Secretary

EVENING SESSION, APRIL 12, 1933, 6:15 p.m.

Commandant: Rise, please, the Court is coming.

The President: Please be seated. The session is resumed. Accused Gussev. [*Gussev comes to the witness stand.*] The court has no questions to put to Gussev just now. Has the Prosecution any questions?

Vyshinsky: Yes, if you please. Citizen Gussev, will you be kind enough to tell us your biography in brief.

Gussev: I was born in 1898, in the city of Penza, in the family of a railroad foreman. Shortly after my birth, two or three years later, my father together with his family moved to the city of Zlatoust. There in Zlatoust with the exception of a few short intervals I passed my whole life.

Up to 1918 I studied—first in an elementary city school, then in a grammar school and then in a secondary technical school.

Vyshinsky: From what school did you finally graduate?

Gussev: I graduated in 1922 from the Zlatoust Practical Institute.

Vyshinsky: What branch?

Gussev: This institute issued diplomas for electrical installation engineers.

Vyshinsky: And since 1922 you have been engaged in practical work?

Gussev: Yes.

Vyshinsky: What posts have you occupied and where?

Gussev: I graduated from the Institute in 1922 and went to work at the power station of the Zlatoust works, first as assistant foreman, which post I filled for a year.

Vyshinsky: Who was the chief of the station at that time?

Gussev: Engineer Morganov. Then I was senior foreman for

two years, I do not remember exactly how long. After that I was assistant to the chief of the station also for about two to two and a half years. And since March 1929 I have worked in the capacity of chief of the station up to the moment when I was arrested, to January 24, 1933.

Vyshinsky: As chief of the power station, what have you been managing? All the departments or any special department?

Gussev: The power station combined all the power installation of the works. I had charge of the power station, the blast engine station which fed air to the blast furnaces, then the water supplying station and the lowering transformer sub-station for getting the current from the Chelyabinsk Power Station.

Vyshinsky: Consequently, all the power installations of the Zlatoust Power Station were in your charge?

Gussev: I had charge of all the power installations of the Zlatoust Metallurgical Works.

Vyshinsky: Were the power station and the Zlatoust Metallurgical Works organically combined from the point of view of management and technique?

Gussev: This was the power station of the works; territorially it was situated in the centre of the works.

Vyshinsky: Have the Metallurgical Works been supplied by any station other than this one?

Gussev: Since October or November 1930 the Zlatoust Mechanical Works passed over to the use of energy from the Chelyabinsk Power Station, but up to that moment all the three plants in Zlatoust were fed by the Zlatoust Power Station.

Vyshinsky: Entirely?

Gussev: Yes.

Vyshinsky: Tell us, where were you in 1918, after the October Revolution?

Gussev: In 1918? At that time I went to the White army without having graduated from the Secondary Technical School.

Vyshinsky: To the White army, where?

Gussev: I joined the Volunteers' Training Company of the 22nd Zlatoust Regiment.

Vyshinsky: Did you enter the Training Company as a volunteer, or was it the Volunteers' Training Company that you entered?

Gussev: I joined the Volunteers' Training Company as a volunteer.

Vyshinsky: You were not conscripted?

Gussev: No.

Vyshinsky: How do you explain that? Why did you join the Kolchak army at that time? How old were you then?

Gussev: I was twenty years old.

Vyshinsky: How was it to be explained? Why did you take that step?

Gussev: It came as a result of my convictions and the sentiments which I had at that time.

Vyshinsky: How could you characterize these convictions in a few words?

Gussev: As hostile to the October Revolution.

Vyshinsky: What have you to say about your services in the ranks of the White army?

Gussev: During that period I served in the White army for about five months. I left the army owing to bad eyesight. During that period I took part in fighting.

Vyshinsky: Against . . .?

Gussev: Against the Red Army during the offensive in the Ufa Gubernia: in the Zlatoust uyezd, in Birsk uyezd. Afterwards, owing to bad eyesight I was discharged from the army and I took advantage of this discharge to complete my course in the secondary school.

Vyshinsky: Where?

Gussev: In Zlatoust. After that I went to work at the Zlatoust Mechanical Works as constructor in the machine-building department. Here I worked for several months, as owing to the advance of the Red army, the Zlatoust plant, was evacuated to the city of Tomsk.

Vyshinsky: And you?

Gussev: I evacuated with the Whites also to Tomsk.

Vyshinsky: What year was that?

Gussev: 1919.

Vyshinsky: Thus, in the period of 1918-19, you were part of the time in the White army, part of the time outside, at any rate you were on the territory which was occupied by Kolchak?

Gussev: Yes.

Vyshinsky: Did you continue to work at this plant in Tomsk?

Gussev: In Tomsk there was practically no opportunity to work because after its transfer to Tomsk the plant could not develop its work.

Vyshinsky: What did you do then?

Gussev: I and a number of my comrades were discharged from the factory owing to lack of work.

Vyshinsky: And then?

Gussev: Then I was again conscripted by the White army.

Vyshinsky: That means that from the plant you again went into the White army? Was that by conscription or voluntarily?

Gussev: By mobilization. In the first armoured-car training division. There I served from August to the beginning of December 1919.

Vyshinsky: What posts did you occupy in this armoured-car division?

Gussev: I was private in a platoon of automobile drivers. They had courses there which prepared drivers.

Vyshinsky: And did you complete the course?

Gussev: I almost completed it but I did not go through the practical school of driving. At that time I had the rank of technician-mechanic.

Vyshinsky: But a technician-mechanic is not a driver. Apparently you went through other drivers' courses?

Gussev: I went through the drivers' courses of the armoured detachment. They were attached to the First Armoured-Car Training Division.

Vyshinsky: That means that you also took a special military course?

Gussev: This course was organized by the division.

Vyshinsky: You completed the course, and what then?

Gussev: At that time Omsk fell. The front moved to the east and came nearer to Tomsk. Tomsk was already being evacuated.

Vyshinsky: And your unit?

Gussev: I, together with my unit, began to retreat further east.

Vyshinsky: Were there any battles, did your unit at that time participate in battles?

Gussev: No.

Vyshinsky: Now how was that, did it only retreat?

Gussev: Yes.

Vyshinsky: How far did you retreat?

Gussev: From Taiga station to the east, about 200 to 250 kilometres.

Vyshinsky: Then?

Gussev: Then I and two of my comrades deserted from the column.

Vyshinsky: Where to?

Gussev: To the woods.

Vyshinsky: Why? Perhaps you will first tell us of whom this column consisted?

Gussev: There were officers.

Vyshinsky: There were officers everywhere, but what officers?

Gussev: White officers.

Vyshinsky: Perhaps there were foreign detachments?

Gussev: No, our column did not contain any foreigners. The foreigners were retreating along another route.

Vyshinsky: What are the motives, under what circumstances did you desert?

Gussev: The situation of the White army was absolutely hopeless.

Vyshinsky: The situation was hopeless and therefore you deserted?

Gussev: Yes.

Vyshinsky: If the situation had been hopeful, in that case, we might say, you would have remained?

Gussev: I cannot say at present how I would have acted.

Vyshinsky: At any rate you deserted because you saw that it was hopeless?

Gussev: This I can say.

Vyshinsky: And what were your ideological impulses? Perhaps they were shaky? Perhaps your White convictions began to assume other colours?

Gussev: To tell the truth I cannot say that my convictions changed sharply. It is true that those facts, those scenes which I witnessed during the retreat, that to a certain extent they. . .

Vyshinsky: What scenes?

Gussev: I saw the whipping of peasants.

Vyshinsky: By whom?

Gussev: By Polish Legionaries. I saw shootings of peaceful inhabitants.

Vyshinsky: By whom?

Gussev: Also by them. I saw the maltreatment of peaceful citizens.

Vyshinsky: On whose part?

Gussev: Also on the part of the Polish Legionaries.

Vyshinsky: And did this influence your convictions?

Gussev: My anti-Soviet sentiments and my hostility lost something of their sharpness. Although, of course, I cannot say at present that this hostility disappeared entirely.

Vyshinsky: The sharpness of your hostility was softened and you deserted. Where did you desert to?

Gussev: At first, in order not to be caught by our people and shot, we proceeded again eastward away from the column. After we had walked for some time, we simply turned into the woods, and there, far away from the highways, we lived in a forest hut for two weeks until the arrival of the Red Army. When the front crossed the place where we had been staying we went to the commissar of one of the Red Army regiments; we were examined and after the examination we were set at liberty.

Vyshinsky: What year was that?

Gussev: December 1919.

Vyshinsky: Where did you go then?

Gussev: I returned to Zlatoust, which at that time was in the hands of the Red Army.

Vyshinsky: What was your occupation there?

Gussev: I entered the Practical Institute.

Vyshinsky: Again to study?

Gussev: Yes, again to study.

Vyshinsky: For the third time. You went to study in the intervals between your fighting activity?

Gussev: Yes, this was the third period.

Vyshinsky: How long did you study then?

Gussev: Two and a half years. In the autumn of 1922 I graduated from the Practical Institute as candidate for engineer.

Vyshinsky: Where did you go then?

Gussev: I went to work at the Zlatoust Metallurgical Works, at the power station.

Vyshinsky: In what capacity?

Gussev: At first in the capacity of assistant foreman.

Vyshinsky: What were your political views at that time? After you had studied for two and a half years and the sharpness of your former experiences had somewhat softened, during that period, what were your political views and your attitude towards Soviet reality, towards the revolution?

Gussev: My views and convictions remained essentially the same as before.

Vyshinsky: That is?

Gussev: That is, anti-Soviet and counter-revolutionary.

Vyshinsky: So during these two and a half years the environment in which you found yourself, the circumstances under which you lived, all that you had seen during the civil war did not confirm the change in you, which to a certain degree was manifesting itself when you deserted from the Whites to the Reds, but on the contrary your anti-Soviet views became strengthened. You even called them counter-revolutionary. Under what influence did this happen? What were the causes?

Gussev: Obviously there were no causes which would make me entirely change my former convictions.

Vyshinsky: Well, so we might say that essentially the impressions which made you desert the Whites for the Reds were entirely fleeting, casual and transitory, and did not affect your convictions at the root.

Gussev: On the whole, I cannot say that my convictions have changed diametrically. Fundamentally, these convictions remained.

Vyshinsky: So, fundamentally, the line of your political convictions had remained the same during all this period of time from 1918 practically up to the day of your arrest?

Gussev: Fundamentally, yes.

Vyshinsky: So, fundamentally, your convictions have been the same with slight deviations dependent on various circumstances —when the cause of the Whites is hopeless you desert, when you remain in your old environment your old sentiments remain. Do I understand correctly?

Gussev: Almost so.

Vyshinsky: During the period, when you became assistant to the chief of this Zlatoust station, that is, from 1925 to 1929 and then from 1929 up to the date of your arrest, during which time you were chief of the Zlatoust station, did the people with whom you were coming in touch influence your attitude towards Soviet reality and in what way? Or, did you remain outside of politics, entirely neutral, indifferent to questions of political importance?

Gussev: During this time also I associated primarily with people with anti-Soviet sentiments.

Vyshinsky: For instance—concretely?

Gussev: Some of these people were subsequently convicted for wrecking activities.

Vyshinsky: Who are they?

Gussev: For instance, Shalayev, Bogoslovsky, and others.

Vyshinsky: You have associated with this circle. Has that influenced in any way your attitude to the Soviet Government and towards socialist construction?

Gussev: Of course this did not change my anti-Soviet convictions, they remained the same as before.

Vyshinsky: They remained the same as before? Did they become stronger, or did they remain the same as before?

Gussev: At this moment I must say that they became stronger.

Vyshinsky: Is it precisely under the influence of this environment that they became stronger?

Gussev: Under the influence of this environment.

Vyshinsky: How did it happen that you turned to more active counter-revolutionary work? What was the stimulus? In connection with what did you make yourself active, and in what form has the activization of your counter-revolutionary work taken?

Gussev: I must count the beginning of my active counter-revolutionary work from the moment when I started to engage in espionage work.

Vyshinsky: In what year?

Gussev: At the beginning of 1930.

Vyshinsky: Perhaps a little earlier. More exactly?

Gussev: No, it was in 1930.

Vyshinsky: At the beginning of 1930. What circumstances made you engage in such an honourable business—espionage?

Gussev: At that time, in December 1929, I became acquainted with MacDonald, the engineer of the English firm, Metropolitan-Vickers.

Vyshinsky: Under what circumstances?

Gussev: Engineer MacDonald arrived at Zlatoust to install the turbo-generator of the firm, Metropolitan-Vickers, in the power station which I managed. Our first acquaintance was on a business basis because I had charge of this installation.

Vyshinsky: As chief of the station?

Gussev: As chief of the station. As I said, we met on a business basis, then I received an invitation from engineer MacDonald to visit him. Our acquaintance became more intimate. The conversations which we carried on at that time concerned not only business but touched upon general political questions.

Vyshinsky: In particular, what questions were these?

Gussev: In particular, these were questions concerning the living conditions of the technical intelligentsia and in general the rights enjoyed by the technical intelligentsia. Then questions of industry.

Vyshinsky: What do you mean by questions of industry?

Gussev: To be more exact, questions of industrialization.

Vyshinsky: What do you mean, questions of industrialization, to be still more exact?

Gussev: The question of the development of heavy machine building in the Soviet Union, of its own industry in general, large-scale industry.

Vyshinsky: This subject is quite understandable. But what was the anti-Soviet character of these conversations?

Gussev: The anti-Soviet character of the conversations consisted in that, while touching upon the living conditions of the technical intelligentsia, we talked about how badly it fares under the Soviet regime.

Vyshinsky: This is understandable. Well, regarding industrialization, what was the nature of the anti-Soviet conversations in this case?

Gussev: We were saying that the Soviet Union does not need to develop its own machine building industry.

Vyshinsky: Does not need. And you thought so?

Gussev: I shared these views.

Vyshinsky: Very well, and did the matter stop at this, or did your acquaintance with MacDonald become more intimate, or, on the contrary, did you not go beyond these little talks?

Gussev: Our acquaintance became more intimate in the course of time and later it turned into and assumed a shade of friendship.

Vyshinsky: So you state now that you established relations of friendship with MacDonald, but how much time was required for these relations to become friendly?

Gussev: About two to two and a half months.

Vyshinsky: What did these friendly relations lead to further?

Gussev: They led to my receiving proposals from engineer MacDonald to give him information on the production of the Zlatoust works.

Vyshinsky: What proposals did MacDonald make to you?

Gussev: They were formulated by him as proposals to furnish him information on the functioning of the Zlatoust works.

Vyshinsky: Concretely, what information?

Gussev: Subsequently I gave . . . .

Vyshinsky: I am not interested in what you gave but in what information was required of you. Tell us first what was proposed to you.

Gussev: To give information concerning the electric supply of all plants.

Vyshinsky: Including the mechanical works?

Gussev: Including the Zlatoust Mechanical Works which produces munitions.

Vyshinsky: That means, works of military significance?

Gussev: Of military significance. Then also on the work of the metallurgical plant which produces automobile and tractor springs, aeroplane steel, steel for ball-bearings, *i.e.*, high grade steels.

Vyshinsky: For what purpose are these used?

Gussev: They are used in munition works.

Vyshinsky: That is, both in the first and in the second instance it was a matter of information concerning war munitions?

Gussev: Yes. This was the scope of the questions on which it was proposed to me to furnish information.

Vyshinsky: In the material of the preliminary investigation it is said that it was proposed to you that you should furnish information concerning the output of shells.

Gussev: I have already said what I meant when speaking of the production of the Mechanical Works.

Vyshinsky: When you speak of the production of the Mechanical Works, do you mean everything including the production of shells?

Gussev: Yes.

Vyshinsky: Did MacDonald ask for that information too?

Gussev: He said that he needed information on the quantity of shells produced, on the types of the shells and on the expansion of the output of shells.

Vyshinsky: Did MacDonald put these questions of a military nature at the very beginning of your acquaintance, or later, when your friendly relations had been strengthened?

Gussev: At first I furnished information on power supply, then I passed over to information of the kind I have just mentioned.

Vyshinsky: This is the way I understand it: first there was general information and then military information?

Gussev: Correctly speaking, when I gave information on power supply I was giving information on the power supply of the departments producing munitions, consequently I gave information of a military nature.

Vyshinsky: I understand.

Vyshinsky: Permit me to interrupt the questioning of Gussev and to put one question to MacDonald.

The President: Certainly.

Vyshinsky: Accused MacDonald. You heard the testimony of Gussev? Do you corroborate what he said regarding your acquaintance in 1929?

MacDonald: Regarding our acquaintance, yes.

Vyshinsky: You corroborate that during this time, from 1929 and on, your relations with Gussev were of friendship, of intimacy?

MacDonald: From 1930 on.

Vyshinsky: You did indeed ask Gussev to furnish you the information of which he just spoke?

MacDonald: Yes, in my personal interests.

Vyshinsky: Perhaps you will explain more exactly what you mean by your own interests? Did you ask Gussev for information on the power supply?

MacDonald: I did.

Vyshinsky: Military information?

MacDonald: I did.

Vyshinsky: This is all I wanted.

The President: Sit down.

Vyshinsky: Permit me to proceed with Gussev. So originally your counter-revolutionary activity, starting with the year 1930, was expressed in gathering information which you have now qualified as espionage. Correct?

Gussev: Yes.

Vyshinsky: Was your counter-revolutionary activity confined to the gathering of this and similar information, or did you choose some other forms of counter-revolutionary activity besides? In such case, what were these forms?

Gussev: Having entered upon this road I went further and subsequently I was given and carried out the task of engineering breakdowns of equipment in the Zlatoust works.

Vyshinsky: Tasks of engineering breakdowns? Now, did you figure on carrying out these tasks single-handed or in company with others?

The President: The accused has not said on whose orders?

Vyshinsky: I am not putting this question for the time being. What I want to find out now is: did Gussev figure on carrying out the task of engineering breakdowns single-handed or with the complicity of other persons?

Gussev: These breakdowns were carried out with the assistance of other persons. One of the accused in this case, Vassily Andreyevich Sokolov, at first my assistant and then electrical engineer, participated in bringing about the breakdowns; then the works foreman, Patrin; then Nikolai Matveyevich Rossman took part in concealing the traces or rather the true causes of the breakdowns....

Vyshinsky: How did it happen that these persons, particularly Sokolov, came to be in your group, in your company?

Gussev: Sokolov, like myself, took part in this work under the influence or rather on the proposal of engineer MacDonald.

Vyshinsky: How do you know that?

Gussev: When I discussed with engineer MacDonald the plan which I had outlined for causing breakdowns and when the question arose of the means of carrying out the plan, among those who could be utilized, MacDonald named this Sokolov. Afterwards, Sokolov took part in working out the plan and in discussing it.

Vyshinsky: With whom?

Gussev: With me.

Vyshinsky: Did you propose this to him or did he propose it to you?

Gussev: I proposed it to him.

Vyshinsky: Why did you propose to him to discuss the plan?

Gussev: I said that on the one hand I received information or a communication from MacDonald that Sokolov could be used for this work. This was sufficient for me to bring him to participate in working out this plan.

Vyshinsky: And you began to discuss this plan?

Gussev: Yes.

Vyshinsky: What did this plan consist of?

Gussev: When I agreed to engineer breakdowns this task was subsequently concretized in the following manner: I was to cause such breakdowns as a result of which it would be possible to curtail or to stop entirely the production of shells and non-firing weapons at the Zlatoust works. In order to carry out this kind of task I mapped out the course of disrupting the power supply and, on the other hand, of putting out of commission the large-shaping rolling mill in the rolled steel department. This motor set into motion . . .

Vyshinsky: Is this the 1,400 h.p. motor?

Gussev: Yes.

Vyshinsky: Why did you choose this motor?

Gussev: I chose this one because the open hearth department turns out ingots weighing 1,000 tons. This ingot is shingled on the large-shaping rolling mill and then it comes to the other mills in the form of billets for refining.

Vyshinsky: We are not all technicians here. Tell us what part did this rolling mill play in the production of munitions?

Gussev: When this rolling mill is not working then all the other mills which turn out finished products including shell billets and automobile and tractor springs cannot work either.

Vyshinsky: On what did the work of this mill depend?

Gussev: The mill was set in motion by the 1,400 h.p. motor.

Vyshinsky: Consequently it was your plan to strike at this motor?

Gussev: This motor, yes.

Vyshinsky: By striking at this motor you hit also at the mill and at the production of munitions?

Gussev: Yes, and at the production of munitions.

Vyshinsky: This is clear. Now, how did you decide to accomplish this thing?

Gussev: At the time when the question of putting the rolling mill out of commission was discussed, the plan was not yet definitely outlined. It was indicated that the motor must be put out of commission. Subsequently this question was decided according to the circumstances. At present I can only say in what manner this motor was put out of commission.

Vyshinsky: Please.

Gussev: In 1932, in the month of April, during the control inspection of this motor I left a small piece of sheet iron in the ventilation intake of the motor. Then I went away. Subsequently, when the motor was set in motion, this piece was sucked into the air gap, as a result of which there occurred a displacement of a part of the iron of the stator and rotor. This displaced iron passed into the mechanite bushings where the windings of the stator are located which caused the perforation in the insulation of the windings of the stator.

The first time the motor was put out of commission owing to wrong repairing or rather owing to the circumstance that the displacement of the iron occurred in several places along the circumference of the stator and was not eliminated. There were several such breakdowns.

Vyshinsky: So it appears to have been thus: You started by leaving a certain iron object in this motor. As a result there occurred a displacement in the iron of the stator, *i.e.,* of the stator iron. Following this . . . ?

Gussev: Following this there occurred a perforation in the insulation of the windings of the stator.

Vyshinsky: What were the consequences of this?

Gussev: The motor being put out of commission for a period (I do not remember exactly at present) of six, seven, eight days.

Vyshinsky: As a result it turned out that the motor was put out of commission for a certain number of days?

Gussev: Yes.

Vyshinsky: Was this act the first act of wrecking which you carried out at that period?

Gussev: No, it was not the first act from the point of view of time.

Vyshinsky: That means that some others preceded it?

Gussev: Yes.

Vyshinsky: Why did you not start with them?

Gussev: I thought that you so put the question that I should tell about this breakdown which I caused at the large-shaping rolling mill.

Vyshinsky: And a number of other breakdowns preceded it?

Gussev: Yes, a number of breakdowns at the power station.

Vyshinsky: Of what character?

Gussev: During the winter of 1931-32—the freezing of boiler No. 8 at the power station, putting the coal conveyor out of commission also at the power station, and finally (this cannot be referred to a definite time, it was carried on over a long period) delaying the setting up of boiler No. 11 and delaying the converting of the Sterling boilers Nos. 1 and 2.

Vyshinsky: That means we can count now a whole series of these wrecking acts. If I begin from the end, then it is: one, Sterling boilers Nos. 1-2; then two, intentionally delaying the setting up of the U.M.T. boiler No. 11; three, sabotage in the form of conscious intentional dismantling of the coal conveyor. Further?

Gussev: Boiler No. 8.

Vyshinsky: The freezing of boiler No. 8 by not closing the damper. Then the 1,400 h.p. motor. And after this a series of still other breakdowns caused by the incorrect arrangement of the ventilation.

Gussev: Yes, there were more breakdowns which were caused by myself and by Sokolov.

Vyshinsky: These were more the speciality of Sokolov?

Gussev: Yes, and that is why I did not dwell on that.

Vyshinsky: So during this time no less than about ten intentional breakdowns and damagings were caused at the power station. Is this correct?

Gussev: Yes, I caused several breakdowns at the power station and in the rolled steel department during this period.

Vyshinsky: So. Now tell us, please, these breakdowns were not engineered by you single-handed, but also, as you said, by Sokolov. Is that correct?

Gussev: Yes.

Vyshinsky: (Turning to the President) Perhaps I may be permitted to put one question to Sokolov?

The President: Certainly.

Vyshinsky: Accused Sokolov, do you corroborate this or not?

Sokolov: Yes, I corroborate it.

The President: Regarding the breakdowns?

Sokolov: Yes.

Vyshinsky: Now I have a question to put to MacDonald. Do you corroborate Gussev's testimony in this part?

MacDonald: I do.

Vyshinsky: (to Gussev): Accused Gussev, were you doing that as an enemy of the Soviet Government, as an enemy of socialist construction, or were you doing that owing to material incentives, or owing to both?

Gussev: Since I received money for the breakdowns caused by me it follows that I did not do it purely from ideological motives. However, I must confess that the basic motive was my convictions.

Vyshinsky: And the one not basic?

Gussev: This was the material side of it.

Vyshinsky: Was this a sort of paid supplement to your convictions, or what?

Gussev: This formulation does not change the essence of the matter.

Vyshinsky: It is important for me to know whether money has played a part in this or not; whether money matters were involved or not; whether you were given bribes for this or not?

Gussev: I was paid.

Vyshinsky: From whom did you receive money?

Gussev: From engineer MacDonald.

Vyshinsky: How much did you receive?

Gussev: During the whole period I was connected with him I received at various times remunerations amounting to about 3,000 rubles.

Vyshinsky: At various times?

Gussev: Yes.

Vyshinsky: Did Sokolov receive money through you or directly, if he received any? Did Sokolov receive any?

Gussev: I do not know whether he received any outside of the money that he received from me. I only can say that he received money once through me.

Vyshinsky: From the amount which you received from whom?

Gussev: From engineer MacDonald.

Vyshinsky: When MacDonald gave you this money how did he explain the payment?

Gussev: At the very beginning when it was proposed to me to engage in this work I was told that the work would also be paid. And afterwards I received this money as a remuneration for me personally and for those people who participated in this work.

Vyshinsky: How much were you receiving in your capacity as chief of the station?

Gussev: At what time?

Vyshinsky: During that period.

Gussev: I find it hard to remember.

Vyshinsky: What I am interested in is whether the question of material gain was of any importance to you or whether it was secondary.

Gussev: At the moment of my arrest I was receiving 800 rubles, and at that time 500-600 rubles. I have no family and therefore the material side did not play any particular role in my case.

Vyshinsky: MacDonald, when he gave you that money, what did he say?

Gussev: He said that the money was for myself and to pay those people who participated in carrying out the work.

Vyshinsky: Accused MacDonald, do you corroborate Gussev's testimony in this part or not?

MacDonald: I gave him money.

Vyshinsky: How much?

MacDonald: About 2,500 rubles.

Vyshinsky: Where did you get it?

MacDonald: From the firm. From the Moscow office.

Vyshinsky: From whom personally?

MacDonald: Through chief engineer Thornton.

Vyshinsky: Now let us proceed. Tell us how you produced the breakdown of the coal conveyor?

Gussev: It was indicated in the plan of disrupting the power supply to put the coal conveyor out of commission. This was carried out in the following manner: the motor which starts the skip-hoist and the belt conveyor was on several occasions installed by me incorrectly. As a result of this incorrect installation the foundation was broken. Then I introduced a piece of a metal gear into the cylindrical transmission. Owing to this the foundation was smashed.

Vyshinsky: The foundation or the transmission?

Gussev: Both the foundation and the transmission.

Vyshinsky: Why did you find it necessary to do this.

Gussev: I said already that putting the coal conveyor out of commission stops the feeding of coal to the boiler room. Consequently it brought about the disruption of the power supply of the Zlatoust plants. This was the most convenient way in the sense that it meant swift action.

Vyshinsky: And simplicity?

Gussev: And simplicity.

Vyshinsky: Both swift and simple? Tell us, when you decided on this question were you not afraid as to whether you would succeed in carrying out the smashing of the coal conveyor so simply and smoothly?

Gussev: Of course there were apprehensions, there were also waverings.

Vyshinsky: Caused by what?

Gussev: Caused by the fear that all this activity might be found out.

Vyshinsky: Comparatively easily.

Martens: Describe how you did it?

Gussev: The installation is situated above, on the bunkers. The mechanic in charge has charge of two motors, one above and one below, the one below at the crusher and the one above which I put out of commission. When there was nobody near the motor, when the mechanic went down, I inserted in it a piece of metal, a piece of round iron.

Vyshinsky: What then—you damaged the foundation and the transmission—and then?

Gussev: Then I gave orders to dismantle the mechanism of the coal conveyor and I reported to the management of the works that this coal conveyor was out of commission and that the whole mechanism must be rebuilt. I proved this to the management of the works and I received permission for the rebuilding.

Vyshinsky: What prompted this action—reporting to the management of the works, getting permission, and so on?

Gussev: It was prompted by the same motives, *i.e.,* I wanted to have this coal conveyor out of commission for a sufficient long period.

Vyshinsky: Very well, but you were the chief of the power station, from whom then did you ask permission?

Gussev: I had no independent right to dismantle the coal conveyor and to rebuild it since this was connected with the expenditure of means for alterations.

Vyshinsky: What then finally happened to this coal conveyor?

Gussev: It was dismantled. I ordered a design for rebuilding it and at present I cannot be exact about it because before my arrest the coal conveyor was still dismantled.

Vyshinsky: When did the first dismantling take place?

Gussev: It was in 1931.

Vyshinsky: When were you arrested?

Gussev: During the night of January 25, 1933.

Vyshinsky: That is, from 1931 to January 1933 this coal conveyor was dismantled?

Gussev: It was dismantled.

Vyshinsky: Why did you not succeed in assembling it? Owing to any insurmountable technical difficulties or owing to some other circumstances?

Gussev: I already said that this was a wrecking act engineered by me.

Vyshinsky: I understood it this way: That first you smashed the foundation, then the transmission, then you used this as a pretext and started rebuilding the coal conveyor and you dismantled it but did not rebuild it, and you dragged the matter out over a period of about two years. That means that there was not one wrecking act but a whole series of them. At first smashing the foundation, then the conscious wrecking proposal for rebuilding the coal conveyor, then the dismantling of the coal conveyor and finally leaving it dismantled for two years. Do I understand it right?

Gussev: Yes, I said that I put the coal conveyor out of commission, and all the rest was conscious action on my part directed towards destroying.

Vyshinsky: Of what significance was this coal conveyor for your power supply?

Gussev: Without normal feeding with coal, without adequate feeding, no normal work of the power station is possible.

Vyshinsky: Besides this coal conveyor, was there any other at the station?

Gussev: There were two coal conveyors.

Vyshinsky: One was working?

Gussev: One was working.

Vyshinsky: The other was dismantled?

Gussev: Yes.

Vyshinsky: What was the significance of the withdrawal of one coal conveyor?

Gussev: One was insufficient.

Vyshinsky: With the dismantling of the second coal conveyor you had an insufficient feeding of the power station. Do I understand correctly?

Gussev: The boiler room of the power station got an inadequate quantity of coal.

Vyshinsky: Consequently, the station was fed more weakly than was necessary. Necessary for what, for full load or for normal?

Gussev: For normal.

Vyshinsky: But the station was working at full load?

Gussev: Not at full load.

Vyshinsky: Consequently, by taking away the second coal conveyor you immediately lowered the work of this station?

Gussev: It did not work at full power.

Vyshinsky: Thus, what active significance for the fate of your electric power station had the breakdown of the second coal conveyor?

Gussev: The second part of the wrecking carried through by me consisted in the fact that according to the plan for mobilization, the Zlatoust works was to pass over completely to being supplied with energy from the power station at which I was working, but in that case the power station would not provide the quantity of energy which was necessary.

Vyshinsky: Consequently, we come up against the same military question. Am I to understand it so?

Gussev: Yes.

Vyshinsky: That is to say, in destroying the second coal conveyor you acted in the direction of weakening the producing capacity for war purposes?

Gussev: Yes.

Vyshinsky: And you thereby achieved your aims?

Gussev: I did.

Vyshinsky: The plan consisted in this?

Gussev: Yes.

Vyshinsky: You worked out this plan with Sokolov, or was there somebody else as well who took part in the working out of this plan?

Gussev: Sokolov took part in the details of the working out of this plan and in certain parts of the plan. After that I communicated the plan in its entirety....

Vyshinsky: To whom?

Gussev: To engineer MacDonald.

Vyshinsky: Engineer MacDonald discussed this plan?

Gussev: He did.

Vyshinsky: Consequently, this plan was worked out and discussed by you with Sokolov and MacDonald?

Gussev: Primarily by these three persons.

Vyshinsky: One question to MacDonald. Accused MacDonald, do you or do you not confirm the evidence of Gussev that the plan for dismantling the coal conveyor was known to you?

MacDonald: It was not known to me.

Vyshinsky: Did Gussev discuss it with you?

MacDonald: No.

Vyshinsky: But he told you about it?

MacDonald: I heard about it afterwards.

Vyshinsky: You heard about it afterwards?

MacDonald: Yes.

Vyshinsky: When?

MacDonald: When I met him.

Vyshinsky: And you were acquainted with this question?

MacDonald: It was news to me.

Vyshinsky: When you met him and he had told you, then from that time you were acquainted with the question?

MacDonald: Yes.

Vyshinsky: And until then you knew nothing?

MacDonald: No.

Vyshinsky: But Gussev maintains that you did know. *(To Gussev.)* Perhaps you remember where you discussed this, under what circumstances?

Gussev: This plan was discussed several times in the apartment of Vassily Vassilievich MacDonald, afterwards in my apartment and further this plan was again discussed on the arrival of engineer Thornton in Zlatoust. Thus engineer MacDonald knew the whole plan.

Vyshinsky: This whole plan concerned only the coal conveyor, or something else as well?

Gussev: Under the plan I understood all the plans for breakdowns, *i.e.,* the coal conveyor, boilers Nos. 1 and 2, boiler No. 8, boiler No. 11, the 1,400 h.p. motor in the rolled steel department and, further, a whole number of separate equipments.

Vyshinsky: You assert that this whole plan in its whole extent was known to MacDonald?

Gussev: Yes, I do assert this.

Vyshinsky: In regard to the 1,400 h.p. motor MacDonald confirms it, but in regard to the coal conveyor, MacDonald says he only learned about this when it was told to him.

Gussev: No, he knew before.

Vyshinsky: Very well, we will go on to the other breakdowns.

Gussev: The breakdown of boiler No. 8 was carried out in the winter of 1931-32—the month I do not exactly remember—it was January or December. The boiler was left with water in it in a very cold period and the damper on the flue was not closed. Cold air got into the interior of the boiler. In consequence, the super-heater and part of the tubes of the boiler were frozen.

Vyshinsky: What happened as a result?

Gussev: As a result the boiler went out of commission and there was a prolonged repair. The time needed for repair I do not exactly remember, but it was more than one and a half months.

Vyshinsky: This was also included in your plan?

Gussev: Yes, I already said so.

Vyshinsky: The Sterling boilers Nos. 1 and 2 and the boiler No. 11—what happened to them?

Gussev: Boilers Nos. 1 and 2 were altered for pulverized fuel. The installation was carried out by the Rema firm. This installation, thanks to the measures which I undertook, was dragged out for two to two and a half years.

Vyshinsky: How long was it dragged out?

Gussev: The whole process of this work occupied about two years.

Vyshinsky: They began to re-install the coal conveyor but they did not finish it—two years passed. The Sterling boiler could not be repaired during two years, and the boiler No. 11 . . . ?

Gussev: This was a new boiler, the mounting of it extended over a period of two years.

Vyshinsky: It comes to this, that whatever you undertake is dragged out for two years. Why was it that matters were so ordered, or more correctly, so disordered during two years?

Gussev: I find it difficult to answer anything to this question because I can say that it was brought about by me, but why precisely two years . . . .

Vyshinsky: Perhaps it was two years because you did not succeed in making it three years and perhaps it will become three years if your substitutes have remained on the spot. You dragged this out deliberately and consciously, or was it dragged out owing to circumstances not depending on you?

Gussev: I have already said that the delay in the mounting of boilers Nos. 1 and 2 and also No. 11 was foreseen in the plan of breakdowns, as also boiler No. 8. All this was brought about by me.

Vyshinsky: All this you produced consciously and deliberately according to the plan which you had then worked out?

Gussev: Yes.

Vyshinsky: But the other breakdowns such as the putting of the oil switches out of commission? Were you connected with that? That was not your speciality?

Gussev: I know that there were such breakdowns. I knew of the carrying through of these breakdowns but I did not take any immediate part in their execution.

Vyshinsky: They were included in the plan?

Gussev: They were.

Vyshinsky: According to the plan who had to carry them out?

Gussev: Sokolov had to carry them out.

Vyshinsky: But your plan was not overfulfilled, was it?

Gussev: You must ask Sokolov.

Vyshinsky: We will question Sokolov in due course. Consequently, the oil switches were also put out of commission according to your plan. Is that so?

Gussev: Yes.

Vyshinsky: I have no more questions.

The President: Has Comrade Roginsky any questions?

Roginsky: Yes. You mentioned three lines of your counter-revolutionary wrecking work. In the first place, the collection of information of a secret character. Is that so?

Gussev: Yes.

Roginsky: Next, the organization and carrying through of damage to machinery.

Gussev: Yes.

Roginsky: And, finally, a third line—this was the delay in the mounting of various equipment with the object of holding up the extension of the Zlatoust Power Station.

Gussev: Yes.

Roginsky: Besides these lines, what kind of functions in addition were imposed on you as a member of the counter-revolutionary group for causing breakdowns in the Zlatoust Power Station?

Gussev: Besides this I also served as a connecting link between different persons who were connected with MacDonald.

Roginsky: Consequently, there was a fourth line—connection between the separate members of the counter-revolutionary group and, as you assert, MacDonald.

Gussev: Yes.

Roginsky: Can you name the persons who through you were communicating with MacDonald?

Gussev: Engineer Nikolai Petrovich Vitvitsky.

Roginsky: Where did this engineer Vitvitsky work?

Gussev: As chief engineer of the Chelyabinsk Regional Electric Power Station .

Roginsky: Anyone else?

Gussev: Sokolov.

Roginsky: And Patrin? You remember him?

Gussev: Yes, also Patrin.

Roginsky: These were the definite persons who had connection with MacDonald through you?

Gussev: Yes.

Roginsky: This connection was established through you in the period of time when MacDonald was still in Zlatoust, or was it after the departure of MacDonald from Zlatoust?

Gussev: I served as connection after the departure of engineer MacDonald from Zlatoust.

Roginsky: And before that? With Patrin, for example?

Gussev: Before that I had relations with Sokolov.

Roginsky: And with Patrin?

Gussev: And with Patrin.

Roginsky: From your answers we can establish the following: both at the time of MacDonald's stay in Zlatoust and after the departure of MacDonald from Zlatoust, you also brought about the connection of definite persons with MacDonald, by handing him letters from these persons.

Gussev: Yes.

Roginsky: Did you hand over anything from MacDonald to these persons?

Gussev: I handed over money from MacDonald to Sokolov.

Roginsky: You handed over money to Sokolov, and next?

Gussev: I handed over money to Vitvitsky.

Roginsky: You handed over money to Vitvitsky. Was this the limit of your mutual relations with MacDonald in regard to connections?

Gussev: Afterwards I handed over and sent on letters from engineer Vitvitsky to engineer MacDonald.

Roginsky: Very well. Now tell me, at the time of MacDonald's stay in Zlatoust, did any more of the engineers of Metro-Vickers come to Zlatoust?

Gussev: Engineer Thornton came.

Roginsky: Engineer Thornton? When did he come?

Gussev: He came twice.

Roginsky: When?

Gussev: The first time in the summer of 1930 in June-July, I do not remember exactly, and afterwards in the winter of 1930-31.

Roginsky: In the summer of 1930 and in the winter of 1931. At the time of his first arrival in Zlatoust, had you already begun the practical carrying out of your counter-revolutionary activity?

Gussev: At this time I was collecting information about the various Zlatoust works.

Roginsky: That means, at the time of this arrival of Thornton you were in practice carrying out espionage?

Gussev: Yes.

Roginsky: And what was the character of the information which you provided for MacDonald at this time?

Gussev: At this period the information concerned both power supply and war production.

Roginsky: It means that at this time also the information was of a clearly secret character. Is that so?

Gussev: Yes.

Roginsky: It concerned the work of war production of the Zlatoust works?

Gussev: Yes, that is correct.

Roginsky: Did you have conversations with Thornton when he arrived?

Gussev: Yes, I spoke with him.

Roginsky: Why did he come to Zlatoust?

Gussev: He came to control the work of mounting.

Roginsky: To control whom?

Gussev: Engineer MacDonald.

Roginsky: Did your encounters with Thornton take place while at work or apart from your work?

Gussev: They took place only while at work.

Roginsky: And were your conversations with him solely in relation to work or did they bear another character?

Gussev: In so far as we had business relations, we spoke also of business.

Roginsky: Of what business?

Gussev: Of the business of mounting. But already at the first time I was recommended to him by engineer MacDonald as their man for espionage work.

Roginsky: You were recommended by engineer MacDonald to Thornton as their man for espionage, is that the case?

Gussev: Yes.

Roginsky: In what circumstances was this recommendation made, where?

Gussev: That was in my office.

Roginsky: Who was there at that time?

Gussev: Engineer MacDonald, Thornton and myself.

Roginsky: So there were three of you?

Gussev: Yes.

Roginsky: What did MacDonald speak to Thornton about?

Gussev: He said, "He is our man."

Roginsky: And then?

Gussev: Before that he told me that he had informed Thornton that I was acting for him as an Intelligence agent.

Roginsky: So that at the time you had this conversation with Thornton, MacDonald had already informed Thornton that you were "our man"?

Gussev: Yes.

Roginsky: Did you personally, apart from MacDonald, convey any information to Thornton on this visit of his?

Gussev: No.

Roginsky: Consequently your conversation with Thornton, in the presence of MacDonald, was only to the effect that you were recommended as a man who was acting in their interests?

Gussev: Yes.

Roginsky: Was Thornton informed about the nature of your work, about the nature of what "our man" was doing? Did you have a conversation with him on this point?

Gussev: I have already stated that MacDonald spoke to him about my espionage work and on that occasion I had no detailed conversation with Mr. Thornton. I had a detailed talk with him later on.

Roginsky: On that occasion you were only recommended? And when did your second meeting with Thornton take place?

Gussev: The second meeting took place in the winter of 1930-31.

Roginsky: The first meeting took place in July 1930; when did the second meeting take place?

Gussev: In January or February 1931.

Roginsky: Was MacDonald at Zlatoust at that time?

Gussev: Yes.

Roginsky: What was the nature of your counter-revolutionary work at that time?

Gussev: At that time we had drawn up a plan of breakdowns in Zlatoust.

Roginsky: Are we to understand that by that time you had passed from espionage to the immediate organization of concrete acts of wrecking?

Gussev: Yes.

Roginsky: So the plan of these wrecking activities had been outlined and Thornton arrived just at that time?

Gussev: Yes.

Roginsky: Thornton knew at that time that you were their man?

Gussev: Yes, he knew it.

Roginsky: Did you have a talk with Thornton concerning your work as one of their men?

Gussev: Yes, on the second occasion this plan was discussed by all three of us, *i.e.,* by myself, Thornton and MacDonald.

Roginsky: So the plan of these activities was discussed by the three of you—yourself, MacDonald and Thornton?

Gussev: Yes.

Roginsky: Where did that take place?

Gussev: At the power station, in my office.

Roginsky: Would it be correct to say that all meetings during Thornton's stay took place only in your office and that you did not meet him outside of your office?

Gussev: I was warned by engineer MacDonald that meetings with Thornton outside my office would be unwise.

Roginsky: Did Thornton make any comments when he examined this plan to proceed to acts of diversion? Did he indicate any direction which such acts of diversion were to take, or did he approve the measures you had worked out?

Gussev: Mr. Thornton scrutinized the main features of this plan and commented on the work of the Chelyabinsk Power Station, because as I have already stated, the Zlatoust Metallurgical Works was partly supplied with power from the Chelyabinsk station and this rather disturbed us.

Roginsky: About action?

Gussev: Yes. Mr. Thornton said that the plan must be carried out, that the fact that the Chelyabinsk Power Station supplied energy should not disturb us, because that station was under their influence.

Roginsky: Under their influence? So, apart from discussing the plan itself and the acts of diversion which you communicated, Thornton gave you to understand that there were people at the Chelyabinsk Power Station who were under their influence?

Gussev: I cannot say what he thought, but I understood that something must be up over there, that the work of the Chelyabinsk Power Station was not reliable.

Roginsky: And did you, as the man who was actually carrying out the plan agreed upon, subsequently establish contacts with the people who were performing the same tasks at the Chelyabinsk Power Station that you were performing at the Zlatoust Power Station?

Gussev: I was connected with Vitvitsky with regard to passing on information, but I had no specific knowledge about the wrecking work.

Roginsky: And did Vitvitsky, during his conversations with you, indicate with whom he was connected and the circumstances under which he joined or organized the counter-revolutionary group?

Gussev: During one of the meetings I had with him, Vitvitsky said that at Mr. Thornton's suggestion he had promised to give him information concerning the work of the Chelyabinsk Power Station.

Roginsky: Apart from the plan of acts of diversion did you get any other instructions from Thornton during his stay in Zlatoust?

Gussev: During that stay, the plan was approved. Afterwards, in reply to his question as to the role of the Zlatoust Power Station in time of war, I told him what I knew about the mobilization plan in connection with the supply of power to the Zlatoust works.

Roginsky: That is, you supplied information concerning the mobilization plan in connection with the power supply of the Zlatoust station in the event of war?

Gussev: Yes.

Roginsky: Was the plan of acts of diversion, the mobilization plan of the Zlatoust Metallurgical Works in case of war and generally the question of how to organize your counter-revolutionary activity in case of war taken up when this plan or program was drawn up, or was this question raised subsequently?

Gussev: This question had already been raised at that time.

Roginsky: What was the plan?

Gussev: The mobilization plan specified a normal capacity for the Zlatoust works of 12,000 kw., and according to this plan the capacity of the power station was to be reduced to 6,000-6,500, at the maximum, 7,000 kw. Thus, this plan provided for disruption of the power supply to the metallurgical works in case of war.

Roginsky: Consequently the diversion activities, which you have already mentioned in reply to the questions put by Comrade Vyshinsky, were aimed at maintaining the capacity of the power station at the reduced level you have just spoken about?

Gussev: As a result of all the breakdowns which were caused at the station, the original capacity of the turbine generator of 12,000 kw. was reduced to a maximum capacity of 7,000 kw. This was at the time when I was arrested.

Roginsky: And so by your wrecking activities you brought about a state of affairs in which the capacity of the power station was reduced to almost half?

Gussev: Yes, that is so.

Roginsky: When did MacDonald leave Zlatoust?

Gussev: He left in the second half of April 1931.

Roginsky: Did MacDonald's departure from Zlatoust break your relations with him or was the connection ensured?

Gussev: My connections with MacDonald were not severed with his departure from Zlatoust.

Roginsky: How were they kept up?

Gussev: They were kept up by various means: through the medium of a certain Ryabova; then I sent letters by mail to this Ryabova's address; then I took advantage of the journey of Ryabova's sons, and then my own journey to the Zuevka Power Station.

Roginsky: And so, after MacDonald's departure, the connections were maintained through the following channels: Ryabova, Ryabova's sons and your own visit to MacDonald in Zuevka?

Gussev: Yes.

Roginsky: Did you keep up connections with MacDonald before his departure for Zuevka, or were they interrupted and re-established after MacDonald's arrival at Zuevka?

Gussev: I received a letter from him in September 1931.

Roginsky: Where from?

Gussev: I do not remember now.

Roginsky: Was he in the U.S.S.R. or abroad at that time?

Gussev: In the U.S.S.R.

Roginsky: Did you get any other news from MacDonald apart from this letter, later on?

Gussev: Later, about August 1931, I received a parcel.

Roginsky: From whom?

Gussev: On the parcel the name of the sender was given as Ivanova, but the parcel contained a letter from engineer MacDonald.

Roginsky: So the sender's name on the parcel was Ivanova, while the letter inside the parcel was from MacDonald?

Gussev: Yes.

Roginsky: Was it agreed between you and MacDonald before his departure from Zlatoust that pending his arrival at Zuevka he would, in one way or another, keep up his connections with you, or were the connections accidental?

Gussev: When he was leaving Zlatoust it was agreed that the main channel for contact was to be Ryabova. Then he said that if I wanted to find him I might apply to the office.

Roginsky: In Moscow?

Gussev: Yes. Then he gave me an address which I do not now recollect and even before, when I wanted to make use of it, I could not find it.

Roginsky: And so he gave you an address which you do not recollect and another address—the office. Did he tell you exactly to whom you might apply in the office?

Gussev: He said I might apply to the secretary, Kutuzova, or to engineer Monkhouse.

Roginsky: Did he not name Thornton?

Gussev: I do not remember now.

Roginsky: You received a parcel from Ivanova. Was there such an Ivanova, or was there not?

Gussev: I cannot say. I received it from Ivanova, but now I do not remember either of the addresses.

Roginsky: One more question to the accused Kutuzova. Can you explain how this Ivanova appeared on the scene and what parcel the accused Gussev received?

Kutuzova: In the autumn of 1931, engineer MacDonald asked me to send a parcel to Gussev in Zlatoust and asked me not to give the name, the firm or the address of the firm. He asked me to put down the name Ivanova and the address, I do not remember very well—either Neglinny, or Petrovka, a fictitious address.

Roginsky: And you did so?

Kutuzova: Yes.

Roginsky: It was done at the request of engineer MacDonald?

Kutuzova: Yes.

Vyshinsky (To Gussev): Accused Gussev, just now, in reply to Comrade Roginsky's question, you said that a parcel was sent in the name of a person, who turned out to be a fictitious person. Was this the only case when fictitious names were used? Or were there several cases of this kind?

Gussev: I, personally, resorted to this method when sending letters.

Vyshinsky: What was this method?

Gussev: I wrote letters which were meant for engineer MacDonald, but addressed them to Ryabova and gave the name of the sender as Mochalov. I wrote to Ryabova in the name of Mochalov.

Vyshinsky: Did you use the name Utkin; didn't that name ever appear?

Gussev: I used to sign letters in this way.

Vyshinsky: And so you used the name of Utkin too?

Gussev: Yes.

Vyshinsky: And so you used the fictitious names Mochalov, Utkin, Ivanova and a fictitious address, Neglinny Prospect?

Gussev: Yes.

Vyshinsky: And in your information did you write plainly "shells" or perhaps some other word? For instance, so many and so many shells have been manufactured and the weekly output is so much and so much?

Gussev: Of course, the word "shells" was never used.

Vyshinsky: What word did you use?

Gussev: In one of the reports the word "tins" was used.

Vyshinsky: And so you wrote so many and so many tins are being produced?

Gussev: Yes.

Vyshinsky: Did the members of your group go only by their own names or did they have pseudonyms for the sake of secrecy?

Gussev: Some of them had pseudonyms.

Vyshinsky: For instance?

Gussev: Kotelnikov was known as "Fedor."

Vyshinsky: And what is his name?

Gussev: Fedor.

Vyshinsky: That is his real name and not a pseudonym. Fedor is Fedor. If he were called Fedot then it would be: Fedot, but not the one you mean.* And how was Ryabova called?

Gussev: "Derevo."

Vyshinsky: Were there other pseudonyms?

Gussev: Yes, there were.

Vyshinsky: So it may be stated that in your communications with MacDonald, as well as in MacDonald's communications with you and also with Kutuzova and the others, pseudonyms, fictitious adresses and fictitious names were used. Is that right?

Gussev: Yes, that is right.

---

* In the original: *Fedot, da ne tot*—a popular Russian saying.—Ed.

Roginsky: When did you visit MacDonald in Zuevka?

Gussev: In the middle of September 1932.

Roginsky: What wrecking activities had you actually accomplished by that time?

Gussev: Those of which I have spoken, Sterling boilers Nos. 1 and 2.

Roginsky: The delay in installing boilers Nos. 1 and 2. And after that?

Gussev: The delay in installing boiler No. 11. The breakdown of boiler No. 8. Breakdown of the coal conveyor.

Roginsky: And the breakdown of the 1,400 h.p. motor?

Gussev: Yes.

Roginsky: And all these acts were practically carried through by that time?

Gussev: Yes, they were carried through.

Roginsky: Why did you go to Zuevka, what was the object of that journey?

Gussev: I had received an invitation from MacDonald to come to see him on business.

Roginsky: What business could that invitation have referred to?

Gussev: There was only one matter of business that concerned us.

Roginsky: What was it?

Gussev: To cause breakdowns at the Zlatoust works.

Roginsky: That is your work as a member of a counter-revolutionary group of wreckers, is that so?

Gussev: Yes.

Roginsky: Previous to your journey in September 1932, you used the connection which you had through Ryabova and her sons in order to inform MacDonald of the wrecking activities. Or perhaps MacDonald did not know of these?

Gussev: He didn't know all the details. I was afraid to write about them in letters. However, indirectly I informed him that the work was going on.

Roginsky: You informed him in a veiled way, but MacDonald did not know exactly when and exactly which machines were put out of action?

Gussev: No, he did not know.

Roginsky: Not before your arrival?

Gussev: No.

Roginsky: Did you go to Zuevka via Moscow, or by some other route?

Gussev: I went via Moscow.

Roginsky: How many days did you stay in Zuevka?

Gussev: I stayed four days, perhaps five days, in Zuevka, I don't remember exactly.

Roginsky: You were informing MacDonald?

Gussev: Yes, I made a detailed report about all the breakdowns which were carried out by myself and our group. I also informed him about the situation that was created as a result of these breakdowns.

Roginsky: So during that visit to Zuevka you gave MacDonald detailed information on the results of the activity of the group of wreckers that was organized at the Zlatoust Power Station. Did you inform him about the coal conveyor, the motors and the boilers?

Gussev: Yes.

Roginsky: A question to MacDonald. Do you confirm Gussev's evidence about his visit to you at Zuevka and the detailed information he gave you about the wrecking activities carried out by him at the Zlatoust Power Station?

MacDonald: Yes, he said that such breakages did take place.

Roginsky: He informed you that there was a breakdown of the coal conveyor, and the boilers, that there was delay in the installation of the boilers?

MacDonald: Only about the breakages.

Roginsky: Do you confirm that you asked him by a special letter to come to Zuevka?

MacDonald: Not on this business.

Roginsky: On what business then?

MacDonald: I wanted to see him.

Roginsky: What for, and on what matter?

MacDonald: On no definite matter.

Roginsky: Have you heard Gussev's evidence that he went with the object of giving you information about the counter-revolutionary work which he carried out in Zlatoust? Is that evidence correct?

MacDonald: No, he received no such invitation from me.

Roginsky: But he gave you this information upon his arrival?

MacDonald: Yes.

Roginsky: I have no more questions to put to MacDonald.

The President: The Court will adjourn for twenty minutes.

* * *

Resumption of proceedings.

Commandant: Rise, please, the Court is coming.

The President: Please be seated.

The Prosecutor still has some questions to ask. Accused Gussev.

Roginsky: On your departure from Zuevka did you meet any other representatives of the Metro-Vickers firm apart from MacDonald?

Gussev: At the time of my departure from Zuevka, I met Mr. Thornton at Khartsisk Station.

Roginsky: Did this meeting take place at the moment of your departure, or did you stay on in Zuevka after that?

Gussev: It was at the moment of my departure. It was when I was going to the station to take the train.

Roginsky: Did you have a talk with Thornton?

Gussev: Yes, I spoke with Mr. Thornton in the restaurant at the station.

Roginsky: Was it a long talk?

Gussev: No, a short one, about twenty to thirty minutes.

Roginsky: What was the conversation about?

Gussev: I briefly informed Mr. Thornton about the situation in Zlatoust, *i.e.,* about the breakdowns which occurred there, and then replied to his questions concerning the work that was being done at the Zlatoust works.

Roginsky: Tell us exactly what you communicated to Thornton regarding these breakdowns which occurred at the Zlatoust Power Station.

Gussev: I told him about the breakdowns, as well as about the 1,400 h.p. motor, about the wrecking and the converting of the boilers.

Roginsky: Who was present during that conversation with Thornton?

Gussev: Mr. MacDonald.

Roginsky: Who else?

Gussev: At the same time, in the restaurant there was an engineer, likewise of the Metro-Vickers firm, who arrived from Makeyevka, whose name I do not know. He, however, was sitting at another table in the restaurant and was not present at that conversation.

Roginsky: There were three of you, yourself, Thornton and MacDonald?

Gussev: Yes.

Roginsky: Where did you go after that?

Gussev: Zlatoust.

Roginsky: Via Moscow?

Gussev: Yes.

Roginsky: Did you carry any messages to Moscow from MacDonald?

Gussev: I received a note from him to Mr. Monkhouse, which I was to take to their office in Moscow.

Roginsky: What sort of note was that? Did you read it?

Gussev: No, I did not read it. The note was in English and I cannot read English.

Roginsky: Did not MacDonald tell you verbally why you had to go to the office and on what matter you were to see Monkhouse?

Gussev: No, I did not know that.

Roginsky: May I put a question to Thornton?

The President: Yes, certainly.

Roginsky: Accused Thornton, do you confirm Gussev's evi dence about his meeting you at Khartsisk Station?

Thornton: Yes, I do.

Roginsky: This meeting did take place?

Thornton: Yes, it did.

Roginsky: Do you confirm having met him twice at Zlatoust?

Thornton: Yes, I do.

Roginsky: So your testimony, so far as it concerns your meetings with Gussev, is correct?

Thornton: Yes, it is correct.

Roginsky: I have no more questions to put to Thornton.

Accused Gussev, your departure from Khartsisk to Zlatoust was connected with some new tasks or instructions in connection with your wrecking activities?

Gussev: I was to take measures to keep the capacity of the power station at the level to which it was reduced in consequence of our wrecking activities, *i.e.,* half the normal, and then, in the event of military complications, in the event of war, to cause breakdowns in the power stations and in the installation of the works, breakdowns which should bring about a stoppage of production at the Zlatoust works affecting the output of high grade steel as well as the output of shells.

Roginsky: So the task set was to keep the station running at half of its capacity and prepare a number of very serious wrecking acts against the event of war. Is that so?

Gussev: That is so.

Roginsky: I have no more questions to ask.

Vyshinsky: I have a question to put to the accused Gussev.

Accused Gussev, I am interested in the following question. First you said that the information you supplied about the Zlatoust works was being transmitted to MacDonald. Is that so?

Gussev: Yes, that is what I said.

Vyshinsky: Did Thornton know you were passing on information to MacDonald?

Gussev: I have already said that on Mr. Thornton's first visit he knew that I was engaged in espionage work on the instructions of Mr. MacDonald.

Vyshinsky: So Thornton knew about it when he paid his first visit?

Gussev: Yes, he did.

Vyshinsky: Allow me to put a question to Thornton. Accused Thornton, do you confirm Gussev's evidence in this part?

Thornton: No.

Vyshinsky: Consequently, you did not know that Gussev was supplying MacDonald with information?

Thornton: Allow me to ask—information about breakdowns?

Vyshinsky: No, spying information.

Thornton: Spying information—no; but information about the general condition of the station—yes, in so far as it interested the firm.

Vyshinsky: We do not say, in so far as it interested the firm, we say in so far as it interested you. You and the firm are not one and the same thing. I am asking whether you knew that Gussev had connection with MacDonald through which he, Gussev, gave MacDonald information of a nature that he described as spying information. Do you understand my question?

Thornton: I do not confirm the word "spying."

Vyshinsky: Let us leave this word out for the moment. Accused Thornton, is Gussev's evidence that you, Thornton, knew that he, Gussev, was giving MacDonald information about the Zlatoust works, correct?

Thornton: Yes.

Vyshinsky: Well, was the evidence which you gave when you were confronted with Gussev on March 15 correct or not? Do you remember the occasion, or shall I remind you of that?

Thornton: I would like to be reminded.

Vyshinsky: Let me remind you. Page 71 of the dossier, Volume XVIII, a question put to Thornton: "In your deposition of March 12, you stated that engineer Gussev of the electric power station of the Zlatoust works was connected with MacDonald, who for a period of several years transmitted to you detailed information regarding the situation in the Zlatoust district and regarding the technical condition of the power station and power installations. Do you confirm this? Reply: 'Yes, MacDonald transmitted to me such information, received by him from Gussev.' "

Do you confirm this?

Thornton: This I confirm.

Vyshinsky: We can say, then, that you confirm this part of the record of the investigation of March 15 when you were confronted with Gussev?

Thornton: Yes.

Vyshinsky: The second question. You know that Gussev's connection with MacDonald was not accidental, but was of a regular nature and he was regularly and systematically supplying him with various information?

Thornton: I didn't know that.

Vyshinsky: Then perhaps I should remind you of what you said during that confrontation?

Thornton: Yes, please.

The President: The same confrontation?

Vyshinsky: Yes.

Page 71, Volume XVIII. "Do you admit that engineer Gussev was your and MacDonald's agent in the Zlatoust district as you deposed?" You replied: "Yes, I think it is right."

Do you confirm this?

Thornton: No.

Vyshinsky: Why did you say it then?

Thornton: I do not say that I was forced to say it.

Vyshinsky: Then permit me to ask—did you say it?

Thornton: Yes, I did.

Vyshinsky: That is to say, what is written in the records is actually what you said?

Thornton: Yes, that is what I said.

Vyshinsky: Did you speak the truth or was it an untruth?

Thornton: In this case it was an untruth.

Vyshinsky: Do you usually speak the truth or not?

Thornton: In this case I did not speak the truth, I was excited.

Vyshinsky: That is to say, when you are excited you don't speak the truth?

Thornton: Yes.

Vyshinsky: You are not excited now?

Thornton: No, I am not excited.

Vyshinsky: That is to say, you are now speaking the truth?

Thornton: Now, I am speaking the truth.

Vyshinsky: Why then did you write this and not something else? You said: "I think, it is right." You did not affirm, but you thought. I ask why, when you were excited, you thought precisely this and not something else? Were you forced to do it?

Thornton: No.

Vyshinsky: You said this voluntarily?

Thornton: Voluntarily.

Vyshinsky: Perhaps some special methods were applied to you?

Thornton: No.

Vyshinsky: Were you tortured?

Thornton: No.

Vyshinsky: Third degree?

Thornton: No.

Vyshinsky: I have no more questions.

The President: Has the Prosecution any more questions to put to the accused Gussev?

The Prosecution: No.

The President: Does the Defence wish to put any questions to the accused Gussev?

Kaznacheyev (To Gussev): You spoke about your counter-revolutionary activity during a fairly long period of time. Tell me, please, were there occasions on which you wished to leave this counter-revolutionary work, to discontinue it, or were there no such occasions?

Gussev: There was such an occasion in 1932; it was at the time when I was at Zuevka, giving information about the break-downs and receiving instructions from MacDonald, confirmed by Mr. Thornton, to proceed further with my work. When I saw that I was driving further and further along this road I felt the desire to leave this business altogether. That is why I did not take the note I received to the Vickers' firm in Moscow, I did not deliver it to Monkhouse but went straight to Zlatoust.

Kaznacheyev: What gave rise to this desire to leave this business? Was it fear of being discovered, or were there other reasons, and what exactly were they?

Gussev: The main reason was that I saw that the path upon which I had entered, the path on which my work proceeded was a wrong one.

Kaznacheyev: But still, you did not succeed in abandoning this work altogether?

Gussev: I found no way out of the position I was in, because my connections had gone so far that it seemed to me that there was no way out.

Kaznacheyev: Did you talk to MacDonald or anybody else about this desire to give up this work? Didn't any one of them notice some wavering on your part? Can you recall that?

Gussev: There was such a moment at Zuevka.

Kaznacheyev: What happened there?

Gussev: There was some talk about the dangerous character of this work. In particular, there was some talk in Zuevka about my being called to the O.G.P.U. in Zlatoust, in the spring of 1932, in connection with a breakdown. This incident was communicated by Ryabova to Mr. MacDonald upon his arrival. On my arrival, MacDonald asked me whether this was really so. I confirmed that. He then began to talk about the danger of the thing, that it was necessary to exercise extreme caution, that in case of being found out I would have to deny all connection with him. At this time he said that in case of need he could arrange my escape abroad.

The President: Just abroad, or to some definite country?

Gussev: Just abroad.

Kaznacheyev: Were there no cases when MacDonald, or some one else, threatened to expose you deliberately?

Gussev: There was such a case.

Kaznacheyev: Tell us about it.

Gussev: It was at the time when I was instructed to proceed to cause breakdowns. I hesitated for a time. It was not a direct threat of exposure but was told as an example of how it might happen. As I was engaged in spying for them, they, as foreign subjects, in case of discovery, would not, in their opinion, be held responsible, whereas I, as a Soviet citizen, would be held strictly responsible.

Kaznacheyev: If it is not possible to consider the example you give as a direct threat, could it not be considered as a desire to bring psychological pressure to bear on you?

Gussev: That was how I interpreted this conversation.

Kaznacheyev: You interpreted it in just this way?

Gussev: Yes.

Kaznacheyev: And it could not be interpreted in any other way?

Gussev: No.

Kaznacheyev: A short while ago you told about your own political convictions and views, about your hostile attitude towards the Soviet Government. Well, at the present moment today, have your convictions and views changed, or do they remain the same?

Vyshinsky: What do you mean by today—April 12?

Kaznacheyev: No, not on April 12, but of late.

Gussev: Yes, my views have changed.

Kaznacheyev: How would you characterize this change? What could you say in regard to this change?

Gussev: I now am fully aware of the whole enormity of the crimes which I have committed, I recognize that these actions were wrong.

The President: Only wrong?

Gussev: Criminal.

Kaznacheyev: I would like to hear from you a more exhaustive estimation of what you have committed. How you estimate it all subjectively. Could you formulate this?

Gussev: That is to say, what did I do?

Kaznacheyev: Yes. Could you say how you, personally, estimate the change in your convictions?

Gussev: I can formulate it this way: I am a man who received his education under the Soviet power. Instead of using all my knowledge for a useful, common cause, I engaged in espionage. I engaged in wrecking, thus undermining State industry. Through the breakdowns that I carried out I undermined the military strength of the Soviet Union. All these of course, are crimes of colossal dimensions, crimes which for a citizen of the U.S.S.R. are absolutely impermissible. I now admit my guilt. I am telling here about all I have done, without hiding anything.

Kaznacheyev: Do you consider your admission, as you formulate it, sincere repentance?

Gussev: I have the feeling now, as I have already said, that this change began earlier. When I was arrested and when I was presented with the circumstances condemning me, I made no attempt to hide my crimes and at the examination I told all that had happened. Further, I can only say that if I am permitted to live, if that is possible, then the rest of my life will be spent in redeeming my guilt, in making up for the crimes I have committed.

Kaznacheyev: Allow me to ask you to make more precise one point in regard to your biography. In answering a question asked by the Prosecutor, you said that your father was a railway clerk. What was his material position?

Gussev: My father was absolutely non-propertied.

Kaznacheyev: How is it that you, who came from a non-propertied family, have come to this pass; under the influence of what facts did your counter-revolutionary outlook and convictions take shape?

Gussev: I explain it as the influence of the environment in which I found myself during 1916 and 1917 and ever since then.

Kaznacheyev: That is to say, you explain it as the influence of your environment during all the years of your conscious life. And what was the environment in which you moved and lived?

Gussev: First of all, when I joined the White army as a volunteer, it was an environment made up of sons of merchants and factory owners, and later, after finishing at the Institute, when I worked in the electric power station, as I have already said, I moved among the anti-Soviet section of engineers and technicians. Some of these engineers were subsequently convicted of wrecking. In general I moved among the anti-Soviet section of engineers.

Kaznacheyev: I understand. But, at the time when you went as a volunteer into the White army, obviously some convictions had already formed themselves in your mind. In what circles did you move before this voluntary entry into the White army?

Gussev: When I was studying and went as a volunteer, I was among sons of merchants and factory owners.

Kaznacheyev: A last question. You said that you finished at the Higher Practical Institute. Is this a higher educational institution?

Gussev: Yes.

The President: Have the other Counsel for the Defence any more questions?

Smirnov: Tell me this, accused. MacDonald left Zlatoust in April 1931. What was the cause of his departure from Zlatoust? Do you know?

Gussev: His work had come to an end.

Smirnov: Tell me, were any English mechanics left at Zlatoust after MacDonald left?

Gussev: No.

Smirnov: Nobody remained. That is to say, after MacDonald left Zlatoust, not a single English engineer was left?

Gussev: No.

Smirnov: Tell me, please, when was the first breakdown with, say, the 1,400 h.p. motor?

Gussev: In April 1932.

Smirnov: This was the first breakdown in chronological order?

Gussev: Yes.

Smirnov: The second was in May and the third in June 1932?

Gussev: Quite correct.

Smirnov: Then there was the breakdown with boiler No. 8, which took place in the winter of 1932, that is to say, later still?

Gussev: Yes.

Smirnov: And finally, when did the dismantling of the reserve coal conveyor take place?

Gussev: In December 1932.

Smirnov: It follows that all these breakdowns took place after MacDonald had left Zlatoust and approximately a year later?

Gussev: Yes.

Smirnov: Tell me, how do you account for the fact that all these cases of wrecking took place when MacDonald was not at the works?

Gussev: That is quite understandable. I had received instructions from Mr. Thornton and from MacDonald to the effect that all the breakdowns that had been planned must absolutely take place in their absence.

Smirnov: You say that you had received instructions from Mr. Thornton and MacDonald to the effect that all breakdowns should be carried out in their absence?

Tell me, what make is the 1,400 h.p. motor?

Gussev: As far as I remember, it was made by a Russian firm Siemens-Schuckert.

Smirnov: This firm was functioning in pre-revolutionary days?

Gussev: Yes.

Smirnov: It follows that this motor was installed at the works before 1917?

Gussev: It was put into operation, if my memory does not deceive me, in 1923.

Smirnov: That means it was standing idle between 1917 and 1923?

Gussev: I cannot say that. I was not employed at the works at that time. I began working there in 1922 and can say nothing about it.

Smirnov: What approximately was the amount of wear amortisation of the motor, in 1931?

Gussev: I am not sure. This question should be given to the Commission of Experts.

Smirnov: But you are an engineer? What is your personal opinion?

Gussev: In any case, I must say that the motor was in working order, and that the breakdowns which took place were brought about by me.

Smirnov: I understand that, but maybe the motor was of an old type of construction, out of date and worn out to a sufficient degree. Or was it not?

Gussev: The motor is not new, but it is perfectly capable of working. If you want to have it more exact, I cannot take this upon myself. I can say approximately. If the motor was put into exploitation in 1923, worked till 1932—8 years—and if you figure its term of service to be 25 years, then it had done one-third of its work. The extent of wear was figured at 30 per cent.

Smirnov: Tell me, who was chief engineer in the Zlatoust works at the time when MacDonald arrived?

Gussev: I am afraid to say exactly, for the reason that at that period of time the chief engineers were frequently being changed. While MacDonald was there, there was Popov, at one time there was Titorovsky.

Smirnov: This name interests me. Do you know whether MacDonald, soon after his arrival at the works, had a conversation with Titorovsky, the chief engineer, about it being advisable to change this motor and, consequently, to place an order for a motor of the Metro-Vickers firm?

Gussev: I know nothing about this conversation.

Smirnov: Allow me to ask you this: when, approximately at what period of time, or perhaps you remember exactly—when and how many times did MacDonald give you money and approximately how much? This sum of 2,000-2,500—in how many instalments did he give it to you and over what period of time?

Gussev: I cannot say now, because all this period of my connection lasted from December 1929 to the day of my arrest, that is three years, during which a fair amount of money passed through my hands and I cannot remember the dates.

Smirnov: Allow me to put the question in another way. Was money passing through MacDonald's hands these three years, or perhaps it was only given out the last time, if so, when?

Gussev: The last time he gave it out was a few days before his departure, 5,000.

Smirnov: What departure?

Gussev: From Zlatoust.

Smirnov: You say he left 5,000, but what are the 2,500?

Gussev: I was speaking about the 2,500 which I received for myself.

Smirnov: That means he gave you 2,500 before his departure from Zlatoust, and 5,000 when he actually left Zlatoust?

Gussev: Yes.

Smirnov: You do not know where he went from Zlatoust?

Gussev: To England.

Smirnov: And he returned to Zuevka in August 1931?

Gussev: I do not know, Mr. MacDonald should be asked about this.

Smirnov: When did you go to Zuevka?

Gussev: In September 1932.

Smirnov: So he gave you this new 5,000, about which during the preliminary examination you made no mention, gave you money before his departure from Zlatoust?

Gussev: Before his departure from Zlatoust.

Smirnov: In other words, after his departure from Zlatoust, *i.e.*, when he was in Zuevka, he didn't give you money?

Gussev: He did.

Smirnov: How much did you receive?

Gussev: 1,500.

Smirnov: That is 1,500; so it was 2,500, plus 5,000, and in Zuevka 1,500 rubles, is that a fact?

Gussev: Yes.

Smirnov: Tell me, please, you were connected with MacDonald, as you say, were on relations of friendship and intimacy with him, you were a guest at his house? He first of all lived in a hotel? Is that so?

Gussev: You had better ask him, three years have passed since. I know he lived in one of the apartments belonging to the works and I used to visit him there.

Smirnov: Only in one of the works' apartments? Can you say whether his way of life was extravagant or not?

Gussev: To my mind extravagant enough.

Smirnov: What did he have—wine?

Gussev: There was wine.

Smirnov: Was there any special food?

Gussev: What does special food mean? What do you understand by special food? Put the question more exactly, as to what you understand by special food.

Smirnov: If my questions annoy you, although I see nothing in particular in them to annoy you, you need not reply.

Gussev: I will answer what I can with pleasure. You asked about wine and I told you. You ask, was there any special food, and I ask you to make more clear what you mean by special food.

Smirnov: Then tell me what you understand by extravagant living.

Gussev: Extravagant living means, to my mind, that there is wine, all kinds of delicatessen as part of the food, fruits, etc.

Smirnov: That is to say that extravagant living is expressed in wine and delicatessen. It is important that I fix the point as to the kind of life MacDonald lived in Zlatoust. This is essential for me as MacDonald's Counsel for the Defence. Did he live extravagantly in his own personal life? Would it have been possible in Zlatoust, in the works atmosphere, in one of the works' apartments, to live extravagantly?

Gussev: The main thing may be that there is a difference in what you understand as extravagant living and what I understand it to mean. To my mind it was extravagant living. I could not live in this way, nor could any of our engineers live as Mr. MacDonald lived. I take the average, definite standard in the circumstances in which we live and compare it with the standard of living of Mr. MacDonald and several other foreign installation engineers whom I knew. Hence I draw the conclusion that his life was more extravagant.

Smirnov: Not only than yours, but than that of the other foreign engineers?

Gussev: Yes.

Smirnov: And so this was expressed in the fact that MacDonald had wine and delicatessen?

Gussev: Yes.

Smirnov: Tell me, please, this extravagant life could give reason to suppose that MacDonald was free to dispose of such sums of money as 2,500, 5,000, 1,500 rubles and so on, that he had at his disposal private means, I emphasize the point private, and not received from somewhere else, which enabled him to lead an extravagant life.

Gussev: The question needs to be made more exact. You want to talk about private means. I do not know exactly how much money he had, and consequently whether he gave this money from his own private means or from some other sources. To my mind, he should be asked, I can only say that I received money; I have named the sums.

Smirnov: Please tell me if you know whether MacDonald himself was ever in Chelyabinsk?

Gussev: I know nothing about his having been in Chelyabinsk.

Smirnov: When he was working in Zlatoust, apart from the times when he went to Irkutsk, was he ever absent?

Gussev: As far as I remember, he was never absent.

Smirnov: Did he know Vitvitsky personally?

Gussev: As far as I know, no.

Smirnov: You said in Court that Vitvitsky, in your opinion, saw Thornton and agreed with him personally on the question of his giving information.

Gussev: I did say so.

Smirnov: Then why was MacDonald necessary in connection with the passing of information to Thornton? You pointed out that Thornton met Vitvitsky and agreed with him about information being passed on to him.

Gussev: I state that Vitvitsky told me that he had had an interview with Thornton.

Smirnov: You assert that here MacDonald as well acted as an intermediary?

Gussev: You are confusing something.

Smirnov: I believe that I wrote down your testimony.

Gussev: I said that Vitvitsky told me that Thornton, while he was at the Chelyabinsk Electric Power Station, proposed to Vitvitsky that he give information on the work of the Chelyabinsk Power Station; that Vitvitsky agreed to this.

Smirnov: And MacDonald has nothing to do with it? You know nothing about MacDonald having played any role in this?

Gussev: That is another point. I handed Vitvitsky money to the extent of about 4,500 out of the 5,000 MacDonald had provided.

Smirnov: Why, if Thornton came to an agreement with Vitvitsky, and Vitvitsky told you that Thornton had come to an agreement with him, did MacDonald, for some reason or other, give you the money to give to Vitvitsky? Why not directly, but through someone else?

Gussev: I can say what I know, but the chief explanations, in my opinion, you can get from Thornton and MacDonald. When MacDonald left I received 5,000; moreover I was told that a small part of the money I could spend for myself and for the business, but the greatest part I must spend according to instructions which I should receive later. These were instructions I received from MacDonald in September 1931—to hand over the money—which I did.

Smirnov: It amounts to this, that Thornton made an agreement with Vitvitsky direct, that Vitvitsky should give him information, and then MacDonald gave you money and said: "When I send you instructions as to how to hand over the money, you will hand it over"; and you received instructions to hand the money over to Vitvitsky?

Gussev: Yes, and allow me to add that Vitvitsky told me that Thornton told him that the information that Vitvitsky would give Thornton should be handed over to Mr. MacDonald through me.

Smirnov: Tell me, please, the department of the mechanical works where high grade steel and shells are made is undoubtedly a secret department?

Gussev: Here a division must be made: the production of high grade steel, including auto-tractor springs, shell billets and aviation steels, is in the metallurgical works. Purely shell billet production is done in the mechanical works. All this production in the mechanical works is secret. As for the metallurgical works, it is also secret.

Smirnov: You are the chief of the electric power station. As a matter of fact, what connection have you as chief of the power station with these departments? Is not all that is done there a secret for you as well? Ought it not to be?

Gussev: I have already said that I covered not only the electric power station, but also the pump station, the boiler room, the blast air station, *i.e.*, all the energy supply of the works. Thus in compiling control figures, in determining the monthly production program, in order to draw up a balance sheet of steam and energy supplies, I had to know the size of production.

Smirnov: I allow that as regards the size. But was it necessary to know the type of shells?

Gussev: For the production program?

Smirnov: Yes.

Gussev: No, it was not necessary.

Smirnov: Not necessary. And yet you received information also about the types of shells?

Gussev: Yes, I received it.

Smirnov: In other words, the chief of the department passed on to you secrets which he had no right to tell you?

Gussev: I was a member of the staff with access to secret information.

Smirnov: Is it true that every such member of the staff has the right to know all the secrets, even those which have nothing to do with his functions?

Gussev: I received such information.

Smirnov: What does it mean, you received it? How did you receive it: through the collaboration of the chief of the department or by deceit, or in some other way?

Gussev: Without any collaboration.

Smirnov: Then how?

Gussev: In certain cases, I simply made use of the confidence of the chiefs of the departments, and in some cases I made use of the right I enjoyed as staff member with access to secret information.

Smirnov: In order to understand the type of shell in detail, it is not necessary to be a specialist yourself. What do you mean by a type of shell? Blueprints and so on. You understand all that?

Gussev: I cannot call myself a specialist in this field.

Smirnov: You do not consider yourself a specialist. What sort of information did you hand over in these circumstances? What did it consist of? What was it: blueprints, designations?

Gussev: There were no blueprints, there were designations.

Smirnov: Only designations?

Gussev: Designations and the amount of output.

The President: You are not to mention the designations and amount of output here in Court.

Smirnov: I have no more questions.

The President: I draw the attention of Smirnov, Counsel for the Defence, to the fact that he has made the following mistake: The accused Gussev in reply to one of the questions of the Counsel for the Defence, Smirnov, stated that MacDonald before his departure gave him 5,000 rubles. The Counsel for the Defence surprisingly remarked that he was hearing this for the first time, and that during the preliminary examination the accused Gussev allegedly had not said this. I draw attention to the fact that in Gussev's testimony of March 23, Volume III, page 73, there is the statement: "Before MacDonald's departure he gave me money amounting to 5,000 rubles, saying that a small part of it I could take for myself and spend as I thought fit for our business. More than half the money I was to keep and spend as per his instructions, which I received later."

Smirnov: I beg to be excused. I understood at first that this 5,000 was also given for Gussev himself.

The President: Has the Counsel for the Defence any more questions?

Braude: Tell me, accused, when did you hear from Vitvitsky that he had met Thornton?

Gussev: If my memory does not deceive me, it was at the end of July 1931.

Braude: At the end of July 1931. Did you go to him, or did he come to you?

Gussev: I went to the Chelyabinsk Electric Power Station.

Braude: On what business?

Gussev: I don't remember now.

Braude: Nevertheless, were you sent by your firm or did you go on your own account? If you were sent, who sent you?

Gussev: It is hard to tell.

Braude: In what circumstances did Vitvitsky tell you about his interview with Thornton, why did he decide to speak about it, were you connected with him only through your work, or did you know of his participation in the organization?

Gussev: I was on friendly terms with Vitvitsky when in Zlatoust. He was chief of that electric power station for three and a half years and I was his assistant.

Braude: Were you in any counter-revolutionary organizations before that time?

Gussev: No.

Braude: And before then, you knew nothing compromising about him, and he knew nothing about you?

Gussev: I knew Vitvitsky as a man who was anti-Soviet, counter-revolutionarily inclined. Vitvitsky knew the same of me. That was enough.

Braude: That was enough for him to tell you that he had been given the task of performing acts of diversion, wrecking and breakdowns—that is what I am to understand?

Gussev: In my opinion you are saying more than I said.

Braude: Make it more precise yourself.

Gussev: When we met, Vitvitsky told me that at the suggestion of Thornton he had agreed to give information concerning the work of the Chelyabinsk Electric Power Station.

Braude: Only information. Then I was a little mistaken. I have no more questions to Gussev. Allow me to ask Thornton a question.

Accused Thornton, do you confirm that you met Vitvitsky and had a conversation with him as Gussev has just stated?

Thornton: I was in Chelyabinsk and saw him. . .

Braude: Did any conversations take place in the nature of those mentioned?

Thornton: Absolutely none.

Braude: The accused Gussev testifies that you gave instructions and tasks of a wrecking character. Did this take place or not? Had you any information to the effect that wrecking actions of this kind were being done by Gussev, and in connection with whose tasks?

Thornton: I did not know this.

Braude: You did not know it, because you did not give such instructions?

Thornton: No.

Braude: During the examination did you say anywhere, at any time, that you knew, or that you gave instructions, or had been informed about wrecking acts, or did you say nothing anywhere?

Thornton: I never said anything.

Braude: You said nothing. In this respect your testimony does not differ from your previous testimony?

Thornton: I never said that I gave instructions or knew anything concerning wrecking.

Braude: In the beginning, you mentioned here that you were aware of the fact that information was being collected by Gussev for your employees. State more precisely what sort of information, what kind of data, and why it was collected.

Thornton: Information about electric power stations.

Braude: 'About what in particular? Not about the painting or about their outward appearance. What sort of information?

Thornton: The work of our equipment. About the work of that which feeds our equipment, namely, the boilers. About that which takes the energy from our equipment, *i.e.*, the construction of the transformers. This was necessary so that, should there be a breakdown with a machine, we should have every opportunity of finding the cause.

Braude: Who received this information?

Thornton: I received it from MacDonald.

Braude: So certain types of information were received by you, but it was limited to the sort of which you have just informed us?

Thornton: Yes.

Braude: Did you hand money over to the apparatus for this information?

Thornton: For the information, no. I only once gave money to MacDonald.

The President: I do not understand the character of the questions to the accused. We have not yet finished examining the accused Gussev. We have not yet examined MacDonald and Thornton. The questions you are asking concern MacDonald and Thornton.

Braude: In connection with Gussev's deposition I have no other questions.

Vyshinsky: Since a question connected with Thornton has been touched upon here, I would ask to be allowed to put a few questions to Thornton.

The President: Granted.

Vyshinsky: Accused Thornton. I did not quite comprehend your answer to the question put by Braude, Counsel for the Defence, as to whether Zlatoust interested you or not?

Thornton: It interested me.

Vyshinsky: You personally, or as a representative of your firm?

Thornton: As a representative of the firm.

Vyshinsky: Perhaps you would explain why during the preliminary examination you said that you were not much interested in Zlatoust. You said that?

Thornton: I did say so.

Vyshinsky: It would appear that the one contradicts the other.

Thornton: Of course, I was more interested in the big power station.

Vyshinsky: I am asking you how do you explain the fact that at the preliminary examination you said that in the interests of your firm, Zlatoust was not of much interest to you.

Thornton: Allow me to speak through an interpreter.

The President: All right.

Vyshinsky: How is it that Mr. Thornton at the preliminary examination stated the following. Allow me to read the passage from his deposition: "I was not much interested in receiving information from Zlatoust."

Thornton: Please translate this: I want to say that Zlatoust is of comparatively small interest.

Vyshinsky: In comparison with what? I am now interested in the degree to which the information which Thornton collected about Zlatoust interested him and whether it interested him at all. Here there are two testimonies. In one place it says that it interested him as a representative of the firm, and in the other place it says that it was not of much interest to him as a representative of the firm. How do you explain this?

Thornton: Any contradictions? There is, yes. There is, yes.

Vyshinsky: How do you explain this contradiction.

Thornton: The contradiction is this: that what is written in the Russian is apparently that I took no interest in the Zlatoust station.

Vyshinsky: You said not much interested.

Thornton: At all power stations, one and the same information is interesting to my firm.

Vyshinsky: I know that it is the same information.

Thornton: Since there was only one small turbo-generator station in Zlatoust, it interested me less than a station of a larger size.

Vyshinsky: True. There was only one small turbine there, consequently you were less interested in Zlatoust than in the others. Is that so?

Thornton: Yes.

Vyshinsky: Then there is the next question. Did you give MacDonald 1,500 rubles in connection with the information received from Zlatoust?

Thornton: Yes. During the preliminary examination I did not know the exact sum, but since then I have been able to check up the sum paid.

Vyshinsky: How much money did you give MacDonald in connection with Zlatoust?

Thornton: I gave 2,000.

Vyshinsky: You said before 1,500, we will make a correction, not 1,500, but 2,000. You gave this money for receiving information about Zlatoust?

Thornton: That is not correct. I said during the examination that it was different.

Vyshinsky: Then what?

Thornton: It was like this. First of all it was . . . (tries to read from notes).

Vyshinsky: Can you not answer without notes?

The President: What notes?

Vyshinsky: Thornton is answering from notes.

The President: The question does not refer to figures or statistics so I see no reason for the notes. Are you tired?

Thornton: No.

Vyshinsky: Why did you give this money if Zlatoust did not interest you?

Thornton: I gave MacDonald the money for Zuevka.

Vyshinsky: Then I do not understand what you said before.

Thornton: I said that I gave MacDonald 1,500 rubles, but I gave 1,900 rubles, and I made that correction when the examination took place with Assistant Prosecutor Vyshinsky. I gave this money in 1932 for Zuevka.

Vyshinsky: This is of no interest to me. I am interested in something different. I will read the deposition of March 27:

Volume XVIII, on page 338 of the dossier. You said the following: "I gave 1,500 rubles to MacDonald at his request. Since Zlatoust was not of much interest to me as representative of the firm, I cannot explain why MacDonald required so much money and where and on what he spent it." Do you confirm this?

Thornton: I confirm that.

Vyshinsky: I am through.

Thornton: I wanted to explain the affair in more detail.

Vyshinsky: You will explain this in more detail later.

Counsel for the Defence, Libson: Tell me, accused Gussev, in your official work in Zlatoust were you in any way connected with Zuevka and did you know any of the engineering staff working at Zuevka?

Gussev: No.

Libson: This means that you went there only when summoned by MacDonald?

Gussev: Yes.

Libson: For what length of time were you in Zuevka?

Gussev: About four days.

Libson: During those four days, besides the persons enumerated by you, did you chance upon anyone else?

Gussev: That is to say, how . . . chance upon?

Libson: Did you meet . . . or did you converse. . . ?

Gussev: I met Ryabova, and don't remember any other meetings in the sense in which, apparently, you understand them.

Libson: That is to say, you add only the name of Ryabova. You have already said that you met MacDonald, Thornton and another engineer whose name you did not mention and who sat at a table in the station.

Now another question: when you, having received the note at Zuevka, had to go to the Moscow office, whom did you see in Moscow? For you were in Moscow, were you not?

Gussev: No, I travelled through Moscow, but did not call at the firm's office.

Libson: When your relations with MacDonald first began, your personal relations, was not the money offered to you at first in the form of a loan?

Gussev: I don't remember that.

Libson: And were there established between you and MacDonald personal, friendly relations?

Gussev: There were.

Libson: Who took the initiative in this rapprochement?

Gussev: In my opinion, Mr. MacDonald.

Libson: I have no more questions.

Kommodov: I have a question to Kutuzova.

Did you know what were the contents of the parcel which you sent under the name of Ivanova?

Kutuzova: I knew at the time, but now I do not remember. I only know that it was food—butter and other food. I do not remember exactly.

Kommodov: I have no more questions.

The President: Has the Prosecution any questions?

Vyshinsky: Accused Gussev, there are a few questions of interest to Smirnov, Counsel for the Defence, connected with your attitude towards Vitvitsky. The question caused some perplexity as to why you informed him of data which, within the confines of your counter-revolutionary work, was of a conspirative character; how did this come about? You said—as a result of your friendly relations which made it possible for you to be frank with him. And later you said: I knew that his frame of mind was the same as mine.

Gussev: Yes.

Vyshinsky: Did you know only about his anti-Soviet inclinations, or perhaps you knew about certain of his anti-Soviet actions?

Gussev: I knew that he was in a wrecking organization.

Vyshinsky: Well, and before? Did you know, for example, about his participation in the Kronstadt events?

Gussev: Yes, I knew.

Vyshinsky: What did you know?

Gussev: That he took part in the Kronstadt mutiny.

Vyshinsky: In which—the whiteguard . . . .?

Gussev: Yes, in the whiteguard.

Vyshinsky: That gave you the right to consider him your brother?

Gussev: I have spoken about this, and again confirm: when we exchanged this information, our mutual knowledge about each other excluded any possibility of danger or fear.

Vyshinsky: It was not here only a question of a frame of mind, but of more.

Gussev: We had quite a fixed impression about each other.

Vyshinsky: How long have you known him?

Gussev: I became acquainted with him for the first time approximately in 1925.

Vyshinsky: That means you have been acquainted for several years.

Gussev: Since 1925 or 1924.

Vyshinsky: Excellent.

The second question. Had MacDonald at his disposal private means of such extent and size as to allow of his giving you 5,000 rubles before his leaving Zlatoust? I am not quite clear as to why the question is raised of MacDonald's private means. Did he tell you that he was giving it from his private means?

Gussev: I have already said that I know nothing of the source from which this money came.

Vyshinsky: In return for what did he give the money?

Gussev: In return for my giving him intelligence information and later for carrying out the breakdowns.

Vyshinsky: Did you imagine that you were doing this in the private interests of MacDonald?

Gussev: Certainly not.

Vyshinsky: Consequently, is it in order, in this case, to raise the question of the private means of MacDonald?

Gussev: I should think that it is certainly not in keeping, but our positions are too different: Counsel for the Defence and accused. I can be asked a question in any way, and I have to answer. But if I could ask questions, I should find questions to raise *(laughter).*

Roginsky: The question to accused Gussev is connected with the question asked of him by Smirnov, Counsel for the Defence. In your official capacity as chief of the electric power station, you had free access to the metallurgical works?

Gussev: I had a pass in which was written: valid for all departments, at all times, day and night, both for open and closed entrances.

Roginsky: It follows that you had absolutely free access to all departments, secret and non-secret, of the metallurgical works.

Gussev: Yes.

Roginsky: And to the mechanical works?

Gussev: I had no permanent pass.

Roginsky: But access?

Gussev: Access was secured for me on each particular occasion.

Roginsky: Including the secret departments of the mechanical works?

Gussev: Yes.

The President: Has the Counsel for the Defence any questions?

Smirnov: When you received money from MacDonald, you were quite clear as to the fact that he was giving you the money not from his own private means, or was this not clear to you? Answer briefly.

Gussev: Allow me to answer as I am able to. At the time when I agreed to give information on the functioning of the works, I was told that it would be paid for. Then I can say that I received money, but from what sources this money was given to me, ask Mr. MacDonald. I cannot tell you that. How can I tell you where he got his money?

Smirnov: You considered that the question was not clear as to the source from which the money was given.

Gussev: I do not know exactly and can only make a guess. As an engineer, the information I gave him was unnecessary to him.

Smirnov: That is to say, it was also a question to you as to where he got the money?

Gussev: It means that the conclusion must be made that it was not from his private money—but that is only my supposition.

Smirnov: You are not sure?

Gussev: I am not sure.

The President: Has the Prosecution any more questions?

The Prosecution: No.

The President: Has the Counsel for the Defence any more questions to the accused?

Defence: No.

The President: Have the accused any questions?

Accused: No.

The President: The order of procedure will be as follows: the session begins at 10 o'clock, the dinner recess is from 3 to 6 p.m. and the adjournment at 10 p.m.

It is now 10 p.m. I declare the session adjourned until 10 o'clock on the morning of April 13, 1933.

(At 10 p.m. the Court adjourns until 10 a.m., April 13, 1933.)

[Signed] V. V. ULRICH
President of the Special Session of the Supreme Court of the U.S.S.R.

A. F. KOSTYUSHKO
Secretary

MORNING SESSION, APRIL 13, 1933, 10:15 a. m.

Commandant: Please rise. The Court is coming.

The President: Please be seated. The session is resumed. Accused Sokolov, please tell us, very briefly, your biography, the main points.

Sokolov: I was born on January 1, 1899, in the village of Ostyn, in the Birsk region, in the family of a cobbler, an artisan who worked by himself. Up to the age of 14 I lived in Ostyn village with my father and family. I went through an elementary city school, then I studied in a grammar school. I showed good progress in mathematics and a leaning towards mathematical sciences. . . .

The local teachers advised my father to give me an opportunity to continue my studies. But since he had no means to keep me in a city which had a structural engineering school my father was compelled to move to Zlatoust. In 1914, on July 10, our family came to Zlatoust. In August I entered the Zlatoust secondary mechanical-technical school from which I graduated in 1918. During the time I studied in the technical school I had to work in the evenings at the Zlatoust Mechanical Works, since the family had not sufficient means of subsistence. My father was frequently sick. I worked at first in the pattern department on patterns, then in the tool room, and afterwards in the munitions shop of the Zlatoust Mechanical Works where I worked up to the day of my conscription into the White army. At that time the White army did not yet exist as such. There was only an order for the conscription of the intelligentsia.

Vyshinsky: Whose order?

Sokolov: I think it was General Boldyrev's. It was on the 8th or 9th. This was the first order for the conscription of the intelligentsia. We—students who had not graduated from their schools—were also conscripted. A city company was formed which did guard service in the city. When general conscription was started, the city company was the nucleus for the organization of the 22nd Zlatoust Regiment. Later on the city company was renamed the training company of the 22nd Zlatoust Regiment. It was in this training company that I served in the White army.

The President: On the basis of what qualifications was the training company organized?

Sokolov: According to education. All those who had an education were in the training company. Afterwards, when they began to form the regiment, this company was included in the regiment in order to bring the latter up to its full numerical strength. Later I participated in military expeditions.

The President: Have you met anyone of the accused in the present case in the 22nd Regiment?

Sokolov: I met Gussev in the same training company.

The President: In the same training company.

Sokolov: I took part in the expeditions of the White army in action against the Red Army. My service in the White Army was in the rank of private, since I sought to evade the military school. I resorted to all kinds of methods in order to escape the military school, as was done also by many of my comrades. I served in the White army up to December 1919.

In December, the city of Tomsk was taken by the Red Army and, after all the Whites who remained in the city had been registered, I was sent to the Irbit hospital as an orderly, since I had both typhoid fever and recurrent typhus. I held my post as orderly for about three weeks. Soon after, it was early in January 1920, there was an enlistment to military schools. I expressed my desire to go to a military school. I was sent to the Radio Division which was attached to the Third Radio Base. In 1920 in the month of April, I graduated from the radio school in the class of electro-mechanics before I had completed my term. After my graduation I was sent to work as technician in a radio-telegraphy shop. In the radio-telegraphy shop I worked at first on assembling internal combustion engines, afterwards I expressed the desire to work in the electrical department. My request was granted by the commanders of the division and I was transferred to the electro-technical department. Here I began to specialize in electro-technics. While in the radio-telegraphy shop in the post of junior commander, which post is equal to that of platoon commander, I worked on the repair of the electric parts of radio stations and on the installation of newly built and repaired radio stations.

In 1923, when the civil war was over, the radio base began to be reduced numerically. The radio-telegraphy shop also began to reduce its staff. I was transferred to a communication regiment in the capacity of chief of a training and repair shop, with the rank of assistant company commander. This post I held up to October 1924. Then I was demobilized. After demobilization, in 1924, I began to work at first as electric repairer in order to attain a deeper knowledge of my speciality. I worked at the State mills in Tomsk, mills No. 1 and No. 2, until February. After finishing the installation and repair works at the State mills I was given my discharge. I registered at the labour exchange. But since I was too far back in the line for getting a job I decided to go to Zlatoust. I arrived in the city of Zlatoust in 1925. On March 8 I started work temporarily as rate-fixer at the Zlatoust Mechanical Works. Then, in July 1925, I was transferred to work at my speciality as foreman at the electric power station of the Zlatoust Metallurgical Works. I worked in this capacity until the spring of 1929. Then I was appointed assistant to the chief of the Zlatoust Electric Power Station. At this post I worked until May 1932.

The President: As assistant to Gussev?

Sokolov: Yes.

In 1932, in the month of May, I was appointed assistant chief mechanic for electric installations, virtually chief electrician of the Zlatoust Metallurgical Works, reckoned according to my actual post. Officially there is no such post on the rolls of Spetz-Stahl, there is the post of assistant mechanic for electric installations. At any rate, I was in charge of the electric installations of the metallurgical works. At this post I worked until the day of my arrest.

The President: What was your salary during the last period?

Sokolov: 700 rubles.

The President: When and under what circumstances did you begin to engage in wrecking activities and in espionage?

Sokolov: My first wrecking work was done in 1927, but this work was not connected with any organization. I did not know of the existence of any organization. I delayed two jobs at the power plant. That was with Vitvitsky. I did not know of the existence of any organization and did not belong to any organization.

In 1930, approximately June or July, I became connected with the installation engineer of an English firm, MacDonald, through the assistance of Gussev, the chief of the power station. That was the moment when my counter-revolutionary work began, from that time on I was counted as a member of a counter-revolutionary organization.

Vyshinsky: You just said, accused Sokolov: "That was the moment when my counter-revolutionary work began." What moment?

Sokolov: The moment when I became connected with the English installation engineer MacDonald.

Vyshinsky: Consequently, you regard all your activity prior to 1930 as not being counter-revolutionary activity?

Sokolov: It was counter-revolutionary activity, but I did not belong to any counter-revolutionary organization and did not know of the existence of any.

Vyshinsky: Let us make it more precise.

The first question: You apparently went through several periods. The first period—when you served in the White army, occupied a certain post in the training company and took part in the fights against the Bolsheviks. That period began from the moment of the October Revolution. When did that period end, in what year?

Sokolov: I did not participate in armed clashes, I took no part in battles.

Vyshinsky: But you were in the White army?

Sokolov: I was.

Vyshinsky: And it was armed?

Sokolov: It was.

Vyshinsky: Did the White army just look at the Bolsheviks or did it fight them?

Sokolov: It fought.

Vyshinsky: You were in the ranks of the White army?

Sokolov: I was.

Vyshinsky: You were in the White army, you carried the arms appropriated by the White army?

Sokolov: Yes.

Vyshinsky: So I am justified in saying that you were actively, with arms in your hands, opposing the Red Army?

Sokolov: Yes.

Vyshinsky: Whether you happened to participate in one battle or another—this is a separate question. You answer that question in the negative.

Sokolov: I did not happen to participate.

Vyshinsky: How long were you in the White army?

Sokolov: From June 1918 to December 1919.

Vyshinsky: Almost a year and a half; and during this time you were in the reserve or rearguard units, or in an active service unit?

Sokolov: In an active service unit.

Vyshinsky: In which unit?

Sokolov: In the 22nd Zlatoust Infantry Regiment.

Vyshinsky: In what capacity?

Sokolov: As a private in the training company.

Vyshinsky: Usually the best from among the privates are recruited into the training company.

Sokolov: Yes.

Vyshinsky: The more reliable, not only the more literate, but the more stable ones—those that can be relied upon.

Sokolov: Yes.

Vyshinsky: And was Gussev there?

Sokolov: Yes.

Vyshinsky: Did the Zlatoust Regiment take part in fighting?

Sokolov: Yes.

Vyshinsky: How was it then that the 22nd Regiment went into battle while the company, composed of the more reliable, stable persons, did not take part? There can be only one answer to this—either that unit took part in battles, or it was intended for other operations of an internal kind.

Sokolov: When the Zlatoust Regiment went to the front and came face to face with the Red Army, I, being inclined. . . .

Vyshinsky: Did the training company take part in the battles at the front?

Sokolov: Yes.

Vyshinsky: And you?

Sokolov: It so happened that I did not.

Vyshinsky: And Gussev?

Sokolov: I do not know, he wasn't there any more.

Vyshinsky: When it came to fighting, Gussev wasn't there any more?

Sokolov: He was not.

Vyshinsky: And you were not there?

Sokolov: I tried to get away from the front. I made an artificial wound on my left leg and was discharged from the front.

Vyshinsky: Why?

Sokolov: Because it was obvious that the army had collapsed, that the army would go back to the old order of things. The new reinforcements, chiefly from Altai and Akmolinsk, told us of what was going on in Siberia.

Vyshinsky: That was the time when the White army became demoralized, and you tried to desert at the moment when the army began to collapse?

Sokolov: Yes.

Vyshinsky: And before that? When the army was strong you were in its ranks and you made no attempts to leave it?

Sokolov: That is so.

Vyshinsky: That was in December 1919?

Sokolov: Yes.

Vyshinsky: What came after that?

Sokolov: After that I served in the Red Army.

Vyshinsky: You were conscripted?

Sokolov: Yes, conscripted.

Vyshinsky: And served in the Red Army until 1924?

Sokolov: Yes.

Vyshinsky: Where did you serve in the Red Army?

Sokolov: First of all I served in an ambulance hospital.

Vyshinsky: How did you come to be there?

Sokolov: I was weak, and was transferred to a convalescent unit. As I had been sick with typhoid and recurrent typhus, I was assigned to the medical corps as an orderly.

Vyshinsky: Were those who had been sick with typhus appointed as hospital orderlies?

Sokolov: I was very weak.

Vyshinsky: And you yourself tried to get there?

Sokolov: I made no attempt to get there.

Vyshinsky: How long did you serve there?

Sokolov: About three weeks.

Vyshinsky: Where were you at that time?

Sokolov: In Tomsk in the Verbitsk hospital. In the early part of January I was sent to the military school in Tomsk, to the radio division. I finished the radio school in April. On getting my commission, I was sent to work in the radio-telegraph workshop as a technician.

Vyshinsky: During the time when you were in the Red Army, from 1920-24, were the units to which you were attached ever in action?

Sokolov: The unit was not in action.

Vyshinsky: Consequently, you too could not be active?

Sokolov: Yes, and I was not in action.

Vyshinsky: Where was Gussev at that time?

Sokolov: I do not know.

Vyshinsky: And did you never serve in the armoured car division? Or meet Gussev?

Sokolov: No.

Vyshinsky: When did you meet him first?

Sokolov: In Zlatoust in 1925.

Vyshinsky: What was his work there, and what was yours?

Sokolov: I was a foreman in the power station. He was assistant chief. Before this I had met him when working in the mechanical works as rate-fixer.

Vyshinsky: During that period did your counter-revolutionary activity find expression in any way?

Sokolov: At that time I had not yet engaged in counter-revolutionary activities.

Vyshinsky: That means that after 1920 there was a break. Is that so?

Sokolov: Yes.

Vyshinsky: And until when?

Sokolov: Until 1927.

Vyshinsky: It follows that the second period of your counter-revolutionary activities begins from 1927. Is that correct?

Sokolov: Yes.

Vyshinsky: Why and in what circumstances did you begin your counter-revolutionary activities during that period and what form did they take?

Sokolov: I was not inclined towards the Soviets. In other words, I had anti-Soviet inclinations. I held up a series of operations in the electric power station.

Vyshinsky: On your own initiative?

Sokolov: No.

Vyshinsky: No? Then on whose?

Sokolov: The proposal was made to me by the former chief of the electric power station, Vitvitsky.

Vyshinsky: Thus the second period of your counter-revolutionary activities brought you into contact with Vitvitsky.

Sokolov: Yes.

Vyshinsky: Did you work alone with Vitvitsky, or were there other people as well?

Sokolov: I know of no one else.

Vyshinsky: There were two of you?

Sokolov: Yes, I know of only two.

Vyshinsky: Did Vitvitsky give you commissions or did you yourself carry out various acts without any preliminary commission from Vitvitsky?

Sokolov: Vitvitsky told me that I should hold up this or that work.

Vyshinsky: Why did he tell you to?

Sokolov: He knew of my anti-Soviet attitude.

Vyshinsky: How did he know?

Sokolov: From our frequent conversations in the office.

Vyshinsky: How long had you known him?

Sokolov: From the time when he came to the power station. Approximately from the end of 1926. Approximately for about a year.

Vyshinsky: And as a result of your conversations with Vitvitsky, he, recognizing in you a suitable person, indicated to you the necessity of committing . . . what?

Sokolov: Committing wrecking acts.

Vyshinsky: How?

Sokolov: By holding up a number of jobs.

Vyshinsky: What work was held up by you?

Sokolov: I held up work with regard to the connection of the transformers in the power station, and the transfer on the auxiliary excitor of the Westinghouse turbo-generator; and also the minor hold-up of the Zelli turbine.

Vyshinsky: You did all this with the knowledge, or maybe on the proposal, of Vitvitsky?

Sokolov: On the proposal of Vitvitsky.

Vyshinsky: Did you accept the proposal at once?

Sokolov: No, not at once.

Vyshinsky: Why not at once?

Sokolov: Because I considered that the affair would be discovered.

Vyshinsky: You were afraid that the affair would be discovered?

Sokolov: I was afraid of that, but Vitvitsky used repressive measures against me.

Vyshinsky: What measures?

Sokolov: He turned me out of the apartment I occupied and went to live there himself, putting me into an apartment situated on a swamp.

Vyshinsky: And this caused you to obey his instructions?

Sokolov: Yes.

Vyshinsky: When you began to obey his instructions, your position improved?

Sokolov: Yes, his attitude towards me improved.

Vyshinsky: And the apartment affair—that passed off?

Sokolov: The question of the apartment was settled afterwards with the help of Gussev.

Vyshinsky: You mean your apartment was restored to you?

Sokolov: Yes.

Vyshinsky: The same one, or another?

Sokolov: No, another.

Vyshinsky: Gussev helped to arrange it?

Sokolov: Yes, I asked him to.

Vyshinsky: Thus, had it not been for Vitvitsky's pressure, you would have maintained your neutral position?

Sokolov: Yes.

Vyshinsky: You put this down definitely to the activity of Vitvitsky?

Sokolov: Yes, to the activity of Vitvitsky.

Vyshinsky: During what period of time were these acts committed?

Sokolov: In 1927.

Vyshinsky: During the course of one year?

Sokolov: In one year, I imagine, I do not remember exactly. These acts followed one after the other.

Vyshinsky: And in 1928?

Sokolov: Perhaps in 1928. I think the turbine was transferred in 1928—I do not remember the exact date.

Vyshinsky: Thus, 1927, 1928 were marked by acts of this kind?

Sokolov: Yes.

Vyshinsky: And 1929?

Sokolov: I did not carry out any counter-revolutionary acts then.

Vyshinsky: You committed none. And after the 1929 break, what was there?

Sokolov: After the 1929 break there was passivity. I took no part in counter-revolutionary activities until 1930, approximately until June or July, until the time when I came into contact with MacDonald, the English installation engineer.

Vyshinsky: Had you any connection with Gussev before your connection with MacDonald, the English installation engineer?

Sokolov: I always had connection with Gussev.

Vyshinsky: Perhaps Gussev played a definite role earlier than MacDonald, or did both together?

Sokolov: Gussev was anti-Soviet, and so was I. We understood each other perfectly well, but we did not engage in wrecking acts and counter-revolutionary activities then, as far as I know at any rate.

Vyshinsky: And who introduced you to MacDonald?

Sokolov: I became linked up with MacDonald through Gussev.

Vyshinsky: Gussev was first, after all, or was MacDonald first?

Sokolov: I was introduced through Gussev. When MacDonald came to the power station at the end of 1929 and beginning of 1930, Gussev introduced me to MacDonald.

Vyshinsky: How did he introduce you?

Sokolov: He said: "My assistant in charge of the electrical work."

Vyshinsky: Electrical or wrecking?

Sokolov: Electrical. "The assisant with whom you will have to work." It was in his office.

Vyshinsky: And he did not say, this is "my assistant in the sphere of wrecking?"

Sokolov: In the sphere of electricity.

Vyshinsky: At that time you were connected with Gussev in your counter-revolutionary sentiments?

Sokolov: I did not know of Gussev's activities in connection with counter-revolutionary work.

Vyshinsky: When?

Sokolov: Before 1930.

Vyshinsky: And in 1930 you found out?

Sokolov: Yes, I found out in 1930.

Vyshinsky: In what circumstances?

Sokolov: It happened as follows. When I was introduced to MacDonald, Gussev recommended me to MacDonald as a man with anti-Soviet inclinations. MacDonald made use of this and began to hold conversations with me which were more frankly anti-Soviet, saying, you live very badly, the technical personnel is paid badly, is fed badly, your material position is much too poor. The standard of living of your workers is very low. All this construction work that you have undertaken, it is all useless.

Vyshinsky: That is common anti-Soviet talk. What did it lead to?

Sokolov: These conversations strengthened the anti-Soviet leanings I already had. My friendship with MacDonald developed when I visited him in his apartment, in June or July. At that time no questions of a counter-revolutionary nature had yet been discussed. There were just anti-Soviet conversations.

Vyshinsky: Therefore, you connect this new period of your anti-Soviet activities with the moment when Gussev introduced you to MacDonald, recommended you as an anti-Soviet person, and when MacDonald made some proposals to you?

Sokolov: At that time, before I visited his apartment, he had not yet made any proposals to me. Only after I did so were there any proposals made.

Vyshinsky: Tell me, was this visit to his apartment made in the daytime or in the evening, and under what circumstances?

Sokolov: In the evening.

Vyshinsky: What was it, a meeting?

Sokolov: It was just a drinking party. Tea, drinks and snacks.

Vyshinsky: Was he in the habit of having evenings of this kind, or was this an isolated case?

Sokolov: No, not an isolated case.

Vyshinsky: He is fond of drinking?

Sokolov: Yes, he frequently drinks.

Vyshinsky: Did he drink alone or invite the engineers?

Sokolov: It was a gathering of engineers.

Vyshinsky: Besides you, who was there?

Sokolov: I was there and Gussev.

Vyshinsky: In a word, your own crowd.

Sokolov: Yes.

Vyshinsky: How did your evening go off? You drank, and gave some toasts?

Sokolov: Yes.

Vyshinsky: What toast did MacDonald give?

Sokolov: Gussev said: "For the Five-Year Plan in Four," and MacDonald said: "For the Five-Year Plan in Ten Years."

Vyshinsky: And why did Gussev make the toast "For the Five-Year Plan in Four"?

Sokolov: It was said with sarcasm.

Vyshinsky: And MacDonald also spoke with sarcasm?

Sokolov: Yes, he spoke with sarcasm and irony.

Vyshinsky: Sarcasm here and irony there and, in general, an anti-Soviet drinking party?

Sokolov: I supported the affair.

Vyshinsky: What sort of talk was there?

Sokolov: On abstract topics.

Vyshinsky: About how to wreck?

Sokolov: There was no talk of this on that particular evening.

Vyshinsky: And what conversation was there? What do you mean by abstract?

Sokolov: Anti-Soviet conversation of a general kind.

Vyshinsky: Abstract talk about the Soviet Government?

Sokolov: Yes, about the Soviet Government, but there was no concrete solving of any questions at the party that evening.

Vyshinsky: And was there any talk, for instance, about the fact that certain capitalist countries and certain capitalist circles are planning intervention, and similar talk, or was there nothing of the kind?

Sokolov: I do not remember any such talk.

Vyshinsky: Perhaps I might remind you. Allow me. In Volume XVI, page 38 of the dossier, is the following: "The conversation was of an open anti-Soviet nature." Do you confirm this? Then: "Gussev gave a toast for the Five-Year Plan in Four. . . MacDonald corrected him: 'For the Five-Year Plan in Ten Years.' Moreover, he said again that the Soviet Union would not be able to free itself from foreign dependence anyhow . . . would not be able to manage the production of machines, etc."

Sokolov: Yes, that was so.

Vyshinsky: And there was no talk of intervention?

Sokolov: No.

Vyshinsky: But perhaps there was, later?

Sokolov: There was. That was when Gussev and I discussed the plan of wrecking activities.

Vyshinsky: What was said there on the subject?

Sokolov: It was said that should the Soviet Union find itself in difficulties, in the event of intervention, we would have to be prepared for this business in some way or another, and a plan of wrecking was drawn up—to disrupt the normal supply of electricity to the Zlatoust works, to put the station out of commission.

Vyshinsky: Was this conversation at the party that evening or after it?

Sokolov: It was after the party.

Vyshinsky: Consequently, there was no drinking then?

Sokolov: No.

Vyshinsky: All this took place while you were all sober?

Sokolov: Yes, sober.

Vyshinsky: Then who talked about intervention, about preparations for intervention being the undermining of the functioning of the works for the purpose of weakening the economic strength of the Soviet Union?

Sokolov: Gussev and I talked about this.

Vyshinsky: And MacDonald?

Sokolov: There was some talk with MacDonald also.

Vyshinsky: What was the meaning of your conversation with Gussev?

Sokolov: The meaning was that we should fulfil the instructions and tasks given us by MacDonald.

Vyshinsky: And what tasks did MacDonald give you?

Sokolov: To cause breakdowns, to commit acts of diversion and to give information of espionage character.

Vyshinsky: That is, causing breakdowns and acts of diversion on the one hand, and on the other, the receiving of spying information. Whose task was this?

Sokolov: MacDonald's.

Vyshinsky: Did he give you this task while alone, or in the presence of Gussev?

Sokolov: It was like this. MacDonald received information from me personally about the number of workers at the Zlatoust

Metallurgical Works, then about the output of high-grade steel, auto-steel, aviation, ball-bearing and instrumental steel.

Vyshinsky: And did you give information about ingots?

Sokolov: Not to MacDonald personally.

Vyshinsky: Then to whom?

Sokolov: I gave it through Gussev.

Vyshinsky: Why?

Sokolov: It turned out that way. MacDonald said, "You will hand over the information required by me through Gussev." I agreed, and from then on I began to work in contact with Gussev.

Vyshinsky: Who gave you these instructions, MacDonald or Gussev?

Sokolov: On the first two questions, about the number of workers and about high-grade steel, I gave the information directly to MacDonald.

Vyshinsky: As regards the commissions you were given to do by MacDonald in connection with causing breakdowns, acts of diversion and the information you procured—did you get these commissions directly from MacDonald personally or through Gussev?

Sokolov: I received them from Gussev, but knew that the information was from MacDonald. .

Vyshinsky: And MacDonald did not give you this sort of task?

Sokolov: MacDonald said that Gussev and I were entrusted with the work of causing breakdowns and performing acts of diversion. He said, "you must talk it all over with Gussev."

Vyshinsky: Allow me to put a question to Gussev on this point.

The President: You may.

Vyshinsky: Accused Gussev, are you following the examination?

Gussev: Yes.

Vyshinsky: You heard what the accused Sokolov said about giving commissions in connection with breakdowns, acts of diversion and the collection of spying information?

Gussev: Yes.

Vyshinsky: What have you to say?

Gussev: I do not know the content of the conversation between engineer MacDonald and Sokolov. I can only say that, after the general plan had been outlined, a conversation took place with engineer MacDonald and the latter told me that Sokolov could be used for carrying out the plan, *i.e.*, for bringing about the breakdowns.

Vyshinsky: Did you speak with Sokolov about MacDonald's having some sort of mission, some task?

Gussev: Afterwards, I spoke with Sokolov about this.

Vyshinsky: Excellent. Now allow me to put a question to the accused MacDonald.

Accused MacDonald, did you hear Sokolov's testimony?

MacDonald: Yes.

Vyshinsky: What have you to say about Sokolov's testimony to the effect that you gave out commissions for the organizing of breakdowns and acts of diversion and the collection of espionage information?

MacDonald: To whom?

Vyshinsky: To Sokolov and Gussev.

MacDonald: No.

Vyshinsky: Then to whom did you give them?

MacDonald: I had dealings with Gussev.

Vyshinsky: That means you said this to Gussev?

MacDonald: Yes.

Vyshinsky: It follows that you here confirm your deposition at the preliminary investigation, where you deposed to this effect.

MacDonald: I do not understand.

Vyshinsky: At the preliminary investigation, you were asked whether you gave Gussev commissions to perform in connection with the organization of breakdowns and the collection of espionage information.

MacDonald: Perhaps we could continue through the interpreter?

Vyshinsky: Let us do it another way; let the interpreter read out the deposition made in English by MacDonald; and MacDonald will answer whether it is so or not.

The President: You may.

Vyshinsky: On page 205, Volume XIX, April 2, 1933, Sheinin, the Investigating Judge on Important Cases, questioned MacDonald, who deposed: "In addition to the testimonies I have given before, I state as follows: I confirm that in my conversation with Sokolov at the end of 1930 I have not given him definite instructions on wrecking of equipment but I told him that he and Gussev had to undertake the taking out of service of plant and that he (Sokolov) had to come to an understanding directly with Gussev."

MacDonald: What do you mean by saying that Sokolov was to be charged with the wrecking of equipment?

Vyshinsky (Reads the Russian text of the same deposition): Did you say this and do you confirm the deposition you made?

MacDonald: I did not give Sokolov orders to carry out breakdowns.

Vyshinsky: Then why did you depose to this effect at the preliminary investigation?

MacDonald: Because I considered that it was convenient to make that statement under those circumstances.

Vyshinsky: And when was this examination?

MacDonald: I do not remember the date.

Vyshinsky: In which language did you make your deposition, in Russian or in English?

MacDonald: The script was made in Russian by the investigator and after this translated.

Vyshinsky: Did you not translate it into English yourself?

MacDonald: No.

Vyshinsky (To the Court): I ask permission to call MacDonald over here and confront him with the original dossier. On page 204, Volume XIX, there is an original record of MacDonald's own deposition. On the left side of the page in this record is the signature of MacDonald. Is it in his handwriting or not? The deposition was made at the examination by the Public Prosecutor, and not in the O.G.P.U.

The President (To MacDonald): Please come here. [MacDonald goes to the table of the Special Session.] Was the deposition on page 204 written by you in your own handwriting?

Vyshinsky (To MacDonald): Read this please.

MacDonald: Yes, I signed this.

Vyshinsky: Under what circumstances, why did you sign it?

MacDonald: I considered it convenient under those circumstances.

Vyshinsky: Under what circumstances? Were any special methods of examination applied to you?

MacDonald: No.

Vyshinsky: Were you forced to write this?

MacDonald: No, but I signed it because it was not the open court.

Vyshinsky: Were you compelled to do so?

MacDonald: In the beginning I refused to do it.

Vyshinsky: Where?

MacDonald: Before the investigator—when the investigator said: "Sign," I said, "No." But he did not allow me to do otherwise.

Vyshinsky: He forced you to?

MacDonald: (No answer.)

The President: The record of the examination of the accused MacDonald, made by the Public Prosecutor of the Republic on April 2 and written in MacDonald's handwriting in the English language, will now be read out.

(To the interpreter): Please read out MacDonald's deposition in the English language.

The Interpreter (Reads the following full text of the deposition by MacDonald):

"In addition to the testimonies I have given before, I state as follows:

I confirm that in my conversation with Sokolov at the end of 1930 I have not given him definite instructions on wrecking of equipment but I told him that he and Gussev had to undertake the taking out of service of plant and that he (Sokolov) had to come to an understanding directly with Gussev.

Besides this, I told Sokolov that for this work he should receive monetary remuneration.

Gussev informed me that the 1,400 h.p. motor was taken out of service.

April 2, 1933 W. L. MacDonald."

The President: And is there the signature and the date?

The Interpreter: There is the signature and the date. April 2, 1933.

The President: That is to say, only ten days ago.

Vyshinsky: I want to establish a few points. I ask the Court to pay attention to the following facts: 1. the examination in question took place on April 2 and was carried out by the Investigating Judge on Important Cases under the Public Prosecutor of the Republic. On the right hand side, on page 204, there is the translation, written in MacDonald's own handwriting, of the deposition, given by him orally in the Russian language, and countersigned with his own signature, and in this deposition, certain facts, which have just been read out, were confirmed. 2. MacDonald declared that under "those circumstances" he considered it necessary to say what he did. 3. In reply to my question as to whether any special methods were applied to him which would force him to give this testimony, he answered in the negative.

Now, I should like to put one more question to MacDonald. Accused MacDonald, after April 2, did you make any declaration to anybody to the effect that your deposition does not correspond to the facts, or did you not make any such declaration?

MacDonald: No such statement.

Vyshinsky: At the close of the preliminary investigation, did you receive the record from the Public Prosecutor where you were declared accused; and was it proposed to you at the same time, according to the law, to make any statement, if you so cared to do, about the procedure of the preliminary investigation?

MacDonald: Yes.

Vyshinsky: You were notified that you have the right to put forward any claims you may have in connection with the preliminary investigation. Did you make any statement to the effect that your deposition does not correspond to the fact?

MacDonald: No.

Vyshinsky: And why didn't you tell anyone?

MacDonald: As I didn't want to state to anybody.

Vyshinsky: Why didn't you want to make statements you are prepared to make now?

MacDonald: I do not want to discuss this point.

Vyshinsky: Do you understand the significance of this written deposition?

MacDonald: Yes.

Vyshinsky: Perhaps you will at least answer one question. Yesterday, in reply to the question as to whether you consider yourself guilty of the charges brought against you, you declared: "Yes, guilty." Do you deny this today, or do you confirm that you are guilty?

MacDonald: According to the testimony given by myself, I plead guilty; in actual fact, not guilty.

Vyshinsky: I am not asking about that. Yesterday, did you say that you consider yourself guilty or didn't you? Perhaps I dreamed it all.

MacDonald: Yesterday I pleaded guilty.

Vyshinsky: And today?

MacDonald: Today in accordance with what I have just said, not guilty.

Vyshinsky: It follows that we may expect that perhaps tomorrow you will do the opposite.

MacDonald: No.

Vyshinsky: Yesterday you said that you gave Gussev instructions about the breakdown of the 1,400 h.p. motor. Did you give Gussev such instructions, or not?

MacDonald: The remarks that I made to Gussev about the motor were to the effect that the motor was in such a bad condition, it needed replacement. How he interpreted this, I cannot answer.

Vyshinsky: It is definitely known how Gussev interpreted it. He obtained direct instructions from you to the effect that the motor should be put out of service by means of a breakdown. In reply to my question to you as to whether you confirm this or not (this is fixed in the stenogram), you declared yesterday: "Yes, I confirm it." I now ask, do you confirm this now or not?

MacDonald: I agree, that was written in my testimony. What I wrote was in agreement with my statement of yesterday.

Vyshinsky: True. Do you agree with it?

MacDonald: Yes.

Vyshinsky: In order to finish the dialogue on this question, I want to know whether you received information from Sokolov or not?

MacDonald: What sort of information?

Vyshinsky: That about which you spoke yesterday, about which Gussev spoke yesterday, and about which Sokolov spoke today.

MacDonald: Sokolov told me of a number of people employed in the various works, and general remarks of such a nature.

Vyshinsky: Let us stop at that. Did you pay for this?

MacDonald: No.

Vyshinsky: Accused Sokolov, did you receive any money from MacDonald?

Sokolov: I received a thousand rubles through Gussev.

Vyshinsky: Accused Gussev, did you hand a thousand rubles to Sokolov?

Gussev: Yes.

Vyshinsky: Accused MacDonald, did you hand a thousand rubles to Gussev?

MacDonald: In general I gave money to Gussev.

Vyshinsky: What did you give Gussev money for?

MacDonald: At various times the workmen employed on the erection of the Metro-Vickers turbine worked very much overtime, sometimes 24 hours.

Vyshinsky: So it was for overtime work?

MacDonald: Yes.

The President: Accused MacDonald, was Gussev in your service?

MacDonald: No.

The President: Why, then, do you speak of overtime work?

MacDonald: For overtime work, for work 24 hours on end.

Vyshinsky: Were they paid wages?

MacDonald: Yes.

Vyshinsky: Besides this, you paid them also?

MacDonald: Yes.

Vyshinsky: Through Gussev?

MacDonald: Yes.

Vyshinsky: And you paid big sums of money?

MacDonald: As far as I can remember, for the whole time, I used about 2,500 rubles.

Vyshinsky: Then you confirm that you paid 2,500 rubles for so-called overtime work?

MacDonald: Yes.

Vyshinsky: Where did you get the 2,500 rubles for overtime work?

MacDonald: Part of the money was my own and part of it I received from the Moscow office of Metro-Vickers.

Vyshinsky: From whom precisely in the Moscow office of Metropolitan-Vickers?

MacDonald: From the chief engineer of the erection department, Mr. Thornton.

Vyshinsky: So part came from Thornton and part from your personal funds?

MacDonald: Yes.

Vyshinsky: So in order to pay for overtime work put in by the mechanics at the Zlatoust Station, you used your own money and paid for the work of the mechanics out of your pocket?

MacDonald: Yes.

Vyshinsky: And you think that this is a plausible explanation, that you paid with your money?

MacDonald: Yes.

Vyshinsky: Very good. Did you have a great amount of such personal funds?

MacDonald: No, I cannot remember.

Vyshinsky: But did you have a great deal?

MacDonald: All the money I had was 600 or 700 rubles.

Vyshinsky: So out of 600 to 700 rubles you paid 2,500?

MacDonald: The 600 to 700 rubles was my own money.

Vyshinsky: And then?

MacDonald: I also had money which I obtained from the office of Metro-Vickers.

Vyshinsky: From Thornton?

MacDonald: Yes.

Vyshinsky: And did Thornton give you much?

MacDonald: No, I cannot remember exactly, but I think I had about 1,500 rubles.

Vyshinsky: About 1,500 rubles and a further 600 makes 2,100. Is that right?

MacDonald: Yes.

Vyshinsky: The six hundred rubles of your own money that you paid the workers out of your own pocket, were they refunded by the Moscow office or were they lost?

MacDonald: They were lost. *(Murmur in the Court.)*

Vyshinsky: When were you arrested?

MacDonald: The 11th of March.

Vyshinsky: When were you questioned for the first time?

MacDonald: The following day.

Vyshinsky: May I show you one of your depositions and ask you to give an explanation?

MacDonald: Yes.

Vyshinsky: This is the deposition in Volume XII, page 14. This deposition is written in English and is the original. I request that the deposition be shown to MacDonald and let him be asked whether he wrote it himself or not. (Original deposition written in English is handed to MacDonald for inspection.)

Vyshinsky: Is that your deposition?

MacDonald: Yes.

Vyshinsky: So you confirm that this deposition was written by you personally?

MacDonald: I do.

Vyshinsky: Please listen to this part of the deposition—the second paragraph of the first page. I will ask the translator to read it in English.

The Interpreter (Reads the above-mentioned deposition in English): "Whilst I was there I made it my business to find out all I could about the political, economical and military state of the country. In this I was greatly helped by engineer Gussev of the power station and various men employed by him, Sokolov and others."

Vyshinsky: What have you to say about it?

MacDonald: What I said before, that under the circumstances, I considered it was necessary to make the statement after other testimony was presented.

Vyshinsky: What testimony?

MacDonald: The first testimony which I saw was written by Mr. Thornton.

Vyshinsky: So you spoke under the influence of the deposition of Thornton?

MacDonald: I was shown the deposition of Mr. Thornton. . . .

The President: Of what date?

Vyshinsky: He was arrested on the 11th; evidently it was the 12th. I do not yet know what your answer to my question is: "Under whose influence did you make such a deposition?"

MacDonald: After reading the text of Mr. Thornton's testimony which was shown to me in the dossier, and after having seen all this, I decided that under those circumstances, having so much evidence against me, it was necessary to give such deposition.

Vyshinsky: So it was Thornton's deposition which made you give such a deposition?

MacDonald: Not the evidence given by Mr. Thornton, but the fact that there was such evidence.

Vyshinsky: What depositions of Thornton were shown to you? As the question is now centering around MacDonald, perhaps the accused Sokolov can be asked to sit down and MacDonald be asked to come forward.

The President: Accused Sokolov, be seated. Accused MacDonald.

Vyshinsky: Accused MacDonald, you made a deposition on March 13 owing to the fact that you were confronted with the deposition of Thornton. Will you please tell us what was contained in this deposition of Thornton?

MacDonald: In Thornton's deposition it is written that Thornton had used me to gather information in the Zlatoust district, and that Gussev was also used for the same purpose. The names of some English engineers were also mentioned.

Vyshinsky: In the deposition of March 13, MacDonald says: "Whilst I was there I made it my business to find out all I could about the political, economical and military state of the country. In this I was greatly helped by engineer Gussev of the power station and various men employed by him, Sokolov and others."

I am interested in this part—about the military situation of the country. Why did you make this deposition on March 13? It would seem that you were first shown Thornton's deposition which exposed the same thing. Have I understood you right?

MacDonald: I wish to be understood in this way: I saw the deposition of Mr. Thornton, and I also saw a large book which was said to contain other depositions and so decided that it was no use on my part to deny the charges.

Vyshinsky: You decided that it was useless to deny any longer. Is that right?

MacDonald: Yes.

Vyshinsky (To the Court): I wish to question the accused Thornton.

The President: Certainly.

Vyshinsky: Accused Thornton, did you hear the interrogation?

Thornton: Yes, I heard it.

Vyshinsky: MacDonald here stated that when he was examined on March 13 regarding the military situation of the country, and when he made his deposition, he did it under the impression of your deposition, the deposition of Thornton. Did you make such depositions in which you said that you or MacDonald gathered military information?

Thornton: There was such a deposition: page 26, March 13.

Vyshinsky: So it was not the day before, March 12, but the same day.

Thornton: It was late at night or early in the morning.

Vyshinsky: The 14th.

Thornton: No, I think it was the 13th.

Vyshinsky: Did you make such a deposition?

Thornton: I made it, but I wish to state that this deposition was not correct.

Vyshinsky: And under whose influence did you make this deposition? MacDonald made it under your influence and you evidently did so under his influence? Why did you make an untrue deposition?

Thornton: Because I was very excited and lost my courage.

Vyshinsky: Why did you loose your courage?

Thornton: Under the influence of events.

The President: What events?

Thornton: My arrest.

Vyshinsky: An unpleasant event, certainly.

The President: You were kept under arrest for one day and you lost your nerve?

Vyshinsky: You are an officer, I think?

Thornton: No.

Vyshinsky: Have you served in the army?

Thornton: Yes.

Vyshinsky: In what rank?

Thornton: In the army supply train.

Vyshinsky: Service in the army supply train. Did you fight in the army supply train?

Thornton: Yes, I did.

Vyshinsky: So, you were arrested and the arrest made an impression on you.

Thornton: Not the arrest, but this terrible charge.

Vyshinsky: Yesterday you gave three replies to three of my questions as to whether you were compelled to make a deposition? You said—no.

Thornton: Nor do I say it now.

Vyshinsky: And were you shown depositions previously?

Thornton: Summaries of depositions were read to me.

Vyshinsky: Whose?

Thornton: Monkhouse's.

Vyshinsky: Did he also give you away?

Thornton: And MacDonald's.

Vyshinsky: So MacDonald made a deposition under the impression of your deposition which was shown to him. But you made a deposition under the impression of MacDonald's deposition which was shown to you. Which of these depositions came first?

Thornton: I don't quite understand.

The President: In other words, who gave the other away? Did Thornton betray MacDonald, or MacDonald, Thornton?

Thornton: I don't know.

Vyshinsky: Let me record the following fact: MacDonald explains his deposition of March 13 by saying that he was previously confronted with the deposition of Thornton. Under the influence of this deposition, he decided that there was no use in denying the matter any longer and began to say what he did say. Is that true, MacDonald?

MacDonald: Yes.

Vyshinsky: Thornton states that he gave his deposition under the influence of the deposition of MacDonald which was presented to him. Is that so?

Thornton: And other depositions.

Vyshinsky: At present I am interested in MacDonald. Is that true?

Thornton: Not entirely.

Vyshinsky: In this part? In the military part?

Thornton: I gave a plainly false deposition.

Vyshinsky: We shall examine later whether it was false or not.

Thornton: I say that it was false. You can say what you like.

Vyshinsky: I shall say nothing more than you do. MacDonald says that he made his deposition on March 13 under the influence of your deposition. Did I understand you rightly that in this part you made your deposition under the influence of MacDonald's deposition which was shown to you?

Thornton: And others.

Vyshinsky: Quite so. Is that right?

Thornton: Right.

Vyshinsky: It remains undecided which deposition was first. It seems that you influenced each other. But something preceded something. Can you explain this?

Thornton: It was not given into my hand. A dossier was taken and read out to me.

Vyshinsky: Accused MacDonald, in this same deposition of March 13, you confessed to having received . . . "secret information relative to: 1) the work of military shops of the mechanical and metallurgical works, including the production of the shell shops, the quality, the quantity of the shells made, their types and other data; 2) the development of military shops. . . ." Do you confirm that you said this?

MacDonald: Yes, I said so.

Vyshinsky: Correct, you said so. But that was not really the case? You did not receive this information?

MacDonald: Gussev said that they make large shells and small ones.

Vyshinsky: So in this part you confirm that you received information on shells from Gussev. Am I correct?

MacDonald: Correct.

Vyshinsky: And so you really received this information about shells from Gussev?

MacDonald: Yes, he told me that they were being made there.

Vyshinsky: Has this information about shells any relation to the Metro-Vickers Company or not?

MacDonald: None whatever.

Vyshinsky: None whatever. Why then did you, an employee of the Mero-Vickers Company, receive information which has no relation to the Metro-Vickers Company? For whom did you receive it?

MacDonald: For no one. For myself.

Vyshinsky: Why were you interested in shells?

MacDonald: Out of curiosity.

Vyshinsky: Curiosity is a great vice.

I have no further questions for MacDonald at present.

The President: I have a question. Why did you decide to make yourself ridiculous today in the eyes of the Court and the public present?

MacDonald: I do not think that I look ridiculous.

The President: I have another question wherewith to check the accused Thornton this time. You stated in reply to the question of the Public Prosecutor that you made your deposition on March 12, the second day after your arrest, because you lost your courage. Do you remember when your courage returned and on what date?

Thornton: My courage returned on April 4.

The President: At what hour?

Thornton: At six o'clock. *(Murmurs and laughter in Court)*

The President: We will continue the examination of Sokolov.

Vyshinsky: Accused Sokolov, in connection with what has just passed, what can you say concerning your spying activities? Did you really give information of a military nature or not?

Sokolov: I gave information of a military character also.

Vyshinsky: When you received the money from Gussev, did

you hear from him or could you guess for what you received the money and from whom, whose money it was, although money in general does not smell?

Sokolov: I received the money from Gussev with the remark: "Here is a premium for you from Vassily Vassilievich."

Vyshinsky: Who is that?

Sokolov: MacDonald.

Vyshinsky: That is what you called MacDonald?

Do you confirm this, accused Gussev?

Gussev: Yes, I gave the money.

Vyshinsky: And so, Sokolov received 1,000 rubles from Gussev, Gussev received 1,000 rubles and over, from MacDonald. Sokolov Gussev and MacDonald confirmed it.

Secondly, Sokolov gave information of a military character, of State and military importance. This is confirmed by Sokolov and MacDonald, that he received such information, Am I right?

Sokolov: Yes.

Vyshinsky: Gussev, is that right?

Gussev: Yes.

Vyshinsky: MacDonald, is that right?

MacDonald: Yes.

Vyshinsky: I have no further questions.

The President: Has the Defence any questions to ask Sokolov?

Defence: No.

The President: Have the accused any questions to ask Sokolov?

The Accused: No.

The President: The Court will take a recess for twenty minutes.

* * *

The Commandant: Please rise. The Court is coming.

The President: Please be seated. We will consider the examination of Sokolov closed.

Vyshinsky: I have no more questions.

Kaznacheyev: I have two questions.

You spoke here of some periods in your counter-revolutionary activity. In the last period, you mentioned that you received money. But in the previous periods, particularly when you had relations with Vitvitsky, did you receive any remuneration or not?

Sokolov: No.

Kaznacheyev: Then the material aspect did not play any role?

Sokolov: No.

Kaznacheyev: The material aspect did not play any role in the first stage of your work either?

Sokolov: It did not play a big role.

Kaznacheyev: So it did play some role?

Sokolov: To some extent only, because my salary was quite a good one.

Kaznacheyev: The last question. When Gussev introduced you to MacDonald, was his role that of a simple intermediary or something else?

Sokolov: The role of Gussev was simply that of an intermediary, because the chief factor which impelled me to undertake counter-revolutionary work, the motivating factor, was the frequent conversations I had with MacDonald.

Kaznacheyev: Did you ever ask MacDonald why he was collecting information?

Sokolov: No, I did not ask, but I understood that it was not for his personal interests. If he asked about the work of a turbine, this would interest his firm, but a question about the number of workers. . . .

Kaznacheyev: You are speaking about suppositions, but I am asking you whether you had concrete talks with him on this subject?

Sokolov: There were no concrete talks about what this information was wanted for.

Kaznacheyev: Did you think it embarrassing to start such conversations, or did you think that he would not reply?

Sokolov: I thought it would be embarrassing.

Kaznacheyev: I have no more questions.

The President (To the Public Prosecutor): Have you any questions?

Vyshinsky: No.

The President: Accused MacDonald, come forward please. The Court has no questions at present.

Vyshinsky: Accused MacDonald, please be good enough to tell us when you first came to the U.S.S.R.

MacDonald: At the beginning of 1928.

Vyshinsky: And what position did you occupy when you arrived in the U.S.S.R.?

MacDonald: Installation engineer on turbines.

Vyshinsky: In what town did you live?

MacDonald: In Moscow.

Vyshinsky: So you came to Moscow in 1928 and took up the position of installation engineer here in the Moscow office of the Metropolitan-Vickers Company? Or was it somewhere else?

MacDonald: At the First Moscow State Electric Power Station.

Vyshinsky: How long did you occupy this position?

MacDonald: Nine or ten months.

Vyshinsky: To whom were you subordinate in this work in the Metro-Vickers firm?

MacDonald: To Monkhouse, the chief engineer.

Vyshinsky: Had you any official business relations with Thornton at the time?

MacDonald: No.

Vyshinsky: When did you begin to have official business relations with Thornton?

MacDonald: Towards the end of 1928 or the beginning of 1929.

Vyshinsky: Where did you go when you left the First Moscow Electric Power Station and Moscow?

MacDonald: After leave of absence spent in London, I went to Leningrad.

Vyshinsky: You arrived in Leningrad towards the end of 1928. or in the beginning of 1929?

MacDonald: At the end of 1928.

Vyshinsky: Where did you work in Leningrad?

MacDonald: At the Fifth State Electric Power Station.

Vyshinsky: Had you any connection at all with the "Krassny Oktyabr"?

MacDonald: Yes.

Vyshinsky: The Fifth State Electric Power Station is actually the "Krassny Oktyabr"?

MacDonald: The Fifth Power Station is called "Krassny Oktyabr".

Vyshinsky: When in Leningrad, did you collect any information?

MacDonald: Yes.

Vyshinsky: What information?

MacDonald: As indicated in my depositions.

Vyshinsky: Perhaps you will allow me to state what it was If necessary, it will be translated. You said that you engaged in systematic economic espionage. Do you confirm this?

MacDonald: I confirm it.

Vyshinsky: Political—do you confirm that?

MacDonald: I confirm it.

Vyshinsky: And military?

MacDonald: I confirm it.

Vyshinsky: And where did you get the information of a military character?

MacDonald: Near our electric power station there was the "Bolshevik" Works.

Vyshinsky: What information did you get from the "Bolshevik" or about the "Bolshevik"?

MacDonald: Aeroplane motors are made there, and tested there.

Vyshinsky: And besides aeroplane motors, did you receive information about the firing ranges where artillery is tested?

MacDonald: Whatever there was to hear.

Vyshinsky: So you obtained information about the testing of guns. Is that so?

MacDonald: Yes.

Vyshinsky: For what purpose did you collect this information, what was it required for?

MacDonald: These inquiries were of interest to me.

Vyshinsky: Very well. At the preliminary investigation you testified that not you alone and not only you personally were engaged in this intelligence work, but that you carried on this intelligence activity under the guidance of certain other persons Do you confirm this?

MacDonald: All that I found out there I passed on in conversation to Mr. Thornton.

Vyshinsky: Including the information about the firing range guns, aeroplane motors? You communicated this also to Thornton?

MacDonald: Yes, this also.

Vyshinsky: It follows then that you confirm your testimony to the effect that intelligence work was carried on in the U.S.S.R. under the guidance of Thornton?

MacDonald: Yes.

Vyshinsky: Do you also confirm that besides Thornton, several other engineers of the Metro-Vickers firm were participants in this intelligence work?

MacDonald: I did not know, but I assumed as much.

Vyshinsky: In particular, did you presume that engineer Cushny, ex-officer in the British army, also took part in this work?

MacDonald: I did.

Vyshinsky: You presumed this also. Then on this point we do not disagree.

Now permit me to put the following question: when did you first go to Zlatoust?

MacDonald: Early in 1930.

Vyshinsky: Whom did you meet there?

MacDonald: What?

Vyshinsky: With whom of the Russian engineers did you first become acquainted?

MacDonald: From the very beginning I became acquainted with the chief engineer. I have forgotten his name.

Vyshinsky: When were you introduced to Gussev?

MacDonald: To Gussev, later on.

Vyshinsky: What sort of relations existed between you and Gussev?

MacDonald: Friendly ones.

Vyshinsky: I have this question: did you speak to Gussev about wrecking equipment? Your preliminary deposition about the 1,400 h.p. motor, do you confirm it or not?

MacDonald: I confirm what I deposed.

Vyshinsky: You deposed that you gave Gussev instructions to wreck this 1,400 h.p. motor. Do you confirm this or not?

MacDonald: Yes.

Vyshinsky: Very well; accused Gussev, do you confirm your

explanation of yesterday as to the circumstances under which you received this instruction from MacDonald?

Gussev: Yes, I fully confirm it.

Vyshinsky (To MacDonald): Please tell me, in what manner you received information from Gussev which contained data of a military character? Did you receive it over his signature or in some other way?

MacDonald: We only had talks.

Vyshinsky: And the information that he sent through Ryabova, did you receive it?

MacDonald: Yes.

Vyshinsky: Why did you make use of Ryabova?

MacDonald: Because she was my housekeeper.

Vyshinsky: Did you find that convenient?

MacDonald: Of course, if she went from Zlatoust to Zuevka, she could take along a letter.

Vyshinsky: When you transmitted the information you received from Gussev, to Thornton, did the information that Thornton received from you satisfy him; was he glad to get it, and was it sufficient?

MacDonald: Yes.

Vyshinsky: Did Thornton give you any instructions to carry out?

MacDonald: What instructions?

Vyshinsky: That you should collect various information.

MacDonald: Yes, he spoke about that to me.

Vyshinsky: Permit me to ask you this now: at the preliminary investigation you testified that Thornton was interested in certain questions—political, economic, military, and that you had collected information about the food situation, about the functioning of the "Bolshevik" Works, about aeroplane motors, about the production of guns, and that all this information you passed on to Thornton in December 1929, is that right?

MacDonald: Yes.

Vyshinsky: That is, you confirm that in December you transmitted information to Thornton about aeroplane motors, about the functioning of the "Bolshevik" Works, about the production of guns?

MacDonald: Yes.

Vyshinsky (To Thornton): You have heard MacDonald's testimony, where he says that in December 1929 he gave you information about aeroplane motors, about the functioning of the "Bolshevik" Works. Do you confirm this?

Thornton: I do not remember him having said that, but I knew myself that the "Bolshevik" Works makes guns.

Vyshinsky: And you do not remember whether there was any conversation with MacDonald about guns, motors, etc.?

Thornton: I do not remember.

Vyshinsky: So, when he says that he informed you. . . .

Thornton: He is not telling the truth.

Vyshinsky: Then you say. . . .

Thornton: I do not remember him saying that.

Vyshinsky: But you cannot say that he is not telling the truth; you cannot assert that this is not true.

Thornton: I say that I do not remember that, but I say that I knew about the functioning of the "Bolshevik" Works and about the firing range. When they shoot there all the windows shake in the power station.

Vyshinsky: But not all those who hear the shooting know all that is to be known about these guns.

Thornton: They know what I know. I know that there is a firing range there, and nothing more.

Vyshinsky: That is rather little.

Thornton: Yes, that is very little.

Vyshinsky: MacDonald tells a different story. Of course, when it is a question of guns, well, all right, everybody hears them. But when it is the question of an aeroplane motor?

Thornton: The motor is tested opposite the power station on the other side of the Neva, and these motors make a lot of noise, so that everybody can hear that noise as well.

Vyshinsky: So you only heard the noise, and nothing more?

Thornton: Nothing more.

Vyshinsky: Then MacDonald gave you no information?

Thornton: No.

Vyshinsky: And yet MacDonald asserts that he did. [To MacDonald] You did say that, did you not?

MacDonald: Yes, we had such a conversation.

Vyshinsky (To Thornton): So that besides the noise of the motor, there was also a quiet talk?

Thornton: I do not confirm this.

Vyshinsky: But you remember Voykov Street in Leningrad?

Thornton: Yes.

Vyshinsky: Do you remember house No. 13?

Thornton: Yes.

Vyshinsky: Perhaps you had a talk with MacDonald before his departure for Zlatoust in this street, in this house? Did you have any conversation there before MacDonald set out for Zlatoust?

Thornton: I think that at that time it was not known that MacDonald was going to Zlatoust. However, I do not remember very well.

Vyshinsky (To MacDonald): Was it known, or was it a secret?

MacDonald: Of course I knew where I was going.

Vyshinsky: You knew. And did your other comrades know or not? Thornton, for example? Or did you keep it from them?

MacDonald: Everybody knew.

Vyshinsky: And Thornton knew?

MacDonald: I think he knew.

Vyshinsky (To Thornton): And yet you say you did not know.

Thornton: I cannot say for sure. I thought that he was appointed to Zlatoust from England. Perhaps I did know.

Vyshinsky: So you do not remember. Perhaps you knew. Is your memory usually poor?

Thornton: I have a poor memory for dates.

Vyshinsky: For dates and facts.

Thornton: It is you who are adding the word "facts."

Vyshinsky: I am only asking you concerning the fact of the conversation and the fact of your knowledge of MacDonald's departure: these are not dates, but facts. Is your memory weak on facts?

Thornton: I do not remember very well.

Vyshinsky: So, you do not remember the conversation you had with MacDonald about Zlatoust?

Thornton: If I did not know that he was going there, then I do not remember the conversation either.

Vyshinsky: I want to refresh your memory. In that conversation, did you not ask MacDonald to get you information about the manufacture of munitions at the Zlatoust works?

Thornton: That is an absolute lie.

Vyshinsky: MacDonald, at the examination you deposed that: "Thornton asked me to obtain information about the manufacture of munitions." Do you confirm this?

MacDonald: I confirm it.

Vyshinsky (To Thornton): Perhaps you will recollect?

Thornton: I never asked for military information to be collected.

Vyshinsky: At the preliminary investigation you spoke of this when confronted with MacDonald, didn't you?

Thornton: Yes, I did. The investigator asked whether MacDonald informed me about the firing range.

Vyshinsky: And did you have any conversation about means of military defence, about information concerning defence and offence, or about the military defensive and offensive possibilities of the Soviet Union? Did you have such a conversation?

Thornton: No. There is my evidence.

Vyshinsky: Repeat it.

Thornton: If it is dated March 26, then I deny it.

Vyshinsky: No, it is not the 26th. Do you deny this too?

Thornton: I deny it.

Vyshinsky: Were you confronted with MacDonald or not?

Thornton: I was.

Vyshinsky: When confronted with MacDonald, he declared that you were interested in and obtained information from MacDonald concerning matters of military defence and offence characterizing the military defensive and offensive possibilities of the Soviet Union.

Thornton: As far as I remember, MacDonald did say that

Vyshinsky: And you confirmed it?

Thornton: No.

Vyshinsky: You did not confirm it then?

Thornton: No.

Vyshinsky: Here is the tenth question to Thornton, on page 121, Vol. XVIII: "You stated that you received from MacDonald information regarding the offensive and defensive possibilities of the Soviet Union. Do you confirm this testimony?" And Thornton's reply: "Yes, I confirm that I received from Mr. MacDonald information regarding the offensive and defensive possibilities of the Soviet Union."

What have you to say?

Thornton: I had in mind that MacDonald told me. . . .

Vyshinsky: I read out what he said. And you confirmed it?

Thornton: Yes.

Vyshinsky: You confirmed it; then how can you now say that you did not confirm it?

MacDonald, you were asked a question as to whether you had given information to Thornton concerning the defensive and offensive possibilities, and which precisely. You answered: "Yes." Is this so? Do you confirm it?

MacDonald: It is true.

Thornton: And what did I say?

Vyshinsky: And you said: "I confirm that I received from MacDonald information concerning the offensive and defensive possibilities of the Soviet Union."

Thornton: I absolutely deny the point about the shells.

Vyshinsky: You only said that motors make a noise, guns shoot and nothing more?

Thornton: Yes.

Vyshinsky: Why did you speak otherwise before?

Thornton: I have already explained that to you.

The President: You lost your courage?

Thornton: Yes.

Vyshinsky: Next you were asked: "Do you confirm that MacDonald gave you this information?" Your answer was: "He told me that in general they are making shells at Zlatoust." Did he say that?

Thornton: I knew that myself.

Vyshinsky: That is not written down; further on it says: "He told me that many troops were concentrated in Leningrad."

Thornton: That is true.

Vyshinsky: And did he talk about shells?

Thornton: Perhaps, as gossip.

Vyshinsky: Really—he passed on common gossip about shells? So we can say that a conversation took place between you and MacDonald about the Zlatoust works and in particular about the manufacture of shells? Is that so?

Thornton: Perhaps that was so. I do not remember very well.

Vyshinsky: But you say that conversations did take place?

Thornton: I confirm that there was some gossip.

Vyshinsky: Was there any such gossip with anyone else?

Thornton: There were many people.

Vyshinsky: For example, with Monkhouse about war shells?

Thornton: No, with Russians.

Vyshinsky: And so, there was special gossip with the Russians about shells?

Thornton: No, with MacDonald. He said that they made shells. I knew that myself.

Vyshinsky: Hence, being interested in it, you tested your knowledge? All right. Now tell me, did you know that Gussev was connected in his spying work with MacDonald?

Thornton: I knew that Gussev was MacDonald's friend.

Vyshinsky: But that he was his friend in spying?

Thornton: I did not know that.

Vyshinsky: And were you asked about this at the preliminary investigation?

Thornton: It is written there that Gussev was a "resident," if I am not mistaken.

Vyshinsky: And you said that you confirm this?

Thornton: No.

Vyshinsky: You don't confirm it now?

Thornton: We don't do any spying work at all.

The President: It does not matter what it is called. It can be called by a different name.

Vyshinsky: Let us check up a few facts again. Gussev is MacDonald's friend; Gussev collects certain information for MacDonald. Did you know about that?

Thornton: Information that might be of interest to our firm.

Vyshinsky: I do not know what information might interest

your firm. We shall discover that later with your assistance. I ask you whether you knew that Gussev was collecting certain information for MacDonald?

Thornton: MacDonald received information from Gussev thanks to their friendly relations.

Vyshinsky: And also thanks to money? Money was paid, was it not?

Thornton: I have heard here that money was paid.

Vyshinsky: Aha! Here! But you did not hear of it before? Did you give 2,000 odd rubles to MacDonald?

Thornton: I gave MacDonald 2,000 rubles to straighten out his unfavourable balance.

Vyshinsky: Well then, did he squander the money?

Thornton: No, he did not squander it.

Vyshinsky: Why then, did he have an unfavourable balance?

Thornton: Because he took a lot of money in advance.

Vyshinsky: Why?

Thornton: I don't know why. He owed several thousand rubles.

Vyshinsky: And you wanted to straighten out his financial affairs?

Thornton: I will tell about this in detail.

Vyshinsky: And so, when Gussev gave information to MacDonald, you did not know that Gussev received money from MacDonald?

Thornton: I did not know it.

Vyshinsky: But you knew what information Gussev gave?

Thornton: The most ordinary information about the station.

Vyshinsky: That is to say?

Thornton: How the machines were working.

Vyshinsky: Why did Gussev have to give this information? MacDonald was there and he could give it.

Thornton: When MacDonald himself was there, it was another matter.

Vyshinsky: But you do not deny that the information he gave covered more than merely the work of the station?

Thornton: Perhaps he gave it a little more extensively. He spoke about Zlatoust in general and, also, about the stability of the local government.

Vyshinsky: The local Soviet Government in Zlatoust, or in general?

Thornton: General and local.

Vyshinsky: Perhaps you were interested in the weak spots of the power station, from the point of view of breakdowns?

Thornton: I was very much interested in this, but allow me to say why.

Vyshinsky: We will clear that up later on.

Thornton: That won't do. I want to finish what I have to say.

Vyshinsky: Very well.

Thornton: I had to know the weak spots so as to judge, if there should be a breakdown on the generator, what kind of switchboards there were, the transformer lines and, in general, what was the state of the internal wiring.

Vyshinsky: Were you not interested in the weak spots so that you could conceal these spots somehow?

Thornton: Why should I cover up their equipment?

Vyshinsky: Yours.

Thornton: We were not speaking of the weak spots in our equipment.

Vyshinsky: But your equipment was there?

Thornton: There were turbines and switchboards.

Vyshinsky: Perhaps you were interested in the weak spots so as to conceal them?

Thornton: Of course, we had to know these as well, not to conceal them, but to put them right.

Vyshinsky: Did you know the mechanic Marin?

Thornton: Yes.

Vyshinsky: Where did you meet him?

Thornton: At the First Moscow Power Station.

Vyshinsky: Did you give any money to this Marin?

Thornton: Yes.

Vyshinsky: A lot?

Thornton: Three hundred or four hundred rubles, perhaps.

Vyshinsky: And why did you give it?

Thornton: To put right some small defects, possibly without the knowledge of the management, and, in general, for our equipment.

Vyshinsky: Perhaps it was because Marin did not inform the management about these defects?

Thornton: That is saying too much.

Vyshinsky: You said this.

Thornton: I might have said anything, but the trial is taking place here.

Vyshinsky: The Court does not examine anything detached from the rest. The court examines what went before. In Volume XIX, p. 337, you said that "the erector Marin of *Moges* has received from me a total of about 4,000 rubles. I gave him this money so that if small defects arose in our equipment or plant he would not inform his superiors; the firm would not receive complaints and claims."
Do you confirm this?

Thornton: Yes.

Vyshinsky: Was that actually the case?

Thornton: It is a little stretched.*

Vyshinsky: And who stretched it?

Thornton: I did it myself. I am not so much concerned with what I wrote there because this is the trial and it is here that the matter will be cleared up.

Vyshinsky: Well, that is exactly what we are doing.

The President: Evidently he deliberately stretched it so as to provide more work for the Court.

Vyshinsky: You said this about Marin in your depositions. Let us proceed further. You wrote at the same time: "I confirm that money was given to all the engineers and technicians mentioned in the deposition of March 13, so that they would conceal various defects found in our equipment." Did you so depose?

Thornton: Yes.

Vyshinsky: Is it true?

Thornton: Not altogether.

Vyshinsky: But it is written in the record and definite persons are mentioned there.

Thornton: Not engineers, this one is an engineer.

---

* Thornton uses here the Russian idiomatic expression "zagnuto" which cannot be translated literally into English.—*Ed.*

Vyshinsky: To which engineer did you give money?

Thornton: I did not give it to any engineer.

Vyshinsky: You said there was one engineer.

Thornton: I gave it as a loan.

Vyshinsky: What was the name of this engineer?

Thornton: Dolgov.

Vyshinsky: How much did you lend him?

Thornton: Three thousand rubles.

Vyshinsky: Your own money?

Thornton: No, the company's.

Vyshinsky: How did you enter this money in the books? Did you write—loaned to Dolgov?

Thornton: It was not entered that way.

Vyshinsky: These were the "suspense" accounts?

Thornton: Yes. *(Murmur in the court)*

The President: "Suspended," no doubt pending their passage from one pocket to another?

Vyshinsky: Does that mean, accused Thornton, that you had a system in the office by which, when you gave loans, you entered in the books something which was not actually the case? Why did you enter it in the suspense account?

Thornton: Because we thought it was a loan.

Vyshinsky: You ought to have opened an account to Dolgov—loaned three thousand rubles.

Thornton: That would have been better.

Vyshinsky: Perhaps it would have been better, but more dangerous. It is less dangerous to put it to the suspense account.

Thornton: If you wish I will tell you about it.

Vyshinsky: You'll tell it later at your examination.

Thornton: But at present it works out that you have your say but I don't have mine.

Vyshinsky: At present I am the one who is examining and, therefore, I have my say. We shall return to Dolgov and then you will give exact testimony. So we can say that engineer Dolgov received three thousand rubles from you under the guise of a loan which you then entered in the books to the suspense account?

Thornton: Yes.

Vyshinsky: Which technicians received money?

Thornton: Erectors. Technicians did not receive any.

Vyshinsky: So that is also correct. What is it that is not correct in this deposition? Dolgov received money, the erectors received money, so everything is correct?

Thornton: No engineers except Dolgov received anything.

Vyshinsky: I am speaking only of Dolgov. Dolgov received money, the erectors received money; perhaps they received the money for overtime work?

Thornton: That was the case with erector Marin.

Vyshinsky: So it was for overtime work?

Thornton: No, for being sent out on special work and for overtime work.

Vyshinsky: And was Dolgov also sent out on special work?

Thornton: No, he was not.

Vyshinsky: Did he work overtime?

Thornton: Perhaps. He did a lot of work. Allow me to explain.

The President: Comrade Vyshinsky, you are wandering away from the examination of MacDonald.

Vyshinsky: The accused insists on this.

The President: Have you any more questions to put to Thornton?

Vyshinsky: No, I have a question to put to MacDonald.

Thornton: Comrade President: I want to complete my say because otherwise the press would not get the full meaning. I ask you to allow me to state how things were.

The President: In half an hour you will tell us, but at present we must finish with the examination of MacDonald.

Vyshinsky: So you partly confirm and partly deny the deposition you gave when confronted with the other accused?

Thornton: Yes.

Vyshinsky: And you, accused MacDonald, do you confirm the deposition made when confronted with Thornton?

MacDonald: Yes.

Vyshinsky: I have no more questions to put to MacDonald.

Roginsky: I have some questions to ask. Were you confronted with Gussev?

MacDonald: Yes.

Roginsky: Do you remember your deposition on this occasion on the question of the nature of the information given to you by Gussev?

MacDonald: I confirm this deposition.

Roginsky: You confirm this deposition?

MacDonald: Yes.

Roginsky: I ask permission to read out this deposition of MacDonald and to ask a number of questions in connection with it.

The President: You may.

Roginsky: This is Volume XII, p. 29, of the MacDonald dossier. "Question to MacDonald: 'Please tell us exactly what information of a military nature you gathered through Gussev'." Were you asked that question?

MacDonald: Yes.

Roginsky: "MacDonald replied: '*Gussev* had the commission from me to gather—and he actually systematically secured—secret information relative to: 1) The work of military shops of the mechanical and metallurgical works; including the production of the shell shops, the quality of shells made, their types and other data; 2) The development of military shops; 3) Data about the production of special steels used by works for making military materials; 4) The energy supply to the works, and questions related to an uninterrupted work of the military shops."

Is this the deposition which you gave when confronted with the accused?

MacDonald: Yes.

Roginsky: Do you confirm it?

MacDonald: Yes.

Roginsky: Did you receive this information from Gussev?

MacDonald: Yes.

Roginsky (To Gussev): Did you collect information of such a nature?

Gussev: Yes.

Roginsky: And gave it to MacDonald?

Gussev: Yes.

Roginsky (To MacDonald): Do you remember your deposition on the question of organizing the damaging of machines at the

Zlatoust works, which you gave when confronted with the accused?

MacDonald: I remember it.

Roginsky: Were you asked the question whether it was at your direct instructions that Gussev damaged the motor of the large-shaping rolling mill in the metallurgical works with the object of hindering the production of shells?

MacDonald: Yes.

Roginsky: Is your deposition correctly given here? You replied:

"It seems that it happened in my or engineer *Gussev's* house. I told *Gusev* after getting closely befriended with him that for the purpose of a struggle with the Soviet power one must use also such means as the organization of breakages in the works and especially in their most important points. I requested him, considering it to be a very important undertaking in order to stop the production, to organize a breakage of the above-mentioned motor, being aware that it will lead to most definite effective consequences. *Gussev* first hesitated but afterwards agreed to it and in such a way that the stoppage of the motor occurred in May. And later this act was repeated several times in June and August 1932 after my departure from the Urals to the Ukraine."

Is this deposition correct?

MacDonald: Yes.

Roginsky: You confirm it?

MacDonald: Yes.

Roginsky (To Gussev): Was there such a conversation?

Gussev: Yes.

Roginsky: Under the circumstances as indicated here?

Gussev: Yes.

Roginsky (To MacDonald): And did you have any talk with Gussev about damaging other machines besides the motor?

MacDonald: Yes.

Roginsky: When confronted with Gussev, do you remember the deposition which you gave on the question of damaging other machines—delaying the installation of boilers Nos. 1, 2 and 11. and the freezing of boiler No. 8?

MacDonald: Please repeat the question.

Roginsky: You were asked the question: "Do you confirm that you gave engineer Gussev a number of other assignments for bringing about breakdowns?" Were you asked such a question?

MacDonald: Yes.

Roginsky: At the preliminary investigation you gave the following reply: "As means for it I chose the reducing of the power output of the power station from 12,000 kw. to 6,000 kw., that means to cut it by a half. In such a state the smallest breakage on the station would fully paralyse and stop the work of the plant. Taking this into consideration I gave to *M. Gussev* the commission to organize the stoppage of boilers Nos. 1, 2, 8 and 11 and also of the coal conveyor." Is this deposition correct?

MacDonald: Yes.

Roginsky (To Gussev): Were such instructions given?

Gussev: Yes.

Roginsky: A question to the accused MacDonald. Did these breakdowns take place while you were at Zlatoust, or after you left?

MacDonald: After I left.

Roginsky: When did you know that these breakdowns had been brought about?

MacDonald: When Gussev came to visit me in September, 1932.

Roginsky: After Gussev came to visit you at Zuevka?

MacDonald: Yes.

Roginsky: Did you inform Thornton about the breakdowns which occurred?

MacDonald: I told him that Gussev had told me that there had been such breakdowns.

Roginsky: When did you tell Thornton about this?

MacDonald: I don't remember now. It was when we next met.

Roginsky: Wasn't it in Zuevka?

MacDonald: Yes, it was.

Roginsky: Were you confronted with Thornton?

MacDonald: Yes.

Roginsky: Do you remember what deposition you gave on this question when confronted with him?

MacDonald: I don't remember now.

Roginsky: On page 123, Volume XVIII, we have the following question and reply: "Question to MacDonald: 'Did you tell about the breakdown at Zlatoust and what was Thornton's attitude towards this matter?' Reply: 'I think that this was done well and Thornton was pleased with everything I told him.' "

Was this the case?

MacDonald: That was when confronted with Thornton?

Roginsky: Yes.

MacDonald: At present I cannot remember.

Roginsky: Did you have such a conversation with Thornton?

MacDonald: Yes, I told him that such breakdowns had occurred.

Roginsky: You told him that Gussev told you that such breakdowns had occurred. Is that right?

MacDonald: Yes.

Roginsky: And was this in Zuevka?

MacDonald: Yes.

Roginsky: Did you pass on to Thornton the information which Gussev gave you?

MacDonald: Yes. Gussev told me and I passed it on to Thornton.

Roginsky: A question to Thornton. In reply to Comrade Vyshinsky's question, you stated that you did not collect any information of a military nature.

Thornton: I did not.

Roginsky: What deposition did you make on this question, not on March 13, not on the 15th and not on the 19th, but on the very day when, according to your statement to the President your courage returned to you? You do not remember? When you were being examined by the Investigating Judge on Important Cases on April 4?

Thornton: By mistake I signed that I was guilty.

Roginsky: I am not speaking of whether you signed by mistake. I ask you about the nature of the information which you collected. You spoke about this: Volume XIX, page 343 on reverse side.

Thornton: I do not understand the question.

Roginsky: I ask you, do you confirm your words: "I obtained espionage information of a military character about the Putilov works."

Thornton: Yes, but this does not apply to MacDonald.

Roginsky: Is that right?

Thornton: The Putilov works? Yes.

Roginsky: And from the Mytischy works?

Thornton: Yes.

Roginsky: That means that you collected information of a military nature?

Thornton: This was common gossip.

Roginsky: Did you collect this common gossip that had State and military importance?

Thornton: No, I did not collect it. It came casually.

Vyshinsky: From whom?

Thornton: Honest to God, I don't know. To speak in detail. . .

Vyshinsky: State briefly from whom.

Thornton: Simple answers won't do. Can I speak in somewhat greater detail?

Roginsky: For the time being we can record the following: that you obtained casual information of State and military importance and you collected such information about the Putilov works.

Thornton: They just came to me and nothing more.

Roginsky: About the Putilov works, the Mytischy works, and from Gussev through MacDonald the same kind of information came to you also about Zlatoust?

Thornton: No.

Roginsky: Ten minutes ago you confirmed this when replying to a question by Vyshinsky.

Thornton: I only knew that shells were made there and nothing else.

Roginsky: Let us go on to other facts. The Investigating Judge wrote, dated April 4: "The accused Thornton was charged on four counts. The first count—engaging in economic and military espionage. Second count—procuring a number of Soviet engineers and technicians for espionage and paying them various sums of money for the information supplied. Third count—both personally and through the medium of MacDonald and other engineers of the aforementioned firm under him systematically giving bribes to a number of Soviet engineers for concealing defects in the equipment supplied by the Metro-Vickers Company. Fourth count—giving instructions to MacDonald and other engineers of the firm and organizing and carrying out, through the agency of specially recruited Soviet engineers and technicians, the damaging of equipment and the causing of breakdowns in a number of electric power stations and enterprises in the U.S.S.R.."

Were you charged on these counts?

Thornton: Yes.

Roginsky: After this the following is written by Thornton:

"I admit that I am guilty according to the charge presented to me, with the exception of paragraph four, in which it is stated that I gave instructions to wreck installations." Consequently, you pleaded guilty to economic and military espionage.

Thornton: In that document, yes.

Roginsky: You pleaded guilty to paying money for economic and military espionage?

Thornton: In that document, yes.

Roginsky: You pleaded guilty to giving bribes for concealing defects in equipment?

Thornton: In that document, yes.

Roginsky: This is a document dated April 4, not drawn up at the O.G.P.U., but before the Investigating Judge on Important Cases, in the presence of the Assistant Public Prosecutor of the Republic.

I will pass on. Another examination on March 20 by the Assistant Public Prosecutor of the Republic, Roginsky, in the presence of the Public Prosecutor of the Republic, Vyshinsky; do you remember your deposition on this same question?

Thornton: Was that in the O.G.P.U.?

Roginsky: The examination was made in the O.G.P.U. by the Assistant Public Prosecutor in the presence of the Public Prosecutor of the Republic. Here is what is stated in the records:

"It is hereby declared to me that the prosecution against me initated by the State United Political Administration (O.G.P.U.)

is transferred to the office of the Procuror.*" You were told that from this moment the whole case in the hands of the Public Prosecutor and the examination would be carried on by the Public Prosecutor. Is that so?

Thornton: Yes.

Roginsky: "The testimonies given by myself in the O.G.P.U. were presented to me during this enquiry." Were your depositions presented at this examination?

Vyshinsky: Were you shown this deposition of March 11?

Thornton: I don't remember exactly. Perhaps I was.

Vyshinsky: You discussed them in our presence, these three previous records. Try to remember.

Thornton: I don't know.

The President: Evidently when the accused's courage returns, he loses his memory.

Vyshinsky: That is to say, we are not getting a reply from you to this question. Do you remember, on March 19, about 6 o'clock in the evening, you were presented by Comrade Roginsky in the presence of the Public Prosecutor of the Republic with some of the depositions you made in the O.G.P.U.? You examined them and after that you were asked a number of questions. Do you remember?

Thornton: Yes, I remember.

Vyshinsky: So we can set down that you were presented with your previous depositions by Comrade Roginsky in the presence of the Public Prosecutor?

Thornton: Yes.

Roginsky: According to this record, when this was presented to you, you admitted the following: "1) That being the chief erection engineer of Metropolitan-Vickers Company, in the U.S.S.R. I carried out espionage."

Did you say this?

Thornton: Yes.

Roginsky: Further: "2) That for carrying out of the above mentioned spying activities I drew in certain Russian engineers technicians whose names I enumerated in previous testimonies."

---

* Public Prosecutor—*Ed.*

Is that your deposition?

Thornton: Yes.

Roginsky: "3) That financial remuneration was given to the persons recruited by me for carrying on espionage."

Is that your deposition?

Thornton: Yes.

Roginsky: "That this work I have carried out in conjunction not only with Russian engineers and technicians whom I drew in, but I have carried out and organized it in conjunction with certain employees of the Metropolitan-Vickers Company—MacDonald, Cushny, Monkhouse and others whom I mentioned in the protocol of March 13, 1933." Is that right?

Thornton: Yes.

Roginsky: This deposition was made by you?

Thornton: Yes, you wrote it.

Roginsky: Quite right. Was it taken down from what you said?

Thornton: But you wrote it.

Roginsky: But you said it.

Thornton: I don't speak Russian so well.

Roginsky: Very well, when we finish this examination we will see who wrote this deposition.

Vyshinsky: Did you say everything that is written here or not?

Thornton: I said it, but I deny it, of course.

Roginsky: Further: "I plead guilty to the charge that I gave bribes to Russian engineers and technicians for concealing defects and discrepancies in the operation of plant and equipment which had been supplied by us." Did you make this deposition?

Thornton: Yes, I did.

Roginsky: Finally, the seventh point: "That I gave bribes for passing me information on plant and equipment to be imported from abroad." Is that so?

Thornton: I said this, but I did not give anything.

Roginsky: I beg leave to show these depositions to Thornton and to ask him who wrote them. He said that I wrote them. (Shows them to Thornton.) Is that your handwriting?

Thornton: It is my handwriting. It is a translation of what you wrote.

Vyshinsky: Who conducted the examination? Who asked questions and to whom did you answer?

Thornton: The Assistant Public Prosecutor, citizen Roginsky.

Vyshinsky: So he questioned you?

Thornton: Yes.

Vyshinsky: Did he write down what you said or what you did not say?

Thornton: It was this way. He collected all the statements which I wrote in the O.G.P.U.

Vyshinsky: Did he show them to you?

Thornton: Yes.

Vyshinsky: Did you look them over and read them?

Thornton: Yes.

Vyshinsky: And then you replied?

Thornton: And then he wrote them down.

Vyshinsky: Is what Roginsky wrote here what you said to him or is it not what you said to him?

Thornton: I don't speak Russian very well.

Vyshinsky: How long did the questioning recorded here last? —Five minutes, ten minutes or an hour?

Thornton: Very little indeed.

Vyshinsky: About an hour?

Thornton: Not longer.

Vyshinsky: Did he write down what you said, or did he speak and you agreed?

Thornton: He spoke and I agreed.

Vyshinsky: But why did you agree?

Thornton: I agreed on the basis of these false documents.

Roginsky: But on April 4, you confirmed this deposition. Why did you confirm it?

Thornton: I confirmed it on April 4, in the O.G.P.U.

Roginsky: But when you were handed the indictment, did you make any statement regarding this deposition?

Thornton: I did not, because I did not know that I could do so.

Vyshinsky: But were you not told that you could make comments?

Thornton: We came into the room, we were handed a document and told to sign. That's all.

Vyshinsky: But you read what you signed in the office of the Public Prosecutor of the Republic, didn't you?

Thornton: I have not been in the office of the Public Prosecutor of the Republic, except once when I came for my belongings.

Roginsky: Here is the record of the announcement that the preliminary investigation was completed. I will read it: "On April 4, 1933, Sheinin, the Investigating Judge on Important Cases under the Public Prosecutor of the Republic, on the basis of Article 207 of the Criminal Proceedings Code, announced to Thornton that the preliminary investigations of his case were completed, and Thornton stated: 'I have nothing to add to my depositions, I wish to study the case and I wish to have a counsel for defence.' "

This was on April 4.

Thornton: Yes.

Roginsky: So on April 4, when you were informed of the completion of the investigation, you made no statement. On April 5, when you were no longer in the O.G.P.U. you made no statement. On April 6, you made no statement and on April 7, you made no statement.

Thornton: I did not understand that I could, I knew that the Court would investigate the matter.

Roginsky: The Court is investigating. So you made no statement before the opening of the trial?

Thornton: I was told I could not.

Roginsky: Were you asked whether you wished to add anything to the completed preliminary investigation or whether you had any statement to make?

Thornton: I did not want to add anything, but to withdraw it. *(Murmur in Court)*

Vyshinsky: So we can place on record: first, that Thornton at all the interrogations made depositions on all the episodes about which he was asked. Everywhere, in every succeeding deposition, he confirmed his previous deposition. Is that right? Nowhere and at no time, either in the presence of the Investigating Judge on Important Cases or in the presence of the Public Prosecutor, or his assistant, did he make any attempt to discredit these depositions. Nor did he show dissatisfaction with these depositions. Is that right?

Thornton: Yes, I thought that ought to be done in Court.

Vyshinsky: And moreover, on March 19, when the question was specially asked as to how he had made his depositions at the preliminary investigation at the O.G.P.U., he gave the following reply, which I ask leave to read out so that I can question Thornton about it.

Thornton stated on March 19: "These testimonies were given by me wholly on my own free will without outside influence or pressure. The testimonies were given by me in the English language and were written in my own handwriting.

The protocols of interrogations first in Gussev's, mine, and each other's presence and then in Kutuzova's, mine, and each others presence that were shown to me during this interrogation and in which I confess facts about my spying activities and my connections with other persons I have read. I can make no additional remarks about the records of these protocols. The protocols are taken down correctly and are confirmed by my signature.

This protocol was read by me, and I confirm its accuracy."

19/3/1933. (Signed) Leslie C. Thornton

Do you confirm this?

Thornton: No, it was written, and I signed it.

Vyshinsky: Do you confirm that you made it voluntarily without being influenced, without any pressure?

Thornton: Yes.

Vyshinsky: Everything that you read?

Thornton: Yes.

Vyshinsky: Then you signed?

Thornton: Yes, and now the Court will examine it.

The President: But why did you give such information? Was it only to take up everyone's time, the Court's and the Public Prosecutor's? Or did you have some special reason? What you are saying is absurd. You have been making depositions for three weeks so as to deny them now.

Thornton: I merely....

The President: Decided to provide work for the Court?

Thornton: I did it because, as I have said, I was frightened.

The President: How were you frightened? By whom were you frightened? Where and when were you frightened?

Thornton: I was not frightened by arrest and by the consequences, but simply this way . . . .

The President: No, you give a straight reply so that it will be clear and plain to everybody: who frightened you, when did they frighten you, in what room?

Thornton: I want to speak through the interpreter.

The President: When you find it difficult to reply you always resort to the aid of the interpreter. But very well, you may.

Thornton: No, I will speak in Russian. I was simply afraid, but of what I do not know myself.

The President: And you were afraid on March 11, March 12, March 13, and April 4. You were evidently afraid also on April 10, the day before the trial, because you made no statement.

Thornton: Some of the points there are right, but some of them I want to withdraw and I was told that this would have to be done during the trial.

The President: Who told you that? Give his name.

Thornton: I was told by . . . (tries to remember).

Vyshinsky: Well, let that pass. Let me ask something else. I am interested in the circumstances in which you were questioned in the office of the Public Prosecutor of the Republic by my assistant Roginsky, in my presence. Were the facts which are set down here, written down exactly as you told or not?

Thornton: As I spoke. Yes, correctly.

Vyshinsky: Nothing was distorted?

Thornton: No, you did not change anything.

Vyshinsky: But perhaps Roginsky did?

Thornton: No.

Vyshinsky: Perhaps the O.G.P.U. distorted it?

Thornton: No, I signed it with my own hand.

Vyshinsky: And with your head? When you were writing, did you consider and think?

Thornton: (Does not reply.)

The President: And whose head is thinking for you now?

Thornton: At present I feel different.

Vyshinsky: Let us finish with this record. It is important to establish the facts. We will draw conclusions later; at present, it is important for me to confirm from the deposition which was made on March 19 that the facts which are here set down were really told by you, that there was no falsification and no juggling.

Thornton: That is so.

Vyshinsky: The depositions which you made before were given quite freely and voluntarily, without any pressure or coercion. Do I understand you correctly?

Thornton: Correctly.

Vyshinsky: I have no further questions.

Let us pass on to MacDonald. In January 1932, Ryabova came to visit you at Zuevka. What did Ryabova bring when she came to Zuevka?

MacDonald: A letter.

Vyshinsky: From whom?

MacDonald: From Gussev.

Vyshinsky: Did you read this letter?

MacDonald: Yes, I read it.

Vyshinsky: What was in the letter?

MacDonald: News and information which....

Vyshinsky: Which were generally given you?....

MacDonald: Yes.

Vyshinsky: What happened to the letter?

MacDonald: I threw it into the stove.

Vyshinsky: You burnt it?

MacDonald: Yes.

Vyshinsky: Why did you burn this letter?

MacDonald: I always burn all letters.

Vyshinsky: All the letters from Gussev?

MacDonald: Not only from Gussev, but all of them.

Vyshinsky: You burned all correspondence?

MacDonald: Yes.

Vyshinsky: And this letter in particular?

MacDonald: No, just like the others.

Vyshinsky: Who else did you correspond with?

MacDonald: In Russia?

Vyshinsky: Yes.

MacDonald: With no one.

Vyshinsky: Only with Gussev?

MacDonald: Yes.

Vyshinsky: And did you throw into the stove all the letters you got from Gussev?

MacDonald: Yes.

Vyshinsky: I have no more questions.

The President: Has the defence any questions?

Braude: How much money did you receive from Thornton?

MacDonald: I cannot remember.

Braude: But was there not an occasion when you sent Thornton some money?

MacDonald: No.

Braude: You transferred 66 pounds for Thornton from England, do you remember this case?

MacDonald: No.

Braude: There was no such case, or you do not remember?

Vyshinsky: He said he does not remember.

Braude: A question to Thornton. Please tell us what sums of money, how much in all, you gave to MacDonald and under what circumstances.

Thornton: I paid him 2,000 rubles. MacDonald gave a cheque for 66 pounds which I sent to my bank.

Braude: From where did you receive this money? From where did he remit it? Through what bank?

Thornton: I shall have to look.

Braude: Have you the documents?

Thornton: Yes.

Braude: An official document which we will submit to the court?

Vyshinsky: The question of the defending counsel, Braude, refers to some document which has not been submitted to anybody. I think a different procedure would be more correct. The document should be submitted first, and then questions put about it.

Braude: I agree. I intended to submit it at the end of the interrogation.

We are now finishing with the examination of the accused MacDonald. The Prosecutor has questioned the accused Thornton.

I think that I can question him in connection with the examination of MacDonald.

Vyshinsky: But you should first submit the document and then carry on the examination.

Just now some document was produced. The defending counsel, Braude, asked a question in connection with the document and therefore I ask to be given the opportunity to examine this document. After this, it would be advisable to consider whether it is necessary to supplement or repeat a number of questions that were asked on this account. I request that this be done.

The President: You will receive the document in a moment and be able to examine it.

Smirnov: Tell us, citizen MacDonald, what is your education? Did you attend a secondary school?

MacDonald: No.

Smirnov: Why not?

MacDonald: When I was 11 years old, I met with an accident and became crippled and so was unable to go to school.

Smirnov: What accident?

MacDonald: With my leg.

The President: What was the matter with your leg?

MacDonald: The hip joint was dislocated.

Smirnov: And then you studied at Sheffield University?

Mac Donald: During the time I was unable to go to school, I studied at home.

Smirnov: What does that mean? I don't quite understand. Is it what is called in Russian an external student *(volno-slushatel)* or a regular student?

MacDonald: I was a regular student of the University.

Smirnov: You were a regular student? Are you allowed to enter an English University without a certificate from a secondary school?

MacDonald: Considering my special circumstances it was possible.

The President: What special circumstances?

MacDonald: That I had been unable to attend an ordinary school.

Smirnov: Did you pass any examination or test, when you entered the university?

MacDonald: Yes, I passed the entrance examination.

Smirnov: How old were you when you entered?

MacDonald: Sixteen.

Smirnov: When you left the university, what was your age?

MacDonald: I left after the first year, I was 17 years old.

Smirnov: So you were at the university for one year?

MacDonald: Yes.

Smirnov: In that case, are you an engineer in the Russian sense of the term, *i.e.,* one who has a university diploma or, as at present, one who has long practical experience.

MacDonald: I consider myself an engineer by practical experience.

Smirnov: Are you what we call a senior mechanic, or technician, or should you be classed higher? You know Russian mechanics and technicians. Do you think that you have had a better education than they, or not?

MacDonald: I think that my education is higher than that of the ordinary erector.

Smirnov: In any case, we may say that in the Moscow office or, in general, in the Metropolitan-Vickers Company you were a plain installation engineer?

MacDonald: Yes.

Smirnov: Can you say what salary you received in England when you went to work after leaving Sheffield University?

MacDonald: I started to work as an apprentice in the Metropolitan-Vickers works and received two pounds ten shillings a week.

Smirnov: That would be about 25 rubles in our money? Before you came to Russia, what was the highest salary you received when working in England?

MacDonald: At the time I left for Russia my salary was raised to three pounds a week.

Smirnov: What salary did you get in Russia?

MacDonald: Twelve pounds a week.

Smirnov: Twelve pounds a week. Was that all you received from the Vickers Company in money?

MacDonald: That was the agreed standard salary.

Smirnov: How was this paid to you? In foreign currency, or not?

MacDonald: I received 189 rubles a month in Soviet currency and the remainder of the money I received in English currency which was deposited to my account in England.

Smirnov: So, all the money you received, except twenty pounds which on the Russian exchange is 189 rubles, was deposited in a bank in England. Was that so?

MacDonald: Yes.

Smirnov: These 189 rubles were paid to you in Soviet currency? Was that the case?

MacDonald: It was.

Smirnov: Did you receive any additional pay when you were sent on a job at some distance, what we call allowances for travelling expenses and hotel bills? Was your apartment paid for and how did you get it?

MacDonald: The apartment, light, coal, etc. was supplied by the Russian authorities.

Smirnov: By the factories where you worked?

MacDonald: Yes.

Smirnov: Did you receive any food parcels, clothing or boots from England through the Metro-Vickers office, or directly?

MacDonald: Yes, I did.

Smirnov: So you had an apartment with heating and light from the factory. You received food parcels, clothing and boots from England. Then you had 189 rubles, *i.e.,* twenty pounds, which in Russian currency is 189 rubles. Is that so?

MacDonald: Yes.

Smirnov: This was all the income you had. Tell us please, why you got into debt to the office, as Thornton says you had big debts. If this was the case, why was it?

MacDonald: I spent a lot of money.

Smirnov: On what? On your needs?

MacDonald: Yes.

Smirnov: Or did you spend it on giving money to Gussev and the mechanics?

MacDonald: I spent the money which was on my account on myself, and in addition to that, I gave money to the mechanics.

Smirnov: Tell us, when the examination in the O.G.P.U. was concluded, were you also questioned by the Investigating Judges on the present case?

MacDonald: Yes.

Smirnov: In the presence of the Public Prosecutor of the Republic and the Assistant Public Prosecutor of the Republic?

MacDonald: Yes.

Smirnov: Did you confirm all the depositions which you had made earlier?

MacDonald: Yes.

Smirnov: But in addition, did you not make any personal statement to the President of the Supreme Court or to the President of the State Political Administration?

MacDonald: Please repeat the question.

Smirnow: I ask whether you made an application to the Public Prosecutor of the Supreme Court and the President of the O.G.P.U.?

MacDonald: Yes.

Smirnov: Can you say approximately what was written in the application?

The President: If necessary it can be read out.

MacDonald: At the present time I do not wish to repeat this application.

Smirnov: Then I have no further questions.

MacDonald: I do not want this application to be read now.

Smirnov: Very well. I have no more questions.

The President: Have the other Counsel for the Defence any questions?

Kommodov: MacDonald, tell us now, you have admitted that you gave information of a secret political, economic and military nature; you have admitted acts of diversion and bribery. Did you receive any instructions on this, or the second, or the third count of the indictment directly from Monkhouse?

MacDonald: No.

Kommodov: Did you ever give information directly to Monkhouse on the acts performed on the first, second or third main counts of the charges?

MacDonald: No.

Kommodov: In reply to the question put by the Public Prosecutor of the Republic, you said that you only presumed that the other engineers of Metro-Vickers participated. Do you confirm this?

MacDonald: Yes.

Kommodov: I have no further questions. Allow me to call the attention of the Court to the fact that MacDonald's testimony corresponds to MacDonald's deposition at the preliminary investigation in Volume XII, page 64.

The President: Has the Defence any more questions?

Vyshinsky: I have a question to MacDonald concerning Monkhouse. Did Monkhouse take part in the illegal work which was carried on by a group of spies, including Thornton?

MacDonald: I do not know that.

Vyshinsky: What did you think?

MacDonald: All of us employees of the firm thought that since one of them is taking part in this business, then all of them must be doing so.

Vyshinsky: I wish to recall this to make matters clear. In Volume XII, page 10, you said: "The head of the representation was *Mr. Monkhouse* who also took part in this illegal work of *Mr. Thornton.* The assistant of *M. Thornton* for travelling purposes and his associate in the espionage work was engineer *Cushny,* officer of the British army, now an engineer of the Metropolitan-Vickers firm. This is the main group of reconnaissance workers which did the espionage work in the U.S.S.R." etc.

Here you say that Monkhouse was in charge of the office and evidently also participated in illegal work. In reply to the question about Cushny, you say that you presume that Cushny also participated. Do you confirm this?

MacDonald: Yes, I presumed. . . .

Vyshinsky: That Monkhouse participated in espionage?

Kommodov: I must call the attention of the Court to the fact that this is part of the depositions of MacDonald that the Prosecutor of the Republic has read out just now. In this deposition of March 12, page 10, there is also the following passage:

"All data secured were submitted by me only to Thornton." In the deposition of March 13, page 14, there is the following:

"When I was in Zlatoust, I was visited twice by Thornton and all information I had procured was given to him."

On March 19, page 64, he replies once more on the question which you asked him: "That I carried out these crimes against the U.S.S.R. not only together with the Russian engineers and technicians enlisted by me, but also in collusion with employees of Metropolitan-Vickers named by me in my former depositions, acting directly with Thornton and presuming that Monkhouse and Cushny were participating in this work."

Volume XIII, page 64, on the same question: "I consider it necessary to enter into the report of this examination that I received all the directions and instructions on the carrying on of espionage, the engineering of breakdowns and the damaging of machines, from Thornton.

"I consider it also necessary to point out that the espionage information which was given to Thornton was passed on by him to the Intelligence Service."

Vyshinsky: Let us register the following two facts: 1) that MacDonald mentions Monkhouse not once, but twice; he pointed out that Monkhouse participated in this activity, *i.e.,* activity connected with military and other espionage, along with other persons.

He deposes on page 10 and on page 64, as Counsel for the Defence, Kommodov, correctly stated. So it was not once, but twice.

Kommodov: Only with a correction—"presumed."

Vyshinsky: Now let me speak about the document which the Defence asks to be admitted as evidence.

Braude: This document is submitted for the following reasons: in the Prosecutor's questions with regard to Thornton having given money to MacDonald, reference was made to 2,000 rubles. To explain what these 2,000 rubles were, Thornton submits a document to show that this was money to cover debts.

Vyshinsky: Here three documents are presented. The first document contains something written in English with the seal, if I am not mistaken, of the British Embassy, and stating that the Foreign Office is enclosing some telegram or other.

The second document contains a translation of the text of this telegram.

The third document contains some explanation without any signature. The explanation is evidently that of the accused.

Without casting any doubt on the genuineness of the first two documents, I think it absolutely impossible to submit as evidence an unsigned document.

Braude: The last document got in by accident. It was my mistake.

Vyshinsky: Let us correct the mistake. I object to the admission of any unsigned document, *i.e.,* this explanation, as evidence.

Braude: Nevertheless, I request that this document in English be submitted to MacDonald. And I beg leave to ask him what it means.

Vyshinsky: I think it would be more correct to proceed as follows: first of all, to put the following question to him—had MacDonald and Thornton any financial transactions between them through an English bank?

MacDonald: Yes.

Vyshinsky: They had. The second question: were these transactions connected with payments to various engineers for their services or were they not?

MacDonald: Not connected at all.

Vyshinsky: And do not these transactions therefore concern certain personal relations between Thornton and MacDonald in no way connected with the present case?

MacDonald: They are in no way connected.

The President: If that is so, why admit the document as evidence?

Braude: I thought that it was my right to question MacDonald now. Comrade Vyshinsky has taken my privilege. I ask leave to exercise my right. The question is decided not only by MacDonald's testimony but by Thornton's testimony as well.

Vyshinsky: Let me now exercise my right. I had three questions to which I have received exhaustive replies. The fourth question is: were sixty-six pounds remitted to Thornton through an English bank in August 1932, or don't you remember?

MacDonald: Repeat it.

Vyshinsky: Did you, in August 1932, remit to Thornton's account sixty-six pounds through an English bank?

MacDonald: Yes.

Vyshinsky: Under what circumstances? Why did you transfer this money to him?

MacDonald: I bought Soviet money from him and gave him a cheque for it.

Vyshinsky: And why did you buy this Soviet money?

MacDonald: My personal account was overdrawn.

Vyshinsky: How did this overdraft arise?

MacDonald: I spent a great deal of money.

Vyshinsky: On whom? On yourself, or for some needs?

MacDonald: On myself.

Vyshinsky: Do you mean to say your salary was insufficient?

MacDonald: Yes.

Vyshinsky: I have no further questions.

Braude: Tell us, please, MacDonald, what was the amount of the overdraft?

MacDonald: About 2,500.

Braude: Did you obtain this Soviet money yourself or did Thornton obtain it for you?

MacDonald: I obtained it from Thornton.

Braude: How are we to understand this? Did you first receive this money, then obtain a remittance of the English equivalent from London, or was the one directly connected with the other? Was this in England or in the U.S.S.R.? Where did you receive this money?

MacDonald: I received it in the U.S.S.R.

Braude: So you admit that you received some money, as Thornton testified, in settlement of your overdraft. Was that the case or not?

MacDonald: Yes.

Braude: I have no more questions to put to MacDonald.

Vyshinsky: Permit me to ask a question to make things clear. Was this to settle a debt connected with your personal needs?

MacDonald: Yes.

Vyshinsky: And the 2,500 which you gave to Gussev, was this the same money, or some other?

MacDonald: An entirely different matter.

The President: What has this information to do with the case?

Braude: I have to consider the explanation given by my client, and he explains that he gave money once, and precisely in this case. I submit the document that is produced by my client.

Thornton, be good enough to explain what you meant by this document that you gave me.

Thornton: I meant that this is the only sum that I gave to MacDonald.

Vyshinsky: I have a question to Thornton. Why did you pay sixty-six pounds for 2,000 rubles? How much did sixty-six pounds cost at that time on the official exchange and not on the so-called Black Exchange? About 500 rubles?

Thornton: About 500 rubles.

Vyshinsky: So for 500 rubles you bought 2,000 rubles?

I have no more questions.

Braude: I have a question to put to the accused Thornton. You have heard MacDonald admit to the Court, and at the preliminary investigation, that he undertook a series of wrecking acts to cause breakdowns, that he participated in espionage. Did he do this on your orders or on his own responsibility?

Thornton: I gave no instructions.

Braude: So he did it on his own responsibility?

Vyshinsky: And did you know that he was doing it?

Thornton: No, or I would have dismissed him. If I had known that he was wrecking, I would have dismissed him.

The President: And if he had engaged in military espionage, would you have dismissed him?

Thornton: I would also have dismissed him.

Vyshinsky: And for gossip about shells, would you have dismissed him or not?

Thornton: Why for gossip?

Vyshinsky: For information about shells. You remember that you received what you call gossip information about shells. Would you have dismissed him for that?

Thornton: Of course not. Anybody could have got this information.

Vyshinsky (To MacDonald): Did Thornton know of these breakdowns or not?

MacDonald: I confirm my deposition.

Vyshinsky: Did he know or not?

MacDonald: He knew.

Vyshinsky: I have no further questions to put to MacDonald.

The President: Have the accused any questions to MacDonald?

Accused: No.

The President: Has the Defence any questions to put to MacDonald?

Defence: No.

Braude: Now permit me. The accused wishes to present further evidence corroborating his version of the origin of this sum of money.

The President: Very well.

Vyshinsky: On the first question, has the Court decided to admit the telegram?

The President: Not yet.

Braude: Allow me to produce a ledger. Here is an entry of 2,000 rubles.

The President: What ledger is that?

Braude: From the bookkeeping department of Metropolitan-Vickers.

Thornton: It is the personal accounts ledger.

The President: Is it certified by anyone? Are there any signatures?

Braude: It is the ledger which is kept in their office.

Vyshinsky: May I examine it?

The President: Certainly. I presume the questions to MacDonald are finished.

Smirnov: I ask to be allowed to put a question to Thornton in connection with this incident concerning MacDonald.

The President: You may.

Smirnov: Citizen Thornton, do you confirm the testimony of MacDonald, that his salary was paid partly in English currency and that twenty pounds was paid in the U.S.S.R. in Russian currency?

Thornton: Yes, I confirm it.

Smirnov: Then, if he earned twelve pounds a week, *i.e.,* forty-eight to fifty pounds a month, about thirty pounds would remain in his current account in the bank in London.

Thornton: That remains in England.

Smirnow: I understand that Metropolitan-Vickers paid thirty pounds every month into a London bank on MacDonald's account.

Thornton: The employees themselves settle that.

Smirnov: But can you explain: if MacDonald's account was overdrawn and you could not give him your own money, but took it from the funds of the Moscow office, why was it impossible to get in touch with your London office and ask them to stop paying the thirty pounds to his current account, and thus cover the overdraft?

Thornton: That could have been done, had the overdraft not been so large.

Smirnov: If you gave him your own money, I understand that you would demand that he transfer money through the bank when he went to London. That can be understood. But this money which, according to you, was wanted by MacDonald for his personal needs, you took from the funds of the Moscow office. At the same time, in London the same firm, Metropolitan-Vickers, continued to pay thirty pounds a month to MacDonald's account. Would it not have been simpler to stop the payment for two months and thus cover his debt? In reality it comes to the same thing. You go to London and through the same bank you transfer these sixty pounds to be covered in two months, by giving instructions to transfer it from his current account.

Thornton: Had MacDonald sent the money here, he would have had to pay 200 pounds in order to pay off 2,000 rubles, because we were going by the old rate of exchange; but the way I did it, he paid only sixty-six pounds. True, this was illegal, I do not dispute that.

Smirnov: And for sixty-six pounds you bought, on what we call the Black Exchange, 2,000 rubles. Is that so?

Thornton: Yes.

Smirnov: Very well. You were acting illegally, but why did you get a remittance from London instead of stopping payments until the overdraft had been paid?

Thornton: It had nothing to do with our business. MacDonald sent a wire asking for a remittance.

Smirnov: That is, he asked for money for the installation work but failed to put in an account of how he spent the money?

Thornton: Yes.

Smirnov: This is what we call embezzlement.

Thornton: That is not so, it was not embezzlement.

Smirnov: Very well, we shall call it a deficiency.

The President: It is not our business to investigate as to how the firm's funds were spent.

Smirnov: I want to elicit the reason why this complicated transaction was necessary in order to repay this sum.

Vyshinsky: I have not quite understood the accused Thornton. Whose money was it, after all; was it the firm's or not?

Thornton: No, I gave it personally.

Vyshinsky: If I heard the answer to the question put by the Counsel for the Defence, Smirnov, correctly, you bought that 2,000 somewhere. From whom?

Thornton: From a German specialist, who was returning to Germany. He had apparently received a great deal of Soviet currency.

Vyshinsky: That means you bought it privately?

Thornton: Yes.

Vyshinsky: Then the affair had nothing to do with the firm?

Thornton: No.

Vyshinsky: And the money had nothing to do with the firm at all?

Thornton: That is so.

Vyshinsky: In order to repay this money, you obtained Soviet currency through private channels. Why did you enter this money in your firm's ledger? Why did you enter it in the ledger? Do you usually enter private sums of money in your books? The books have to reflect the operations of the office. What sort of book is this?

Thornton: Personal accounts.

Vyshinsky: Fixing the relation between whom, between the firm and its employees?

Thornton: Yes.

Vyshinsky: Then your attitude to MacDonald in that case does concern the firm?

Thornton: No.

Vyshinsky: Why was this sum entered in the books, the accounts of which should reflect only the relations between the firm and its employees? Perhaps it was something like Dolgov's suspense account?

Thornton: No. I want to explain. Suppose I need a thousand rubles in order to travel.

Vyshinsky: On the business of the firm?

Thornton: On any business. I take a thousand rubles. I go to the accountant, take out a cash order, and 1,000 rubles is entered on the debit side. On my return, in order to write off this sum I must repay the thousand rubles, or enumerate in detail all the items of the trip and then the sum will be balanced. But in the given case, MacDonald took 2,000 rubles and paid it back.

Vyshinsky: He took this money from you?

Thornton: No. He accumulated a big debit balance.

Vyshinsky: Then, let us say that he embezzled the money.

Thornton: No.

Vyshinsky: Then he borrowed the money with your permission?

Thornton: Yes.

Vyshinsky: But what has this to do with your personal transactions?

Thornton: In order to pay off the account, I could have given MacDonald a bonus, or raised his salary.

Vyshinsky: Or perhaps you might have assigned the sums which are paid in London to MacDonald's account to cover this sum?

Thornton: I might have done that.

Vyshinsky: You might have done that?

Thornton: Yes.

Vyshinsky: Why didn't you?

Thornton: His overdraft was large.

Vyshinsky: Sixty-six pounds in all.

Thornton: If it were not for the sixty-six pounds he would have to pay 300 pounds at the new rate of exchange.

Vyshinsky: You paid sixty-six pounds.

Thornton: If it had been paid through the firm, it would have been 300 pounds.

Vyshinsky: Does the firm grow rich as a result of your transactions?

Thornton: No. To me it is quite obvious.

Vyshinsky: But it is not at all obvious to me.

Thornton: I admit that this transaction—the purchase of currency at a cheap rate—was illegal.

Vyshinsky: Yes, not at all the proper thing to do.

Thornton: I do not know how it is regarded as far as foreigners are concerned.

Vyshinsky: Are foreigners permitted to do anything they like?

Thornton: No.

Braude: In the middle of the ledger there is an item: 2,000 rubles received through Thornton.

Vyshinsky: When was that?

Braude: You must ask him that question.

Vyshinsky: It was August 7 when the 1,500 rubles, to which Thornton referred, were received.

Thornton: I said that it was 1,500, but actually it was 2,000.

Vyshinsky: When was that? When did MacDonald receive 2,000 from you?

Thornton: It is in the ledger.

Vyshinsky: Yesterday we established that in 1931, in connection with MacDonald's journey to Zlatoust, he received money which was first put down at 1,500, and yesterday it was stated to be 2,000. We know that MacDonald was not in Zlatoust in 1932. Is that so?

Thornton: Yes.

Vyshinsky: Then he received this money while in Zlatoust in 1931, and the entry in the ledger refers to the 7th of August of what year?

Thornton: 1932.

Vyshinsky: Let me sum up. In view of the fact that it is clear from all the data that the sum of 2,000 rubles, which was first put at 1,500 rubles, was received according to MacDonald's and Thornton's own admission by the former, and given by the latter in June 1931 during MacDonald's visit to Zlatoust, and that this entry refers to a transaction dated August 7, 1932. I take it that it has nothing whatever to do with the episode in question. Therefore, the Prosecution objects to the admission of this document as evidence.

The President: Let us turn to the examination of the accused Thornton. Please tell us your biography briefly.

Thornton: I was born in 1887, in Leningrad, formerly St. Petersburg. As a child I was taken to England. My father was a member of the Thornton family which owned a woollen mill. The firm was called The Thornton Woollen Manufacturing Company. My father was the youngest son and had few shares in the company. I went to school in England and came to St. Petersburg on vacations.

My father left this factory, I think, in 1903. He went to Germany, bought a carpet factory, and went bankrupt. I studied for two years in Freiburg University.

After this I studied for two years in England. I worked in several places. I have no diploma, but I have the certificate of the Institute of Electrical Engineers. I did not finish any higher educational institution, but I am styled an electrical engineer.

In 1905, I was in Domodedovo, where my father, after his bankruptcy, was manager of a hose factory. This was in the Moscow district. I was there for perhaps a year or a little less. Then I went to England and worked in electrical engineering and mechanical works.

In 1911, I came here to work in connection with the installation of the Moscow tramways.

I worked on the Moscow tramways with Monkhouse. After this I worked in Domodedovo in a stone works. I worked as a mechanic.

The President: And where were you during the war?

Thornton: During the war, I was at the stone works.

The President: And were you never in the army?

Thornton: After Brest-Litovsk, I was for one year in the army in Mesopotamia.

The President: As a private?

Thornton: Yes, I was the lowest rank—electrician . . .

The President: You were not an officer?

Thornton: No. After that I worked in different places. I had a hard time after the war because there was no work to be got.

The President: You came to Russia in 1911. And when did you leave?

Thornton: After Brest-Litovsk.

The President: In 1918?

Thornton: Yes.

The President: After the revolution?

Thornton: Yes.

The President: What do you mean—after Brest-Litovsk? After the Brest-Litovsk treaty?

Thornton: Yes. I worked here for five months under Bolshevik rule. In 1924, Vickers engaged me to do engineering installations in the Soviet Union. I arrived in November 1924. The rest you know.

The President: You have worked here for nine years?

Thornton: Yes, nine years.

The President: During this period were you frequently in England? Did you go for long periods, or only for a few days?

Thornton: When I was an installation engineer, I went once a year. Then, when I was appointed to take charge of everything, three times a year, each time for two weeks.

Martens: Are you a member of the British Electrical Engineers' Association?

Thornton: Yes.

Roginsky: In what year did you come to the U.S.S.R. on behalf of Metro-Vickers?

Thornton: In November 1924.

Roginsky: Who invited you to work for the firm?

Thornton: Richards.

Roginsky: Did Monkhouse have anything to do with your invitation?

Thornton: Yes. He approved, because he was my senior.

Roginsky: Before this, did you work with Monkhouse in Russia?

Thornton: Yes.

Roginsky: In 1911?

Thornton: Yes.

Roginsky: How many years, approximately, did you work together with Monkhouse?

Thornton: Before the revolution about a year, and after the revolution it will soon be nine years.

Roginsky: You were in Russia together with Monkhouse from 1911, if I understand you rightly, up to the time of your departure after the October Revolution?

Thornton: That is correct. Only we did not arrive together in 1911.

Roginsky: Yes. But from 1911 to 1918, you worked together?

Thornton: Yes, only in different companies.

Roginsky: In different companies—correct. Your mutual relations with Monkhouse were friendly, close, intimate?

Thornton: Very.

Roginsky: Very friendly and very close.

In 1924, when you were invited to work for Metro-Vickers, was this invitation connected with a special commission to go to work in the U.S.S.R.?

Thornton: Yes, the firm, apparently, considered that I was experienced, that I could speak Russian fairly well.

Roginsky: You knew the Russian language, had been in Russia before, and, therefore, you were invited to go to the U.S.S.R. to work. Is that so?

Thornton: Yes, I agreed to go.

Roginsky: Did the agreement you signed cover your work in the U.S.S.R.?

Thornton: Yes.

Roginsky: Was Monkhouse already in the U.S.S.R. at that time?

Thornton: I think Monkhouse was there in May. He had been to Shatura, with Alexander Vassilievich Winter, who was the chief of construction at that time.

Roginsky: He arrived a few months before you did?

Thornton: He went back, and then came a second time. When I was there he had his wife and two children with him.

Roginsky: In what capacity did you arrive in 1924?

Thornton: Installation engineer.

Roginsky: Where did you work?

Thornton: First at Shatura.

Roginsky: At the Shatura Electric Power Station. Is that so?

Thornton: Yes.

Roginsky: How long did you work there?

Thornton: A very short time at first, a few months.

Roginsky: And then?

Thornton: Then I was sent to Moscow to the Shatura sub-station. At the same time I was taking part in the installation of the Nizhni and Moscow sub-stations.

Roginsky: That means you were working at the Nizhni Electric Power Station. How long did you work on the Shatura sub-station and on the Nizhni Power Station—up to what year?

Thornton: I arrived in Leningrad in December 1925. So I finished with Nizhni and Shatura in December 1925.

Roginsky: So you came in 1924, and finished in 1925?

Thornton: Yes.

Roginsky: After the Nizhni Power Station and Shatura, where did you work?

Thornton: At the Volkhovstroy near Leningrad.

Roginsky: How long were you there?

Thornton: I was there approximately a year.

Roginsky: One year approximately, in 1926?

Thornton: Yes.

Roginsky: And after Volkhovstroy?

Thornton: Again Shatura.

Roginsky: Again Shatura—until what year?

Thornton: There were intervals when I worked in the office, before my second turn at Shatura and after that. After the second Shatura installation I was in Moscow, at the Moscow sub-station, but in 19298 I worked at the Moscow-Mytischy Electric Power Station, on the electric railway.

Roginsky: That was in 1928. After this job, you worked in the office?

Thornton: Yes.

Roginsky: From what date?

Thornton: From 1929.

Roginsky: From 1929. To what post were you then appointed?

Thornton: Chief installation engineer.

Roginsky: Now tell me: as chief installation engineer, were all the installation engineers subordinate to you?

Thornton: Yes.

Roginsky: Those who worked at various electric power stations?

Thornton: Yes.

Roginski: In what way were they subordinate? What were your duties in relation to those engineers?

Thornton: I gave them all necessary instructions.

Roginsky: So you gave instructions. And what further?

Thornton: I was responsible for discipline. All the correspondence between the works and the engineers passed through my hands, if there was any direct correspondence.

Roginsky: And the inspecting?

Thornton: I made inspections.

Roginsky: Did they receive wages from you or directly through your office?

Thornton: We have this system. They are paid fully in sterling. They can receive it all here or there. They can have it all in foreign currency. But usually about 200-300 rubles are received here in the office, and the remainder is either paid to their families in England, or deposited in the bank.

Roginsky: Who arranged for the payment of salaries at your office, you or some other persons?

Thornton: The bookkeeping department saw to that.

Roginsky: Who gave instructions to the bookkeeping department?

Thornton: When a new installation engineer arrives, he is asked how much he wants to receive in rubles. He says: "I do not know." We tell him: "You go to Shatura and we will send you 180 rubles a month there." Then I would write a note to the bookkeeping department and it was done.

Roginsky: This means that the bookkeeping department made remittances of money on your instructions.

Thornton: Yes.

Roginsky: Any correspondence from these installation engineers about their work or on any other questions connected with their work was usually addressed to you direct?

Thornton: They had no right to deal directly with the works management.

Roginsky: They had no right to do so, except through you. through your office?

Thornton: Yes.

Roginsky: But you were the chief engineer and director in the office?

Thornton: Yes, but there was also Monkhouse. I demanded, of course, that they should send things to me, and in my absence, to him.

Roginsky: What were the relations between you and Monkhouse? Did he supervise your work? Were you his subordinate?

Thornton: Yes.

Roginsky: And did he give instructions to the installation engineers directly, or did they come to you, and did you report or communicate their statements to Monkhouse?

Thornton: They were directly subordinate to me.

Roginsky: It was in your capacity of inspector that you travelled to the various localities?

Thornton: Engineer Monkhouse also travelled.

Roginsky: It was Monkhouse who was in charge of finances in the offices?

Thornton: Yes.

Roginsky: And money could be paid out only after Monkhouse had given his sanction, isn't that so?

Thornton: Usually he gave his sanction post factum.

Roginsky: Who signed the cheques?

Thornton: Engineer Monkhouse, always.

Roginsky: Nobody else had the right?

Thornton: No.

The President: Is is now already 3 o'clock. It is clear that the examination will be a lengthy one.

Roginsky: Yes.

The President: The Court will now adjourn until 6 p.m.

(Court adjourns at 3:05 p.m. until 6 p.m.)

[Signed] V. V. ULRICH

President of the Special Session of the Supreme Court of the U.S.S.R.

A. F. KOSTYUSHKO

Secretary

EVENING SESSION, APRIL 13, 1933, 6:10 p.m.

The Commandant: Please rise. The Court is coming.

The President: Please be seated. The proceedings are resumed. We shall continue the interrogation of the accused Thornton.

Roginsky: Tell me, please, accused Thornton, when you sent your installation engineers to the various electric power stations, did you or any other leading person in the office of Metro-Vickers in Moscow instruct them to collect information, data, facts, and so forth?

Thornton: Did I instruct them to collect information? Did I understand you correctly?

Roginsky: I ask you, did you personally or anybody else in your office instruct the installation mechanics or engineers, who were sent to work at various electric power stations, to collect any information or data of any kind? Is the question clear?

Thornton: Yes. Yes, they gave me information.

Roginsky: And did you instruct them to collect such information?

Thornton: I think not, but they supplied me with such information.

Roginsky: Did they supply it on their own initiative, or by your orders?

Thornton: When I asked them they gave me information.

Roginsky: And when they left for their place of work did they know that you would subsequently ask for such information?

Thornton: All our installation engineers working abroad would have collected such information as I require anyhow.

Roginsky: Accused MacDonald, you heard Thornton's evidence?

MacDonald: Yes, I heard it.

Roginsky: Is it in accordance with the facts? Or was the case otherwise when you arrived at Leningrad and Zlatoust? Did Thornton instruct you to collect information?

MacDonald: Yes.

Roginsky (To Thornton): Is MacDonald's evidence correct?

Thornton: No.

Roginsky: Were you confronted with MacDonald?

Thornton: Yes.

Roginsky: At the confrontation between you and MacDonald, did you corroborate MacDonald's testimony to the effect that you instructed him to collect information?

Thornton: At the confrontation I did corroborate it.

Roginsky: At the confrontation did you corroborate Gussev's deposition?

Thornton. I do not remember.

Roginsky: I will refresh your memory. It is in Volume XVIII of the Thornton dossier. Confrontation between Thornton and Gussev, March 15, 1933, on page 71. Thornton was asked:

> "In your testimony of March 12, you stated that engineer Gussev of the electric power station of the Zlatoust works was connected with MacDonald who for a period of several years transmitted to you detailed information regarding the political situation in the Zlatoust district and regarding the technical condition of the power station and power installations.
>
> "Do you confirm this?"
>
> And Thornton's reply: "Yes, Mr. MacDonald submitted me this information, received from Mr. Gussev."

Thornton: Yes, but I should like to add that I received information from MacDonald regarding Zlatoust while MacDonald was at Zlatoust, but when he left Zlatoust I received no information.

Roginsky: I am not asking now what happened before, or what happened after. I ask you, were you aware of the fact that MacDonald was receiving information from Gussev? I also ask, did you confirm that during the confrontation with Gussev?

Thornton: I knew that MacDonald was receiving information from Gussev.

Roginsky: Did MacDonald receive such information from Gussev systematically? I will put it in another way: Did he receive information frequently?

Thornton: Whenever I saw MacDonald.

Roginsky: That is to say, whenever you saw MacDonald he supplied such information?

Thornton: I saw MacDonald there twice.

Roginsky: Are these depositions correct?

Thornton: It is stated there—for a period of several years.

Roginsky: It is stated here: "Yes, Mr. MacDonald submitted to me this information, received from Mr. Gussev."

Thornton: That is correct.

Roginsky: Let us establish the following fact before the Court: MacDonald was the person who collected information and data for you concerning the Zlatoust district?

Thornton: Concerning the Zlatoust Electric Power Station.

Roginsky: Gussev was the person who collected information concerning the Zlatoust Power Station for MacDonald, and that was known to you?

Thornton: Yes, I knew it.

Roginsky: If MacDonald was the person who transmitted information to you concerning the Zlatoust Electric Power Station, it follows that that information was the information to which MacDonald referred here. Is that so?

Thornton: In my opinion, that is so.

Roginsky: Accused MacDonald, do you corroborate the fact that the information which you collected concerning Zlatoust and which you transmitted to Thornton, as he admits, was information concerning the manufacture of munitions, the work of the munitions shops, information regarding the manufacture of ammunition, information concerning shell billets, information concerning types of shells, information regarding enlargement of munitions shops, etc.?

MacDonald: Yes.

Roginsky. Is that correct?

MacDonald: It is correct.

Roginsky: That is the very information you received from Gussev and which you transmitted to Thornton?

MacDonald: That is so.

Roginsky: (To Thornton): Did you receive this information from MacDonald?

Thornton: That is not true, I did not receive any military information.

Roginsky: You just said that MacDonald was the person who supplied you with this information; you also said that it was the information of which MacDonald spoke. In order that it may be clearer to you, I asked MacDonald what kind of information that was.

Thornton: I understand how it was, but I did not receive any military information from MacDonald.

Roginsky: What kind of information did you receive?

Thornton: Information that could be obtained for our firm.

Roginsky: What kind of information was of interest to your firm?

Thornton: Information of the following kind: regarding new business, new construction works, also whether there was any intention of placing new orders at the Zlatoust Station, how machinery was being handled, such as machinery received from us, what condition they were in and also what was the condition of the installation which supplied steam to the turbines. Also gossip such as how the workers were living.

Roginsky: Was your firm interested in gossip, but uninterested in factual information that was not gossip?

Thornton: Gossip is information that may or may not be correct. I used the wrong word. By "gossip" I meant information that was not a State secret.

Roginsky: Were you interested in the way the workers are living from the point of view of the interests of your firm?

Thornton: Yes.

Roginsky: Was there any other kind of information, or only such as you mentioned?

Thornton: I think that was all.

Roginsky: Very well. Let us take each kind of information in turn. What kind of machinery did the Metro-Vickers supply for the Zlatoust Electric Power Station?

Thornton: It supplied one 6,000 kw. turbine and several oil switches.

Roginsky: Was that a large order or a small one?

Thornton: A small one.

Roginsky: A small order. Metro-Vickers supplied a very small quantity of equipment for the Zlatoust Station, isn't that so?

Thornton: Yes.

Roginsky: Very well. Was it or was it not intended to extend the Zlatoust Electric Power Station?

Thornton: I have no information about that. Perhaps it was intended.

Roginsky: And did you perhaps have information to the contrary, in view of the work on the Chelyabinsk Electric Power Station?

Thornton: I heard that the Chelyabinsk Power Station would work parallel with Zlatoust.

Roginsky: Was the Zlatoust district included in the area to be supplied with electricity by the Chelyabinsk Station?

Thornton: When I was there that was not so.

Roginsky: I say, subsequently.

Thornton: I do not know.

Roginsky: There was one small turbine. In that case would you be interested in the condition of your machinery, or doesn't that apply to the Zlatoust district?

Thornton: Of course we would be interested in knowing, because sometimes there can be more trouble in connection with a small installation than with a large installation.

Roginsky: Suppose we make the testimony you gave on this subject on March 27, 1933, to the Assistant Public Prosecutor, more precise.

Thornton: To Sheinin.

Roginsky: No, not to Sheinin, but to Roginsky, where you wrote as follows: "I was only interested in information of economic and political nature, which would be of interest to the firm, *i.e.*, future business in connection with orders for the plant; we did not expect business from this quarter." Did you so depose?

Thornton: Yes. MacDonald told me that there would be no orders.

Roginsky: I just asked you whether you knew that there would be no orders for the Zlatoust Station. You replied that you did not know. It follows that your reply was not true.

Thornton: The latest information I had was that there would be no orders, that the station would not be enlarged.

Roginsky: That is to say, you knew from MacDonald that it was not intended to place orders for machinery for the Zlatoust Electric Power Station. Is that so?

Thornton: Yes, as far as he knew. He told me this when he returned.

Roginsky: Is that correct?

Thornton: Yes.

Roginsky: Very well. Let us take your next words. You say that you were interested in the "treatment of our machinery; we had only one set at Zlatoust." Is that correct?

Thornton: That is correct.

Roginsky: Consequently, that part of the questions which might interest your firm regarding the Zlatoust district also was not of great interest for your firm?

Thornton: I repeat that there is sometimes more trouble in connection with these small machines than with large installations.

Roginsky: I am not asking you about these troubles.

Vyshinsky: What troubles have there been?

Roginsky: We shall speak about these troubles later when we come to speak particularly about the Chelyabinsk Power Station. Was there any row in connection with Zlatoust?

Thornton: There was none.

Roginsky: If there was no row, then information and interest regarding such information is excluded?

Thornton: It would appear then that if information is to the affirmative it is information, but if it is to the negative then it is not information.

Roginsky: When there is no information, then indeed there is no information. That is perfectly clear.

Thornton: No, it would appear that if somebody stated that there would be orders, that is information; but if there will be no orders, that is not information.

Roginsky: If it is said that there will be no orders, that is also information. But it seems to me we have settled the point about orders. You have confirmed your testimony and we have made it clear to the Court that there was no intention of placing additional orders for machinery at the Zlatoust Electric Power Station.

Thornton: That was when MacDonald was leaving Zlatoust.

Roginsky: Yes. That was when MacDonald left Zlatoust. Everything that is said here is being recorded in the stenographic report—every word. But we are now speaking of information that might have interested you regarding the turbines you supplied. There you supplied a small turbine. There was no row of any kind. Isn't that right? No claims were presented to your firm. Is that right?

Thornton: Yes.

Roginsky: And you also heard nothing about any defects or about claims of any kind?

Thornton: No.

Roginsky: Therefore, is it true or not that that part of the information which might have interested you is, in this case, also excluded?

Thornton: No, that is not so, because we have even smaller units than the Zlatoust one.

Roginsky: I am now referring specifically to Zlatoust. We shall speak about other units later. At present regarding Zlatoust specifically. Is it or is it not true that part of the information which might have been of interest to your firm, commercial information one might say, had no importance as far as Zlatoust was concerned, since the turbine installed there is working?

Thornton: I do not agree; it of course had importance.

Roginsky: To proceed: "The general condition of the Zlatoust Power Station"—is that correct?

Thornton: Correct.

Roginsky: What does that mean—"the general condition of the Zlatoust Power Station"?

Thornton: We have already spoken about that. It means everything that feeds the turbines and everything that is fed by the turbo-generators. It means the general state of the power station.

Roginsky: And precisely by whom the power station is supplied and precisely whom the power station is serving—that does not interest you?

Thornton: No, that does not interest us.

Roginsky: And the load of the power station?

Thornton: The load does interest us.

Roginsky: If the load interests you, if the general situation interests you, then you must also know whom the power station is serving.

Thornton: I do not understand—what do you mean: whom it is serving?

Roginsky: What factories, what industries the power station is supplying.

Thornton: No, that is not so. It is a matter of indifference where the power is going. As far as the firm is concerned, it does not give a hang.

Roginsky: What then does interest you? At the preliminary investigation you were much more precise in your answers, in this respect, and much more intelligible, because you said you were interested in the load of the power station and therefore in the electric power supply of the Zlatoust works, which gave you a picture of the work of those factories. That was your deposition.

Thornton: May I have an interpreter?

The President: Granted.

Thornton: That part of my deposition was suggested to me by the Investigating Judge.

Roginsky: Which investigator questioned you on these depositions—the investigator of the O.G.P.U. or the investigator of the Public Prosecutor?

Thornton: I think it was you.

Roginsky: And what did I suggest to you?

Thornton: It was you who said "and works fed by the station."

Roginsky: And you denied that?

Thornton: I think that, well. . . [makes a gesture].
If I have been rude, I apologize, "suggested" is a legitimate term.

Vyshinsky: In the depositions which Roginsky took on March 27, you had some questions concerning that which interested you. First, as to whether there would be orders for equipment. Were you really interested in that? Weren't you prompted to say that?

Thornton: I think it would not be right to use the Russian word meaning "prompted," but the English word "suggested."

Vyshinsky: By what methods was it suggested to you? Am I suggesting anything to you now?

Thornton: No.

Vyshinsky: Was it different then?

Thornton: While the investigator of the Prosecution was writing, the Assistant Prosecutor proposed that I say, "the load of the Zlatoust works." However, I am interested only in the total amount of energy distributed.

Vyshinsky: That is to say, in the first place, you withdraw the expression that you were prompted to say that. You say that it was suggested?

Thornton: Yes.

Vyshinsky: Well, how was it suggested? By hypnotism?

Thornton: No.

Vyshinsky: Hypnotism was not applied?

Thornton: I think not.

Vyshinsky: Let us take it point by point. It is said here there will be new orders for equipment, although no such orders were expected for the Zlatoust works. Was there such a question?

Thornton: There was.

Vyshinsky: Without any suggestion?

Thornton: Without any suggestion.

Vyshinsky: How the machinery was handled, you confirm that?

Thornton: I do.

Vyshinsky: "The general condition of the Zlatoust Power Station, particularly its weak places, liable to break down." You confirm that? This makes it worse?

Thornton: No, it is not worse. I know what technical expert opinion is. It is necessary to know that for our machines.

Vyshinsky: "The general condition of the Zlatoust Power Station, particularly its weak places, liable to break down." Was that said?

Thornton: That was undoubtedly said, but it can be understood this way or that.

Vyshinsky: How do you understand it? I understand it this

way, that there might be weak spots in the electric power station, and because of these weak spots, and in these weak spots, breakdowns might occur; and that you were interested to know whether there were such weak spots which might lead to breakdowns?

Thornton: Breakdowns of our generator?

Vyshinsky: Not of your generator, but of the whole power station. Is that so?

Thornton: Yes. But you see, that is not so. That does interest me. If it is so stated there, then it follows that I am interested in weak spots, whether the roof leaks or whether a tube might break.

Vyshinsky: The roof has nothing to do with it; but perhaps whether a blade breaks off.

Thornton: It is our machine.

Vyshinsky: Well, the coal conveyor, the oil switches and so forth?

Thornton: If oil switches are bad, it would be dangerous to our generator.

Vyshinsky: That interested you.

Thornton: Yes.

Vyshinsky: I will quote once again: "Not only of individual units, but also the general condition of the Zlatoust Power Station." That interested you?

Thornton: Yes.

Vyshinsky: That is to say the third point has also been safely passed. The fifth point—the living conditions and political state of mind of the workers. That is also written correctly?

Thornton: Correctly.

Vyshinsky: Why did you or your firm want to know, if you say that you collected information for your firm; why did you want to know the political state of mind of the workers?

Thornton: I will soon tell you.

Vyshinsky: Very well, I will wait. Why did you want to know the political state of mind of the workers? Did the work of the oil switches depend upon the political state of mind of the workers?

Thornton: No.

Vyshinsky: Or of the turbo-generators?

Thornton: No.

Vyshinsky: Or of the turbine?

Thornton: No.

Vyshinsky: Then what did you need it for?

Thornton: The firm of Vickers grants tremendous credits to this country for the purchase of machinery.

Vyshinsky: Then it is for the soundness of credits?

Thornton: I do not understand.

Vyshinsky: That is to say, whether your credits are sufficiently protected?

Thornton: The firm wants to know not what is written in the newspaper, but what is actually going on here, so as to be able to decide whether to grant credits or not.

Vyshinsky: That is to say, you verified the solvency of the Soviet Union through your agents? Have you set yourself the task of verifying the solvency of the Soviet Government?

Thornton: Yes.

Vyshinsky: Can it not be understood thus: to verify the stability of the Soviet Government?

Thornton: If you prefer that, yes.

Vyshinsky: It is not what I prefer, but what you say.

Thornton: Do you understand why it is necessary?

Vyshinsky: You said in order to establish how far the credits were protected by the stability of the Soviet State? Is that so?

Thornton: Yes.

Vyshinsky: Permit me to draw the conclusion: through your agents, Gussev, Sokolov and the like, you verified the stability of the Soviet Government. Is that so?

Thornton: Yes.

Vyshinsky: That is to say, you investigated "the living conditions and the political state of mind of the workers" in order to judge of the stability of the Soviet Government. Is that correctly written?

Thornton: Yes.

Vyshinsky: Then all four points are written correctly?

Thornton: Yes.

Vyshinsky: There remains one point which you do not like—that is the load of the electric power station and the state of the supply of electricity of the Zlatoust works which gave a picture of the work of those factories.

Thornton: I do not like that at all.

Vyshinsky: But that it what is written. Permit me to take into account the fact that this is what is written and you cannot explain away that this is what you said.

Thornton: That document is signed by me.

Vyshinsky: Perhaps we will put it differently: that document is not only signed by you, but written in your own handwriting.

Thornton: And translated in my own handwriting.

Vyshinsky: Yes, translated in your own handwriting.

Thornton: Yes. I can explain more precisely what interested me. The other works in Zlatoust did not interest me.

Vyshinsky: But you wrote that they interested you.

Thornton: I want to say that it is not so.

Vyshinsky: Why did you write what is not the case?

Thornton: It had been written as was said.

Vyshinsky: But this is your document?

Thornton: I said that this did not interest me.

Vyshinsky: At that time you said that it did interest you and now you say that it did not interest you.

Thornton: I was not interested in the condition of the Zlatoust works.

Vyshinsky: You say that now, but then you said what you wrote.

Thornton: Yes, then I said it.

Roginsky: May I put a question?

The President: Certainly.

Roginsky: That was the case with Zlatoust. If we take Zlatoust as a basis, perhaps you will tell the Court if it was not a general thing with you that a number of your installation engineers, in addition to their work, were engaged in the special work of collecting data and information?

Thornton: Yes, they transmitted such information to me.

Roginsky: Who?

Thornton: Those who worked.

Roginsky: But who particularly, for instance, among those sitting here?

Thornton: Cushny.

Roginsky: In other words, Cushny fulfilled the same role as MacDonald.

Thornton: But as I say, and not as MacDonald said.

Roginsky: MacDonald gave his testimony and you gave your testimony. Your testimony as regards the part about which MacDonald spoke we read here today. But now I ask you: were your instructions to Cushny similar to the instructions you gave MacDonald?

Thornton: I gave Cushny no instructions. There is the confrontation.

Roginsky: The confrontation is recorded. I am asking you now: did Cushny fulfil the same role as MacDonald or not?

Thornton: MacDonald speaks about espionage information. . . .

Roginsky: You have already given your explanations on that point. According to your explanation, Cushny fulfilled the same role as MacDonald.

Thornton: Cushny was my assistant and like me travelled about on construction work.

Roginsky: Cushny has been your assistant since what year?

Thornton: Two years, but he was ill about a year.

Roginsky: During 1932?

Thornton: Yes.

Roginsky: And prior to 1932 he worked at various electric power stations?

Thornton: He was in Baku and in Shterovka.

Roginsky: Consequently he was connected with definite districts. Was he supposed to act exactly like MacDonald in these districts?

Thornton: I was not the chief installation engineer at that time, and do not know how he acted. Lately, he spoke to me about the power stations.

Roginsky: When he travelled about later, did he bring you information?

Thornton: Yes.

Roginsky: That is to say, Cushny also participated in supplying information. Who else participated—Nordwall?

Thornton: Yes.

Roginsky: Oleinik also?

Thornton: Also.

Roginsky: And Gregory?

Thornton: I saw Gregory only once. Gregory did not speak Russian. Gregory did not give information.

Roginsky: Consequently, of those sitting here—Cushny, Oleinik and Nordwall. But in your testimony, you mentioned a number of other persons engaged in collecting information.

Thornton: Yes, a good many.

Roginsky: Consequently it would be correct to conclude that the installation engineers working under your direct guidance, instructed by you, supervised by you, having direct connection with you alone, in addition to their immediate work of installing various kinds of machinery, were also obliged to collect definite information and transmit that information to you?

Thornton: They were not obliged to, but they did it.

Roginsky: You received that information from them?

Thornton: Yes.

Roginsky: Did you get this information from them?

Thornton: Yes.

Roginsky: That is, you received that information from them. Do you follow me?

Thornton: Yes.

Roginsky: And to whom did you transmit that information?

Thornton: I did not transmit all that they said, but obtained a general picture, and when I was in England, transmitted it to my Board, to certain members of the Board.

Roginsky: In the light of this testimony, explain to me the following point in your deposition where you say that you and Monkhouse collected information of an espionage character.

Thornton: I reject the word espionage.

Roginsky: . . . you and Monkhouse collected definite information— is that correct?

Thornton: Yes, information.

Roginsky: That is to say, that not only you yourself and your engineers, but also Monkhouse, engaged in the work of collecting this kind of information.

Thornton: Yes, that was his business and my business.

Roginsky: That was your business and his, but you said jointly with Monkhouse.

Thornton: Yes.

Roginsky: Consequently your joint business?

Thornton: Yes, otherwise our firm could not work here.

Roginsky: If your firm did not know the weak places in Zlatoust, those liable to have breakdowns, it could not work here?

Thornton: Technically weak places.

Roginsky: Yes, of course, technically weak places. In order to place a piece of iron into a motor, one must be technically trained and know the technically weak spots.

I want to put one question to Monkhouse. Accused Monkhouse, you just heard the evidence of Thornton regarding the collection of definite information. Is that evidence correct?

Monkhouse: It is correct in part.

Roginsky: Information was collected?

Monkhouse: Information that might be useful to the firm concerning future orders was collected.

Roginsky: In what respect is Thornton's testimony incorrect?

Monkhouse: In what sense?

Roginsky: You said that the testimony was correct in part. Perhaps you will explain to the Court in what part the testimony was incorrect.

Monkhouse: In my opinion almost everything he said was correct.

Roginsky: That is to say, there is no partly incorrect testimony?

Monkhouse: I do not agree with the word "espionage" information.

Roginsky: He does not say espionage information. And where he spoke of Zlatoust, of the information collected at the Zlatoust works, did that information interest you?

Monkhouse: That he was interested in such information is true. We have to know about the state of our equipment here.

Roginsky: For instance, the information about Zlatoust, when he said that the load of the electric power station interested him?

Monkhouse: The load of the electric power station did interest us.

Roginsky: The political sentiments of the workers?

Monkhouse: The political sentiments of the workers and, in general, the situation of the country interested me, because every time I went to London I had to report to my Board in order to verify the information given in the English newspapers. My Board would ask me whether that information was right or not.

Roginsky: That is to say, through the mediation of Cushny, MacDonald and Oleinik, you verified the information given by the English press regarding the situation in the Soviet Union?

Monkhouse: I sometimes questioned Cushny when he returned from his trips. I had practically no talks with MacDonald.

Roginsky: We are not speaking about MacDonald. You just said that when you went to London you informed the Board of your firm regarding the political situation of the Soviet Union on the basis of the information you received, in order to establish the true state of affairs.

Monkhouse: But that was information which I received not only from Cushny and Thornton, but also from the other workers with whom I dealt.

Roginsky: I took Cushny and Oleinik as an example. In addition to Cushny, Oleinik and Nordwall, there were a number of other persons who gave information?

Monkhouse: They were persons whose official duty it was to give such information.

Roginsky: Whose business was it to give such information? Was it engineer Levinson's business to supply information?

Monkhouse: That was as far back as 1926.

Roginsky: That is all the same.

Monkhouse: That is not all the same.

Roginsky: It was his business to supply such information?

Monkhouse: Of course.

Roginsky: Did Alexeyev-Popov supply information as a part of his duties?

Monkhouse: That was apart from his business duties.

Roginsky: Did engineer Schlegel supply information as part of his duties?

Monkhouse: That was in 1924.

Roginsky: This was in 1924, and that was in 1926. Let us quote a few more names. Here we have Alexeyev-Popov who gave information apart from his official duties. I am referring to the information which you collected through a whole circle of individuals, information of the most diverse kind.

Monkhouse: That was not on my instructions. They simply knew that I was interested in such things and had conversations about them.

Roginsky: They knew that you were interested and gave such information. Thornton was interested, and all the installation engineers, or a majority of the installation engineers, were engaged in collecting information. Monkhouse is interested, and a whole group of people are engaged in collecting information and transmitting it to him.

Monkhouse: As loyal employees of our firm.

Roginsky: As loyal employees of your firm, and as a definite group of persons having no relation to your firm at all.

Monkhouse: I know nothing about that.

Roginsky: And what about Alexeyev-Popov?

Monkhouse: He was a former employee.

Roginsky: And now an employee?

Monkhouse: No.

Roginsky: Did he give information?

Monkhouse: Yes.

Roginsky: Was Gussev an employee of your firm? Did he supply information?

Monkhouse: No.

Roginsky: Accused Thornton, did Gussev supply information?

Thornton: He supplied it through MacDonald.

Roginsky: Was Vitvitsky an employee of your firm? Did he supply information?

Monkhouse: Not as far as I know.

Roginsky: Accused Thornton, did he supply information?

Thornton: No.

Roginsky: Accused Kutuzova, did Vitvitsky supply information?

Kutuzova: Yes.

Roginsky: Did the accused Thornton supply this information?

Kutuzova: He received information from Vitvitsky.

Thornton: This information is absolutely wrong.

Roginsky: Did Sukhoruchkin give information?

Thornton: No.

Roginsky: Is he an employee of the firm?

Thornton: No.

Roginsky: Accused Monkhouse, is Sukhoruchkin an employee of your firm?

Monkhouse: No.

Roginsky: Is this the group of people about whom you told the Court?

Monkhouse: I do not know.

Roginsky: Did Sukhoruchkin supply information?

Monkhouse: I do not know.

Roginsky: Is Zorin an employee of the firm?

Thornton: No.

Roginsky: Did he give information?

Thornton: What you said must be made more explicit.

Roginsky: We shall make it more explicit later. I am only clearing up this question. Was Zorin supplying information?

Thornton: He spoke about the regulator, if you call this information.

Roginsky: Did Krasheninnikov supply information?

Thornton: I was not very well acquainted with him.

Roginsky: Perhaps the accused Krasheninnikov will tell us whether he supplied information or not.

Krasheninnikov: Not to Thornton. I spoke with Oleinik and Jolley.

Roginsky: Did Oleinik supply information that interested him as fitter of this firm?

Krasheninnikov: I do not know, perhaps he did.

Roginsky: Accused Oleinik, did you get information from Krasheninnikov?

Oleinik: I do not know what information you are referring to.

Roginskg: The information you mentioned when confronted with Thornton.

Oleinik: About the condition of the station? Yes.

Roginsky: You gave him that information?

Krasheninnikov: Yes.

Roginsky: Accused Thornton, is Krasheninnikov an employee of the firm?

Thornton: No.

Roginsky: Do you know Volkhovsky?

Thornton: Yes.

Roginsky: Did you receive information from him? Is he an employee of your firm?

Thornton: No.

Roginsky: Perhaps this will do. Now we shall sum up. So apart from your employees, there was a whole group of persons not working at your office who were collecting particular information for you. Is that so?

Thornton: Yes, they were.

Roginsky: They were giving you particular information and you were receiving that information?

Thornton: Yes, we were getting information.

Vyshinsky: Permit me to put a question to accused Oleinik in connection with this question. Accused Oleinik, when questioned by Roginsky you asked him what information he was referring to. I want to make this point clear. I want to ask you, did you or did you not give Thornton information which might be called espionage information in the real sense of the word?

Oleinik: Yes.

Vyshinsky: Explain what sort of espionage information this was.

Oleinik: About the condition of the munitions works, about the mood of the population, about railway transport.

Vyshinsky: And in particular, what things are happening on the transport system?

Oleinik: About the work of the transport system and what condition it is in.

Vyshinsky: This is not much. What about military transport?

Oleinik: Yes, about that too.

Vyshinsky: About movement of troops?

Oleinik: Yes.

Vyshinsky: About military supplies?

Oleinik: Yes.

Vyshinsky: You reported all you knew? Accused Thornton, did you hear this story, is it true?

Thornton: No.

Vyshinsky: You didn't get that information?

Thornton: No.

Vyshinsky: No information whatsoever?

Thornton: Only the information about which I spoke.

Vyshinsky: Such as interested the firm?

Thornton: Yes.

Vyshinsky: Now what was said about the movement of troops, did that interest the firm too?

Thornton: As I was told—that is so.

Vyshinsky: The political sentiments, in order to determine the stability and firmness of the Soviet Government? Was there information of that kind?

Thornton: Yes, there was.

Vyshinsky: Did you get information from the Zlatoust station?

Thornton: Yes.

Vyshinsky: You said previously that this was common gossip about shells. Do you remember?

Thornton: The phrase "common gossip" just fits in when we speak about shells.

Vyshinsky: Please bear in mind, gossip precisely about shells, but not the things that gossips talk about when standing in queues.

Thornton: I think that it is exactly what the folks are talking about.

Vyshinky: At any rate, you are not denying the fact—information concerning the output of shells at Zlatoust.

Thornton: I emphatically deny that.

Vyshinsky: What then did they say about shells?

Thornton: That shells are being manufactured in Zlatoust.

Vyshinsky: Probably you knew that without being told. What information did they give you then?

Thornton: I do not know. Sorts and quantities—I do not know.

Vyshinsky: Accused Oleinik, permit me to ask you, did you get direct instructions from Thornton to collect this information?

Oleinik: Yes.

Vyshinsky: Perhaps you will say definitely: when, under what circumstances were these instructions given to you by Thornton?

Oleinik: Which instructions? I received instructions several times.

Vyshinsky: You can confine yourself to a general statement.

Oleinik: This was chiefly in 1932, when we were staying in the country.

Vyshinsky: Did Thornton know about the wrecking work?

Oleinik: Yes, he knew.

Vyshinsky: And what kind of wrecking work?

Oleinik: Are you referring to military or general wrecking work?

Vyshinsky: I do not know how you class it.

Oleinik: There was work of both kinds.

Vyshinsky: What will Thornton say about that? Accused Thornton, did you hear that?

Thornton: I did.

Vyshinsky: Do you deny it?

Thornton: Yes, I do.

Vyshinsky: Accused Kutuzova, were you present at any conversations where the necessity of causing these breakdowns was discussed?

Kutuzova: I was present many times.

Vyshinsky: Tell us in detail what kind of conversations they were and who carried them on.

Kutuzova: These conversations were carried on between engineers Thornton and Monkhouse.

Vyshinsky: What were they about?

Kutuzova: They planned the destruction of stations, damaging of installations and breakdowns.

Vyshinsky: But why did they choose such an excellent occasion to talk about these things in your presence?

Kutuzova: They didn't mind my presence. I was quite at home with them.

Vyshinsky: They were both well disposed towards you? Both liked you?

Kutuzova: Yes.

Vyshinsky: You were on friendly terms?

Kutuzova: Yes.

Vyshinsky: Accused Thornton, do you confirm that you were on friendly terms with Kutuzova, that you considered her as one of your own people?

Thornton: Yes.

Vyshinsky: You didn't mind her presence?

Thornton: I do not understand.

The President: You didn't mind speaking in her presence about your affairs?

Thornton: I didn't mind because there was nothing to mind, since we never spoke about wrecking activities. I never spoke with Monkhouse about wrecking activities.

Vyshinsky: At any rate, you had conversations with Monkhouse which were not to be heard by outside parties.

Thornton: We had business conversations.

Vyshinsky: And during these conversations you didn't mind the presence of Kutuzova?

Thornton: Sometimes. But of course we sometimes spoke with no third person present. We spoke sometimes, the two of us, about the business of the firm and sometimes she may have heard our talk, but she couldn't hear these things because we never spoke of wrecking activities.

Vyshinsky: But Kutuzova maintains that there had been such conversations, Oleinik says that there had been such conversations and Gussev says the same.

Thornton: Gussev says the same?

Vyshinsky: He spoke about the 1,400 h.p. motor and that you knew about this and that you were pleased.

Thornton: I deny that. I never spoke about breakdowns.

Vyshinsky: I know you deny it. I will remind you. Oleinik said so, Gussev said so, Kutuzova said so—Kutuzova who was trusted, who has lived in your house several years, whom you considered as one of your own people. Is that true?

Thornton: Yes.

Vyshinsky: Besides this, you trusted her to such an extent that you carried on in her presence conversations which were not to be heard by outside parties. Is that true?

Thornton. Yes, but I never spoke with Monkhouse about the things referred to by Kutuzova.

Vyshinsky: Tell me please, who is Olgin?

Thornton: Olgin was the director of the Cable Works, formerly Podobedov's Factory.

Vyshinsky: In what way were you connected with the ex-Podobedov Factory?

Thornton: I worked there as a mechanic.

Vyshinsky: And afterwards?

Thornton: I lived there about seven or eight years.

Vyshinsky: What was Olgin's position in Moscow?

Thornton: He was managing director.

Vyshinsky: Was he not a partner in these works?

Thornton: He owned some shares, but the chief shareholders were the Volga-Kama Bank, Gukasov and Debour.

Vyshinsky: Olgin owned some shares. Would it be correct if I say that Olgin belonged to a group of capitalists who formerly owned factories, works and shares?

Thornton: At first he was more an employee.

Vyshinsky: And subsequently became the owner. Do I understand correctly that this Olgin was the owner or partner in one of the enterprises subsequently confiscated from the capitalists and transferred to the Soviet Government? Is that true?

Thornton: Yes.

Vyshinsky: Where was this Olgin after the October Revolution? In the same place where Gukasov was?

Thornton: He was in England.

Vyshinsky: What position did that former Russian capitalist occupy there? What position did Olgin get in England?

Thornton: He didn't get any situation in England. He lived there and after a year or two, in 1924, he left for Berlin and became an adviser.

Vyshinsky: Whose adviser?

Thornton: Metro-Vickers.

Vyshinsky: So we can put it this way. This Olgin, a former partner in the Podobedov Factory, after the property rights of those works were abolished, left for London and became a Metro-Vickers adviser?

Thornton: Yes, he was adviser in Berlin.

Vyshinsky: Is he still adviser at the present time?

Thornton: He died.

Vyshinsky: But there remains a brother of his, I think?

Thornton: A son.

Vyshinsky: Does this son continue to have connections with Metro-Vickers?

Thornton: Yes, he is a young engineer in the London office.

Vyshinsky: You arrived in Russia as chief installation engineer?

Thornton: I came to Russia as an ordinary, common installation engineer.

Vyshinsky: You came to work as a technician and then occupied the post of chief installation engineer?

Thornton: Yes.

Vyshinsky: And, as we have now discovered—for the moment I shall not use the word "spying"—you, as well as Monkhouse and MacDonald and a number of other persons, attempted to obtain, through various engineers and technicians, all sorts of information of an economic, political and even military nature, as MacDonald told us.

Thornton: As MacDonald says, yes.

Vyshinsky: And as you say, common gossip about shells?

Thornton: Common gossip, yes.

Vyshinsky: Common gossip about shells?

Thornton: Well, as far as I can understand you—yes.

Vyshinsky: And as far as I can understand you—I think so too. I am interested now in this activity of yours in a close circle of persons connected with Metro-Vickers. Was this activity really kept in that close circle, or did it also touch other institutions? The information, which, as we agree, was concentrated in your hands and obtained by you, did it remain the knowledge of definite persons connected with Metro-Vickers? Or was it transmitted outside of this circle in some other direction?

Thornton: It is very difficult to answer that question because I do not know. I consider that this information was kept only within our group.

Vyshinsky: Of course, in your group, but what kind of a group was yours? Who exactly in England was personally receiving this information?

Thornton: Richards, Turner.

Vyshinsky: Let us deal with Richards. Who is Richards?

Thornton: Richards is managing director of the Metropolitan-Vickers Electrical Export Company.

Vyshinsky: Has he been in the U.S.S.R.?

Thornton: Yes.

Vyshinsky: Many times?

Thornton: Yes.

Vyshinsky: How many times? Let me remind you: was he here in 1923?

Thornton: Yes.

Vyshinsky: And in 1925?

Thornton: Yes.

Vyshinsky: In 1926?

Thornton: Yes, I think he was.

Vyshinsky: 1927?

Thornton: Yes.

Vyshinsky: In 1928?

Thornton: Probably, yes.

Vyshinsky: In 1929?

Thornton: He came almost every year.

Vyshinsky: Every year beginning with 1923?

Thornton: I think he did not come over in 1924.

Vyshinsky: Was he here before 1923, for instance in 1917?

Thornton: He was here in 1911.

Vyshinsky: And in 1917-18?

Thornton: Yes, he was here in 1917.

Vyshinsky: Where?

Thornton: He was representative of the British Westinghouse Co.

Vyshinsky: Where?

Thornton: In Moscow and then in Leningrad.

The President: Does this refer to 1917 or to 1918?

Thornton: In 1917.

Vyshinsky: And in 1918, did he stay in Leningrad or in Moscow?

Thornton: In Leningrad.

Vyshinsky: Was he in Archangel?

Thornton: He was in the expeditionary force.

Vyshinsky: What expeditionary force?

Thornton: That is what I call the British Expeditionary Force in Archangel.

Vyshinky: It is the expeditionary force which occupied Archangel and fought against the Red Army?

Thornton: Against the Soviet Government.

Vyshinsky: Oh, is that so?

Thornton: Yes.

Vyshinsky: What was he in Archangel?

Thornton: I was not there.

Vyshinsky: I understand. You were in Mesopotamia.

Thornton: I can only say what I heard.

Vyshinsky: But he is your representative? You confirm it?

Thornton: Yes, it is a fact.

Vyshinsky: Consequently, we may say that in 1918, Richards, the present director of the export department of Metropolitan-Vickers, was in Archangel with the British forces, which were fighting against the Soviet Government at that time.

Thornton: Yes.

Vyshinsky: Perhaps you will tell us what position he occupied there.

Thornton: As far as I know he was an "intelligence officer."

Vyshinsky: How would you say it in Russian?

Thornton: An officer.

Vyshinsky: An officer of what? What was the institution called in which he served as an officer?

Thornton: It is not an institution, it is a unit.

Vyshinsky: Would it be correct if I say that it was called the Intelligence Service

Thornton: I think that is something different. He was an intelligence officer. There is no Intelligence Service in the army, but there is an intelligence officer who is in charge of this business.

Vyshinsky: What business?

Thornton: He is in charge of all information about the enemy and examines prisoners.

Vyshinsky: Is he in charge of arrests?

Thornton: Yes, not of our soldiers, however, but of others.

Vyshinsky: Of the other side?

Thornton: Yes.

Vyshinsky: Bolsheviks?

Thornton: In the present case, probably, yes.

Vyshinsky. Probably. We may say that he is an officer of the counter-espionage?*

Thornton: I do not know how to say "scout" in Russian.

Interpreter: "Scout" in Russian is *"razvedchik."*

Thornton: I regret that I do not know this part of the army very well. A scout, as far as I know, is attached to a special unit. But this was an office job.

Vyshinsky: Razvedchik, not in the sense of scouting on the battlefield, but a razvedchik who does his work from a swivel chair.

Thornton: This, of course, concerns principally the enemy.

Vyshinsky: I understand. I want to ask Monkhouse. Accused Monkhouse, at that time were you too in Archangel, in the same corps, and were you connected with this Richards?

Monkhouse: I was in the Engineers.

Vyshinsky: Was Richards there?

Monkhouse: I myself was not in Archangel. I was in Vysokie Gori.

Vyshinsky: And where was Richards?

Monkhouse: In Archangel.

Vyshinsky: What was his position?

Monkhouse: He was an intelligence officer at military headquarters.

Vyshinsky: So you see, it turns out to be the Intelligence Ser-

* In the original: *Contre-razvedchik.—Ed.*

vice. Now after the Archangel Expedition, which ended in failure, did this Richards return to England?

Monkhouse: Yes.

Vyshinsky: And then he came secretly to the U.S.S.R.?

Monkhouse: No.

Vyshinsky: But in 1918, he crossed the Finnish frontier illegally?

Monkhouse: In the middle of 1918.

Vyshinsky: In the middle of 1918, he crossed the Finnish frontier illegally.

Monkhouse: I cannot say he crossed illegally.

Vyshinsky: How then, did he have a passport?

Monkhouse: He had a passport, but he crossed secretly. May I say why he crossed secretly?

Vyshinsky: I shall ask you about that later. Now I have a question to Thornton. Would you please permit me to submit Thornton's deposition made by him on March 13 written in his own hand? Is this your deposition? Take it please and examine it carefully from beginning to end, and then we shall have it read.

Is it your deposition?

Thornton: Yes.

Vyshinsky: In your own hand?

Thornton: Yes.

Vyshinsky: Did you write it?

Thornton: Yes.

Vyshinsky: So we shall have to read it in full. If necessary, in English first.

The President: We shall read the deposition written by Thornton himself on March 13, 1933.

Member of the Court, Martens (Reads the following deposition written and signed by Thornton):

"All our spying operations on U.S.S.R. territory are directed by the British Intelligence Service, through their agent, C. S. Richards, who occupies the position of Managing Director of the Metropolitan-Vickers Electrical Export Company, Ltd.

"Spying operations on U.S.S.R. territory were directed by myself and Monkhouse, representatives of the above-mentioned Brit-

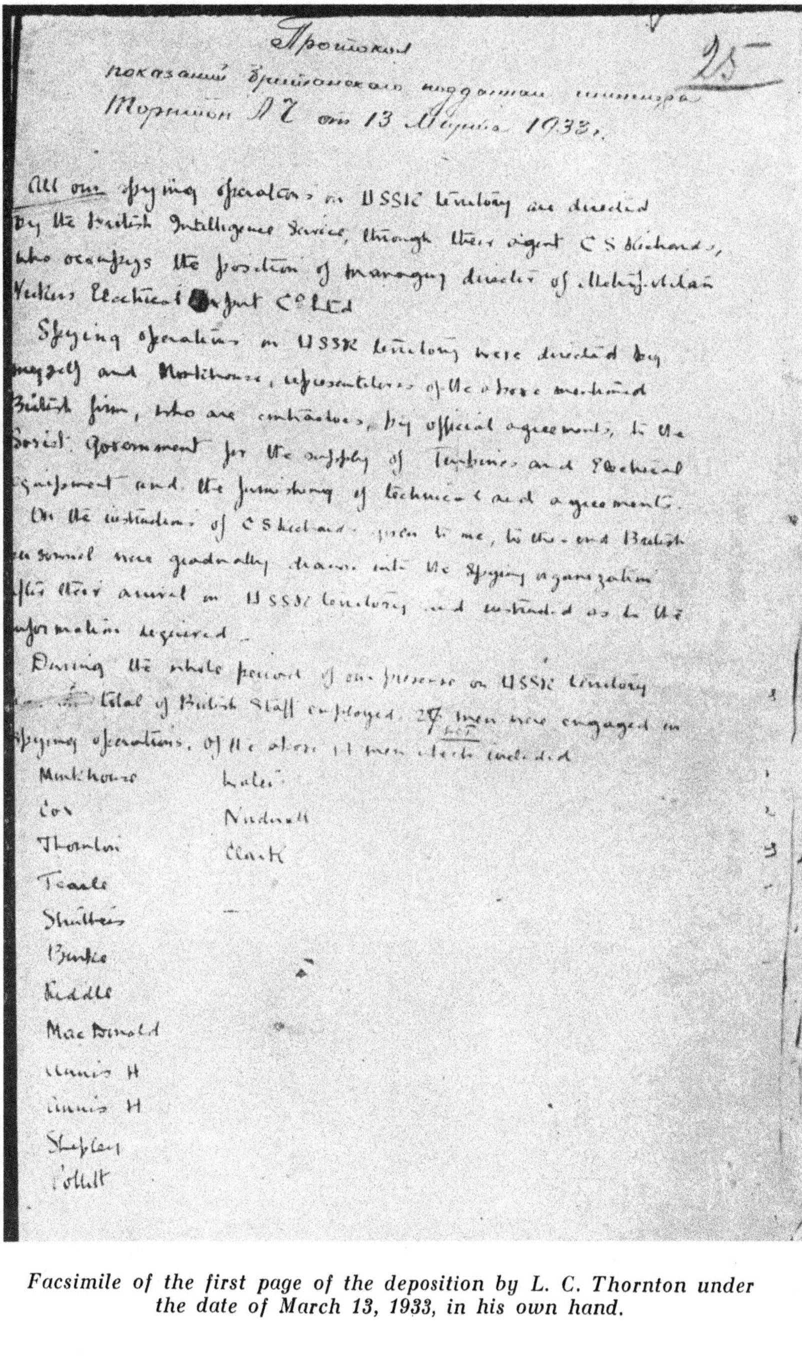

Протокол
показаний британского подданного инженера
Торнтон Л.Ч. от 13 Марта 1933 г.

25

All our spying operations on USSR territory are directed by the British Intelligence Service, through their agent C S Richards, who occupies the position of managing director of Metrop. Vickers Electrical Export Co Ltd

Spying operations on USSR territory were directed by myself and Monkhouse, representatives of the above mentioned British firm, who are contractors, by official agreements, to the Soviet Government for the supply of Turbines and Electrical equipment and the furnishing of technical aid agreements.

On the instructions of C S Richards given to me, the British personnel were gradually drawn into the spying organization after their arrival on USSR territory and instructed as to the information required.

During the whole period of our presence on USSR territory [illegible] total of British Staff employed, 27 men were engaged in spying operations. Of the above 27 men [illegible] included

Monkhouse — Lalee
Cox — Nordwall
Thornton — Clark
Teasle
Shutters
Burkie
Riddle
MacDonald
Annis H
Annis H
Shepley
Pollitt

Facsimile of the first page of the deposition by L. C. Thornton under the date of March 13, 1933, in his own hand.

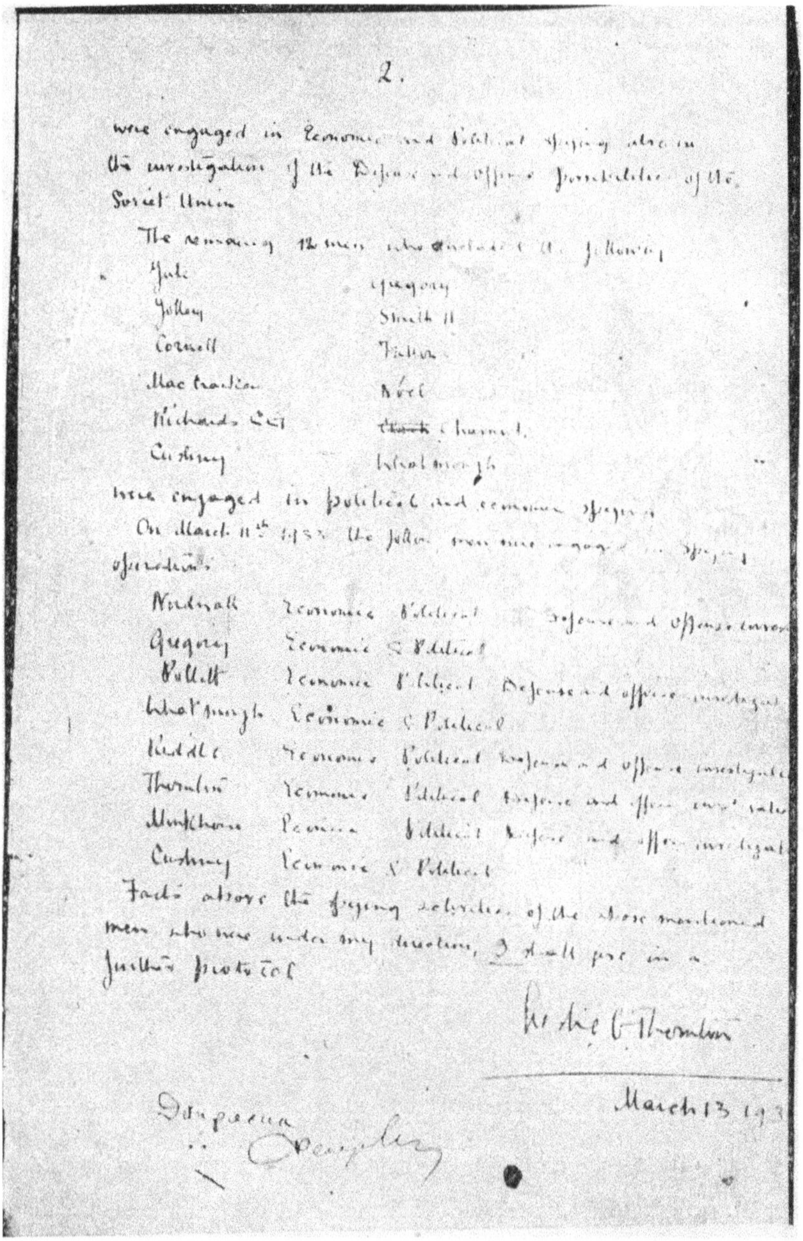

2.

were engaged in Economic and Political spying also in the investigation of the Defense and Offense possibilities of the Soviet Union

The remaining 12 men who included the following

Gale	Gregory
Jolley	Smith II
Cornell	[illegible]
Mac Cracken	Noel
Richards Cecil	~~[illegible]~~ Chennell
Cushny	Whatmough

were engaged in political and economic spying

On March 11th 1933 the following men were engaged in spying operations:

Nordwall	Economic Political Defense and Offense investigation
Gregory	Economic & Political
Pollitt	Economic Political Defense and offense investigation
Whatmough	Economic & Political
Riddle	Economic Political Defense and offense investigation
Thornton	Economic Political Defense and offense investigation
Monkhouse	Economic Political Defense and offense investigation
Cushny	Economic & Political

Facts about the spying activities of the above mentioned men who were under my direction, I shall give in a further protocol

Leslie C Thornton

March 13 193[illegible]

Допрашивал [illegible]

Facsimile of the second page of the deposition by L. C. Thornton under the date of March 13, 1933, in his own hand.

ish firm, who are contractors, by official agreements, to the Soviet Government, for the supply of turbines and electrical equipment and the furnishing of technical aid agreements. On the instructions of C. S. Richards given to me to this end, British personnel were gradually drawn into the spying organization after their arrival on U.S.S.R. territory and instructed as to the information required. During the whole period of our presence on U.S.S.R. territory, from the total of British staff employed, 27 men were engaged in spying operations. Of the above 15 men which included

Monkhouse	Waters
Cox	Nordwall
Thornton	Clark
Teasle	
Shutters	
Burke	
Riddle	
MacDonald	
Annis, A.	
Annis, H.	
Shipley	
Pollitt	

were engaged in Economic and Political spying, also in the investigation of the defence and offence possibilities of the Soviet Union.

"The remaining 12 men who included the following

Jule	Gregory
Jolley	Smith, A.
Cornell	Fallows
MacCracken	Noel
Richards, C. G.	Charnock
Cushny	Whatmough

were engaged in political and economic spying.

"On March 11, 1933, the following men were engaged in spying operations:

Nordwall—economic, political, defence and offence investigation
Gregory—economic and political
Pollitt—economic, political, defence and offence investigation

Whatmough—economic and political
Riddle—economic, political, defence and offence investigation
Thornton—economic, political, defence and offence investigation
Monkhouse—economic, political, defence and offence investigation
Cushny—economic and political

"Facts above [about?] the spying activities of the above-mentioned men who were under my direction, I shall give in a further protocol.

(Signed) Leslie C. Thornton"

March 13, 1933.

Vyshinsky: Accused Thornton, in your deposition which has just been read, you say: "All our spying operations on U.S.S.R. territory are directed by the British Intelligence Service through their agent, C. S. Richards, who occupies the position of Managing Director of the Metropolitan-Vickers Export Company, Ltd." That is the first part.

Thornton: I wish to repudiate this document entirely.

The President: Your wish alone is not enough.

Vyshinsky: I want to take it up part by part, and then we shall get the whole. This is the first part. And so you repudiate it?

Thornton: Yes.

Vyshinsky: In reality there was nothing of the kind?

Thornton: No.

Vyshinsky: But you wrote it.

Thornton: Yes, I did.

Vyshinsky: For the same reason—you were excited?

Thornton: At the time I wrote that, it was a matter of indifference to me what I wrote.

Vyshinsky: But why was it a matter of indifference?

Thornton: I was in such a frame of mind.

Vyshinsky: You were upset?

Thornton: Yes.

Vyshinsky: Why then blab on Richards?

Thornton: I know I have slandered him.

Vyshinsky: The second paragraph: "Spying operations on U.S.S.R. territory were directed by myself and Monkhouse, representatives of the above-mentioned British firm, who are contractors, by official agreements, to the Soviet Government, for the supply of turbines and electrical equipment and the furnishing of technical aid."

Do you repudiate this?

Thornton: Yes.

Vyshinsky: What exactly? That it is a firm that supplies turbines?

Thornton: That is well known.

Vyshinsky: In this paragraph you do not deny that your firm was supplying turbines, that it offered technical aid. You do not deny that?

Thornton: No.

Vyshinsky: But you deny that you, in conjunction with Monkhouse, were directing spying operations.

Thornton: Spying I deny.

Vyshinsky: If we throw out the word "spying," then it will be like this—the information of which you spoke, and within the limits which you have admitted. Does this correspond to what you said?

Thornton: Yes.

Vyshinsky: Here it says "spying operations," but I bear in mind that you have all the time obstinately repudiated the word "spy"; therefore I throw this word out. I am not speaking of spying operations but of operations concerning which quite a number of persons have spoken, operations the secret character of which is the only thing you deny—were there such operations?

Thornton: Yes.

Vyshinsky: Consequently, the whole paragraph, with that reservation, was written down correctly.

Thornton: Yes.

Vyshinsky: Consequently, although you were upset, it didn't hinder you writing it down correctly.

Thornton: Yes, but not spying.

Vyshinsky: I have already made that reservation. Then here it is written: "On the instructions of C. S. Richards given to me to this end, British personnel were gradually drawn into the spying organization after their arrival on U.S.S.R. territory and instructed as to the information required."

What do you admit and what do you deny here?

Thornton: I deny it. I didn't speak the truth. What I said about instructions is not true.

Vyshinsky: There were no instructions?

Thornton: No.

Vyshinsky: Was there information?

Thornton: What was required for the firm, yes.

Vyshinsky: That which you transmitted to Richards, was there such?

Thornton: Yes.

Vyshinsky: So you admit that?

Thornton: Subject to correction.

Vyshinsky: Let us make the following correction to this paragraph: "The information received by me here I transmitted to Richards, but without his instructions."

Thornton: The information about which I spoke here?

Vyshinsky: Yes. The second paragraph is partly admitted, the third paragraph is partly admitted.

Further: "During the whole period of our presence on U.S.S.R. territory from the total of British staff employed, 27 men were engaged in spying operations. . ." How many employees were there during that time, about twenty-seven?

Thornton: As far as I remember, that is what I wrote down.

Vyshinsky: Here is the figure 27.

Thornton: I wrote 27.

Vyshinsky: But were there 27?

Thornton: I think not.

Vyshinsky: How many were there then?

Thornton: From what date?

Vyshinsky: First of March. [passes the dossier to Thornton] Are they all included?

Thornton: All are included.

Vyshinsky: You have put the right figure?

Thornton: Perhaps 26 or may be 28, but approximately correct.

Vyshinsky: There may be a mistake in one person more or less?

Thornton: They were all here.

Vyshinsky: They were all here. Perhaps we shall enumerate them: Monkhouse, Cox, Thornton, Teasle, Shutters, Burke, Riddle, MacDonald, Annis A. and Annis H., Shipley, Pollitt, Waters, Nordwall, Clark. Is that right?

Thornton: Yes.

Vyshinsky: Further you wrote that apart from their work they were all engaged in spying operations. Is that right? Did you write that?

Thornton: I wrote that, but it isn't so.

Vyshinsky: Very well. How were they distributed? I have enumerated fifteen people who were engaged in economic and political spying as well as in investigating the defensive and offensive possibilities of the Soviet Union. You wrote that?

Thornton: I wrote that, but it is not so.

Vyshinsky: Do you always write the other way about?

Thornton: In the present document, yes.

Vyshinsky: And it was the same with a number of other documents. The remaining twelve people: Jule, Jolley, Cornell, MacCracken, Richards C. G., Cushny, Gregory, Smith A., Fallows, Noel, Charnock, Whatmough were engaged in political and economic spying. Did you write that?

Thornton: Yes, I did.

Vyshinsky: And was it so?

Thornton: Only not in spying.

Vyshinsky: What then?

Thornton: In collecting information, which we have specified today.

Vyshinsky: Consequently, we shall say about these people that all these twelve men were really engaged in collecting information which you consider was not spying, but which MacDonald, for instance, considers is spying.

Thornton: MacDonald considers it spying?

Vyshinsky: Exactly.

Thornton: MacDonald spoke of military spying. This I deny.

Vyshinsky: And the first fifteen people were engaged in military espionage as well?

Thornton: I say this is a lie.

Vyshinsky: They collected no information?

Thornton: Perhaps information that was required for the firm.

Vyshinsky: Information which MacDonald considered to be military information, but which you do not regard as military and secret information, but as common gossip?

Thornton: No.

Vyshinsky: Did the first fifteen engage in military espionage?

Thornton: I say that is a lie.

Vyshinsky: They did not collect any information at all?

Thornton: Perhaps they collected information, as we have defined it, that was of interest to the firm.

Vyshinsky: Now this coincidence for instance: you name MacDonald among those fifteen people, and MacDonald confirms that he really collected information of a secret military nature. Did you hear that?

Thornton: Yes, I did.

Vyshinsky: MacDonald confirmed that he collected information of a military and secret nature. Is that right?

Thornton: Yes.

Vyshinsky: You wrote on March 13 that MacDonald collected information concerning offence and defence possibilities. Does it coincide?

Thornton: That was on the same date.

Vyshinsky: It coincides. MacDonald said here as well as at the preliminary examination that he collected information of a military espionage nature.

Thornton: Yes.

Vyshinsky: And you, on the 13th, pointed to MacDonald as a man who collected information of a military nature concerning offence and defence possibilities. I ask you, does this agree with what you said then and what MacDonald says here in court?

Thornton: It does, but I did not speak the truth then.

Vyshinsky: You did not speak the truth, but this "untruth" agrees with what MacDonald says here in Court.

Thornton: Yes, it does.

Vyshinsky: If you wrote an untruth, how does it happen that in your evidence we come across points which found confirmation here in the evidence given by MacDonald and Kutuzova?

Thornton: It would seem this is all one case.

Vyshinsky: Why did you in that evidence, although as you say you were excited and upset, give with such precision the number of people as 27, a circumstance which equally coincides with the data which you have further deciphered?

Thornton: I do not think that this....

Vyshinsky: You have just verified this and you said the figure was right—27. If you were really excited and upset, how could you remember the figure, and since you remembered the exact figure, then permit me to doubt whether you were so excited and upset then.

Thornton: I was really upset.

Vyshinsky: But not to such an extent as to forget the figure.

Thornton: I do not know. These figures, I think, are right.

Vyshinsky: I think so too.

Thornton: But I deny military spying.

Vyshinsky: You deny, but this will not convince me that it was not so.

Thornton: I say that my deposition is false.

Vyshinsky: But we must find out. You say you were upset, but the figure 27 is an exact figure, and you divided it so exactly—15 and 12 people.

Thornton: I had a list and I simply ticked them off at random.

Vyshinsky: Answer the last question. What were you guided by when you put some into the category of economic and political spying, and the others into the category of economic and political as well as military, that is to say, spying as to offence and defence possibilities? Here is Nordwall—economic and political espionage, Pollitt—the same, Whatmough—no military spying, Cushny—no military spying, but to Monkhouse you have added military spying.

Thornton: This is only accidental.

Vishinsky: Also at random?

Thornton: Yes.

Vyshinsky: So you put one into the economic-political spying and the other into the military, at random?

Thornton: Yes.

Vyshinsky: And what was your object in doing that? I ask—for what purpose?

Thornton: I simply didn't know, but I was asked to confess.

Vyshinsky: And you have gratified that request?

Thornton: Yes, I gratified that request.

Vyshinsky: I have no more questions to ask.

The President: The Court will adjourn for twenty minutes.

* * *

The Commandant: Please rise, the Court is coming.

The President: Be seated. Accused Thornton, take your place. Has the Public Prosecutor any questions?

Vyshinsky: No.

The President: Has the Defence any questions to ask?

Braude: Yes. Accused Thornton, I want to ask you to explain to the Court, what you understand by the word "spying information." What did you imagine at that time was implied by the phrase "spying information"?

Thornton: Spying information is information collected by a man who is in the service of those states who need that information, *i.e.*, the obtaining of all sorts of secrets in an illegal way.

Braude: You did not always give evidence in the way you did on March 13. In your depositions of March 12, there is this statement:

> "It is known to me that certain of our erecting engineers and erectors have reported from time to time on future orders for electrical equipment to be installed which was to be purchased abroad, either verbally or in writing."

And further you wrote:

> "According to Soviet law the collection and passing of such information is equivalent to economic spying, which in effect has been carried out by certain members of our erection staff, to wit,"

Then follows a list of names. In this deposition you speak of spying information. Did you have in view only military information, or this information?

Thornton: After it was explained to me that this is spying information, I wrote everywhere in my deposition—spying.

As to all sorts of military information, I deny it, although I wrote it.

Braude: What did you mean by the term offensive and defensive, which you mentioned in the deposition read today?

Thornton: I do not know myself what it is.

Braude: Do you write what you do not know?

Thornton: I wrote it after long questions and moral pressure.

Braude: Because of the fatigue of which you spoke?

Thornton: These phrases are not mine. They were suggested.

Braude: You wish to say that that was a bad formulation of your ideas?

Thornton: I wrote that document under moral pressure.

Braude: May we put it that you were interested in the question of the stability of the Soviet Government? Can it be interpreted that way?

Thornton: No, it was different. This is that very spying, military information, only under a different name.

Braude: On page 140 of the dossier, in the depositions of March 20, in referring to this kind of information which was communicated to you by your comrades, you incidentally say:

> "Nordwall was for a short time at Kuznetsk with MacDonald and was chiefly employed in the modification of the "R" motors in the power station. He gave me no information about Kuznetsk, except about our equipment.
>
> "Nordwall maintained the soundness of the Soviet Government."

How is this to be interpreted? What was the object of that sort of information? Does that confirm your idea of the stability of the Soviet Government?

Thornton: In that sense, yes.

Braude: And as regards wrecking? You have already stated that you have never in your evidence admitted your guilt in organizing breakdowns and acts of wrecking. Do you confirm it now?

Thornton: I do confirm it.

Braude: And according to your convictions regarding the Soviet Government, the Soviet Union, could you organize wrecking work in the sense of engineering breakdowns, collisions, etc.?

Thornton: I never could have done it.

Braude: Why?

Thornton: All my life I have been making things, but I never destroyed things, and moreover, to do that in a foreign country, I would consider it extremely immoral and I would never do it.

Braude: One more question. Tell me please, during the time you have been working with Metro-Vickers in connection with the contract with the Soviet Government, have you personally taken part in a large number of installations, you yourself working?

Thornton: Yes, I installed transformers.

Braude: You have been to different places. Cite one or two instances where you have personally worked on installations. There were no breakdowns in your work?

Thornton: Barring the last breakdown, there were none.

Braude: Was there a single instance of a breakdown, or collapse on the installation works which you personally carried out?

Thornton: There was one case in Leningrad.

Braude: It doesn't figure in this case?

Thornton: No, it doesn't.

Braude: There were no others?

Thornton: No.

Braude: Another question of a biographical nature. Your father was one of the proprietors of an industrial enterprise? What share did he have in that enterprise?

Thornton: There were twenty-five to thirty people in the Thornton firm.

Braude: So there were from twenty-five to thirty people? He had a small number of shares?

Thornton: He was the youngest in the family.

Braude: You said that you have worked in a number of enterprises. Have you personally owned property—houses, estates, etc.?

Thornton: No. I have always worked for my living.

Braude: How many years have you worked for your living?

Thornton: Roughly, twenty-six years.

Braude: Did the revolution deprive you personally of a lot of capital, estates, etc.?

Thornton: Yes, approximately 20,000 Kerensky rubles. You can buy this for a couple of rubles.

Braude: So you personally had no reason to have an immediate grudge against the revolution?

Thornton: No.

Braude: Did you find Soviet conditions favourable for your work?

Thornton: Very favourable.

Braude: Was the treatment you received from the Soviet Government and its representatives and from business people with whom you came in contact, good? Were there any grounds for dissatisfaction?

Thornton: There were no grounds for that at any time.

Braude: So there was nothing that would prompt you to commit a crime?

Thornton: No.

The President: Has the Defence any more questions to ask?

Lidov: When you were receiving information from Cushny, did you hand over sums of money for it?

Thornton: I have never given Cushny any money for information and I never sanctioned his bills, which contained suspiciously large sums.

Lidov: So you didn't sanction them?

Thornton: I never sanctioned and never gave money, I never sanctioned a bill which had abnormal figures.

Lidov: So the information which you obtained from him did not go beyond that which he communicated to you upon his return from his travels without him getting any payment for it or any money for expenses?

Thornton: Quite so.

Lidov: You were asked about this also during the preliminary investigation. Do you remember that?

Thornton: Yes.

Lidov: You gave the same answer also at the investigation?

Thornton: Yes.

Lidov: I draw the attention of the Court to the fact that indeed, on page 96, Volume XVIII, in the record of the examination of Thornton, there is a question which was put to him in relation to the accused Cushny, and he really asserts that he never paid and never sanctioned any expenses which seemed suspicious and were not in the nature of ordinary expenses.

I have no more questions to ask.

The President: Any more questions?

Kommodov: In connection with Thornton's evidence allow me to put some questions to the accused Gussev, Sokolov, Oleinik and Kutuzova.

The President: Perhaps some of the other Counsel for the Defence have some questions?

Dolmatovsky: (To Thornton) The information concerned your business relations with clients?

Thornton: Yes. I do not know what the law says about it. Sometimes it is said that this is spying information. He told me that they would order new transmission for their shaping rolling mill.

Dolmatovsky: May I ask leave of the Court to have this translated to accused Gregory, who does not understand?

The President: Yes.

(The interpreter translates.)

Gregory: Could I add something to it?

The President: You may.

Gregory: I obtained this information from an engineer who worked there.

Dolmatovsky: Apart from this information did you get any written or verbal information?

Thornton: (Inaudible)

Dolmatovsky: Did Nordwall give such information? Where and when? When you used to meet him, what kind of information did he give you? Couldn't you specify it in detail?

Thornton: The information which I obtained from Nordwall was ordinary information and could in no way be suspected of being spying.

Dolmatovsky: Spying in what sense? There is a great difference. Ordinary information which conerns his work and their mutual relations in connection with the work?

Thornton: It could be called information about his work and local gossip.

Dolmatovsky: In what sense "gossip"? Was it about the conditions of work in the given locality or more concrete?

Thornton: Of a general character.

Dolmatovsky: Did you consider Nordwall to be a man who could give information which was harmful for the Soviet Union?

Thornton: No. I may say that Nordwall was very well disposed towards the Soviet Government.

Dolmatovsky: Tell me, was the sum of 112 rubles, which was entered in the record of March 13, given as remuneration for illegal information?

Thornton: I inspected the books and it turns out that it was not 112 rubles but 120.

Dolmatovsky: What money is that? Remuneration for illegal work?

Thornton: I do not know. I passed it. I signed it. It was a bill of Nordwall's for 120 rubles, and he gave that sum for dismantling and repairing the induction motor of the Tomsk works.

Dolmatovsky: So this is expenditure in connection with work?

Thornton: This is a legitimate expenditure.

Dolmatovsky: Why then did you call that an illegitimate expenditure by an employee?

Thornton: I did not know what it was for.

Dolmatovsky: Why then did you say this was remuneration to employees?

Thornton: Yes, he did pay. I thought it was so. I think somewhere in my depositions I said that I supposed that it was for repairs.

Dolmatovsky: I would ask the Court to ascertain that in Thornton's depositions of March 20, it is stated that this sum was paid not for wrecking, but to workers for work done.

Schwartz: Permit me to put a question of a general nature but which concerns two of the accused.

Mr. Thornton, you replied to the Public Prosecutor's question that you knew Zorin?

Thornton: Yes.

Schwartz: Permit me to ask you, in what year did you first make his acquaintance and under what circumstances?

Thornton: I think that it was in 1931 at a committee meeting which was called to discuss the units installed on the First Moscow Power Station.

Schwartz: You first made his acquaintance in 1931 at a meeting of a committee. Where did that meeting take place?

Thornton: At the Moscow Power Station. I do not quite remember, but I think it was there.

Schwartz: This was your first acquaintance, and on that occasion you had only a business conversation?

Thornton: Yes.

Schwartz: Then when did you meet him again?

Thornton: I was at his office at the Moscow Power Station and spoke with him about the breakdown at Orekhovo-Zuevo. This was our second meeting. And our third meeting, if I am not mistaken, was at the Electro-Import.

Schwartz: I am interested to know in what year and on what occasion you carried on conversations of a different nature other than business conversations.

Thornton: The only conversation I had with Zorin, as I stated in my depositions, was one concerning the regulators made by other firms, regulators which were on the turbine.

Schwartz: What year was that?

Thornton: That was quite recently.

Schwartz: And that was?

Thornton: That was in 1933.

Schwartz: Where?

Thornton: It was after the meeting at the Electro-Import. I brought him to our office and he asked for literature.

Schwartz: There were no other conversations apart from business conversations?

Thornton: Only concerning the regulators and nothing more.

The President: Has the Defence any more questions?

Libson: Tell me, please, how many years has the accused Kutuzova worked in the firm with you?

Thornton: She came to work at the end of 1926, or at the beginning of 1927.

Libson: And has she been secretary all the time?

Thornton: All the time.

Libson: Was there no employee above her in the office?

Thornton: She had the highest post.

Libson: And she enjoyed special confidence?

Thornton: She did.

Libson: Was Monkhouse always in the office?

Thornton: Yes.

Libson: Did Monkhouse, who was the head, have a separate room?

Thornton: Not quite a separate room; it was supposed to be a separate room.

Libson: Did Kutuzova work in that room?

Thornton: No, she worked in the general office.

Libson: But she had the right to enter the room where Monkhouse worked?

Thornton: Yes.

Libson: Apart from the fact that you worked in the Moscow office together with accused Kutuzova, you also lived in the same house?

Thornton: She lived in a separate apartment which was on the floor above my apartment.

Libson: Is this house a hostel?

Thornton: This is one of the sections of the hostel.

Libson: You were together constantly, you, Monkhouse and she?

Thornton: Yes.

Libson: Consequently all conversations outside of the office were carried on together?

Thornton: Not always, but sometimes we were together. She has a separate apartment.

Libson: In reply to a question put by the Assistant Prosecutor Roginsky, you said that you felt no constraint in her presence. How is this to be understood—you felt no constraint?

Thornton: I am not sure myself, I meant that we trusted her.

Libson: Tell me please, when you spoke with Monkhouse, you spoke in English?

Thornton: Always.

Libson: Does she know English well?

Thornton: She knows it well. Perhaps certain special terms not so well.

Libson: She may not know some special technical terms, but generally she knows the English language?

Thornton: Yes.

Libson: And you always spoke in her presence in English?

Thornton: Sometimes Russian, but mostly English.

Libson: Do you know other languages?

Thornton: I speak German.

Libson: And so does she, I believe?

Thornton: Very little, she speaks French.

Libson: You have one estimate of your activity and the Public Prosecutor has another. We shall not call it spying, collecting military information, but shall call it just information. Now your conversations concerning the information which you were receiving, when you talked with Monkhouse, were they carried on in the presence of Kutuzova?

Thornton: If we knew that something was going to be built, we might have said it in her presence.

Libson. You did not conceal that?

Thornton: No.

Libson: And, in general, were there any subjects which you concealed from her in these conversations?

Thornton: Yes, perhaps. She did not know our business affairs.

Libson: You presume she did not know?

Thornton: Yes.

Libson: One more thing. Have you yourself been to Zuevka?

Thornton: Yes.

Libson: Did you know any of the Russian engineering staff personally? For example, did you have occasion to meet engineer Kotlyarevsky?

Thornton: When I saw him here I remembered him, but over there he was not working on the installation—he was on the operating staff.

Libson: So you had no conversation with him?

Thornton: No.

Braude: Tell us, please, you said that you trusted Kutuzova. There are different kinds of confidence. To what degree did you trust her? If you had been talking to Monkhouse concerning your firm's secrets, would you do it in her presence?

Thornton: No.

Braude: She is a Soviet citizen?

Thornton: Yes.

Braude: And how long has she been working for you?

Thornton: Since 1927.

Braude: Did she know the business affairs of the firm?

Thornton: She was informed on many matters of business.

Braude: But was she informed on matters which you would not want other employees to know?

Thornton: There were many things that I did not know myself.

Braude: Suppose you had plotted some crime, would you have taken her into your confidence?

Thornton: Of course not!

Libson: Were you carrying on any secret business correspondence?

Thornton: No.

Libson: All kinds of confidential letters, confidential correspondence which was carried on with London—was that carried on through Kutuzova?

Thornton: We have two kinds of confidential letters. There are letters addressed to department managers. This correspondence is put in separate envelopes. This concerns salaries, increase of salary to employees. These letters always passed through the hands of Anna Sergeyevna Kutuzova.

Libson: So you trusted her to carry on this correspondence?

Thornton: With this kind of confidential correspondence we trusted her.

Libson: Accordingly, what secrets do you refer to? You said before that you were reserved in her presence. In what cases?

Thornton: For instance, regarding the salaries of our Board. She did not know what salary I was receiving.

Libson: You considered this kind of thing confidential and you kept it from Kutuzova?

Thornton: We did not consider it particularly confidential but abroad it is not done. People do not know how much each gets.

Libson: This was kept secret from her. You did not conceal the rest?

Thornton: My personal brief case was sometimes kept in her desk drawer.

Libson: Anything that concerned Russian life was not kept secret from her?

Thornton: No, it was not.

Libson: I have no more questions to ask.

Smirnov: You said that it is not the custom in English firms to know what salaries were paid. But you knew how much MacDonald was receiving?

Thornton: Yes, I am his chief.

Smirnov: Did he state correctly that his salary was 12 pounds a week?

Thornton: When he was in Zlatoust?

Smirnov: Yes.

Thornton: Correct.

Smirnov: Was it correct when he testified that out of these 12 pounds, if we count 50 pounds a month, 30 were deposited in a bank?

Thornton: I do not understand.

Smirnov: Is it your custom to deposit part of your employees' salaries in a bank to their account and pay part here in Soviet currency?

Thornton: Sometimes it is paid out here also in foreign currency. It is as they want it. There is the Torgsin here now.

Smirnov: You have attested here that you gave 2,000 rubles to MacDonald for his personal needs. Did he run up a large debt to your office?

Thornton: Yes.

Smirnov: Tell us please, how do you explain that he was in debt to the office? How do you explain this, and how could this debt have occurred?

Thornton: Very simply. He asked for 500 rubles, then for 500 rubles more. He did not want to take 200 rubles, or even 300.

Smirnov: In general, has the system of such advances been customary in your firm?

Thornton: Yes, of course. I must say that in general MacDonald does not understand the value of money.

Smirnov: What does that mean? That he is a man who is very free with money?

Thornton: Yes. Very free.

Smirnov: Squanders it on trifles?

Thornton: To tell the truth, that's so. When he was in Zlatoust his postal and telegraph expenses... (inaudible)

Smirnov: That is, he did not usually present accounts of his expenses on various small items.

Thornton: Yes.

Smirnov: In this way he ran up personal debts to the amount of 2,000 rubles?

Thornton: I think even more than that.

Smirnov: Approximately during what period of time?

Thornton· This went on for several years.

Smirnov: For several years?

Thornton: Yes, his debt grew larger and larger.

Smirnov: He started to work at the end of 1929, or in the beginning of 1930. Accordingly, all this went on for about three years, 1930, 1931, and 1932?

Thornton: Yes.

Smirnov: And it was during this time that he ran up this debt?

Thornton: I do not know the exact amount.

Smirnov: I am interested to know whether it is true that he ran up such a debt (personal, as you say) during this period of time. And that accordingly, whether he is, in general, a man who spends more than he receives?

Thornton: More than is necessary.

Smirnov: In this way the debt was accumulated?

Thornton: Yes.

Smirnov: I have no more questions to ask.

Kommodov: I have a question. How many employees were there on the staff of Metro-Vickers on March 11?

Thornton: English employees?

Kommodov: Yes, English. Perhaps Monkhouse knows better?

Thornton: I think thirteen.

Kommodov: Thirteen British subjects?

Thornton: Yes.

Kommodov: I have no more questions. Permit me to put a question to Gussev. Gussev, yesterday you testified quite frankly to the crimes you committed both in espionage and in wrecking. Tell us, in this criminal activity did you have any direct contact with Monkhouse?

Gussev: No, I did not.

Kommodov: Did you receive any instructions from him personally?

Gussev: No.

Kommodov: Did you give him any information?

Gussev: No.

Kommodov: When you passed through Moscow, did you pay him any visits?

Gussev: No.

Kommodov: And MacDonald even gave you the address?

Gussev: I had a note.

Kommodov: Nevertheless, you did not see each other?

Gussev: No.

Kommodov: Sokolov, you also frankly spoke of your espionage and wrecking crimes. Have you personally had any occasion to come in touch with Monkhouse directly?

Sokolov: No.

Kommodov: Did you give him any information?

Sokolov: No.

Kommodov: Did you receive any money?

Sokolov: No.

Kommodov: Did you meet him?

Sokolov: No.

Kommodov: Oleinik, tell us concretely. . .

The President: We are at present completing the examination of the accused Thornton.

Vyshinsky: Concerning Monkhouse there will be a special question.

Kommodov: Comrade Vyshinsky has been putting questions to Monkhouse and asked what information he had been receiving through other persons. Here Oleinik, Gussev, Sokolov and MacDonald were mentioned. I consider this proceeding impermissible for the defence of Monkhouse, because I cannot disclose my argument beforehand, but if you wish I shall say it.

Vyshinsky: No, I do not wish.

Kommodov: I shall tell the Court. Thornton is acting on his own responsibility. Therefore permit me to establish the direct relations of Monkhouse with the wreckers who are sitting here. Since Vyshinsky was asking Oleinik about Monkhouse, permit me also to ask what concrete instructions he received from Monkhouse in the matter of espionage.

Oleinik, tell us what concrete tasks of a spying nature you have received from Monkhouse—one or several?

Oleinik: In 1928, when I was going to the Nadezhdinsky Works, I was instructed to ascertain the condition of the station, about the intended expansion of the works.

Kommodov: Correct.

Oleinik: About the attitude of the workers, about the program of the works—to what extent it was being fulfilled, and about the state of railway transportation.

Kommodov: Correct. So you stated in your deposition when answering the concrete questions. What other instructions were there along these lines?

Oleinik: From Monkhouse?

Kommodov: Yes.

Oleinik: Along the lines of espionage?

Kommodov: Yes.

Oleinik: In the sense of getting orders it was necessary to collect all information in general.

Kommodov: I am not speaking in general. The investigation quite correctly formulated the question thus: What tasks of a spying and diversional nature were received from Monkhouse? This is a very concrete question. Now you were telling us here about the case that occurred in 1928. Were there any other cases or not?

Oleinik: I do not remember any of a diversional nature

Kommodov: Concerning instances of a diversional nature you said this: "Concerning diversional acts, I did not receive any instructions from Monkhouse." Do you confirm this deposition in the part concerning diversional acts?

Oleinik: Concerning diversional acts I do not remember.

Kommodov: You did not receive any instructions. In the part concerning diversional acts you do not know of any more instances except this one?

Oleinik: No, because I was dealing with Thornton.

Kommodov: Now in this instance did you consider it an espionage act or not?

Oleinik: I did not think of it at all. I thought that I was obliged to do it.

Kommodov: Why?

Oleinik: As an employee of the firm.

Kommodov: You thought that this was in the interests of the firm?

Oleinik: Yes.

The President: I thought that you were going to put only a cursory question?

Kommodov: Very well, he confirmed what I needed. Now tell us, please, this: When you were giving information concerning the movement of troops during your trip to the Urals, did you receive this information from someone, or was it the result of your personal observations?

Oleinik: I did not give such information to engineer Monkhouse.

Kommodov: I am interested in something else. Did you receive this information from some source or was it from your personal observation?

Oleinik: From my personal observation and from the conversations which I carried on in the train.

Kommodov: You passed this information on to Thornton?

Oleinik: Yes.

Kommodov: Now the last question, which concerns Kutuzova. Comrade Roginsky put to you the question: Did anybody in the firm tell you that they thought it was necessary to be on the lookout and that there was an agent of the O.G.P.U. in the office?

Oleinik: There was talk about that. I was warned that there was an agent.

Kommodov: And was there any talk concerning Nordwall's wife?

Oleinik: They told me to be careful, because Nordwall's wife is also an agent of the O.G.P.U.

Kommodov: Did you say that they were always on the look-out?

Oleinik: Yes, I said so.

Kommodov: I have a question to Kutuzova.

The President: We are completing the examination of Thornton, and here you are putting questions all the time to Oleinik.

Kommodov: In that case I reserve the right to put these questions later. There remain two questions to be put to Kutuzova.

The President: The Defence have exhausted all their questions. Has the Prosecution any questions?

Vyshinsky: One question to Oleinik in connection with Kommodov's examination of Oleinik.

The President: Kommodov referred to the fact that Roginsky had put questions and therefore he began to put questions.

Roginsky: I did not put such a question.

Vyshinsky: Permit me to put not six questions but one.

The President: You may.

Vyshinsky: Accused Oleinik, do you recall your depositions about Shterovka? Did you not say that Monkhouse gave you certain instructions?

Oleinik: I remember very well.

Vyshinsky: What were these instructions?

Oleinik: When everything was ready for testing the machines, I received a letter from engineer Monkhouse to the effect that I should inform the customer that not everything was ready for the test. He said that it was not in the interests of the firm to have the test made then, but it was impossible to tell that to the customer, and he wrote that I should inform the customer in this way, that at present the personnel which takes charge of the testing is very busy and that the apparatus for these tests is also engaged.

Vyshinsky: And how was it in fact? Was the testing apparatus engaged?

Oleinik: I do not know.

Vyshinsky: How then did you write if you did not know?

Oleinik: Engineer Monkhouse wrote to me about this.

Vyshinsky: That means that you gave information which you had not verified.

Oleinik: Only on the basis of the instruction.

Vyshinsky: At the investigation did you say: "Monkhouse's instructions were to drag out the term . . . because this was not in the interests of the firm"?

Oleinik: Yes.

Vyshinsky: Is this correct?

Oleinik: Correct.

Vyshinsky: I have no more questions to put to Oleinik. Now a question to Kutuzova, one directly concerning Thornton. Accused Kutuzova, the Defence was trying to establish a fact which is of great importance. I ask you, in developing what I asked you yesterday, how you can explain the fact that Thornton trusted you with such confidential matters as required a great deal of trust in the person to whom they were communicated. Please explain the nature of your relations with Thornton?

Kutuzova: I was on friendly terms with engineer Thornton as well as with engineer Monkhouse. The relations were quite the same, only during one period I spent more time with engineer Thornton when he was in Moscow, first, because we lived in the same house. Then, engineer Thornton at my request taught me how to drive a car; he taught me to do mechanical work. Therefore I spent my evenings more often with him; engineer Monkhouse was busy in the evenings. He was engaged in writing some scientific book.

Vyshinsky: Is that all?

Kutuzova: That is all.

Vyshinsky: Your relations did not develop further?

Kutuzova: No.

Vyshinsky: The status remained the same?

Kutuzova: I may add that I was compelled by my fate to be with them.

Vyshinsky: Compelled by your fate? But how was that?

Kutuzova: Because I worked for a foreign firm there was

practically no one who wanted to become acquainted with me, and I was too proud to seek the acquaintance of strangers and to go around with strangers.

Vyshinsky: That is a different question. I am interested in the degree of your friendship with Thornton. Perhaps I shall remind you of your depositions at the preliminary investigation?

Kutuzova: Certainly, do.

The President: Is it necessary?

Vyshinsky: It is of essential importance to me. You testified: "On November 11, 1932, owing to the fact that I continued to suffer and be apprehensive, I again started a conversation with Thornton in my room. . . ."

Was there any illegal work?

Kutuzova: There was.

Vyshinsky: You remember this deposition.

Kutuzova: I do.

Vyshinsky: Well then?

Kutuzova: I was apprehensive for myself and my relatives and I wanted to ask. . .

Vyshinsky: Why were you apprehensive? Did you have any reason to be apprehensive for Thornton?

Kutuzova: I was apprehensive for myself.

Vyshinsky: And why did you link your fate with that of Thornton?

Kutuzova: Because I was connected with him through the organization.

Vyshinsky: Through the organization? Perhaps also in some other way?

Kutuzova: I consider that I was not connected with Thornton in any other way.

Vyshinsky: How shall we understand you? You could say more but you do not consider it possible here?

Kutuzova: Yes.

Vyshinsky: This is evading an answer.

Kutuzova: (Silent)

The President: The accused has a right not to answer the question.

Kutuzova: I gave detailed depositions regarding the whole of my life at the preliminary investigation and this is known to the Court.

Vyshinsky: Do you confirm them?

Kutuzova: I do.

Vyshinsky: Once you confirm them, then the question is clear to me.

The President: Are there any more questions?

Roginsky: I have a question to Kutuzova in connection with the examination of Thornton. Tell us, please, you knew about the payments for that illegal activity which Thornton was carrying on?

Kutuzova: Yes. He told me.

Roginsky: What did he tell you?

Kutuzova: He told me in a general way that he was enlisting Russian engineers, technicians and mechanics to collect information. Of course he paid them.

Roginsky: And how were these payments made to the Russian engineers and technicians enlisted by Thornton? Did he tell you that?

Kutuzova: Yes, he did.

Roginsky: In what way?

Kutuzova: Of course these payments were not entered in the books by the bookkeeping department—except one sum.

Roginsky: Which sum?

Kutuzova: 3,000 rubles.

Roginsky: And the other sums?

Kutuzova: The other sums were not entered in the books.

Roginsky: And where were they entered?

Kutuzova: Engineer Thornton entered them into his own notebook.

Roginsky: Did he do his own bookkeeping?

Kutuzova: Bookkeeping or accounts, I do not know.

Roginsky: Did you yourself see that notebook?

Kutuzova: Yes, I did.

Roginsky: Did you see those accounts which Thornton drew up?

Kutuzova: I cannot say in detail, but in general I saw and asked him about them.

Roginsky: What did Thornton tell you, what kind of accounts and sums did he enter in his notebook?

Kutuzova: He did not tell me at once. At first he was evasive and said that this did not concern me, but then gradually he began to tell me that he was entering expenditures for payments to Russian citizens who furnished him with information.

Roginsky: And did you make depositions on these questions at the confrontation with Thornton?

Kutuzova: Yes.

Roginsky: This testimony that you are giving here does not conflict with the depositions you made at the confrontation?

Kutuzova: I think not.

Roginsky: Did Thornton object to these depositions at the confrontation?

Kutuzova: Thornton objected there at first, but later he signed them.

Roginsky: Did he corroborate your deposition in the part of which I am talking now?

Kutuzova: He confirmed it in writing.

Roginsky: You reminded him of the facts, the concrete circumstances, and after that he confirmed them, or was it under other circumstances?

Kutuzova: He admitted this almost immediately.

Roginsky: Without hesitation?

Kutuzova: Yes.

Roginsky: The notebook in which Thornton entered the accounts, where was it kept—in the office or at the apartment?

Kutuzova: The notebooks are not kept in the office.

Roginsky: So they are kept at the apartment?

Kutuzova: Yes.

Roginsky: And where are these notebooks at present?

Kutuzova: In England. But this was not one notebook, there was a number of them.

Roginsky: How were these notebooks sent there?

Kutuzova: He took them with him himself on December 20, 1932.

Roginsky (To Thornton): You heard these depositions by Kutuzova?

Thornton: I did.

Roginsky: Are these correct depositions?

Thornton: I do not remember all of them.

Roginsky: I can remind you of them in parts: Confrontation of Kutuzova and Thornton. Question to Kutuzova: "Were the spying operations paid for and if so, how did you know about it?" Answer by Kutuzova (the one that was given there and put on record): "Yes, the spying was paid for; Thornton told me about it, and besides, I heard it in the conversations between Thornton and Monkhouse, as I had their confidence and it often happened that I entered the room while they were talking."

Here is a question that was put to Kutuzova in your presence and her answer to it. Tell me now, what was your reply to this deposition by Kutuzova? Did you confirm it?

Thornton: As far as I can remember I confirmed it at the confrontation.

Roginsky: Do you confirm it at this confrontation which we are having now?

Thornton: No. I do not confirm the word "spying."

Roginsky: We know that you disclaim this word. But you admit that you paid the Russian engineers and technicians for information furnished by them.

Thornton: A Russian engineer, not engineers.

Roginsky: A Russian engineer—whom have you in mind?

Thornton: Dolgov.

Roginsky: No, we will speak later of Dolgov. The question at present is: were there any payments made for the spying operations that were carried on?

Thornton: I did not give anything to any engineer except Dolgov.

Roginsky (To Kutuzova): Did this question relate to Dolgov, or did it relate to Thornton's general illegal work?

Kutuzova: It related to the general illegal work.

Roginsky: Accordingly, the sums given to Dolgov have nothing to do with this?

Kutuzova: No.

Vyshinsky: At that time, during the confrontation, when you were asked: "What will you say in regard to these statements by Kutuzova, does she speak the truth or not?" What did you answer then?

Thornton: I said: "Except the receipt of money from the Consulate."

Vyshinsky: We are not talking of that now.

Thornton: No, but it was so.

Vyshinsky: You replied: "Yes, Kutuzova is speaking the truth. As I have already testified, the money to the Russian engineers was paid out by me for information received from them."

Thornton: It should be "a Russian engineer."

Vyshinsky: One?

Thornton: Yes.

Vyshinsky: And a fitter?

Thornton: That is so.

Vyshinsky: Perhaps we should correct it this way: one engineer and several fitters.

Thornton: Yes, that will be correct.

Roginsky: Will it be correct to say that citizen Kutuzova said: to Russian citizens—fitters and an engineer? Is that so?

Thornton: Yes.

Roginsky: Now about the manner in which these payments were made. You heard Kutuzova's evidence?

Thornton: Yes.

Roginsky: Do you confirm it?

Thornton: I do not confirm that I received the money from the Consulate.

Roginsky: I am not asking you about that. It was not at the confrontation.

Thornton: Yes, it was.

Roginsky: I am asking about Kutuzova's depositions. Question to Kutuzova: "In what way was the money spent on spying operations covered in the accounts?" Kutuzova answered: "The sums paid for this work were not officially entered in the books. Engineer Thornton kept his accounts at his villa." Do you confirm these depositions made by Kutuzova?

Thornton: No, they were in my expenditure sheets.

Roginsky: Do you confirm the deposition that besides the entries in your official bookkeeping accounts you entered your accounts in your own notebook?

Thornton: Yes.

Roginsky: To the question: "Do you confirm this?" you answered: "I did not carry any official books, but I made entries into a diary to aid my memory in order later to write these sums off. This I did by entering these sums in the books of the firm as some non-existent expenses."

Thornton: That is correct.

Roginsky: And these notes you later sent to England?

Thornton: These notebooks are at present in England. Nine books.

Roginsky: You sent nine books to England?

Thornton: Yes.

Roginsky: You sent to England those books in which you entered the payments to the fitters and to the engineer for the information which you had been receiving? Is that correct?

Thornton: Yes.

Roginsky: I have no more questions.

Vyshinsky: You said that you made this entry in your diary or notebook in order to write it off later as an expense?

Thornton: That is correct.

Vyshinsky: I am interested in the sum of 3,000 rubles which you loaned to Dolgov. If it was a loan, was it repaid later?

Thornton: No.

Vyshinsky: Was if written off as expense?

Thornton: It was.

Vyshinsky: With whose permission?

Thornton: Monkhouse and Richards.

Vyshinsky: How did it occur? Do you remember that?

Thornton: At first it was in my account, then it was in the suspense account, then, I don't know, in some way it was transferred to valuta. I don't know the details.

Vyshinsky: When Richards arrived was a special report made to him on this question?

Thornton: Yes, we asked what to do.

Vyshinsky: And he permitted you to write it off?

Thornton: Yes.

Vyshinsky: And you confirm that the sum was written off?

Thornton: Yes.

Vyshinsky: And at the same time you assert that this sum was a loan, or perhaps it was not a loan?

Thornton: It was lent.

Vyshinsky: For something?

Thornton: No. I should like to explain in detail how it was, because I was promised today that I would be given the opportunity to do it.

Vyshinsky: I first want to clarify the question completely. You assert that this sum was a loan?

Thornton: Yes, a loan.

Vyshinsky: I wanted first to question Monkhouse about this. [To the Court] Permit me to do so. [To Monkhouse] Tell us, please, do you also assert that this sum was a loan?

Monkhouse: This was the sum which Dolgov himself asked for as a loan.

Vyshinsky: And you gave him this sum as a loan?

Monkhouse: No, I did not give this sum.

Vyshinsky: Of whom did he ask it?

Monkhouse: He approached Thornton and asked for money as a loan.

Vyshinsky: And how did you learn about it?

Monkhouse: Thornton, before the arrival of our board here last summer....

Vyshinsky: How was it that you found out about the fact that Dolgov asked for this sum as a loan?

Monkhouse: Thornton told me that Dolgov asked for it.

Vyshinsky: Did he consult you?

Monkhouse: He told me.

Vyshinsky: On the 26th of March you were already released?

Monkhouse: I was.

Vyshinsky: You were questioned about this on the 26th of March.

Monkhouse: Yes.

Vyshinsky: And do you remember what you said then?

Monkhouse: I said that Thornton told me that he did that.

Vyshinsky: You did not say so there. Permit me to read page 233. Perhaps Comrade Martens will be kind enough to read it.

The President: The deposition of April 1 written in his own hand in English will be read. You do not deny that you wrote this yourself?

Monkhouse: I did not write it. Sheinin wrote it.

Vyshinsky: Sheinin wrote in English? Here are depositions in English.

The President: Comrade Commandant, will you please show it to him?

Monkhouse: I apologize. This was not during the deposition to the Public Prosecutor.

Roginsky: This was when it was announced that the investigation was completed.

Vyshinsky: After that you wrote your deposition?

The President: You do not deny that this deposition of April 1 was written by you in your own hand?

Monkhouse: I wrote it.

Vyshinsky: (To Martens) Please, read what Monkhouse wrote in his own hand.

Martens: (Reads the deposition): "I do not recognize myself guilty of the charge made against me, with the exception of point 4 of the resolution containing the said charge, in which point I plead guilty since I shared in the special sum, *i.e.,* the sum of 3,000 rubles given as a bribe by Thornton to Dolgov."

Monkhouse: There was no bribe.

Vyshinsky: What do you mean—there was no bribe?

Monkhouse: It was a present.

Vyshinsky: Let it be a present. You call it a present, we call it a bribe. And now permit me to show you another deposition of March 26. "I presume that Thornton, when he gave Dolgov the money, allegedly as a loan, wanted in this way to secure Dolgov's favourable disposition to the firm in those cases when Dolgov, as the manager of the installation department, would be called upon to decide on disputes which occurred in connection with compensation claims for defects in the equipment which we are supplying." Did you make this deposition?

Monkhouse: I said that.

Vyshinsky: You did not say but you wrote it. It is written in your hand. Please show it.

(The Commandant shows the deposition to Monkhouse)

Monkhouse: This is not my handwriting.

Roginsky: But you have read the deposition?

Monkhouse: This is a translation written by Sheinin.

Vyshinsky: And is your signature there?

Monkhouse: It is.

Vyshinsky: That means that you signed it?

Monkhouse: This is a translation into Russian.

Vyshinsky: We are at present conferring with you also in Russian and nothing untoward is happening. I am asking, did you make the deposition that the money given to Dolgov, allegedly as a loan, was in reality given by Thornton with the aim that Dolgov, who is the manager of the installation department, should take a favourable attitude in cases where he would be called upon to decide on questions of claims for defects against the firm. Did you say that?

Monkhouse: I did not say that. Read what I said there.

Vyshinsky (reads): "I presume . . . ."

Monkhouse: I presumed.

Vyshinsky: Here it says: "I presume that Thornton, when he gave Dolgov the money allegedly as a loan, wanted in this way to secure Dolgov's favourable disposition to the firm in those cases when Dolgov, as the manager of the installation department, would be called upon to decide on disputes which occurred in connection with compensation claims for defects in the equipment which we are supplying." Did you say that?

Monkhouse: You wrote it and I signed it.

Vyshinsky: I did not write it. It was written from your words by the Investigating Judge on Important Cases.

Monkhouse: More or less so.

Vyshinsky: Now do you admit this more or less?

Monkhouse: I admit that Thornton gave the money to Dolgov as a loan.

Vyshinsky: You admit that this money was given as a loan, but before you said it was given as a present.

Monkhouse: I gave it as a loan. I have never in my life given bribes.

Vyshinsky: This is beside the point. But we may record that the sum given to Dolgov is nowhere entered in the documents as a sum given as a loan, but on the contrary it is artificially covered up by some reference to a suspense account. Is that correct?

Monkhouse: When we decided to write this sum off.

Vyshinsky: How did you decide to enter it in the books?

Monkhouse: We decided to enter it as a commercial transaction.

Vyshinsky: Under what account did you enter this in the books as a transaction? How was it entered in the books?

Monkhouse: At first it was Thornton's personal account. This is his personal affair. Then Thornton wanted to close his account and this sum was written off in the suspense account. And there it was suspended for five months.

Vyshinsky: One more question, so that we will not have to return to this any more. This question is connected with the 3,000 rubles. How did you cancel this 3,000 rubles? It is true you wrote it off. But what was the transaction with the Torgsin checks?

Monkhouse: I don't know these transactions in detail.

Vyshinsky: And who knows?

Monkhouse: I think Kutuzova knows.

Vyshinsky: You permitted this transaction?

Monkhouse: I did.

Vyshinsky: What was this transaction of the Torgsin checks for clearing off this expenditure?

Kutuzova: I got permission to get 250 rubles in the Torgsin and sold them for 3,000 rubles which I put in the treasury.

Vyshinsky: I have no more questions to ask.

I have a request in the name of the Prosecution to summon Dolgov as a witness and to make an examination of all the data which are connected with the expenditure of these 3,000 rubles. According to my information, Dolgov is in Moscow and so he can be summoned to the Court at any moment.

The President: Has the Defence any objections?

Braude: I wish to ask that the examination of Thornton be timed to take place when the witness Dolgov is questioned.

The President: The accused does not object?

Thornton: I do not understand.

The President: The Prosecution asks that Dolgov be summoned as a witness in order to clear up the question about the expenditure of these sums.

Thornton: Thank you. It would be just as well.

The President: The request of the Prosecution that Dolgov be summoned as witness is granted.

The Court will now adjourn till 10 o'clock tomorrow morning.

(At 10 p.m. the Court adjourns until 10 a.m., April 14, 1933)

[Signed] V. V. ULRICH
President of the Special Session of the
Supreme Court of the U.S.S.R.

A. F. KOSTYUSHKO
Secretary

MORNING SESSION, APRIL 14, 1933, 10:15 a.m.

Commandant: Please rise, the Court is coming.

The President: Please be seated. The session is resumed. Comrade Commandant, please call witness Dolgov.

Commandant: He is here.

The President: Your name is Dolgov?

Dolgov: Yes.

The President: First name and patronymic?

Dolgov: Alexei Nikolayevich.

The President: Where do you work?

Dolgov: At the Electro-Import.

The President: In what capacity?

Dolgov: As manager of the Control Department.

The President: You've been called as witness at the request of the Prosecution. You must give correct evidence, for any false evidence you make yourself liable to proceedings under a criminal charge. (Dolgov signs a statement to this effect presented to him by the Secretary.)

One question: Under what circumstances did you receive the 3,000 rubles from one of the employees of the Metro-Vickers firm?

Dolgov: The bribe was given in the office of Mr. Thornton, I believe on July 1 or 2, 1932, in the following circumstances: Mr. Thornton came as usual into my office on some business and asked . . .

The President: Where was that?

Dolgov: In my department. He asked me to come to see him in his office in connection with some business. As I often had occasion to attend at the office of the firm in order to present and discuss various questions in connection with claims, I went there this time to settle some questions. Thornton opened a drawer where there were 3,000 rubles and offered me the money. At first I felt my blood mounting to my head; then I decided that if Mr. Thornton, a British subject, wished to buy me, a Soviet engineer, I would take this money and hand it over to the prosecuting authorities; which I did the very same day.

The President: What did Thornton wish to obtain from you?

Dolgov: By the nature of my work it was within my duty to present claims and watch the quality of the imported electric power equipment in general. Quite naturally all the data as to the concrete defects of the imported equipment, including the equipment of the Metro-Vickers firm, was concentrated in my hands.

The equipment supplied by the firm was not always of the proper quality. I was very insistent in presenting my claims, demanding that the legitimate requests of our clients should be satisfied, and besides this, quite naturally I used to draw my own conclusions in regard to the quality of the installation. An engineer who is in charge of the placing of orders, was able to recommend one type of equipment or another. To my mind the money was given so that I should keep quiet about the bad quality of the equipment supplied by Metro-Vickers. I repeat again that I was always firm in my demands and used to ask not only the representatives of Metro-Vickers, but also the representatives of other firms that they should satisfy our legitimate demands without any beating about the bush and without befogging us with theoretical talk. I treated the Metro-Vickers firm in the same way.

Therefore, I think that the money was given me presumably to conceal defects in the imported equipment coming from the Metro-Vickers firm.

Vyshinsky: Witness Dolgov, please tell us, how long you have known Thornton?

Dolgov: I have known Mr. Thornton since 1930.

Vyshinsky: And when did that incident take place?

Dolgov: That incident took place in 1932, I believe in July.

Vyshinsky: Consequently it happened after a long acquaintance, an acquaintance lasting for about two years.

Dolgov: An acquaintance of two and a half years.

Vyshinsky: What were your relations with Thornton during these two and a half years?

Dolgov: At first, when I worked as an engineer of the Control Department (I may say I was a pioneer, I was the first engineer), Mr. Thornton and Mr. Monkhouse hardly noticed me at all, because my duties were those of presenting claims, but not the placing of orders, which was of much more interest to the representatives of the firm. So that was quite understandable. In any case, however, in 1930-31 they scarcely noticed me.

Vyshinsky: Well continue. When did they begin to take notice of you?

Dolgov: About November 1931, when I became manager of the Control Department.

Vyshinsky: How was this change of attitude towards you expressed?

Dolgov: Well, outwardly, these people began to notice me, to greet me.

Vyshinsky: To greet you?

Dolgov: Of course, to greet me.

Vyshinsky: To come in to have a chat?

Dolgov: Yes, they came in to have a chat. And then, the following little incident. The firm usually circularizes its technical magazine. Formerly I never received it. From that moment, however, I began to receive it regularly, like all the engineers of the Electro-Import.

Vyshinsky: As a definite sign of attention?

Dolgov: Yes.

Vyshinsky: And what was Thornton's attitude to you? How did it appear to you? Was it the attitude of an intelligent, responsive and considerate man, or something different, the attitude of a harsh and insistent man?

Dolgov: On the one hand, I noticed that from this time, they began to be very amiable to me. On the other hand, this made me nevertheless insist on what it was necessary to demand. The amiability, however, undoubtedly increased. It was as if we had been acquainted a long time, and the fact that they never noticed me in 1930—this was something of the distant past.

Vyshinsky: What conversations did you have with them?

Were they only of a business nature, only within the limits of your business relations?

Dolgov: I had conversations with Mr. Thornton, who was also dealing with claims in regard to Metro-Vickers, that is, he used to receive these claims and discuss them. I had many talks with him about these claims. Apart from this, there were conversations on subjects of a purely technical order. I am a young specialist and have graduated recently, in 1929. Mr Thornton has great practical experience. It is quite natural that it is very useful to speak with an experienced man—there is always something to learn. We spoke on technical subjects, discussed questions of various equipment.

As to Mr. Monkhouse, who by his position had less connection with my work, my conversations with him were very rare. They too, however, touched on claims. Or I used to speak with him as with a prominent specialist on questions of insulation, which interest me very much. We discussed these questions in connection with concrete facts.

Vyshinsky: Did you have any conversations with Thornton and Monkhouse on questions not concerning your immediate duties and technique, that is, conversations in the nature of common gossip?

Dolgov: It is quite understandable that in the course of long conversations there was such talk too. There were conversations precisely in the nature of common gossip, because the representatives of the foreign firms used to surprise me by their judgments and questions which proved that they did not understand our Soviet life. Of course, there were such conversations.

Vyshinsky: What about personal matters? Questions of your personal life, of your personal position, including your material position? Was this matter touched upon either by you or by them?

Dolgov: If you put in that category such questions as asked by Mr. Thornton—"Where are you going for your holidays? Are you going to a sanatorium or to a rest home?"—then, there were such questions.

Vyshinsky: Was the question put directly as to whether you were in need of money?

Dolgov: The question was not put directly.

Vyshinsky: It may seem to you indelicate, but I wish to know, didn't you put to Thornton the question of your difficult material position.

Dolgov: Comrade Prosecutor, I am a Soviet engineer, and I know the limits where one may speak on this question.

Vyshinsky: I do not wish to embarrass you, but it is important for me to get an answer as to whether you did not speak to Thornton, as to a representative of the firm with which you were connected—perhaps quite unconsciously because of your inexperience, or lack of caution—that your position might have been better if you were to receive a higher salary, if you had a different apartment, something of this kind? Perhaps accidentally and incautiously you touched on this question?

Dolgov: I was very busy with my work and in the process of work perhaps there was such a time when Thornton came into my room and I often nervously spoke about all this mountain of papers. Perhaps this, my heightened nervousness, gave the possibility of speaking about my being dissatisfied, but it was not necessary to speak directly to the representative of the firm about my being in need, because I was not in such need.

Vyshinsky: What is your salary?

Dolgov: 550 rubles, besides literary work, translations, reviews and articles.

Vyshinsky: What is your family position?

Dolgov: I have a wife and child.

Vyshinsky: Does your wife work?

Dolgov: Yes, she does.

Vyshinsky: How much does she earn?

Dolgov: 190 rubles.

Vyshinsky: Consequently you earn. . . .

Dolgov: On the whole 750-800 rubles, apart from my literary earnings.

Vyshinsky: And what do your literary earnings amount to?

Dolgov: On the average I easily earned from 100-150 rubles a month, in 1932. I have plenty of material for such literary work, namely, defects in quality of material and of imported equipment—things that are of value not only to Russian engineers and technicians, but also to our entire industry. Properly speaking, I am working in this branch, but this is also in accord with my work of self-education.

Vyshinsky: Did you ever meet anyone else from Metro-Vickers, apart from Monkhouse and Thornton, someone from England?

Dolgov: Very seldom, but of course I met Cushny, since in the absence of Thornton he frequently took his place.

Vyshinsky: Did Cushny offer you any money, by hints and so on?

Dolgov: No.

Vyshinsky: And Monkhouse?

Dolgov: No.

Vyshinsky: Did Thornton at that time offer you the money right away, or was there some preparation for it?

Dolgov: I would say the extreme amiability was the preparation. He was exceedingly amiable to me, even obliging. Thus, perhaps a day or two before this he asked me whether I was going to a sanatorium or to a rest home, because it was summer. As far as I remember, I said that I was taking my holidays in the country.

Vyshinsky: Didn't he tell you that some of their employees get money in advance, or in some other way, for their needs in general?

Dolgov: Yes, he did.

Vyshinsky: What did you say to that?

Dolgov: I certainly said nothing at all. I showed that it did not concern me.

Vyshinsky: And soon after that conversation were you handed these 3,000 rubles?

Dolgov: In about a day after that, or several days later.

Vyshinsky: Under the circumstances as described by you to the President?

Dolgov: I forgot to say that when Mr. Thornton gave me the money he reassured me, telling me that I need not worry, that only he and Mr. Monkhouse knew about it, so that there was no need to worry, and everything was in order.

Vyshinsky: Were you presented with any demands of a general or a concrete nature, by way of compensation?

Dolgov: No, there were no demands.

Vyshinsky: How was the money offered—take it and you will return it afterwards, or some other way?

Dolgov: I heard nothing about returning the money.

Vyshinsky: But you personally took it as a loan?

Dolgov: Absolutely not.

Vyshinsky: Or as an ordinary simple bribe?

Dolgov: I took it as an ordinary bribe.

Vyshinsky: When did you make your statement to the O.G.P.U. about the fact that you were given a bribe?

Dolgov: The same day.

Vyshinsky: And you enclosed the money with your statement?

Dolgov: Yes.

Vyshinsky: Are you a member of the Communist Party?

Dolgov: No, I am not a Party member.

Vyshinsky: A member of a trade union?

Dolgov: Since 1918.

Vyshinsky: Allow me to put some questions to Thornton.

The President: You may.

Vyshinsky: You have heard the evidence of Dolgov. You do not deny the fact of giving the money?

Thornton: No.

Vyshinsky: You confirm that you have actually given 3,000 rubles to Dolgov in your office?

Thornton: Yes.

Vyshinsky: Second, do you or do you not deny the conversation that preceded the handing over of the money, a quite insignificant conversation in the nature of common gossip?

Thornton: No.

Vyshinsky: You confirm that you told Dolgov that he need not worry, that only Monkhouse knows about these 3,000 rubles—do you confirm that?

Thornton: Yes.

Vyshinsky: Do you also confirm that you were obliging and quite amiable to Dolgov before that?

Thornton: I was always on very good terms with Dolgov.

Vyshinsky: There were no misunderstandings between you?

Thornton: No.

Vyshinsky: Did Dolgov show any particular lack of tact towards you?

Thornton: No. He carried out his duties very well.

Vyshinsky: Do you confirm that you did not give this money to him as a loan, but exactly as Dolgov understood it, that is, as a bribe?

Thornton: No.

Vyshinsky: And you still affirm that this money was given as a loan?

Thornton: He asked for the money himself. But, at first, he asked whether we could give it to him in foreign currency because he had relatives abroad through whom he could return it. I refused.

Vyshinsky: So you gave it as a loan?

Thornton: Yes.

Vyshinsky: For what period?

Thornton: We did not speak about that.

Vyshinsky: So it was given for good?

Thornton: Never.

Vyshinsky: When you give a loan, don't you state the time of repayment?

Thornton: This was to buy an apartment, because he had a very poor and damp apartment.

Vyshinsky: And how did you know that he had a poor apartment?

Thornton: He said so himself.

Vyshinsky: Possibly he said where he intended to buy an apartment?

Thornton: I did not ask him. I asked Monkhouse whether I could give him money and he gave his consent very reluctantly, but when I spoke later with Dolgov and said that it would be better to get a receipt, he said that it was quite impossible to do anything of the sort.

Vyshinsky: Why?

Thornton: I don't know.

Vyshinsky: So Monkhouse warned you not to get a receipt?

Thornton: Not at all. Monkhouse said it was better to get a receipt.

Vyshinsky: And who said that in no case must a receipt be given?

Thornton: Dolgov said that the receipt was not necessary.

Vyshinsky: Comrade Dolgov, were you asked to give a receipt?

Dolgov: I absolutely deny everything which Thornton has said. I have no relatives abroad. All my relatives live here, and I could not have spoken about this. How could I speak of it when I have no relatives abroad?

Vyshinsky: Thornton says so.

Thornton: I have forgotten whether it was relatives or acquaintances.

Vyshinsky: Have you some acquaintances abroad, who are in close relations with you?

Dolgov: No. Merely some of my colleagues from Electro-Import work abroad.

Vyshinsky: Accused Thornton, possibly Dolgov mentioned the names of his acquaintances abroad?

Thornton: He did not.

Vyshinsky: So, what were they, acquaintances or relatives?

Thornton: I have forgotten.

Vyshinsky: You have forgotten? So no date was mentioned?

Thornton: No.

Vyshinsky: When was this?

Thornton: In the middle of 1932.

Vyshinsky: Did you remind him that the money had to be returned?

Thornton: I did not ask him.

Vyshinsky: You lent him money so you should have asked.

Thornton: Not a very long time passed—six months.

Vyshinsky: Was it your personal money?

Thornton: No.

Vyshinsky: So we can record one more fact—that the money belonged to the firm. Who was responsible for it?

Thornton: I was.

Vyshinsky: And then, for an entire half year you were not interested and did not ask for the return of the debt?

Thornton: I did not know that he could not return it.

Vyshinsky: But the longer you leave a debt, the harder it is to repay it.

Thornton: Not enough time had passed to ask him, and I did not ask.

Vyshinsky: So half a year passed, and during this time you did not ask?

Thornton: I did not.

Vyshinsky: And did he say anything?

Thornton: He did not.

Vyshinsky: Of course he did not say anything, because he took this money to the authorities. Did you know what had happened to the money?

Thornton: I read about it in the indictment but before that I did not know.

Vyshinsky: All the same, I cannot make out whether Dolgov got the money for an apartment, or for something else.

Thornton: He asked for the money to buy an apartment.

Vyshinsky: And what has that to do with acquaintances abroad?

Thornton: First of all, he asked for foreign currency, because he could buy an apartment in Moscow for foreign currency. I did not give him any. We had little of it but plenty of rubles.

Vyshinsky: Therefore you offered him rubles?

Thornton: Yes, I said that it was only possible in rubles.

Vyshinsky: So it was all about obtaining an apartment for these rubles?

Thornton: Yes.

Vyshinsky: Well, did he get the apartment?

Thornton: I don't know.

Vyshinsky: Didn't you ask later?

Thornton: No.

Vyshinsky: How does that come about? You were not interested in his apartment, and he lived in such a damp apartment?

Thornton: I never was at his house and the only thing I knew was that he had a poor apartment.

Vyshinsky: That was what he said, but possibly he had a good apartment?

Thornton: Possibly.

Vyshinsky: Was it enough for you that he said that he had a poor apartment and wanted to get a better one, for you to give him these 3,000 rubles, and, in passing, to put it through the books, to the suspense account?

Thornton: At first it was on my account.

Vyshinsky: And then on the suspense account?

Thornton: Yes.

Vyshinsky: Excellent. There remains just one conflicting statement. All the other facts fit in and do not give rise to doubt. The conversation, the money, the failure to get the money back, the failure to remind him about this money, and your lack of knowledge about the apartment. There remains one conflicting statement, or rather, two. The first is that you did not give it of yourself, but he asked for it; and the second that you gave it as a loan. Is that so?

Thornton: Yes.

Vyshinsky: Dolgov denies this. We have heard him and I now want to question Monkhouse.

Accused Monkhouse, you have heard the explanation of Dolgov? Do you still insist on what you said before?

Monkhouse: Yes.

Vyshinsky: Do you confirm what you said: "I suppose that the money given to Dolgov in the form of a loan was given so that he . . ." and so forth.

Monkhouse: It was written down this way.

Vyshinsky: You confirm that it was so written?

Monkhouse: I wrote it because I saw that Dolgov regarded it as a bribe.

Vyshinsky: You confirm that Dolgov regarded this as a bribe?

Monkhouse: It had to be understood that way, because he did not want to give it back.

Vyshinsky: And do you confirm that you gave him this money as a bribe?

Monkhouse: No.

Vyshinsky: When the preliminary examination ended, and the record of the accusation was received by you, you wrote: "I do not admit myself guilty of the charges made against me, except point 4 in the indictment and in this I admit my guilt inasmuch that I assisted to write off the amount—*i.e.*, 3,000 rubles which was given as a present to Dolgov by Thornton." Did you write that?

Monkhouse: Did I write that? I did not write that it was a bribe.

Vyshinsky: In your deposition you wrote exactly that. Volume XII was read out in Court yesterday and I think it unnecessary to return to it at present. At that time we could not agree on one point—you, Monkhouse, said that this was not a bribe but a present, I replied then—according to you, a present, according to us, a bribe.

Monkhouse: I said that I considered it as a loan all the time, but if he did not give it back, that means that it was a present.

Vyshinsky: But you did not know whether he would repay it or not, Thornton says that six months is a short time. Possibly he would have paid within two months, and then it would not have been a bribe.

Monkhouse: As he had not paid after six months, I decided that this was a bribe and informed our chief, Richards, about it.

Vyshinsky: We know that Richards gave you permission to write this sum off.

Monkhouse: Yes.

Vyshinsky: Consequently, for the reason that the money was not paid within six months, you decided that it was a bribe.

Monkhouse: I decided that it smacked of bribery.

Vyshinsky: I ask the Court to pay attention to these two examinations of the accused Monkhouse on this matter—the first examination on March 26, when Monkhouse stated definitely that, under the pretence of a loan, a present was really made so that Dolgov, as head of the installation department through which the decision on questions of claims and complaints passes, should support the firm, so that the firm should be in a more favourable situation when questions of claims and complaints are decided.

The second deposition is in the same Volume XII, on April 1, where Monkhouse states directly that among the four points in the charge made against him, he pleads not guilty to three, but

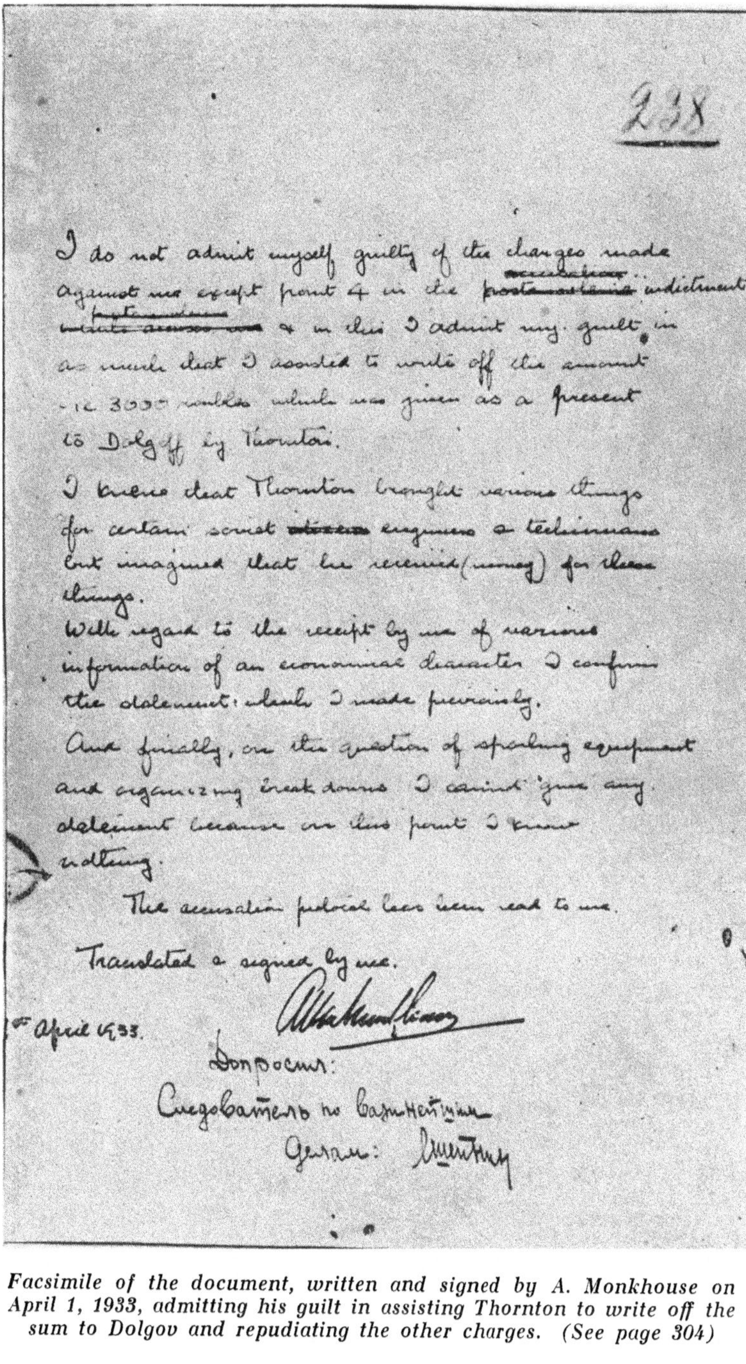

238

I do not admit myself guilty of the charges made against me except point 4 in the indictment & in this I admit my guilt in as much that I assisted to write off the amount i.e. 3000 roubles which was given as a present to Dolgoff by Thornton.

I knew that Thornton brought various things for certain soviet engineers & technicians but imagined that he received (money) for these things.

With regard to the receipt by me of various information of an economical character I confirm the statement which I made previously.

And finally, on the question of spoiling equipment and organizing break downs I cannot give any statement because on this point I know nothing.

The accusation protocol has been read to me.

Translated & signed by me.

1st April 1933.

Допросил:
Следователь по Важнейшим Делам:

Facsimile of the document, written and signed by A. Monkhouse on April 1, 1933, admitting his guilt in assisting Thornton to write off the sum to Dolgov and repudiating the other charges. *(See page 304)*

guilty to the fourth as: "I assisted to write off the amount. . . which was given as a present to Dolgov by Thornton."

Roginsky (To Thornton): Did I correctly understand your reply to Comrade Vyshinsky, that when you gave these 3,000 rubles as a loan to Dolgov, you had in view that the repayment of this sum would take a long time, about six months?

Thornton: Possibly even longer.

Roginsky: Consequently, you were to wait approximately six months before it was repaid?

Thornton: Yes.

Roginsky: At least, six months?

Thornton: Yes.

Roginsky (To Monkhouse): And did you also have the impression that you had to wait at least six months?

Monkhouse: I spoke to Thornton repeatedly about it during the six months. I asked all the time. I asked Thornton about it every month.

Roginsky: Then how can you explain that this sum was written off to the suspense account before six months?

Monkhouse: Thornton did not want to have this sum on his account and I transferred it to the suspense account.

Roginsky: But you ought to have waited a certain time, and if Dolgov repaid the money, then Thornton's account would have been cleared. (To the Court) I ask permission to read out an extract from the books of Metro-Vickers, which shows when the 3,000 rubles were given and when the account was closed. There was no mention of any six months. Volume XIX, page 340: "Record of inspection of March 29. Investigating Judge on Important Cases, Sheinin, in his office inspected the personal account ledger of the Moscow office of Metro-Vickers and discovered the following: On page 12 of this book there is an entry in the debit column of the personal account of Thornton on the payment of 3,000 rubles in cash to him." That is to say, the very day on which, according to the witness Dolgov, he was given 3,000 rubles. In the same year, on June 22—only twenty days later, and not six months—this sum was transferred from Thornton's account to the suspense account. Accused Thornton, where are the six months?

Thornton: A suspense account is the same as a pending account.

Roginsky: Was your account closed?

Thornton: No, it was not.

Roginsky: How was that?

Thornton: It is still there.

Roginsky: Of course your account is still there, but the 3,000 rubles do not appear now in your account. They appear as "suspended" on July 22. They were written off your account and put on the suspense account, not six months later, but twenty days later, that is, on July 22. Is that right?

Thornton: Yes.

Roginsky: Were they written off in the way the accused Kutuzova spoke yesterday?

Thornton: No, they were written off this year.

Roginsky: They were written off to the suspense account on July 22.

Thornton: Just the same, it was money in suspense. It had to be accounted for. It hardly makes any difference. It is an uncovered sum.

Roginsky: Obviously, it was uncovered, but was it taken off your account?

Thornton: It was.

Roginsky: Now let us take up another point. Do you remember your deposition given in connection with this at the examination by the Investigating Judge on Important Cases? In this same Volume XIX, page 336, you make a deposition: "I confirm that I gave the manager of the Control Department of Electro-Import, Dolgoff, 3,000 rubles. I would state that I did this with the agreement of Monkhouse, without the consent of whom I could not give this amount."

Thornton: Yes.

Roginsky: Accused Monkhouse, was the payment of these 3,000 rubles agreed upon with you?

Monkhouse: About June 29, on the day of my departure, I was very busy. Thornton told me that Dolgov was asking for money. I said that I did not feel very inclined to give him any. He said that he, however, was asking. I said—very well, then.

Roginsky: Did you make the same deposition at the preliminary investigation?

Monkhouse: I said that I did not know the sum.

Roginsky: Let us remind you of what you said at the preliminary investigation.

Monkhouse: I did not write.

Roginsky: Didn't you depose that you only knew about this when you returned from your vacation?

Monkhouse: Not from my vacation but from Dnieprostroy.

Roginsky: Here is your deposition of March 26: "I learned when I returned from my vacation and when I found a sum of 2,000 rubles on my account that Thornton had taken 3,000 rubles in Soviet currency from the office. Thornton had entered 1,000 rubles to some other account. I don't know exactly which. When I asked Thornton for an explanation, he told me that he had lent this money, that is, 3,000 rubles, to Dolgov, an employee of Electro-Import."

Monkhouse: That is correct.

Roginsky: This was after you returned from vacation?

Monkhouse: It was after I had visited Dnieprostroy.

Roginsky: After your return from your journey. Now, did you agree about giving this money or not?

Monkhouse: There was no agreement on the actual sum.

Roginsky: But about giving a loan?

Monkhouse: There were preliminary conversations.

Roginsky: So you change your deposition made at the preliminary investigation?

Monkhouse: I supplement it.

Roginsky: You change it, because at the preliminary investigation you stated that you only knew about it when you returned from a business trip. Later, at the second investigation, you made the following correction: "My statement that the 3,000 rubles lent by Thornton to Dolgov were put to my account proved to be incorrect. I discovered from the bookkeeper that the whole 3,000 had been put to Thornton's account. A different sum of 2,000 had been put to my account, which, however, related to expenses for a trip in the U.S.S.R. of directors of Metro-Vickers, who had come from England at that time."

Further you state that you asked Thornton for an explanation of why this sum was given to Dolgov. Do you remember this deposition?

Monkhouse: It is correct.

Roginsky: If you knew that this money had been lent, why did you ask Thornton for an explanation?

Monkhouse: I asked why it was needed.

Roginsky: But wasn't the money given as a loan?

Monkhouse: He said that Dolgov wanted to buy himself a new apartment.

Roginsky: If you knew that Dolgov wanted to buy an apartment, that the money was given to get Dolgov out of some difficulty, why did you ask Thornton for an explanation of why he gave this money?

Monkhouse: I don't know why.

Roginsky: Then what has the explanation to do with the matter?

Monkhouse: You are taking advantage of my poor knowledge of Russian.

Roginsky: I don't want to take advantage of anything. I don't want to take advantage of your poor knowledge of Russian. I ask you a question and I want an answer. If it is difficult for you to reply in Russian, and you do not understand my question in Russian, there is an interpreter who can translate for you.

Monkhouse: I don't want to talk through an interpreter.

Roginsky: Then there is no need to claim that you know Russian badly. I will read out, page 226, Volume XIX: "When I asked Thornton what he had spent this sum on," etc. Is that your deposition?

Monkhouse: Yes.

Roginsky: Did you ask Thornton?

Monkhouse: Yes.

Roginsky: Why did you want to know on what Dolgov spent this money?

Monkhouse: If a person asks for 3,000 rubles, it is unexpected.

Roginsky: What interest was it to you what he spent it on?

To buy an apartment, an automobile or a motorcycle? What interest had you in the question?

Monkhouse: I asked Thornton why Dolgov needed the money. Thornton replied that he wanted to buy an apartment.

Roginsky: This is how you replied to this question at the preliminary investigation: "I asked Thornton what he had spent this sum on. He replied that it was better for me not to know."

Monkhouse: Oh, no.

Roginsky: Then we shall have to submit your deposition at the preliminary investigation.

The President: Accused Monkhouse, please come here. These are the depositions spoken about.

Roginsky: I call your attention to the fact that there are signed texts both in Russian and in English.

Monkhouse: Yes, but here, about 250 rubles in Torgsin money was involved.

Roginsky: I ask you to attest that this was written in his own hand by the accused Monkhouse.

Monkhouse: That is correct. When Thornton said that it was better for me not to know about this money, this did not refer to the 2,000 rubles, but to 250 rubles, and I have explained that to you.

Vyshinsky: But is this 250 rubles in Torgsin checks the very same sum?

Monkhouse: The very same.

Vyshinsky: Then, what is the matter?

The President: Perhaps we can conclude this examination?

Vyshinsky: I ask to continue the examination because we have still a whole series of questions. Accused Monkhouse, will you please tell us if you remember your deposition of March 26, when you said that you did not know why 3,000 rubles had been given to Dolgov. Or shall we remind you?

Monkhouse: I said that I did not know for what purpose they were given. Thornton said it was for an apartment.

Vyshinsky: You did not say so. We asked you why 3,000 rubles were given to Dolgov. You wrote, and afterwards signed, the document which has just been shown you, as follows: "I do not know for what reason 3,000 rubles were given to Dolgov, and why Richards gave instructions to write off the debt of 250 rubles in Torgsin money." So you did not know on March 26?

Monkhouse: On March 26 I wrote that I did not know, but personally I said what Thornton had told me, that it was for an apartment.

Vyshinsky: Accused Monkhouse, was everything that you said at the examination written in the record?

Monkhouse: No.

Vyshinsky: If not, you ought to have made a suitable proviso, otherwise you are now expressing a supposition that a distortion of your deposition was allowed to take place at the examination under my direction.

Monkhouse: I do not say that, but everything which I said was not written there.

Vyshinsky: You provide a clause yourself—"written by me in my own hand and correct in its facts."

Monkhouse: Yes, but. . .

Vyshinsky: There is no "but." The question is quite clear. Let us pass on. Do you know of a case when a gift was made to a certain Wagner?

Monkhouse: No.

Vyshinsky: Let me show you your deposition of March 26, where it says: "In the same way I explain the gift made to Wagner."

Monkhouse: You showed me the deposition of Thornton, where he speaks of a gift to Wagner.

Vyshinsky: Quite correct, and you explained this gift to Wagner in the same way as the gifts made by Thornton to various engineers.

Monkhouse: Correct.

Vyshinsky: In that case, do you or do you not confirm this part of your deposition: "I explain the gifts made by Thornton to these engineers precisely by the fact that they gave information to me and Thornton about future orders for electrical equipment, or rather, I suppose this." Do you confirm this?

Monkhouse: I confirm it.

Vyshinsky: Let us consider that we have established that

Thornton gave gifts to various Russian engineers and technicians for giving information about future orders for electrical equipment.

Monkhouse: You showed me the deposition of Thornton, where he spoke of gifts, and I said what I supposed.

Vyshinsky: So, you used to do this? To give gifts for such information?

Monkhouse: I personally never gave anything.

Vyshinsky: If this had been in England, how would these gifts have been described according to English law? May we say that according to English law it would be a bribe?

Monkhouse: This is a small present, and not a bribe.

Vyshinsky: And a big present?

Monkhouse: There is a big difference.

Vyshinsky: I know that there is always a difference between a small gift and a large one.

Monkhouse: If a person helps you, you give him a present. Our installation mechanics on construction work receive rewards. These are not bribes.

Vyshinsky: I do not ask about your men; I ask about our men. When presents are made for concealing defects, for getting information, do you consider that normal?

Monkhouse: If a person has helped you to do something, I consider it as a present.

Vyshinsky: Do you think such kinds of presents are normal? It is important for me to establish your point of view. Do you consider such presents to be normal?

Monkhouse: If this is done with the aim of corrupting a person it is not normal, but if it is done on account of assistance, I consider it normal.

Vyshinsky: And if it is done so that a person will not make a claim, then what is it? It means corruption.

Monkhouse: It is not corrupting him. If I made a mistake and he helped me to put it right, it is a gift.

Vyshinsky: The question is quite clear.

The President: Has the Public Prosecutor any other questions?

Vyshinsky: No.

The President: Has the Defence any questions?

Braude (To Monkhouse): Will you be so kind as to explain the transfer of these 3,000 rubles from the personal account of Thornton to the suspense account?

Monkhouse: Thornton is a very accurate person. He checks up his personal account every month. It is natural that he did not want this money to be on his account. Therefore, he applied to have this money transferred to the suspense account and consequently I applied to the chief, who gave permission to write off the sum.

Kommodov (To Monkhouse): Let us establish the following fact. Thornton says that when he spoke to you about this, you asked him to get a receipt. The money was given in your absence while you were at Dnieprostroy. When you returned you were faced with a *fait accompli.* So the receipt which you had asked to be obtained was not taken.

Monkhouse: It was not.

Kommodov: The money had been given, and was not returned. You asked for a receipt to be obtained, and it was not obtained. Did you yourself have the impression that the money was given as a gift?

Monkhouse: At first, I did not. I knew Dolgov very well. I went with him to the Chelyabinsk Power Station, and we were six days in the train together. I looked on him as a very straightforward man who worked well. I trusted him and thought that he would return the money.

Kommodov: There is no doubt that Dolgov is an honest man and works well. You know yourself that he returned to you the cost of the railway tickets. Let us return to the established facts. You asked for a receipt to be obtained, and it was not obtained. The money was taken in your absence, and the money was not returned. Didn't this give you the impression that a gift had been made?

Monkhouse: Not at first. I never looked on this sum as a gift, but when the money was not returned, I thought that it plainly smacked of a gift. Therefore, when Richards was here, we decided to write off this money. That was five months after the money was given.

Kommodov: So, during this time, there was already an impression created in your mind that it was really a gift?

Monkhouse: I got the impression that Dolgov regarded it as a gift.

Kommodov: Dolgov regarded it as every honest man must have done, but in your own mind, was there not the impression that this was a gift? You asked for a receipt to be obtained. The receipt was not obtained. The money was given in your absence. You came back again, and were confronted with an accomplished fact. Every month you asked when it would be paid back; it was not paid back. Was this not bound to create a definite impression?

Monkhouse: I trusted Thornton.

Kommodov: The impression was not created, because you trusted Thornton?

Libson: Accused Monkhouse, were there in the Moscow office of your firm other cases when sums of 3,000 rubles were lent to Russian engineers who were in touch with the work of your firm?

Monkhouse: No.

The President: Has the Defence any questions for the witness?

Kommodov: Comrade Dolgov, do you confirm your deposition given at the preliminary investigation [Volume XIX, page 359], in the part where you speak of the railway ticket?

Dolgov: Yes, I confirm it.

The President: Have the accused any questions to ask the witness? [Accused: No.] Has the Prosecution any questions for the witness? [Prosecution: No.] Witness Dolgov, you may go.

We will proceed to Kotlyarevsky. Accused Kotlyarevsky, give us your biography briefly.

Kotlyarevsky: I was born on April 21, 1904, in the town of Bodrintsy in the family of a fitter. My father was a wage worker in various handicraft and industrial enterprises. Then in 1912, he had his own mechanical workshop. In 1914 he was conscripted into the army as a private.

In 1914, I entered the parish school where I remained for one year. Then, I entered the higher elementary four-year school, which I finished in 1919. In 1919, I went to a secondary school in the same town of Bodrintsy. In 1920, I was promoted from the fifth class to the sixth. The school was closed. From 1920-21 I did not do anything, I did not go to school. I 1921, in Odessa, I joined the preparatory course of the Odessa Polytechnical Institute, I completed this course in 1922, and then entered the Institute. In 1927, I graduated from the Institute. I received a diploma as a mechanical engineer. This was in June 1927. In September 1927, I went to work at the Shterovka Power Station as technician in charge of the boilers, where I worked until March 1929. From March 1929, until about May or June 1930, I worked as engineer on duty at the station. Then, I became senior engineer of the boiler department and was manager of the engine house of the Shterovka Power Station. In connection with the flooding at the Shterovka Power Station in July 1931, I was removed from my job. I lived at Shterovka for a month, having given an undertaking not to leave, to the O.G.P.U. authorities of the Krasno-Lug district. Then I was transferred to Kharkov to work in Donenergo as engineer of a turbine group. At the end of October 1931, I was sent for three months to the Zuevka Power Station. I spent nine months at the Zuevka Power Station because they would not release me earlier. I left it on July 29, 1932. I was in Odessa, then in Moscow with my family, then I took my family to Odessa and returned to Moscow, and on November 25, 1932, I began to work in the Orgenergo as chief engineer. I worked there until the day of my arrest, though I was on a business trip to the Kazan Electric Power Station for two and a half months.

The President: Are you married?

Kotlyarevsky: I am married and have a child.

Roginsky: In what capacity did you work at the Zuevka Electric Power Station?

Kotlyarevsky: As manager of the turbine department.

Roginsky: From which year and which date?

Kotlyarevsky: From November 1, 1931. But it would be difficult for me to give the exact time because I returned from my vacation to Zuevka on July 23, 1932, and the order to release me from my post was given in my absence on July 11, of the same year. It was pointed out that this was done with my consent, and this is really the case because I was trying all the time to get away from there.

Roginsky: So your stay at the Zuevka Electric Power Station lasted about nine months?

Kotlyarevsky: About nine months, or even less, because I was actually not there at all for the last two months.

Roginsky: In your work as head of the turbine department, did you frequently come into contact with the engineers who were installing turbines?

Kotlyarevsky: Yes, of course, because they were working in the turbine department, installing machines, and I was the head of the department.

Roginsky: With whom did you come into contact most frequently?

Kotlyarevsky: With MacDonald.

Roginsky: Did you know which firm MacDonald represented?

Kotlyarevsky: Of course I did.

Roginsky: Did you meet him only at work, or did your meetings afterwards occur at other times too?

Kotlyarevsky: At first it was at work, later at his house, more rarely at my house.

Roginsky: You visited him at his house and he came to your house?

Kotlyarevsky: Yes, but the latter was less frequent. I was much more often at his house.

Roginsky: And these meetings took place frequently?

Kotlyarevsky: Yes, frequently.

Roginsky: Your relations became friendly and close?

Kotlyarevsky: Yes.

Roginsky: On what basis did you get friendly with MacDonald?

Kotlyarevsky: I was living alone at Zuevka. My family remained behind in Kharkov; I had practically no acquaintances. I had to go to MacDonald's regarding the drawing up of the first preliminary instructions for looking after the turbines during operation. MacDonald had a gramophone with very good records. I am very fond of music and on these grounds, and later in general, he made a very good impression on me and I began to visit him more and more frequently.

Roginsky: At first you got friendly on musical grounds, and then perhaps on somewhat different grounds?

Kotlyarevsky: Yes.

Roginsky: On deeper grounds. Did you have political conversations with MacDonald?

Kotlyarevsky: When?

Roginsky: At the time when you were becoming friendly?

Kotlyarevsky: Probably I had, because I cannot imagine. . .

Roginsky: From what time did the political talks and conversations which you held with MacDonald lead to your rendering certain services to MacDonald which were outside your business relations?

Kotlyarevsky: It is difficult to reply in that form. In my deposition at the preliminary investigation I told how everything took place; most probably all the conversations we had led up to this, but it would be difficult for me to say how this influenced me.

Roginsky: What proposals did MacDonald make, or what commissions did he give to you at the beginning of your friendly relations, and what commissions did you carry out at his request?

Kotlyarevsky: He asked me first to tell him in what way it was proposed to enlarge Zuevka in the future.

Roginsky: The expansion of the Zuevka Power Station? Then?

Kotlyarevsky: Then he asked me to get him the layouts, which had been made at the power station, of the oil pipe lines, turbines, then pipe lines to the compressors, then for the water circulation to the condensers, and he asked me to obtain the plans of the station building. I obtained all this for him.

Roginsky: You carried out these requests of MacDonald?

Kotlyarevsky: Yes.

Roginsky: Besides these commissions, were there also any other commissions of a more active nature?

Kotlyarevsky: Yes.

Roginsky: What were they?

Kotlyarevsky: MacDonald proposed that I should not pay attention to defects in the equipment and give a false estimate of the breakdowns which might take place with the turbines.

Roginsky: Concealing defects in the equipment, and giving a false estimate of the breakdowns which might take place with the turbines?

Kotlyarevsky: Correct. Then MacDonald suggested that I should damage one of the turbines in such a way that the turbine would be put out of action for as long a time as possible.

Roginsky: So, at first, it was information, the concealment of defects in the equipment, a false estimate of breakdowns which took place, and afterwards, proposals to carry on direct acts of diversion? Is that so?

Kotlyarevsky: Yes.

Roginsky: Which of your last acts related to your concrete work of wrecking?

Kotlyarevsky: The breakdown on generator No. 3.

Roginsky: And further?

Kotlyarevsky: Nothing further.

Roginsky: What did you do to generator No. 3?

Kotlyarevsky: I put a bolt in the air gap of the generator.

Roginsky: What was the result?

Kotlyarevsky: The result was that the rotor of the generator was damaged, that is, deep grooves were made on its surface and the iron laminations of the stator of the generator were injured. This caused the work of the turbine to be held up for about ten days, because, during these ten days, the rotor was taken out and the defects which had been caused were rectified as far as possible.

Roginsky: Is this the act of diversion committed by you?

Kotlyarevsky: Yes.

Roginsky: And in the matter of concealing the wrecking acts committed by other members of the wrecking group which was organized at the Zuevka Station?

Kotlyarevsky: Are you asking whether I concealed the acts which other people committed?

Roginsky: Yes.

Kotlyarevsky: I am not aware of that.

Roginsky: And did you know about the breakdown of the oil pumps?

Kotlyarevsky: I know that MacDonald said that the material in the oil pumps was of low quality and breakdowns were possible, and he warned me that another appearance should be given to this—it should be explained differently.

Roginsky: Did he warn you that breakdowns would take place?

Kotlyarevsky: It was said in such a form that breakdowns could take place, and would do so.

Roginsky: You understood it as meaning that breakdowns would take place?

Kotlyarevsky: I did.

Roginsky: And didn't you take any steps to remove these defects?

Kotlyarevsky: No.

Roginsky: You concealed them?

Kotlyarevsky: Yes, practically.

Roginsky: In connection with this testimony, I have a question to MacDonald. Accused MacDonald, did you hear the testimony of Kotlyarevsky?

MacDonald: I did.

Roginsky: I your depostition of April 3, 1933, you say: "There was at the first and third turbine a breakdown of the oil pumps owing to their being left in a dirty condition."

MacDonald: Yes.

Roginsky: The very same?

MacDonald: Yes.

Roginsky: Accused Kotlyarevsky do you also have in view the breakdown of these oil pumps?

Kotlyarevsky: Yes.

Roginsky: So there is no disargreement with the testimoney of MacDonald.

Kotlyarevsky: In my opinion, there is not.

Roginsky: And there is no discordance between the statement of MacDonald and the testimony of Kotlyarevsky?

MacDonald: No.

Roginsky: Accused MacDonald, you have heard the testimony of Kotlyarevsky on the breakdown of generator No. 3. Here is what you deposed: "This breakdown took place as a result of leaving a bolt in the air gap of the generator." Do you confirm this?

MacDonald: I do.

Roginsky: So Kotlyarevsky was the person who did it?

MacDonald: I do not know whether he did it himself, but it was done.

Roginsky: That was what you deposed: "This was done under my instruction by Fomichev or Kotlyarevsky"—we have cleared this up.

Accused Kotlyarevsky, did you receive financial remuneration for your activity at the Zuevka Electric Power Station?

Kotlyarevsky: 1,000 rubles.

Roginsky: Was the 1,000 rubles given to you in a lump sum, or in several installments?

Kotlyarevsky: In two installments of 500 rubles.

Roginsky: I have no further questions.

The President: Has the Defence any questions?

Libson: I have a question.

The President: Very well.

Libson: You are now 29 years old?

Kotlyarevsky: Yes.

Libson: You told the Court that you received all your education under the Soviet Power, in Soviet schools. Is that so?

Kotlyarevsky: Not exactly. Only my higher education.

Libson: Do you come from a working class family?

Kotlyarevsky: Yes.

Libson: Did you live with your family all the time?

Kotlyarevsky: Except for a short time when I lived in Odessa, for about one and a half or two years, during which time I lived in lodgings. Then my parents also came to Odessa, in 1923, and I lived with them again.

Libson: Did you live all the time in working surroundings, in an atmosphere of work?

Kotlyarevsky: Yes.

Libson: Be so good as to explain to the Court what motives guided you in these actions which you have so openly spoken about. What drove you to this? How can this be explained?

Kotlyarevky: It took place as follows. The first time when

MacDonald asked me to give information about the expansion of the station, I gave him this at once, since as head of the engine house and one of the highest technical employees at the station this information was known to me.

Shall I speak in greater detail?

The President: Tell us what motives drove you to this activity?

Libson: Allow me to make the question more exact. Be so good as to tell the Court how you first got into conversation with MacDonald. Under what circumstances did the conversation take place which terminated in the first gift of money? What happened later, and how did it come about that, with your life history, you decided to do this?

Kotlyarevsky: MacDonald asked me to give him information about the expansion of the station. I immediately told him the things which interested him. He asked me to give him exact figures because I had not spoken quite definitely to him. A day or two later, the next time I came, I told him. The same evening, in the course of a general conversation, the talk turned on to my difficult financial situation, because I was living in Zuevka and my family was in Kharkov. We had spoken of this before and he knew my position. He offered me a loan of 500 rubles; I did not see anything wrong in this and took the money.

The President: You took the money definitely as a loan?

Kotlyarevsky: Yes, as a loan.

Libson: And whose was the initiative?

Kotlyarevsky: It is difficult for me to remember now.

Libson: What happened further?

Kotlyarevsky: Then, after that, he asked me to get him the plans of the station building. I obtained them for him because I did not see anything particular in this, and then, as I had his money in my hands, I felt somewhat under an obligation to him. When I brought the plans, he gave me a second 500 rubles. I did not want to take them, because I had not yet returned the first sum. Then he opened my eyes to the whole business, explaining that in giving him information I had done what I should not have done. I took the money.

Libson: Tell me, have I understood you rightly? It follows

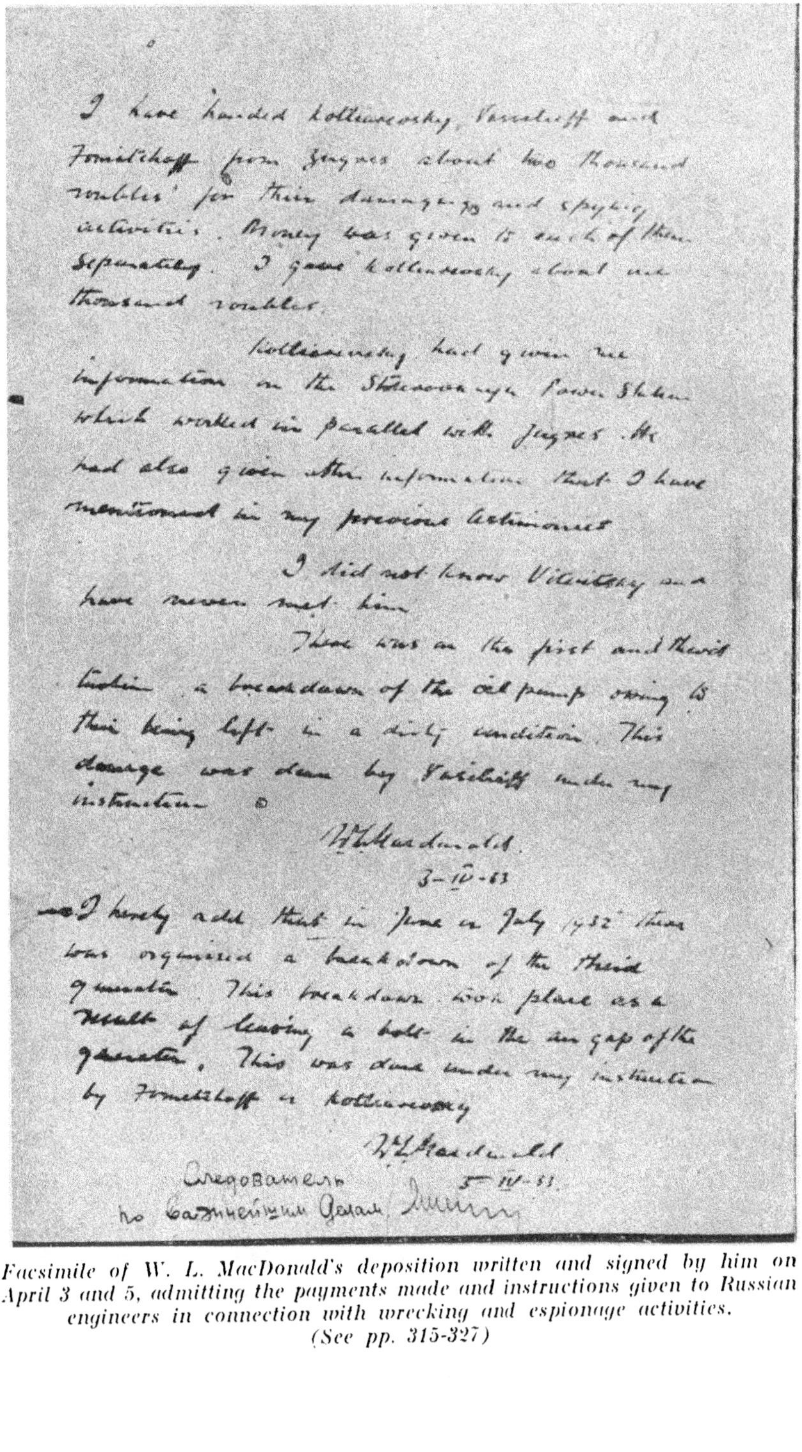

I have handed Kotliarevsky, Vassilieff and Fomitcheff from Zuyres about two thousand roubles' for their damaging and spying activities. Money was given to each of them separately. I gave Kotliarevsky about one thousand roubles.

Kotliarevsky had given me information on the Shterovskya Power Station which worked in parallel with Zuyres. He had also given other information that I have mentioned in my previous testimonies.

I did not know Vitvitsky and have never met him.

There was in the first and third turbine a breakdown of the oil pump owing to their being left in a dirty condition. This damage was done by Vassilieff under my instruction.

W L MacDonald
3-IV-33

I hereby add that in June or July 1932 there was organised a breakdown of the third generator. This breakdown took place as a result of leaving a bolt in the air gap of the generator. This was done under my instruction by Fomitcheff & Kotliarevsky

W L MacDonald
5-IV-33

Следователь
по важнейшим делам [signature]

Facsimile of W. L. MacDonald's deposition written and signed by him on April 3 and 5, admitting the payments made and instructions given to Russian engineers in connection with wrecking and espionage activities.
(See pp. 315-327)

that before you received the first 500 rubles you did him a service simply owing to your friendly relations?

Kotlyarevsky: Yes, before.

Libson: You supplied the information about the expansion of the station.

Kotlyarevsky: Yes, this was given before I received the money.

Libson: Was this information of a secret character, or information which simply should not be published? How did you understand it?

Kotlyarevsky: I did not see any secret in it at the time.

Libson: Was it a direct request addressed to you to supply this information?

Kotlyarevsky: Yes.

Libson: Apart from you, could he have officially received information about the proposed enlargement of the station?

Kotlyarevsky: Maybe he could.

Libson: But you understood that MacDonald was appealing to you for a friendly service?

Kotlyarevsky: Yes, I did not suspect anything in it.

Libson: Did you bring the plans of the building after you had received the loan?

Kotlyarevsky: Yes.

Libson: What time passed between the moment when he first offered you a loan of 500 rubles, and when he asked you to bring the plans of the building?

Kotlyarevsky: A few days.

Libson: Were the plans of the building a secret for MacDonald, or rather from MacDonald, or not? How did you understand it?

Kotlyarevsky: I don't know. Perhaps he could have received them from the chief engineer, but he asked me to get them.

Libson: But how did you understand it—was this request a secret commission or simply a request for a friendly service so as not to apply to the chief engineer, with whom it was difficult for him to talk?

Kotlyarevsky: It may be put so; I did not attach any importance to it at the time.

Libson: Very well. When you gave the plans of the building, how did you look on this action? Did you think that in the given case you were committing, if not a crime, at any rate, an unethical action, doing something which you should not have done in your position? Or had you no such suspicions?

Kotlyarevsky: No, I had no such suspicions. I was friendly with MacDonald.

Libson: Did you see each other every day?

Kotlyarevsky: Every day at work.

Libson: And then you lived together in one apartment?

Kotlyarevsky: At first we were together in a hotel, and then he went into a separate apartment.

Libson: So two days passed. After that he asked you to bring the plans? When you gave him the plans, how did he give you the money—at once?

Kotlyarevsky: At once.

Libson: You did not ask?

Kotlyarevsky: No.

Libson: And when you tried to decline the money, what did he say?

Kotlyarevsky: I don't remember exactly. But in any case, he told me that I was giving information to a foreign subject and that a Soviet engineer should not do so, and that if it became known, it would have unpleasant consequences for me.

Libson: What did you reply to this?

Kotlyarevsky: I don't remember what I replied, because it was a very difficult conversation.

Libson: But you took the money?

Kotlyarevsky: Yes, I took the money.

Libson: Perhaps you will explain to the Court why you did not give information at once about this to the proper authorities, that you had got into such a serious mess—first, friendly favours, then, all this had turned into crime.

Kotlyarevsky: Because I was afraid of the consequences.

Libson: Consequences, in what sense?

Kotlyarevsky: In the sense that I should be called to account for the information which I had given, and, in general, for this connection.

Libson: And after this, didn't he give you any money?

Kotlyarevsky: No.

Libson: You carried out all the succeeding measures without receiving any more money?

Kotlyarevsky: Yes.

Libson: You came to Zuevka in November?

Kotlyarevsky: November 1.

Libson: When did you first get money from him?

Kotlyarevsky: I don't remember exactly, probably in January. Somewhere about that time.

Libson: So, from November to January you had no conversations?

Kotlyarevsky: We gradually became more friendly.

Libson: I see. But were there no conversations like the one when this request was made to you?

Kotlyarevsky: No.

Libson: For how long did your criminal activity continue? During what period did the breakdowns which you concealed continue, and the breakdowns which you carried out?

Kotlyarevsky: About four or five months.

Libson: You left Zuevka in July?

Kotlyarevsky: On June 1, I was given a vacation of eight or ten days. On the 12th I returned, and on the 20th I went for my official vacation. I returned on the 23rd of July, and, on the 29th, I left altogether.

Libson: You told us that, after Zuevka, you began to work in Moscow. Did you meet MacDonald here?

Kotlyarevsky: I met him once in the office.

Libson: Did you have any conversation with him here or not?

Kotlyarevsky: There was no conversation on any similar subjects.

Libson: Wasn't there any talk of where you were being sent to work, where you would work?

Kotlyarevsky: No, I did not know.

Libson: You didn't know yet? Now, another question. When giving your biography, you said that you did not leave as you had given an undertaking to the O.G.P.U. not to leave. Where, when and why was this?

Kotlyarevsky: On July 13, 1931, the Shterovka Electric Power Station was flooded owing to which the station stood idle for eleven hours. In connection with this, five people were removed from their work: I, Fomichev, who, at that time, was foreman of my department, the engineer on duty, the chief of the station, and someone else—I don't remember. On the 15th, I was summoned to the Krassno-Lug department of the O.G.P.U. There the investigator talked to me, interrogated me, and I gave an undertaking not to leave the place. Two days later I was summoned again. I came, but the investigator was not there. The next day he summoned me to Shterovka, and asked me a number of questions which were written down in the office. I gave him replies and he did not call me any more. There was no further examination. I went several times because I was interested in knowing how the matter would finish, and, on August 14 or 15, I think, I was released of my undertaking not to leave the place.

Libson: The question was fully settled, and no accusation was made against you?

Kotlyarevsky: No charge was made.

Libson: Allow me to ask MacDonald a question. Accused MacDonald, you have heard the testimony of Kotlyarevsky. Do you confirm this testimony in every part?

MacDonald: As a whole, yes.

Libson: And in particular? I am interested in knowing whether you confirm every part, whether everything which Kotlyarevsky has testified is true, and whether everything which he said really occurred.

The President: In the parts referring to MacDonald?

Libson: Of course, as far as concerns MacDonald.

MacDonald: Yes.

The President: Who has any further questions for Kotlyarevsky?

Smirnov: Tell me whether this information, the plans of the building of the station, the expansion of the electric power station, was secret or not?

Vyshinsky: Allow me, with the consent of the Defence, to make a statement which will simplify the investigation of this episode. Here Comrades Libson and Smirnov are conducting the examination as to the part referring to secret information and espionage. I want to call attention to the fact that the accused Kotlyarevsky is charged under Articles 58-7 and 58-11, while the Prosecution does not make a charge of espionage against Kotlyarevsky.

Smirnov: But does this apply to MacDonald in the given episode?

Vyshinsky: On this point MacDonald is not under this charge either.

Smirnov: Then this question is clear. But I have another question. What firm supplied generator No. 3?

Kotlyarevsky: Metro-Vickers.

Smirnov: And turbines Nos. 1 and 3?

Kotlyarevsky: The same firm. All three turbines were made by this firm.

Smirnov: So it turns out that it was a matter of damaging their own machines, that is, the machines of their firm?

Kotlyarevsky: Yes.

Smirnov: What did you understand to be the aim with which this damage was proposed to you? Do you understand my question? I can understand a proposal to damage a different machine, one of a different firm, to put it out of action so as to get an order to supply one's own machine.

Kotlyarevsky: By putting out of action the machines installed in a power station which supplies current to the mines and factories of Donbas, injury was obviously caused to the industry of the Soviet Union.

Smirnov: You understood it in that way, that its purpose was direct wrecking to cause detriment to the industry of the Donbas?

Kotlyarevsky: Yes, because it is much bigger than the direct injury to the generator.

Smirnov: When was the damage done to these oil pumps on turbines Nos. 1 and 3?

Kotlyarevsky: It was about March or April.

Smirnov: At that time, was MacDonald in Zuevka or had he left?

Kotlyarevsky: I don't remember exactly, but I think he was not there. Apparently he was on vacation in England from the beginning of March to April 17 or 18.

Smirnov: So you carried out this wrecking act in the absence of MacDonald?

Kotlyarevsky: The breakdowns took place in his absence.

Smirnov: But had he warned you previously that such breakdowns might take place?

Kotlyarevsky: Yes.

Smirnov: Did he warn you as the engineer in charge of the machine house?

Kotlyarevsky: Of course. He gave me concrete instructions on the matter.

Smirnov: Let us take absolutely objective facts at present. Before MacDonald left on vacation he warned you that all was not well in regard to generators Nos. 1 and 3. He warned you that a breakdown of the oil pumps might take place on them.

Kotlyarevsky: Yes.

Smirnov: When MacDonald went to England, were any English mechanics left in Zuevka?

Kotlyarevsky: Yes, Cornell was there, and Elliott, and Ogney. There were several installation engineers.

Smirnov: And were there English fitters?

Kotlyarevsky: Yes.

Smirnov: Were they obliged to watch these generators in the absence of MacDonald?

Kotlyarevsky: Of course.

Smirnov: It follows from this that Cornell and the others were also aware that this breakdown was to be allowed to happen?

Kotlyarevsky: I don't know this.

Smirnov: Who actually allowed it? Whose carelessness, whose direct action caused this breakdown? The facts are as follows: MacDonald had left for England. Before his departure he warned you as head of the engine house that everything was not in order on two particular turbines, that a breakdown might take place, because the oil pumps on them were not in order. Three English mechanics remained, one of them an engineer, and two, ordinary fitters. Who then actually permitted this breakdown to take place?

Kotlyarevsky: First, I permitted it because I did not give information in the proper place; and, secondly, I do not know, maybe somebody else knew that the oil pumps were out of order, but permitted it.

Smirnov: I do not know your functions, but as chief of the engine house, was it your duty to see to the condition of the oil pumps on the turbines, or are there special people assigned for this?

Kotlyarevsky: There is a definite organizational structure. I am the manager; under me is the foreman; he has an assistant; but I supervise all their work also.

Smirnov: But who, first of all, should anticipate that something is wrong with the oil pumps? Who should first give the signal that steps should be taken, or who should demand that orders be given for steps to be taken—the manager of the engine house, or some other person closely and directly on the job?

The President: Does the Counsel for the Defence know that a whole group of people were arrested in connection with this, and are under preliminary examination? This should be known from the indictment in this case.

Smirnov: I know it.

The President: Then why do you still talk here about the English engineer Cornell? What did you require that for? I repeat that you know that a number of Soviet employees have been arrested in connection with this matter, charged with a series of crimes. These people are being questioned. Therefore, your question about those who are not present here is purposeless.

Smirnov: Then permit me to ask one more question. (To the accused Kotlyarevsky) You say that this money—500 rubles, and a further 500 rubles—was given to you before you gave information about the expansion of the station, and after you handed over the plans of the building?

Kotlyarevsky: No, I did not say so. I said something else. If you wish, I will repeat it. I gave this information and received 500 rubles. I was asked to give the plans, I gave them, and received the second 500 rubles.

Smirnov: So the 1,000 rubles were given to you after you supplied the information, and money was not given you at all for carrying out acts of diversion? Is that so?

Kotlyarevsky: It is.

Smirnov: I have no further questions.

Libson: I have a question. Tell us, Kotlyarevsky, did some of the breakdowns at the Zuevka Station, which are being spoken about, take place owing to the poor quality of the equipment and the bad installation work? Was that the case or not?

Kotlyarevsky: Yes, the breakdown of the pumps.

Libson: Can you say that definitely?

Kotlyarevsky: Yes.

Libson: When you came to work in November, was the installation finished?

Kotlyarevsky: It was not entirely finished, but I had nothing to do with it.

Vyshinsky: Allow me to ask a question. You say that the installation work was bad. But if the installation was ideal and you put an iron object into the air gap, could an accident have taken place?

Kotlyarevsky: Yes.

Vyshinsky: Then the reference to the poor installation work does not play any role—the fact of wrecking remains.

Kotlyarevsky: We are talking about different things. The bolt was left in the air gap of the generator. We are not speaking here about the installation of the generator.

Vyshinsky: The installation work does not enter into the matter?

Kotlyarevsky: That is so.

Libson: Then allow me to ask another question. You damaged the generator, putting a bolt into the air gap. But all the other breakdowns took place on the basis of bad installation work?

Vyshinsky: Which breakdowns?

Libson: The oil pipes, the oil pumps.

Kotlyarevsky: You speak about the oil pumps. The oil pumps went wrong owing to relatively bad installation and owing to bad material.

Roginsky: And owing to bad treatment? I speak of the clogging.

Kotlyarevsky: Clogging did take place.

Vyshinsky: Does that depend on the installation?

Kotlyarevsky: No.

Libson: Did you have anything to do with the clogging?

Kotlyarevsky: No. Allow me to say what clogging is being spoken about. What I am speaking about is this. While the installation of the machines was going on, construction work was going on in the same place in the building, and, owing to this, there was always dust in the machine house.

Zelikov: Accused Kotlyarevsky, did you know about this clogging?

Kotlyarevsky: Yes.

Zelikov: Should you, as chief of the engine room, have taken steps and informed the chief?

Kotlyarevsky: I informed my immediate chief; then I spoke to the manager, unofficially, it is true.

Zelikov: Was it your duty to take immediate measures?

Kotlyarevsky: I was in charge of the operation of the turbines, while the building work was carried on by the building department of Orgenergo.

Zelikov: You should have given definite information about this?

Kotlyarevsky: I informed the engineer in a definite manner that further work in such a form would lead to the breakdown of the machines.

Roginsky: Was this before your talk with MacDonald, whereas, after your talk, these warnings ceased?

Kotlyarevsky: I don't remember. If I spoke after these conversations, it was by chance.

Roginsky: After the conversation with MacDonald, did your demands for suitable conditions for the operation of the oil pumps cease? Did you close your eyes to the defects which existed?

Kotlyarevsky: I don't exactly remember when I wrote the notes, but probably it was as you say.

Roginsky: I have no further questions.

The President: Are there any further questions?

Vyshinsky: I am interested in making clear one point only. At the preliminary investigation, accused Kotlyarevsky, you deposed as follows: "I know that a breakdown took place on turbines Nos. 1 and 3 owing to the poor work of the oil pumps, as a result of which one turbine stood idle for about two weeks.

and the other turbine, a little less. The breakdowns took place after my conversations with MacDonald. I did not really make any fuss, either after the first or the second breakdown. I know that soon after the breakdown a commission of six or seven engineers was formed, which came to the conclusion, without my assistance, that the cause of the breakdown on the turbine was the poor construction of the main oil pump. Under such circumstances, I had to agree to the decision of the commission *post factum.*"

Kotlyarevsky: That is all true.

Vyshinsky: I have no further questions for Kotlyarevsky.

The President: Has the Defence any questions?

Defence: No.

The President: Have the accused any questions to ask Kotlyarevsky?

Monkhouse: I have a question. Did Citizen Kotlyarevsky conceal this defect in the oil pumps?

Kotlyarevsky: Yes.

Monkhouse: Then how can he explain that a telegram was sent to Moscow about it and we immediately communicated with England, from where two new oil pumps were sent, which were sent to the Zuevka Station and unpacked?

Kotlyarevsky: I do not understand what telegram you are speaking about.

Monkhouse: The telegram which I think MacDonald sent himself.

Kotlyarevsky: But that was after the breakdown.

Vyshinsky: But you discovered the defects also after the breakdown?

Kotlyarevsky: After the breakdown I agreed with the opinion of the commission.

Vyshinsky: After the breakdown took place, could the defects have been concealed?

Kotlyarevsky: No, they spoke about them there.

Vyshinsky: Did your commission sit immediately after the breakdown, or later?

Kotlyarevsky: I don't remember; I think it was immediately.

Monkhouse: He says that he gave the plans of the station

building to MacDonald. Can he say exactly what plans he handed over?

The President: That is not important. The accused Kotlyarevsky is not charged with espionage.

Monkhouse: Then, another question about this bolt which was found in the air gap of the generator. Can he say what size this bolt was?

Kotlyarevsky: I don't remember. You see, I took the first bolt I found in the workshop, which, in my opinion, would go in —about a half inch bolt, with a nut and a head. It was found later broken in two.

Monkhouse: Can you explain how you inserted the bolt there?

Kotlyarevsky: That is very simple. When the cover was open (I sometimes was delayed at the station until late at night), this was in the evening or at night. In any case, there was nobody at the third machine. The other machines were working, and I put the bolt in this machine. That is not a hard thing to do.

Monkhouse: Did you see that a bolt was missing on the cover? Where is the bolt which had been taken out of the cover?

Kotlyarevsky: I don't know exactly what he is speaking about. I think he is speaking of the following. We found a bent edge on one of the covers. I do not know whether it was found that some bolt was missing there. I only know that MacDonald and Elliott and Taylor—electricians—went over the whole generator and did not find that a bolt was missing anywhere, as far as I know. I do not know what Mr. Monkhouse is speaking about now. It is known that the edge was bent. You can see it from the photograph.

Vyshinsky: Was there a case when all kinds of extraneous objects were found in the generator, besides a bolt?

Kotlyarevsky: Yes.

Vyshinsky: For example?

Kotlyarevsky: I think there was a lot of dust. I know that a brush for sweeping the bus-bars was found there.

Vyshinsky: A piece of board?

Kotlyarevsky: Exactly.

Vyshinsky: Some stone or other?

Kotlyarevsky: Possibly a stone. I don't know about a stone.

Vyshinsky: I have no more questions.

I request that the following statement be put on record. In the material from the Commission of Experts, we have a statement which speaks of the case in which various extraneous objects, such as bolts, a piece of board, a stone and so forth, were found in generator No. 3, which can only be looked on as the result of criminal negligence on the part of the installation staff or of some direct malicious intent, of which Kotlyarevsky speaks here.

I ask the Court to take note of this.

The President: No more questions? The Court will adjourn for twenty minutes.

*
* *

Commandant: Please rise. The Court is coming.

The President: Please be seated. We come to the examination of the accused Lobanov. Accused Lobanov, tell us the main details of your biography.

Lobanov: I was born in 1897. My father had a flour mill which he rented; at the same time he had an oil factory, a steam flour mill and he also engaged in trade. My father died when I was studying in secondary school. I then lived with my brother who also rented a flour mill. I finished the secondary school in 1918.

The President: In what city?

Lobanov: In Rostov—Yaroslavsky. In 1918-19 I worked together with my brother in my brother's mill. From 1920 to the beginning of 1928 I studied in the Ivanovo-Voznesensk Polytechnical Institute, from which I graduated in 1928. During my stay in the Institute, I worked for about two years in various establishments. In 1928, after I graduated from the Institute, and even a few months prior to my graduation, I went to work at the Ivgres (Ivanovo District State Electric Power Station). At first I worked as a draughtsman on sub-stations in the electrical division. Shortly afterwards I became constructor on sub-stations and then an engineer on the sub-stations. In the beginning of 1930 I was sent to Leningrad to attend courses for raising the qualifications of power station engineers. After I completed these courses I returned to the Ivanovo Power Station and was sent to work in the District Station. Up to that time I worked in the management which was not located at the station itself, but in 1930, I was sent to direct the testing operation of the Ivanovo District Station. There I spent a short time and then I was appointed manager of the electrical operating department of the Ivanovo Power Station. Afterwards, up to the moment of my arrest, I filled the post of director of the thermo-mechanical group of the technical department, and before that I worked as an engineer in the rationalization department. I think this is about all.

The President: Has the Prosecution any questions?

Vyshinsky: Yes. When did you become acquainted with Nordwall?

Lobanov: Some time towards the end of 1930.

Vyshinsky: Under what circumstances?

Lobanov: He used to be at the station and, together with Chopin, who at the time was also employed as an English fitter, at the Ivanovo Station, he worked on the installation of the equipment which was being supplied by the Metropolitan-Vickers firm.

Vyshinsky: What post did you occupy?

Lobanov: That of manager of the operation department and afterwards director of the thermo-mechanical group of the technical department up to the time of my arrest.

Vyshinsky: Who was the chief of the station at the moment of your arrest?

Lobanov: Director Byelov.

Vyshinsky: At the time when you became acquainted with Nordwall, who was director?

Lobanov: I do not remember, it might have been Glebov, but I am not certain.

Vyshinsky: You became acquainted with Nordwall in 1930 only in connection with your work?

Lobanov: No, not only in connection with my work. I do not remember how and in what connection our very first meeting took place, but generally speaking our closer acquaintance went on, both at work and during train rides, between the Ivanovo Station and Ivanovo. There was a special train in which I very often travelled as my family lived in Ivanovo. Nordwall also very often was in the train with me, and here it was that I became acquainted with him more or less intimately.

Vyshinsky: This was at the end of 1930. How about 1931?

Lobanov: It continued also in the beginning of 1931.

Vyshinsky: Now, how did you subsequently pass over to illegal relations? That is to say, relations which were based on your illegal work?

Lobanov: One fine moment, some time in February 1931, in my office, Nordwall, after a conversation on some general topics, approached me with a proposal to carry on acts of wrecking and diversion at the Ivanovo Power Station.

Vyshinsky: Weren't you surprised at this proposal?

Lobanov: Yes, of course I was very much surprised at this.

Vyshinsky: And why did he make that proposal to you?

Lobanov: It seems to me, our relations were fairly close, not so much as to be intimate, but we knew each other quite well. He knew perfectly well my anti-Soviet sentiments.

Vyshinsky: And why did you have such anti-Soviet sentiments? In what form did they express themselves?

Lobanov: They expressed themselves in utterances of dissatisfaction with the existing order, in all kinds of complaints regarding hardships in my personal life, particularly material hardships.

Vyshinsky: Did Nordwall carry on conversations with you concerning your attitude to Soviet reality, or was it you who carried them on?

Lobanov: Both I and he did so.

Vyshinsky: What considerations and judgments did he express?

Lobanov: Sometimes he himself even provoked me to indulge in all kinds of anti-Soviet talk, but I, of course, was not loath to carry on conversations on this subject.

Vyshinsky: Why this "of course I was not loath"?

Lobanov: Such were my convictions at that time.

Vyshinsky: Under what influence did you form those convictions?

Lobanov: In the first place, the family.

Vyshinsky: That is?

Lobanov: My brother who was a private entrepreneur. He did not work, he rented a flour mill.

Vyshinsky: He rented a flour mill, where?

Lobanov: In the Gavrilov Posad, Vladimir Gubernia. This was my own brother.

Vyshinsky: What was your father's occupation?

Lobanov: I said already that my father also rented a flour mill, then he had an oil factory, then a steam operated flour mill. He also engaged in trade.

Vyshinsky: And what did your father trade in?

Lobanov: Flour, groceries, I think. I do not know exactly what it is called.

Vyshinsky: When did your father die?

Lobanov: About 1907.

When I was attending secondary school two of my close friends were shot during the Yaroslawl uprising in Poshekhonya.

Vyshinsky: So your friends participated in an uprising against the Soviet Government?

Lobanov: Yes.

Vyshinsky: And did you participate?

Lobanov: I did not.

Vyshinsky: Why not, if you had such convictions?

Lobanov: I was not one who would participate in action of a military character. I never went through military service.

Vyshinsky: Under the influence of all these circumstances, you began to form definite opinions?

Lobanov: Yes. Then, when I worked in the Ivanovo Power Station, I found myself in an environment which was not very favourable—in an environment where my views were shared.

Vyshinsky: Did you carry on any social work?

Lobanov: None.

Vyshinsky: Now it is clear. You met Nordwall, you became friends of a fashion, at any rate to such an extent that you had the opportunity to carry on with him quite frank political conversations. What happened under these circumstances?

Lobanov: Under these circumstances, some time around February, I cannot say exactly, he proposed that I carry out acts of wrecking and diversion at the Ivanovo Power Station.

Vyshinsky: With what object?

Lobanov: With the object of undermining the economic strength of the Soviet Union.

Vyshinsky: What motives did he advance?

Lobanov: The fact that I had expressed to him my convictions, my hostile sentiments. He did not talk to me about the final aims, but I understood him.

Vyshinsky: And then you passed from words to deeds?

Lobanov: Yes. He said, "If you desire personal well-being, then let us pass from words to deeds." This is the way he said it.

Vyshinsky: What kind of deeds were these?

Lobanov: Of course I was somewhat surprised and I did not want to get mixed up in this affair, because it was an affair which could have grave consequences.

Vyshinsky: Only could have? Perhaps it did?

Lobanov: This is the proof. *(Commotion in the court)*

The President: I would ask the audience to express their sentiments more quietly.

Vyshinsky: Tell us concretely what breakdowns took place at the Ivanovo Power Station. In which did you participate, of which did you know, who else took part in these and what were the consequences of these breakdowns?

Lobanov: It was pointed out to me by Nordwall at the time when he enlisted me that it was necessary to hit at trifles so as not to get caught, but these trifles should be such as to bring about quite heavy consequences. He pointed out that as a rule it was necessary to hit at the imported equipment in order to pump out the foreign currency reserves of the Soviet Union and in this way to undermine its economic strength. He also pointed out that it was necessary to spread out these acts of diversion, to damage intentionally the equipment, including the equipment of the Metro-Vickers firm and not only that of other foreign firms, but at the same time he pointed out that this should be done in such a way as to make it impossible to lay the blame on the firm, that is, that the causes of the breakdowns and of the acts of diversion should be of such a nature as not to implicate the firm and that the damaging of the equipment should not affect the terms of guarantee, that is, if some equipment is put out of service for any reason, this should be done only to equipment of the Metro-Vickers firm for which the terms of guarantee have already expired.

Vyshinsky: What were the concrete facts of wrecking, of acts of diversion?

Lobanov: Putting the motors of the chain grates out of service, disconnecting the house feeders, damaging the bearings of the feed pumps, clogging the bearings, causing short circuits.

Vyshinsky: And did something happen to the motor of boiler No. 5?

Lobanov: Yes, we burnt it out.

Vyshinsky: Why? How?

Lobanov: We shut down the ventilation and since these motors are ventilated, the winding of the motor became overheated.

Vyshinsky: And then?

Lobanov: We struck at the machine-cut peat. In this I participated myself. We hit at the feeding of the boilers, but we were not quite successful in that.

Vyshinsky: Why not successful? Didn't it come off well?

Lobanov: It did not come off. Of course it might have been carried out well, but it was averted in time by the workers.

Vyshinsky: Further?

Lobanov: We burned out the transformer. The winding was burned out.

Vyshinsky: How about the telephone connections?

Lobanov: That's right. We interfered with the telephone connections. So it was.

Vyshinsky: Let us return to one of these concrete facts and let us see how it was carried out by you. Who participated in this affair? What were the consequences? Let us for example, take the putting out of service of the chain grates of the boilers.

Lobanov: Such things have been.

Vyshinsky: Tell us about it.

Lobanov: Remembering Nordwall's instruction—to hit at trifles but at such as would bring about serious consequences, we figured out a rather simple, but very effective operation. By damaging the cable which feeds the motors of the reductors of the chain grates, these motors were put out of action. Owing to this the grates were stopped, the beams were bent, the furnace was put out of service, the boilers were stopped; thus the load was cut off—sometimes entirely, sometimes partly.

Vyshinsky: What does it mean—"the load was cut off"?

Lobanov: Owing to the fact that the boilers went out of service, when the station was still working at a small capacity, the grates were stopped. The boiler could not supply the steam. The pressure was dropping. Once the pressure dropped the turbines could not work any more with reduced pressure. The turbine was shut off. The consumer load—factories and works—was taken off.

Vyshinsky: The load was taken off—does that mean that the supply of current was stopped?

Lobanov: The supply of current to the industrial districts which are served by the Ivanovo Power Station was stopped. This brought about all the consequences.

Vyshinsky: Who carried out this operation?

Lobanov: We enlisted Lebedev to take part in this affair—he was foreman of the electrical department.

Vyshinsky: Was he in your group?

Lobanov: Yes.

Vyshinsky: What post did he occupy?

Lobanov: He was foreman of the department in which I worked.

Vyshinsky: Accused Lebedev, did you hear this evidence?

Lebedev: I did.

Vyshinsky: What can you say about it?

Lebedev: Yes, I did that.

Vyshinsky: On whose instructions?

Lebedev: On the instructions of Lobanov.

Vyshinsky: With what object?

Lebedev: With the purpose of damaging.

Vyshinsky (To Lobanov): What about cutting off the feeders?

Lobanov: Cutting off the house feeders—this seemed something entirely harmless and we could easily do it.

Vyshinsky: Why was it so easy for you? Were there a number of such cases?

Lobanov: Quite a number.

Vyshinsky: Why did you get off so easily?

Lobanov: You see, all the feeders are protected by relays. It is the kind of mechanism on which you can very easily lay the blame.

Vyshinsky: Can you put the blame on objective causes?

Lobanov: Yes, on objective causes: the mechanism wore out and so on. Nobody could ever explain why.

Vyshinsky: Well, and how do you explain it? How were they switched off?

Lobanov: It was very simple. I was ordered to do this work. In order to avoid clashing with one another I took in the senior electrician Ugrumov, then everything was all right for us.

Vyshinsky: Did he have anything to do directly with these house feeders?

Lobanov: Yes. In general he worked in the electrical division, he was next to me.

Vyshinsky: Your assistant?

Lobanov: He was not considered an assistant but senior electrical technician.

Vyshinsky: And did he assist in wrecking?

Lobanov: Yes.

Vyshinsky: That means we have now Lebedev and Ugrumov. Perhaps there were others in your station?

Lobanov: Lebedev, Ugrumov and then towards the end, but not quite towards the end, Rostov who damaged the telephone connections.

Vyshinsky: Rostov—wasn't there still another one?

Lobanov: There were attempts to enlist the services of another one—that was Kitayev.

Vyshinsky: But you did not enlist him?

Lobanov: No.

Vyshinsky: You did not suceed?

Lobanov: When I thought of recruiting someone because there was nobody of our group in the turbine room, I thought of enlisting the services of Kitayev who was the foreman. At that time he was not foreman, but something in the way of senior mechanic on the turbines. I thought of enlisting his services to carry out wrecking work in the part connected with the installation of turbines. When I tried to tell him what it was all about he reported that I was somewhat late with my proposals as he had already been working in this direction.

Vyshinsky: So there was no occasion for enlisting his services?

Lobanov: That is so.

Vyshinsky: And what else were you doing, let us say, with the house generators, with the shakers?

Lobanov: When I got into the rationalization department, I was not immediately concerned with the work of the station, but my position was well suited for carrying out wrecking acts. Behind the guise of rationalization, I carried out a series of wrecking acts.

Vyshinsky: That is, wrecking represented as rationalization?

Lobanov: Yes, represented as rationalization.

Vyshinsky: That is, you misused the rationalization work? How? In what way?

Lobanov: In the first place, I hit at the machine-cut peat. It was necessary to equip boilers Nos. 3 and 4 with shakers. The shakers were already at the Ivanovo Power Station, but when I began planning, I decided to suggest another system. It was alleged to be better than the existing system. The administration told me—you, they said, as the chief (although at that time I was only just transferred to the post of chief of the thermo-mechanical group) you verify the existing blueprints of the old shakers and start them working. I, for my part, made the proposal for a new construction and insisted quite strongly that this should be carried into effect. After objecting persistently for a long time, the administration agreed to this. I promised that the work would be carried out in the shortest possible time and that it would hardly affect the course of equipping boilers Nos. 3 and 4 with shakers. The administration agreed and I started to design a new system. I spent something like several months on the designing and, by this, the equipping of the two boilers was delayed and the burning of machine-cut peat at the station became impossible with these boilers. There was a considerable setback in the burning of the peat. Of course the new construction turned out to be neither better nor worse than the one we had before. I tried to prove that it was better, but in fact it may have been better and it may have been worse. In some parts it was better, in others it was worse. In a word, I did not weigh the matter fully. As a result there was a delay of about half a year in round figures in the burning of the machine-cut peat in these two boilers.

Vyshinsky: What was your task in this case?

Lobanov: Considering the importance of mastering the use of machine-cut peat, my task was to delay the burning of it at the station, and this could bring about all kinds of consequences in connection with the storing of the machine-cut peat as well as other consequences.

Vyshinsky: One more question: How did matters stand regarding your calculations on the possibility of various war complications? Were these questions being considered?

Lobanov: Certainly, they were. At first it was pointed out by Nordwall in a general way that in the event of war or intervention it would be necessary to put the station entirely out of operation. It was suggested that we think over how and in what way it should be done most conveniently. The last time I met Nordwall, when receiving instructions, it was definitely pointed out that in some such event he promised to inform us in detail how to carry this out, how to blow up the dam which holds the water in the pond supplying the station with water and, thus put the station entirely out of action for a long time, by draining the water from the pond. Besides everything else he also suggested that it would be necessary to arrange for putting out of service the main equipment, the main units of the station, such as the transformers.

Vyshinsky: So this was basically your plan in case of war?

Lobanov: Yes.

Vyshinsky: Did you talk about this to any one of your accomplices?

Lobanov: I talked about it in passing, to Lebedev.

Vyshinsky: And what did he say?

Lobanov: He said that when he received the necessary instructions and explanations from me, it would be possible for him to take part in this affair. He agreed to carry out some such act.

Vyshinsky: A question to Lebedev.

The President: Accused Lebedev.

Vyshinsky: In regard to this part, what have you to say?

Lebedev: In May 1931, Lobanov spoke to me about this.

Vyshinsky: And what did you tell him on this subject?

Lebedev: I did not tell him anything definite.

Vyshinsky: What do you mean, not anything definite?

Lebedev: Lobanov told me that Nordwall had said that in event of war it would be necessary to put the station out of operation but there was no plan worked out in detail.

Vyshinsky: No detailed plan?

Lebedev: And therefore I did not say anything.

Vyshinsky: He said that Nordwall suggested that you should think it over how to put the station out of action in the event of war, and you listened and did not say anything?

Lebedev: Because the plans were not worked out.

Vyshinsky: But how did you react—that it was a bad thing and must not be done, or did you say all right, you would think it over?

Lebedev: I said, that it was possible to carry it out.

Vyshinsky: Did you receive any money?

Lebedev: I did.

Vyshinsky: From Lobanov?

Lebedev: Yes.

Vyshinsky: In installments?

Lebedev: In installments.

Vyshinsky: What for?

Lebedev: For carrying out wrecking work.

Vyshinsky: So, for carrying out wrecking actions, did you, Lobanov, give him money?

Lobanov: I did.

Vyshinsky: In installments?

Lobanov: No, wholly and in full.

Vyshinsky: What does it mean, wholly and in full?

Lobanov: I gave him 1,000 rubles all at once so that he might feel it.

Vyshinsky: And what does Lebedev say?

Lebedev: I got rather less. The first time, in June, I got 150 rubles. The second time I got 100 rubles. When I got that money the second time he seemed dissatisfied with my work . . . then, maybe, he counted in the 50 rubles a month that he added to my salary.

Vyshinsky: Lobanov, did you count that?

Lobanov: No.

Vyshinsky: That means that there is a discrepancy in the sums. You say you received less and Lobanov says that he gave more. Lobanov, from whom did you receive this money?

Lobanov: From Nordwall.

Vyshinsky: How much?

Lobanov: Five thousand rubles.

Vyshinsky: How did you dispose of this money?

Lobanov: I kept a little for myself.

Vyshinsky: How much?

Lobanov: 2,600 rubles.

Vyshinsky: That is about half.

Lobanov: Then I gave 1,000 rubles to Lebedev, 800 rubles to Ugrumov and 600 rubles to Rostov.

Vyshinsky: Under what circumstances did you receive these 5,000 rubles from Nordwall, was it in one lump sum or not?

Lobanov: In two installments. The first was some time in June 1931, the second in the end of 1931 or at the beginning of 1932.

Vyshinsky: What were the circumstances, under what conditions?

Lobanov: The first sum, 3,000 rubles, I received from him after a talk and a report on what I had done in carrying out his instructions.

Vyshinsky: Where was the report given?

Lobanov: As a rule I tried not to meet with him in home surroundings, but at the place of work where it would not attract attention. This was at the control board near the administration office and while going along the machine room over the special platforms which have been built for passing into the service department; it was there that he gave me 3,000 rubles as a premium for this work.

Vyshinsky: Did you count the money in his presence?

Lobanov: Of course I did not count it there; I counted it at home.

Vyshinsky: And you divided it at home?

Lobanov: I divided it the next day when I calculated how much each should get.

Vyshinsky: May I put a question to Nordwall?

The President: You may.

Vyshinsky: Accused Nordwall, you heard this testimony?

Nordwall: I did.

Vyshinsky: What have you to say?

Nordwall: It is partly true and partly not true.

Vyshinsky: Tell us what is true and what is not true.

Nordwall: What Lobanov said about me is not true. As to what he said about himself I don't know.

Vyshinsky: Did you give him any money?

Nordwall: I did not.

Vyshinsky: Did you indulge in anti-Soviet conversations?

Nordwall: There was such a conversation. I once met Lobanov in the train. There were other persons in the compartment and he began to talk about his hard living conditions. I told him what my own views were and told him how I understand the Soviet Union. I said that each employee, engineer and worker in the Soviet Union must reduce somewhat his demands in life under present conditions, because the increased hardships were due to the efforts to fulfil the Five-Year Plan. He said that he was not interested in that. I said that the Russian engineers think that they are very badly off here. Then I said that our engineers at present live better than the Soviet engineers; that is quite understandable.

Vyshinsky: Did you meet several times in the train?

Nordwall: We met several times.

Vyshinsky: And you had a talk, and Lobanov during this conversation showed his lack of interest in the Five-Year Plan and expressed his dissatisfaction.

Nordwall: He expressed his dissatisfaction with the Soviet system.

Vyshinsky: And you did not agree?

Nordwall: I did not.

Vyshinsky: You tried to explain to him that there should be no reason for dissatisfaction, that there were great tasks to perform, that it was necessary to subordinate oneself to these interests, and he disagreed?

Nordwall: He disagreed. I defended the Soviet Union.

Vyshinsky: Accused Lobanov, it turns out the other way. It was you who carried on anti-Soviet conversations, while Nordwall tried to convince you in a Soviet spirit. Is that so?

Lobanov: No. He sometimes provoked such talk. On his part there was no attempt to convince me that I should give up my views. On the contrary, I felt that he was supporting me, he said "yes, yes" and I felt anti-Soviet suggestions; it was not possible to talk very loudly about such things.

Vyshinsky: Accused Nordwall, I understood you as follows: You said in your talk with Lobanov that at present English engineers live better than Russian engineers.

Nordwall: Yes.

Vyshinsky (To Lobanov): Is that how it was?

Lobanov: Yes.

Vyshinsky (To Nordwall): And what did you advise him to do?

Nordwall: I told him that he must understand what the present times were like, that he occupied a big post in the Soviet Union, and that he must behave accordingly. But he said that that did not interest him.

Vyshinsky (To Lobanov): Is that how it was?

Lobanov: I do not quite understand him.

Vyshinsky: He says that you occupied a post which bound you up with the big tasks of the country, and that you must bear that in mind. [To Nordwall] Did I understand you correctly?

Nordwall: Yes.

Vyshinsky (To Lobanov): Well?

Lobanov: That is not quite how it was. What he says about my occupying a responsible post, is true. I do not object to that. Regarding the fact that my official duties obliged me to carry out the work—that is true. But I did not preach my morals to him.

Vyshinsky: And did he preach to you?

Lobanov: He carried on the usual anti-Soviet talk expressing dissatisfaction with the Five-Year Plan, said that the Five-Year Plan would fail, and so forth. I agreed with him, and there was talk on this subject. We did have such conversations. Of course, there were also talks on business.

Vyshinsky: Accused Nordwall, was there any talk about damaging equipment and so on?

Nordwall: None at all.

Vyshinsky: And you gave no instructions at all?

Nordwall: No.

Vyshinsky (To Lobanov): And you affirm the contrary?

Lobanov: I do.

Vyshinsky (To Nordwall): Was there any talk about war?

Nordwall: Not at all.

Vyshinsky: And there was no talk to the effect that the Soviet Union might be faced with the danger of war?

Nordwall: No.

Vyshinsky (To Lobanov): And what do you say?

Lobanov: I do not know why he denies that. Is he thinking of putting the whole blame on me?

Vyshinsky: You insist on your statement that there were such conversations—about putting equipment out of operation by acts of diversion in the event of war?

Lobanov: Yes, they actually took place.

Vyshinsky: You assert this even after the statement Nordwall just made, alleging that that was not the case. You say that it actually took place?

Lobanov: I affirm that I had such a talk with him and received instructions.

Vyshinsky (To Nordwall): Did you ever give any money to Lobanov?

Nordwall: Never.

The President: As a loan, perhaps?

Nordwall: I never gave him any money.

Lobanov: I received from him 5,000 rubles and a fur coat in addition.

The President: Let us get it clear about the money. The accused Lobanov stated that he received 3,000 rubles, and the remaining 2,000 rubles. . . .

Lobanov: 2,000 rubles were given me in 1932 when he came for the last time for the testing at the Ivanovo Power Station, and soon after that, I tried on the fur coat he sent me. Because I had told him before that I would like to receive some clothing, particularly a fur coat.

Vyshinsky (To Nordwall)) Was there a fur coat?

Nordwall: I can tell you about that in detail. A certain citizen Taylor, working for our firm, was at the Ivanovo Power Station testing the turbo-generator. He had come to work temporarily in the Soviet Union, and had bought a new fur coat. He went back to England and seeing that the fur coat soon would not be needed, he wanted to sell it.

Vyshinsky: To whom?

Nordwall: Wait a moment, please, I will explain everything in order.

Vyshinsky: If you please.

Nordwall: One day Taylor said to me: There is a fellow Lobanov. I said: Yes. Do you know where he works? I said: I think I do. Upstairs in one of the departments. Taylor said to me: Go to Lobanov and tell him to come today and try on the coat. He told me that in English. Taylor did not speak Russian at all. I went upstairs to the office where Lobanov worked. At the same time I asked him a technical question, which interested the Commission —regarding the reaction of the generator. I then said to him: Come to our apartment today to try on the coat. He said: Very well. Lobanov already knew about the coat. Lobanov came to our apartment in the evening. I called Taylor and said: Here is Lobanov. I said it to him in English.

At the preliminary investigation I said that the room was Taylor's. I now know definitely: it was my room in our joint apartment. Taylor and I lived together. Taylor brought the coat and showed it to him. They began to discuss the price.

At the preliminary investigation, I said, I think 400 rubles. Now I know definitely. The amount was 500 rubles.

At the preliminary investigation, I said: I think my wife was present. Now I know definitely. When I was confronted with Lobanov, I said: Nordwall's wife was present, and Taylor was present.

Taylor sold the coat. It was agreed that when Taylor left for England we would send Lobanov the coat. The following day, in the corridor of the Ivanovo Power Station building, Lobanov gave me the 500 rubles.

The President: He handed it to you personally?

Nordwall: To me personally.

The President: You corroborate the fact that Lobanov acquired a fur coat?

Nordwall: Bought a fur coat.

Vyshinsky: And you assisted Taylor on the one hand, and helped Lobanov on the other, to acquire a fur coat? You assisted him in that purchase?

Nordwall: Yes.

Vyshinsky: At whose request?

Nordwall: Taylor's.

Vyshinsky: Lobanov paid Taylor the money for the coat?

Nordwall: No, he gave me the money to hand over to Taylor.

Vyshinsky: The very same day, or the next?

Nordwall: The next.

Vyshinsky: Did you receive that money?

Nordwall: Yes.

Vyshinsky: And you handed the money over to him?

Nordwall: Taylor said: I do not need the money just now.

Vyshinsky: Why not give a straight answer?

Nordwall: I did not hand over the money that day.

Vyshinsky: You said that you received the money from Lobanov on the following day and handed it over to Taylor?

Nordwall: But not on the same day.

Vyshinsky: You testified that Taylor received the money at the paying desk of the office from your account?

Nordwall: Yes, that is what I said.

Vyshinsky: And then when the books of the pay office were examined it was found that that amount was not in the books?

Nordwall: That is true.

Vyshinsky: And then you remembered that it happened otherwise and that you paid Taylor by a transfer on London. Was there such a lengthy operation?

Nordwall: That was not a lengthy operation, because Taylor did not wish to put such a large sum through his account.

Vyshinsky: And so that is the only instance when you had any monetary transaction with Lobanov, that of the fur coat?

Nordwall: Yes.

Vyshinsky: Moreover, you denied the testimony you gave at the preliminary investigation?

Nordwall: Not entirely, but in part. I was in error about things which happened a long time ago.

Vyshinsky: Let us record your mistakes. The first mistake is that you, that very day or the day following, having received money from Lobanov, handed it over to Taylor. That actually was not the case. Is that right or not? I will request you to answer my question.

Nordwall: Say it again.

Vyshinsky: With great pleasure. You just stated that at the preliminary investigation you made certain mistakes on this subject. I want now to establish what mistakes you then made, what mistakes you made at the preliminary investigation. First mistake: You stated at the preliminary investigation that you received the money for the fur coat from Lobanov the same day or the following day, and handed it over to Taylor. That was actually not the case. That was your first mistake. Is that right? Yes or no?

Nordwall: Yes.

Vyshinsky: That was your first mistake. Second mistake: You stated that you received 400 rubles, but you now state that you received 500 rubles. That is your second mistake—yes or no?

Nordwall: Is that what I stated?

Vyshinsky: That is your second mistake?

Nordwall: Yes.

Vyshinsky: Third mistake: You stated that the money was written off your account in your office in Moscow. When the Investigating Judge examined your bookkeeper's books in your presence, what was discovered?

Nordwall: The account was not recorded. And I immediately recalled how I sent the money.

Vyshinsky: Fourth mistake: you later remembered that the money was transmitted to Taylor not in Moscow but in London, in corroboration of which you produced a telegram. What was the amount in the telegram?—400 or 500?

Nordwall: 500.

Vyshinsky: Fifth mistake: you say not 400 but 500, that is the amount stated in that telegram. Is that right?

Nordwall: No. When I was released and came home, I asked my wife how much Lobanov paid for the coat. She said 500.

Vyshinsky: The telegram says 500, and you today for the first time declared that it was 500?

Nordwall: Before I said, I think it was 400.

Vyshinsky: The following is stated here: "Thereupon they agreed upon a price of 400 rubles. This amount Lobanov gave me either the same day or the day following; I handed it over to Taylor. Taylor received the money at the pay desk at the office from my account, and it was written off my account at the office."

Nordwall: Look at the testimony I gave before this testimony, where it is stated: "I think it was 400 rubles."

Vyshinsky: Did you mention 500?

Nordwall: No, I said "I think."

Vyshinsky: 500, did you mention that figure?

Nordwall: No. I made a statement, and it is now clear how that sum was transferred to Taylor.

Vyshinsky: We have established several mistakes which you committed.

Now a question to Lobanov. Did you pay him 400 rubles for the coat?

Lobanov: No.

Vyshinsky: How did you receive the coat—from Taylor?

Lobanov: I received the coat from Nordwall.

The President: Have you any other questions?

Roginsky: No.

The President: Has the Defence any questions?

Pines: Yes. You were ten years old when your father died?

Lobanov: About that. Perhaps eleven.

Pines: Did he leave a lot of money?

Lobanov: No.

Pines: At whose expense were you educated at the high school and the Institute?

Lobanov: At the expense of my brother and sister.

Pines: At the Institute?

Lobanov: At the expense of my brother, also at my own expense and at the expense of my wife.

Pines: You state that you studied at the Institute in Ivanovo from 1920 to 1928? Why so long?

Lobanov: I worked two years in a factory.

Pines: How long was the course?

Lobanov: As long as you liked. I do not recall that the course was limited.

Pines: You have stated in what circles you mixed when you were at the Polytechnic Institute. Apart from study, were you interested in social activities and political questions? Were you a member of any circles?

Lobanov: No. I was not a member of any circles.

Pines: Did you read the newspapers?

Lobanov: Rarely.

Pines: One might say that you did not interest yourself in political questions at all?

Lobanov: Yes.

Pines: What were you interested in, apart from your studies?

Lobanov: Technical questions.

Pines: When you went to work at the Ivanovo Power Station after some time you were sent to take courses for raising your qualifications. Why did they send you? What was the system that existed there? Was it at the expense of the power station?

Lobanov: Yes. As a good worker. Of course, as a technical worker and not as a social worker.

Pines: After you returned from the courses to the power

station, how long did you work there as an engineer before your first meeting with Nordwall?

Lobanov: About a year, somewhat less.

Pines: You said that, in general, your inclinations and views were anti-Soviet.

Lobanov: Yes.

Pines: Did those views and inclinations find expression in any way, in conduct, actions and so on?

Lobanov: They did not find expression in actions.

Pines: They were only your state of mind? Didn't you express it in any way, and wasn't it manifested somehow?

Lobanov: No.

Pines: How long were you acquainted with Nordwall and how many, approximately, conversations were there between you, before he proposed to you to pass from words to deeds? What interval of time?

Lobanov: A couple of months.

Pines: During those two months how often did you meet and have conversations unrelated to business?

Lobanov: We met often, and those conversations took place several times a month.

Pines: Were you ever at his apartment except when you went there to buy the fur coat?

Lobanov: Never.

Pines: And he was never at your apartment?

Lobanov: Never.

Pines: You say that he often provoked you into anti-Soviet conversations, knowing your convictions at the time. Why did those convictions subsequently change?

Lobanov: My convictions changed, my anti-Soviet frame of mind altered, I began to repent. It tormented me sometimes to the point of ill health, nevertheless, I returned again to my work, in spite of the fact that moral torments and the consciousness of my wrong position manifested itself during the whole period of my work.

Pines: You mentioned other members of your organization — Lebedev and Ugrumov. Did you inform them of your relations with Nordwall?

Lobanov: No.

Pines: Did Lebedev know that you were meeting Nordwall, and that you were working on his initiative?

Lobanov: When I enlisted Lebedev, I told him that it was on the initiative of Nordwall and Elliott.

Pines: I want to ask Lebedev a question. [To Lebedev] Were you told that?

Lebedev: I was.

Pines: In what way?

Lebedev: I was at Lobanov's apartment and he told me that the work was being carried on, on the initiative of Nordwall and Elliott.

Pines: And with whom were you connected?

Lebedev: With Elliott.

Pines: I have no more questions to ask Lebedev. Now Lobanov. Tell us about the fur coat: did he offer it to you, or were you looking for a coat?

Lobanov: I asked him when he went to England to bring a fur coat back with him. At first I did not ask directly for a fur coat, but for an overcoat, preferably a fur coat. He brought a fur coat.

Pines: You say that your state of mind changed several times and that you wanted to abandon wrecking activities?

Lobanov: Yes.

Pines: Was it before you received money from Nordwall or after?

Lobanov: Continually.

Pines: Did your first vacillations occur before you received money, or after? You testified that the first money you received was 3,000 rubles—in June 1931. Did your vacillations occur prior to June or after June?

Lobanov: There were vacillations during the whole period of this work.

Pines: Were there ever occasions when you told Nordwall that you wanted to stop this work?

Lobanov: No.

Pines: What prevented you?

Lobanov: I thought that it was useless to speak to him about it. What could he tell me? I did not intend to consult him on this question. If I wanted to abandon the work, I could have abandoned it without him.

Pines: Permit me to put several questions to Nordwall. Accused Nordwall, tell me, what in your opinion were your relations with Lobanov? You say that you never talked with him about wrecking. What were your relations—purely official, business relations?

Nordwall: Official business relations, apart from the occasion when I helped to sell the fur coat.

Pines: Were your relations with him the same as with the other engineers of that power station?

Nordwall: The same.

Pines: How do you explain that you took such a keen interest in the purchase of the fur coat which Lobanov needed?

Nordwall: In what way "keen"?

Pines: For the sake of the coat you invited him to your apartment.

Nordwall: I speak Russian well, but Taylor is a man who speaks Russian badly. He was not long in the Soviet Union and I helped him as a man, no more. Anyone in this hall would have done the same.

Pines: I have no more questions to ask.

The President: Are there any other questions?

Dolmatovsky: I have a question to ask Lobanov. Tell me, please, accused Lobanov, did you ever meet Nordwall privately, or did you meet him only at work and in the train?

Lobanov: I met him privately when I tried on the coat.

Dolmatovsky: Apart from the instance of the coat. At work, did you work with him together?

Lobanov: At the same plant.

Dolmatovsky: Since when?

Lobanov: From the autumn of 1930 to the autumn of 1931, about a year.

Dolmatovsky: At first you were manager of the operating department?

Lobanov: I used to meet him at that time.

Dolmatovsky: And when you worked at the Ivanovo Power Station?

Lobanov: He worked at the first sub-station and used to come to us at the Ivanovo Power Station.

Dolmatovsky: That is to say, on the same job?

Lobanov: I was on one, he was on several.

Dolmatovsky: How long did you work together with him?

Lobanov: About half a year.

Dolmatovsky: What was your branch, and what was his, how often did you meet him?

Lobanov: I was manager of the operating department and he worked on the installation of electrical equipment at the Ivanovo Power Station.

Dolmatovsky: How often during work could one hold conversations on questions of a non-business nature?

Lobanov: One could talk as long as one liked.

Dolmatovsky: During the course of the half year you worked together, can you say how many times a day you spoke to him, or how many times a week?

Lobanov: Sometimes ten times a day, and sometimes once a week when he came to visit us.

Dolmatovsky: I am speaking of the time you worked together.

Lobanov: Several times a day. Sometimes we would meet and sometimes we would just go up and start a conversation.

Dolmatovsky: I am interested to know how often you could hold conversations with him on non-business subjects.

Lobanov: Might hold conversations, or actually did hold conversations?

Dolmatovsky: Might hold conversations and actually did hold conversations.

Lobanov: I could have held anti-Soviet conversations from morning to night, but in fact it happened, at any rate, several times a month.

Dolmatovsky: That is to say not very often: it might be three or four times or only twice a month, consequently eighteen times in six months.

Lobanov: I made no record of how many times exactly, but something like that.

Dolmatovsky: How often did you meet on the train?

Lobanov: Also several times a month.

Dolmatovsky: And also during the period of half a year?

Lobanov: Yes.

Dolmatovsky: In the train, were you usually alone together, or were there others present?

Lobanov: Sometimes there were others.

Dolmatovsky: Who exactly, what kind of people, people like Lebedev, Elliott?

Lobanov: Permit me to describe the conditions on the train. There was a special compartment for the employees on the Ingres-Ivanovo train. The foreigners who worked there travelled in this compartment, Nordwall among them. I also enjoyed this privilege, although not all the officials had the right to travel in the compartment—only a few persons. Well, picture the conditions of a noisy rattling train—they were of course not Pullman cars, but clumsy, noisy cars. While the train was in motion, you could say anything you liked, and a person sitting next to you could not hear. As a rule there were not many people—of course there were times when every seat was occupied—but nevertheless, everybody had a place, and nobody stood, so that there was plenty of room.

Dolmatovsky: In a word, the conditions were favourable for conversation?

Lobanov: Quite favourable.

Dolmatovsky: And did Nordwall speak Russian well at that time?

Lobanov: Fairly well.

Dolmatovsky: How long was he in the U.S.S.R.?

Lobanov: I do not know. I began seeing him in the autumn of 1930.

Dolmatovsky: And you say that at that time he spoke Russian well?

Lobanov: Fairly well.

Dolmatovsky: Fairly well—better or worse than now?

Lobanov: Worse than now, but fairly well.

Dolmatovsky: But even now it cannot be said that he speaks Russian well. How was it possible to conduct conversations with him on complicated subjects?

Lobanov: There were no particularly complicated subjects—anti-Soviet talk is sometimes clear from a couple of words.

Dolmatovsky: Tell me, please, when did you begin to repent?

Lobanov: It went on during the whole period of my wrecking activities.

Dolmatovsky: But at first, prior to February, you did not repent?

Lobanov: There were vacillations.

Dolmatovsky: Were you already carrying on this work in September, October and November, 1930?

Lobanov: I do not understand you.

Dolmatovsky: I ask you, when did you begin to repent of your actions of which you spoke?

Lobanov: When I began my wrecking activities.

Dolmatovsky: When did you begin your wrecking activities?

Lobanov: From the time I received instructions in this respect from Nordwall.

Dolmatovsky: Can you say when approximately?

Lobanov: About March, or February.

Dolmatovsky: Consequently, in September, October, November and December you had not repented? You were not yet carrying on wrecking work, and so did not repent?

Lobanov: Of course, I did not repent. There was nothing to repent of.

Dolmatovsky: Why did you need an external stimulus to begin anti-Soviet conversations? You assert that not you but Nordwall was the initiator of those conversations.

Lobanov: I do not assert that. I myself held such conversations and I myself started them.

Dolmatovsky: While at work, did you in fact conduct protracted conversations?

Lobanov: With whom?

Dolmatovsky: With Nordwall.

Lobanov: There were no particularly protracted conversations.

Dolmatovsky: Passing conversations?

Lobanov: What do you mean by passing? Not in the sense that you passed by, said how do you do, and nothing more. There were conversations, but not such conversations where you sat for half a day and talked.

Dolmatovsky: You began wrecking activities about March 1931. Is that so?

Lobanov: Yes.

Dolmatovsky: Did you receive the first money, as you assert. in May or June 1931?

Lobanov: In June 1931.

Dolmatovsky: What sum did you receive?

Lobanov: 3,000 rubles.

Dolmatovsky: Were you receiving such sums all the time?

Lobanov: All the time.

Dolmatovsky: You received 3,000 and then 2,000?

Lobanov: Yes.

Dolmatovsky: And didn't you say that you received 2,000 in order to conceal how much you really got and not share with the others?

Lobanov: That is not how it was.

Dolmatovsky: How was it then?

Lobanov: At the preliminary investigation I said that I gave Kitayev 1,000 rubles. As a matter of fact I did not.

Dolmatovsky: And today you said that you did give it to him?

Lobanov: No, I did not say so.

Dolmatovsky: At how much do you value the fur coat?

Lobanov: Not having sold it, I don't know.

Dolmatovsky: But you received it?

Lobanov: I did.

Dolmatovsky: Did you ask for a fur coat to be brought you?

Lobanov: I did.

Dolmatovsky: Beforehand?

Lobanov: Yes.

Dolmatovsky: In May, you knew of course that you would need a fur coat?

Lobanov: I knew of course that in the winter one needs a fur coat.

Dolmatovsky: But you remembered it as early as May?

Lobanov: Not only in May and in June, but remembered it even in winter.

Dolmatovsky: Did you count the money when you gave it to Nordwall?

Lobanov: How do you mean, count it?

Dolmatovsky: When they presented you with the coat, as you say, did you figure how much it was worth?

Lobanov: Yes, approximately.

Dolmatovsky: How do you mean, approximately?

Lobanov: I did not appraise it. The coat was a fairly good one.

Dolmatovsky: You did not translate it into money value?

Lobanov: There was no particular need.

Dolmatovsky: Consequently, you received not 3,600, but 3,600 plus the coat which costs about 500?

Lobanov: The coat?

Dolmatovsky: Yes.

Lobanov: More!

Dolmatovsky: And so you received more?

Lobanov: No. The talk was about money.

Dolmatovsky: How did the incident with the coat take place? You did not know Taylor, who he was and what he was. You saw Taylor for the first time at Nordwall's apartment?

Lobanov: I don't know who this Taylor is.

Dolmatovsky: It's the one whom you described as the stout Englishman.

Lobanov: If that's the one, then I have seen him.

Dolmatovsky: Describe him in detail.

Lobanov: Stout, I don't remember whether he had a moustache and beard, elderly.

Dolmatovsky: Don't you know any more details?

Lobanov: No.

Dolmatovsky: Permit me to put a question to Kutuzova? Can she describe Taylor and say when he was in Ivanovo-Voznesensk?

Kutuzova: I don't know Taylor's age, but he is about 30, of middle height, a straight ordinary nose, with a fair amount of hair.

Dolmatovsky: Is that the one?

Lobanov: I don't remember about the hair.

Dolmatovsky: Now tell me, please, you say that when Nordwall began to make proposals to you to engage in wrecking, he said—let us pass from words to deeds. Do you say that that is exactly what he said?

Lobanov: Yes, that is what he said.

Dolmatovsky: That is to say, he spoke Russian so well that he could use such expressions?

Lobanov: As you see.

Dolmatovsky: When did you commit the wrecking acts—putting the motor out of action in March 1931, disconnecting the conveyor cables?

Lobanov: That went on continuously.

Dolmatovsky: But approximately?

Lobanov: That happened several times, repeatedly.

Dolmatovsky: In what period?

Lobanov: In the period of 1931. And in 1932, but more in 1931.

Dolmatovsky: Damage to the bearings?

Lobanov: That was in the spring of 1931.

Dolmatovsky: In the spring.

Lobanov: Yes.

Dolmatovsky: Causing short circuits?

Lobanov: In the summer of 1931.

Dolmatovsky: Then the motor of the smoke exhaust pump, which you burnt out?

Lobanov: That was recently.

Dolmatovsky: In what year—1933?

Lobanov: I think in 1933.

Dolmatovsky: And your work on the machine-cut peat, when was that done?

Lobanov: At the end of 1932, in the second half.

Dolmatovsky: Is that when you were working in the rationalization department?

Lobanov: Yes, I was already appointed and worked simultaneously as the director of the thermo-mechanical group.

Dolmatovsky: When did you start work in the rationalization department?

Lobanov: I think in the spring of 1931.

Dolmatovsky: And when were you the director of the mechanical group?

Lobanov: I can't say exactly, I think in the winter.

Dolmatovsky: When was that unsuccessful blow at the boiler feed attempted?

Lobanov: When I worked in the rationalization department.

Dolmatovsky: That is to say approximately in the autumn of 1931. When was the transformer burnt out?

Lobanov: At the end of 1932.

Dolmatovsky: When did you come to an agreement with Rostov over the telephone?

Lobanov: In 1932.

Dolmatovsky: In what period was that?

Lobanov: Almost from the beginning of 1932, the whole year.

Dolmatovsky: Did you engage in wrecking before Nordwall suggested wrecking to you?

Lobanov: No.

Dolmatovsky: Why do you say that if it was necessary to stop wrecking you could have done that without Nordwall? Why in one case is outside initiative required, and here, you display your own initiative? You said so confidently that you could do without him, that his instructions were not necessary.

Lobanov: I could reason for myself. I can think independently, but of course there could be some stimulus. I said that I could think independently, it is not absolutely necessary, that because Nordwall pushed me into this business he had to drag me out. All I said was that in my opinion he could have induced me to stop the wrecking work. There were vacillations. Perhaps, had someone interfered, he could have dragged me out of the situation.

Dolmatovsky: But it was not Nordwall who could help you?

Lobanov: Perhaps he would have taken such measures, or perhaps circumstances would have been such that even Nordwall would have served as a cause.

Dolmatovsky: When he proposed that you start wrecking work did he say that you would receive money?

Lobanov: He did. In any case he said that I would have no cause to complain, and I, of course, expected a great deal.

Dolmatovsky: You expected a great deal and he said that you would have no cause to complain. Were those his exact words?

Lobanov: As for exactness—that is a matter of the past.

Dolmatovsky: About the words "from words to deeds," do you definitely remember that?

Lobanov: Yes.

Dolmatovsky: And "you will have no cause to complain," you don't remember that?

Lobanov: Perhaps this is not an absolutely exact formulation, but that is the sense of it.

Dolmatovsky: What sum did he mention?

Lobanov: He did not mention any sum.

Dolmatovsky: And when you received 3,000, did you think it was too little?

Lobanov: I thought it was little.

Dolmatovsky: For yourself or for the others?

Lobanov: For myself and the others.

Dolmatovsky: Did you know that Lebedev was also receiving money?

Lobanov: No.

Dolmatovsky: When did you get to know about it?

Lobanov: I didn't know at all.

Dolmatovsky: How much did you give Lebedev a second time?

Lobanov: Once I gave him a thousand rubles.

Dolmatovsky: He says that you gave him less. Did you borrow money from his wife?

Lobanov: I don't remember, perhaps I did.

Dolmatovsky: Did he ask you to lend him money?

Lobanov: I don't remember.

Dolmatovsky: Immediately after your conversation with Nordwall you began to organize a group?

Lobanov: What do you mean to organize?

Dolmatovsky: Was it organized already?

Lobanov: You can't say it was organized, but there were people there already, it was not necessary to exert any special effort to get a group together.

Dolmatovsky: The group was there. When did you get it together?

Lobanov: I did not get it together, it got together itself.

Dolmatovsky: When was that?

Lobanov: While I was working at the Ivanovo Power Station.

Dolmatovsky: When did you inform Lebedev for the first time?

Lobanov: Approximately in March.

Dolmatovsky: Did he say at once that he was enlisted?

Lobanov: He did not say that to me.

Pines: Did you have a separate office when you worked at the Ivanovo Power Station?

Lobanov: Yes.

Pines: Was Nordwall able to carry on conversations with you without anybody hearing?

Lobanov: Yes.

Pines: Did such conversations take place?

Lobanov: They did.

Pines: I have no more questions to put.

The President: Has the Prosecution any questions to Lobanov?

Prosecution: No.

The President: Sit down, accused Lobanov. Accused Lebedev come here, please. The Court has no questions. What questions have the Prosecution?

Vyshinsky: Accused Lebedev, tell us when you started work at the Ivanovo Power Station, what was your position, how did you meet Lobanov on wrecking work? Tell us briefly how you did wrecking work, and why.

Lebedev: In 1930, May 8, I started work at the Ivanovo Power Station in the capacity of foreman of the electricians' shop. The manager of this shop was the senior technician, Ugrumov. In December 1930 I made the acquaintance of Lobanov who had arrived at the Ivanovo Power Station. On December 27, by an order of the management, I was transferred to the operating department as a foreman and worked under Lobanov. I struck up an acquaintance with Lobanov and Ugrumov. I used to visit the one and the other at their homes.

When I arrived at the Ivanovo Power Station I held anti-Soviet views. Mixing in the company of Lobanov and Ugrumov, I became strengthened in my anti-Soviet views because both of them held exactly the same views as I held.

In March 1931 I made the acquaintance of the English specialist, Mr. Elliott, who was invited to my flat on the initiative of one Volkova, who arranged a party at our house. Why did she select my flat for a party? Because my flat consisted of two rooms and she lived only in one room and moreover, two other women lived in her room.

Vyshinsky: And who is this Volkova?

Lebedev: She is a typist who works in the office of the Ivanovo Power Station.

Vyshinsky: Were you acquainted with this typist before?

Lebedev: She was acquainted with me and with my family. She was aquainted with Lobanov a long time before that.

Vyshinsky: When Volkova arranged this party, was Lobanov there?

Lebedev: Lobanov was there, Elliott and many strangers. Parties were arranged in Lobanov's flat, but I was not present at those.

After this party Elliott began to visit my flat every evening and always brought drinks with him. In the evenings there were dances with Volkova and he always brought a gramophone with him. A few days later Lobanov asked me to visit him at his flat in the evening. Sometimes I used to visit him without invitation, but this time he asked me to come. When I arrived at his flat in the evening we at first talked about anti-Soviet subjects, he expressed discontent with the system and I supported him. We talked about our material position. At the end of our conversation Lobanov offered to give me material assistance because at that time I was hard up. I want to go back a bit. Before I was transferred from the electricians' shop to the operating department I had supplementary earnings of 110 rubles in addition to my salary of 200 rubles. This satisfied me. When I was transferred to the operating department I lost this 110 rubles because owing to the nature of my work and Lobanov's insistence, I no longer had the opportunity of coaching the apprentices. That evening when Lobanov invited me to join the counter-revolutionary group he wanted to rectify this error, that is to say, of having deprived me of my earnings of 110 rubles, and he told me that instructions had been received from Nordwall and Elliott to damage the equipment and put it out of action and in that way to undermine the working capacity of the Ivanovo Power Station. At first I hesitated a little, and then I agreed. Lobanov told me that Nordwall had promised to pay well for this. Next day I thought over what Lobanov had said and I realized that I had lost sight of the fact that my immediate superior was senior technician Ugrumov. Thinking over the matter I decided that if Ugrumov learned of this, the scheme would be discovered. That is why I wanted to clear this point up with Lobanov. I cleared it up next day. Lobanov said that Ugrumov was our man and there was no need to be afraid of him. In this respect I was almost appeased but nevertheless I wanted to test the one and the other. Just then an opportunity occurred. In March I was working in the pump yard on the motor of the feed pump. Work was being carried on there. Bricklayers were at work mixing concrete. The motor was not covered up and sand and pebbles were being scattered around. The electrician on duty, who was my subordinate, spoke to me about this and said that the motor ought to be covered up. I replied that he ought to go and look for something, a tarpaulin, to cover up the motor. As we had just started operations there was nothing available to cover the motor up with. The motor was not covered up and the sand continued to be scattered over it.

I reported this to Ugrumov, took him to the job, told him that sand was being scattered around and that certain measures ought to be taken. Ugrumov did not give me any definite reply; he said, "Cover it up," and nothing more. But there was nothing to cover it up with, and that is how it was left.

Next day, while it was working, the bearings of the motor became heated. I again reported to Ugrumov. Ugrumov said that it was necessary to test the temperature and if the temperature did not rise then the bearings would do and the motor would continue to work. I took no further measures. The result, however, was that the temperature of the bearings continued to rise and finally we had to stop the motor. On inspection it was found that the neck of the shaft and part of the bearings were damaged.

This was the first wrecking act that I committed on Lobanov's instructions.

My next wrecking work was performed in the boiler house on boilers 1, 2 and 3. There I damaged the cable in order to stop the motors that drove the reductors. There were many breakdowns with these motors. Several of the breakdowns resulted in very long stoppages of the boilers, that is to say, in the main, the motors became overheated, and the furnace of the boiler had to be dismantled, which took approximately a week to do. The boiler was put out of action. There were approximately five such stoppages. There were other stoppages, but of shorter duration, that is to say, the motors were cut off, but they were quickly switched on again.

This was my second piece of wrecking work.

My third piece of work was done on the motor of the fire-brigade pump. In view of the fact that we had not received unpurified-water pumps for the motor, we adapted the fire-brigade pump. This fire-brigade pump was defective: there was a crack from the box and the cable coupling which carried the current to the motor. Lobanov told me about this defect so that I should concentrate my attention upon it. As the motor was of high voltage and had to be handled carefully, I first of all made sure of the state of the contact box. The crack in the contact box was painted over. During the work the crack became larger because the motor became heated and dampness got into the crack.

Before the breakdown which occurred in the evening, about 5 o'clock, I did the following. As the motor was in the charge of the boiler staff I wanted dampness to get into this box. For this purpose, inspecting the motor every day, I tried the pump to see how it worked. I opened the tap. When the tap was opened water spirted on to the motor and as the motor was oval-shaped the water flowed into the box. On flowing into the box the water did not cause a short circuit. But while the motor was working, when the motor had a temperature of about 50 degrees, the water gradually evaporated and caused a short circuit between the bolts of the plug. An explosion occurred. The cover—the weakest spot—blew off. The motor was put out of action for two days.

My fourth act of wrecking was on the centrifugal pump of the house turbine.

I have said that the breakdown with the fire-brigade pump occurred in August. And in the beginning of September the fourth breakdown occurred with the centrifugal pump of the house turbine. A short circuit occurred in the plug box. An explosion occurred. Part of the cable that emerged from the coupling was burnt out. The motor was stopped for about three days.

Vyshinsky: Is that all?

Lebedev: Yes.

Vyshinsky: I have a question concerning the parties that Volkova arranged. Was Baldin there?

Lebedev: Yes.

Vyshinsky: Was there a military department at the power station?

Lebedev: Not at the station.

Vyshinsky: Where was it?

Lebedev: It was not at the station.

Vyshinsky: And where did Baldin work?

Lebedev: At the Fourth Korolev Mechanical Works.

Vyshinsky: Was there a military department there?

Lebedev: Yes, there was a military department there.

Vyshinsky: Do you know whether at these parties anyone asked Baldin about this military department?

Lebedev: I heard some talk, but I do not know who first put the question.

Vyshinsky: Did you hear talk about the military department?

Lebedev: Yes.

Vyshinsky: Between whom?

Lebedev: Elliott was there.

Vyshinsky: With whom was he speaking?

Lebedev: With Baldin.

Vyshinsky: What about?

Lebedev: They were discussing what was being manufactured at the works.

Vyshinsky: Was that about the military department? Did Baldin speak about the work of the military department?

Lebedev: Yes.

Vyshinsky: Did he tell Elliott?

Lebedev: Yes.

Vyshinsky: And how did you hear it?

Lebedev: I was in the room and sat not far from them.

Vyshinsky: By their side?

Lebedev: No, not by their side, but a little nearer than you are to me.

Vyshinsky: Was this a single case, or did it happen often?

Lebedev: It was the only case with me.

Vyshinsky: The only case with you. Well, and what else did they talk about at these parties, besides military talk?

Lebedev: There was no special talk at these parties.

Vyshinsky: Soviet or anti-Soviet talk?

Lebedev: Both the one and the other.

Vyshinsky: Who talked Soviet and who talked anti-Soviet?

Lebedev: Baldin talked and I talked and Lobanov talked.

Vyshinsky: And Elliott?

Lebedev: Also.

Vyshinsky: And Volkova?

Lebedev: Also.

Vyshinsky: And was Volkova previously acquainted with various engineers?

Lebedev: I don't know, because I arrived only on March 8, 1930, and she had been working there several years before.

Vyshinsky: Was she acquainted with Nordwall?

Lebedev: Yes.

Vyshinsky: Permit me to put a question to Nordwall. Accused Nordwall, tell me, please, were you acquainted with this Volkova?

Nordwall: Not under that name.

Vyshinsky: Don't you remember?

Nordwall: No.

Vyshinsky: Was Elliott there?

Lebedev: Yes.

Vyshinsky: Did you meet him?

Lebedev: I met him when I was at the Ivanovo Electric Power Station.

Vyshinsky: About the money. Do you corroborate or do you amend—a thousand rubles, or less?

Lebedev: I received 150 rubles from Lobanov in June, 100 rubles in July, altogether 250 rubles. From Elliott I received 140 rubles in March and 200 rubles in April.

Vyshinsky: What for?

Lebedev: He said it was for drinks.

Vyshinsky: That is what you were to do with the money, but I asked—why did he give you the money?

Lebedev: I received the 140 rubles to cover the expenses connected with the party for which we clubbed together.

Vyshinsky: A question to Thornton. Accused Thornton, will you be good enough to say whether you received any information from Elliott?

Thornton: Of a general character.

Vyshinsky: Did you hear what the accused Lebedev says, that he was a witness to the fact that Elliott collected information about the work of the military department?

Thornton: Yes, I heard.

Vyshinsky: Did you receive any information from this Elliott?

Thornton: Yes, Elliott came to see us.

Vyshinsky: And did you get information from him?

Thornton: Yes.

Vyshinsky: That means that you corroborate the testimony you gave during the investigation—that you received information from Elliott about the Ivanovo Power Station?

Thornton: Yes.

Vyshinsky: I have no more questions.

The President: I have a question to Lebedev. You related in great detail about all this wrecking, but you did not say why it was all done, for what aims. Was it for money? But you got very little for it. Where does this hatred for the Soviet Government come from?

Lebedev: It's like this. I said here that I was hard up. Lobanov promised that I would be rewarded and I thought I would get this money. But in the end I didn't.

The President: Why did you engage in this wrecking? Was it only for the sake of the money, or because you held anti-Soviet views?

Lebedev: It was both.

The President: The Court will adjourn until 6 p.m.

(Court adjourns at 3:10 p.m. until 6 p.m.)

[Signed] V. V. ULRICH

President of the Special Session of the Supreme Court of the U.S.S.R.

A. F. KOSTYUSHKO

Secretary

EVENING SESSION, APRIL 14, 1933, 6:15 p.m.

The Commandant: Please rise. The Court is coming.

The President: Please be seated. The session is resumed. Has the Prosecution any more questions to Lebedev?

Prosecution: No.

The President: And the Defence?

Dolmatovsky: Tell us, Lebedev, did Nordwall take part in the evening parties organized by Elliott?

Lebedev: He did not take part.

Dolmatovsky: Did you consider Nordwall your friend?

Lebedev: I went there several times.

Dolmatovsky: Did you consider him as one of your group?

Lebedev: No. I had dealings with Lobanov.

Pines: Who were your parents?

Lebedev: My father was an office employee.

Pines: When did you begin working?

Lebedev: At the age of 16.

Pines: Right up to the time of your arrest?

Lebedev: I worked in industry for 30 years and served in the navy for 6 years.

Pines: What was your position in the navy?

Lebedev: First a seaman; then I studied in a school and became a petty officer.

Pines: In what capacity did you work all the time? What was your speciality?

Lebedev: An electrician.

Pines: Did you receive a special education?

Lebedev: No, I studied here in Moscow. Then two years in a military school. The rest was practical work.

Pines: Did you work right up to your arrest in the Ivanovo

Power Station, or did you leave before? And if you left, then why? When did you leave work at the Ivanovo Power Station?

Lebedev: On November 2, 1931.

Pines: Where did you go after that?

Lebedev: Still at the Ivanovo Station, but on the power transmission.

Pines: You left on your own?

Lebedev: Yes, because I was transferred from the post of foreman to that of brigadier and I didn't agree to that, and therefore left.

Pines: When you left for the new job, did you keep in contact with Elliot?

Lebedev: No.

Pines: Consequently, your criminal activities ceased?

Lebedev: Yes.

Pines: What wages did you get?

Lebedev: Two hundred rubles, then I received a rise of 50 rubles on the first of March.

Pines: How big was your family?

Lebedev: Four people.

Pines: All dependent on you?

Lebedev: Yes.

Pines: At the party that evening when Elliott was present and Nordwall was absent, was his name mentioned in any conversations?

Lebedev: Yes, because Elliott was a good friend of Nordwall.

Pines: In what connection was it mentioned?

Lebedev: Elliot said that Nordwall would bring from abroad the presents which were promised.

Pines: Were there any references to wrecking activities?

Lebedev: Yes, Elliot spoke about it.

Pines: In the presence of you and Lobanov?

Lebedev: Yes.

Pines: Consequently, there was no doubt?

Lebedev: No.

Pines: I have no more questions.

The President. Has the Prosecution any questions?

Prosecution: No.

The President: There are no more questions. Accused Lebedev, you may sit down.

Accused Nordwall, please come here. (Nordwall comes to the witness stand.)

Roginsky: Did you work at some other power station or works in the U.S.S.R. apart from the Ivanovo Electric Power Station?

Nordwall: After being at the Ivanovo Power Station, I worked at the power station in Minsk for a short time, testing turbines. Then I took part in the testing commission which tested turbines at the Ivanovo Power Station. I left Ivanovo about January 15 and was for a time in the Moscow office of the firm. After a certain time I was sent to the Balakhna-Nizhni Electric Power Station. I worked there with short intervals until close on March 20. After that I was in Moscow a few days and was sent to Kuznetskstroy where I worked till the end of July. From there I was sent to the Tomsky Works at Makeyevka, where I superintended the installation of the electrical equipment of the first Soviet blooming mill. In connection with this work I was presented at the November festivities with a testimonial as the best shock-brigade worker of Makstroy. At that time I gave an emphatic promise to do everything possible to complete my work in connection with the first Soviet blooming mill before the end of the year, bearing in mind that this would be the end of the first Five-Year Plan. We attained that result, and set our unit in operation on December 30. During the gala opening of the Soviet blooming mill the builders and the social organizations recognized my work as shock-brigade work; and when the People's Commissar, Comrade Orjonikidze, came to the works, the builders introduced me personally to him in view of the fact that I assisted in the construction and that I always tried to avoid wasting foreign currency in the construction work. I was the only electrician, but there were three more Englishmen working for my firm. At the gala meeting, at the evening organized after the starting of the turbine, Comrade Orjonikidze was also present. The construction committee invited me to the presidium and asked me to explain the Makeyevka construction, how well it works, that it works just as well as in England and in other countries.

For this work I was officially given a premium of 1,000 rubles.

After that I continued working on this construction right up to the day of my arrest.

Roginsky: Apart from Makeyevka and Minsk, you also worked at the Motovilikha works?

Nordwall: Yes, I did.

Roginsky: When?

Nordwall: While working at Ivanovo I was sent there—to start on my return from England the power station and test it. I was there a few days and then I received a telegram to examine one of the generators at the Chelyabinsk Power Station on my way back from Perm.

Roginsky: Did you have any trouble during your work at the Motovilikha works?

Nordwall: Nothing very serious.

Roginsky: And what about less serious matters?

Nordwall: I shall tell you that at once. There was a synchronizing relay. I had to test it. All the connections had to be re-made. I had to check whether we had properly connected this synchronizing relay. On the first occasion it was all right, but afterwards our turbine did not work. Two turbines were started and then the station was disconnected. We didn't know what was the matter, but on the following day we found out the cause and everything was clear.

Roginsky: Did anyone come from the Moscow office to Motovilikha at that time?

Nordwall: I believe Mr. Thornton came before me.

Roginsky: Who was there at the time when this trouble happened?

Nordwall: Oleinik worked there at the time.

Roginsky (To the Court): May I, in connection with this, put a question to Oleinik?

The President: Accused Oleinik. (Oleinik comes to the witness stand.)

Roginsky: Accused Oleinik, did the incident at Motovilikha occur just as described by the accused Nordwall, or was it different?

Oleinik: Not quite so.

Roginsky: Tell us how it was.

Oleinik: Nordwall came there to check the system of connections of the electric appliances. I fixed the turbine there. My part was mechanical work. Nordwall came to test the electrical part. He tested everything—all the appliances. Upon starting up, there was a shock but not a very big shock. They began to check what had happened, why the shock had occurred. It seemed as if everything was tested, as if everything was in order, and yet there was a shock. When Nordwall tested it, there was also an electrician from Motovilikha—Serebryannikov. And still they found nothing. Finally the fitter on duty at the Novikov shield ascertained that the system of connections of the synchronizing relay was not right. After that Nordwall agreed that it was not right.

Roginsky: Whose fault was it then?

Oleinik: First of all, the system was turned out defectively by the works.

Roginsky: Which works?

Oleinik: By the Metro-Vickers Works in Manchester.

Roginsky: Who was carrying out the work here in connection with this system?

Oleinik: Nordwall.

Roginsky: Is he responsible for the fact that the work was not properly checked?

Oleinik: Of course he is responsible.

Roginsky: Is he responsible for the defects which occurred in consequence at the Motovilikha works?

Oleinik: Certainly he is responsible. This is what he came here for.

Roginsky: Now a question to the accused Nordwall. (To Nordwall) Was it as Oleinik says?

Nordwall: No. There was a shock when we synchronized two or three other machines. Our machine was not there. Our machine was not working at that time. The two other machines were synchronized.

Roginsky: Oleinik describes it somewhat differently. Did you hear what he said?

Nordwall: Yes, I heard it, but he does not speak correctly.

Roginsky: Why were there these defects of which you yourself spoke here? In consequence of a wrong system of connections, or for some other reason?

Nordwall: In consequence of a wrong system.

Roginsky: But you carried out the work here?

Nordwall: I came here to test. I myself tested all the relays. I didn't notice anything. And not only I. All your expert commissions from the Electro-Import which buy our equipment, all the engineers of the Motovilikha works let these defects pass. When new equipment is started for the first time, there is always some infantile disease, as it were. Every engineer knows that.

Roginsky: Consequently, you consider that what happened at the Motovilikha works was an accident and not a premeditated technical oversight?

Nordwall: Quite an incidental oversight.

Roginsky: Now a question to Oleinik. [To Oleinik] You heard Nordwall's evidence as to his work at Makeyevka?

Oleinik: Yes.

Roginsky: Did you go to Makeyevka?

Oleinik: I didn't go to Makeyevka, but I worked with him.

Roginsky: Was everything as smooth there as Nordwall told us here or were there defects there too, similar to those which were discovered at Motovilikha?

Oleinik: There were defects, of course.

Roginsky: What kind of defects?

Oleinik: There were several defects.

Roginsky: Breakdowns or defects?

Oleinik: There was a breakdown.

Roginsky: A serious one?

Oleinik: A pretty serious one.

Roginsky: What has this breakdown to do with Nordwall's work?

Oleinik: Will you permit me to tell you in detail, because I cannot put it briefly.

Roginsky: No, put it briefly, but so that it should be clear.

Oleinik: There was a breakdown in the case of two motor generators. In one motor generator the coupling was broken and also part of the spool on which the winding of the anchor of the generator was wound. This piece, which broke off, weighing about three poods, smashed the winding and then it rebounded and damaged another motor generator. Thus, two motor generators were put out of action at the same time.

Roginsky: What was the connection between this breakdown and the work which Nordwall carried out at Makeyevka?

Oleinik: Nordwall had nothing to do with that officially. There was only the starting relay of Metro-Vickers and, as it turned out afterwards, the relay was wrongly connected.

Roginsky: What effect did this have on the breakdown?

Oleinik: You see, immediately this motor generator was started, everybody could see, including myself, of course, that the motor generator was not being started properly. It tore too quickly. I spoke about it to Nordwall, but he said that that was not our business.

Roginsky: Whose business was it then?

Oleinik: He said that the starting relay of Metro-Vickers was delivered without installation, and the installation was done by the Makstroy under the guidance of Dobrodeyev, and since Metro-Vickers had nothing to do with the installation, therefore Nordwall had nothing to do with it officially either.

Roginsky: Consequently, in so far as you were not formally responsible for these machines, as the representative of Metro-Vickers, therefore although it was clear to you and as you assert, to Nordwall as well, that these machines were not working properly, you did not consider it your duty to prevent the possibility of a breakdown of these machines. I ask, would it be correct to draw such a conclusion?

Oleinik: No, it would be wrong.

Roginsky: Explain to me why it would be wrong.

Oleinik: Even if the installation was by another firm, if I saw that the installation or the start was being made wrongly, and the more so since this is Metro-Vickers and not some other firm, then I would be obliged to draw attention to this.

Roginsky: Did you draw somebody's attention to this case?

Oleinik: I couldn't draw anybody's attention to it, because I am not an electrician.

Roginsky: Who, then, drew, or ought to have drawn, somebody's attention to it?

Oleinik: I drew attention to it at the time the breakdown occurred.

Roginsky: And who had to draw attention to it before the breakdown occurred?

Oleinik: Formally, Makstroy had to.

Roginsky: I do not speak formally.

Oleinik: But morally, ethically, Nordwall had to.

Roginsky: Did he draw attention to it?

Oleinik: No, he expressed malicious joy after the breakdown.

Roginsky: And didn't he draw the attention of anyone of the Makstroy staff to it?

Oleinik: He said that next time they would ask for fitters for installation work.

Roginsky: Consequently, instead of drawing the attention of the Makstroy staff to it, Nordwall maliciously rejoiced at the event?

Oleinik: Yes, he said that next time they would be wiser and woud ask for electricians and not do it themselves.

Roginsky: Accused Nordwall, is that evidence right?

Nordwall: No, it is not right.

Roginsky: Consequently, you deny it?

Nordwall: I deny the main thing of what he said, but I do not deny that there were some breakdowns. There was a breakdown on the unit of the foreman Platt.

Roginsky: Did Oleinik warn you of the possibility of a breakdown?

Nordwall: No.

Vyshinsky: One question to Oleinik. I am interested in the Makeyevka story. It turns out that something was wrong with the blooming mill at Makeyevka?

Oleinik: This is not all yet.

Vyshinsky: I have the following impression. The blooming mill was connected with the relay of the rolling mill. Am I correct in saying that, because it was connected while the circuit-breaker was on, it created a danger of serious breakdowns?

Oleinik: Yes, absolutely.

Vyshinsky: Why was this?

Oleinik: Nordwall said that it was the mistake of the works.

Vyshinsky: Was it necessary to remove it?

Oleinik: Yes, it was.

Vyshinsky: Was it removed?

Oleinik: No.

Vyshinsky: The danger of a breakdown remained?

Oleinik: Yes.

The President: Are there any more questions?

Vyshinsky: No.

The President: Accused Oleinik, you may sit down. Has the Defence any questions?

Dolmatovsky (To Nordwall): Could you tell how the work proceeded with the blooming mill at Makeyevka?

Nordwall: The work at the Makeyevka works proceeded very well.

Dolmatovsky: Allow me to put a question to Oleinik. When you warned Nordwall, did you already consider yourself a member of the counter-revolutionary organization?

Oleinik: Yes, I did.

Dolmatovsky: Did you also consider him a member?

Oleinik: No, Thornton warned me that I must be very cautious with Nordwall because he was, if not a Bolshevik, then almost a Bolshevik.

Dolmatovsky: So you said that something must be done and he maliciously rejoiced, but you knew that he was almost a Bolshevik?

Oleinik: No, not quite so. Thornton told me this, but I didn't consider him a Bolshevik.

Dolmatovsky: Did your organization consider him their man or not?

Oleinik: More than that.

Dolmatovsky: What do you mean?

Oleinik: Because I wasn't trusted as much as he was.

The President: Who did not trust you?

Oleinik: The firm.

Dolmatovsky: Did you consider him one of your people in the counter-revolutionary organization, or didn't you?

The President: Accused Oleinik probably understands the

word organization somewhat differently from you. Will you explain?

Dolmatovsky: I had in mind your organization, but not Metro-Vickers. Why, although Thornton told you to beware of Nordwall, did you nevertheless warn him?

Oleinik: I do not understand your question.

Dolmatovsky: Then it is not worth while putting it. I think it is clear to the Court.

Vyshinsky: It is not clear at all.

The President: Has the Defence any further questions to ask?

Dolmatovsky (To Nordwall): Tell us how long you stayed at the Ivanovo Power Station.

Nordwall: I was doing constant work the first two months after my arrival, and then I worked continuously in Ivanovo-Vosnesensk. It is forty versts from the power station.

Dolmatovsky: Is what Lobanov said correct—that you worked together in one place for six months?

Nordwall: No, it is not correct.

Dolmatovsky: Accused Lobanov, you said that you worked together for six months.

Lobanov: I didn't speak of continuous work. I spoke about work with intervals.

Dolmatovsky: Consequently, you worked altogether six months in contact with one another?

Lobanov: His work was not continuous. He worked at the First Power Station and at the Ivanovo Power Station.

Dolmatovsky: What is the distance between the First Power Station and the Ivanovo Power Station?

Lobanov: Thirty versts, as I said already.

Dolmatovsky: I have no more questions to ask Lobanov.

Now I wish to ascertain certain details about the coat. You received some money from Lobanov. Where did you put it? Did you give it to Taylor?

Nordwall: I gave the money to Taylor in this way. I put this 500 rubles in my pocket. I had in mind that I needed money, because at that time, to be exact, on January 15, I left for the Ivanovo district, while my wife stayed on at Ivanovo and I had to leave her some money until I should get settled at another place.

Dolmatovsky: When did you marry?

Nordwall: I married on September 25, 1931.

Dolmatovsky: When did you learn to speak Russian more or less well?

Nordwall: I began to speak much better after my acquaintance with my wife.

Dolmatovsky: Who is your wife?

Nordwall: She works for the State Publishing House.

Dolmatovsky: Is she Russian?

Nordwall: Yes.

Dolmatovsky: Does she live permanently at Ivanovo-Vosnesensk?

Nordwall: She lived there only two years before I made her acquaintance.

The President: Has the Defence any more questions to ask?

Defence: No.

The President: And the Prosecution?

Prosecution: No.

The President: Have the accused any questions? No. Accused Nordwall, you may sit down.

Dolmatovsky: In connection with this evidence, I have a request. The question of Nordwall's mistakes has come up. I would like to draw attention to the fact that at his confrontation. Nordwall made a mistake as to the cost of the coat and, instead of 500, named the figure 400, he said "Probably 400 rubles."

Then there was the question of another more important mistake. At his confrontation on March 15, Nordwall said: "Lobanov gave me this sum on the following day and I handed it over to Taylor; or, to be more exact, I didn't hand it over, but he received this money from the office from my account."

Then it turned out that he made a mistake, and I want to establish that he personally did not hand over the money but wrote it down to his account.

Vyshinsky: I also ask the Court to ascertain that in the file of Nordwall's case there is a statement to the effect that he made a mistake in saying that he paid Taylor through the Moscow office of Metro-Vickers, and secondly, that he made that statement pointing out his mistakes only after it was established in his presence by the examiner who was inspecting the books of the office and who drew up a note by which Nordwall's statement that this sum was passed through the books of Metro-Vickers was refuted.

These two facts I would ask the Court to fix in their mind.

The President: Accused Zivert. (Zivert comes to the witness stand.) Tell us how you became engaged in wrecking work.

Zivert: I met Thornton for the first time at the Nizhni Power Station, where I worked on the installation of a 115,000 volt substation. At that station we had the equipment of Metro-Vickers—transformers, for instance. Mr. Thornton, engineer from Metro-Vickers, came to install them. Our administration warned us that we must be very polite to all foreigners and all their requests must be complied with without any objections.

At the meeting, the chief engineer expressed the idea that we were getting such equipment as could only be handled by foreigners, by great specialists, and it was best for us Russians not to come near this equipment. These words touched me to the quick. I consider every machine made by human hands to be within the possible comprehension of everyone. I am very interested in machines. I received no technical education. I only received a practical education under the Soviet Government. I made it my aim to understand all the newest machines. Secondly, after Krzhizhanovsky and Lenin raised the question of the electrification of the U.S.S.R. at the Fifth Congress of Soviets, I decided to devote all my life to electrification and I worked for ten years in this sphere. Thornton seemed to me an extremely valuable man. From the very first day, Thornton, as a British engineer, explained to me the structure of the transformers and all the instruments of Metro-Vickers, their installation and the installation of the oil circuit-breakers, and so forth, which we saw for the first time in Russia.

After giving a whole lecture, he gave practical explanations concerning the inspection of the cores, explained every connection, every screw, explained how carefully one must handle things while installing so as not to break anything, and so on.

I began to respect Mr. Thornton very much, firstly because we were told to treat foreign specialists with respect and secondly because he was a man from whom the Russian workers could learn very much. My ardent desire was to learn how to handle these machines and I set myself this task.

We worked in this way in 1925-26. After the Nizhni Power Station was completed, I worked at a 20,000 kw. station. Some other engineers of the firm Thomson-Houston were also working there, putting the whole installation in proper shape. I had to deal with other British firms; there were about eight Britishers, but there was a very sharp dispute going on with them. It even happened that after a few months of work, the Britishers dropped the work on the switchboard and said they were leaving.

Thornton arrived upon the completion of the work at the Nizhni Power Station in 1926.

Excuse me, I forgot to tell you something. When we had worked for two or three weeks, Mr. Thornton invited me and said that he would show me some catalogues and blueprints of transformers. He said they were very valuable things, that he had them at home and he invited me to come. I was very pleased. He lived at that time in the house allocated to foreign specialists, where he had a room to himself. When I called on him, he showed me blueprints of different transformers. After that he said to me: "Shall we have some dinner?" I answered: "Well, why not?" I had nothing at the back of my mind. Dinner was ordered in the dining room. After our meal, he asked: "Do you drink, maybe?" "Well," I said, "sometimes; I'll not refuse." He said: "I have a good bottle of wine here from Moscow." After dinner we had some wine and began to talk.

He said: "Tell me, Comrade Zivert, what do you think, will you be able to tackle the construction work which you have started?" At that time we had very good installation cadres which we had drafted from among the old electricians in 1924. There was only one weak spot, there were not enough tools. Four fitters had to work on one vice.

He asked me: "What do you think is wrong here with you?"

I told him simply that everything was all right, only there was a shortage of tools. But perhaps we would get them through the Sormovo works. We finished with that. After that, another installation engineer arrived and continued this work at the substation. In 1926, when everything was finished, Mr. Thornton arrived to test and pass the transformers. In 1926 Mr. Thornton invited me to enter the service of Metro-Vickers. He said they were getting permission to organize a Russian office in Moscow, that it was difficult to get people, but he would arrange things so that I would be able to serve there. I told him that I had other plans. My aim was to work exclusively on the electrification of Russia. The government raised the question of Dnieprostroy. I told him emphatically that I planned to work on Dnieprostroy, because the work was on a big scale, and I said that I would not serve with him. He said then: "If you do not care to, then I can recommend you to Dnieprostroy. I have acquaintances there. These people are Winter and Karpov, who built the Shatura Station. They have now gone to Dnieprostroy."

In April 1927 I handed in an application to chief engineer Stupin, asking him to let me go to Dnieprostroy. He said: "I am very sorry to part with you, but the case being so, I wish you success." In my presence he called the secretary and asked him to write two letters, one to A. V. Winter, the other to Chizhevsky.

The President: You are not speaking on what you are asked.

Zivert: After the completion of the works when the tests were made, Mr. Thornton expressed his thanks for the work. He gave 25 to 50 rubles to the workers. He gave me 50 rubles for assisting in the work. My help consisted in reconstructing the coolers of two transformers. The construction there was such that each group had one cooler, and I made it so that if one group stopped, then it would be possible to switch over. And there were many things which I altered. With this, my meetings with Mr. Thornton at the Nizhni Power Station ceased.

In 1927 I left for Dnieprostroy. I did not meet Mr. Thornton again after that. In 1930, when all the preliminary work on Dnieprostroy was completed, I found it tedious being without work. I asked through the organization and through the administration to be sent to Energocentre to intall equipment at other power stations, which were in the installation stage. Having obtained such an appointment, I came to Moscow to the personnel department of Energocentre. I was offered three stations—Chelyabinsk, Ivanovo and Nizhni. But as I was bound by the education of my daughter. . .

The President: I call your attention to the fact that you are not speaking on the question which I put to you.

Zivert: I was at the Ivanovo Power Station, where all the equipment was supplied by Metro-Vickers. I arrived at the Ivanovo Station on February 18, 1930. At the Ivanovo Station all equipment was from Metro-Vickers—the turbines, transformers, oil, circuit-breakers and all the switchboards. I met Thornton. He said: "I am very pleased you came here, that a man whom I know will do the installation." He recommended me to the administration of the Ivanovo Power Station as a man to whom the equipment is entrusted. I felt very pleased that he was a man whom I knew and that the work would be pushed on.

At the Ivanovo Station it was necessary in the first case to install a 12,000 kw. transformer to supply current to the peat works. The transformer was one of 38,000 volts. It was necessary to finish the work by May 1, but we did not receive the transformers at the Ivanovo Station until April 15. The question was raised about sending engineers or electricians of the British firm to install these transformers. Instead of this, a message arrived from Moscow that the installation engineers could not be sent, that Zivert was to be entrusted with installation and that they would be answerable for his installation, but on condition that a representative of the firm should be present at the inspection of the cores and at the tests. For me personally it was a great honour that I was considered such a competent man that the firm entrusted me with the installation of 38,000 volt transformers. The administration agreed, seeing that the firm gave its guarantee. I started on the installation of the transformers. We received them at the end of April and put them in the shop. Thornton came to inspect the cores. Having inspected them, Thornton left, and I remained to dry them and set the transformers in the foundation and carry on the installation until the final test. This work was done. After that, Thornton was called and he arrived for the tests. Thornton tested the transformers and at the opening of the sub-station, in the presence of the whole administration, including the chief engineer and director, shook my hand, thanked me saying the work was well done, thanked me very much, and so on. But during the inspection of the internal cores, before the drying of the transformers, he made me an offer, saying: "We will not send any Englishmen. Perhaps you will agree to work without any Englishmen. We shall pay you and you will work." I answered that I would not undertake the responsibility for the group of the 38,000 kw. transformers. He could negotiate with the administration. If the administration was willing, it did not concern me. But I would not work otherwise. I do not know whether he spoke with the administration or not, but after that, two British engineers arrived for the installation.

After that test, when all the people left, we went to the newly opened sub-station and had a talk. He said to me: Comrade Zivert, here is some money; you may be in need of some. Thank you for your work; you will continue to work with me in the sense of giving assistance to the engineers who will come from England, but it is important that you should supply information.

The President: Did you take the money?

Zivert: Yes, I took the money. He said: Give me information and—this is the main thing—you must not work at such a rapid rate as you did at the Nizhni Power Station, but slow up the work and do not examine the quality of the work so carefully because our installation is so reliable that this is not necessary. In short, there is no need for hurry. His words implied that it was necessary to try to hamper the work of construction in one way or another and that all information could be passed on to engineer Elliott in the engine house, who would take my information when he was away. I accepted the money. On taking leave of me, he said: I must leave today. And he left. I counted the money—it was 500 rubles. I wondered what to do with the money. I was in such a position that I simply did not know what to do. I was afraid to hand over the money to the O.G.P.U., out of weakness; questions would be asked, there would be a lot of fuss and he wouldn't admit the fact anyhow. I took the money to the shop and put it on the transformer, on the beams. I didin't take the money to my wife, because she would ask where I got it. Four days after that, I had to go to Leningrad on business. I went away and then kept on wondering what to do. How was I to hamper the installation? How was I to damage everything? I tried various distractions and kept on thinking what am I to do! How am I to obstruct the installation? What shall I do? He would say that I had received money; he would write an anonymous letter and then I would be lost.

The President (To the Prosecutor): Have you any questions for the accused?

Roginsky: Let us start with clearing up the following circumstances. What was your position at the Ivanovo Station?

Zivert: The foreman of the transformer oil system.

Roginsky: Consequently, a Soviet State employee.

Zivert: Yes.

Roginsky: Did you have any formal business standing with Metro-Vickers officially?

Zivert: No.

Roginsky: You were in the Soviet State service. On what grounds did you take money from the representative of a private firm, while in State service?

Zivert: I committed a crime.

Roginsky: Let us see what you were given the money for. Let us pass on at once—what wrecking work did you do at the Ivanovo Power Station?

Zivert: My wrecking work consisted in concealing the defects of the oil circuit-breakers.

Roginsky: And further?

Zivert: Then, when turning the accumulators the head part was not shielded.

Roginsky: Putting out of action the converters?

Zivert: Third, to hamper the installation of the transformers and oil circuit-breakers.

Vyshinsky: And this you carried out?

Zivert: As far as it was possible, this was carried out.

Vyshinsky: Did your wrecking activities satisfy those who afterwards remunerated you for committing them?

Zivert: I do not know. I was not told anything about it.

Vyshinsky: Were you remunerated for it?

Zivert: They gave me a further 300 rubles.

Vyshinsky: That is to say, the commission was carried out and in addition to the 500 rubles you received a further 300 rubles. Is that so?

Zivert: Quite so.

Vyshinsky: This is somewhat different from the stories you told us during the last 15 minutes.

May I now put a question to Thornton?

The President: You may.

Vyshinsky: You heard Zivert's testimony?

Thornton: Yes, I did.

Vyshinsky: Do you confirm his evidence?

Thornton: No, I do not.

Vyshinsky: Not any part of it?

Thornton: I did not say that, and he did not do that. I did not say that the transformers were to be damaged, and he was not concealing the defects in the oil circuit-breakers, because records were drawn up about the defects in the oil circuit-breakers. So therefore I repudiate it.

Vyshinsky: You didn't conceal defects, but did you give instructions to damage installations?

Thornton: No.

Vyshinsky: But you gave him money?

Thornton: I gave him 250 rubles for the installation of a transformer.

Vyshinsky: Was he employed by your firm?

Thornton: Yes.

Vyshinsky: Accused Zivert, were you an employee of the firm?

Zivert: No.

Thornton: He was not our employee.

Vyshinsky: Why did you give him money then?

Thornton: He carried out the work well.

Vyshinsky: Whose work?

Thornton: The work he was doing.

Vyshinsky: Was he doing this work as your employee?

Thornton: He received this for doing his installation work well.

Vyshinsky: Wasn't it his duty to do it as an employee in the Soviet State service?

Thornton: I consider that he could have refused.

Vyshinsky (To Zivert): Could you have refused?

Zivert: I could have refused.

Vyshinsky: Being in State service, in the Soviet State service, carrying out definite duties which also included supervision of the installation, did you have a right to refuse?

Zivert: I don't understand.

Vyshinsky: Were you obliged to do this work because of your position in the State service?

Zivert: Yes, I was obliged to do it.

Vyshinsky: If you were obliged to do it, then how could you refuse?

Zivert: No, I could not.

Vyshinsky: Had you a right to receive money from outside sources, apart from the money which you received in your official position as salary?

Zivert: No.

Vyshinsky: And you didn't have the right to receive that remuneration about which Thornton spoke here?

Zivert: No, I had no right.

Vyshinsky: Did you receive the money because you did the installation well, or because you hampered the work?

Zivert: Probably because I hampered the work.

Roginsky: Let us specify the sum. Thornton says 250 rubles, what do you say?

Zivert: 500 rubles and 300 rubles.

Roginsky: That is. . . .

Zivert: 800 rubles.

Roginsky: Apart from that which you received at the Nizhni Power Station.

Zivert: Yes.

Roginsky: Where and when did you get the 300 rubles?

Zivert: In the Metro-Vickers office.

Roginsky: From whom?

Zivert: From Thornton.

Roginsky: From him personally?

Zivert: Yes, personally.

Roginsky: Where, in his private office?

Zivert: Yes, in his private office.

Roginsky: Was anyone else present?

Zivert: No.

Roginsky: Just between you two?

Zivert: Just between us two.

Roginsky: Did you give any receipt?

Zivert: No. It was this way. He asked, "Are you leaving?" I said: "Yes." After that he said, "Thank you for the work," and gave me 300 rubles more.

Roginsky: Although you were in the State service, you agreed to carry out wrecking actions and here in Moscow you also went to the Metro-Vickers office and received an additional bribe of 300 rubles for your wrecking work.

Zivert: I didn't go to the office to get this 300 rubles.

Roginsky: Then what for?

Zivert: There were matters of business.

Roginsky: What business?

Zivert: When the breakdown took place at the Ivanovo Power Station, it was necessary to order transformers. When I came with the engineer to get an import license to be able to place an order, I was instructed by the board of the Ivanovo Power Station to go to the Metro-Vickers office and ask them to see that we get the equipment speedily.

Roginsky: What did you get the 300 rubles for?

Zivert: For the work at the Ivanovo Power Station.

Roginsky: About which you told us here?

Zivert: Yes, about which I told you.

Roginsky: Accused Thornton, did this take place?

Thornton: I did not give the 300 rubles.

Roginsky: Was he in the office?

Thornton: He was, and borrowed money.

Roginsky: What sum?

Thornton: I do not know. It is in the books.

Roginsky: This may be just these 300 rubles.

Zivert: This is other money.

Roginsky: What money?

Zivert: I went to buy tools. I found a drill socket and took 50 rubles to buy it with, but I returned this money on the following day.

Roginsky: When was that?

Zivert: It was in 1931.

Roginsky: And when did you get the 300 rubles?

Zivert: The 300 rubles I also got in 1931, but the 250 rubles—in 1932, when I was sent to the Moscow Power Station. The Dnieper combine office of the All-Russian Electric Association did not give me money for a ticket or for anything. When I arrived in Moscow, I wrote to the office of the Moscow Power Station to advance me 400 rubles on account of my travelling expenses and on account of my salary. The Moscow Power Station refused because there was no money prior to the November festivities. I went to the Metro-Vickers office and asked for 250 rubles. I wrote a receipt in the bookkeeper's office and upon my return from the Ivanovo Power Station, I paid the money back. I borrowed twice and each time I settled accounts.

Roginsky: But have these 500 rubles and 300 rubles anything to do with that?

Zivert: Nothing whatever.

Roginsky: That is to say, it was direct remuneration to you for wrecking actions which you carried out at the Ivanovo Power Station?

Zivert: Yes. Apart from this I was given a suit of clothes and a pair of boots for which I paid 95 rubles.

Vyshinsky: Accused Zivert, did you also have something to do with the installation of the oil circuit-breakers?

Zivert: Yes.

Vyshinsky: Did you do the installing well?

Zivert: There were a great many defects.

Vyshinsky: And in consequence of these defects were there breakdowns?

Zivert: Yes.

Vyshinsky: Did you work in 1931?

Zivert: Yes.

Vyshinsky: And part of 1932?

Zivert: I went to a sanatorium and then worked part of 1932.

Vyshinsky: According to my calculation, it comes to about ten months. During this time how many breakdowns were there with the oil circuit-breakers?

Zivert: I don't know. I left in August 1931 and was at work in the power station proper for five months.

Vyshinsky: According to the data of the preliminary examination—ten months, and during these ten months you had about fifteen breakdowns in the oil circuit-breakers.

Zivert: No, it was only five months.

Vyshinsky: Well, let us suppose it is so. How many breakdowns were there during that time?

Zivert: I cannot say. I only installed two oil circuit-breakers and there were seven of them.

Vyshinsky: But were there breakdowns?

Zivert: While I was there, there were no breakdowns, but there were cases when the oil circuit-breakers would not disconnect. The celluloid was bad.

Vyshinsky: Perhaps they were being disconnected politically? Politically or technically?

Zivert: They were being disconnected politically.

Vyshinsky: I have no more questions to ask Zivert.

The President: Has the Defence any questions?

Pines: How many years did you work in Russia?

Zivert: I began to work in 1899.

Pines: What is your social origin?

Zivert: I come from a family of agricultural labourers. My father died when I was six months old. He worked as a labourer for a kulak in Kurland. I myself was a swineherd in my childhood, then worked as a boy at an inn, then a coachman. In 1899 I was an apprentice to a fitter.

Pines: So you are fitter by profession?

Zivert: Yes.

Pines: How many years did you work?

Zivert: 34 years.

Pines: Have you been to school at all?

Zivert: As for studies, I went to a village school for three winters; I even write badly.

Pines: How much did you get at your last place?

Zivert: 240 rubles.

Pines: Tell us frankly why you accepted Thornton's offer to commit acts of wrecking. You have been through such a hard life struggle.

Zivert: As I understand now, it happened because I respected Thornton very much. He helped me to understand machines and when I received the money I felt cornered and could not see any way out. In brief, I didn't know what to do.

Pines: How long did your wrecking work continue?

Zivert: Only one year.

Vyshinsky: Is that much or little?

Zivert: A great deal.

Vyshinsky: Consequently, not "only" one year.

Zivert: Now I feel that I am well, now I am at peace, otherwise, all the time I was ill at ease.

Pines: Did you serve at the Ivanovo Power Station prior to your arrest?

Zivert: No, I left that station.

Pines: Why, were you discharged?

Zivert: No, I left because I wished to get rid of all this. I didn't want to meet the engineers of the firm. I already wanted to get away in 1930, but I was tied up with the installation.

Pines: You went in order not to meet Thornton again?

Zivert: In order not to meet the Metro-Vickers firm and particularly Thornton.

Pines: Where did you go?

Zivert: I went to the installation bureau of the All-Russian Electric Association.

Pines: And after that you never met any of the foreign specialists?

Zivert: Englishmen?

Pines: Yes.

Zivert: Unfortunately, I had to meet them again.

Pines: On what basis?

Zivert: In 1932 when Metro-Vickers installed 12 oil circuit-breakers at the Dnieprostroy sub-station. Instead of an installation engineer a letter was sent to the Dnieprostroy administration to the effect that the firm entrusted me with the reconditioning of the oil circuit-breakers, quite a large installation job—to check the oil filling before the arrival of the installation engineer of Metro-Vickers. But I was engaged on a big job in the Zaporozhstal in connection with the first electrical smelting furnace. The question was raised through the Engineering Technical Section and it was decided that I was to commence the installation of the sub-station, as otherwise there would be an explosion at the Dnieprostroy Power Station. Willy-nilly, I had to give my consent, even though I had to work 16 hours on the job. It was agreed with my chief that from 2 to 10 in the evening I would work on the installation of these oil circuit-breakers.

Pines: Did you receive something from Metro-Vickers?

Zivert: There was a very serious affair. There is present here Gregory, the installation engineer of Metro-Vickers, who commenced working for a complete breakdown and for the damaging of the installation. I didn't come out on the side of Metro-Vickers, but, on the contrary. Mr. Thornton received two letters from me. I wrote that if Gregory was not removed, I would make a row. I wanted to kick out Gregory because he tried my patience to the utmost. He, an installation engineer, a British specialist was engaged for 45 days on one isolator. I decided to come out against Metro-Vickers and not in their defence. Gregory started right away to carry on anti-Soviet agitation at Dnieprostroy. I suggested to him that he give me immediately a description of instruments. I invited my comrade who speaks excellent English so that they should both write it down. Let him write anything that's necessary in order to prepare the instruments—so as not to hinder the work. He gave nothing. I thought there was something wrong. I supplied an instrument according to my own plans. We prepared the instrument and began to work. Five insulators in the course of 8 hours, while Gregory installed only one in 12 hours.

Roginsky: For whom did you work?

Zivert: For Dnieprostroy.

Roginsky: Why did you write a letter to Thornton?

Zivert: Because I spoke to the administration about it. I pointed out that it was necessary to write to the firm about an erector but the administration said that it was somewhat embarrassing.

Roginsky: When was that?

Zivert: In 1932, after the Ivanovo Power Station.

Vyshinsky: Why did you all of a sudden decide to fight against such actions?

Zivert: Because my conscience could no longer stand that sort of business. I had pangs of conscience all the time.

Vyshinsky: May we take it, that at the Ivanovo Power Station you were doing wrecking work, but at Dnieprostroy you repented and began to counteract.

Zivert: Even there I felt repentant but I was afraid.

Vyshinsky: That is to say that under the influence of that change which occurred in you, you began to show resistance to Gregory. I would like to ask that this part of Zivert's evidence be translated to Gregory in English, and that I be allowed to put a question to him.

Zivert: Let Gregory recollect how he kept delaying the installation of the oil circuit-breakers.

The President: Simply repeat your evidence, pointing out what Gregory did.

Zivert: Gregory, first of all, deliberately delayed the installation. When the question was put to him, he answered that he had come to Russia not to work but to make money.

(The Interpreter translates for Gregory)

Gregory: I did not say that.

Zivert: Gregory began to tell our workers that here you people have nothing to eat, while in our country, for 25 kopeks, they eat butter, white bread, and so forth. Generally he carried on agitation so that the workers who understood English told me that we must pay attention to this man because he is spreading discontent by saying things like that. *(The Interpreter translates)*

Gregory: But I could not speak Russian.

Zivert: But this was heard by workers who understand English.

The President: In what language did Gregory speak?

Zivert: In English.

The President: Do you understand English?

Zivert: No, but there were three workers who spoke English.

Vyshinsky: Apropos of what Zivert said just now and what Gregory answered, I understood from Zivert's evidence that he received information from a few English workers, who naturally speak English, that Gregory was carrying on anti-Soviet agitation among these Englishmen.

Zivert: Quite so.

The President: So he stated. I do not know how the interpreter translated it.

Vyshinsky: In that case, will you translate to the accused Gregory as my question that, first it is a matter of his conversations with his fellow countrymen in English and not in Russian, and that his reply, that he does not speak Russian, does not contain a reply to the real matter, and let him be so kind as to reply to the point.

(The Interpreter translates for Gregory.)

Gregory: You must remember that these English speaking men there spoke very, very little English and it took all my time to talk about business without my wasting time talking about Soviet politics which I was not interested in.

The President: It seems to me that it is not worth while developing this question, as Zivert is repeating the words of third persons who are not here and whom we cannot call as witnesses. Has the Defence any questions?

Braude (To accused Zivert): Tell us, please, at the moment of your meeting with Thornton, when you were given money, did you belong to any counter-revolutionary organization?

Zivert: No.

Braude: Had you Soviet or anti-Soviet convictions?

Zivert: Soviet ones.

Braude: Then I cannot understand. You, an old worker, not belonging to any counter-revolutionary organization, you a person with Soviet sentiments, for a few hundred rubles undertake to carry on wrecking against the country in which you live. You have said here that it was out of respect for Thornton. What! Do you respect Thornton more than the State in which you live? Or do you respect money more?

Zivert: The Counsel for Defence asks why I all at once became such a counter-revolutionary, how I could take money out of respect for Thornton. If a man respects another man, especially one who has helped you, and you know that in 1925 I did not know transformers at all—they said that this was some strange monster for us, that we could not work—and in 1930 I installed 38,000 volt transformers on behalf of a British firm. Can you imagine what that meant for us, practical workers, without technical education? The situation arose that when I met this man, I received money and took it.

Braude: So, in gratitude for education, because he taught you to work and create, you began to destroy?

Dolmatovsky: Did you install the oil switches together with Gregory?

Zivert: Yes.

Dolmatovsky: What power?

Zivert: Two and a half million.

Dolmatovsky: And which were you installing?

Zivert: One million.

Dolmatovsky: A big difference. Why do you point out that he worked for 45 days and you for 22? Is it of no consequence what the size of the oil switches was?

Zivert: Yes, there was a big difference. The difference here is how a man does it. If a man comes along and keeps his hands in his pockets, snuffs tobacco and says, nobody do anything and I will do it alone. And here nine people stood around him and he alone did it. That is no work. When I installed machines, all the nine men worked.

The President: Has the Defence any more questions?

Defence: No.

The President: Have the accused any questions?—No. Has the Prosecution any questions?

Vyshinsky: And so you, working on State service, as an employee in a Soviet State enterprise, a power station, carried out a series of actions which we are compelled now to qualify, describe and define as wrecking. Is that so?

Zivert: As wrecking.

Vyshinsky: Thy consisted in that you delayed and hindered the installation of the oil circuit-breakers, transformers, that you deliberately acted in such a way that as the result of these actions, the accumulator segments were pierced and it was put out of action?

Zivert: Yes.

Vyshinsky: Thirdly, that during that period you frequently met Thornton privately, and received money from him for this work. Is that right?

Zivert: Yes.

Vyshinsky: So on one side of the scales were your position, your relations with Thornton, your improved material condition, and on the other side of the scales were the interests of the proletarian State, the interests of socialist construction. Which of these did you choose?

Zivert: The worst.

Vyshinsky: Can we say that in essence you betrayed the interests of the proletarian fatherland?

Zivert: Yes.

Vyshinsky: Do you admit it?

Zivert: I admit it.

Braude: How long did Thornton stay at the Ivanovo Power Station after he had given you the money?

Zivert: He left the same day.

Braude: So he was not there during that year when you were committing wrecking?

Zivert: He used to come.

Braude: Did the wrecking activity take place in his absence?

Zivert: Elliot was appointed to look after it.

Braude: What did he do—check up, give instructions?

Zivert: Mr. Elliott was there, who gave instructions.

Braude: But you were afraid?

Zivert: I was afraid.

The President: Be seated, please, accused Zivert.

Gregory: I want the court to listen to my statement.

The President: Certainly.

Gregory: This man Zivert is fouling my reputation and you are taking his statement without proof. Is that fair towards me?

The President: Translate to Gregory that we have heard the testimony of the accused Zivert, and now we will hear the explanation of Gregory. He will know by our decision whom we believe.

Gregory: I went to Dnieprostroy to erect some very large switches. These switches are the largest switches that have ever been made by our company. The largest switches erected in Russia. Now, when I left Moscow office, they told me that they were the largest switches going in Russia and that in the past no switches of ours had broken down. Therefore they wanted me to take every care and see to every part of the erection myself. Although that meant far more work for myself, it meant my getting into the tanks in the very hottest part of the year. But still, for my own reputation, and the reputation of the firm, and the reliability of the plant I went into the switches and saw to every part of the work myself. Now, I am coming to the part which I think affects Zivert. Zivert wanted to do some of these switches himself in another sub-station. I had never met him before and I did not know him. I could not place confidence in him, but found out later that the man was better than I first estimated him. Before leaving, I came down to Dnieprostroy for temporary work. From there I went to Dzerzhinka, which was the plant I really came to work for. While I was at Dnieprostroy I completed one switch. Another switch was completed, and there were two switches half finished. Now, that really amounted to three switches fully completed. That is from the 16th of July 1932, to the 3rd of September. Now I would like to point out to the President this: that in the beginning there was a lot of work being done at Dnieprostroy. The oil filters necessary to the job were very difficult to obtain. So it really amounted to this, that in spite of the delays there were three switches completed in 48 days. These switches were 45 tons each.

So now I will leave that to the technical experts to judge whether those switches were done in good time, and whether if done in a shorter time, they would be done properly. Will you please thank the President for listening to me.

The President: The Court will now adjourn for 20 minutes. *(Court adjourns at 7:50 p.m.)*

* * *

Commandant: Please rise. The Court is coming.

The President: Please be seated.

Accused Sukhoruchkin, come to the witness stand. Give us the main points of your biography.

Sukhoruchkin: I was born in 1894, on May 30, in the village of Novo Pavlovskaya, in the former Tersky Region. My father was a trader. I passed through three grades of the village school after which, at the instructions of the local priest, I was sent by my father to the Missionary Theological Seminary near the town of Vladikavkaz (now Orjonikidze). I spent 8 years there, till 1913. On graduating from the seminary, I was a teacher for two years. After that, at the end of 1915, I came to Moscow, where I became a student at the Moscow Commercial Institute and intended to study. At the beginning of 1916 along with study which I had already started, I began to work. At that time there existed the so-called Zemgor Union, uniting the Zemstvo and the towns, for the organization of engineering and technical detachments. I worked as a sorter in the military stores for about six months, after which I was taken into one of the detachments which worked later round Baranovichi Station near Minsk. In this detachment I worked till the middle of 1917. In the middle of 1917 I returned again to Moscow to continue my studies in the Institute, but owing to financial reasons I had to go to work again. I started working in the Moscow State Savings Bank as accountant. I worked in the Moscow Savings Bank until the beginning of 1919 and took part in public life, particularly in trade union work. Therefore in January 1919 at the All-Union Congress I was elected a member of the Central Committee of the union as a representative of the Savings Bank. In the Central Committee of the union I worked till the end of 1919, and then, as a student, I was called up for service in the Red Army. I was in the Red Army one year in the 5th Reserve Rifle Regiment in Moscow. For three or four months I was in the ranks and the remainder of the time I worked in the office. At the end of 1920 as a student I was released by decree from the

Red Army to continue my education in the Institute. I returned again to the Moscow Commercial Institute which was then called the Karl Marx Institute of National Economy, and instead of continuing my studies in the faculty of economics, where I was registered formerly, and where I previously worked, I changed to a newly organized faculty, the so-called faculty of electrical industry. On this faculty I studied from 1920 to the end of 1924. In February 1925, I received a diploma as engineer and entered the service of the Moges, namely, the First Moscow Power Station. At the First Moscow Power Station I worked from 1925 to the day of my arrest. I consecutively occupied the following positions. I worked one year in the boiler department, and the rest of the time till December 1, 1931, I worked in the electro-technical department, successively occupying the following positions: at first engineer of the electrical department, then from about the middle of 1929 assistant manager of the electro-technical department, and from about the middle of 1930 I worked as head of the electro-technical department. On December 1, 1931, I was appointed chief of the station and on March 1, 1932, in connection with the reorganization which took place at the station, I was appointed chief of the operating department in which I worked till the day of my arrest.

The President: Comrade Vyshinsky, have you any questions to ask the accused?

Vyshinsky: Yes. What was your position when you were arrested?

Sukhoruchkin: I was chief of the operating department.

Vyshinsky: Chief of the operating department in the power station—is that a pretty responsible post?

Sukhoruchkin: Yes, a very responsible post.

Vyshinsky: From the point of view of the work and existence of the power station, how could this responsibility be described?

Sukhoruchkin: Actually, it represented the ultimate authority.

Vyshinsky: It might be said that the fate of the station was in your hands?

Sukhoruchkin: Yes.

Vyshinsky: Were all the main, important levers of the power-station consequently in your hands also?

Sukhoruchkin: Yes, that was so.

Vyshinsky: What more exactly were your duties as head of the operating department of the station?

Sukhoruchkin: Concretely, my duties as head of the operating department were as follows: to see to the reliable and economical working of all the equipment at the station.

Vyshinsky: Did you carry out these duties or not?

Sukhoruchkin: No, I did not.

Vyshinsky: And your second duty?

Sukhoruchkin: My second duty was to look after the work of the staff of the station.

Vyshinsky: The operating work?

Sukhoruchkin: Yes.

Vyshinsky: Did you carry out this duty conscientiously?

Sukhoruchkin: I carried out this duty as far as possible.

Vyshinsky: And were there many possiblities for you?

Sukhoruchkin: In this matter, the possibilities were probably less than in regard to the first point because the selection of the staff was not entirely in my hands.

Vyshinsky: Correct. And the supervision of the work of the staff?

Sukhoruchkin: The supervision of the work of the staff was in my charge.

Vyshinsky: In this matter, did you conscientiously carry out this duty in the interests of the station, in the interests of the State, when directing the work of the staff put under your charge?

Sukhoruchkin: I cannot say that I carried it out in full.

Vyshinsky: Here also not in full. Further, what were your duties connected with the installation?

Sukhoruchkin: As head of the operating department, I was not directly responsible for the installation work. We had an installation and repair department which looked after the installation and repair of equipment.

Vyshinsky: So you had nothing to do with installations?

Sukhoruchkin: Nothing whatever.

Vyshinsky: And how are we to understand your deposition made at the preliminary investigation, that as engineer of the distributing department you superintended the installation of three-phase transformers and supervised the work at the Shatura Station in particular? How is that to be understood?

Sukhoruchkin: There is a misunderstanding here. I was head of the operating department after March 1932. The station was reorganized.

Vyshinsky: And before that?

Sukhoruchkin: Before that I worked in the distributing department and you should remember that before this reorganization, the distributing department and other departments which existed at the station, such as the boiler department and generator department, carried out both the operative work and the installation and repairs.

Vyshinsky: Had you anything to do with installation at that time?

Sukhoruchkin: Yes, I had.

Vyshinsky: So you were directly connected with installation work before March 1932?

Sukhoruchkin: Yes.

Vyshinsky: Further, when did you become assistant manager of the distributing department?

Sukhoruchkin: About the middle of 1929.

Vyshinsky: Then you were occupied with questions of the operation of the station, were you?

Sukhoruchkin: Yes.

Vyshinsky: What did you supervise?

Sukhoruchkin: I looked after the proper operation of the electrical equipment of the station. In particular, I was directly in charge of the distributing station and the frequency converters and the motors. Besides that I took turns on duty at the station.

Vyshinsky: Are all these four duties at the power station, in the operation of the station, responsible duties?

Sukhoruchkin: Yes, they are responsible duties.

Vyshinsky: In giving your opinion of your activity in these duties, can you say that you carried them out conscientiously, or that here also you exhibited shortcomings?

Sukhoruchkin: Of course, I cannot say that I carried them out conscientiously.

Vyshinsky: You cannot say so. Finally, and in particular, as head of the operating department recently were you responsible for the whole of the power station, both the distributing section and the boiler department, although other individuals were at the head of these sections? Who was in charge of the distributing section and who was in charge of the boiler department?

Sukhoruchkin: Do you want their names?

Vyshinsky: Yes, if you can give them.

Sukhoruchkin: We had three departments: the boiler department, the generator department and the distributing department. Engineer Kovalev was in charge of the boiler department. Recently engineer Lukashevsky was in charge of the generator department. From March 1, 1932, to March 1, 1933, it was engineer Krasheninnikov.

Vyshinsky: So Krasheninnikov was head of the generator department? But who was in charge of the distributing department?

Sukhoruchkin: Engineer Yazunsky was in charge of the distributing department.

Vyshinsky: Is this Krasheninnikov the one who is in the dock?

Sukhoruchkin: Yes.

Vyshinsky: And what did Zorin do?

Sukhoruchkin: He worked in Mosenergo.

Vyshinsky: Did his work have any connection with your work?

Sukhoruchkin: It was connected to the extent that he was a turbine specialist and participated in the investigation of breakdowns and planning the repairs required.

Vyshinsky: Now let us pass on to these breakdowns. At the First Moscow Electric Power Station, were there any breakdowns in 1931, let us say?

Sukhoruchkin: Of course there were breakdowns, but I cannot say exactly at present what breakdowns took place.

Vyshinsky: If I remind you of a few dates, you, as head of the operating department, will recollect. Take, for example, the breakdowns at the First Moscow Power Station on March 9, 1931, May 10, 1931, June 16, 1931 and November 1931.

Sukhoruchkin: There were breakdowns, but at present I cannot remember exactly, without the documents, nor can I state what their nature was.

Vyshinsky: Were these breakdowns investigated from the point of view of the causes which gave rise to them, or was no such investigation made? In all the breakdowns, were the causes ascertained or were they not?

Sukhoruchkin: In the majority of cases, the causes of the breakdowns were ascertained, especially in the larger breakdowns, because usually a commission was formed, with the participation of the Mosenergo organization, to discover the causes.

Vyshinsky: It seems to me that the head of the operating department is responsible for analysing the causes and establishing the facts and causes of the breakdowns. Or isn't it his concern?

Sukhoruchkin: Undoubtedly it is his concern.

Vyshinsky: Consequently, in all breakdowns the causes of these breakdowns should have been ascertained, because there cannot be a breakdown without a cause. Or could there be a breakdown without a cause?

Sukhoruchkin: There are sometimes complicated breakdowns.

Vyshinsky: When can't the causes of the breakdowns be ascertained because they are so complicated?

Sukhoruchkin: There were such breakdowns.

Vyshinsky: For example?

Sukhoruchkin: I don't remember just now, but all breakdowns which take place at the Mosenergo Station are recorded and investigated by the breakdown department of the Mosenergo organization and I remember that breakdowns did take place not only at our station but at other stations, when it was pointed out that the causes had not been discovered.

Vyshinsky: So there were a number of cases when the causes of the breakdowns were not discovered by your apparatus, by your staff. Can you say that this was so because they were complicated breakdowns, or because no great interest was taken in the causes?

Sukhoruchkin: I cannot say that no interest was taken.

Vyshinsky: But you also cannot say the opposite?

Sukhoruchkin: (No reply)

Vyshinsky: Can you mention even one case in which the causes were so complicated that it was impossible to ascertain them and in which the official statement declared that these causes had not been discovered owing to their being so complicated?

Sukhoruchkin: It is difficult to remember.

Vyshinsky: Then here is what I wanted to ask you. Do you remember the breakdown on generators Nos. 26 and 27?

Sukhoruchkin: Yes, I remember.

Vyshinsky: Were these breakdowns accidental, not depending on someone's malicious intent, or were they the direct result of malicious intent on the part of someone?

Sukhoruchkin: The breakdowns on turbines 26 and 27 took place before December 1, 1931, and it was only the last breakdown on turbine No. 27 that took place in 1932. Before December 1, 1931, I was not directly in charge of the turbines as I was head of the distributing department, but I remember the breakdowns on these turbines.

Vyshinsky: So I ask you: Were these breakdowns the result of somebody's malicious intent or of some other circumstances?

Sukhoruchkin: Which breakdowns do you mean? I remember the breakdown with the blades.

Vyshinsky: The last breakdown on generator No. 27.

Sukhoruchkin: The last breakdown in 1932?

Vyshinsky: Yes.

Sukhoruchkin: The blades flew off the turbine.

Vyshinsky: Why did they fly off?

Sukhoruchkin: In my opinion, owing to the poor quality of the blades supplied by the firm.

Vyshinsky: So it was not the malicious intent of someone on the staff of the station?

Sukhoruchkin: I cannot give an exact reply to that question because I was not directly in charge of the repair of this turbine. It is possible that some mistakes were made in repairing the turbine.

Vyshinsky: Tell us, please, did you personally carry out any acts of a wrecking nature at this station?

Sukhoruchkin: I did.

Vyshinsky: Possibly it was on just this turbine No. 27, of which I spoke?

Sukhoruchkin: Yes, turbine No. 27.

Vyshinsky: And maybe on turbine No. 26 of which I spoke?

Sukhoruchkin: Yes, turbine No. 26.

Vyshinsky: Perhaps you will be good enough to state exactly what these acts were?

Sukhoruchkin: My wrecking was done not on the turbines but actually on the generators connected with these turbines. These generators were connected with the switchboard by a single-phase cable. In order to damage these cables I personally grounded the sheathing of the single-phase lead-sheathed cable on both machines.

Vyshinsky: How did you do it?

Sukhoruchkin: It is very easy to ground it. It must be admitted that in general the laying of these single-phase lead-sheathed cables was not entirely satisfactory at the station.

Vyshinsky: Who put them up?

Sukhoruchkin: That was back in 1929-1930.

Vyshinsky: Did you take part in it?

Sukhoruchkin: At that time I was assistant manager of the electro-technical department and this had nothing to do with me.

Vyshinsky: Whom did it have to do with?

Sukhoruchkin: At that time the head of the electro-technical department was Yazykov.

Vyshinsky: How did you ground these cables?

Sukhoruchkin: The single-phase cables have a cardboard packing which is put between the cable and the iron shelf. To ground it you either move the cable a little or move the packing a little from under the cable. You move the cable a little bit so that it touches the supports of the shelves and then you can ground it.

Vyshinsky: And what exactly did you do?

Sukhoruchkin: I moved the packing away from the cable.

Vyshinsky: Tell us how you did this so that it will be comprehensible to laymen.

Sukhoruchkin: I simply moved the packing a little so that the cable was no longer lying on the cardboard packing but on the iron shelf.

Vyshinsky: You said at the preliminary investigation: "I personally short-circuited the lead cover of the single-phase cables of generators No. 26 and No. 27 with an iron rod."

Sukhoruchkin: That was not an exact expression. If you take my deposition which I signed, it says there that the grounding was done by making a contact with an iron shelf and not a rod.

Vyshinsky: It was inaccurate editing.

Sukhoruchkin: No, it was simply a typist's error.*

Vyshinsky: Inaccurate editing or a typist's error, but you effected the grounding of the cables by making the single-phase cable touch an iron shelf, didn't you?

Sukhoruchkin: Yes.

Vyshinsky: Did a breakdown take place?

Sukhoruchkin: A breakdown did not take place, but the cable was damaged.

Vyshinsky: And a damaged cable is not a breakdown?

Sukhoruchkin: It is hardly a breakdown.

Vyshinsky: But was it a breakdown in the sense that the work of the station stopped?

Sukhoruchkin: No.

Vyshinsky: Why?

Sukhoruchkin: Because the workers noticed it in time.

Vyshinsky: What did the workers do?

Sukhoruchkin: They informed the foreman of the electro-technical department, and steps were taken to repair the cable.

Vyshinsky: But what were your motives for carrying out this wrecking act?

Sukhoruchkin: I committed this wrecking act on the instructions of engineer Thornton after a conversation which I had with him approximately in October 1931.

Vyshinsky: In October 1931, after a conversation with Thornton, you decided to carry out a diversional act of wrecking, did you not?

Sukhoruchkin: Yes.

Vyshinsky: What was this conversation?

Sukhoruchkin: It was prepared for by my previous connection with Thornton.

Vyshinsky: What connection? Where did it begin? Of how long a time and on what basis?

Sukhoruchkin: My connection with Thornton was formed and

* In Russian, the word for shelf is "polka" and the word for rod is "palka."

my work under his instructions took place at the beginning of 1928.

Vyshinsky: So it was a connection lasting many years?

Sukhoruchkin: Yes.

Vyshinsky: Tell us about it more in detail, but only the part referring to the subject with which we are concerned, namely, your counter-revolutionary work.

Sukhoruchkin: This connection consisted in the fact that from the end of 1927 I carried out Thornton's instructions, especially in regard to wrecking. In carrying out these commissions and on the basis of the conversation which we had in October 1931, when I discussed with Thornton possible wrecking acts, but of a nature which would not be obvious wrecking, he, being acquainted with the working of our power station, suggested that I should carry out this act. I did it.

Vyshinsky: When was this?

Sukhoruchkin: The conversation was in October 1931, and I carried out the act itself in December 1931.

Vyshinsky: Had you such conversations previously which logically resulted in such actions?

Sukhoruchkin: Yes, there were such conversations.

Vyshinsky: Tell us, please. Was the first transformer group installed and tested in December-January 1930-31?

Sukhoruchkin: Yes, it was.

Vyshinsky: What can you tell us about this?

Sukhoruchkin: I can tell you this about it: The installation of the transformer group took place in absolutely abnormal conditions owing to the following causes: This group of transformers should have been put into operation in 1930-31 at the latest. But the firm supplied the equipment with great delay. This delay applied particularly to the transformer regulators and the oil pipe lines. Owing to this delay, this group of transformers was installed in the winter of 1930, and as they were very necessary, it was neverthelesss decided to switch over from the old transformers to the newly installed ones at the end of 1930 and the beginning of 1931. This group of transformers was actually connected up, but under very difficult circumstances.

Vyshinsky: What were your actions in regard to this? Oughtn't you to have examined the condition of the equipment on the completion of the installation?

Sukhoruchkin: Yes, I ought to have examined it.

Vyshinsky: And did you?

Sukhoruchkin: Yes, I did.

Vyshinsky: You examined it? But perhaps you have forgotten? Perhaps you did not examine it?

Sukhoruchkin: With regard to the first transformer group, as far as I remember, there was no breakdown. That took place when connecting up the second transformer group. That was already in October 1932.

Vyshinsky: Let us get clear on this question. Do you remember your deposition of March 23? You probably can remember it. You were asked about the second transformer group. After the completion of the installation of the second transformer group, was there a breakdown or not?

Sukhoruchkin: Yes, there was.

Vyshinsky: What was this breakdown?

Sukhoruchkin: When testing this transformer group, especially when testing the transformer regulator, there was a short circuit inside the oil circuit-breaker and the connections burned out.

Vyshinsky: Why?

Sukhoruchkin: Because oil had not been put into two of the oil circuit-breakers.

Vyshinsky: Nevertheless, was the group put into operation?

Sukhoruchkin: The test was made under such conditions.

Vyshinsky: And the result?

Sukhoruchkin: The result was that a breakdown took place, owing to which this transformer group was put into the circuit with a delay of about a day, on the one hand; and on the other hand, as the bakelite insulators were burned, there is no doubt that the reliability of the transformer group was reduced.

Vyshinsky: So we can sum up your evidence as follows: With regard to generators 25 and 27, by making a contact with the iron shelf you damaged the insulators, owing to which a breakdown would have taken place, had it not been averted by the vigilance of the workers.

Sukhoruchkin: Yes.

Vyshinsky: Was this done deliberately?

Sukhoruchkin: Yes.

Vyshinsky: At the end of the installation of the second transformer group in October 1931, there was a breakdown because the containers were not filled with oil—and was this also the result of your deliberate action?

Sukhoruchkin: Yes.

Vyshinsky: Consisting in that you deliberately did not check up on the condition of the containers?

Sukhoruchkin: Yes.

Vyshinsky: So there are two definite acts of wrecking?

Sukhoruchkin: Yes.

Vyshinsky: Now with regard to the fourth switchboard. How did the matter stand on the work for ventilating the fourth switchboard? What can you tell us about this?

Sukhoruchkin: On this question I can say that in the basement of the fourth switchboard there were many power cables which heated up very much. Ventilation had to be arranged for this. I did not arrange for making such ventilation, or rather I delayed the making of it.

Vyshinsky: For how long?

Sukhoruchkin: According to the latest information I have this ventilation should have been carried out about March.

Vyshinsky: For how long did you delay it?

Sukhoruchkin: For about two months.

Vyshinsky: Is that all, or do you remember anything else deserving the attention of the Court?

Sukhoruchkin: Yes, I can remember a good deal more.

Vyshinsky: Well, let us continue this deplorable list of breakdowns committed by a State employee, by a person responsible for the condition of the power station. Let us continue. The breakdown on November 22, 1932?

Sukhoruchkin: On November 22, 1932, there was really a big breakdown which put out the lights almost everywhere in Moscow. The machine supplying the needs of the station itself went out of action because measures were not taken to put the whole water supply to the station in order. As a result a turbine blade was forced back, the rotor was shifted out of place, the thrust bearing was damaged and the turbine went out of operation.

Vyshinsky: One or two?

Sukhoruchkin: In this accident, one went directly out of operation.

Vyshinsky: What number?

Sukhoruchkin: No. 17. But besides that, owing to the same insufficient water supply the blades were greatly scaled, owing to which the turbines had to be opened up because vibration could be observed. There was turbine No. 24, and as far as I remember, No. 21 or 22.

Vyshinsky: So it was three turbines—17, 22 and 24?

Sukhoruchkin: Yes.

Vyshinsky: That was a big breakdown. The fourth case. In order to finish, perhaps you will tell us of the fifth breakdown on the boiler equipment, when breakdowns were also caused owing to a number of your actions?

Sukhoruchkin: Yes, that took place.

Vyshinsky: And what did it consist in?

Sukhoruchkin: It was as follows: In connection with the fact that a number of new consumers of heat energy were attached to our station, it was undoubtedly necessary to prepare carefully the old boiler equipment for the heating season of 1932-33. As, in my opinion, the 12,000 kilowatt non-condensing turbine which was being installed at the station could not as yet be used during this heating season, these measures were all the more necessary.

But in spite of this I did not take the necessary steps in two respects. On the one hand, as head of the operating department, I did not press the question of the necessity of putting the chemical water purifiers in order, of periodically cleaning the old boilers, and on the other hand I did not raise in time the question of putting the third boiler, the old boiler, into operation.

Vyshinsky: When was the old third boiler installed? Under normal conditions?

Sukhoruchkin: Not normal conditions.

Vyshinsky: Under breakdown conditions?

Sukhoruchkin: Yes. Besides that, this made big repairs necessary, especially to the old boilers after we installed the supplementary third boiler. That is all about the boiler equipment.

Vyshinsky: And was all this done deliberately?

Sukhoruchkin: Yes.

Vyshinsky: Intentionally?

Sukhoruchkin: Yes.

Vyshinsky: For wrecking purposes? To undermine the strength of our economy?

Sukhoruchkin: Yes.

Vyshinsky: To make the supply of electricity more difficult?

Sukhoruchkin: Yes, that was the case.

Vyshinsky: To undermine production?

Sukhoruchkin: Yes.

Vyshinsky: At whose instructions?

Sukhoruchkin: At the instructions of the representative of Metro-Vickers and of engineer Thornton.

Vyshinsky: Did you receive any money?

Sukhoruchkin: Yes, I did.

Vyshinsky: How much?

Sukhoruchkin: As far as I remember, I received in all about 2,500 rubles in Soviet currency and 350 rubles in Torgsin checks.

Vyshinsky: I have no further questions at present.

The President: Comrade Roginsky, have you any questions?

Roginsky: Accused Sukhoruchkin, tell us, in addition to the testimony which you have just given to Comrade Vyshinsky, whether you had planned acts of diversion in case of war?

Sukhoruchkin: Yes, there were such plans.

Roginsky: What acts of diversion were planned?

Sukhoruchkin: To put the switchboards out of action and thus paralyse the work of the station.

Roginsky: To paralyse the work of the whole power station?

Sukhoruchkin: Depending on which switchboard was put out of order, it meant that the paralysing might be partial.

Roginsky: And what did you intend?

Sukhoruchkin: We intended to put either the 6,600 volt switchboard or the 2,200 volt switchboard out of order.

Roginsky: And the result?

Sukhoruchkin: The result was we might have left all consumers attached to the 6,600 volt switchboard or all consumers attached to the 2,200 volt switchboard without current.

Roginsky: Which consumers were attached to the 6,600 volt switchboard?

Sukhoruchkin: Light consumers and also works and factories.

Roginsky: Works, factories, and what else?

Sukhoruchkin: Important consumers were also connected, like barracks and the Government House.

Roginsky: So this plan provided for putting out of order the very part of the power station which supplies current to the most responsible or best guarded sections?

Sukhoruchkin: It would be more exact to say responsible.

Roginsky: Would a factory like the Hammer and Sickle Factory happen to be among these enterprises to be put out of operation?

Sukhoruchkin: Yes, it was connected to the 6,600 volt switchboard.

Roginsky: And the Spartacus Factory?

Sukhoruchkin: I don't remember the Spartacus Factory.

Roginsky: Was the Kremlin connected up?

Sukhoruchkin: It was.

Roginsky: And the Krutitsky Barracks?

Sukhoruchkin: Yes.

Roginsky: And the Central Aero-Hydrodynamic Institute?

Sukhoruchkin: Yes.

Roginsky: The Dzerzhinsky Barracks?

Sukhoruchkin: Yes.

Roginsky: All the radio stations?

Sukhoruchkin: Yes.

Roginsky: That is a total of the enterprises which should have been withdrawn from the sphere of current supply according to your plan.

Sukhoruchkin: That is so.

Roginsky: Tell us, please, whether this plan was drawn up by you personally.

Sukhoruchkin: I drew it up together with Thornton.

Roginsky: Under what circumstances?

Sukhoruchkin: Approximately in this way: I had two conversations with Thornton on this question, namely on the 6,600 volt switchboard.

Roginsky: Where did these conversations take place?

Sukhoruchkin: One conversation took place in the 6,600 volt switchboard building itself, about the beginning of 1930. As far as I remember, it was in February, when we were examining this room.

Roginsky: How was it that the accused Thornton was in the switchboard building?

Sukhoruchkin: He got in in this way: This switchboard was new. He was not acquainted with it and therefore on one of the occasions when he visited the station, as far as I remember, in February, he asked me to show it to him. As the switchboard building can be visited only with the permission of the directors, I asked for permission from the then technical director of the plant.

Roginsky: Who was that?

Sukhoruchkin: Ryazanov. Together with him I went to the switchboard building and showed him every part of it.

Roginsky: Another question in connection with this Ryazanov. What happened to him?

Sukhoruchkin: He was arrested in connection with the trial of the "Industrial Party."

Roginsky: As a wrecker?

Sukhoruchkin: Yes.

Roginsky: So you asked permission for Thornton to go with you to the switchboard building from Ryazanov, who was involved in the "Industrial Party" case and condemned as a wrecker, and went with him to the switchboard room!

Sukhoruchkin: Yes.

Roginsky: Well, did this visit have any concrete practical results?

Sukhoruchkin: The concrete practical results of this visit were that Thornton got a good knowledge of the switch-gear, starting from the bus-bar floor right down to the cable basement and the cable tunnel, after which he mentioned his idea, with which I agreed, that an easy act of diversion was possible precisely in connection with this switchboard.

Roginsky: What do you mean by an "easy" act of diversion?

Sukhoruchkin: I am speaking of an act of diversion easy to carry out.

Roginsky: But with serious results?

Sukhoruchkin: Yes, with serious results.

Roginsky: So this visit of yours together with Thornton to the switchboard building was used to discover the weakest and most vulnerable places in the switchboard arrangements and for planning definite acts of diversion?

Sukhoruchkin: Yes, that was so.

The President: Not "weak" places but vulnerable places?

Roginsky: Yes, vulnerable places?

Sukhoruchkin: Yes.

Roginsky: Had Thornton anything to do with the work of the station at this time?

Sukhoruchkin: Yes, he had. He did not work as installation engineer, but he often visited the station because even at this time it was planned to instal the first transformer group in 1930 for the central sub-station.

Roginsky: But at the time, the Metro-Vickers office or any of its employees had not yet carried out any immediate, practical work on the station, had they?

Sukhoruchkin: They had not.

Roginsky: This was still a plan for the future—the supply of equipment and its installation?

Sukhoruchkin: Yes.

Roginsky: When Thornton visited the power station, particularly the switchboard building, could it be connected in any way with the further work carried on by the Metro-Vickers Co. at this station?

Sukhoruchkin: It had no direct connection.

Roginsky: So this visit was not necessarily connected with the later work of Metro-Vickers?

Sukhoruchkin: No.

Roginsky: When did the second visit to the switchboard building take place?

Sukhoruchkin: I don't remember the second visit with Thornton to the 6,600 volt switchboard building.

Roginsky: What other visit do you remember?

Sukhoruchkin: I remember conversations on the question of this switchboard.

Roginsky: Was there one visit and were there further talks in regard to the switchboard?

Sukhoruchkin: Yes.

Roginsky: Very well. When were the plans for acts of diversion in the event of war prepared? At the time of this visit or during the course of further conversations?

Sukhoruchkin: A preliminary scheme was drawn up already at this visit. These talks were made more concrete at the second visit.

Roginsky: At the second visit? So there was a second visit?

Sukhoruchkin: Yes.

Roginsky: When was that?

Sukhoruchkin: At the end of 1931, in October.

Roginsky: How were the acts of diversion made more precise?

Sukhoruchkin: We had already had conversations on the actual possibilities of carrying them out. Here we decided on the methods by which it could be done.

Roginsky: So on the first visit you decided on the most vulnerable spots, you had a number of talks and finally at the end of 1931 you had a definite talk to discuss the methods of carrying out these acts of diversion. Is that so?

Sukhoruchkin: Yes.

Roginsky: Thus, we have so far established two lines of your wrecking activity. There were direct wrecking acts. Comrade Vyshinsky has established five or six such acts. The second line was the concrete preparation of a program or scheme for acts of diversion in case of war complications. Is that so?

Sukhoruchkin: Yes.

Roginsky: The third line was the deliberate and intentional concealment of defects in the equipment. Did that take place?

Sukhoruchkin: Yes, it also took place.

Roginsky: In order to be more precise, perhaps you will tell us of a few such cases of concealing defects in the equipment?

Sukhoruchkin: I can give the following facts: First, there were defects in the generators supplied by Metro-Vickers, due to unsatisfactory construction; then in the leads of the generator rotor and the oil safety switches of the generator.

Roginsky: Perhaps you will inform the Court more exactly how you managed to conceal these defects?

Sukhoruchkin: We did it by not making any claims on the firm.

Roginsky: You didn't make any claims?

Sukhoruchkin: No.

Roginsky: And were these defects put right? Or weren't they put right altogether?

Sukhoruchkin: They exist right up to the present time.

Roginsky: These defects still exist?

Sukhoruchkin: Yes.

Roginsky: Did the existence of these defects keep the station in a state of breakdown and does it still keep it so?

Sukhoruchkin: Not exactly.

Roginsky: Will you please explain?

Sukhoruchkin: There were such defects only in three generators installed at our station. Apart from this, these defects do not create a direct danger of a breakdown or stoppage.

Roginsky: I do not ask about an immediate danger, but about a dangerous state.

Sukhoruchkin: But the fact that owing to this the generators were frequently stopped for repairs and thus were apparently not entirely reliable of course shows that the new equipment, that is the three generators installed by Metro-Vickers, were unsatisfactory as to these parts.

Roginsky: So they were unsatisfactory? What other defects did you conceal and in what equipment?

Sukhoruchkin : There were also other defects in the transformer groups, especially the defects in the transformer regulators which also are working unsatisfactorily at the station right up to the present. No claim was made about them either.

Roginsky: Further?

Sukhoruchkin: In addition, regarding the transformer groups, no claims were made on the firm about the failure to fulfil contracts or the poor quality of the equipment supplied.

Roginsky: Very well. How did you succeed in your action, how did you cover up these defects?

Sukhoruchkin: Without question, it was easy for me to do it as I was head of the electro-technical department at the time and it depended on me whether the Mosenergo organization was informed of the defects or not.

Roginsky: So if defects were discovered, the presentation of claims had to go through your hands?

Sukhoruchkin: Yes, not only through my hands but it had to be sent by me.

Roginsky: And so you were able to stop the sending of any particular claim or complaint?

Sukhoruchkin: Yes.

Roginsky: And how did you explain the presence of these defects to the various people on the staff of the station?

Sukhoruchkin: They were simply put right as far as possible by the station staff itself.

Roginsky: And thus the defects . . . .

Sukhoruchkin: And thus the defects in reality remained undisclosed.

Roginsky: So there were three lines mapped out: direct wrecking activity, a plan of action in case of war and the deliberate concealing of a number of most serious defects in the equipment supplied, which created a danger of breakdowns. Is that so?

Sukhoruchkin: Yes.

Roginsky: And for all this activity you were paid the sum which you mentioned in reply to Comrade Vyshinsky?

Sukhoruchkin: Yes.

Roginsky: May I put a question to Thornton?

The President: You may.

Roginsky (To Thornton): Did you hear the testimony?

Thornton: Yes.

Roginsky: Were you at the station?

Thornton: Yes.

Roginsky: Were you together with Sukhoruchkin in the switchboard building?

Thornton: I was also there before that.

Roginsky: And were you together with him?

Thornton: Yes.

Roginsky: And did the conversations which have been related here by accused Sukhoruchkin take place?

Thornton: They never took place.

Roginsky: And did you give the money which Sukhoruchkin says you gave?

Thornton: No.

Roginsky: I have no further questions for Thornton and no questions for Sukhoruchkin.

The President: Has the Defence any questions?

Schwartz: Accused Sukhoruchkin. I want to ask you the following: before you went to work in the Moscow State Power Station and Mosenergo, had you carried on a great deal of trade union work? Let us examine the beginning of your work in Mosenergo. Was it in 1925? What was your position?

Sukhoruchkin: Engineer in the boiler house.

Schwartz: Was this work carried on honestly and conscientiously or not?

Sukhoruchkin: Yes, up to that time I worked honestly.

Schwartz: Tell us, about what year did you first meet Thornton?

Sukhoruchkin: I met him in 1926, but I was not acquainted with him.

Schwartz: And when did you become acquainted?

Sukhoruchkin: We became more closely acquainted in 1927, about the middle of the year.

Schwartz: In the middle of 1927 you began to get more closely acquainted. Is it correct to say that before the middle of 1927 you worked honestly and conscientiously?

Sukhoruchkin: Yes, that was the case.

Schwartz: How did you get acquainted with Thornton? Under what circumstances, and who introduced you?

Sukhoruchkin: It was in connection with some business. In 1927 two three-phase transformers of Metro-Vickers Company were installed at the central sub-station of the First Moscow Station. The installation of these transformers was in charge of

Thornton as the installation engineer. I took part in installing these transformers, as engineer in the current distributing department under whose direction this central sub-station was operated.

Schwartz: Tell us, please, had you any other relations with Thornton in 1927 except business relations?

Sukhoruchkin: I had none, unless you consider that I had frequent conversations with him and informed him of various technical matters concerning our station.

Schwartz: Did you do this on your own initiative or at someone's request?

Sukhoruchkin: I replied to the questions which Thornton usually asked in his conversations.

Schwartz: Were these questions and answers of a non-secret character or, on the contrary, did you give him secret information?

Sukhoruchkin: I think it was not quite harmless.

Schwartz: Not quite harmless? Once you began to give such information, will you be so good as to tell us why and on what grounds you decided to give such information?

Sukhoruchkin: I decided to give this information because at that time I already knew Thornton well enough; we knew each other's political views rather well.

Schwartz: Did you continue to meet Thornton in 1928?

Sukhoruchkin: Yes.

Schwartz: And in 1929?

Sukhoruchkin: These meetings took place almost every year, beginning from 1927; but in 1927 he was working as installation engineer, and in the other years he visited our station fairly often and especially often up to about 1930. Up to 1930 they found it quite easy to get into our station because they had a pass to admit them.

Schwartz: Were there cases when Thornton rendered you some services which relieved you of some difficulties or misunderstandings at work? Say the case of the grindstone for grinding down the commutator of the generator.

Sukhoruchkin: There was such a case. It was a case when we had only one grindstone for the commutator of the generator supplied by this firm. We lost this stone, owing to which we could not order similar stones in the Soviet Union on the same pattern.

Schwartz: In short, Thornton got you a grindstone?

Sukhoruchkin: Yes.

Schwartz: The second case with the welding apparatus. Did Thornton get it?

Sukhoruchkin: He did.

Schwartz: Why did he try to render these services? What was the reason? And incidentally, do you remember in what year these two cases took place?

Sukhoruchkin: As far as I remember, the case of the grindstone was in 1931. I don't remember exactly. But the case of the welding apparatus was in 1932.

Schwartz: That is to say, at the time when you were on more or less friendly and close terms.

Sukhoruchkin: Yes.

Schwartz: Did you work for a long time in a trade union organization?

Sukhoruchkin: Yes.

Schwartz: Will you explain how it came about that you became involved in such criminal activity?

Sukhoruchkin: Although I worked in a trade union organization, in reality, my sentiments were anti-Soviet.

Schwartz: Why?

Sukhoruchkin: There were reasons for this. First, when I came to the station I found myself surrounded by engineers who were later either expelled from the station or were arrested in the case of the "Industrial Party" or were simply discharged. On the other hand, this took place at the time of the N.E.P., when, so to say, it seemed that the Soviet Government was making a definite backward move. All this urged me on. Besides that, my dissatisfaction with material conditions had some effect, because the prices in the stores at that time did not correspond to the salary we received.

Schwartz: Tell us—had you any desire to return to your previous work in the trade union, to honest work? Did you have any hesitations in this respect? If so, when, and how did they manifest themselves?

Sukhoruchkin: There were such hesitations, and these hesitations and regrets in my work, in my activities, probably became more pronounced at the time when it was clear that the program of the first Five-Year Plan was being carried out and that everything which had been decided on was being carried into practice. This showed that I had judged the Soviet Power very incorrectly.

Schwartz: Can we say that this criminal work was explained by your disbelief in the Soviet Power, and your hesitations, your turn towards an honest life was caused by the fact that you became convinced by obvious facts of the strengthening of the Soviet Power such as the fulfilment of the first Five-Year Plan and the entrance into the second Five-Year Plan?

Sukhoruchkin: That was so.

Schwartz: I have no more questions.

Braude: Sukhoruchkin, be so good as to explain. I did not quite understand. When you spoke of the causes of your anti-Soviet sentiments, you spoke of the N.E.P., of a turn to the Right. Why should a turn to the Right cause anti-Soviet feeling in you? I should think it would be just the opposite.

Sukhoruchkin: I don't quite understand the question.

Braude: You had anti-Soviet sentiments. These sentiments were not compatible with the N.E.P., but as we have seen, they were compatible with the carrying out of acts of diversion. I ask you, did your convictions agree with the commission of wrecking, of acts of diversion?

Sukhoruchkin: My convictions? Yes, they agreed with it.

Braude: Then why was Thornton necessary? He did not help you technically. Why was Thornton necessary when all this fitted in with your own sentiments?

Sukhoruchkin: I think that in this case, if I had not met with Thornton, probably I should not have taken the path which has brought me to the dock.

Braude: You are contradicting yourself.

Sukhoruchkin: This prompted me on.

Braude: From your point of view, which played the greater role—the meeting with Thornton, or, as you say, the money which Thornton gave you?

Sukhoruchkin: Private conversations with Thornton on general political questions influenced me most of all.

Braude: Did you try to line up with him, with his attitude to the N.E.P.?

Sukhoruchkin: (No reply.)

Schwartz: May I put a question to Thornton?

The President: Certainly.

Schwartz: Citizen Thornton, you have heard the testimony of Sukhoruchkin on the two cases when you gave him assistance at work. The first was when you obtained for him and for his institution two grindstones for grinding down the commutators of the machines.

Thornton: Yes, there was such a case.

Schwartz: The second case was when you obtained a welding apparatus, wasn't it?

Thornton: Yes.

Schwartz: Who ordered these grindstones and welding apparatus?

Thornton: He ordered them. It was done officially, backed up by an official record.

Schwartz: These two cases actually happened?

Thornton: Yes.

Schwartz: I have no further questions.

Sukhoruchkin (To the President): May I ask Thornton a question?

The President: You may.

Sukhoruchkin: Citizen Thornton, at whose request and at whose order were these grindstones and then the welding apparatus sent to the First Moscow Power Station?

Thornton: Apparently at your order. You said that you had no grindstones. We decided to get you the stones. We sent them not only to you but to Krassny Oktyabr. It was a slight act of courtesy. It is better for us, if you have the right tools.

Sukhoruchkin: At whose request was the welding apparatus sent?

Thornton: I think Sukhoruchkin himself asked for it.

Vyshinsky: I have a question for Thornton. Accused Thornton. did I understand you rightly to say that you sent these grindstones and welding apparatus not only to the First Moscow Power Station but also to a series of other enterprises?

Thornton: That is true about the grindstones, but only one welding apparatus was sent.

Vyshinsky: Were grindstones sent to a number of other enterprises?

Thornton: Yes.

Vyshinsky: What for? Why? Did you do it in the interests of your firm or at someone's orders?

Thornton: Not at anyone's order. It is better to send a grindstone to some institution so that they can grind down their commutator than for them to spoil it and say that the commutator was no good.

Vyshinsky: Was the commutator yours?

Thornton: The commutator belonged to the customer.

Vyshinsky: But was it part of the equipment supplied by your firm?

Thornton: Yes, of course.

Vyshinsky: Did you do this in the interests of your firm? Were you interested to see that your equipment was worked on with good grindstones, so that the shortcomings of treatment would not seem to be shortcomings in the equipment? Do I understand you correctly?

Thornton: Yes.

Vyshinsky: It was your interests which made you do it?

Thornton: Yes.

Vyshinsky: Did you send the welding apparatus as an advertisement, because it was in the interests of the firm to make the apparatus widely known?

Thornton: Yes.

Vyshinsky: So you were acting in the commercial interests of your firm?

Thornton: Yes.

Vyshinsky: I have no further questions for Thornton.

A question to Sukhoruchkin. Thornton was acting in the commercial interests of his firm in this case, in other cases he acted in the interests of other institutions. And you, Sukhoruchkin, in whose interests did you act in your wrecking work? You ought to answer this question plainly and clearly. You are a citizen of the Soviet country. In whose interests did you act, or, if you prefer, against whose interests? You are a Soviet citizen in State service. In whose interests did you act?

Sukhoruchkin: I acted against the interests of the Soviet Government.

Vyshinsky: The Government or the working people as a whole?

Sukhoruchkin: The working people as a whole.

Vyshinsky: And the Government?

Sukhoruchkin: Of the Soviet Union.

Vyshinsky: And whose interests did you uphold? In whose interests were you acting in such a way?

Sukhoruchkin: I was acting in the interests of the enemies of the Soviet Union.

Vyshinsky: You understand what responsibility you assumed by so doing?

Sukhoruchkin: Yes, I know.

Vyshinsky: So you consciously entered upon such actions, well understanding the consequences?

Sukhoruchkin: Yes.

Vyshinsky: I have no further questions.

The President: The Court will adjourn until 10 a.m.

[Signed] V. V. ULRICH
President of the Special Session of the
Supreme Court of the U.S.S.R.

A. F. KOSTYUSHKO
Secretary

MORNING SESSION, APRIL 15, 1933, 10.15 a.m.

Commandant: Please rise. The Court is coming.

The President: Be seated, please.

Monkhouse: May I make a statement about Sukhoruchkin's testimony?

The President: You may.

Monkhouse: I want to speak in English so as to be more exact.

The President: You may.

Monkhouse: After hearing the testimony of Sukhoruchkin and other Soviet citizens during yesterday and the day before. . .

The President: Do you want to make some explanation concerning Sukhoruchkin's testimony, or do you want to make a statement? Is it an explanation or a statement?

Monkhouse: An explanation.

The President: Concerning yourself?

Monkhouse: Concerning myself.

The President: Then you may continue so far as Sukhoruchkin's testimony is concerned. But what has the testimony of other Soviet citizens to do with it?

Monkhouse: Well, after the showing which Sukhoruchkin made last night, it is perfectly clear to me that this case is a frame-up against the Metro-Vickers, based on the evidence of terrorized prisoners.

The President: Accused Monkhouse, did Sukhoruchkin refer to you in his testimony or not?

Monkhouse: Yes, he referred to me.

The President: Then speak on that point, and the rest will speak for themselves. You are not a counsel for defence and every one of the accused has his own counsel, who will defend him.

Monkhouse: As I understand the law, I have the right to make a statement.

The President: It cannot be made now, but at the end of the Court's examination—in the final speeches every one of the accused will have the right to make the declarations he desires. This morning Krasheninnikov is to be examined, then Zorin, but not Monkhouse. When your turn comes, you will be able to make statements concerning the charges against you.

Monkhouse: I wish to continue, Sir, and to say that the evidence given by these persons, and I know from my own experience, when I was arrested and subjected to an eighteen hour examination. . .

The President: We shall examine you this evening or tomorrow morning. In so far as you are trying to make a statement on behalf of all the accused, I cannot allow you to speak. Therefore I call upon the accused Krasheninnikov, whom we shall now examine, and this evening, or tomorrow morning, you will have an opportunity to state what you find necessary concerning previous testimony.

Accused Krasheninnikov, will you please come here.

Comrade Vyshinsky, have you any questions to Krasheninnikov?

Vyshinsky: What position have you occupied, and where exactly?

Krasheninnikov: Recently?

Vyshinsky: Yes.

Krasheninnikov: Recently, from March 1, 1932, I was chief of the repair and installation department of the First Moscow State Power Station.

Vyshinsky: From what date?

Krasheninnikov: From March 1, 1932.

Vyshinsky: Until. . . ?

Krasheninnikov: Until the day of my arrest.

Vyshinsky: What were your duties in connection with this position?

Krasheninnikov: In the position I occupied it was my duty to carry out repairs and installations in the power station, in the whole station.

Vyshinsky: Repairs and installations of the whole power station?

Krasheninnikov: Yes.

Vyshinsky: And further?

Krasheninnikov: These were my major duties, as chief of the repair and installation department.

Vyshinsky: Consequently, the responsibility for installing turbo-generators Nos. 26 and 27, of which mention was made yesterday, lay upon you?

Krasheninnikov: I was responsible for the installation of turbines Nos. 26 and 27. At that time I was an engineer at the power station and carried out various commissions in the power station. In particular, since late in 1927 I was charged with the installation of old turbines and new turbines Nos. 26 and 27.

Vyshinsky: When were you entrusted with this work?

Krasheninnikov: Towards the end of 1927 and the beginning of 1928.

Vyshinsky: You were not yet chief of the repair and installation department then, were you?

Krasheninnikov: No, I was merely an engineer.

Vyshinsky: But in 1929?

Krasheninnikov: Some time in the middle of 1929 I was appointed foreman of the generator room of the power station.

Vyshinsky: At that time what were your duties in connection with the post you held?

Krasheninnikov: I was in charge of the repair of mechanical equipment and the operation of the same equipment.

Vyshinsky: And in 1930?

Krasheninnikov: At the end of 1930 I was appointed chief of the generator room of the power station.

Vyshinsky: And what were your duties as chief of the generator room?

Krasheninnikov: It was part of my duty as chief of the generator room to see to the operation and the repairs in the generator room and to control the staff working in the installation department.

Vyshinsky: Who was Ryazanov? What position did he occupy?

Krasheninnikov: Assistant director in charge of the technical section.

Vyshinsky: What was your official relation to him at that time?

Krasheninnikov: I was his subordinate.

Vyshinsky: Does that mean you worked under his immediate direction?

Krasheninnikov: Almost entirely under his immediate direction.

Vyshinsky: Who was your immediate superior?

Krasheninnikov: There was also the chief of the power station to whom I was formally subordinate, but I also carried out the orders of the assistant director.

Vyshinsky: Does that mean you were doubly subordinate: to the assistant director of the power station and to the director himself?

Krasheninnikov: Yes.

Vyshinsky: So that in this sense you were immediately subordinate to them?

Krasheninnikov: Yes.

Vyshinsky: When did Ryazanov leave the First Moscow State Electric Power Station?

Krasheninnikov: I do not remember exactly, but I think it was in the middle or at the beginning of 1931.

Vyshinsky: Under what circumstances?

Krasheninnikov: He was arrested in connection with the "Industrial Party" case.

Vyshinsky: Arrested in connection with the "Industrial Party" case. Did his arrest and prosecution come as a surprise to you, or did you perhaps expect it?

Krasheninnikov: It was unexpected.

Vyshinsky: So you were not aware of his participation in the counter-revolutionary organization of the "Industrial Party"?

Krasheninnikov: No, I was not.

Vyshinsky: And when did you become aware of the fact that there were persons at the First Moscow State Power Station who were carrying on counter-revolutionary wrecking work?

Krasheninnikov: I was brought into this work myself at the end of 1928 or beginning of 1929.

Vyshinsky: Was Ryazanov at the power station at that time?

Krasheninnikov: Yes.

Vyshinsky: Hence, your counter-revolutionary wrecking activities at the First Moscow Power Station began at the time when Ryazanov was still active in the power station. Is that so?

Krasheninnikov: Yes.

Vyshinsky: But you were not aware that he was one of the organizers of the counter-revolutionary group?

Krasheninnikov: No, I was not aware of it.

Vyshinsky: But at the end of 1928 and beginning of 1929 were you already a member of the group, or were you acting on your own?

Krasheninnikov: I was acting on my own.

Vyshinsky: And who was it that brought you into this work, and under what conditions? Under what circumstances did you take this criminal path?

Krasheninnikov: It was like this. I was working on the installation of turbines Nos. 26 and 27. I was in charge of this work. At the same time Jolley and two other engineers from Metro-Vickers, MacDonald and Jule, were engaged on the work. MacDonald and Jule did not speak Russian, but Jolley spoke Russian fairly well, even very well.

Vyshinsky: MacDonald—is he the one who is now being tried?

Krasheninnikov: Yes.

Vyshinsky: That is to say, during this period, 1928 and 1929, you were already acquainted with MacDonald?

Krasheninnikov: Yes.

Vyshinsky: And were you acquainted with Jolley?

Krasheninnikov: Yes. Ryazanov introduced me to Jolley, when he came to the power station, introduced him to me as the firm's engineer who was to carry out the installation of turbines at the power station.

Vyshinsky: I do not understand. What have Jolley and Ryazanov to do with it?

Krasheninnikov: Jolley was introduced to me by Ryazanov who, in his official capacity, called me into his office when Jolley arrived at the power station to carry out the installation work. At first, during the installation work, until the middle of the year, my relations with Jolley were very bad and strained, because Jolley thought that he alone was carrying out the installation work and that he was not obliged to give any consideration to the people at the power station. On these grounds hundreds of misunderstandings cropped up with him. Owing to Jolley's attitude towards me as the one supervising the installations, I on several occasions raised the question of the abnormal relations between us.

Vyshinsky: With whom did you raise the question?

Krasheninnikov: With Ryazanov.

Vyshinsky: And what did Ryazanov say?

Krasheninnikov: He advised me not to start a quarrel with Jolley, his motive being that it might upset the work of installation, for if we raised this question seriously before the firm, it would mean that other engineers of the firm would have to come from England, and that might hold up the installation for some time.

Vyshinsky: How did you interpret this conversation with Ryazanov?

Krasheninnikov: I interpreted it as it should be interpreted, namely, that the installation work itself should not be delayed; I thought that it would really be better for me to hold myself in check, to see to the installation work and thus make it possible to continue it and finish it in the stipulated time.

Vyshinsky: I do not understand you. I asked you the question: under what circumstances did you, Krasheninnikov, begin your wrecking work at the end of 1928 and beginning of 1929? But you have not answered this question.

Krasheninnikov: After that conversation with Ryazanov, I began to hold myself in check and allowed Jolley to direct the installation work.

Vyshinsky: What do you mean when you say, you began to hold yourself in check?

Krasheninnikov: I stopped making a fuss about hitches.

Vyshinsky: Did these hitches hinder the installation? Did you stop making a fuss about these hitches in order to avoid them?

Krasheninnikov: Yes, in order to avoid them.

Vyshinsky: Did Ryazanov say it was not worth while making a fuss?

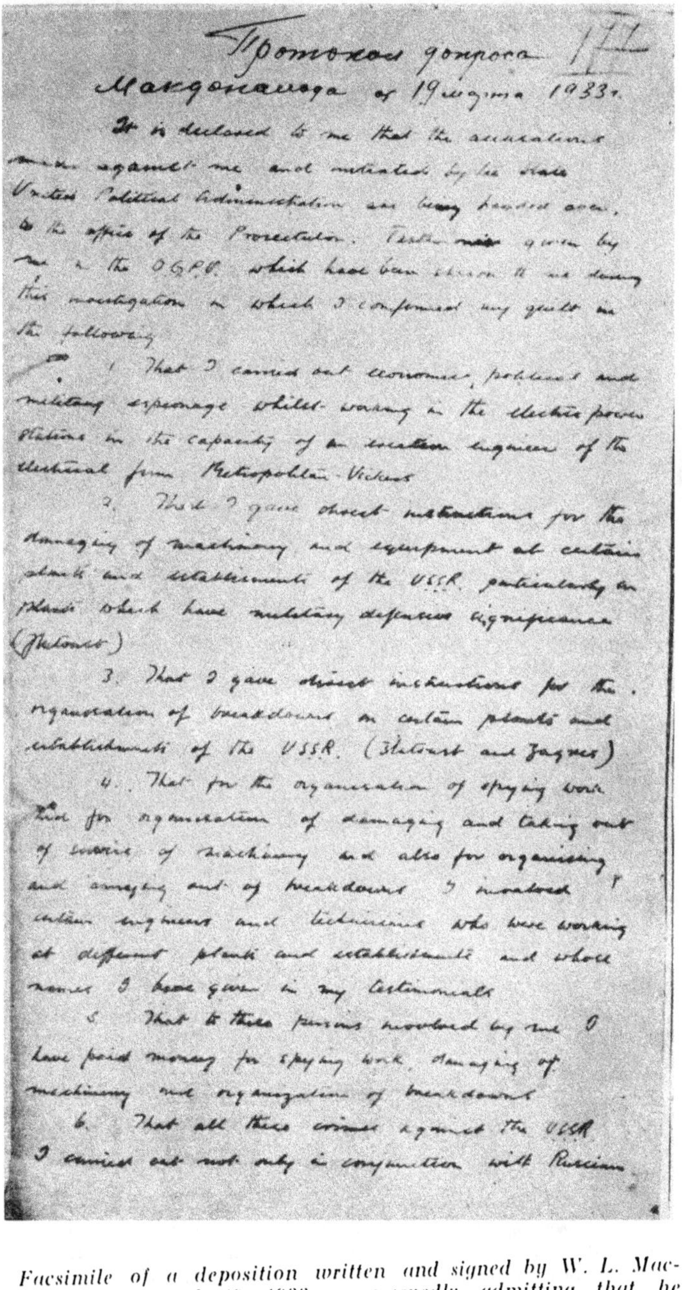

Протокол допроса 17

Макдональда от 19 марта 1933 г.

It is declared to me that the accusations made against me and initiated by the State United Political Administration are being handed over to the office of the Prosecutor. Testimonies given by me in the O.G.P.U. which have been shown to me during this investigation in which I confirmed my guilt in the following:

1. That I carried out economic, political and military espionage whilst working in the electric power stations in the capacity of an erection engineer of the electrical firm Metropolitan-Vickers

2. That I gave direct instructions for the damaging of machinery and equipment at certain plants and establishments of the USSR, particularly on plants which have military defensive significance (Zlatoust)

3. That I gave direct instructions for the organisation of breakdowns on certain plants and establishments of the USSR. (Zlatoust and Zagres)

4. That for the organisation of spying work and for organisation of damaging and taking out of service of machinery and also for organising and arranging out of breakdowns I involved certain engineers and technicians who were working at different plants and establishments and whose names I have given in my testimonials

5. That to these persons involved by me I have paid money for spying work, damaging of machinery and organization of breakdowns

6. That all these crimes against the USSR I carried out not only in conjunction with Russian

Facsimile of a deposition written and signed by W. L. MacDonald on March 19, 1933, unreservedly admitting that he committed acts of espionage, wrecking and bribery.

(Continued on next page)

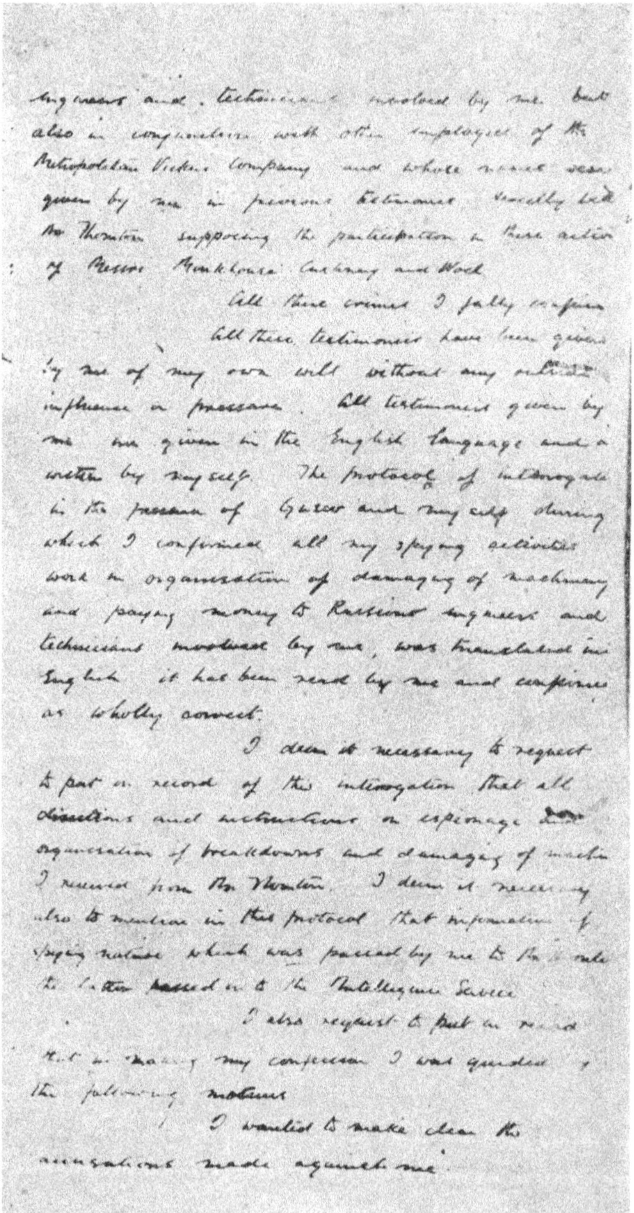

engineers and technicians involved by me but also in conjunction with other employees of the Metropolitan Vickers Company and whose names were given by me in previous testimonies directly tell Mr Thornton supporting the participation in these action of Messrs Monkhouse Cushny and Nord

All these crimes I fully confirm

All these testimonies have been given by me of my own will without any outside influence or pressure. All testimonies given by me were given in the English language and are written by myself. The protocol of interrogation in the presence of Gusev and myself during which I confirmed all my spying activities work in organisation of damaging of machinery and paying money to Russian engineers and technicians involved by me, was translated in English it has been read by me and confirmed as wholly correct.

I deem it necessary to request to put on record of this interrogation that all directions and instructions on espionage and organisation of breakdowns and damaging of machin[ery] I received from Mr Thornton. I deem it necessary also to mention in this protocol that information of spying nature which was passed by me to Mr Thornton the latter passed on to the Intelligence Service

I also request to put on record that in making my confession I was guided by the following motives

I wanted to make clear the accusations made against me.

Facsimile of page 2 of W. L. MacDonald's deposition of March 19, 1933, wherein he inter alia *confirms, that all his depositions have been made by him of his "own will without any outside influence or pressure."*

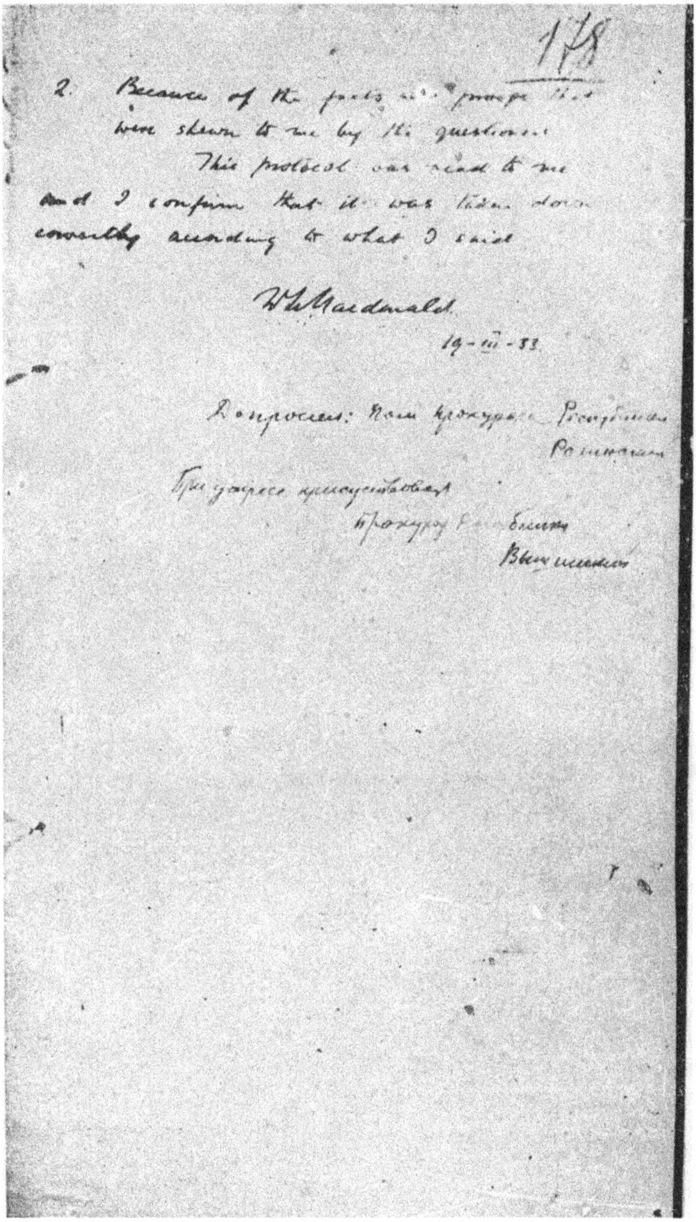

178

2. Because of the facts and proofs that were shown to me by the questioner.

This protocol was read to me and I confirm that it was taken down correctly according to what I said.

W L MacDonald

19-III-33

Facsimile of W. L. MacDonald's signature to his deposition of March 19, 1933, wherein he, inter alia, *put on record that "all directions and instructions on espionage, organization of breakdowns and damaging of machines" emanated from L. C. Thornton.*

Krasheninnikov: He said it was not worth while making a fuss about trifles.

Vyshinsky: So Ryazanov told you it was not worth while making a fuss about trifles, and you decided not to pay any attention to them, to hurry on the work of installation. What is there wrecking in that?

Krasheninnikov: The manner in which the installation work was done.

Vyshinsky: The quality of the work?

Krasheninnikov: Yes, the quality of the work. I ceased to insist upon what I thought should have been done, and as Jolley was in charge of the work, I from that time on began to restrain myself and began to pay heed to him more, because if the question were raised of sending another engineer in Jolley's place, the installation work might have been delayed.

Vyshinsky: However, you did not draw from this the necessary conclusion that the installation work should be hindered, that it should be held up?

Krasheninnikov: I did not draw this conclusion from the conversations with Ryazanov.

Vyshinsky: I asked you something else. You said that at the end of 1928 you embarked on criminal, wrecking activity and that you carried it out alone, without being a member of a counter-revolutionary group. Did I understand you rightly?

Krasheninnikov: Yes.

Vyshinsky: Under what circumstances, what caused you to take the road of individual wrecking activities?

Krasheninnikov: Ryazanov's answer played, to some degree, a definite role in determining my attitude towards this installation work.

Vyshinsky: What role?

Krasheninnikov: I gave Jolley the opportunity of doing everything he thought fit.

Vyshinsky: Consequently, your conversation with Ryazanov had only one meaning—don't poke your nose too much into things that don't concern you. Nothing more?

Krasheninnikov: Nothing more.

Vyshinsky: What circumstances induced you to begin to be

more active, to change from passively tolerating shortcomings to active methods of participation in this work?

Krasheninnikov: I began to conceal defects in the installation work. I began to conceal defects in the equipment.

Vyshinsky: And further?

Krasheninnikov: As a matter of fact it all began from that moment.

Vyshinsky: And how did it end?

Krasheninnikov: It ended in my finding myself in the dock.

Vyshinsky: You found yourself in the dock. This happened in spite of your activities, as a result of the activities of some other institutions. I ask you, what was the direct result?

Krasheninnikov: It brought about several breakdowns in the power station.

Vyshinsky: What brought about several breakdowns? And what breakdowns?

Krasheninnikov: First of all, I learned from Jolley that the blades were defective.

Vyshinsky: We have already spoken about that. Now we are discussing what exactly your active wrecking actions were, if there were any; or did you limit yourself to this role?

Krasheninnikov: I limited myself to concealing defects in the equipment supplied by Metro-Vickers.

Vyshinsky: At that time you were acting on your own responsibility, quite alone, or with other persons?

Krasheninnikov: I did it on Jolley's instructions.

Vyshinsky: Personal and direct instructions?

Krasheninnikov: Personal and direct.

Vyshinsky: And besides Jolley, was there anyone else who prompted you to do this?

Krasheninnikov: Jolley left for England in the middle of 1929.

Vyshinsky: We know that. From among the Soviet engineers or mechanics, or citizens in general?

Krasheninnikov: I knew Oleinik.

Vyshinsky: What did you know about him?

Krasheninnikov: I had known him since 1929.

Vyshinsky: What did you know about him?

Krasheninnikov: He was Thornton's agent.

Vyshinsky: Let us leave Thornton aside for the moment. In connection with what activities did you know Oleinik?

Krasheninnikov: He concealed defects in the equipment supplied by Metro-Vickers and collected economic information about the work of the power station.

Vyshinsky: In your opinion was Oleinik a loyal Soviet citizen, or a counter-revolutionary?

Krasheninnikov: No, he was not a loyal Soviet citizen.

Vyshinsky: Then was he a counter-revolutionary, a wrecker, or just hostile to the Soviet Government?

Krasheninnikov: He was a wrecker.

Vyshinsky: What grounds have you for asserting that Oleinik was a wrecker?

Krasheninnikov: On his arrival at the power station the second time, in 1930, to install turbine No. 28, he had talks with me.

Vyshinsky: On what subject?

Krasheninnikov: He first of all brought me an envelope from Thornton.

Vyshinsky: What envelope?

Krasheninnikov: An envelope with money.

Vyshinsky: With what money?

Krasheninnikov: There were 500 rubles.

Vyshinsky: What for?

Krasheninnikov: For concealing the defects in the equipment which I had noticed and seen.

Vyshinsky: There. That is more interesting. Did you mention the sum of 500 rubles at the preliminary examination?

Krasheninnikov: Yes, 500 rubles.

Vyshinsky: May I ask Oleinik a question?

The President: You may.

Vyshinsky: Accused Oleinik, you heard this part of Krasheninnikov's evidence?

Oleinik: Yes.

Vyshinsky: Which part of it do you corroborate?

Oleinik: It is true that I handed him an envelope.

Vyshinsky: With money?

Oleinik: The envelope was sealed. Engineer Thornton warned me that there was money in it but I did not know how much money there was.

Vyshinsky: You did not count it? Krasheninnikov however counted it. Did you receive money from Thornton?

Oleinik: Yes.

Vyshinsky: With what orders?

Oleinik: To pass it on to Krasheninnikov.

Vyshinsky: What for?

Oleinik: What for—that was understood. He did not tell me, but it was understood. I knew already in 1928 that Krasheninnikov was supporting the interests of the firm.

Vyshinsky: Was it as a bribe?

Oleinik: It cannot be understood in any other way.

Vyshinsky: That is so. What do you mean by the expression: supporting the interests of the firm?

Oleinik: That is to say, concealing the defects in the equipment during installation.

Vyshinsky: What else?

Oleinik: Furnishing information, if necessary.

Vyshinsky: Of a certain nature?

Oleinik: Yes.

Vyshinsky: And so on?

Oleinik: Yes. All that was of interest to the firm.

Vyshinsky: And why did you think it was being done in the interests of the firm? Perhaps it was all being done in the interests of Thornton?

Oleinik: I cannot say definitely. I dealt with Thornton. But that was how I understood it. The equipment was not Thornton's.

Vyshinsky: You understood that Thornton was not working in his own personal interests?

Oleinik: Yes.

Vyshinsky: But perhaps he was working in the interests of some other institution?

Oleinik: I did not know that at the time.

Vyshinsky: Did you learn it later?

Oleinik: Yes.

Vyshinsky: Hence it can be said that Thornton acted in two capacities: as the firm's engineer and also as an individual?

Oleinik: I learned this later.

Vyshinsky: So he could be acting in the interests of the firm and in the interests of another institution. Is that correct?

Oleinik: Yes.

Vyshinsky: Accused Krasheninnikov. Having received this money, were you not surprised to have such a present, as Monkhouse called it here, dropped on you? Not a bribe, but a present?

Krasheninnikov: No, I was not surprised.

Vyshinsky: Why?

Krasheninnikov: Before receiving this money I had spoken to Jolley and Jolley had assured me that he would know how to recompense me for concealing the defects in the machinery.

Vyshinsky: By this time were you and Thornton already acquainted?

Krasheninnikov: I do not remember exactly when I became acquainted with Thornton, but it must have been in the middle or the end of 1928.

Vyshinsky: I ask you whether you were already acquainted with Thornton?

Krasheninnikov: I already knew Thornton.

Vyshinsky: Who introduced you to Thornton?

Krasheninnikov: I think it was Ryazanov again.

Vyshinsky: Ryazanov again. So Ryazanov was a sort or organizing centre: introduced people to each other, gave instructions. As a result of this acquaintanceship you received money. As a result of this acquaintanceship you hid the defects, that is, you criminally violated your duty as a Soviet citizen. Is it correctly stated?

Krasheninnikov: Yes.

Vyshinsky: And what was Oleinik's role in this?

Krasheninnikov: Oleinik's role was to form the link with Metro-Vickers.

Vyshinsky: In his work? How can this work be described? Legal, within the framework of your official duties, or illegal work carried on during the fulfilment of your official duties?

Krasheninnikov: Illegal.

Vyshinsky: Illegal, in violation of your official duties?

Krasheninnikov: Yes.

Vyshinsky: I have a question to the accused Thornton. Accused Thornton, have heard the testimony? You, of course, deny it, don't you?

Thornton: Of course I deny it.

Vyshinsky: I have no more questions to put to Krashenninikov for the time being.

The President: Has the Defence any questions?

Schwartz: You testified here that you were acquainted with Jolley. When did you become acquainted?

Krasheninnikov: In the beginning of 1928.

Schwartz: Tell me, in what capacity did he come to you at the Moscow State Power Station?

Krasheninnikov: As an installation engineer of Metro-Vickers.

Schwartz: Was he there often or did he only come from time to time?

Krasheninnikov: He was there during the whole of 1928 and half of 1929.

Schwartz: I understand, but did he come every day or once a week, or once a month, or merely from time to time?

Krasheninnikov: He used to come every day.

Schwartz: So he was with you every day. You stated to the Court that at first in your attitude towards him you were a little inclined to find fault; that you demanded detailed checking of his installation work and that you even had disputes on this account?

Krasheninnikov: Yes.

Schwartz: Were there any cases when the disputes were carried to Ryazanov in the presence of you and Jolley?

Krasheninnikov: I saw him alone, or perhaps Ryazanov was speaking to Monkhouse and Thornton.

Schwartz: Referring to your complaints?

Krasheninnikov: Yes.

Schwartz: You stated to the Court that Ryazanov was indifferent to your complaints and urged you to be less exacting about the defects in Jolley's work?

Krasheninnikov: As a matter of fact I stopped being so insistent.

Schwartz: What period of time does this refer to? What month and year?

Krasheninnikov: About the middle of 1928.

Schwartz: After you had changed your attitude towards Jolley, did he try to become more intimate with you, to chat more often on subjects not only connected with the work, but on other subjects?

Krasheninnikov: Then our relations considerably improved.

Schwartz: From whom did you learn in detail about the defects of the equipment?

Krasheninnikov: First of all I knew myself, and secondly I knew from Jolley.

Schwartz: When he went to England, you say that Oleinik, a mechanic, came to you to work as a fitter. Did Oleinik bring you nothing from Jolley, did he never speak to you on behalf of Jolley?

Krasheninnikov: No he never spoke on behalf of Jolley.

Schwartz: When Oleinik handed over the envelope, did he say he was bringing it from Jolley or from Thornton?

Krasheninnikov: He said he was bringing it to me from Thornton.

Schwartz: An envelope from Thornton. You have just answered the Prosecution and testified concerning your participation in wrecking acts. What was the main thing about this wrecking? Can the main thing be considered to be the concealing of defects in the equipment and the installation?

Krasheninnikov: Yes.

Schwartz: Permit me to ask, when did you begin to work at the Moscow State Power Station?

Krasheninnikov: At the First Power Station, in 1926.

Schwartz: In what year did you graduate from the university?

Krasheninnikov: In 1925.

Schwartz: After graduating from the university where did you go to work?

Krasheninnikov: Before graduating from the University I went to work at the Moscow State Power Station.

Schwartz: So you worked and studied at the same time?

Krasheninnikov: Yes.

Schwartz: And on graduating did you remain at the Moscow State Power Station?

Krasheninnkov: Yes, I remained there.

Schwartz: So you parted with Jolley in the middle of 1929. In which year did you come into contact with Oleinik?

Krasheninnikov: I became acquainted with Oleinik in 1929.

Schwartz: At the end or in the middle?

Krasheninnikov: At the end. After that, he worked for almost a year with us, installing turbines.

Schwartz: In 1931?

Krasheninnikov: I did not see Oleinik in 1931 nor in 1932.

Schwartz: Tell me, please, did any change take place in your criminal attitude during that period or was there no such change? If a change did take place when was it and how did it express itself?

Krasheninnikov: Yes, there was a change at the end of 1932.

Schwartz: In what direction?

Krasheninnikov: In this direction, that I realized that the work I was doing was criminal work. I was ill at the time, lay sick, alone, and thought a great deal about it; and I considered that the work I was doing of concealing defects, and the breakdowns which were the result of these defects, was betraying the country; and so I considered that I ought to stop the whole business.

Schwartz: I have no other questions to ask.

The President (To the Defence): Have you any questions?

Kommodov: Tell me, please, did Oleinik, when he gave you the envelope from Thornton, tell you that there was money in?

Krasheninnikov: Yes. He said: "The envelope is from Thornton, and he is expecting you to continue your activities."

Kommodov: Did he say just that: "Here is an envelope for you from Thornton and he is expecting you to continue your activities"?

Krasheninnikov: Yes.

Kommodov: I have a question for Oleinik. When Thornton handed you the envelope, did he say anything?

Oleinik: Yes. He said that he expected Krasheninnikov to go on working as he had done before.

Kommodov: Did he mention the sum he was sending?

Oleinik: No.

Kaznacheyev: Tell me, Oleinik, when you handed the envelope to Krasheninnikov, did you converse with him for long?

Oleinik: No, it was in my office, where Krasheninnikov frequently came in connection with his work.

Kaznacheyev: Was it during one of his visits?

Oleinik: I really cannot say exactly whether it was in my office or in his, because he often came to me, and I often went to him; but it is not so important. We were alone, because I could not hand it over in the presence of others. I told him on the spot, briefly.

Libson: Please, tell me, Krasheninnikov, did I rightly understand you to say that your wrecking activities continued for over two years?

Krasheninnikov: Longer.

Libson: Even longer? And during all that period you were, it seems, under the same influence of which you have been speaking. Were you in touch all the time?

Krasheninnikov: I was not in touch with these people all the time, but at any rate I met Thornton, I saw Thornton at meetings, etc.

Libson: You mentioned another English name.

Krasheninnikov: I have not seen Jolley since the end of 1929

Libson: But during the whole of this period, for two and a half years, were you always in touch directly and immediately, or was it through somebody else?

Krasheninnikov: No.

Libson: You mean that there was a period when you carried on independent wrecking work, apart from these influences?

Krasheninnikov: There was such a period.

Libson: A second question interests me. According to your testimony you received only 500 rubles during all this time.

Krasheninnikov: Yes.

Libson: And did you get any other privileges, or anything else?

Krasheninnikov: No, I received nothing but promises.

Libson: What kind of promises?

Krasheninnikov: In 1929, Jolley promised to bring me

certain things from England on his return to the installation work at the power station.

Libson: He promised certain articles, and what else?

Krasheninnikov: Besides this he promised to arrange for me to get good practical work at Metropolitan-Vickers works if I could get an official business commission to go to England.

Libson: So there was talk about the possibility of your being sent on an official business commission and of your being given work with the firm?

Krasheninnikov: Yes.

Libson: Anything else?

Krasheninnikov: And to arrange a comfortable living for me in England.

Libson: Who had this sort of conversation with you?

Krasheninnikov: Jolley.

Libson: So that wider prospects and opportunities were opened up before you, beyond the 500 rubles that you received?

Libson: This had an effect upon you?

Krasheninnikov: Yes.

Libson: I have no more questions.

Schwartz: I have a question. Accused Krasheninnikov, you stated to the Court that in 1931-32 you and Oleinik did not meet. But did you meet anyone else besides Oleinik?

Krasheninnikov: I met Thornton.

Schwartz: Did you have a talk with him?

Krasheninnikov: There was no direct conversation, but I met him at meetings.

Schwartz: At official meetings?

Krasheninnikov: Yes.

Schwartz: You stated to the Court that at the end of 1932 a definite change took place in yourself in the sense, as I understand it, of your desiring to take part in the building of socialism?

Krasheninnikov: Yes. I felt that all that I had been doing was harmful to the Soviet State, and I noticed how I was treated after my illness.

Schwartz: Treated by whom?

Krasheninnikov: By the Soviet Government.

Schwartz: What was this treatment?

Krasheninnikov: I was given a free place at a rest home.

Schwartz: You regarded this as care shown towards you as a Soviet engineer?

Krasheninnikov: Yes, that was how I regarded it.

Schwartz: This did still more to strengthen your attitude in the sense of refraining from doing any further wrecking?

Krasheninnikov: Yes.

Schwartz: And besides the 500 rubles, you got no other material benefits from Oleinik and Jolley for your wrecking activities?

Krasheninnikov: Quite correct.

Schwartz: I have no more questions.

Defence: No.

The President: Has the Defence any more questions?

Vyshinsky: I have a question. From the examination of the accused Krasheninnikov by Counsel for the Defence Schwartz, I draw the conclusion that he was paid and that he wrecked; once he got a free place at a rest home he stopped wrecking.

Krasheninnikov: That is not so.

Vyshinsky: Perhaps not quite so?

Krasheninnikov: Not quite so.

Vyshinsky: The second question: quite irrespective of whether they paid you much or little, you wrecked all the same?

Krasheninnikov: Yes.

Vyshinsky: What were your motives?

Krasheninnikov: I have already said here—primarily for material motives.

Vyshinsky: That is to say, when they paid, you wrecked?

Krasheninnikov: Yes.

Vyshinsky: I have no more questions.

Roginsky: I have a few questions for Oleinik. Tell me, accused Oleinik, when you were sent to work for the Moscow State Power Station, were you told that you would find a group of engineers there whom you could bring into the work of wrecking?

Oleinik: Not who could be brought into it, but who had already been brought into it.

Roginsky: That is to say, you were told that at the Moscow

State Power Station there was a group of engineers engaged in wrecking activities?

Oleinik: That was said.

Roginsky: Who said it?

Oleinik: In 1929, when I first came to the Moscow Power Station—it was in the middle of 1929. . . .

Roginsky: Who said it?

Oleinik: Engineer Monkhouse told me.

Roginsky: What did engineer Monkhouse tell you?

Oleinik: He told me that there were people there who were supporting the intersts of the firm, and mentioned a few including Ryazanov, Sukhoruchkin, Krasheninnikov, Yazykov, etc.

Roginsky: So the accused Krasheninnikov was mentioned by Monkhouse as one of the engineers who constituted the wrecking group that was operating at the Moscow State Power Station.

Oleinik: I can say the following about Krasheninnikov: when I was with Monkhouse in Moscow at the end of 1928—when turbine No. 27 was put into operation and Monkhouse took me with him, I needed a pass for the Moscow Power Station. He told me that Krasheninnikov was working there, and characterized him in two words, saying in English that he was "a good chap." Well, it was obvious for whom he was a "good chap."

Roginsky: And you interpreted it to mean that Krasheninnikov was one of your own crowd?

Oleinik: Of course.

Roginsky: Monkhouse's crowd?

Oleinik: Yes.

Roginsky: So you knew about Krasheninnikov in 1928?

Oleinik: Since the end of 1928.

Roginsky: You also worked for the Moscow State Power Station at the end of 1928?

Oleinik: Not for long.

Roginsky: Did you have occasion to encounter, to observe or to come directly in contact with the practical work of Krasheninnikov?

Oleinik: I had occasion to come in touch with it all the time.

Roginsky: Can you relate some concrete facts regarding the way Krashenninikov reacted to the recommendation which was made to you by Monkhouse?

Oleinik: There were some defects in the turbines but he kept quiet about them.

Roginsky: Tell us more concretely. This is a too general answer.

Oleinik: It is hard to recall now. There were cases when the turbines were stopped, there was trouble with the valves.

Roginsky: You remembered that better on March 3, 1933. Perhaps we should remind you?

Oleinik: If you please.

Roginsky: Perhaps you will tell us of the case which occurred in connection with the installation of the safety valves?

Oleinik: This was later, not in 1929 but in 1930.

Roginsky: Yes. What happened then?

Oleinik: This conversation was held just in passing. It referred to the Metro-Vickers equipment.

Roginsky: Tell us first about your talk with Krasheninnikov, about the substance of the conversation.

Oleinik: The talk was of the following nature: there were no safety valves on the feed water piping of the condensers, and since the level of the water in the Moskva River changes considerably in the spring, it was quite possible that the pressure would rise. Apparently, in order to protect the condensers, it was necessary to have safety valves installed. I reminded Krasheninnikov of this. He replied that it was none of our business.

Roginsky (To Krasheninnikov): Accused Krasheninnikov, was this the case?

Krasheninnikov: Yes, but it is my opinion that no safety valves are needed there.

Roginsky: Was there a case where you replied: "This has not been provided for, better be quiet about that"?

Krashenninikov: Yes, there was.

Roginsky: Another case: What happened in connection with the testing of turbines Nos. 26 and 27?

Oleinik: I examined turbine No. 27 before it was tested. It was necessary to make some changes. To be more exact, I was changing the packing and at the same time I was examining it.

This was in 1929. I discovered that there were large clearances which caused a considerable leakage of steam. Then, in 1930, the testing of turbine No. 26 was to take place after 8,000 hours of work. Before testing in order to find out the condition of the turbine (and it was in the interests of the firm that the machine should be in good condition), I examined turbine No. 26. I found that it was in a considerably better condition than turbine No. 27. Which turbine should be tested? We could have tested either this one or the other, or, more correctly, both. But I recommended that turbine No. 26 should be tested, because it was in better condition.

Roginsky: What was Krasheninnikov's part?

Oleinik: It was his immediate concern. But whether he decided the question independently or not, that I don't know. But he was immediately concerned with this matter, and, according to my opinion, it depended on him.

Roginsky: Accordingly, turbine No. 26 was in better condition than turbine No. 27 which had a number of definite defects, and, therefore, was it at the insistence of Krashenninikov that the testing was made with turbine No. 26?

Oleinik: Yes.

Roginsky: And thereby the defects of No. 27 were covered up, which defects could have been revealed in the testing. Is that so?

Oleinik: Yes.

Roginsky: Accused Krasheninnikov, did this take place?

Krasheninnikov: Partly, yes.

Roginsky: Partly, yes, and in what part didn't it take place?

Krashenninikov: Partly, because this question was being decided not only by this fact but also by the circumstance that it would have been necessary to open turbine No. 27, and there was insufficient time for that.

Roginsky: Was it known to you that turbine No. 27 was in worse condition than turbine No. 26?

Krasheninnikov: It had worked more.

Roginsky: Was it known to you that if the tests were made with turbine No. 26 the results of the test could in no way be applied to turbine No. 27?

Krasheninnikov: Yes.

Roginsky: Did you declare that the turbines were identical?

Krasheninnikov: Yes.

Roginsky: And that, accordingly, the result of the testing of turbine No. 26 could be fully extended to apply to turbine No. 27.

Krasheninnikov: Yes.

Roginsky: So we have two cases. Now, the third case. Accused Oleinik, how did the matter stand with the discovery of cracks in the babbit of bearing No. 1 of turbine No. 28?

Oleinik: This was in 1932, when I came to examine the turbine. I already knew before that in other turbines there were cracks discovered in these bearings. When turbine No. 28 was opened, it was found that there were cracks in this case also. In this connection engineer Thornton was called, the question had already been raised by the operating department, that there was the danger that if a little piece of the babbit should fall out, it would cause the metal of the bearing to melt. Thornton came and brought with him another English installation engineer, I think it was Bell; I had met him once. They assured us that there was no danger. I, of course, also confirmed this.

Roginsky: What was Krasheninnikov's role?

Oleinik: Krasheninnikov permitted this.

Roginsky: Did any talk concerning this take place between him and Thornton?

Oleinik: I do not remember.

Roginsky: And didn't you testify that Thornton came to an agreement with Krasheninnikov that these cracks were not dangerous, and that Krasheninnikov did not raise the question any more?

Oleinik: That is so.

Roginsky: Accused Krasheninnikov, did this take place?

Krasheninnikov: This was in the engine room when there was a whole commission there. I was there also.

Roginsky: Did this circumstance take place about which Oleinik has just told the court?

Krasheninnikov: Yes, it took place.

Roginsky: Accordingly, we can come to the following conclusions, that as manager of the turbine room in 1929, you concealed the defects connected with the equipment of which Oleinik was speaking, that is, those connected with the installation of safety valves—is that so?

Krasheninnikov: Yes.

Roginsky: In 1930, you deliberately did not permit the testing of turbine No. 27 which, as you knew, had a number of defects and you covered up these defects by the testing of turbine No. 26. And in 1932, while already working on repairs, you again consciously permitted the concealment of defects which had been found in the bearings. Is that so?

Krasheninnikov: Yes, that is correct.

Roginsky: I have no more questions to the accused Krasheninnikov.

The President: Comrade Vyshinsky, have you any questions to put to Krasheninnikov?

Vyshinsky: I have one question. I want to ask the following: In your testimony today you emphasized several times that you had been drawn in by Jolley, or that Ryazanov introduced you to Thornton, and so forth. I am interested in the following question. You, engineer Krasheninnikov, a Soviet employee, did you realize the difference between the responsibility of a foreigner, who, if he belonged to hostile circles in foreign countries, had been acting against the Soviet Union, and your responsibility as a Soviet State employee who was acting against the interests of the proletarian State? Have you realized the difference in the degree of responsibility or not, and how do you understand this difference at present?

Krasheninnikov: Yes, I realized this. As I said, I became aware of it particularly when I was sick. Such activity as the one I had been carrying on should be considered as. . . .

Vyshinsky: Treason?

Krasheninnikov: Treason.

Vyshinsky: Which, according to our laws, is punished—you know how treason is punished by our laws?

Krasheninnikov: Yes, I know.

Vyshinsky: I have no more questions.

The President: Has the Defence any questions?

Schwartz: Please tell us, during these years, did you have any talks with Thornton concerning these wrecking acts? With Thornton personally?

Krasheninnikov: No, not with Thornton personally.

The President: Are there any more questions?

Thornton: May I put a question?

The President: You may.

Thornton: The testing committee for testing the turbine was formed by the Moscow Power Station, was it not?

Krasheninnikov: Yes.

Thornton: What defects exactly were established?

Krasheninnikov: In the first place, as Oleinik said, the difference in the clearances was considerable, which unquestionably might have affected the steam consumption of that particular turbine.

Thornton: I am asking about the defects.

Krasheninnikov: There were defects in the governor valves. They caused the stoppage of the turbine.

Thornton: Did the management of the Moscow Power Station know about that?

Krasheninnikov: It knew, but it did not know the actual cause why these valves were sticking. The management of the Moscow Power Station was told that this was so and had to be so, that this is always so.

Thornton: So you did not conceal it?

Krasheninnikov: But I knew that these valves had not been properly heat-treated at the works; this was told to me both by Jolley and by Oleinik.

Thornton: Any other defects?

Krasheninnikov: This was the basic defect. Then there were others. During the testing I already knew that the blades of the turbine were not sufficiently safe.

Thornton: And when the blades flew off, did the management of the Moscow Power Station know about this?

Krasheninnikov: It did.

Vyshinsky: Why did they fly off?

Thornton: In my opinion, owing to defects of construction.

Vyshinsky: I also think so.

Thornton: About the bearings of which Oleinik spoke . . . Did the management know about all three turbines?

Krasheninnikov: Yes.

Thornton: You did not conceal that?

Krasheninnikov: I did not conceal it but I knew the attitude of the firm to every kind of defect. I concealed this attitude of the firm.

Thornton: You said that the management knew.

Krasheninnikov: The management knew that there was this defect. But it did not know the cause of it.

Thornton: Was there at any time a breakdown on account of these bearings?

Krasheninnikov: No, there was not.

Thornton: When were these cracks discovered—after how many thousand hours?

Krasheninnikov: During the first inspection.

Thornton: Say, after about 8,000 hours.

Krasheninnikov: Less.

Thornton: And did these machines work much longer than 8,000 hours?

Krasheninnikov: Yes.

Thornton: Were there no more breakdowns?

Krasheninnikov: No.

Thornton: How long did they work?

Krasheninnikov: About 13,000 to 14,000 hours.

Vyshinsky: Accused Krasheninnikov, you are asked by accused Thornton whether the management knew about the various defects, and so forth. You answered that it knew but did not know the causes, and I want to ask you along somewhat different lines. Was Ryazanov then in the management?

Krasheninnikov: He was.

Vyshinsky: Was he a wrecker?

Krasheninnikov: He was.

The President: Are there any more questions?

Monkhouse: I should like to ask whether Krasheninnikov knew the causes of these defects.

Krasheninnikov: I knew in part the causes of these defects, and partly, I knew from Jolley that in general there were defects in the turbines. I myself knew of such defects: a defect in the piston rod of the governor valve, its thread, its packing rings, the rings on the pumps—I knew and saw all this myself.

Vyshinsky: And the clearances?

Krasheninnikov: And the clearances in the turbines.

Monkhouse: If he knew of these defects why didn't he tell? We were getting together in the committee and finding out these defects. We wanted to find out, but he told us nothing.

Krasheninnikov: I did not say anything because I was instructed not to.

The President: Instructed by whom?

Krasheninnikov: By the representatives of the firm, Oleinik and Jolley.

Monkhouse: I have a statement to make in connection with Oleinik's testimony. I want to make it clear. Oleinik said in his depositions that it was said that a man will come, a "good chap"* which means a "good fellow," but I did not say that he was a wrecker.

The President: But have you the word "wrecker" in English?

Monkhouse: There is the word *"wrecker,"* but *"good chap"* means a "good fellow."

Vyshinsky: From philology to technique. I am interested in whether there really were defects in your equipment?

Monkhouse: There were.

Vyshinsky: And you knew of these defects?

Monkhouse: I knew. I knew after the breakdowns. I did not know before the breakdowns.

Vyshinsky: And who was working there as your representative?

Monkhouse: Oleinik and Jolley.

Krasheninnikov: That means that you had to find out from Jolley and Oleinik about all defects?

Monkhouse: Yes.

Vyshinsky: Accordingly, the fact that Krasheninnikov did not tell you about this is not at all so very surprising; it was not his duty to tell you.

---

* The English words were used. *Ed.*

Monkhouse: It was his duty to tell when we convened the commission.

Vyshinsky: He should have—provided his attitude towards his duties was honest. But how—if it was criminal?

Monkhouse: I do not believe that his attitude was dishonest.

Vyshinsky: But Krasheninnikov believed in his criminal activity. Was there criminal activity?

Krasheninnikov: There was.

The President: Has the Prosecution any more questions?

Prosecution: No.

The President: Has the Defence?

Kommodov: I have a question for Oleinik. Whom of the engineers who worked at the Moscow Power Station did Monkhouse mention personally as people who, according to your expression, have been upholding the interests of the firm?

Oleinik: I have told you already.

Kommodov: Of those who are sitting here?

Oleinik: Two. Krasheninnikov and Sukhoruchkin.

Kommodov: You said that the way you understood it, a "good chap" was one who upheld the interests of the firm. This expression was taken to mean a wrecker. It was taken to mean a desire to serve not the Soviet interests, but the interests of the firm. This kind of personal conclusion on your part justifies me in asking: what did Monkhouse tell you? What was Krasheninnikov supposed to do? What was Sukhoruchkin supposed to do? Or was it that he did not point out concretely, but just said in a general way that there was a group of engineers who uphold the interests of the firm?

Oleinik: It was at various times. About Krasheninnikov I was told separately. Now as to a "good chap." For one who knows English well there can be no doubt about it because when you say "good" it is clear that he is "good" not for my adversaries but that he is good for me. There can be no doubt of this. At least I had none.

Kommodov: We will not go into interpreting this word. I want to establish a fact, and, as to the conclusions, we will make them later. Were you told concretely what kind of wrecking work Krasheninnikov was to carry out? What Sukhoruchkin was to do? Or were there no such words said; or was it simply pointed out that there is a group of engineers who uphold the interests of the firm?

Oleinik: In the event that there would be any need to get somebody's support, I was to approach them. This was the general rule at the installations, and it was not necessary to repeat that to me. It was not the first year I was working. I had worked for about ten years. I knew the rules and, therefore, it was not necessary to explain them to me.

Kommodov: So you were told that there was a group of engineers upholding the interests of the firm whom you could approach.

Vyshinsky: I have a question to ask. Accused Oleinik, were you told that there was a group of engineers whom you would have to approach? In what case?

Oleinik: There could be all sorts of misunderstandings.

Vyshinsky: These misunderstandings are sometimes settled in the interests of the State power stations or of the power plant enterprises of Soviet industry and sometimes in the interests of the firm. Does it ever happen that these interests clash?

Oleinik: They almost always clash.

Vyshinsky: In those cases where these interests clash, what was this group of engineers whom you were to approach supposed to do?

Oleinik: They were to give support.

Vyshinsky: Against whose interests?

Oleinik: There are only two parties.

Vyshinsky: I want you to make it more clear.

Oleinik: Against the interests of the enterprise.

Vyshinsky: Were you given instructions along this line?

Oleinik: I do not remember whether it was formulated this way, but it was very clear to me.

Vyshinsky: The formulation is of no consequence. It is important that it was clear to you.

Oleinik: Yes.

Vyshinsky: I have no more questions for Oleinik.

The President: Accused Zorin.

Roginsky: Tell us, accused Zorin, what post did you occupy?

Zorin: I was senior engineer of the thermo-dynamic group of the rationalization section at Mosenergo.

Roginsky: What were your duties?

Zorin: To carry out rationalization of the turbine operation in the stations of Mosenergo. Then to organize acceptance tests on deliveries from the firm, to present technical claims to the firm, to consult on questions of repair and operation and to take part in examining the causes of breakdowns.

Roginsky: Were you in the wreckers' group which was active in the enterprises of Mosenergo?

Zorin: Yes.

Roginsky: Since when?

Zorin: Since November 1932.

Roginsky: Is it known to you who else belonged to this wreckers' group?

Zorin: It is.

Roginsky: Who?

Zorin: Krasheninnikov and Sukhoruchkin.

Roginsky: Who told you about it?

Zorin: Engineer Thornton.

Roginsky: When did Thornton tell you that?

Zorin: During our last meeting, in November 1932.

Roginsky: These two persons whom Thornton named to you, were they by the nature of their work frequently participating in those commissions which had to establish the defects of the equipment?

Zorin: Yes, they were.

Roginsky: What do you know about the testing of turbines Nos. 26 and 27?

Zorin: I must make a slight correction, namely, that these testings took place before my transfer to Mosenergo and I did not know anything about them. The tests were made in the beginning of 1931 and I started to work there at the end of 1931.

Roginsky: Was the composition of the commission known to you?

Zorin: I read the records but I do not remember exactly.

Roginsky (To Sukhoruchkin): Were you in the commission which participated in testing turbines Nos. 26 and 27?

Sukhoruchkin: No, I was not.

Roginsky: And who was?

Sukhoruchkin: I do not know, because I did not see the records of the testing of these turbines. At that time I worked in the electro-technical department and I had nothing to do with the working of the turbines.

Roginsky (To Krasheninnikov): Who was on this commission?

Krasheninnikov: I was representing the station.

Roginsky: And Ryazanov?

Krasheninnikov: Ryazanov was not a member of the commission.

Roginsky: But he directed the work?

Krasheninnikov: There was a chairman of the commission—Vetchinkin.

Roginsky: And where is Vetchinkin?

Krasheninnikov: He was arrested in connection with the case of the Industrial Party.

Roginsky: And Ryazanov did not take part in the commission?

Krasheninnikov: He used to attend the sessions of the commission but he was not a member of the commission.

Roginsky: That means, the chairman of the commission was arrested in connection with the case of the Industrial Party, your chief, Ryazanov, who attended the sessions of the commission was also a wrecker, who was arrested in connection with the case of the Industrial Party and you are a member of a wreckers' group. There you have the composition of the commission.

Krasheninnikov: There were others.

Vyshinsky: Were all of them of the same kind?

Krasheninnikov: Almost all.

Roginsky: I have no more questions for Krasheninnikov. Now let us pass to Zorin. In November 1932, you had a talk with Thornton during which it was pointed out that there was a wreckers' group in the enterprises of Mosenergo. Is that so?

Zorin: Yes, that is so.

Roginsky: Please, tell us, under what circumstances did this talk take place?

Zorin: The talk was in the offices of the firm, in Kuznetsky Most, at the Electro-Import.

Roginsky: What preceded this talk? What was the immediate reason that prompted Thornton to have this kind of talk with you?

Zorin: I became acquainted with Thornton at the end of 1931 at a meeting which took place at the offices of Mosenergo in connection with breakdowns which had occurred at the Orekhovo Station. Up to November 1932 we met five times. At these meetings we carried on conversations on political subjects, during which he touched upon political questions, mainly on the situation in the Soviet Union, the conditions of Russian specialists and other similar questions which revealed to him my own anti-Soviet sentiments. From these conversations he gathered that I was a person whom it was easy to use and this is what happened at the end of November 1932.

Roginsky: Let us go deeper into both your meetings and those reasons which, as you maintain, gave Thornton the basis for entrusting you with certain tasks. Where did the first meeting take place?

Zorin: The first meeting took place in the offices of Mosenergo.

Roginsky: Was this meeting concerned with strictly business matters?

Zorin: Yes, with business matters.

Roginsky: In what capacity did you take part in this commission or at that conference when this meeting took place?

Zorin: I took part on behalf of the Moscow Power Station, representing its interests.

Roginsky: In dealing with whom?

Zorin: In dealing with Metro-Vickers.

Roginsky: What were you doing? Presenting some claims?

Zorin: There were definite claims presented to the effect that the turbines concerned should be repaired.

Roginsky: Accordingly, at this conference, there occurred a certain clash between you and the interests of the firm, which were defended by Thornton?

Zorin: Correct.

Roginsky: The second conversation?

Zorin: The second conversation took place some time in February 1932, in the offices of Electro-Import, again in connection with breakdowns on the Orekhovo turbines. Here also I had to appear as the defender of the interests of the Moscow Power Station.

Roginsky: And at this second meeting, at the official session, you again participated as one who was defending some definite interests of Mosenergo, against the firm? Is that so?

Zorin: Yes.

Roginsky: During these two meetings did you confine yourself to talks only on business matters; were there any talks of a different order?

Zorin: During the first meeting the talk was only on business matters. During the second meeting, Thornton put several questions regarding the work of the turbines on the stations of Mosenergo and of the turbines of competing firms, as to how they behaved in the matter of regulation. I gave him this information readily, although I should not have given it, because, if not a secret, it was at any rate ethically incorrect to do so. Then I told him about several cases of breakdowns which had occurred, about the most typical cases which had occurred with their competitors' turbines. Then there were talks of an anti-Soviet nature about the conditions of Russian specialists.

Roginsky: Is it correct that in this conversation you yourself, on your own initiative, gave Thornton to understand that your sentiments were anti-Soviet?

Zorin: There was no intention to give him to understand that. But, of course, from what I said, he clearly understood that I had these sentiments.

Roginsky: The next meeting, the third?

Zorin: The third meeting occurred after a rather long interval, in August 1932, in connection with the tests that were to be made at the Orekhovo station. This meeting was at the offices of Mosenergo.

Roginsky: Was there any talk?

Zorin: Yes.

Roginsky: What about?

Zorin: In the first place he was interested in the further plan of development of the Moscow Power Station from the point of view of the capacity and types of the future turbines. And then the conversation again assumed a clearly expressed anti-Soviet character, that is, the talk was to the effect that the Soviet Union was meeting with difficulties on various sections of its economic front. The conversation went on in this vein.

Roginsky: Is it true that after the second meeting you performed a certain number of services for Thornton by furnishing him with information which you should not have given him?

Zorin: It is true.

Roginsky: The fourth meeting?

Zorin: The fourth meeting took place in the offices of Electro-Import, again in connection with the Orekhovo turbines. This was in the firm's offices and it took place in connection with the arrival from London of a designer, engineer Cox, and Thornton attended as interpreter. At the beginning, the talk was purely of a business nature, as to how the changes should be made, and then, after Cox left, I remained with Thornton. Here again the talk was along the lines which I mentioned in connection with the previous meetings.

Roginsky: Finally, the fifth meeting?

Zorin: The fifth, the last decisive meeting was in 1932 in the firm's office in the Electro-Import building. Thornton came there after a session which took place in the office of the control department of Electro-Import.

Roginsky: What task was given you by Thornton during this last, fifth, meeting?

Zorin: Since Thornton had clearly seen during the previous meetings that it was very easy to enlist me in his work, he immediately began with the statement that he intended to use me in the interests of the firm and of those organizations which had been formed at the various stations, both of Mosenergo and in the Soviet Union in general. Then he said, during this conversation, that he noticed that I was not showing up the defects in the equipment of Metro-Vickers as I should, accordingly, to a certain extent I was his ally. Then he said that the breakdowns which had occurred with the turbines of Metro-Vickers at the First Moscow Power Station and at other stations in the Union were not the result of purely accidental and operational causes, but were the result of organic defects which were deliberately allowed to pass during the construction of the turbines at the works. I was surprised at this and I asked how the firm ventured to take such steps. In this way the firm might lose its good name not only in the Soviet Union, but also all over the world, because what happens in the Soviet Union becomes known in other countries.

Roginsky: Let us leave the firm alone for the time being. What concrete proposals were made to you by Thornton?

Zorin: A concrete proposal of the following kind: That, besides continuing to conceal the defects of the firm, I should also cover up the action of the groups which he had organized, in case I should have occasion to participate in examining breakdowns which occurred with their or with other equipment, and to screen the actions, of these groups.

Roginsky: That is, to conceal the defects in the equipment and then, secondly, that you, as one who usually represents Mosenergo in presenting claims, should be less exacting?

Zorin: That is correct.

Roginsky: Thirdly, to assist in the activity of the wreckers' groups which had already been organized in the various power stations belonging to Mosenergo?

Zorin: Yes.

Roginsky: And fourthly?

Zorin: Fourthly, to keep contact with the groups which he had organized.

Roginsky: So, fourthly, to be a link between him and the groups which had been organized in the power stations belonging to Mosenergo?

Zorin: Yes.

Roginsky: Very well. Now let us pass to your concrete acts. What concrete acts have you performed in connection with concealing the defects in the equipment?

Zorin: When turbine No. 2 of the Orekhovo Station broke down in November 1931, owing to a hydraulic shock, I did not point out, during the analysis of this breakdown, that such breakdowns may occur also without any hydraulic shock, because, in my opinion, there was no conformity between the axial pressure which existed and the thrust bearing which was put on this turbine. Then, when I started to look up the material of the analysis of the breakdown which occurred with turbine No. 26, which took place before my arrival, I could conclude from the statements that the cause which was named there was not the real one, that is, was not the real cause of the breakdown and that it was necessary to look for another cause, namely blade resonance.

Roginsky: This is the second act. Now the third act?

Zorin: The third act was of this sort. When the firm proposed to do away with the resonance by attaching an additional wire binding, I did not point out that the installation of this binding was only a palliative and might not give those results which the firm apparently expected.

Roginsky: That means, you mention a whole series of concrete acts of concealing the defects in the equipment?

Zorin: Yes.

Roginsky: What acts have you perpetrated in the way of concealing the direct acts of diversion carried out by the members of the wreckers' group?

Zorin: I knew from Thornton that he had organized the breakdown at the First Moscow Station, the one that took place in November, by filling up the blades with lime and boiler foam. This breakdown had been concealed.

Roginsky: Was that turbine No. 17?

Zorin: Yes.

Roginsky: When did this take place?

Zorin: In November 1931.

Roginsky: What was the substance of this act?

Zorin: It was a wrecking act.

Roginsky: What did it lead to?

Zorin: It led to part of the machines being put out of action for a certain time.

Roginsky: What other wrecking acts are known to you? The one with turbine No. 1 at Orekhovo?

Zorin: Yes, but this breakdown had taken place before I knew that Thornton was doing that. I was informed afterwards that this breakdown had also been engineered at his instructions.

Roginsky: Was there another breakdown at that same

Orekhovo Station with turbine No. 1 in May 1932, when the vacuum dropped?

Zorin: This was a small breakdown which was of no practical consequence.

Roginsky: How about the breakdown of turbine No. 11 at the Shatura station?

Zorin: I heard from Thornton that this breakdown was engineered by him. This breakdown put the turbine out of service for about 14 days. But this happened at the time when I did not know that such an organization was in existence.

Roginsky: How about turbine No. 28?

Zorin: I do not know of this breakdown.

Roginsky: How about the breaking of the downcomer of the water circulation system?

Zorin: With the piping system. Yes, it was pointed out that the breakdown was engineered.

Roginsky: Concerning this act, was it also pointed out that it was a wrecking act?

Zorin: Yes, that these were not wrecking acts but were breakdowns.

Vyshinsky: As a result of the action of a definite wreckers' group?

Zorin: Yes.

Vyshinsky: Did you carry into practice your function as link?

Zorin: No, there was no occasion for that because this conversation took place at the end of November; after that I was sent away on business, then I had my vacation and after the vacation I did not return to work because I was arrested.

Vyshinsky: And were there any acts of diversion planned which you personally were to organize and to carry out?

Zorin: There were no concrete acts of diversion but he proposed that after his return from abroad he would talk to me more in detail, but I think that I should not have been in a position to carry out any acts of diversion because I did not have any direct practical functions.

Vyshinsky: Of what acts of diversion was there talk?

Zorin: Those which were to be carried out by the groups.

Vyshinsky: How so? Diversions were planned and there was no plan?

Zorin: He said that acts of diversion (this referred to the turbines) should occur in such a way as to hit the rotors of the turbines, because such breakdowns are the most serious for the turbines and they are most difficult to repair.

Vyshinsky: Thus, concealment of the defects in the equipment was done by you?

Zorin: Yes.

Vyshinsky: Concealing concrete acts of diversion at various power stations belonging to Mosenergo, was that carried out by you?

Zorin: Partly.

Vyshinsky: Was there also a certain program of action for the future which was to be concretely worked out at your next meeting after Thornton returned from abroad?

Zorin: Yes.

Vyshinsky: Serving as link—you undertook fulfilment of this function, but you had not yet succeeded in realizing it in practice. Is this so?

Zorin: Yes.

Vyshinsky: And, now tell us, did this wrecking activity of yours remain without remuneration?

Zorin: No. During our last meeting I received 1,000 rubles from him.

Vyshinsky: Where?

Zorin: Again in the firm's office.

Vyshinsky: Was that during your last meeting?

Zorin: Yes.

Vyshinsky: Was that all?

Zorin: That was all.

Vyshinsky: Or were there some plans?

Zorin: There was talk that we would continue this sort . . .

Vyshinsky: That if you would continue to do this kind of work then you would receive certain sums of money regularly and that in the meantime you were given 1,000 rubles?

Zorin: Correct.

Vyshinsky: I have no more questions.

The President: Has Comrade Roginsky?

Roginsky: No.

The President: Has the Defence?

Schwartz: Make it clear, please. You just now gave a detailed explanation as to your participation in wrecking acts. Permit me to ask you—you replied to the Presecutor that you were deprived of the opportunity to participate personally in acts of diversion. Why? Were you not directly engaged on the operations?

Zorin: I was not. I used to come to the station when there was some trouble and when it was necessary to remove the trouble. My work was in the nature of consultation and examination of trouble.

Schwartz: So you were outside of the actual operations?

Zorin: Yes.

Schwartz: Where did you work?

Zorin: I worked in Moselectro in the rationalization section of the thermal group. I was transferred to the board at the end of 1932.

Schwartz: So that is why you had no direct connection with the operating.

Zorin: Yes.

Schwartz: When did you start working at the Moscow Power Station?

Zorin: In 1932. And I was transferred to Mosenergo at the end of 1932. Before this I worked at the Second Moscow Station.

Schwartz: You worked there about nine years?

Zorin: Yes.

Schwartz: How was your work there carried on?

Zorin: Entirely honestly.

Schwartz: So you worked more than nine years honestly and since 1932 you started a different period of work?

Zorin: Yes.

Schwartz: How do you explain such a tremendous difference, that more than nine years you have conscientiously and honestly worked as a Soviet engineer and since 1932 you began to work thus?

Zorin: Why this inner change? Partly for general political reasons. Partly it was due to my personal reaction to some of the more difficult aspects of the life in the Soviet Union.

Schwartz: Did the meetings with Thornton contribute to that?

Zorin: They intensified these feelings.

Schwartz: You said that from the end of 1932 you used to meet Thornton?

Zorin: Yes.

Schwartz: That is to say, your wrecking work commenced in November 1932?

Zorin: Yes.

Schwartz: And ceased with your arrest?

Zorin: Yes, it was interrupted by the arrest.

Schwartz: Consequently, it lasted a little over a month

Zorin: Yes.

Schwartz: Concerning the claims, you said that you had to do with technical claims. Did you have anything to do with financial claims?

Zorin: Nothing whatever. If I am being charged on that account, it is not in accordance with the facts.

Schwartz: You had to deal with technical claims? What does that mean?

Zorin: We presented claims to the firm to remove technical defects in the equipment.

Schwartz: What are we to understand by financial claims?

Zorin: If some breakdowns take place, the firm makes good these breakdowns by changing the parts, and these parts during a fixed time, in accordance with an agreement, are supplied free of charge and the work must be done free of charge at the firm's expense.

Schwartz: That is to say there is a guarantee agreement and the firms must within the limits of this agreement carry out everything at their expense. You had nothing to do with these financial claims?

Zorin: Nothing whatever.

Schwartz: Who was negotiating with the firm in regard to financial claims?

Zorin: We had a technical supply department which dealt with this business and sanction had to be given either by the manager or by his assistant.

Schwartz: You personally had nothing to do with these questions?

Zorin: Nothing whatever.

Schwartz: I've no more questions.

Braude: Please tell me how old you are?

Zorin: 49.

Braude: How many years have you worked?

Zorin: 23.

Braude: Were you also engaged in scientific work?

Zorin: Partly.

Braude. Have you the title of professor?

Zorin: No.

Braude: Have you the title of lecturer?

Zorin: Yes.

Braude: How is it that you, a man of middle age, with great experience, upon your second meeting with a foreigner to whom your only relation was, that you had to oppose him as the representative of a firm with which there were differences of a business nature, how is it that you immediately disclose your anti-Soviet sentiments? How is that to be explained?

Zorin: This happened at a time when I had personal troubles which I was inclined to attribute to the existence of a certain regime.

Braude: And you poured out your soul to the first foreigner you came across?

Zorin: Why first?

Braude: You met him and began to pour out your soul?

Zorin: He met me half way.

Braude: How long did your first meeting last—your private chat with him?

Zorin: About twenty minutes.

Braude: And the second?

Zorin: About twenty-five minutes.

Braude: And the third?

Zorin: About the same time.

Braude: The fourth?

Zorin: About forty minutes.

Braude: Consequently, after several separate conversations with Thornton, spread over a long period and lasting altogether two hours, you entered into an agreement of a wrecking and counter-revolutionary nature?

Zorin: He said that he had heard about me, but I didn't ask him from whom.

Braude: Why so? Had you done any wrecking work before?

Zorin: He might have known my sentiments.

Braude: Now be good enough to answer one more question. There is no doubt in my mind, and you yourself spoke about it, that you committed acts of wrecking, but what had that to do with Thornton? Did you have counter-revolutionary convictions?

Zorin: Yes.

Braude: Sharply defined, or of an ordinary grumbling nature?

Zorin: No, sharply defined.

Braude: Active?

Zorin: Active.

Braude: Explain to me why you, who had active counter-revolutionary convictions and turned every personal offence into an offence at the hands of the Soviet Government, were in need of Thornton to give effect to these convictions?

Zorin: I was not in need of him. But he happened to work in the same direction as myself.

Braude: Wouldn't you have joined the wrecking organization without Thornton?

Zorin: I didn't know it existed.

Braude: But if you had known?

Zorin: It is difficult to say what would happen in the case of an "if."

Braude: Well, then, money played a part?

Zorin: To a certain extent.

Braude: May I understand you in this way, that quite apart from Thornton, you would have committed acts of wrecking just the same because these acts and acts of diversion were in accord with your convictions?

Zorin: Well, I said so before.

Braude: I have no more questions.

Libson: Tell me, did you have occasion to go abroad?

Zorin: No.

Libson: And you did not go abroad under the Soviet Government?

Zorin: No.

Libson: Did you write any scientific work?

Zorin: No.

Libson: I've no more questions to ask.

The President: The Court is adjourned for twenty minutes.

(Court adjourns at 12:30 p.m. until 12:50 p.m.)

*

* *

Commandant: Please rise. The Court is coming.

The President: Please be seated. Accused Cushny, come to the witness stand. The Court has no questions to ask you. Has the Prosecution any questions?

Vyshinsky: Yes. Accused Cushny, when did you arrive in the U.S.S.R.?

Cushny: In 1925.

Vyshinsky: To which town?

Cushny: Shterovka.

Vyshinsky: In connection with the work at the Shterovka Power Station?

Cushny: I was in charge of the installation of two turbines there.

Vyshinsky: For how long?

Cushny: Almost two years.

Vyshinsky: From 1925 to 1927?

Cushny: Yes.

Vyshinsky: And then, from 1927?

Cushny: I also went to Baku to install some turbines.

Vyshinsky: And were you in Baku in 1928?

Cushny: Yes.

Vyshinsky: How long did you stay in Baku?

Cushny: Three years.

Vyshinsky: Up to 1931?

Cushny: No. From 1927 to 1930.

Vyshinsky: And where were you in 1931?

Cushny: In Moscow.

Vyshinsky: At the Metro-Vickers office?

Cushny: Yes.

Vyshinsky: In what capacity?

Cushny: Assistant chief installation engineer.

Vyshinsky: Who was your immediate superior?

Cushny: Mr. Thornton, the chief installation engineer.

Vyshinsky: Is Thornton chief installation engineer?

Cushny: Yes, here in Russia.

Vyshinsky: Did you keep in touch with Thornton while at Shterovka and Baku? Did you correspond with him? Did you make any reports to him? Did you send him any communications?

Cushny: Certainly, otherwise how could I direct the installation work under his supervision?

Vyshinsky: May I put it in this way, that all the time, and not only while you were in Moscow, you acted as installation engineer under the direction of Thornton?

Cushny: No, not all the time. At first, Monkhouse was chief installation engineer.

Vyshinsky: At first under the direction of Monkhouse and then under the direction of Thornton. Did you supply both Monkhouse and Thornton with various information connected with your work?

Cushny: Yes.

Vyshinsky: Did you send information?

Cushny: Certainly.

Vyshinsky: But did this information concern only your duties in connection with installation, or was there perhaps some political information also?

Cushny: In a written form, there was usually only business information.

Vyshinsky: And what about the unwritten form, that is, verbally?

Cushny: When we met we certainly spoke about all sorts of things.

Vyshinsky: You conversed for instance about politics?

Cushny: Probably we spoke about politics too, about things that are common knowledge.

Vyshinsky: But you spoke about politics?

Cushny: Possibly.

Vyshinsky: What exactly did you discuss about politics?

Cushny: The usual talk.

Vyshinsky: What is this usual talk? Tell us what usual talk did you have?

Cushny: We spoke about the price of bread.

Vyshinsky: Is that politics—bread? That is economics.

Cushny: This is both economics and politics. I don't know which is which. It was both at the same time.

Vyshinsky: Because economics passes into politics and politics is based on economics.

Cushny: Quite so.

Vyshinsky: May I understand you thus: that you discussed bread from a political angle?

Cushny: I do not say that.

Vyshinsky: But that's how I understood you.

Cushny: If the price of bread is politics, then, yes.

Vyshinsky: That is what I want to say, that you regarded the question of the price of bread from the point of view of politics.

Cushny: No, I do not say that. I said that if the price of bread is a political question, well, then we spoke about this question.

Vyshinsky: You see, accused Cushny, I am asking what talk you had about politics, and you answer "about the price of bread."

Cushny: I cited this, as an example of our conversations.

Vyshinsky: Of the political talks.

Cushny: I didn't say that it was political talk.

Vyshinsky: I asked about politics.

Cushny: About politics I said that we had general talks about what was in the papers. Perhaps we spoke about this, perhaps about the beginning of the Five-Year Plan, and so on. This is general conversation such as everyone carries on.

Vyshinsky: Let us remove this misunderstanding. I am asking you and you are answering. I was asking you whether you spoke about politics. You said, I believe—we discussed politics with Thornton. Is that so?

Cushny: I said that it was possible.

Vyshinsky: Then I asked, what did you speak about concretely? You replied—about the price of bread. Is that how it was?

Cushny: Yes. That's it.

Vyshinsky: Now, let us pass from this to another question. Apart from general political talk, didn't you speak with Thornton about something else?

Cushny: I can't say that. We spoke about various things.

Vyshinsky: Concerning the Soviet State?

Cushny: Concerning the Soviet State we discussed things of common knowledge.

Vyshinsky: For instance, about political sentiments?

Cushny: Yes, about political sentiments.

Vyshinsky: Yes?

Cushny: We spoke about the sentiments of the workers.

Vyshinsky: About the political sentiments of the workers?

Cushny: I do not know whether this would come under political sentiments or not.

Vyshinsky: What were you interested in, for instance, their attitude towards to the Soviet Government?

Cushny: Their attitude towards work, how they lived.

Vyshinsky: And then?

Cushny: Just such things.

Vyshinsky: Were there conversations about their attitude to the Soviet Government, to the Five-Year Plan?

Cushny: Yes, there were.

Vyshinsky: So you confirm it. On the basis of what data did you have such talks with Thornton?

Cushny: On the basis of the data that I have eyes and ears.

Vyshinsky: Exactly. The eyes saw, the ears heard.

Cushny: Yes.

Vyshinsky: From whom did they hear?

Cushny: From various people.

Vyshinsky: From various people. Name, for instance, someone, if you remember, of your acquaintances who served your ears.

Cushny: There was no special collecting of data from anybody, but general talk when meeting somebody. I passed on to Thornton my impressions which I gathered not from somebody in particular, but in general.

Vyshinky: "General" impressions?

Cushny: Yes, general impressions.

Vyshinsky: And, for instance, did you happen to know Yemelyanov?

Cushny: Yes, I know him.

Vyshinsky: You spoke with him on these questions?

Cushny: It is possible.

Vyshinsky: Did you hear something from him about these questions—about sentiments, the Soviet Government, the attitude to the Five-Year Plan, and so forth, and so on.

Cushny: It's possible, I don't remember.

Vyshinsky: So that was not something general but an individual acquaintance with Yemelyanov. You do not deny that?

Cushny: I was acquainted with him in connection with business. He was a fitter engaged on work which was in my charge.

Vyshinsky: And was your conversation with him only a business conversation?

Cushny: Possibly there may also have been conversations of a different nature.

Vyshinsky: Of the kind of which you spoke just now?

Cushny: Yes.

Vyshinsky: Under what circumstances did you meet Yemelyanov?

Cushny: I said that I used to meet him on business.

Vyshinsky: Where?

Cushny: At the power station at Baku.

Vyshinsky: Did he call on you at your home?

Cushny: No, he did not.

Vyshinsky: Didn't you say in your depositions that he used to call on you at your home?

Cushny: I don't think I made such depositions. I said that I called on him only once at his place.

Vyshinsky: All right. What was his position?

Cushny: He was a fitter.

Vyshinsky: So you were so well acquainted that you even called on him at his home?

Cushny: No, it is not to be understood in this way. I called on him at his home when I had completed my work in Baku and it was necessary to leave. Then all the workers invited me to a party one evening and Yemelyanov and others were there and I came too. So that it was not a case of acquaintance with Yemelyanov but it was my last meeting with him.

Vyshinsky: What was it then, a friendly gathering or a business meeting?

Cushny: Not a business meeting.

Vyshinsky: But you said just now that your relations were only business relations?

Cushny: I do not think that I used the word "only."

Vyshinsky: I believe I heard it so. But this is not important, this is a small thing.

Cushny: Of course it's not important.

Vyshinsky: The fact remains that you met Yemelyanov at his home, not in the course of business.

Cushny: Yes.

Vyshinsky: Didn't you meet him in the restaurant?

Cushny: Possibly he may have been in the restaurant at that time, that is, at the time of the starting of the first turbine.

Vyshinsky: So this is another time?

Cushny: Perhaps he was there. I do not remember.

Vyshinsky: But if somebody should remind you, you may perhaps recollect?

Cushny: I do not know.

Vyshinsky: And you knew no one else apart from Yemelyanov? I do not mean "generally" but particularly. If we search, we may perhaps find some more?

Cushny: If we search long enough, then you may find a couple of hundred.

Vyshinsky: But if we make quite a short search? Do you know the name Medvedev?

Cushny: Yes.

Vyshinsky: Who is he?

Cushny: The manager of the Baku Station.

Vyshinsky: Under what circumstances did you meet him?

Cushny: In the course of my business duties and afterwards I called on him at his place.

Vyshinsky: Not during office hours?

Cushny: No.

Vyshinsky: On what business?

Cushny: At his invitation, particularly because his wife spoke English.

Vyshinsky: How is that? Where did she study?

Cushny: I don't know.

Vyshinsky: So, you used to meet Medvedev outside of office hours?

Cushny: Certainly, as the manager of the station.

Vyshinsky: No, I am asking whether the meetings at his place were of a business nature or not?

Cushny: No.

Vyshinsky: You can't remember anyone else from among your personal, individual acquaintances?

Cushny: Yes, I can.

Vyshinsky: Did you call on any of them at their homes, after office hours?

Cushny: I visited Bochkarev at Baku.

Vyshinsky: Who is he?

Cushny: A fitter.

Vyshinsky: Did he also arrange parties?

Cushny: Yes, he too.

Vyshinsky: And so the fitters arranged parties and you were invited everywhere.

Cushny: I didn't say everywhere, there were only two cases.

Vyshinsky: One case with Bochkarev, the other with Yemelyanov. And did you know Samoylov? Who is he?

Cushny: An electrical engineer.

Vyshinsky: What did he do at the station?

Cushny: He was assistant manager in charge of the distributing department.

Vyshinsky: Did you visit him?

Cushny: I do not remember. I believe I never called on him.

Vyshinsky: You believe so, but if I should remind you that you called on him, would you remember then?

Cushny: No. I am almost certain that I was not at his place, but you must remember that it was a few years ago.

Vyshinsky: All right. That is enough. So we can put it this way, that you had quite a large circle of personal acquaintances —Yemelyanov, Samoylov, Bochkarev, Medvedev—and, as you say, if we search long enough, we shall find a couple of hundred.

Cushny: I said that if you search you will find more, but I didn't say that I was acquainted with a couple of hundred people. But even if I were, I don't consider it a crime.

Vyshinsky: So it will be right if I assert that you did not live isolated, that you enjoyed a large acquaintance and particularly with those people whom you named and whom you visited after office hours, whom you visited at their homes, and, it may be, met in restaurants.

Cushny: Quite definitely in restaurants.

Vyshinsky: And even definitely? And possibly you took part also in a drinking bout?

Cushny: Both occasions were celebrations. The first was upon the starting of the turbines. And the second, upon my departure.

Vyshinsky: But at these celebrations in the houses of these fitters, were there engineers and workers, in general, or was there a limited circle of people?

Cushny: There were those who worked under me on the installation.

Vyshinsky: Was there any drinking on these occasions?

Cushny: Yes.

Vyshinsky: You did not refuse a drink?

Cushny: Why should I?

Vyshinsky: Do you know where Medvedev has gone to?

Cushny: I heard that he was arrested.

Vyshinsky: What for?

Cushny: I don't know.

Vyshinsky: And Samoylov?

Cushny: I heard that he is no longer at the station.

Vyshinsky: And where is he?

Cushny: I don't know.

Vyshinsky: And you do not know that he is arrested?

Cushny: No.

Vyshinsky: Tell me, please, when meeting these people did you have only business conversations?

Cushny: Not only business.

Vyshinsky: But also on general things?

Cushny: Yes, on general things.

Vyshinsky: Did you, for instance, let us say, carry on conversations about the Red Army?

Cushny: No. It is possible that somebody said that he was going to be called up. I remember something of the kind on one occasion when a fitter who was working under me said that he was called up to the Army. But this I do not call a conversation about the Red Army.

Vyshinsky: Certainly, this is a conversation about him and not about the Red Army. But such conversations about the Red Army as to whether it was true to its duty and to what extent it is equipped for war—did you carry on such conversations?

Cushny: No.

Vyshinsky: Perhaps, you will recollect?

Cushny: No, I don't remember.

Vyshinsky: Perhaps you were interested in whether they are well fed in the Red Army?

Cushny: I did not take an interest in the Red Army.

Vyshinsky: You were not interested?

Cushny: No.

Vyshinsky: Neither in the Red Army itself, nor in the way in which it is supplied, nor in what its supply consists of. You were not interested in that?

Cushny: I don't remember. I understand that the Red Army is being supplied.

Vyshinsky: How is it being supplied and what is it being supplied with?

Cushny: I didn't try to find that out.

Vyshinsky: You didn't ask anyone.

Cushny: No.

Vyshinsky: You didn't ask Yemelyanov about it?

Cushny: Yemelyanov? No.

Vyshinsky: Perhaps he told you himself?

Cushny: I don't know. I don't remember.

Vyshinsky: Did you give any presents to Yemelyanov?

Cushny: Never.

Vyshinsky: Did you give presents to any others?

Cushny: To whom exactly? I gave presents to my wife.

Vyshinsky: To your acquaintances among the fitters in the station, and so forth?

Cushny: No, I didn't give any.

Vyshinsky: You gave no presents. Perhaps you lent some money?

Cushny: Some of them sometimes used to borrow petty sums from me.

Vyshinsky: So they only borrowed small sums.

Cushny: I wouldn't give big sums. I must say that they never asked for large sums.

Vyshinsky: They were satisfied with petty sums?

Cushny: Sometimes they asked me to give them five rubles, perhaps ten, till pay day.

Vyshinsky: Ten, twenty, fifty?

Cushny: It never reached fifty.

Vyshinsky: Did they return the money?

Cushny: I don't remember cases when they didn't return it, but maybe one forgot to return it once.

Vyshinsky: You testified at the preliminary investigation that Yemelyanov took some money from you.

Cushny: Would you please read this deposition to me?

Vyshinsky: I shall read it to you: "I remember having lent some money to Kislyakov, it is possible that I gave some to Yemelyanov also."

Cushny: It is possible that I gave some to Yemelyanov.

Vyshinsky: And now you say that you do not remember?

Cushny: It is not a denial, if I say it is possible that I gave money.

Vyshinsky: Consequently it is possible that you gave money to Yemelyanov?

Cushny: It is possible, yes.

Vyshinsky: And it is possible that the money was not returned?

Cushny: I said that if that happened, it was not more than once.

Vyshinsky: So this is also possible?

Cushny: I didn't want to throw money away.

Vyshinsky: Did you lend the money to oblige or because people were obliging you? Did you lend the money to those who asked for it?

Cushny: I gave them the money just to oblige.

Vyshinsky: And they were also obliging you?

Cushny: They always worked well.

Vyshinsky: So you gave money for good work?

Cushny: No, for their kindness.

Vyshinsky: For "kindness," very fine. Tell me, please, do you remember the case of the breakdown of the turbine in 1928 in connection with the over-filling?

Cushny: Yes, I remember.

Vyshinsky: Was this breakdown an accident or was it brought about deliberately, intentionally?

Cushny: I know that water got into the turbine and in consequence, there was a breakdown. The water got inside because of the faulty working of the boilers. The boilers were not my business. They were not supplied by Metro-Vickers. It was soon after the starting up of the first of our turbines. The boilers were new and all the equipment was new. The boilers were different from those which the staff of the station had charge of before, so that it is possible that someone of the staff committed an error, a big error, in regard to the boilers. But this was not my business and I do not know how this mistake occurred, if it was a mistake in the boiler house.

Vyshinsky: May I put a question to accused Oleinik?

The President: You may.

Vyshinsky (To Oleinik): You too worked at Baku at that station?

Oleinik: Yes.

Vyshinsky: Do you remember this breakdown in 1928?

Oleinik: I do.

Vyshinsky: And the cause of this breakdown?

Oleinik: The over-filling with water.

Vyshinsky: Was this over-filling with water accidental or deliberate?

Oleinik: At the time I thought it was accidental. There was this talk—the stokers assembled for the morning shift, at 7 o'clock. There were permanent stokers assigned for duty at the new boilers, they were skilled and well instructed. They earned about 150 rubles and the rest earned about 90. These other stokers started on a shift on their own without the knowledge of the mechanic, and soon after that, about half past seven in the morning, the boilers were found to be full of water. The water ran into the steam tube and not only into the Metro-Vickers turbine which was the nearest, but rushed into all the steam tubes, so that the entire station was put out of action.

Vyshinsky: Of course these are questions which relate to the case but deviate somewhat from the immediate subject of my question. I am asking whether the breakdown in 1928 at the Baku Power Station was accidental or, whether it was organized by someone deliberately?

Oleinik: At the time all thought that it was accidental.

Vyshinsky: At that time, in 1928? And subsequently it turned out that it was not accidental?

Oleinik: I learned that in 1932.

Vyshinsky: From whom?

Oleinik: When Thornton gave me instructions about acts of diversion. At first I couldn't make up my mind to take up these acts of diversion, I said that acts of diversion with our machines are very dangerous because first of all the firm will be held responsible. This is one thing. Then, secondly, I was afraid. He told me that one must know how to organize things, and, as an example, he referred to the case of the breakdown in Baku and said that Cushny knew how to organize it in such a way that there could be no suspicion and that no connection could be established with the personnel of Metro-Vickers.

Vyshinsky (To Cushny): Did you hear this evidence?

Cushny: I heard it. Oleinik is lying.

Vyshinsky: All right. Are you speaking the truth?

Cushny: I am speaking the truth.

Vyshinsky (To Thornton): Thornton, is Oleinik lying?

Thornton: He is not telling the truth.

Vyshinsky: I have no more questions to put to Cushny.

The President: Have you served long in the British Army?

Cushny: Somewhat less than two years.

The President: Were you an airman?

Cushny: I was.

The President: During what years?

Cushny: 1917-19.

The President: Then you left and served no more in the army?

Cushny: I served temporarily. Only during the war.

The President: On what front?

Cushny: In France.

The President: Were you wounded?

Cushny: Yes, I was.

The President: You therefore left the army?

Cushny: I did not leave then, but after I recovered from my wounds, I was not sent again to the front, but was instructing new airman until the end of the war.

The President: Are you in the reserve or retired?

Cushny: I have no connection whatever with the army now.

The President: Are you now retired?

Cushny: I am not in the reserve at all. I am altogether free.

The President: Has the Defence any questions?

Lidov: According to your explanation, you have received a technical education.

Cushny: Yes.

Lidov: But in another place you say that you graduated from a university. From where did you graduate?

Cushny: From London University.

Lidov: Is there a technical department in London University?

Cushny: Yes. There is an engineering department and a chemical department.

Lidov: To put it briefly, you graduated and received a higher technical education in London University?

Cushny: Yes.

Lidov: What year did you graduate?

Cushny: I studied until 1917, then I gave up my studies to go to the war. After the war, after 1919, I had only one year to finish.

Lidov: These details are not important to me. So, at the outbreak of war you were a student in the University?

Cushny: Yes.

Lidov: Did you go to the army straight from the University?

Cushny: I did.

Lidov: In the indictment which you received and which you heard and read, you figure as a shareholder of the British firm, Metro-Vickers.

Cushny: Yes.

Lidov: Are you really a shareholder?

Cushny: I hold shares to the amount of 120 pounds.

Lidov: Small shares?

Cushny: Pound shares. They can be bought for a pound each.

Lidov: We are to understand that you, properly speaking, have a small number of shares.

Cushny: 120 shares.

Lidov: Is the invested capital a large one?

Cushny: A few million—three or four—I don't know.

Lidov: Millions of pounds?

Cushny: Millions of pounds.

Lidov: When you came here to the U.S.S.R. to work and went to Baku—you said in your reply to the Public Prosecutor that you had held conversations and twice gone to parties to which you were invited by the fitters. Tell us why you took an interest in the details of the life of the workers, and so on. Under the conditions of British capitalist society, you as an engineer, as a man with higher education, kept quite at a distance from the working masses. I understand that you can work together, but the sentiments of the workers, why did they interest you?

Cushny: I always take an interest in what is going on around me. And since I was closer to these workers than the others, because they worked directly under me, I dealt directly with them, and had less to do with other people, was further removed from them. And furthermore they all liked me very much.

Lidov: So we are to understand you in this way—that you were connected with them in the course of your work; your relations were such, so to say, that to a considerable degree, they brought you together in this situation and destroyed the difference between you.

Cushny: Yes.

Lidov: And that party to which you were invited, which took place at Yemelyanov's house—who arranged this party and why were you invited?

Cushny: Just because it was at the time when I was leaving Baku for good and there would be no other possibility of seeing me. They wished to take leave of me.

Lidov: Consequently, it was a farewell party at which they took leave of you in view of your departure?

Cushny: Yes.

Lidov: Did the workers and fitters invite you, or did you say that you would arrange it, or was it done jointly?

Cushny: It was done jointly by general wish.

Lidov: To pass an evening?

Cushny: Yes.

Lidov: You said that you remember two occasions, one at Yemelyanov's and another at some one else's. But apart from these occasions, was there any occasion when you came for a visit to chat together, to pass time, at Yemelyanov's place? Or perhaps Yemelyanov came to see you?

Cushny: There was one occasion when I and other British electricians were entertained by Bochkarev.

Lidov: But apart from this, didn't you visit one another in an informal way, as guests?

Cushny: No.

Lidov: So we may establish that these were the only two occasions when you passed your time in the company of the fitters and workers who worked together with you. Were there many people?

Cushny: On the first occasion, there were certainly about thirty people.

Lidov: Consequently, there was a big company?

Cushny: It was in a restaurant. It was at a time when the

installation of the second machine was not yet completed and the staff was in full muster.

Lidov: Hence, all those who worked on the starting up of the machine got together?

Cushny: Possibly some may not have come.

Lidov: But, in general, was the whole staff expected?

Cushny: Yes, all were invited.

Lidov: Where did that take place?

Cushny: In a restaurant.

Lidov: And when was it that you visited Yemelyanov?

Cushny: At a time when there were fewer people working on our turbine—about 15 of them.

Lidov: Consequently, there was still quite a company?

Cushny: It was very difficult to find place for them.

Lidov: Was there general talk all through that evening? Did all take part? Were there toasts, toasts to your health and toasts on your part to their health, or was there private talk or was there a discussion of some events, were all talking together?

Cushny: There were toasts, there was general talk, but nothing special.

Lidov: Was there any special discussion of some questions?

Cushny: No.

Lidov: So you assert that all the time you stayed in Baku, you maintained some personal relations with the fitters and workers who surrounded you; you took an interest in and conversed about general questions of life, but you did not specially collect information through them—you emphatically deny that?

Cushny: Quite true.

Lidov: Now, as regards the office as such, did you get any requests or instructions from any of the persons who worked there or with whom you came in contact, to collect information—not with any definite aim in view—but simply to collect information as to the living conditions about you, around the place where you worked, the sentiments of the people, whether the workers were pleased or not?

Cushny: Never. Maybe they asked me to explain technical questions concerning our installation, but what you said—never.

Lidov: You said that when you met in Moscow and so on, you had some conversations of a general nature with Thornton and other persons.

Cushny: Conversations of a kind which I might have with you, if we were to meet a week hence.

Lidov: Was it a conversation, or some report?

Cushny: Not a report.

Lidov: A simple conversation?

Cushny: Yes. I may have given my impressions and the one with whom I conversed may have given his impressions.

Lidov: Perhaps during these conversations special questions were put to get an answer from you on some definite questions, or was it ordinary conversation about how you live, etc.?

Cushny: It is possible that sometimes somebody wanted to know something.

Lidov: In what respect? What questions were of interest?

Cushny: In the technical field, concerning our equipment, then, some other equipment which is connected with ours.

Lidov: Were any questions put as to how your work was proceeding in different branches of industry, whether many troops of the Red Army were concentrated, what regiments, etc. Were such questions put?

Cushny: No. Such questions were not put.

Lidov: Let me turn to the question of the breakdown in 1928. What actually happened? Do you emphatically deny having anything to do with it?

Cushny: With the breakdown, or with the cause of the breakdown?

Lidov: Of course with the cause, because we all know that there was a breakdown, but what about the cause?

Cushny: I had nothing to do with this.

Lidov: But Oleinik said that some stoker took the place of another without being authorized. Do you confirm that?

Cushny: I heard that.

Lidov: What exactly?

Cushny: That there was some change of stokers and I heard that the stoker who committed the error was on duty at the new boilers for the first time.

Lidov: Were the stokers in your charge?

Cushny: No. They had nothing to do with me.

Lidov: Did you have anything to do with the operating of these boilers, even indirectly?

Cushny: Nothing whatever.

Lidov: Consequently, if some stoker took the place of an experienced stoker, it was done within the precincts of the boiler house and had nothing to do with your work personally?

Cushny: No. Even if the steam pressure was faulty, I should have reported about it not to the head stoker but to the manager of the station.

Lidov: You understand that if an unauthorized stoker started working instead of a skilled one, this from a technical point of view is inadmissible. It could not remain without a definite investigation being made, some punishment or other had to follow that. Isn't that so?

Cushny: There was an investigation after that and that stoker, as I heard, was arrested.

Lidov: So there was an investigation and proceedings were taken against the stoker?

Cushny: Yes.

Lidov: Tell me, please, did you ever return to Baku after your departure?

Cushny: I visited Baku twice after that, the first time in connection with the testing of our turbines. . . .

Lidov: But you were not on permanent work there?

Cushny: No.

Lidov: Consequently, you left to take up some other work and then you went to the Moscow office?

Cushny: Yes.

Lidov: Then you travelled mainly on a mission of inspecting and testing installations?

Cushny: Yes.

Lidov: I have no more questions to ask.

Kaznacheyev: Citizen Cushny, tell us please. You emphatically declared a few minutes ago that Oleinik was telling lies. What do you think—is everything he says a lie, or is only some part a lie?

Cushny: He is lying when he says that I had something to do with this breakdown, as far as causing it is concerned.

Kaznacheyev: But what about that part where he tells about the conversation with Thornton? Is he lying or not?

Cushny: I am convinced that he is lying.

Kaznacheyev: That is your conviction?

Cushny: Yes.

Kaznacheyev: Do you know anything about whether Oleinik had any conversation with Thornton on that subject or not?

Cushny: I do not know.

Kaznacheyev: Consequently, you cannot say either yes or no. But can you tell us what is your presumption or conviction?

Cushny: I was not with them, I do not know whether that took place or not, but I do not admit the possibility of such a thing.

Kaznacheyev: Only that, but you cannot deny the fact?

Cushny: Since I was not with him all the time, I cannot affirm it.

Kaznacheyev: I have no more questions.

The President: Has the Defence any questions?

Defence: No.

The President: And the Public Prosecution?

Public Prosecution: No.

The President: Accused Cushny, you may sit down.

Cushny: I wish to make a statement concerning the evidence.

The President: Your evidence is in no way different from the evidence given before. Perhaps not all the accused among the British subjects know the mode of procedure of our courts. Our procedure is as follows: There is an examination by the Court; the accused are examined in a definite order fixed at the first session. In the course of this examination the accused may make any statements. After the examination of all the accused, there follow the speeches by the Public Prosecutor, then the speeches of Counsel for Defence, and after that each of the accused is allowed to put in his final plea, in the course of which he can make any statement he wishes; after that the verdict is pronounced. This is our procedure. So to make any statements now in violation of the established court procedure would be inopportune.

Cushny: So I will be given the opportunity. . .

The President: This is our procedure as laid down in the Code of Procedure in Criminal Cases. I repeat in case you did not understand properly. This evening or tomorrow morning, we shall complete the examination of all the accused, because there are only four persons to come. Then probably there will be an adjournment to prepare the speeches and we shall probably hear the experts. Then there will be the speech by the Public Prosecution. After that the speeches of Counsel for Defence, followed by the final pleas of all the accused. Then the Court will retire to deliberate on the verdict. This is always the procedure and there will be no exception in this case.

Cushny: Thank you, I have understood.

The President: Now allow me to pass on to the next accused. Accused Oleinik. The Court has no questions. Has the Public Prosecution any questions?

Roginsky: Are you employed by Metro-Vickers?

Oleinik: Yes, I was, until the last moment.

Roginsky: Since what year have you been employed by this firm?

Oleinik: In the Metro-Vickers Company, since 1926.

Roginsky: Where did you work before 1926?

Oleinik: In the Westinghouse Company, the predecessor of Metro-Vickers.

Roginsky: For how long?

Oleinik: I began work in America in 1908.

Roginsky: Where?

Oleinik: At first in San Francisco, and then in Chicago. In 1911, I returned to Russia and again began to work at the St. Petersburg branch of the Russian Westinghouse Company. I was a chief mechanic until 1914. At the beginning of 1914, after the liquidation of the Russian Westinghouse Company, the British Westinghouse Company, or rather its representative in Russia, invited me to work for it and go to England to study turbines. I was sent there for a year. I was there until May. In 1915 I returned to Russia and worked on the installation of turbines until 1920. The Englishmen all left at the end of 1917, but as the

Dynamo Company was the representative of the British Westinghouse Company, I, nevertheless, continued to work until 1920. In that year my work ended. From 1920 to 1926, I served as assistant manager of the power station at the Tambov Powder Works. Then I was assistant head of the mechanical department in the Tambov rail wagon shops. Then I was technician on turbines in the Moscow division of the Electro-Technical Trust, central district. Later, I was appointed head of the turbine department in the State Electro-Technical Trust. Up to 1926, I remained there, and in 1926 at the invitation of engineer Monkhouse who was representing Metro-Vickers here I went to work for Metro-Vickers, that is, in reality the same Westinghouse Company.

Roginsky: Did you know engineer Monkhouse before 1926?

Oleinik: I did. He approached me in 1925. I have known him since then.

Roginsky: Did you know him before that, during your work in 1911?

Oleinik: No, I did not.

Roginsky: So you first met him in 1925?

Oleinik: Yes.

Roginsky: What was your education?

Oleinik: Officially, I have no education because I did not even finish the parish school. I had no opportunities but I afterwards tried to complete my education. While I lived in Russia, I studied and worked at the same time. Then, in America, I went to a so-called higher technical school, took a correspondence course in electrical engineering but did not complete it. I have no diploma.

Roginsky: What is your speciality?

Oleinik: Up to 1914, that is, before I left for England, I worked as chief electrical mechanic, but after 1914, as I was expected to work entirely on turbo-generators in Russia, I was sent by the firm to England to study steam turbines and since then, that is, since 1914, up to the day of my arrest, I have worked entirely on steam turbines.

Roginsky: What work did the Metro-Vickers office give you?

Oleinik: Installing steam turbines.

Roginsky: Were you in the same position as the other mechanics and installation engineers, working in the Metro-Vickers office?

Oleinik: They were not all in the same position. Compared with some of them, I enjoyed a better position.

Roginsky: Why?

Oleinik: Because I received a higher salary, but less than some others. The salaries were not the same and the qualifications were not the same.

Roginsky: How much did you earn?

Oleinik: Lately, I have been earning 600 rubles. In Makeyevka, I received an additional 150 rubles to make up for high prices. Among these 600 rubles I received 50 rubles in Torgsin checks like the other employees of the firm.

Roginsky: Have you any savings abroad?

Oleinik: Yes.

Roginsky: How did they originate?

Oleinik: It was in 1930. I was working in Moscow. Engineer Thornton began to talk to me saying that the situation of the Soviet Government was unstable, the value of money was falling, and maybe the Government would fall any day. If I had any savings it would be better to put them into an English bank. I told him that I had saved 2,000 rubles. I gave this money to Monkhouse, because Thornton was not in the office when I came, and he put it into an English bank when he was in England and brought me a cheque-book from there, but he said that it was dangerous to have a cheque-book at home in case of a search. Therefore it would be better for the cheque-book to remain with him. So I left it at that.

Roginsky: What search was he speaking about?

Oleinik: In case one took place.

Roginsky: Why were you expecting a search?

Oleinik: Because it might be expected. Our activity was not so legal.

Roginsky: What year was that?

Oleinik: The end of 1930.

Roginsky: So Monkhouse brought you a cheque-book?

Oleinik: Not Monkhouse, but Thornton.

Roginsky: When was that?

Oleinik: In 1931.

Roginsky: Why did he warn you of a possible search?

Oleinik: He did not say why, but judging by our activity, it could be expected that it might be discovered and a search be made.

Roginsky: Judging by what activity?

Oleinik: Espionage and wrecking.

Roginsky: Espionage and wrecking?

Oleinik: Yes.

Roginsky: So it would be correct to say that in 1930 or thereabout you sent all your money to England through the agency of Thornton and Monkhouse?

Oleinik: Yes. In addition, I forgot to say that engineer Thornton said to me at the time that it would be better not to draw all my salary here, but to make arrangements to have about 100 rubles, or 10 pounds per month, put to my current account in England.

Roginsky: I intended asking you this question. So you sent your savings to England and in addition, by agreement with Thornton, a certain part of your salary also was to be paid to your current account in England?

Oleinik: Yes.

Roginsky: Furthermore, such a measure was caused, as you say, by some conversations or talks concerning the possibility of a search and the discovery of your crimes.

Oleinik: I don't follow you.

Roginsky: You prepared for your retreat?

Oleinik: I prepared for it?

Roginsky: Yes.

Oleinik: No. I did not have that in mind.

Roginsky: You did not have that in mind? Very well. So you had in mind only the possibility of political complications, and owing to this you left your savings in England?

Oleinik: Yes.

Roginsky: And not from fear of a search?

Oleinik: No. I did not intend to take refuge abroad.

Roginsky: And after your talk with Thornton in 1931, when he warned you not to keep the cheque-book at home?

Oleinik: Just the same I did not intend to leave.

Roginsky: You intended only to leave your money there and you yourself stay here?

Oleinik: No, that is not so.

Roginsky: Let us now concretely go on to your wrecking work. What concrete wrecking work did you do?

Oleinik: Concealing defects in the equipment.

Roginsky: That is one.

Oleinik: Collecting information.

Roginsky: That is two.

Oleinik: The engineering of breakdowns.

Roginsky: Three. And the fourth?

Oleinik: In my opinion, that is all.

Roginsky: And recruiting?

Oleinik: That is what I call organizing breakdowns.

Roginsky: So there were four lines. We will count them over and write them down: concealing defects—first; the engineering of breakdowns—second; recruiting (let us name it separately) and consequently the organization of wrecking groups at the various power stations—third; finally, espionage—the fourth. Is that correct?

Oleinik: Correct.

Roginsky: Very well. With whom in the office were you directly connected in this work of yours?

Oleinik: Recently, after Thornton was appointed chief installation engineer, I dealt only with him.

Roginsky: To speak concretely, what do you consider recently?

Oleinik: Since the end of 1929.

Roginsky: And before 1929?

Oleinik: Before that I dealt with engineer Monkhouse.

Roginsky Tell us more precisely when did you start on your career as a wrecker?

Oleinik: Are you talking about collecting information or concealing defects? If you will permit me, I will speak in chronological order.

Before the beginning of 1928, I worked in Zlatoust and Shterovka and did not meet either Monkhouse or any of the firm's staff. I only corresponded with them. I sent reports on my work and received my salary by telegraph. I did not meet anyone and therefore I was given no tasks. In 1928 I was sent to Kitlin to put new blades in the first wheel in the first disc of the turbine which had been damaged by the check-pin flying out of the nozzle box. These loose pins were the fault of the fitter who had assembled this turbine. According to the instructions, they should have been firmly fixed, and every fitter should have known it anyhow. They were not caulked, they flew out and caused damage. It was lucky that only two rows of blades were affected. I concealed this and did not tell anybody.

Roginsky: What year was that?

Oleinik: At the beginning of 1928.

Roginsky: Did you do this on your own initiative?

Oleinik: Yes, on my own initiative.

Roginsky: Did you get advice from anybody?

Oleinik: No.

Roginsky: So nobody from Monkhouse's office influenced you?

Oleinik: No.

Roginsky: Was that your effort to be of some service to the office which employed you?

Oleinik: It was a very small thing to which I attached no importance.

Roginsky: And you concealed it?

Oleinik: Yes, I did.

Roginsky: Further.

Oleinik: In Shterovka there was a breakdown in 1928 in the middle of the summer. There was a breakdown of the circulating pump on the turbines, which is fairly big. It might have been much worse. The temperature of the bearings rose to 99 degrees. A little more and the whole turbine might have been gone. After this the cause of the breakdown was investigated. The basic original cause was that on the auxiliary turbine, which should work when the motor is switched off, the design of the valve was so poor that it was sufficient to touch the lever and the valve closed. It was established that the mechanic on duty was in a hurry and without noticing it, he touched the valve and it closed. Owing to this the pump was again put into operation, was started wrongly, and broke. This, of course, I concealed.

Roginsky: From whom did you conceal it?

Oleinik: From our authorities and from those who had ordered the equipment.

Roginsky: And what ought you to have done?

Oleinik: I can now see that I ought to have gone immediately to inform the representative of Shterstroy that the firm was to blame, but in that case I could not have continued to work for the firm.

Roginsky: But were you given instructions that you must conceal all defects?

Oleinik: Yes, of course.

Roginsky: By whom?

Oleinik: By my chiefs, Monkhouse and Thornton.

Roginsky: I ask you whether the act which you refer to in 1928 and the second one at Shterovka were the results of your independent action or the result of definite instructions which were given to you?

Oleinik: Excuse me, I did not understand you. The instructions were general, not about this particular breakdown or any other, not about any particular defect, but general instructions that defects must be concealed.

Roginsky: In any case, you had to look after the interests of the firm in every way.

Oleinik: Yes.

Roginsky: That is understood; you were an employee of the firm; were such intructions given to you?

Oleinik: Yes.

Roginsky: And did you carry out these instructions zealously and energetically?

Oleinik: I carried them out very conscientiously.

Roginsky: But when conscientiously concealing defects, were you told or given instructions or did you act on your own initiative, so as to engineer, in addition, some action for wrecking the machines?

Oleinik: I could not do anything on my own initiative.

Roginsky: But you did it?

Oleinik: Yes, I tried to organize it but I did so reluctantly.

Roginsky: Reluctantly or not is a different question. Did you do it?

Oleinik: Yes:

Roginsky: If it was not on your own initiative, then on whose was it?

Oleinik: On the instructions of engineer Thornton.

Roginsky: When did you receive these instructions?

Oleinik: In 1932.

Roginsky: And before 1932 were there no such instructions?

Oleinik: I do not remember.

Roginsky: And before 1932 you had nothing to do with the organization of breakdowns?

Oleinik: I think not, I do not remember.

Roginsky: We will remind you later. Up to 1932, therefore, you had nothing to do with various wrecking groups in the various electrical power stations?

Oleinik: In the sense of concealing defects, of course, I had something to do with them, but I don't remember organizing breakdowns.

Roginsky: Did you have anything to do with concealing defects which those who concealed them knew were bound to cause breakdowns?

Oleinik: Possibly I had.

Roginsky: I ask you whether you had or had not.

Oleinik: It is hard for me to tell you.

Roginsky: But the evidence which you gave today. What does it say?

Oleinik: Here, now?

Roginsky: When confronted with Krasheninnikov. This was not 1932, it was earlier.

Oleinik: But I did not engineer this breakdown. I didn't try to organize it. I saw that something was wrong, but this had nothing to do with the Metro-Vickers machines and I do not consider that I engineered it.

Roginsky: What have the Metro-Vickers machines got to do with it? It was a question of bringing about definite breakdowns.

Were you given instructions only to cause breakdowns on Metro-Vickers machines, or possibly just the opposite?

Oleinik: No. But chiefly, of course, on the Metro-Vickers machines, because it would be difficult for me otherwise.

Roginsky: And did you take part in the acts committed by Krasheninnikov?

Oleinik: Will you please tell me which acts?

Roginsky: They were read out here today and you yourself mentioned them and pointed them out to Krasheninnikov.

Oleinik: I do not remember.

Roginsky: May we question Krasheninnikov?

The President: You may.

Roginsky: Perhaps you will remind Oleinik.

Krasheninnikov: About the bearings, the valves, the clearances on the blades.

Roginsky: Did that take place?

Oleinik: That about the bearings took place in 1932.

Roginsky: And what about the valves?

Oleinik: That was when I was installing the turbine in 1930.

Krasheninnikov: The clearances in the blades?

Oleinik: Not in the blades, but in the labyrinth box.

Krasheninnikov: Yes.

Oleinik: Yes, but I cannot call that a breakdown. This could only cause extra expenditure of steam, or did cause it.

Roginsky: Was this the case?

Oleinik: Yes.

Roginsky: That was before 1932?

Oleinik: Yes.

Roginsky: So before 1932 you equally took part in the organization of those wrecking acts which were carried out at the power stations?

Oleinik: Yes, I don't deny it.

Roginsky: Now take 1932. What acts were organized by you, were carried out by you, or were participated in by you?

Oleinik: I cannot say which.

Roginsky: Were there none?

Oleinik: I could speak about acts which took place, but were not discovered, about breakdowns. In 1932 I tried to engineer them, however, I don't know whether they took place or not.

Roginsky: I asked what acts you tried to engineer in 1932. What did you try to arrange then?

Oleinik: I did not give concrete instructions and could not give them, because this depended on the conditions, but I tried to get hold of several people to carry out these acts.

Roginsky: Speak concretely.

Oleinik: Shall I mention the persons?

Roginsky: Are they among those who are sitting here?

Oleinik: No.

Roginsky: At present tell us the facts and name the places and the power stations.

Oleinik: This was at the First Moscow Power Station.

Roginsky: What act did you try to engineer?

Oleinik: I have already said that I could not give definite instructions in advance, because I did not know. To do it casually was impossible, or, in any case, dangerous; after my talk with engineer Thornton, it was necessary to do it very cautiously. So I had to select people and wait for a convenient moment.

Roginsky: To select people and wait for a convenient moment?

Oleinik: Yes.

Roginsky: What was the aim of your wrecking blow?

Oleinik: Destruction.

Roginsky: In what section of the station precisely? You said that you tried to engineer a definite wrecking act?

Oleinik: Yes.

Roginsky: And I am asking.

Oleinik: I have already said that I don't know what you mean by "section."

Roginsky: You don't understand what is meant by a section? Then let me put the question this way: Did you plan some definite wrecking acts or did you only organize a wrecking group, selecting people and having the intention of passing on to concrete wrecking acts?

Oleinik: Yes, only that way.

Roginsky: Very well. Was your activity in carrying out the instructions of Thornton only limited to the organization of a wrecking group?

Oleinik: Yes.

Roginsky: At the Moscow Electric Power Station?

Oleinik: Not only at the Moscow Power Station, but wherever the opportunity presented itself.

Roginsky: Was it organized at the Moscow Station?

Oleinik: Yes.

Roginsky: By you?

Oleinik: Yes.

Roginsky: In 1932?

Oleinik: Yes.

Roginsky: And where besides the Moscow Power Station?

Oleinik: Besides the Moscow Power Station, I cannot remember anywhere else.

Roginsky: But you said not only at the Moscow Station?

Oleinik: The instructions were to organize it not only at the Moscow Station.

Roginsky: Exactly where was it organized?

Oleinik: At the Moscow Power Station.

Roginsky: Was it organized by you personally at the Moscow Power Station?

Oleinik: Yes.

Roginsky: So you took part in carrying out breakdowns organized by the Krasheninnikov group at the Moscow Power Station. In the same way you yourself organized a wrecking group at the Moscow Power Station in 1932 and intended to proceed to concrete wrecking acts. Is that so?

Oleinik: Yes.

Roginsky: With regard to the other power stations, were actions carried on similar to those of which Krasheninnikov spoke?

Oleinik: In organizing wrecking groups?

Roginsky: In concealing defects which were bound to cause breakdowns.

Oleinik: I wanted to relate it in proper order.

Roginsky: Tell us, were there any?

Oleinik: Yes.

Roginsky: Where were they?

Oleinik: At Shterovka.

Roginsky: So it was at Shterovka and the Moscow Power Station. Where else?

Oleinik: At Belovo in Siberia.

Roginsky: And further?

Oleinik: I don't remember.

Roginsky: You remember these three stations, but you don't remember any others?

Oleinik: I give my deposition willingly, but I cannot remember everything.

Roginsky: Add to this the actions connected with Nordwall which you spoke of yesterday. Was this your wrecking work?

Oleinik: With Nordwall—it was wrecking work.

Roginsky: At the Makeyevka and Motovilikha Works?

Oleinik: Yes.

Roginsky: Also deliberate wrecking?

Oleinik: Yes.

Roginsky: Now tell us please whether these actions were carried out, as you say, on the direct instructions of Thornton?

Oleinik: Yes, mostly. Some cases were on the instructions of engineer Monkhouse.

Roginsky: So on the instructions of engineer Monkhouse too. He also gave you instructions to organize wrecking acts?

Oleinik: I don't remember that, but I knew that he was involved in the matter.

Roginsky: How did you know?

Oleinik: From what Thornton said and from the instructions which he gave me that the people whom I recruited should come to talk to Monkhouse as he was closely concerned with the matter, and engineer Thornton often left Moscow.

Roginsky: Which people?

Oleinik: Those whom I intended to recruit.

Roginsky: So that they could have direct relations with engineer Monkhouse?

Oleinik: Yes.

Roginsky: But personally, did you get from Monkhouse the same kind of instructions which you had from Thornton?

Oleinik: The only instructions I got personally from Monkhouse were not to run the tests, and not only not to run them but by all means to persuade the customers to delay the testing of the turbines, which, he later explained at our next meeting, could not stand the guaranteed steam consumption. I received such written instructions from engineer Monkhouse.

Roginsky: But this is nothing like the instructions which Thornton gave you?

Oleinik: No, this is different.

Roginsky: I am asking you about the kind of instructions that you received from Thornton.

Oleinik: From Thornton I received all kinds of instructions, and as I have already said, I had little to do with Monkhouse after Thornton became chief of the installation work.

Roginsky: So you had most to do with Thornton and received instructions directly from Thornton?

Oleinik: Yes.

Roginsky: But do you confirm that it was plain to you that Monkhouse knew all about this business?

Oleinik: Thornton told me so and even gave instructions to that effect.

Roginsky: You said here that you also engaged in espionage. What information interested you?

Oleinik: I was not interested in any, but I carried out the instructions which were given me.

Roginsky: Very well. What information had you to gather according to the instructions you received?

Oleinik: Information on the technical condition of electric power stations, the enlargement of stations and works, proposed orders, the sentiments of the masses. Also information about the movement of troops and munitions.

Roginsky: So you also had to collect military information according to the instructions you received?

Oleinik: I received such instructions in 1932.

Roginsky: About gathering military information?

Oleinik: Yes.

Roginsky: From whom?

Oleinik: From Thornton.

Roginsky: You accepted the task?

Oleinik: Yes.

Roginsky: Did you take any steps to carry it out?

Oleinik: I partly carried it out.

Roginsky: And this work which you did at the instructions of Thornton and Monkhouse was carried out quite conscientiously, wasn't it?

Oleinik: Yes, like all my work.

Roginsky: Was this work paid for above your salary?

Oleinik: I consider that it was.

Roginsky: And was this activity called forth by the fact that your whole well-being was linked up with Metro-Vickers, that your whole well-being depended on the interests of this firm?

Oleinik: Yes, that was so.

Roginsky: And you did this while being a citizen of the Soviet Union?

Oleinik: Yes.

Roginsky: And did you conscientiously defend the interests of the firm?

Oleinik: Yes.

Roginsky: Dealing wrecking blows at the interests of the Soviet Union?

Oleinik: Yes.

Roginsky (To the Court): I have a question for Thornton.

The President: Accused Thornton.

Roginsky (To Thornton): Do you deny the evidence of Oleinik?

Thornton: I deny it.

Roginsky (To the Court): I have a question for Monkhouse.

The President: Accused Monkhouse.

Roginsky (To Monkhouse): And do you also deny the evidence of Oleinik in the part affecting you?

Monkhouse: I deny it and I ask the Court to allow me to produce some documents.

Roginsky: You can ask the Court later, but now let us return to the evidence which Oleinik gave about you. Do you deny it?

Monkhouse: I deny it.

Roginsky: I have no further questions.

Kaznacheyev: Accused Oleinik. Were you appreciated as an installation engineering specialist in the firm?

Oleinik: I think they appreciated me greatly.

Kaznacheyev: You were considered a good spezialist?

Oleinik: Yes, better than many of the Englishmen.

Kaznacheyev: Then I don't quite understand. If you were a good specialist, if you could have found work when and where you chose under the same conditions, then how was it that you were materially so closely bound up with the firm? You replied to the question of the Public Prosecutor that it was this material connection which drove you on to wrecking work.

Oleinik: I would say that it was not only material connections.

Kaznacheyev: And what else?

Oleinik: Habit. I had worked so long with the firm that it was easier for me to work under those conditions, because exact instructions are given.

Kaznacheyev: So here a certain and possibly the dominating role was played by habit, by close relations, close acquaintance?

Oleinik: Yes.

Kaznacheyev: Now on the question of your current account abroad. Through whom personally had these operations to take place? Who had to deposit the money to your account?

Oleinik: According to engineer Thornton, the firm had to do this.

Kaznacheyev: But you talked with Thornton on this subject?

Oleinik: Only with him.

Kaznacheyev: You did not have conversations on this subject with anybody else?

Oleinik: No.

Kaznacheyev: Did he carry out his promises or not?

Oleinik: He showed me a cheque-book.

Kaznacheyev: So you were sure that this promise did not remain a mere promise but was carried out?

Oleinik: Yes, I believed him.

Kaznacheyev: Still I don't understand. For many years of your work you did not take part in wrecking activities. Under the influence of what factors did you become active and start on the road of active wrecking and espionage? Under what influence particularly in the last few years? You had worked before, hadn't you?

Oleinik: Yes, I had worked before.

Kaznacheyev: Why was it particularly in the last few years that you passed over to action?

Oleinik: It was always customary to get information on the state of factories, proposed extensions and so forth, things in which the firm was interested. Under the old regime, bribes were also a usual thing. Nothing could be done without bribes.

Kaznacheyev. Therefore, you continued the habits which you learned when working with the firm?

Oleinik: Yes, I should say that it was habit.

Kaznacheyev: So, let us go further. You began to tell how you gathered information, and so on. But it is one thing to gather information in general, and another thing to collect definite information of a spying nature, of a military nature. I am interested in the moment when you changed. Do you understand me?

Oleinik: I understand you. At the end of 1930, engineer Thornton approached me about my future, saying that at my age there was not much time left to work. I would work perhaps five or at most ten years and after that I would have to think of how to get along further. Soviet currency, he said, was unstable and if I had any savings then they could arrange for me to bank them in England, and besides that, put in ten pounds every month out of my salary. This would be a guarantee for my old age. Of course, this seemed very good to me. But this was done as a preliminary, and after this, our conversation took on an anti-Soviet character. I should add that there was not merely conversation but I also got some reading material. The Englishmen brought magazines, books and newspapers.

Kaznacheyev: Do you know English?

Oleinik: Fluently.

Kaznacheyev: So Thornton confronted you with the question of your immediate future?

Oleinik: I saw that he was taking a very great interest in me, and when he began to set tasks, it was very difficult for me to refuse.

Kaznacheyev: So he won you over in that way?

Oleinik: Yes, by taking an interest in my future.

Kaznacheyev: But you must have realized what responsibility you undertook by obtaining such information of the nature of military espionage; or did you not understand at that time, or not think about it?

Oleinik: I understood.

Kaznacheyev: You understood?

Oleinik: Yes.

Kaznacheyev: Then how can you explain why you undertook this with such comparative ease?

Oleinik: I tried to fulfil it as little as possible.

Kaznacheyev: You tried to fulfil it as little as possible?

Oleinik: Yes, because all the same a struggle was going on within me.

Kaznacheyev: On the one hand, the feeling of approaching grave responsibility and on the other hand, what?

Oleinik: Not only the feeling of responsibility, but I would say a moral feeling.

Kaznacheyev: That factor also interests me. Tell us about the moral side of the case.

Oleinik: There could be nothing more despicable, of course.

Kaznacheyev: Then how did you reconcile yourself to it?

Oleinik: I have said that it was with reluctance.

Kaznacheyev: It was with reluctance. Now tell us, when you were thinking about your immediate future, were you interested in yourself or in other people—your family, your relatives? Have you a big family?

Oleinik: I have quite a number of people dependent on me.

Kaznacheyev: Who are they?

Oleinik: My own family is not large but I have a mother.

Kaznacheyev: How old is she?

Oleinik: She is eighty-six years old, but she is still active.

Kaznacheyev: Completely dependent upon you?

Oleinik: Yes, entirely.

Kaznacheyev: Who else is there?

Oleinik: I have a sister with children.

Kaznacheyev: How old is she?

Oleinik: Forty-eight years.

Kaznacheyev: Who else?

Oleinik: I often help my other sisters, but they are not dependent upon me.

Kaznacheyev: Have you an adopted child?

Oleinik: Yes, a girl.

Kaznacheyev: How old?

Oleinik: Ten years.

Kaznacheyev: Also completely dependent upon you?

Oleinik: Yes.

Kaznacheyev: So when you undertook this matter, settling the question in a criminal way, you were not thinking so much about yourself as your relatives. Do I understand you rightly?

Oleinik: Yes, of course, I linked up my own fate with that of my relatives.

Kaznacheyev: I ask you, did their fate also play a definite role?

Oleinik: I was the eldest son in the family; the family was a big one and all my life it has relied on me. All my life I have helped to support my brothers and sisters.

Kaznacheyev: One more question. We know that you had a current account. Besides that, during the past years had you saved up money, had you accumulated any means or not?

Oleinik: In the last few years?

Kaznacheyev: No. Had you property in general at any time?

Oleinik: At one time I owned a house. I had savings. I received a good salary.

Kaznacheyev: Big savings or not?

Oleinik: Yes, about 5,000 rubles.

Kaznacheyev: Did you receive anything from your father?

Oleinik: What could I have received when he only earned ten rubles a month?

Kaznacheyev: So his material situation was extremely bad. I have no further questions.

Braude: I want you to make clear the extent of the criminal activity which you attributed to Thornton. You say that Thornton instructed you to organize a group of wreckers?

Oleinik: Yes.

Braude: One group, or as many as possible?

Oleinik: Wherever possible.

Braude: Did you organize many?

Oleinik: I had no time.

Braude: But where did you succeed?

Oleinik: I succeeded in Moscow.

Braude: But in other places?

Oleinik: But besides me, Nordwall was also there.

Braude: Did you reply to the question of the Prosecution that you did not remember or that you did not organize them?

Oleinik: I did not organize them.

Braude: So it was only in the Moscow Power Station? Whom did you draw in there?

Oleinik: Those people are not here.

Braude: Very well. You informed the Court in detail of the wrecking acts personally carried on by you. Did these also occur in many places?

Oleinik: I don't know what to say. I was in many places.

Braude: Did you organize them there?

Oleinik: Yes.

Braude: You mentioned two places, Shterovka and what other place?

Oleinik: Belovo and the Moscow Power Station. But it was not on many jobs.

Braude: So it was only in two places? You replied that you did not remember the others.

Oleinik: I have already spoken of the case in the Urals.

Braude: And no others?

Oleinik: I think not.

Braude: Is it every day you organize wrecking acts that you don't know? This is not a thing which people can forget. You gathered military information on the instructions of Thornton. What kind of military information did Thornton instruct you to gather?

Oleinik: First, it was at a military factory near Perm.

Braude: What kind and what military information?

Oleinik: The volume and kind of production.

Braude: Was it secret production?

Oleinik: Naturally.

Braude: Were you allowed in there?

Oleinik: No.

Braude: Then how could you find out?

Oleinik: If I could have got into contact with the people who worked there, I could have found out, of course.

Braude: But you did not get into connection with them, and so you did not find out and did not give the information?

Oleinik: I gave information of what I saw myself and what I heard by chance.

Braude: So in general there was nothing secret about it? Whatever you could see, anyone could see. Is that so?

Oleinik: No, not everybody. I worked in a factory, and came across people who worked in various departments.

Braude: And did you question them?

Oleinik: It was not convenient to question them. There are strict rules about that; but things which I heard by chance I passed on.

Braude: What concrete information did you send on? What was it about? Were you mentioning figures or exactly formulating the information?

Oleinik: When I went to the Far East, I also sent information about the movement of troops and munitions.

Braude: But did you have instructions to obtain information about the movement of troops? Were you at the railway station as a passenger?

Oleinik: Yes.

Braude: So you saw what every passenger saw.

Oleinik: Yes.

Braude: And is that all the information you sent?

Oleinik: Yes.

Braude: I have no further questions.

Vyshinsky: So we can establish without question that there was military espionage. Did Thornton give you instructions to obtain information on the military work in the factories near Perm when you were sent there, or did he not give you such instructions?

Oleinik: He not only gave instructions, but he came there himself in 1931.

Vyshinsky: He came himself in 1931 to collect information?

Oleinik: He went to Chelyabinsk and on the way he called on me at the place where I worked although there was no need for it.

Vyshinsky: (To Thornton). Accused Thornton, were you there?

Thornton: I was.

Vyshinsky: The fact that you did not succeed in getting the information which interested Thornton does not in the least affect the question that you were given instructions. Did the instructions remain in force?

Oleinik: Yes.

Vyshinsky: Excuse me if my expressions are rather pointed, but they are true. Do spies always carry out instructions capably and successfully?

Oleinik: I think not.

Vyshinsky: To get information about the movement of troops, you tried to get into contact with suitable passengers, people, managers; to listen, to piece things together, to keep a lookout, to smell things out, or didn't you try to do so?

Oleinik: I cannot say that I tried, because it would have been necessary to select suitable people and how could I know the opinions of these people?

Vyshinsky: And what were your instructions?

Oleinik: The instructions were to find out.

Vyshinsky: Did you carry out this task conscientiously?

Oleinik: Yes.

Vyshinsky: Had all this information any importance for the Metro-Vickers Company? Was Metro-Vickers interested in this information?

Oleinik: They were not.

Vyshinsky: I also think they were not, but perhaps one of their employees was interested?

Oleinik: If he had not been interested, he would not have given instructions. That is obvious.

Vyshinsky: And it was Thornton who gave the instructions?

Oleinik: Not only Thornton, but also Nordwall when he was in Motovilikha.

Vyshinsky: They were all serving interests which were not

only those of the firm for which they were working. Perhaps they were hiding behind the firm?

Oleinik: I don't know that.

Vyshinsky: Didn't they entrust that to you?

Oleinik: They did not entrust that to me.

Vyshinsky: Was your standing that of an employee or a full member of this spy organization?

Oleinik: More of an employee.

Vyshinsky: So it was—find out, bring it here, and tell us.

Oleinik: Yes.

Vyshinsky: You would get material benefits according to how much you brought; a cheque on the bank in London, so many pounds, and so forth.

Oleinik: No, they did not give me money for separate pieces of information.

Vyshinsky: But for the lot?

Oleinik: Yes.

Vyshinsky: You were paid according to how you worked.

I have no further questions.

The President: I declare the session adjourned until 6 p.m.

(The Court adjourns at 3 p.m. until 6 p.m.)

[Signed] V. V. ULRICH
President of the Special Session of the
Supreme Court of the U.S.S.R.
A. F. KOSTYUSHKO
Secretary

EVENING SESSION, APRIL 15, 1933, 6 p.m.

Commandant: Please rise. The Court is coming.

The President: Please be seated. Has the Defence any more questions to put to the accused Oleinik?

Kommodov: I have.

The President: Accused Oleinik.

Kommodov: Citizen Oleinik, on the basis of this morning's examination we may take the following facts as having been established; kindly state whether you confirm them or not. First, your direct relations with Monkhouse ended in 1929. Is this correct?

Oleinik: No, this is not correct. Engineer Monkhouse has been the chief engineer of the office of the Metro-Vickers Company in Moscow all the time. I maintained relations with him.

Kommodow: I speak of direct relations.

Oleinik: There were also direct relations.

Kommodov: Then, how are we to understand your answer to the Public Prosecutor when you stated that up to 1929 you were directly in contact with Monkhouse and when Thornton was appointed chief installation engineer, you began to deal with him?

Oleinik: In relation to the installation work, this is so.

Kommodov: Precisely, I am asking in relation to the installation work. This means that here the border line is 1929?

Oleinik: Yes.

Kommodov: And up to that time?

Oleinik: I do not remember the exact date, but it really seems that this was actually at the end of 1929, when Thornton was appointed installation engineer.

Kommodov: Up to 1929 was there any single act of wrecking—not the concealing of defects in the equipment in the interests of the firm—but, of wrecking as wilful destruction or definite breakdowns which followed? Prior to 1929?

Oleinik: In my opinion there was not.

Kommodov: It means that no such acts took place?

The third question. At the preliminary investigation, and I believe, also here, you mentioned two cases: the collection of information on the definite instructions of Monkhouse at the time you went to the Nadezhdinsk Works in 1928 and, if one may express it so, the dragging out of the testing dates of the turbines up to the moment when the guarantee limit for the Shterovka State Power Station had expired.

Oleinik: More correctly, obstruction of the tests so that the tests should not be made at all. If the test is dragged out and the guarantee period has passed, then the test is futile . . . so I understood.

Kommodov: In order to drag out the tests so that they should not take place at all, or only to delay them?

Oleinik: Once the guarantee period has passed, the purchaser has no right to demand a test.

Kommodov: But can the test take place?

Oleinik: Yes, it can take place, but it would not be valid.

Kommodov: The last instructions, you state, were in writing.

Oleinik: Yes.

Kommodov: Do you remember approximately the month when this letter was written?

Oleinik: I think it was about August or September.

Kommodov: And did you write an answer to this letter of Monkhouse?

Oleinik: It seems to me I did, I am not certain.

Kommodov: Outside of these two cases to which you testified, do you remember any other cases of such instructions?

Oleinik: At present, no.

Kommodov: Now I would like you simply to confirm a certain part of your deposition given at the preliminary investigation, page 83, Volume XV. You were asked the question: "State in detail how you were drawn into the espionage work." This is what you answered: "I worked for the firm a long time. At first I was given the task of gathering information about the state of industry in connection with the orders, this being connected with the work of the firm. This was in 1928. I considered that I was obliged to do so in the interests of the firm. In 1931, Mr. Thornton told me that it was necessary to obtain information about the state of industry, transport and electrical energy. And in 1932, Mr. Thornton quite clearly told me that it was necessary to select people for espionage and acts of diversion." Do you confirm this part of your testimony?

Oleinik: Yes.

Kommodow: One more statement—page 82, Volume XV. You were asked the question: "What tasks in the nature of espionage and diversion were given you by Monkhouse?" You answered: "In 1928, when I went to the Urals, I was instructed to find out about the condition of the works to which I was going, namely the Nadezhdinsk Works, and, in general, about the state of transport and industry in the Urals. I was not given any tasks by Monkhouse in regard to acts of diversion." Do you confirm this?

Oleinik: Yes, I do.

Kommodov: Comrade President, I have no further questions for Oleinik.

I beg leave in virtue of Article 272, to admit as evidence two documents after having them examined by the Public Prosecutor and the Court. I ask that you examine them and if you find it possible and expedient for the case, to admit them in evidence. At the same time, I must explain that the first document, inasmuch as it is a copy of a letter, is not certified and, in accordance with Article 272, it depends entirely upon the Court whether it should be admitted or not.

(Counsel for the Defence hands the documents to the President for inspection.)

Dolmatovsky: When did you get acqainted with Thornton?

Oleinik: It was in 1931, in Motovilikha.

Dolmatovsky: Did you, at that time, already have instructions from Thornton, as to how you must conduct yourself?

Oleinik: What do you mean by how to conduct myself?

Dolmatovsky: As you have stated today—that it was necessary to carry out acts of diversion, etc.

Oleinik: No, at that time I did not have such instructions.

Dolmatovsky: And when you were together with him at Makeyevka—did you have such instructions at that time?

Oleinik: At that time I already had them.

Dolmatovsky: Have you had instructions about wrecking acts, espionage activities, and so forth, from Nordwall?

Oleinik: I did not get instructions, but was asked questions and received assistance.

Dolmatovsky: Did you ask him for assistance, or did he ask you?

Oleinik: He asked me.

Dolmatovsky: What did his requests consist of?

Oleinik: When he came to Motovilikha, he asked me the following: first, he asked me several questions in relation to the production of the works and then, as I had been there for a long period of time and he had just arrived, he asked me to introduce him to local engineers from whom we could receive information.

Dolmatovsky: It means that you did not have instructions from Thornton?

Oleinik: What do you mean—did not have?

Dolmatovsky: You stated that you became acquainted with him in Motovilikha and that you had no instructions from him at that time.

Oleinik: I did have instructions. There were several. First, there were instructions about obtaining information simply of an industrial character.

Dolmatovsky: That which you considered necessary and in the interests of the firm and in which there was nothing illegal. In your opinion does information about production and the needs of industry by itself constitute illegal information?

Oleinik: It depends on where and when. I am able to distinguish where it is legal and where illegal.

Dolmatovsky: It means that Nordwall demanded illegal information; you understood this and you gave it to him?

Oleinik: Yes, I gave it to him.

Dolmatovsky: Knowing that this was illegal information?

Oleinik: Yes, I was aware of it.

Dolmatovsky: Consequently, at that time, there was already illegal information being given?

Oleinik: You do not put the question in the right way.

The President: The Counsel puts the question in the way that he finds necessary and you have to answer.

Oleinik: He confuses two questions. If the question refers to acts of diversion, then I had not yet received information.

Dolmatovsky: What information had you already received?

Oleinik: The task was to obtain information about the production of the military works. It was approximately a month and a half prior to the arrival of Nordwall at Motovilikha.

Dolmatovsky: This means that you already had tasks of an espionage character?

Oleinik: I had.

Dolmatovsky: But you stated that you did not have.

Oleinik: No, I didn't say that.

Dolmatovsky: Consequently Nordwall, in fulfilling the instructions which were given by Thornton, had already put to you certain questions in Motovilikha. Is that so?

Oleinik: I do not know whether it was in accordance with instructions from Thornton. This he did not tell me, he put his questions on his own behalf.

Dolmatovsky: But you understood that they came from one source?

Oleinik: I was not convinced of this. I know that he asked questions, but that they came from one source—I didn't think about that.

Dolmatovsky: And the fact that they coincided with the instructions given by Thornton—did you think that was simply a coincidence?

Oleinik: I didn't think about it.

Dolmatovsky: And when you were in Makeyevka, did you know already that Nordwall was your man?

Oleinik: No, I did not know it.

Dolmatovsky: And when did you find out that he was one of your people? Did he give you tasks of an espionage nature?

Oleinik: Yes.

Dolmatovsky: You knew that he was your man?

Oleinik: In Makeyevka I did not know. I stated that regarding Nordwall—I had had a warning.

Dolmatovsky: What kind?

Oleinik: I thought that this was simply camouflage because Nordwall impressed me as a very experienced spy. From his actions in both Motovilikha and Makeyevka he gave the impression of being very experienced.

Dolmatovsky: Then I absolutely cannot understand you. You had a task from Thornton of an espionage nature. Then Nordwall came and duplicated tasks of the same nature.

Oleinik: He gave his own and did not duplicate theirs. He asked me to acquaint him with the personnel which could give him information.

Dolmatovsky: You considered him an experienced spy?

Oleinik: There I did not, but in Makeyevka I already considered him one.

Dolmatovsky: You have just stated that you did not. But let us suppose that you did. Were you in Makeyevka?

Oleinik: Yes.

Dolmatovsky: Were you in a counter-revolutionary organization at that time? Did you already have at that time tasks given to you by Thornton?

Oleinik: I did.

Dolmatovsky: Did you consider that Thornton assigned these tasks of his own accord or that there was a whole organization?

Oleinik: I knew about engineer Thornton and also about Monkhouse, but I did not know about the others.

Dolmatovsky: May I remind you that you knew in detail which tasks were given to which engineers. In Makeyevka you knew that Nordwall was not an ordinary spy but a very experienced one. At that time you were in the organization and were connected with Monkhouse and others.

Oleinik: With Thornton.

Dolmatovsky: Did you have definite tasks?

Oleinik: Yes.

Dolmatovsky: Why then was it necessary to be afraid of Nordwall?

Oleinik: I was not afraid of him.

Dolmatovsky: Then what were your apprehensions?

Oleinik: I repeat I was not afraid of him, but Thornton told me that I must beware of him. If you wish I can tell you much more.

Dolmatovsky: It means that in Makeyevka you were not connected with him because you did not know whether he was an experienced spy or a Bolshevik. Was it because of this that you did not establish connections with him?

Oleinik: Because I had not yet made out at that time who Nordwall was and how far he could be relied upon. I did not know exactly what intentions he had.

Dolmatovsky: What did Thornton tell you?

Oleinik: I explained it to you just now. Besides, I was troubled by the words of Thornton that Nordwall is the sort of fellow who in case of anything happening would report to the institution. and so on.

Dolmatovsky: What institution?

Oleinik: Even to the Workers' and Peasants' Inspection, and so on.

Dolmatovsky: What a man!

Oleinik: This is word for word. I believe that engineer Thornton would confirm this at once.

Dolmatovsky: Now tell me the following. Did you have any misunderstandings with Nordwall in Makeyevka? Were you on hostile terms with him?

Oleinik: Hostile—no. I did not like him but my attitude towards him was not hostile.

Dolmatovsky: And what was the attitude of the local workers towards you and him?

Oleinik: In this respect I would like to state: he disorganized the work there—carried on underground work and bribed the workers.

Dolmatovsky: With what?

Oleinik: With money. I know this definitely.

Dolmatovsky: And from whom did you know it?

Oleinik: From him, and I saw with my own eyes how he was paying out.

Dolmatovsky: So, it means that you were connected with him in your illegal work.

Oleinik: Which illegal work?

Dolmatovsky: Were you in the same organization with him?

Oleinik: In no organization. I had to deal with Thornton.

Dolmatovsky: It means that Thornton gave you tasks of an illegal nature—to commit acts of diversion and to gather espionage information.

Oleinik: Thornton warned me that I should not get entangled with him because when there are two people it is possible to bungle up things, and inasmuch as Nordwall was more experienced, I ought to stand aside and Nordwall ought to do everything that was necessary.

Dolmatovsky: For this reason you did not like him?

Oleinik: Not because of this.

Dolmatovsky: Then why?

Oleinik: Simply because he is a repulsive, even a vile person.

Dolmatovsky: In Makeyevka what was the attitude towards Nordwall—and towards you?

Oleinik: This was the basis on which Nordwall carried on agitation all the time. When I wanted to carry on work, Nordwall incited the workers against me. The job superintendent, a friend of Nordwall's, carried on espionage work. He is not here and perhaps he should not be named, he brought in very much information and this information was very important. He was a friend of Nordwall's and Nordwall maintained this friendship with him just for this purpose and paid him money. Through this job superintendent he acted—bribed the workers and not only bribed, but also agitated.

Dolmatovsky: In what sense did he agitate?

Oleinik: He agitated that they should not submit to or carry out my orders, that they should delay the work. Here he talked about shock brigade work. This was pulling wool over the eyes, because the work which we put out in four and a half months could easily have been done in two months with a smaller expenditure of labour, with half the labour. Now if this work was completed, and in Dzerzhinka they were still behindhand, it means that the wrecking was even greater there than in Makeyevka.

Dolmatovsky: But was this part of your task?

Oleinik: No, it was not.

Dolmatovsky: And in what did your task consist—to carry on good work for the Soviet Government in Makeyevka?

Oleinik: I kept quiet and carried on wrecking work together with Nordwall.

Dolmatovsky: And why did you hate Nordwall?

Oleinik: I did not say I hated him. I said I did not like him.

Dolmatovsky: Why didn't you like him?

Oleinik: No matter what my behaviour was, I never committed vile acts.

Dolmatovsky: Now it is quite clear what value your evidence regarding Nordwall has.

Oleinik: I can tell still more.

Dolmatovsky: When was Nordwall last in Novorossiisk?

Oleinik: He left in September 1932.

Dolmatovsky: After Novorossiisk did you have any conversations with Nordwall?

Oleinik: I did.

Dolmatovsky: And your attitude towards him was as towards an unsympathetic person who might go to the Workers' and Peasants' Inspection to complain?

Oleinik: At that time I knew very little of him inasmuch as he was at Motovilikha only ten days.

Dolmatovsky: Were you given tasks of an espionage nature?

Oleinik: He did not have time to give tasks.

Dolmatovsky: Did Nordwall assign tasks at Motovilikha?

Oleinik: He did.

Dolmatovsky: Did he assign tasks in Novorossiisk, or did you gather the information on your own initiative?

Oleinik: I did not gather information—but I told Nordwall what I observed and saw.

Dolmatovsky: You told what you were asked?

Oleinik: Yes.

Dolmatovsky: You reported what you saw and what you gathered?

Oleinik: I must say that engineer Thornton came to Makeyevka three times during four months, and he appeared at the works only once but he went to Nordwall's apartment twice.

Dolmatovsky: You reported that you were gathering information in Novorossiisk?

Oleinik: I reported to Nordwall and Nordwall transmitted this information to Thornton.

Dolmatovsky: You reported to Nordwall and Nordwall to Thornton, but you yourself could not report to Thornton?

Oleinik: I did not see him. Nordwall was the person assigned for this purpose in Makeyevka. Besides this, I can say something else about Nordwall if you put the question in this way, and not because I hate him but because there are many proofs of this. Nordwall knew the Makeyevka works better than any other engineer working at Makeyevka. He knew both the output and the plan. This I know for certain.

Dolmatovsky: And because of this, you don't like him?

Oleinik: I didn't say because of this. Do not paraphrase my words.

Dolmatovsky: How do you know that he knew the plan?

Oleinik: From conversations which were partially carried on in my presence.

Dolmatovsky: Among what persons did the conversations take place?

Oleinik: Between him and those from whom he personally received the information.

Dolmatovsky: That is to say, you were connected with him since such things were spoken of in your presence, things which one does not speak of in the presence of a third person.

Oleinik: I do not suggest that I have nothing to do with all this; I have no intention of hiding my own guilt.

Dolmatovsky: Were you or weren't you afraid of him as a man who might go to the Workers' and Peasants' Inspection and complain?

Oleinik: I was not afraid that he would go to the Workers' and Peasants' Inspection and complain. I stated that I was warned about this by engineer Thornton, but I was not afraid because I saw that this was simply a bluff, a mask.

Dolmatovsky: Who was subordinate to whom in Makeyevka?

Oleinik: Nordwall, as electrical engineer, was chief.

Dolmatovsky: You were subordinate to him?

Oleinik: What shall I call it—it is rather a strange subordination. Considering my long experience in the work, it is strange.

Dolmatovsky: It is strange that you were subordinate to him, it should have been the other way round. Is that right?

Oleinik: On this job, no.

Dolmatovsky: And in general, on other jobs?

Oleinik: Yes, of course.

Dolmatovsky: And you considered yourself offended?

Oleinik: No—it was known here that I worked on turbines and this was a mechanical job.

Dolmatovsky: A last question—did they treat him better than you in Makeyevka?

Oleinik: Only certain persons, but not all.

Dolmatovsky: And did you hear that he was given a premium there and invited to take his seat in the presidium?

Oleinik: This is correct, but I also received a premium.

Dolmatovsky: The same as his?

Oleinik: He received a thousand rubles while I received four hundred rubles, but the premium is not always received by those who actually do the work.

Dolmatovsky: Consequently, did you receive the premium deservedly or undeservedly?

Oleinik: I consider that this is a futile question and I do not wish to answer.

Dolmatovsky: That is your affair. But tell me, did Nordwall receive the premium deservedly or undeservedly?

Oleinik: Undeservedly.

Dolmatovsky: You spoke about Gregory. On March 24, you gave evidence and cited data touching on the subject, of which engineers were occupied with what. Among others you placed in one group Cushny, Gregory, a certain Noy and Nordwall. Did Gregory have contact with you in your work?

Oleinik: If Nordwall has any sense of decency left, let him step out here and tell what he said about the wrecking work of Gregory.

Dolmatovsky: Did he tell you?

Oleinik: Yes, he told me.

Dolmatovsky: You, of course, can ask Nordwall about it. I am asking you—did you know Gregory?

Oleinik: I knew him—he came twice.

Dolmatovsky: Or did you give your evidence about Gregory on the basis of what Nordwall said?

Oleinik: I knew Gregory in Makeyevka.

The President: Pardon me, Comrade Dolmatovsky, Gregory hears his name all the time and does not understand what is the matter. It is necessary to have an interpreter.

Dolmatovsky: Very well. I am asking Oleinik if he knows Gregory.

Oleinik: I know him. Gregory came twice.

(The Interpreter translates for Gregory.)

Dolmatovsky: Do you know his wrecking work? Did he carry out any definite wrecking act?

Oleinik: Tell me, first of all, what you call wrecking work.

The President: Accused Oleinik, prior to the adjournment you spoke for a whole hour about wrecking activities and now you ask what is wrecking work.

Oleinik: The Counsel for the Defence speaks so unclearly that against my will I am compelled to ask him to speak concretely.

Dolmatovsky: You know very well what wrecking work is.

Oleinik: And I am asking you to put it concretely.

The President: I consider it advisable to end the examination of Oleinik.

Dolmatovsky: As you please.

Schwartz (To the Court): Permit me to ask Oleinik a few questions.

Thornton (From his seat): I want to ask Oleinik some questions.

Vyshinsky: I would like to support the request of Thornton regarding his right to put a few questions to Oleinik. It seems to me that this is of importance in the interests of this case. We can only limit this so that there shall be no repetition.

The President: Oleinik answers all questions at such length and with such confusion that this only drags out the Court's examination unnecessarily.

Braude: Thornton wants to ask Oleinik a few technical questions.

The President: The Court considers it superfluous to continue this examination.

Accused Monkhouse, tell us the main facts in your biography.

Monkhouse: I was born in 1887, in New Zealand. At the age of 15, I came to England to study. I graduated from Manchester University. I received a diploma as Mechanical Engineer and a second diploma as Electrical Engineer. After this I was employed at the Dick Kerr and Co. Works till 1911. In 1911 I came to Moscow as the installation engineer of Dick Kerr and Co. I came for the installation of the Moscow city tramway system. I worked here approximately a year. After that, I was employed at the Dynamo Factory as chief of the tram-car and railway department. I worked at the Dynamo Factory and at another factory connected with Dynamo up to March 1918. At that period, during the war, I had connections with another small factory which produced electrical measuring instruments here in Moscow.

In March 1918, I left Moscow for Vladivostok through Siberia. From there I went to America and joined the Canadian Army. The Canadian Army was sent to England where I was transferred to the British Army. Inasmuch as I knew the Russian language, I was assigned as a translator to the Second Expeditionary Force in Archangel. In September 1918, I arrived in Archangel and at once on the next day, I was sent to the Vysokiye Gorky Station, twelve versts from Archangel. I served there as a translator at the locomotive depot. I had the rank of non-commissioned officer.

In February 1919, the officer who was in command of the depot (chief of traffic on the Northern Railway) was sent back to England. For this reason I was appointed an officer and given the rank of captain.

The President: From non-commissioned officer you were at once promoted to the rank of captain?

Monkhouse: I was promoted from non-commissioned officer to the rank of captain within two weeks.

The President: You arrived as a non-commissioned officer?

Monkhouse: Yes.

The President: Within two weeks you became a captain?

Monkhouse: I arrived in September. In February I was given officer's rank. And within two weeks I was appointed captain. This was done because the post of traffic chief was one which had to be occupied by a captain.

I remained in Archangel up to the last moment, as long as the British Army remained there. After this I obtained employment in the Metro-Vickers Works.

The President: One question in connection with your stay in Archangel. What were your duties?

Monkhouse: My duties in Archangel were the organization and equipment of the locomotive depot and the installation of railway equipment.

The President: Did you serve in the railway troops?

Monkhouse: Yes.

The President: How many soldiers were subordinate to you?

Monkhouse: About 86 Englishmen and about 800 Russians, including the entire railway crew and those who tended the locomotives and the railway depot. In addition, there was a Russian chief of traffic, so that we did parallel work and there was a double command.

The President: The Russians—who were they—railway employees or soldiers?

Monkhouse: Railway employees.

The President: Were they militarized?

Monkhouse: Yes. One might say they were almost militarized.

The President: And to whom were you directly subordinate?

Monkhouse: I was under Col. Graham who was stationed in Archangel on the General Staff. He was assistant director of railways.

The President: How long did you remain in that district?

Monkhouse: I was in the district almost 12 months.

The President: Consequently, a whole year?

Monkhouse: Yes—I arrived on September 2, left Archangel

on September 23, and left Murmansk on October 11. That makes a little more than 13 months.

The President: Were you one of the last to leave Archangel?

Monkhouse: Almost the last. This was by order of the Commander-in-Chief. He wanted me to be on the last train to make sure that everything was in order.

The President: And where was General Miller?

Monkhouse: In Archangel, but I did not see him.

The President: When did he leave?

Monkhouse: I do not know when he left.

The President: Did you meet your schoolmate, Richards?

Monkhouse: I visited Archangel once a month and almost every time met Richards, who was attached to the General Staff. There was an officers' mess room there, I had my lunch there, and met him. He was a good friend of mine and so I almost always saw him.

The President: Was he an officer of the Counter-Intelligence Service?

Monkhouse: Counter-Intelligence or Intelligence, I don't know.

The President: How is it that you don't know? There is a difference between Intelligence and Counter-Intelligence.

Monkhouse: In my opinion, it was Counter-Intelligence.

The President: Intelligence seeks information and Counter-Intelligence seeks Intelligence agents. What was Richards looking for—information or Russian Intelligence agents?

Monkhouse: It seems to me that he did both. I don't know whether Richards did this work personally or not.

The President: Well, of course not personally. What was his rank?

Monkhouse: Captain.

The President: So you both had the same rank?

Monkhouse: Yes.

The President: Did you happen to help him in his work?

Monkhouse: No.

The President: Were you occupied only with the railway business?

Monkhouse: Yes.

The President: And so you met frequently?

Monkhouse: I was always at the officers' mess at the General Staff and I met him there.

The President: Did you leave together with him, or did he leave before?

Monkhouse: He left a few days earlier—I think it was one day ahead. He left on the steamer with the General Staff, and I on a freighter.

The President: And what did you do after that? Did you leave the Army, were you demobilized?

Monkhouse: Yes. I was employed at the Metro-Vickers Works in Manchester and after a few months I was appointed Assistant Chief of the Department of Scientific Research and I remained in this work until the end of 1923. When in the end of 1923 a commission from Moscow came to Manchester to purchase equipment for the Shterovka and Shatura Stations, they asked to see the works. After this they asked me to come here to instal the equipment. At first I didn't want to do this because I had interesting work, but after a conversation which I had at the railway station with Winter, who was on this commission, I decided to come, and arrived for the first time in February 1924. I was here only one month, after which I was at our works for three months where I looked after the shipping of equipment to the Chita and Shterovka Power Stations. Then I finally came here in August 1924, and lived in Shatura. I was in Shatura for 14 months and after this went to Volkhovstroy for the installation of a sub-station in Leningrad. I lived in Leningrad until 1929, and then when Electro-Import was organized and our firm was invited to assist in the formation of the technical bureau of Electro-Import, to clear up various technical questions in connection with enquiries and orders, I settled in Moscow.

The President: In what year?

Monkhouse: This was in 1929, and since then I have lived almost the whole time in Moscow, but three times a year I travel to England to the head office.

The President: How many years have you spent in the U.S.S.R. altogether?

Monkhouse: As a whole, 17 years.

The President: And in the U.S.S.R., after the Archangel affair?

Monkhouse: I came here in 1924—nine years ago.

Vyshinsky: Inasmuch as we have exhausted a number of questions in the course of the Court proceedings, I beg to declare to the Court that we shall limit ourselves to certain supplementary questions in order not to repeat what has already been covered.

Accused Monkhouse, I am interested in several questions in order to throw light on the charges against you.

First question: Did you gather information or receive it from various persons connected with you through service and other relations?

Monkhouse: I received information; perhaps it would be more correct to say, not information, but impressions.

Vyshinsky: You received information; perhaps we should call it information.

Monkhouse: Information. This, of course, I needed because every time I come to London I report to my head office. . .

Vyshinsky: On various questions connected with your work?

Monkhouse: On various questions connected with our work and our head office always asks us to report on the situation in the country.

Vyshinsky: Can we take as established that you are corroborating your entire deposition where you confirm that you received various kinds of information just within the limits of which you have now spoken?

Monkhouse: Just within those limits, as I state. That is to say, I received such information as could be useful for our head office when it had to decide a question on whether or not to grant credits.

Vyshinsky: It means that you received the information which you considered useful and necessary for you?

Monkhouse: That is correct.

Vyshinsky: From whom did you receive this information? Particularly, did you receive it from Thornton?

Monkhouse: When Thornton arrived after his trips he always reported what he saw and from this I received the impressions which remained in my memory.

Vyshinsky: But from whom did you receive it mainly?

Monkhouse: This is very difficult to state. I read all the Russian papers every day, all the technical papers.

Vyshinsky: And besides newspaper information?

Monkhouse: I knew many leaders. . .

Vyshinsky: In a word, you utilized all opportunities to gather information?

Monkhouse: Of course, this was my business.

Vyshinsky: Of course it was your business to utilize all information, every meeting, conversations, and so on.

Monkhouse: To utilize it only in that sense of which I have spoken—in order to carry on our business here.

Vyshinsky: It's clear, to carry on business here. Was Thornton among your informants and your sources of information?

Monkhouse: Of course Thornton was, because I saw him every day.

Vyshinsky: At the preliminary examination you deposed that this information was supplied by Thornton and Cushny who frequently travelled to the construction jobs.

Monkhouse: Quite so.

Vyshinsky: What you deny is only its espionage nature?

Monkhouse: I deny the espionage nature of this information.

Vyshinsky: You deny this except for a few depositions to which we shall return. This information you obtained in different ways from different sources, chiefly from Thornton and Cushny?

Monkhouse: It is difficult to say that it was chiefly, but from among the Englishmen it was so.

Vyshinsky: That is exactly what I wished to establish. We shall not speak about the Dolgov story.

Monkhouse: I have already said that he could not get money anywhere. The money was given as a loan and when Dolgov did not pay back the money, I assisted in the writing off of this sum.

Vyshinsky: You admit that?

Monkhouse: I admit only that my mistake was that I assisted in this writing off.

Vyshinsky: You admit your guilt in this part?

Monkhouse: I admit I made a mistake.

Vyshinsky: You first spoke about a present and then you wanted it returned.

Monkhouse: Since he didn't return the money, it was necessary to write it off.

Vyshinsky: Consequently, he made a present of the money to himself?

Monkhouse: If you wish, you can put it that way. I thought that he was a straightforward man.

Vyshinsky: The third question. Were there defects in the installation supplied by your firm?

Monkhouse: Yes, there were defects.

Vyshinsky: Perhaps you will specify what defects, where and in what cases? Let us say at Orekhovo-Zuevo.

Monkhouse: There were defects there.

Vyshinsky: Something wrong with the turbine or, to be more exact, the turbine was defective?

Monkhouse: The turbine was defective.

Vyshinsky: Well, were they satisfactory or not satisfactory in regard to their construction or in regard to the installation?

Monkhouse: At the preliminary investigation I said that the turbines in Orekhovo-Zuevo were poorly chosen.

Vyshinsky: And were they poor in execution also?

Monkhouse: They were poor in execution also.

Vyshinsky: Consequently, you confirm what you said at the preliminary investigation in this respect?

Monkhouse: Yes, I do.

Vyshinsky: Let us take Moges and particularly the First Power Station. Now what was wrong there?

Monkhouse: There were defects there, too.

Vyshinsky: Grave defects?

Monkhouse: Grave enough with the blades.

Vyshinsky: And in consequence of these defects, there were breakdowns?

Monkhouse: There were breakdowns.

Vyshinsky: Serious breakdowns?

Monkhouse: To my mind they were not very serious. I do not know what you call serious. I consider it a serious breakdown when the turbine flies through the roof. *(Commotion)*

Vyshinsky: But if it does not fly through the roof and is only put out of action—this is not a serious breakdown? Our conceptions of seriousness are somewhat different.

Monkhouse: When the turbine has to be stopped for two or three days and the blades repaired, this is not a very serious breakdown.

Vyshinsky: I do not say that this is very serious, but between two days of stoppage and a turbine flying through the roof there is a big difference.

Monkhouse: Of course, for the reputation of the firm it is serious, but, in general, the breakdown is not serious.

Vyshinsky: Your firm is not on trial, we are speaking here to you. Therefore the reputation of your firm is of little interest to me, but what I am interested in is your deeds.

Monkhouse: I said at the preliminary examination that if you consider this turbine which works at the First Power Station, you have to compare the number of kilowatt hours the turbine is working and the number of kilowatt hours that it is idle. Then the result is not at all bad.

Vyshinsky: Not very bad?

Monkhouse: Not at all bad.

Vyshinsky: But can we say, quite good?

Monkhouse: We can say that, bearing in mind that this turbine was ordered as a peak machine which works 2,000 hours per annum.

Vyshinsky: Perhaps it is necessary to bear in mind that it was ordered for our country and for us it is good enough.

Monkhouse: We don't do that in general.

Vyshinsky: Well, thanks for that. There are defects at the First Moscow Power Station which you consider of a sufficiently serious nature although not of a very serious nature.

Monkhouse: Unpleasant defects. Not very serious but unpleasant.

Vyshinsky: And at the Zuevka Power Station, were there any defects?

Monkhouse: I spoke about this at the preliminary examination; there were defects there.

Vyshinsky: With the diaphragm?

Monkhouse: Yes, and we sent a new diaphragm; this thing was settled.

Vyshinsky: Further—at Baku?

Monkhouse: At Baku there were defects in the blades.

Vyshinsky: Again blades? And at the Ivanovo Power Station?

Monkhouse: The defects which were at Baku were also to be found at the Ivanovo and at the Chelyabinsk Power Stations. These were all defects in the blades.

Vyshinsky: And as a result of this, the turbines shot through the roof?

Monkhouse: No.

Vyshinsky: But they broke?

Monkhouse: No, we stopped the turbines in time.

Vyshinsky: But there were stoppages?

Monkhouse. Not long stoppages. We repaired all the defects either in the course of the annual repairs or during the second stoppage of the turbine.

Vyshinsky: Now, what was wrong, aside from these defects, with specific parts? What was wrong with the regulation?

Monkhouse: Here there were also. . .

Vyshinsky: Defects?

Monkhouse: Not defects, but some incidents. But this too, we put right immediately.

Vyshinsky: At the preliminary investigation you were more outspoken. You said straightforwardly that there were also defects.

Monkhouse: Defects in the regulation.

Vyshinsky: You said: "At Baku, at the Ivanovo Power Station, at the Chelyabinsk Power Station and at the Zuevka Power Station, defects were disclosed in the regulation." Is that so?

Monkhouse: Correct.

Vyshinsky: You confirm that?

Monkhouse: I confirm it, but all these defects were removed.

Vyshinsky: At the Chelyabinsk and at the Zuevka Power Stations, cases were disclosed of varnish dripping off the rotor winding of the 11,000 volt machines.

Monkhouse: It is a fact, but I took part in a committee which went out there and decided that there was no danger.

Vyshinsky: I am not speaking about danger, but were there such cases?

Monkhouse: Yes, there were.

Vyshinsky: You confirm that at a number of stations—Ivanovo, Zuevka, Chelyabinsk, and the First Moscow Power Station—there were a number of defects in the regulation as well as in the turbines and the diaphragms.

Monkhouse: Quite true, but I must say that all these defects we repaired ,and repaired very quickly. These were all defects which depended either on the material or on the design, but not on the installation.

Vyshinsky: In short, these were defects in some cases of greater importance and in others of less importance. Is that so or not?

Monkhouse: You may put it that way if you wish.

Vyshinsky: In consequence of these defects there were breakdowns, and stoppages of machines?

Monkhouse: There were stoppages.

Vyshinsky: And were there any breakdowns?

Monkhouse: There were no important breakdowns.

Vyshinsky: I do not say important breakdowns. Will you please, if it is not inconvenient for you, answer my question. Have there been any breakdowns?

Monkhouse: What is a breakdown?

Vyshinsky: It is a disruption of work.

Monkhouse: If the turbine is stopped for twenty-four or forty-eight hours would that be a breakdown?

Vyshinsky: I consider that that is a breakdown. What do you think?

Monkhouse: If a machine is stopped for a year, this is a breakdown, but if it is for one or two days . . . I do not know the Russian language well.

Vyshinsky: You know Russian as well as I do.

Monkhouse: I am very pleased it is so. There were small breakdowns.

Vyshinsky: And were there stoppages, or not?

Monkhouse: There were small stoppages, but at Orekhovo-Zuevo, there was really a long stoppage.

Vyshinsky: Now we have come to Orekhovo-Zuevo, where there was an important stoppage.

Monkhouse: But the important stoppage was neither the fault of Metro-Vickers nor mine.

Vyshinsky: I repeat again that I do not accuse Metro-Vickers here. I accuse Monkhouse.

Monkhouse: But I am not responsible for this at all.

Vyshinsky: We shall see. In the end, it will be made clear who is responsible.

Thus, we have established that the stoppage at Orekhovo-Zuevo was a considerable one. Is that true?

Monkhouse: Yes, a considerable one.

Vyshinsky: And at Chelyabinsk, in consequence of the defect in the diaphragm, there was even an accident, wasn't there?

Monkhouse: What accident was there?

Vyshinsky: I am asking whether there was any accident.

Monkhouse: What is an accident?

Vyshinsky: Somebody injured.

Monkhouse: A man?

Vyshinsky: Certainly. Perhaps also a building.

Monkhouse: No. In Chelyabinsk one diaphragm was touching the rotor wheel. We stopped the machine.

Vyshinsky: And prevented an accident?

Monkhouse: Yes, so that there was not a very serious breakdown there.

Vyshinsky: Not a very serious breakdown, but all the same there was a breakdown?

Monkhouse: Yes, but there was no accident.

Vyshinsky: At the preliminary investigation you deposed: "At Orekhovo-Zuevo the machines did not give the guaranteed power and required a change of blades. At the Chelyabinsk Power Station there was an accident in consequence of the change of the diaphragm."

Monkhouse: I beg pardon. I speak Russian badly. This accident I spoke about was a breakdown.

Vyshinsky: You had in mind a breakdown?

Monkhouse: Yes.

Vyshinsky: We shall correct it and say that there was a breakdown. Very well. Now, to proceed further. What have you to say to this deposition: "Five turbines were installed in the U.S.S.R. of a nominal capacity from 46,000 to 80,000 kw., whereas they could not stand such a load."

Monkhouse: I do not remember. I said—five turbines—46,000 kw.

Vyshinsky: Of various capacities from 46,000 to 80,000 kw. They were installed but could not stand such a load?

Monkhouse: I said that at Zuevka there were three turbines, and here—two turbines where we had to change the diaphragms in order to give the full load.

Vyshinsky: Consequently, because of the faulty diaphragms, the turbines could not work at full load.

Monkhouse: But, as a matter of fact, they did work.

Vyshinsky: If they worked, then can they work at full load?

Monkhouse: Yes, they can.

Vyshinsky: But you said that they could not.

Monkhouse: We asked the station as far as possible not to work the turbines at full load until we had changed the diaphragms. This was a precautionary measure.

Vyshinsky: Quite so. Consequently, we may say that the defect, the fault in the diaphragms was such that for the sake of precaution the turbines could not work at full load?

Monkhouse: There were two such cases.

Vyshinsky: This concerned at least three turbines. perhaps five?

Monkhouse: I believe four turbines.

Vyshinsky: To my mind this too is a serious defect.

Monkhouse: When a station is not working at full load, then it is not harmful.

Vyshinsky: Of course, it depends on the point of view. There is a time when it is harmful and a time when it is not, but each turbine must be capable of working at full load. Is'nt that so?

Monkhouse: Certainly.

Vyshinsky: And consequently since they couldn't work at full load, it is already a defect, isn't it?

Monkhouse: This is clear. It is already a defect.

Vyshinsky: This is what I would like to ask you—for instance, at a number of stations there are a series of turbines, separate units, with definite defects, is that so?

Monkhouse: Yes.

Vyshinsky: If some people should appear who for some reason wished to conceal these defects, would they be able to do so? Is there something to conceal?

Monkhouse: I do not think so. It is impossible to conceal the defects in the blades.

Vyshinsky: Let us take the diaphragms, the regulation.

Monkhouse: Neither can these be concealed. The defects in the blades and the diaphragms could not be concealed.

Vyshinsky: Could the defects in the blades lead to a breakdown? I know that a blade is not reliable, I should have stopped the turbine or not have started it. I know that it is not reliable, nevertheless I let it work and as a result there is a breakdown. Could there be some malicious intent?

Monkhouse: Of course, if the blades were in such a grave state, but we had no such cases.

Vyshinsky: How is that? We see that for a certain period you had fully twenty breakdowns and all of them because of blades.

Monkhouse: Yes.

Vyshinsky: Consequently, if there were defects, then there were breakdowns?

Monkhouse: There were defects, but we had our mechanics; we sent blades post-haste to the works and did the repairs. For instance, when we discovered the defects in the diaphragm at Chelyabinsk we changed all the diaphragms of the rest of the turbines first.

Vyshinsky: So we can state that there were defects, and in consequence of these defects there were breakdowns, and in consequence of these breakdowns there were stoppages.

Monkhouse: Yes, there were stoppages, but when you are discussing these stoppages, you must bear in mind the relation to the whole work, the number of kilowatts.

Vyshinsky: That is correct, but I am interested in establishing facts which you do not deny. I am asking—if there were people who would have liked to take advantage of the defects, not in order to prevent breakdowns, but to hush up these defects and cause breakdowns, then were conditions favourable for that?

Monkhouse: There could not be such people.

Vyshinsky: Well, that is a different matter.

Monkhouse: But even if they wished to do it, they couldn't, because all the defects which the turbines had were immediately reported by us to the Electro-Import.

Vyshinsky: But there were breakdowns with the blades. Why weren't they prevented?

Monkhouse: This could not be done.

Vyshinsky: For instance, couldn't you put a binding on it?

Monkhouse: Let the technical commission decide that.

Vyshinsky: Your firm did it with wire?

Monkhouse: Yes, it tried to.

Vyshinsky: And you say it cannot be done. Is it possible then?

Monkhouse: It is possible, but as soon as we learned that there was some weakness here, we reported it.

Vyshinsky: It is another matter if nothing comes of it, but were there such attempts?

Monkhouse: These are not attempts, this is being done.

Vyshinsky: Nevertheless, it does not yield results at the First Moscow State Power station.

Monkhouse: At the First Moscow State Power Station, these measures are insufficient, and we are now discussing the question of what must be done in the future.

Vyshinsky: So this is correct?

Monkhouse: In this case, correct.

Vyshinsky: So we have established a number of defects, a number of breakdowns, a number of stoppages.

Monkhouse: It would not be fair to say that.

Vyshinsky: You say so.

Monkhouse: These are the defects in the First State Moscow Power Station.

Vyshinsky: There was a breakdown at Zuevka. As to what is fair our conceptions are different. You will please speak about facts. We have just enumerated them. Was there a breakdown at Orekhovo-Zuevo?

Monkhouse: Yes, there was

Vyshinsky: As a result of defects?

Monkhouse: No. The first was not a result of defects.

Vyshinsky: And the second?

Monkhouse: The first was because of the overfilling of the boiler. The second—cause unknown. It is said that there was also overfilling of the boiler. At Orekhovo-Zuevo, it was quite a different thing. There it was necessary to rebuild the turbine.

Vyshinsky: For fifteen minutes you have been answering a number of questions. Everything your have done (and I was only repeating your answers and asking you whether you confirmed them) you have confirmed, but when it comes to the final conclusion, you say that it is not so. Now, listen to me once more, so that there should be no useless disputing, and either tell me that I am mistaken or confirm what I have said. The following question: in a whole series of your equipment—turbines, diaphragms, and so forth, were there or were there not defects?

Monkhouse: Yes, there were.

Vyshinsky: The second question: in connection with these defects at a number of stations—the Ivanovo, Chelyabinsk, Zuevka, First Moscow Power Station, were there stoppages and were the machines put out of action for some time?

Monkhouse: Yes.

Vyshinsky: Third question: could people who wished to take advantage of these defects act in such a way as not to divulge these defects in time but, on the contrary, to hush them up. Could there or could there not be such a case?

Monkhouse: In my opinion it would be very difficult.

Vyshinsky: But the possibility is not excluded?

Monkhouse: In my opinion it is almost impossible.

Vyshinsky: But still possible, if you say "almost"?

Monkhouse: If a man knew. . .

Vyshinsky: Here you give a different answer from that which could be given according to the laws of logic. Now in one part of your deposition, in estimating the defects of a number of machines and equipment, you said the following: "If I were. . ."

Monkhouse: Wait a moment, I retracted that deposition.

Vyshinsky: I didn't hear that.

Monkhouse: I told you when I was with you at the Public Prosecutor's office.

Vyshinsky: I don't remember that.

Monkhouse: You yourself agreed. I said that I gave my evidence after being examined for eighteen hours, when I was very tired.

Vyshinsky: We shall see first what you said and secondly why you said it.

Monkhouse: You agreed to destroy that deposition.

Vyshinsky: It is not possible for me to appear here as a witness in your case, therefore, I cannot say what you may have told me at some time.

Monkhouse: I said that this deposition was made after an examination of eighteen hours' duration.

The President: What is the deposition in question?

Vyshinsky: The one of March 13.

Monkhouse: Does that refer to the Orekhovo turbine?

Vyshinsky: No, to an employee of the Commissariat of Heavy Industry. Since the accused declares that there was an examination of eighteen hours' duration, I must say that I have no right to appear here as witness in his case, but I must emphatically deny his reference to myself as a witness. You said here that if you had been in the service of the Commissariat of Heavy Industry you would not have bought these machines.

Monkhouse: I said that, in relation to the Rykovo machine.

Vyshinsky: But what has that to do with an alleged eighteen hour examination, with being compelled and so forth?

Monkhouse: But I spoke about something else. . .

Vyshinsky: I am not speaking about something else, I say that this has nothing to do with the case.

The President: Accused Monkhouse, how many hours were you in confinement in Moscow?

Monkhouse: Only 48 hours.

The President: And you became panicky so soon?

Monkhouse: It was enough under such methods of examination.

Vyshinsky: And so if you had been in the service of the Commissariat of Heavy Industry you would not have taken these machines?

Monkhouse: I would not have taken them.

Vyshinsky: And who sent these machines?

Monkhouse: Our firm.

Vyshinsky: So your firm was selling. . .

Monkhouse: We did not select the machines.

Vyshinsky: So our people were taking and your people were getting rid of?

Monkhouse: We did everything that was possible.

Vyshinsky: Did you do all that was possible that our people should not take them, and did they take them nevertheless?

Monkhouse: We did everything to satisfy our clients in regard to machines.

Vyshinsky: But which you yourself as a representative of the firm would decline?

Monkhouse: We did everything to satisfy the demands of our clients. We sent machines which we guaranteed and these machines we shall rebuild.

Vyshinsky: What you will do is one thing, but what you did is another. And, however unpleasant, it is a fact with which we have to reckon.

Monkhouse: Every firm which undertakes such business may have to reckon with that.

Vyshinsky: It is clear to me now that there were such machines which you were selling but which you yourself would not have bought.

Monkhouse: This is my personal opinion.

Vyshinsky: True, it is your opinion, not mine. I want you to confirm once more at the open trial, whether this is correct or not.

Monkhouse: I personally would not have bought these machines, would not have selected them.

Vyshinsky: Why?

Monkhouse: That would be a long technical talk.

The President: Because they are good or bad?

Monkhouse: It is a new system.

Vyshinsky: But a new system may also be good, or perhaps you are against new things? I have no more questions.

The President: Has the Defence any questions?

Kommodov: That machines may have defects, we know. Did the duty to repair these defects devolve upon you, as the representative of the firm?

Monkhouse: Yes.

Kommodov: When these defects were reported to you, did you have to put them right?

Monkhouse: Certainly.

Kommodov: Each time defects were revealed did you consider yourself obliged to send your people and have them repaired?

Monkhouse: Yes, we did it immediately.

Kommodov: Was it your duty as the representative of Metro-Vickers in Moscow?

Monkhouse: It was my duty, as well as that of the installation engineer.

Kommodov: But the main duty was yours?

Monkhouse: Yes.

Kommodov: So we can come to this conclusion: you do not deny that there were defects, but when they were brought to your attention, you tried to put them right?

Monkhouse: I can describe the following case. When the first breakdown occurred at the Orekhovo-Zuevo Station, we knew that the Moscow Power Station was in a difficult position in regard to the load on the machines, and in order to put everything right as soon as possible, so that the Moscow Power Station might have energy, we drove in our motor lorry to Orekhovo-Zuevo and went along the main road to Leningrad. In two-and-a-half days we finished the job at the metallurgical works in Leningrad, so that we put everything right and helped, at our expense.

Kommodov: Should we always consider that a motor or a turbine is useless or defective only because it is badly designed or because the system, in a particular case, let us say for a particular station, is not suitable?

Monkhouse: It is difficult for me to explain. I consider this machine was an unfortunate selection.

Kommodov: Because of the system?

Monkhouse: It is a complicated system.

Kommodov: I have no more questions.

Lidov: You said here that some of your turbines had defects.

in design, in the form of irregular blades which were liable to fracture. Tell us, was the fault to be traced to the manufacture, to the inspection, to the assembly, or to the installation on the spot?

Monkhouse: It depends on the choice of material and on the construction at the factory.

Lidov: Consequently, the material was not quite of the quality which was necessary for these blades?

Monkhouse: The material was of good quality but this question of the vibration of the turbines is a very complicated one. It is what is called fatigue of the metal.

Lidov: The premature wearing out of the metal?

Monkhouse: This is what is called fatigue of the metal.

Lidov: This you could not help, no matter how you assembled it, because that is how it was made in England?

Monkhouse: Yes.

Lidov: Why then didn't you write to England that a turbine of such a type revealed fatigue of the metal and therefore the blades break?

Monkhouse: We cabled to England. Our experts came over here and had a conference at the metallurgical works both in Leningrad and here, at the Moscow Power Station. They immediately made a full investigation of the defects on the spot. This was done immediately.

Lidov: So you wrote to London after the first occasion?

Monkhouse: We didn't write, but we cabled to London.

Lidov: So specialists came from there and you had a series of conferences, experts and investigations which discussed and examined the question? What were the final conclusions of these experts?

Monkhouse: At the Moscow Power Station, we came to the conclusion that it was sufficient to install a permanent wire.

Lidov: This is what the Public Prosecutor said?

Monkhouse: The very same thing.

Lidov: This proved insufficient?

Monkhouse: We are in doubt. This question is still being discussed.

Lidov: Consequently, this is such a complicated thing that at the present moment you do not know how to do it?

Monkhouse: It is very complicated.

Libson: Please tell us, did you work for a long time at Volkhovstroy?

Monkhouse: I did not work at Volkhovstroy itself, but I worked at the Leningrad sub-station.

Libson: How long?

Monkhouse: Almost a year.

Libson: At the same time as Kutuzova?

Monkhouse: She was secretary to the technical director of Volkhovstroy.

Libson: You made her acquaintance there?

Monkhouse: Yes.

Libson: When, later on, Kutuzova joined your staff did you accept her because you knew her from Volkhovstroy?

Monkhouse: When we ceased to work at Volkhovstroy, the majority of the Volkhovstroy employees went to the Electrotyaga, but not all of them. Kutuzova was left without a position. At that time my secretary married one of our engineers and I invited Kutuzova to take her place.

Libson: And was she your secretary?

Monkhouse: Yes.

Dmitriev: Accused Monkhouse, you said that the vibration of the blades had its origin in the fatigue of the metal?

Monkhouse: No, I didn't say that. I speak Russian badly and perhaps you didn't understand me. I said that that question was connected with the fatigue of the metal. When there is a vibration of the blades, if it is a very strong one, we get as a result the fatigue of the metal.

The President: Any more questions to Monkhouse? (No more questions)

(To Monkhouse): You may sit down.

There are two more of the accused to be examined: Kutuzova and Gregory. Whom are we going to question first?

Vyshinsky: I ask that Kutuzova be examined first.

Defence: We join in this request.

The President: The Court will adjourn for twenty minutes.

* * *

Commandant: Please rise. The Court is coming.

The President: Please be seated. Accused Kutuzova, take your place.

Recount the main points of your biography. Tell us in greater detail how you joined the office of Metro-Vickers and what duties you performed.

Kutuzova: I was born in Leningrad in 1895 in the family of an artisan. Upon finishing the Demidov Women's High School, I received a gold medal. I attended the eighth general course at the same school and studied stenography. I lived there as a boarder. I began to work immediately upon finishing school at the age of seventeen.

My first work was that of a teacher. I taught a junior preparatory class in a private commercial school. I then took up clerical work.

I worked in the following places successively: six months, in 1913, in a private German engineering office. I then joined the "Treugolnik" Russian-American Rubber Manufacturing Company. I worked there four years. After the October Revolution the factory was closed down and I went to work in the Automobile Department of the Admiralty, where I remained four months in the capacity of a typist.

From the Automobile Department I went over to the Inspectorate of Infantry of the Leningrad Region. I worked these a little over a year—the end of 1918 and during 1919.

In the middle of 1919 I went to the city of Toropetz in the Pskov Gubernia and worked eight months in the Military Engineering Department as chief office clerk.

In the autumn of 1920, I returned to Leningrad and went to work at the Svir Construction Works [Svirstroy]. I worked four years at Svirstroy, beginning as a clerk of the third category and finishing as assistant office manager of Svirstroy.

When Svirstroy was temporarily closed down I was invited to work at Volkhovstroy as the secretary to the chief electrical engineer. I worked there four years.

About six months before work at Volkhovstroy came to an end, I began to study English with the purpose of joining the office of some private English firm.

At Volkhovstroy I became acquainted with representatives of Metropolitan-Vickers: engineer Monkhouse, engineer Thornton and engineer Sutherland. Engineer Monkhouse invited me to work with him. On April 7, 1929, I began work in the Leningrad Bureau of the firm as secretary to the representative of the firm in the Soviet Union, engineer Monkhouse. I continued at this work until my arrest on March 11, 1933.

The President: Has the Public Prosecutor any questions?

Roginsky: Yes. Accused Kutuzova, your investigation was in the main exhausted during the Court proceedings, during the examination of a number of the accused. I will, therefore, ask you only a few questions, largely by way of summing up the evidence you gave in the course of the proceedings.

First question: Do you confirm your evidence to the effect that you were aware of the criminal, or as you called it in your evidence, illegal activities of Thornton and Monkhouse?

Kutuzova: Yes, I confirm it.

Roginsky: Do you confirm that the substance of those criminal activities was espionage?

Kutuzova: Yes, espionage was part of that work.

Roginsky: Do you confirm that, in addition to espionage, the substance of those criminal activities was the organized damage of machinery, as you testified you had learned from conversations between Thornton and Monkhouse?

Kutuzova: Yes, I also confirm the acts of diversion of that group.

Roginsky: Do you confirm your evidence to the effect that you were aware of the bribing of several Russian engineers and technicians for committing such criminal actions as you have just mentioned to the Court?

Kutuzova: Yes.

Roginsky: Among the engineers sitting here as accused, can you name those who, according to your information, received monetary compensation for wrecking activities?

Kutuzova: I can.

Roginsky: Please do so.

Kutuzova: Engineer Gussev received bribes.

Roginsky: May I put a question to the accused Gussev now?

The President: You may.

Roginsky: Accused Gussev, did you receive bribes?

Gussev: I did.

Roginsky: For wrecking work?

Gussev: Yes.

Roginsky: For espionage?

Gussev: Yes.

Roginsky: That is all I have to ask Gussev.

Who else?

Kutuzova: Further, I learned from the conversations that one of Gussev's foremen also received bribes.

Roginsky: Who?

Kutuzova: Sokolov.

Roginsky: May I question Sokolov?

The President: You may.

Roginsky: Accused Sokolov, did you receive bribes?

Sokolov: Yes.

Roginsky: For wrecking?

Sokolov: Yes.

Roginsky: For espionage?

Sokolov: Yes.

Roginsky: I have no more questions to ask Sokolov.

I desire the Court to certify that in Vitvitky's depositions there is direct mention of his having received money for supplying information and for wrecking activities, and, in connection with Kutuzova's evidence, I would request permission to put one question to the accused Gussev.

The President: You may.

Roginsky: Accused Gussev, are you aware of Vitvitsky's having received money?

Gussev: Yes.

Roginsky: What do you know about this?

Gussev: I transmitted money to Vitvitsky.

Roginsky: What amount?

Gussev: About 4,500 rubles.

Roginsky: From whom did you receive that money?

Gussev: From MacDonald.

Roginsky: I have no more questions to ask Gussev. Can you name any other engineer among those present who, according to your information, received money?

Kutuzova: Engineers Krasheninnikov, Zorin, Sukhoruchkin, Ryazanov, Yazykov.

Roginsky: I mean from among those sitting here.

Permit me to put a question to Sukhoruchkin.

The President: You may.

Roginsky: Is that evidence correct?

Sukhoruchkin: Yes.

Roginsky: Did you receive money?

Sukhoruchkin: Yes.

Roginsky: For doing wrecking work?

Sukhoruchkin: Yes.

Roginsky: Accused Zorin, is that evidence correct?

Zorin: Yes.

Roginsky: Did you receive money?

Zorin: Yes.

Roginsky: I have no more questions to ask Zorin. Accused Krasheninnikov, is that evidence correct?

Krasheninnikov: Yes.

Roginsky: Did you receive money?

Krasheninnikov: Yes.

Roginsky: I have no more questions.

Accused Kutuzova, do you also confirm that part of your evidence where you refer to the manner in which these sums were recorded in the respective books?

Kutuzova: That is not quite correct. There were no books; engineer Thornton kept the records in diaries in his apartment.

Roginsky: That means that the records of sums spent in payment of espionage and wrecking activities were entered by Thornton in special books kept in his apartment.

Kutuzova: Yes.

Roginsky: Where are those books?

Kutuzova: I know that he took them away with him to England.

Roginsky: When?

Kutuzova: About December 1932, when he went away for Christmas.

Roginsky: I have a question to ask Thornton. Do you deny Kutuzova's evidence?

Thornton: I do.

Roginsky: I have no questions to ask Thornton. I have no more questions to ask Kutuzova.

The President: Does the Defence desire to put any questions?

Braude: How did you know about the wrecking activities and acts of diversion organized by Monkhouse and Thornton? Did you learn it from conversations, or did they confide in you?

Kutuzova: I lived in one house with them for about four years.

Braude: Did they have separate rooms?

Kutuzova: Thornton had a separate apartment. I lived above.

Braude: Were you on good terms?

Kutuzova: Yes, we were on very good terms.

Braude: How did they speak about these matters in your presence?

Kutuzova: They did not talk about them at once.

Braude: You know them both, how would you characterize them? Monkhouse, is he garrulous, frivolous, or is he a serious-minded business man of the English type?

Kutuzova: Monkhouse is a serious-minded person, but you cannot say that espionage work is comic.

Braude: That is why I ask you. I should like to know why serious-minded persons should confide in you regarding serious and not comic work. Tell us, did you yourself participate directly in this wrecking work?

Kutuzova: I did. I received and transmitted money.

Braude: But did you take part in the acts of diversion themselves?

Kutuzova: No, I did not, because I understand very little about machinery.

Braude: Now explain to us why serious-minded, not garrulous persons found it possible to speak in your presence about work in which you could not and did not participate, and in which you did not assist them.

Kutuzova: Because it so happened that we lived together.

Braude: And couldn't they go anywhere else away from you?

Kutuzova: No.

Libson: It appears from your statements that you have been working with these people since 1926.

Kutuzova: Since 1927.

Libson: But you worked at Volkhovstroy?

Kutuzova: I did work there, and they knew me.

Libson: Apparently they knew you well enough to consider it possible, when that work ended, to invite you to Moscow.

Kutuzova: I do not think they knew me personally. They came to me as the secretary to the assistant chief engineer. But they had apparently heard about me and what they heard was not bad.

Libson: Since that was a reason for inviting you, it follows that they knew you. You worked for them seven years?

Kutuzova: Eight years.

Libson: During these eight years, you worked together?

Kutuzova: Yes.

Libson: You not only worked with Monkhouse and Thornton all the time, but you lived in one house with them?

Kutuzova: Yes.

Libson: You were Monkhouse's secretary?

Kutuzova: Yes.

Libson: So that you came into particularly close contact with him?

Kutuzova: I was in close contact with the whole office on business matters.

Libson: But since you began to observe "their work," as you call it, your conduct gave them reason to be cautious in regard to you?

Kutuzova: I said I was afraid.

Libson: In what sense?

Kutuzova: I was afraid of arrest.

Libson: That is to say, it alarmed you?

Kutuzova: It alarmed me to some extent.

Libson: But might it not occur to them that it was not safe?

Kutuzova: I don't know. We were great friends.

Libson: Were you together with them in the evenings also?

Kutuzova: Yes.

Libson: Did you live in Perlovka or in Losino-Ostrovskaya?

Kutuzova: At first we lived in Losino-Ostrovskaya, in a small house, and then we built three houses in Perlovka.

Libson: That is to say, everyone that came to visit them or came on business came to that place?

Kutuzova: They came to the house where engineer Monkhouse lived.

Libson: Be good enough to explain the following. When did you first notice their criminal conduct, at the very beginning, or later?

Kutuzova: About the end of 1930.

Libson: You had no occasion for suspicion prior to 1930?

Kutuzova: No.

Libson: You were alarmed, naturally. Did you express your alarm to them frequently?

Kutuzova: I was not alarmed at the end of 1930. At first, I was not alarmed.

Libson: Why?

Kutuzova: Because one can be alarmed only when one is certain.

Libson: You were not certain?

Kutuzova: No.

Libson: When did you begin to become alarmed? Or rather when did you understand it?

Kutuzova: Towards the end of 1931, I endeavoured to find out the truth about the matter and to some extent succeeded.

Libson: I should like to know the approximate time, at least the year.

Kutuzova: 1931.

Libson: That is to say, you became certain after 1931?

Kutuzova: I learned definitely in 1932.

Libson: Now tell me, seeing that you knew this secret, had become an involuntary accomplice, did the thought occur to you that it was necessary to put an end to it, as far as you personally were concerned?

Kutuzova: The thought occurred to me, but I could not put an end to it.

Libson: What prevented you from taking definite steps?

Kutuzova: First, I was tied to them organizationally; secondly, I had given my word, and when I give my word I keep it.

Libson: You considered it necessary to keep that word?

Kutuzova: Yes.

Libson: You say that you were an accomplice. Permit me to put the question concretely. In what respect do you consider yourself an accomplice? You continually refer to the matter of the parcels.

Kutuzova: I sent parcels and transmitted money.

Libson: To whom did you send parcels?

Kutuzova: To engineer Gussev.

Libson: What parcels?

Kutuzova: Provisions.

Libson: Did you know Gussev personally or not?

Kutuzova: Only by name.

Libson: Had you never met him?

Kutuzova: No.

Libson: Did you have a clear idea of the character of his work, acts of diversion, espionage and other activities?

Kutuzova: I knew that he belonged to our group.

Libson: You knew that?

Kutuzova: Yes.

Libson: And did you know the details?

Kutuzova: No.

Libson: Did your active participation consist in the fact that you sent parcels?

Kutuzova: Yes, and moreover transmitted money.

Libson: What was the general arrangement with money? Was handling the money part of your duties?

Kutuzova: Yes. All the Torgsin money was in my hands. Moreover, I always had from five to six thousand rubles at my disposal.

Libson: When you received instructions, was it this money you gave?

Kutuzova: No, I did not give this money. This was money belonging to the firm, and money of the firm was not given for this purpose.

Libson: I understand.

Kutuzova: But Torgsin money was also given as loans, which were later repaid in rubles.

Libson: Upon whose instructions?

Kutuzova: Upon the instructions of engineers Thornton and Monkhouse.

Libson: Did you pay out money personally?

Kutuzova: There were occasions when I paid out personally.

Libson: Were you aware that these people were committing criminal deeds?

Kutuzova: Generally speaking, I knew.

Libson: Only in general?

Kutuzova: Yes.

Libson: You knew, but you did not have sufficient courage to report the matter to the authorities for the reasons which you have mentioned?

Kutuzova: Yes.

Libson: I have no more questions to ask.

Schwartz: Permit me to ask you about Krasheninnikov. You heard him admit that he received money. You recall Thornton's reply denying that he transmitted money to Krasheninnikov through you. Please tell us who transmitted the money to Krasheninnikov.

Kutuzova: I did not transmit any money to Krasheninnikov.

Schwartz: Who did?

Kutuzova: I think it was Thornton, but I do not know the details. I heard the name, I heard their talk in general and I heard them consulting each other.

Schwartz: So there was no transmission of money through third persons in your presence?

Kutuzova: No.

Schwartz: And wasn't there any talk either about the sending of parcels?

Kutuzova: There was some talk.

Schwartz: On whose part?

Kutuzova: Engineer Thornton spoke to engineer Monkhouse.

Schwartz: Were you present at that conversation?

Kutuzova: No. I entered the room when they were finishing the discussion of the matter.

Kommodov: Did you live in the same house as Monkhouse, in Perlovka?

Kutuzova: Next door.

Kommodov: Where Thornton lived?

Kutuzova: Yes.

Kommodov: Did Monkhouse have a separate study?

Kutuzova: Yes.

Kommodov: And Thornton?

Kutuzova: He had one also.

Kommodov: Whose study was adjacent to Monkhouse's?

Kutuzova: There was no study adjacent, only his bedroom.

Kommodov: Wasn't there another engineer who lived there?

Kutuzova: There was daily coming and going of engineers and mechanics.

Kommodov: So there was no engineer living next door to Monkhouse?

Kutuzova: There was engineer Becky, but he didn't live next door, but across the hallway.

Kommodov: That is to say, each of the three engineers had a study to himself?

Kutuzova: Yes, one might say so.

Kommodov: Your defending counsel asked you about your direct participation as a member of the wrecking and espionage organization. You said that you transmitted money and Gussev admitted that he received money. Who transmitted the money to him?

Kutuzova: I think it was Thornton or MacDonald who transmitted the money to him.

Kommodov: But didn't you hand it to him personally?

Kutuzova: No.

Kommodov (To Gussev): Did you receive money?

Gussev: Yes.

Kommodov: From whom?

Gussev: From MacDonald.

Kommodov (To Kutuzova): Did you give money to Sokolov?

Kutuzova: No.

Kommodov (To Sokolov): From whom did you receive money?

Sokolov: From Gussev.

Kommodov (To Kutuzova): Did you give money to Krasheninnikov?

Kutuzova: No.

Kommodov (To Krasheninnikov): From whom did you receive money?

Krasheninnikov: From Oleinik.

Kommodov (To Kutuzova): Did you give money to Zorin?

Kutuzova: No.

Kommodov (To Zorin): From whom did you receive money?

Zorin: From Thornton.

Kommodov (To Kutuzova): Did you give money to Sukhoruchkin?

Kutuzova: No.

Kommodov (To Sukhoruchkin): From whom did you receive money?

Sukhoruchkin: From Thornton.

Kommodov: In his deposition at the preliminary investigation Vitvitsky declared that he received money from Gussev.

[To Kutuzova] To whom did you give money?

Kutuzova: I have already stated in my evidence to whom I gave money.

Kommodov: I am referring to those who are sitting here as accused.

And so we were the fact indisputably established that a parcel was sent addressed to Ivanova?

Kutuzova: No, from Ivanova.

Kommodov: From Ivanova. Did you say that it contained butter and provisions?

Kutuzova: True. As far as I remember, that is so; but I sent cases of provisions every day.

Kommodov: So, that parcel contained butter and other provisions?

Kutuzova: Yes.

Kommodov: I have no more questions.

The President: Has the Defence any more questions?

Defence: No.

The President: Have the accused any questions?

Thornton: Can you give us details of the wrecking work regarding which I am alleged to have given instructions?

Kutuzova: I cannot give details, I heard general conversations.

Thornton: Perhaps you will tell us which?

Kutuzova: I heard how you together with engineer Monkhouse planned to damage the turbines at the Baku, Nizhny, and Zuevka Power Stations. I remember your explaining to me that if one throws a foreign object into a turbine, a rag or a piece of wood, the turbine may blow through the roof. That was of course spoken allegorically.

Thornton: Are you aware that no such thing happened?

Kutuzova: I said that it was spoken allegorically, that is, figuratively.

Thornton: Perhaps in this way: If one threw something into a turbine the cover would fly off?

Kutuzova: No, not necessarily.

Thornton: You said that I spoke to Monkhouse about Zuevka, about the Baku Power Station, and thought of throwing a bolt. There was no such wrecking work there.

Kutuzova: I don't know. I know nothing about machinery. I relate what I heard and what I understood.

Thornton: Regarding espionage work, were there any concrete cases?

Kutuzova: I heard general talk. I have already told the Court, and the details are recorded in my evidence.

Thornton: Give us these details.

Kutuzova: I refuse to give there details, since they are a State secret.

Thornton: One last question. You say that I received money from you?

Kutuzova: I did not say that.

Thornton: So I did not receive money from you?

Kutuzova: I do not know.

Roginsky: Accused Kotlyarevsky, was a bolt put into the generator at Zuevka?

Kotlyarevsky: Yes.

Roginsky: Accused Thornton, do you hear this evidence?

Thornton: Yes.

Roginsky: Was a bolt put into the generator at the Zuevka Power Station?

Thornton: Yes, into the generator; not into the turbine.

Roginsky: Another question to Kotlyarevsky. Was the bolt left there deliberately?

Kotlyarevsky: Yes.

Roginsky: With intent to wreck?

Kotlyarevsky: Yes.

Roginsky: I have no more questions to put to Thornton or to Kotlyarevsky. One question to Kutuzova. Have you ever stated during a preliminary investigation that you personally handed money to Gussev, Krasheninnikov, Zorin and others, namely, to those enumerated by Kommodov?

Kutuzova: No.

Roginsky: During the preliminary investigation did you indicate other persons?

Kutuzova: Yes.

Roginsky: Not present here?

Kutuzova: They are not present.

Vyshinsky: Accused Thornton, you have heard Kutuzova's answers to your questions. Did this happen or not?

Thornton: I don't understand.

Vyshinsky: I will explain. Kutuzova says that she heard a conversation of yours, which contained information that a turbine or some unit of machinery could and should be put out of action by throwing into it some sort of metal or other object such as, for example, as Kotlyarevsky said, a bolt. Did you have a conversation of this kind with Kutuzova? Is she correct in saying this, or not?

Thornton: I didn't say that.

Vyshinsky: And did you speak to Monkhouse about it?

Thornton: I never spoke to Monkhouse on the subject of wrecking.

Vyshinsky: She is wrong in what she says?

Thornton: She is wrong.

Vyshinsky: Perhaps you said it in this way: "You see, Anna Sergeyevna, if it is thrown in, then this is what happens."

Thornton: At first I thought that she had once asked: "If it is thrown in?" But, as I recall, she did not say that.

Vyshinsky: And you didn't say it to her either?

Thornton: No, there were no discussions* about how to wreck.

Vyshinsky: There were no discussions?

Thornton: No.

Vyshinsky: And why should there be discussion, if there is unanimity?

Thornton: Perhaps I used the wrong word.

Vyshinsky: The word discussion means an argument, a dispute.

Thornton: May I have an interpreter? [Continues in English through the interpreter] Discussion in English means a conversation.

Vyshinsky: We shall not argue. The accused in this instance means—a conversation. Then there were no such conversations either in the positive form or in a hypothetical form; consequently she is drawing on her imagination.

Thornton (Continues in Russian): Yes, she is confusing things.

Vyshinsky: What is she confusing?

Thornton: Perhaps she thought it was so.

Vyshinsky: Very well, she thought that you and Monkhouse were talking about wrecking. She could have thought that. But why do you believe she might have thought it?

Thornton: Because she says so.

Vyshinsky: No, she does not say that. She says: "I heard Thornton and Monkhouse having a conversation of this kind," and you say that there were no such conversations, but that perhaps Kutuzova thinks that you held such conversations. What reason was there to think so?

Thornton: But there were no such conversations.

Vyshinsky: Then there is no reason for thinking that she thought so. There are no more questions.

Roginsky: Didn't you tell the accused Kutuzova that besides your duties to the firm, you had others?

---

* Thornton used the Russian word "diskusia" which means dispute.

Thornton: No, I deny ever saying it.

Roginsky: Did you also deny this at the confrontation?

Thornton: I denied it.

Roginsky: May I read that deposition?

Vyshinsky: I have a question for Thornton. Here in Court the record of the confrontation was read to you. You were sitting over there before the microphone. It was during your examination. You declared that you confirmed it. That was only two days ago. Now you are denying it?

Thornton: That I have other work?

Vyshinsky: Yes. So the record of your confrontation with Kutuzova shows. Here again we questioned you and Kutuzova and you confirmed this record in various points.

Thornton: No, I didn't confirm it.

Vyshinsky: Then let us read it again.

Roginsky: Record of the confrontation between Thornton and Kutuzova, March 16, 1933: "Question to Kutuzova: 'Were you aware of the fact that Thornton is engaged in spying activities?' " The answer at first was general, and continued as follows: "Yes, I knew that; I noticed that certain persons, Russian engineers, had begun to come, and that they had mysterious conversations with him. That set me thinking. That was at the end of 1930 and the beginning of 1931. In reply to my question Thornton said that besides his business duties he had others." "Question to Thornton: 'Do you confirm Kutuzova's tesimony?' Answer: 'Yes, I confirm it.' Signed — Thornton."

Vyshinsky: Now I put the question to Thornton—do you confirm this or not?

Thornton: All the same, I have no other work.

Roginsky: You confirm the record. Then everything written here is correct, your tesimony is correct?

Thornton: It may have been written, all the same I have no other work.

Roginsky: I am asking you whether what is written here is what you deposed.

Thornton: It was a mistake on my part to sign it.

Roginsky: Secondly. in the same record. "Question to Kutuzova: 'Was payment made for the spying work carried on?' Answer: 'Yes, payment was made for the spying work. Thornton told me so, and, moreover, I heard it from the conversation between Thornton and Monkhouse, since I was fully trusted by them and was often in the room during their conversations. My presence did not embarrass them. The conversations went on in the English language, and I know enough to understand.' Question to Thornton: 'What have you to say about these statements by Citizen Kutuzova? Is she speaking the truth or not?' Answer: 'Yes, Citizen Kutuzova is speaking the truth.' "

Vyshinsky: How about this question?

Thornton: Spying work?

Roginsky: Spying work was paid for by you according to the testimony of Kutuzova and confirmed by you at the confrontation with Kutuzova. It is signed—Thornton. Did you make this deposition?

Thornton: Yes, I signed it.

Roginsky: But did you make this deposition?

Thornton: Yes, since it is signed.

Vyshinsky: Was this so?

Thornton: Actually it was not so.

Roginsky: Third question. "Question to Kutuzova: 'In what way was the money spent on spying operations covered in the accounts?' Answer: 'The sums paid for this work were not officially entered in the books. Engineer Thornton kept his accounts at his villa. He told me about this himself and besides I saw him sitting at night writing up these accounts.' Questions to Thornton: 'Do you confirm this?' Answer: 'I did not carry any official books, but I made entries into a diary to aid my memory in order later to write these sums off. This I did by entering these sums in the books of the firm as some non-existent expenses. This diary has been sent to England.' "

Roginsky: Did you give this testimony also when confronted with Kutuzova?

Thornton: Yes, only I want to make an explanation.

Vyshinsky: One question more, then the explanation. You kept a diary, in which you wrote down expenses which did not go through the books. Is that so?

Thornton: Yes.

Vyshinsky: You despatched it to England?

Thornton: I took it all with me.

Vyshinsky: Nine books?

Thornton: Yes.

Vyshinsky: Does this correspond with the truth?

Thornton: I want to make an explanation to the effect that these small sums I wrote. . .

Vyshinsky: Small or large—we shall clear that up later. What is important to us is the fact that when confronted with Kutuzova on March 16, with regard to your expenses in connection with payment of various persons entered into the books unofficially by you, in the manner in which you have written it here—in connection with non-existent expenses—you confirmed that you kept special diaries, of which nine exist, and that you carried them off to England in time. Is that correct?

Thornton: Nine books—nine years.

Vyshinsky: Perhaps more, according to the number of years you have been engaged in this work. Is Kutuzova telling the truth?

Thornton: She is right when she says I took them away.

Vyshinsky: Is it correct that these expenses are written there?

Thornton: They were written there.

Vyshinsky: So you confirm that you took them away?

Thornton: That I took them away—yes. The sums which I gave to Zivert were written there.

Vyshinsky: Zivert said here that you gave him money for spying and wrecking work.

Thornton: I did not give it for spying and wrecking work.

Roginsky: Next is the record of the decision of the Investigating Judge dated April 4, 1933, the record of the charges presented. It contains:

1. The charge that Thornton engaged in economic and military espionage.

2. He enlisted a number of Soviet engineers and technicians for spying work and paid them various sums of money for the information supplied.

3. Both personally, and through the medium of MacDonald and other engineers of the firm in question, who were subordin-

ate to him, he systematically gave bribes to a number of Soviet engineers for concealing defects in the equipment supplied by the firm of Metropolitan-Vickers.

4. Gave instructions to Monkhouse and other of the firm's engineers to organize and carry out, through the medium of specially chosen Soviet engineers and technicians, the damage to equipment and also breakdowns in a number of power stations connected with enterprises in the U.S.S.R., which breakdowns and damage to equipment were subsequently carried out; for which Thornton paid various sums to the persons directly carrying out his tasks of diversion.

This is from the record of the charges brought against you by the Investigating Judge of the Public Prosecution.

Thornton: Who wrote that?

Roginsky: The Investigating Judge on Important Cases. "Thornton [answer]: 'I admit that I am guilty according to the charge presented to me as the accused with the exception of paragraph 4.' " That is to say, you admit that you drew a number of Russian engineers and technicians into economic and military espionage, and admit giving bribes to Russian engineers and technicians for concealing defects in equipment, and only do not admit the organization and carrying out of breakdowns.

Thornton: I withdrew the part about espionage in connection with military information.

Vyshinsky: You withdrew it here, before the Court. And why?

Thornton: It is not true.

Vyshinsky: And why did you say what is not true?

Thornton: That was not in the office of the Public Prosecutor, but in the O.G.P.U.

Vyshinsky: But it was the Investigating Judge on Important Cases of the Office of the Public Prosecutor of the Republic. Did you say that there?

Thornton: He wrote it.

Vyshinsky: But did you say it?

Thornton: I signed it.

Vyshinsky: Did you say it or not?

Thornton: He wrote and I signed.

Vyshinsky: Were you shown it?

Thornton: Yes, it was shown to me.

Vyshinsky: Did you read it through?

Thornton: Yes.

Vyshinsky: Signed it?

Thornton: Yes.

Vyshinsky: You wrote that you admit your guilt on three points but not on the fourth. You could just as well have written that you admit two points but not the other two; and yet you wrote that you admit yourself guilty on three points but not on the fourth. Is that correct?

Thornton: Yes, and I explained that I wanted to take it back, but I was told that that was impossible and that I could do it in the course of the Court proceedings.

Vyshinsky: You may take back everything you like, but you must explain why you want to take it back.

Thornton: It is not true.

Vyshinsky: Why?

Thornton: It is based on the depositions of March 26.

Vyshinsky: It is based on your own depositions.

Thornton: On the basis of the depositions of March 26.

Vyshinsky: And what is wrong with the record of your depositions of March 26?

Thornton: They were taken from me under great pressure.

Vyshinsky: For example . . .

Thornton: I was interrogated for a very long time.

Vyshinsky: On what date?

Thornton: On the 13th.

Vyshinsky: And then?

Thornton: I cannot find the word.

Vyshinsky: You can speak through the Interpreter.

Thornton (Continues in English): I was questioned for a very long time. It was suggested to me that if I confessed, "Vsyo budet khorosho," that everything would be all right.

Vyshinsky: And if you did not confess?

Thornton: Further, if I did not confess I should be of no use in Soviet Russia or England. Then I was so tired and browbeaten by the whole thing that I signed this.

The President: Wrote it or signed it?

Thornton: They dictated it in Russian, and I wrote it in English.

The President: You were so tired that you could translate from Russian into English on the spot? Do you know the Russian language so well that when you were tired you could write in English straight away when dictated to in Russian?

Thornton (Continues in Russian): It was so in this instance.

Vyshinsky: Then?

Thornton: Since this was so, I had to sign.

Vyshinsky: This is your whole explanation. Allow me to ask a few additional questions on this explanation.

My first question concerns your deposition, which contains your exposure of the spying network.

Thornton: Oh . . . about the twenty-seven persons?

Vyshinsky: Do you also deny the other records?

Thornton: There is one more.

Vyshinsky: Tell me which one it is, immediately—although it is four days late.

Thornton: Where it speaks about defence and offence possibilities.

Vyshinsky: That is the same document we just mentioned where there is a division into fifteen and twelve men, according to what they were engaged in—whether economic, political, or military spying.

Thornton: That is in another one.

Vyshinsky: There is no other. Do you deny this one?

Thornton: Yes.

Vyshinsky: Were you examined only on the 13th?

Thornotn: No, many times.

Vyshinsky: When were you arrested?

Thornton: On the 11th.

Vyshinsky: Were you interrogated on the 12th?

Thornton: Yes.

Vyshinsky: Were you tired?

Thornton: Yes.

Vyshinsky: Were you interrogated on the 13th?

Thornton: Yes.

Vyshinsky: Were you tired?

Thornton: Yes:

Vyshinsky: Were you interrogated on the 14th?

Thornton: Yes.

Vyshinsky: Were you tired?

Thornton: I was very depressed.

Vyshinsky What depressed you? Can't you say concretely?

Thornton: (No answer)

Vyshinsky: Were you in a bad mood?

Thornton: (No answer)

Vyshinsky: Were you interrogated on March 15?

Thornton: Yes.

Vyshinsky: Were you in the same mood?

Thornton: Better.

Vyshinsky: Were you interrogated on the 17th?

Thornton: Yes.

Vyshinsky: Was your mood better?

Thornton: A little better.

Vyshinsky: Were you interrogated on the 18th?

Thornton: I was interrogated, I think, every day, exept one.

Vyshinsky: Allow me to ask you then when your mood improved, did you at any time anywhere make a declaration to anyone that you intended to deny your deposition of March 13, or didn't you make such a declaration?

Thornton: I was waiting for the trial.

Vyshinsky: Excuse me, please. I have made the question quite clear, and we must finally settle this. In one hour's time the Court examination will come to a close and then it will be too late to examine the circumstances of the case. Be so kind, therefore, as to listen to me and answer the questions I put to you, only in definite order. Be so kind as to answer this question. Did you make a declaration at any time after the examination in the days after your interrogations, on the 14, 15, 16, 17, 18, 19, 20, 21, 22, 23, 24, 25, 26, 27, 28, 29, 30, 31 and the 1st, to the effect that you were annulling this record of March 13?

Thornton: No.

Vyshinsky: Here at the Court when I examined you during the

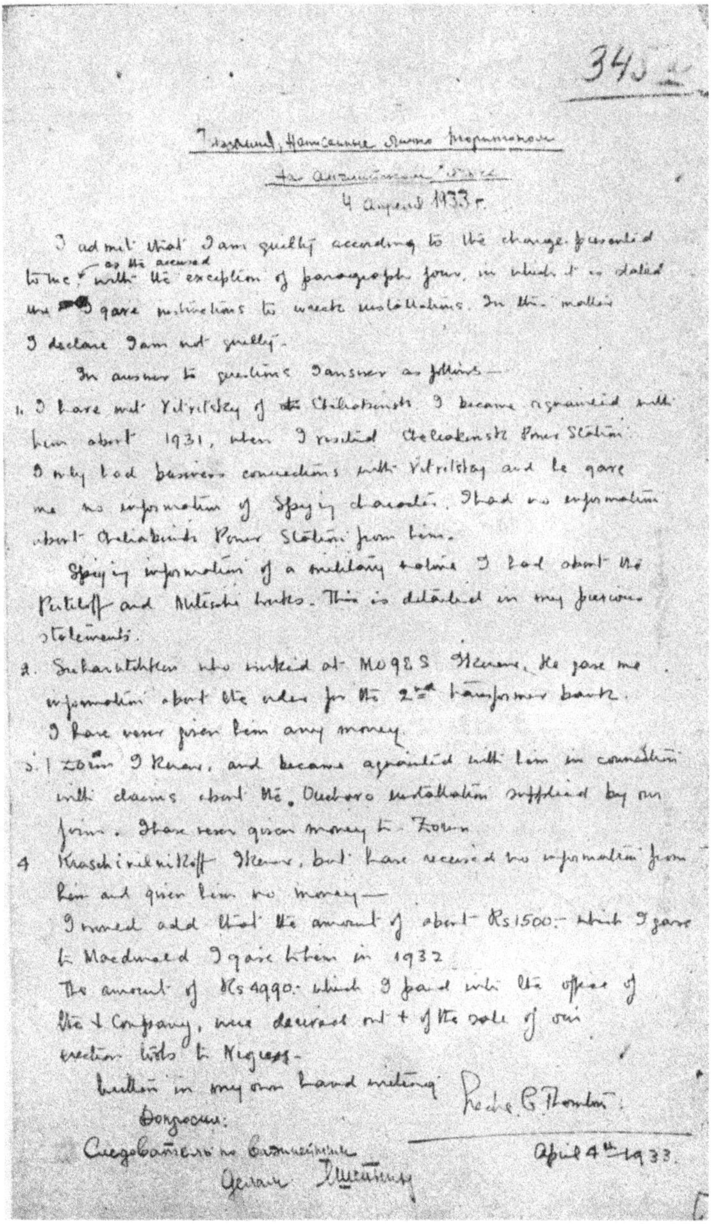
345

[illegible]

4 апреля 1933 г.

I admit that I am guilty according to the charge presented to me as the accused with the exception of paragraph four, in which it is stated that I gave instructions to wreck installations. In this matter I declare I am not guilty.

In answer to questions I answer as follows—

1. I have met Vitvitsky of the Chelyabinsk. I became acquainted with him about 1931, when I visited Chelyabinsk Power Station. I only had business connections with Vitvitsky and he gave me no information of spying character. I had no information about Chelyabinsk Power Station from him.

Spying information of a military nature I had about the Putiloff and Metrovick works. This is detailed in my previous statements.

2. Sukhrutchkov who worked at MOGES I know. He gave me information about the orders for the 2nd transformer bank. I have never given him any money.

3. Zorin I know, and became acquainted with him in connection with claims about the Ouchoro installation supplied by our firm. I have never given money to Zorin.

4. Krasheninnikoff I know, but have received no information from him and given him no money—

I must add that the amount of about Rs 1500.– which I gave to Macdonald I gave him in 1932.

The amount of Rs 4990.– which I paid into the office of the Company, were derived out of the sale of our erection tools to Nigress.

Written in my own hand writing. Leslie C. Thornton

Допросил:

Следователь по [illegible]

[illegible]

April 4th 1933.

Facsimile of a document written and signed by L. C. Thornton on April 4, 1933, admitting his guilt on three counts of the charges against him presented by the Public Prosecution (1. Economic and military espionage, 2. Procuring Soviet engineers for espionage, and 3. Bribery) and repudiating the charge of having engaged in wrecking activities. (See page 557)

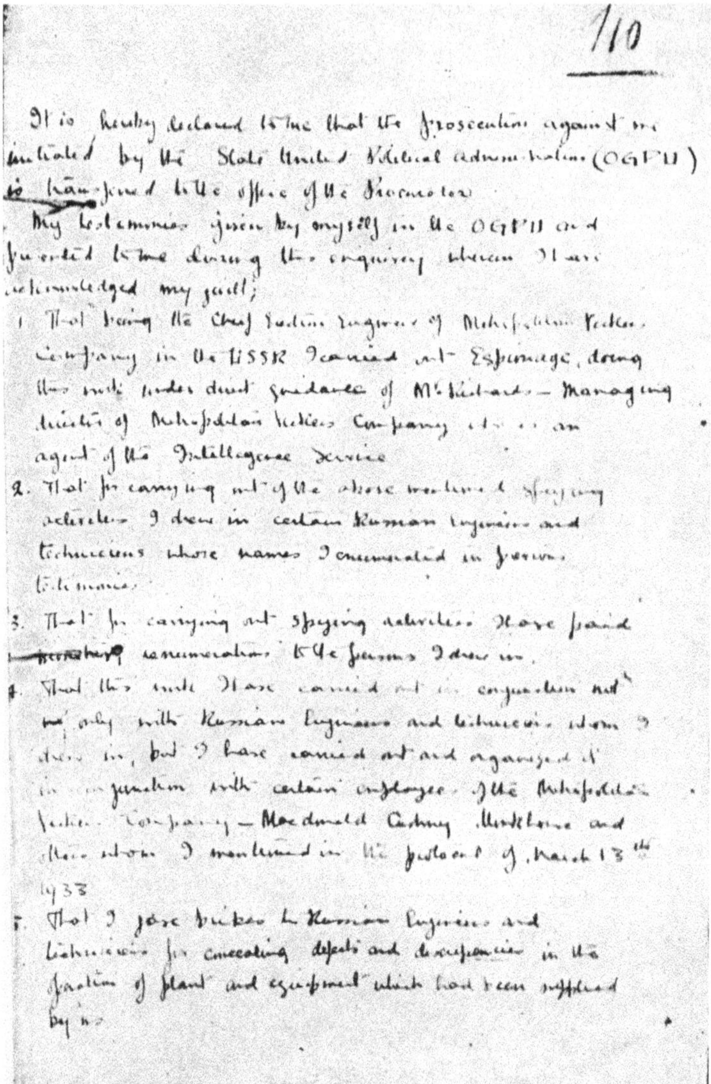

1/10

It is hereby declared to me that the prosecution against me initiated by the State United Political Administration (OGPU) is transferred to the office of the Procurator.

My testimonies given by myself in the OGPU and presented to me during this enquiry wherein I have acknowledged my guilt;

1. That being the Chief Erection Engineer of Metropolitan Vickers Company in the USSR I carried out Espionage, doing this work under direct guidance of Mr Richards – Managing director of Metropolitan Vickers Company who is an agent of the Intelligence Service
2. That for carrying out of the above mentioned spying activities I drew in certain Russian engineers and technicians whose names I enumerated in previous testimonies.
3. That for carrying out spying activities I have paid ~~[illegible]~~ remuneration to the persons I drew in.
4. That this work I have carried out in conjunction not only with Russian engineers and technicians whom I drew in, but I have carried out and organized it in conjunction with certain employees of the Metropolitan Vickers Company – Macdonald Cushny Monkhouse and others whom I mentioned in the protocol of March 13th 1933
5. That I gave bribes to Russian engineers and technicians for concealing defects and discrepancies in the operation of plant and equipment which had been supplied by us

Facsimile of L. C. Thornton's deposition of March 19, 1933, written and signed in his own hand, wherein he fully admits his spying activities and confirms that this deposition was made of his own "free will without outside influence or pressure." *(See page 558)*

(Continued on next page)

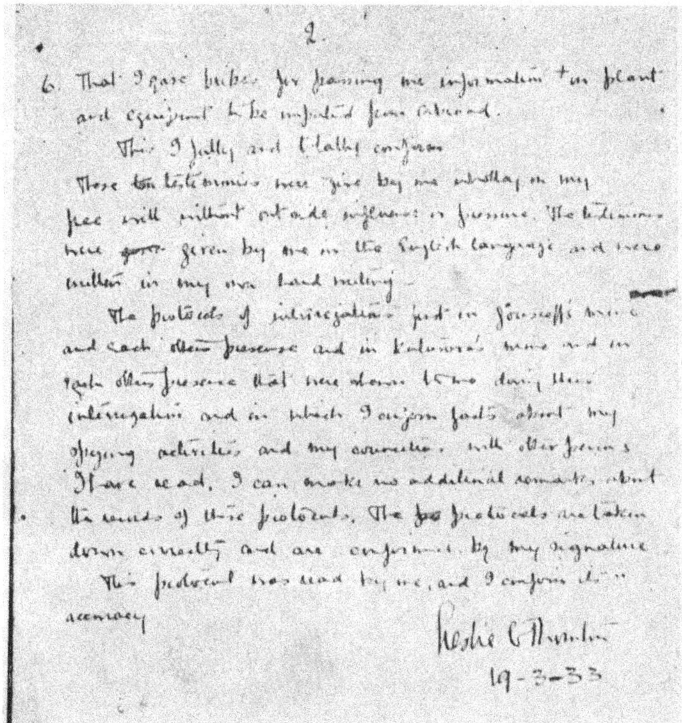

2.

6. That I gave bribes for passing me information on plant and equipment to be imported from abroad.

This I fully and totally confirm

These testimonies were given by me voluntarily on my free will without outside influence or pressure. The testimonies were given by me in the English language and were written in my own hand writing.

The protocols of interrogation put in Gousseff's name and each other presence and in Kutusova's name and in each other presence that were shown to me during their interrogation and in which I confirm facts about my spying activities and my connection with other persons I have read. I can make no additional remarks about the records of these protocols. The protocols are taken down correctly and are confirmed by my signature.

This protocol was read by me, and I confirm its accuracy

Leslie C Thornton

19-3-33

Facsimile of page 2 of L. C. Thornton's deposition of March 19, 1933, showing his signature.
(See page 558)

first days of the trial about the explanation you wished to make, did you declare that this record was written under pressure? Answer my question.

Thornton: No, I didn't.

Vyshinsky: I put three questions to you; was pressure brought to bear on you? You answered—no.

Thornton: I answered no.

Vyshinsky: I asked you—were you tortured? You answered—no.

Thornton: That is so.

Vyshinsky: I asked you—were you subjected to the third degree during your interrogation? What did you answer?

Thornton: No.

Vyshinsky: And now what do you say?

Thornton: I understood it to mean—was I tortured physically.

Vyshinsky: Physically or morally—torture is torture. I ask you, who of the Englishmen in Moscow has taught you not to tell the truth now?

Thornton: I am speaking the truth.

Vyshinsky: I understand who could teach you and who has taught you, and why you are now saying this.

I have no more questions for Thornton.

The President: Accused Thornton, be seated. Are there any questions for Kutuzova?

Monkhouse: I want Kutuzova to tell us about how the money was transmitted through the Consulate . . . (Remainder inaudible)

Kutuzova: I never made such a deposition.

Monkhouse: That document, the deposition which she signed about receiving money from the British Consulate, can be produced.

Kutuzova: I never made such a deposition.

Vyshinsky: Even if Citizen Kutuzova had given such testimony anywhere, concerning the activities of any official institution of any foreign State located on our territory, this document cannot be made public at a public session. Therefore, I categorically object to the reading of such a document.

The President: Quite correct. Are there any more questions for Kutuzova? (There are none)

The President: Accused Gregory, take your place. Your biography, please.

Gregory: To begin with, I finished my term in the secondary school. From there I was apprenticed in the electrical engineering. From there I went to various firms in England. I was employed by various firms in England. Then later I was employed with a German firm in England. I was with them when the war broke out. Then I went to North of Scotland during the war, from there to a Government factory, a munitions factory in England. After that I went to Metro-Vickers and have been with them ever since. Came to Russia.

The President: What year?

Gregory: I think it would be about 1920 or 1921. I arrived in Moscow July 16, 1932. Spent a day in Moscow, then went to Dnieprostroy. Stayed at Dnieprostroy until September 3, and then went to Dzerzhinka in Kamenskoye. It was intended I should go to Kamenskoye in the first place, only that Dnieprostroy wanted a man for the mounting. At Dnieprostroy I was employed on the erection of oil switches. From there to Kamenskoye where I was employed in the erection of a rolling mill.

The President: Has the Prosecution any questions?

Roginsky: Did you hear the testimony of Zivert that you allowed sabotage in the work?

Gregory: Yes, but I don't attach any importance to that.

Vyshinsky: This testimony is not correct then?

Gregory: They turned that man down on his own evidence. Surely this is a Court of Justice. If they turned it down I must do that.

Vyshinsky: And you claim that you worked conscientiously?

Gregory: I put it up to the technical experts yesterday, let them judge.

Vyshinsky: And what is your opinion?

Gregory: Of course I worked conscientiously. That's what I came here for.

The President: Has the Defence any questions?

Defence: No.

The President: Have the accused any questions?

Accused: No.

Vyshinsky: I have a statement to make about the documents handed in. Yesterday a request was made but no definite decision concerning it was given by the Supreme Court, although I had given my conclusion.

Secondly, two documents were handed in today. One of them is a letter, obviously authentic, brought from the papers of the Metro-Vickers office and signed by Oleinik. Before saying anything about this, I would ask to be allowed to show the letter to Oleinik so that he may certify whether it is his signature or not. It depends upon his answer what conclusion I will draw. (Shows the letter to Oleinik.)

Oleinik: Yes, it is my letter.

Vyshinsky: In view of the fact that Oleinik confirms his signature and there is no cause to doubt the authencity of this document, I have no objections to its being admitted.

The second document, handed in by Thornton's counsel, consists of two typewritten pages, beginning with the words: "Testing the Shterovka turbine, Shterovka—to Oleinik." But this document is not only not certified by anybody, but bears no signature and on account of this, and not because of any formal considerations, it can carry no weight as proof and, therefore, the Prosecution objects to admitting it as evidence.

Kommodov: I have to state that I made a reservation to the effect that it was not certified. The document which was written by Monkhouse can be signed now.

Vyshinsky: It is typewritten.

Kommodov: This letter is an answer to the other letter.

Vyshinsky: I do not know to whose letter it is an answer.

Kommodov: I have said.

Vyshinsky: You are not a witness.

I have still one more statement, as follows. In the first place, at the end of today's session before the adjournment, Monkhouse mentioned, as if accidentally, that he had felt tired and he referred to the 18-hour interrogation. Although I do not attach any serious political importance to this, nevertheless, since it is possible that this motive may be used for organized attempts to discredit certain acts in connection with the preliminary investigation—and the further behaviour of Thornton (about which of course before the interval I could know nothing) shows that such attempts have already taken place—I have already obtained the files concerning the accused, taken from the O.G.P.U. prison, and which contain first of all the warrant for arrest and the order committing the accused to the prison.

Also some forms containing not only the dates, but also the hours of leaving for and returning from the interrogation of each accused who was taken from his cell to the place of investigation.

On examination of this material, which I shall have the honour of presenting to the Court with the request that it be admitted as evidence and included in the files up to such time as there shall be no further need for it, since it has to be returned to its proper place, I find it necessary to draw attention to the fact that Monkhouse's statement today concerning his 18-hour interrogation is a false statement, as is equally the statement made by Thornton about the prolonged interrogation as a result of which he was seized with extreme fatigue, which is also false. The proof of this lies in the following: Monkhouse was arrested at night, between the 11th and 12th, and at 3:15 a.m. was placed in his cell. He was called up for interrogation on the 12th, at 11:15 a.m. Consequently he had full opportunity to rest. The interrogation continued until 3:15 p.m. after which there was an interval for dinner, which was brought there into the Investigating Judge's room to the accused Monkhouse, and which took him a very considerable time, since it consisted of three courses. The interrogation was renewed at 5:10 p.m. It was brought to a close at 1:10 a.m. During this interrogation there was also an interval of 40 to 45 minutes for supper, in the same room. Monkhouse dare not deny these facts.

Moreover, during this period of time, Monkhouse was not only interrogated for the number of hours indicated, but his interrogation was translated by him into English in his own handwriting, after it had been originally taken down in Russian by the Investigating Judge. That is to say, a three-fold process took place in this period of time: the interrogation in Russian, the record written in Russian, and Monkhouse's translation of the interrogation into English. For all this a period of time was required, which may be calculated at 12 hours and 30 minutes as the maximum including the intervals indicated by me.

I take it that these facts are sufficient to refute this entirely objectionable attempt to discredit the preliminary investigation by allegations of any kind of abnormal conditions in connection with it, not to mention the fact that there remained always the possibility of making a concrete declaration, so that by direct investigation, facts could be established which would contradict the explanation given by me just now to the Court.

As for Thornton, inasmuch as I obtained all the files in order to be sufficiently equipped to meet any declarations that might be made after Monkhouse's sortie, the matter stands in this case just as unfavourably for the statements of the accused.

Thornton, as can be seen from his dossier, No. 597, was arrested and put into his cell at the same time. His first examination took place also on March 12 at 11:45 a.m. It lasted for 4 hours and 15 minutes. The second interrogation was at 5 p.m. and finished at 1. a.m., that is, it lasted for 7 hours 55 minutes, in all 12 hours.

This is the maximum period of time during which any interrogation took place, including all the intervals for dinner, for supper, for breakfast, the time required to go from the cell to the Investigating Judge's office and from there back to the cell, which distance requires an eight to ten minute walk. These data prove that the organized attempt of the accused, both Thornton and Monkhouse, to try in this manner to get out of the evidence presented to them, must be rejected as unscrupulous and completely overthrown by all the existing data.

I ask the Court to include these files in the file of the present investigation until no longer required, when they should be returned to their proper place. (He hands the files to the President.)

The President: Has the Defence any objection?

Kommodov: No objection.

Monkhouse: May I speak on this question?

The President: You may.

Monkhouse: I do not want to deny the exact figures which have been presented by the Prosecutor, because when I was in the cell I had no watch and did not know exactly how long I was being interrogated, but in the deposition there is a slight inaccuracy. First of all, he stated that the interrogation was taken down in Russian and then translated into English. This is not so.

Vyshinsky: How was it then?

Monkhouse: It was only in English.

Vyshinsky: According to my information, it was written first in Russian and then translated.

Monkhouse: That was not so.

Vyshinsky: First you were spoken to in Russian, and then it was translated into English? Is that so?

Monkhouse: Yes.

Vyshinsky: I accept that correction. But then, if you had no watch, why did you assert that you were examined for eighteen hours?

Monkhouse: It is quite simple. When I left the cell, I supposed the time was 8 o'clock, and when I returned to the cell in the night and asked the young officer, he said it was about 2 o'clock.

Vyshinsky: You were called up for interrogation at 11:15 a.m. Add it up, it does not come to eighteen hours.

Monkhouse: I see I made a mistake and I tender my apologies.

Vyshinsky: You apologize for your mistake; I am very glad to hear it.

The President: Has the Defence any more requests concerning the documents to be admitted as evidence, so that they all may be decided on together.

Kommodov: Monkhouse asked me to submit as evidence four documents characterizing his attitude to the Soviet Union in his capacity as respresentative of the firm. It is an original in English and there are newspapers in Russian. I would ask you to look at them.

The President: Has anyone from either side any questions for the Commission of Experts? Has the Prosecution any questions?

Vyshinsky: The Prosecution considers that the questions which were subjected to examination have been sufficiently investigated without special questions being put to the Commission of Experts, therefore, we have no need of it.

The President: What is the opinion of the Defence? Will you give any questions to the Commission of Experts?

Braude: Allow me to ask the accused. [Asks Thornton] Thornton has no objections.

Defence: The accused Nordwall wishes to ask a few questions.

Kommodov: Monkhouse wishes to ask the Commission of Experts a few questions.

The President: So Monkhouse and Nordwall wish to ask questions. Do the other accused wish to do so?

Defence: No.

Vyshinsky: According to the law, these questions to the Commission of Experts on the part of the accused have to be presented in writing. The Commission of Experts will consider them and give a reply.

The President: Yes. Shall we be able to finish the Court investigations today.

Vyshinsky: We shall not be able to finish the Court investigations today.

The President: Formally we shall not be able to, but we can sketch out the further course of our work.

Have the accused prepared their questions?

Defence: No.

The President: Perhaps we should adjourn for a short time to decide upon the question of the documents to be admitted as evidence.

Vyshinsky: If the Defence is able to arrange for the questions of the accused to be handed in in writing during the adjournment.

The President: The Court will adjourn for 15 minutes.

*

* *

Commandant: Please rise. The Court is coming.

The President: Please be seated.

Dolmatovsky: Nordwall declines to give his questions to the Commission of Experts. I have three characterizations of Nordwall here, which I would ask the Court to admit as evidence. Then there is the information in *Za Industrializatsiu* of January 4, concerning Gregory and the shock-brigader's diploma.

Kommodov: I have a list of questions from Monkhouse, but since they were written in the form of separate notes, I was compelled to rewrite them rapidly. Allow me either to get them typewritten, or to read them in the form in which they are written.

Monkhouse submits the following questions to the Commission of Experts:

1. Page 30 of the indictment: "Could a piece of metal under the valve pass into the turbine, since there is a safety-net guard on the steam chest?"

2. Page 31 of the indictment: "Can it bring about the cause of the varnish running out, in circumstances when all the stators were wound in the works?"

Vyshinsky: Excuse me, "Can it bring about the cause of the varnish running"—what does that mean? It is an entirely unedited phrase.

Kommodov: By this is meant—can the installation be the cause of the varnish running, if all the stators were wound. . . .

There are in all 23 questions. I have made 6 questions out of them. I request the Court to allow me to edit them and get them typed, or perhaps we might carry them over to the morning session, and then we shall hand these questions in their final edited form to the Experts tomorrow morning.

The President: What is the opinion of the Prosecution?

Vyshinsky: I think the only way out is to postpone the presentation of questions to the Commission of Experts until tomorrow morning.

Schwartz: Perhaps we should arrange an adjournment of 15 to 20 minutes, so that the Counsel for the Defence, Kommodov, may hand in the edited questions to the Commission of Experts, and tomorrow morning hear the opinion of the Commission.

The President: The Court will now adjourn until 10 o'clock tomorrow morning.

(At 8:35 p.m. the Court adjourns until 10 a.m., April 16, 1933)

[Signed] V. V. ULRICH
President of the Special Session of the
Supreme Court of the U.S.S.R.
A. F. KOSTYUSHKO
Secretary

MORNING SESSION, APRIL 16, 1933, 10:30 a.m.

Commandant: Please rise. The Court is coming.

The President: Please be seated. The session is resumed.

We have heard the request of both sides to include a number of documents in the exhibits of the Court. The Special Session has come to the following conclusion: The request of the Defence to include the notebook of the office of Metro-Vickers from 1928 is not granted, because the documents in this notebook have no signatures.

The other requests, by the Prosecution to include a number of certificates and personal dossiers of various accused in connection with their imprisonment, and by the Defence to include the other documents—are granted.

What questions has the Defence to put to the Commission of Experts?

Kommodov: May I read them out?

The President: You may.

Kommodov: Questions put by accused Monkhouse:

1) Could a piece of metal found under a valve get into a turbine when there is a safety net on the steam chest?

2) Could the quality of the installation work on a generator be the cause of the varnish dripping from the stator, since the winding of the stator is done at the works and the stator is sent complete?

3) Does the Commission of Experts consider that the heating of the generator at the Chelyabinsk Electric Power Station was normal and in agreement with technical norms; if we take into account the investigation made by the All-Union Electrical Institute?

4) Does the Commission of Experts consider that the Metro-Vickers 24,000 kw. turbo-generators, installed at the Ivanovo Elec-

tric Power Station showed, on testing, the steam consumption guaranteed by the firm?

5) Does the Commission of Experts consider that the measures taken by the staff of the firm to remove defects in the blade setting were sufficient?

6) Does the Commission of Experts know that the safety valve arrangement on the regenerative feed-water heater for Metro-Vickers turbines is used in foreign stations and works satisfactorily?

7) Can it be considered big damage if the pressure regulator on the second transformer group of the First Moscow Power Station was put into operation within eight hours after the breakdown?

8) Are the representatives of the firm who instal a turbo-generator responsible for the state of the drain channel at the Orekhovo-Zuevo Station?

9) Can the representatives of Metro-Vickers be regarded as being responsible for the bad condition of the insulation in the rotor leads on the generators at the First Moscow Power Station, if it is remembered that all the electrical connections were made by Russians and from Russian materials?

10) Does the Commission of Experts know that house turbine No. 17 at the First Moscow Power Station was not supplied by Metro-Vickers?

These are the ten questions.

The President: Has the Defence any further requests?

Libson: To establish the social origin of Kotlyarevsky, I request that a document testifying to the origin of Kotlyarevsky's father be added to the documents in the case.

The President: Have the other Counsel for the Defence any request?

Defence: No.

The President: Have the accused any request?

Accused: No.

The President: Are there any more questions to put to anyone? Have the other Counsel for the Defence any questions for the Commission of Experts?

Defence: No.

The President: How much time does the Commission of Experts require to give its opinion?

Experts: It depends on the questions. If it is to be an opinion on all the questions which we have heard here, we shall have to obtain additional material and this will determine the amount of time required for the reply.

Vyshinsky: Ten questions have been put to the Commission of Experts. The Prosecution do not object to eight of them. With regard to two questions, the Prosecution object on the following grounds. Point 8—"Are the representatives of the firm who install a turbo-generator responsible for the state of the drain channel at the Orekhovo-Zuevo Station?" (p. 52) In the first place, there is an inaccuracy in the formulation—not "who install," but "who installed," because we are not discussing installation work carried on at the present time by the representatives of the firm. If it means "who installed" then it should state what installation work, where, when, and in what period of time. There is a reference to page 52 of the indictment. There is no reference at all there to the representatives of the firm, and besides, the main thing is that we are not trying the representatives of the firm as such, or the firm itself.

Kommodov: I have in view individual representatives.

Vishinsky: Counsel Kommodov is violating the order of procedure—individual persons employed by the firm on installation work are being tried here. For the reasons that I have had the honour to submit to the Court, the Prosecution object to an answer being given to point 8.

Point 9. "Can the representatives of Metro-Vickers be regarded as being responsible for the bad condition of the insulation in the rotor leads on the generators at the First Moscow Power Station, if it is remembered that all the electrical connections were made by Russians and from Russian materials?" (p. 53) There are two facts to which attention must be directed. First, a question cannot be put conditionally without first examining the facts, etc. It is necessary to establish what equipment there is and who installed it. Secondly, on page 53 of the indictment it says literally regarding these facts: "The bad insulation on the rotor leads systematically led to the stoppage of the generators." Consequently this question is not repeated and is not identical with the question in the indictment put as a definite thesis. It does not raise the question as to who is responsible and whether the representatives of Metro-Vickers are responsible, but it states a fact that was established by the Commission of Experts, and therefore, it is necessary to examine the dossier which contains the report of the investigation and which refers to the breakdown.

On these grounds the Prosecution object to point 9.

Kommodov: All these are general remarks. It was not at all my intention to speak about the firm as such. I spoke of individual representatives, who are being tried in the present case.

Vyshinsky: Representatives are not being tried. Citizens are being tried.

Kommodov: But their official position is that of representatives, especially Monkhouse. I understand, of course, that individual representatives cannot compromise the whole firm. That is quite clear. Therefore, I did not speak of the firm as such.

As for question 8, at the investigation, as you will remember, the condition of the drain channel depended to a considerable degree on building work. That is why this gave me grounds to support the request of accused Monkhouse to put this question. The Commission of Experts will understand this question. A mistake in formulation or a typist's error does not change the general nature of the question. It is clear and plain, and material on this question was presented at the trial. Therefore, it seems to me, such a question may be put.

As for question 9, it was put in a conditional form. We expected that the experts would have material on this question and that they would know, or could find from the documents, who did the installation work. Therefore, I think that in the present case the request of accused Monkhouse can be granted and all the ten questions be submitted to the Commission of Experts.

Dmitriev (Member of the Court): Accused Monkhouse, you asked this question: "Does the Commission of Experts consider that the Metro-Vickers 24,000 kw. turbo-generators, which were installed at Ivanovo Power Station showed, on testing, the steam consumption guaranteed by the firm?" Were these turbo-generators tested?

Monkhouse: Yes.

Dmitriev: Is there a report on these tests?

Monkhouse: Yes.

Dmitriev: Accused Monkhouse, on the fourth question, the Court wishes to know which part of the indictment you refer to when you ask the question: "Does the Commission of Experts consider that the Metro-Vickers 24,000 kw. turbo-generators installed at the Ivanovo Power Station showed, on testing, the steam consumption guaranteed by the firm?"

Monkhouse: It is page 39.

Dmitriev: Read it out, please.

Monkhouse (Reads): "The work of the unit when the regulation was not in order," concludes the Commission of Experts, "could either lead to serious breakdowns or increase their number."

Dmitriev: But this is under a heading which says: "Unreliable regulation of the turbines which from the time they were put into operation did not attain the required efficiency and did not ensure normal operation," that is, the turbine did not conform to the guarantee on steam consumption and did not conform to the guarantee on regulation.

You evidently understand the regulation guarantee as a guarantee of the dependence of steam consumption on load.

Monkhouse: Perhaps it was somewhat improperly formulated, because on testing for steam consumption, we simultaneously tested the regulation, from all sides.

Dmitriev: How would you like to alter the formulation?

Monkhouse: You could just leave it as it is or simply say: "Was the guarantee for steam consumption conformed to?"

Dmitriev: If you leave this formulation, will it be correct? It would be more exact to say: "Does the Commission of Experts consider that the Metro-Vickers 24,000 kw. turbo-generators installed at the Ivanovo Power Station, passed the regulation tests?" because the indictment speaks only of the regulations.

Monkhouse: I must explain why this is so. In English, "consumption" tests mean testing the consumption of steam. That is why the mistake in the formulation occurred.

Dmitriev: You don't object to this formulation?

Monkhouse: I don't mind.

The President: The Court puts the following questions to the Commission of Experts.

1) Could a piece of metal found under a valve get into a turbine when there is a safety net on the steam chest? (p. 30)

2) Could the quality of the installation work on a generator be the cause of varnish dripping from the stator, since the winding of the stator is done at the works and the stator is sent complete? (p. 31)

3) Does the Commission of Experts consider that the heating of the generator at the Chelyabinsk Electric Power Station was normal and in agreement with technical norms, if we take into account the investigation made by the All-Union Electrical Institute? (p. 31)

4) Does the Commission of Experts consider that the Metro-Vickers 24,000 kilowatt turbo-generators installed at the Ivanovo Electric Power Station passed the regulation tests? (p. 39)

5) Does the Commission of Experts consider that the measures taken by the staff of the firm to remove defects in the blade setting were sufficient? (p. 39)

6) Does the Commission of Experts know that the safety valve arrangement on the regenerative feed-water heater for Metro-Vickers turbines is used in foreign stations and works satisfactorily? (p. 41)

7) Can it be considered big damage if the pressure regulator on the second transformer group of the first Moscow Power Station was put into operation within eight hours after the breakdown? (p. 50)

8) Does the Commission of Experts know that house turbine No. 17 at the First Moscow Power Station was not supplied by Metro-Vickers Company? (p. 53)

Questions 8 and 9, as originally enumerated by Counsel for the Defence, are deleted because the Court is not trying the firm, nor is it trying individual representatives of the firm but is trying individual British and Soviet citizens on charges of committing definite actions provided against by our Criminal Code.

How much time does the Commission of Experts require?

Experts: Replies can be formulated and given to the Court on all questions except 3 and 4, in an hour's time. On questions 3 and 4, as there is no report of the test of the generators or turbines, the reply can be given within an hour after we obtain those documents.

The President: Where will the documents be obtained?

Experts: From Orgenergo and the Soviet Electric Institute.

Vyshinsky: Perhaps the Supreme Committee on Power Supply could be applied to at once?

Experts: An hour after we receive the documents, we can give the reply.

The President: So as not to drag out the Court procedure today, if there are no further questions, the Court proposes without declaring the Judicial Investigation closed, to adjourn until 7 o'clock in the evening. After this the conclusions of the experts will be heard, and after a short recess we can take the pleas of the parties at eight o'clock.

Vyshinsky: I have no objections.

Kommodov: We would like an adjournment until tomorrow morning so as to give us time to prepare.

The President: Are there any additional questions to put to the accused?

Vyshinsky: I have none.

Schwartz: I have one question for Zorin.

Accused Zorin. You explained to the Court that Thornton suggested you should join a counter-revolutionary organization and become a member of it during the fifth and last meeting. Do you confirm that?

Zorin: Yes.

Schwartz: This happened in November 1932?

Zorin: Yes.

Schwartz: When did you receive 1,000 rubles from him?

Zorin: At that meeting.

Schwartz: You mean. . . ?

Zorin: It was about the middle of November.

Schwartz: When did you take your vacation in 1932?

Zorin: December 27.

Schwartz: Did you return to your work?

Zorin: I did not, I was arrested.

Schwartz: You did not return to your work and you were arrested. Let me ask the last question. Were the thousand rubles given you for concrete wrecking work which had already been carried out, or for future work?

Zorin: For future work.

Schwartz: You received 1,000 rubles for wrecking work in the future. Had you time to carry it out?

Zorin: No.

Schwartz: This is a question of connections. Thornton had not returned?

Zorin: No.

Schwartz: So after his departure you did not see him?

Zorin: No.

The President: Are there any more questions?

Vyshinsky: No.

The President: The Court is adjourned until 7 o'clock.

(At 11:00 a.m. the Court adjourns until 7 p.m.)

[Signed] V. V. ULRICH
President of the Special Session of the
Supreme Court of the U.S.S.R.

A. F. KOSTYUSHKO
Secretary

EVENING SESSION, APRIL 16, 1933, 7:20 p.m.

Commandant: Please rise. The Court is coming.

The President: Please be seated. The session is resumed. Has the Commission of Experts formulated its opinion?

Commission of Experts: We have the minutes.

The President: Read them, please.

Golubtsov: The Commission of Experts were given eight questions on which they have come to the following conclusions.

Question No. 1: Could a piece of metal found under a valve get into a turbine when there is a safety net on the steam chest? (page 30)

Answer: The Commission considers that under very unfavourable conditions it is possible that pieces of metal found under the valve and in front of the safety net, could in time under the influence of the passing current of steam, partially destroy the net and penetrate the turbine. Nevertheless, the Commission considers that the main danger from the iron entering under the valve lay in the fact that the iron did not permit the complete closing of the stop valve. In the case of the main regulating arrangement refusing to work, when the load was being thrown off (which is not unusual with the Metro-Vickers turbine) the speeding up of the machine must be forestalled by means of the closing of the stop valve. The impossibility of its closing on account of the pieces of metal finding their way into it, could be a reason for a large speeding up of the turbine and even a breakdown.

Question No. 2: Could the quality of the installation work on a generator be the cause of the varnish dripping from the stator, since the winding of the stator is done at the works and the stator is sent complete?

Answer: The quality of the installation of the generator, in conditions where it has been sent complete from the works, cannot be the cause of the varnish dripping out. Nevertheless, errors in the assembly and installation of the generator ventilation and of the equipment connected with the ventilation may cause the temperature of the stator winding to rise, as a result of which the drip of varnish will increase.

Question No. 3: Does the Commission of Experts consider that the heating of the generator at the Chelyabinsk Electric Power Station was normal and in agreement with technical norms, if we take into account the investigation made by the All-Union Electrical Institute? (page 31)

Answer: According to the agreement between Arcos and Metro-Vickers in regard to the generator of the Chelyabinsk Station, the maximum increase in temperature above the temperature of the surrounding air (35° C.) with a maximum protracted load of 24,000 kw. (30,000 kw. amperes), should not exceed: for the stator winding, when measured with a thermometer, 50° C. and when determined by the resistance method—80° C. (for the rotor winding when determined by the resistance method—80° C.).

During the testing of generator No. 2 at the Chelyabinsk Power Station, carried out by the All-Union Electrical Institute from June 11 to 27, 1932, it was ascertained that, in regard to the heating of the copper of the rotor and the iron of the stator, the generator came up to the standards of the Association of German Engineers (VDE) but in regard to the heating of the copper of the stator the generator does not comply with these standards of the Association of German Engineers (VDE): also in regard to the heating of the copper of the stator, the generator does not satisfy the technical conditions of the agreement since the temperature increase of the winding of the stator when measured with a mercury thermometer instead of the 50° permitted by the agreement, reached 60° at a stator current of 1,541 amperes. Consequently, for a nominal stator current of 1,578 amperes, the temperature increase would be even larger.

Question No. 4: Does the Commission of Experts consider that the Metro-Vickers 24,000 kw. turbo-generators installed at the Ivanovo Power Station passed the regulation tests? (page 39 of the Indictment)

Answer: On the basis of the materials examined, which were placed at the disposal of the Commission of Experts, the latter has ascertained that:

1. According to the agreement the change in the number of revolutions for an instantaneous throwing-off the load from full load to no load should not exceed + 5 per cent and + 3 per cent for the steady state.

2. For an instantaneous throwing-off or for change of 25 per cent from full load, the number of revolutions should not exceed + 5 per cent and + 2 per cent for the steady state.

3. On October 22, 1931 (see the record of November 12, 1931), representatives of the Ivanovo Power Station in the presence of the firm's representative Shiply, carried out tests of the regulation of turbine No. 2 for the throwing-off of the load and in all cases the number of revolutions rose approximately to 3,000 R.P.M. and the safety valve came into action.

4. At the technical conference on December 11, 1931, in the presence of the firm's representative Thornton, the following defects were noted in the regulation of the turbines:

a) The necessity of hand regulation by means of the by-pass valve on the steam pipe at no load, for the maintenance of a constant number of revolutions.

b) The increase in the number of revolutions above 5 per cent for a partial throwing-off of the load (10-15,000 kw.) and the switching off of the machine by the automatic safety device.

5. In the report regarding the tests of turbines Nos. 1 and 2 carried out by the Orgenergo in January 1932, the following was pointed out in regard to the regulation of the turbine.

a) When throwing off 17,000 kw. of turbine No. 1 the automatic safety devices began to act. The increase in the number of revolutions during this test amounted to 7 per cent.

b) During the test of the automatic speed regulating device for the same machine, by means of an artifical increase in the number of revolutions through tightening the valve sleeves, the automatic safety device began to act when the number of revolutions increased by 9.5 per cent.

c) On turbine No. 2 for a load throw-off of 60,000 kw. the increase in the number of revolutions amounted to 7 per cent.

d) For a load throw-off of 11,600 kw., for the same machine, the number of revolutions increased by 6 per cent.

The measurements of the increase in the number of revolutions for the throwing-off of the loads, as well as during the test of the automatic safety device was carried out by means of a previously calibrated tachograph (recording tachometer). (The tachograms of these tests are in the materials.)

On the basis of the above, the Commission of Experts notes the unsatisfactory work of the regulation of both machines and considers that the "guarantee in regard to the regulation has not been carried out."

Question No. 5: Does the Commission of Experts consider that the measures taken by the staff of the firm to remove defects in the blade setting were sufficient? (page 39 of the Indictment.)

Answer: On the basis of the memoranda and materials examined, which record the breaking of the blade setting of the turbines at the Ivanovo Power Station and other stations, and also on a basis of the examination of the materials relating to the design and stress analysis, the Commission comes to the conclusion that the measures which were taken for the elimination of these defects were not sufficient. The design of the blades is unsafe, since the blades are weak, have excessive stresses due to steam loading and break as the result of metal fatigue caused by resonance vibrations. The introduction of a restraining wire serves only as a palliative measure directed to the bettering of the working conditions of the blades by preventing the resonance of one of the types of tangential vibrations of blades (*i.e.,* one definite order of tangential vibrations).

Having in mind the possible resonance of axial vibrations, the excessive stresses in the blades of the given design due to axial vibration and the insignificant effect of the wire on the axial vibration, it is necessary to recognize that the installation of blades with wire bindings, as well as the installation of new blades of the same design, in place of the broken ones (which has been practised several times) is an insufficient measure.

The Commission would consider an effective measure to be the radical redesigning of the blade setting in the direction of a considerable reduction of the stresses in the active blades in order to avoid the fatigue of the metal with the existing vibrations of the turbine blades.

Question No. 6: Does the Commission of Experts know that the safety valve arrangement on the regenerative feed-water heater for Metro-Vickers turbines is used in foreign stations and works satisfactorily? (Page 41 of the Indictment.)

Answer: The Commission of Experts does not have at its disposal documents corroborating the reliable and irreproachable work at foreign stations of the safety valve arrangement for the feed-water heater of the Metro-Vickers turbines. Nevertheless, the available materials regarding the work of the safety valve arrangement of the feed-water heater No. 2 for the 24,000 kw. turbine at the Ivanovo Power Station testify to cases when the device refused to work during the filling-up of the heaters with water (the float of the device filled up with water and did not work).

This circumstance testifies to the unreliable work of the safety device at the Ivanovo Power Station.

Question No. 7: Can it be considered big damage if the pressure regulator on the second transformer group of the First Moscow Power Station was put into operation within eight hours after the breakdown?

Answer: During the breakdown with the regulator of the second 47,000 kw. transformer group at the First Moscow Power Station which took place on October 1, 1932 (Mosenergo memorandum of April 16, 1933), four bushings of the oil throw-over switch, the throw-over switch contacts and the contacts of the oil circuit breaker were damaged. The transformer was equipped with Translay's safety device. The relay was tightened up too much and during the breakdown the transformer safety device did not work and the generator, used in the test, was switched off by hand.

The Commission of Experts finds that:

1. The damage to the equipment at the breakdown did not assume extensive proportions.

2. The interruption in the work of the transformer group was approximately 8 hours.

3. Part of the damaged equipment was replaced from stock at

the station and a part, due to the lack of parts in stock, was remounted after being cleaned and repaired.

Nevertheless, the Commission of Experts considers that:

(1) An interruption in the work of such a large unit as the 47,000 kw. transformer group even for a few hours may cause great disorganization in the electric power supply system.

(2) If the transformer group, during its trial connection to the circuit, had not been gradually loaded from a specific generator but had been directly placed under a load, the extent of the breakdown would have been considerably larger, the damage to the equipment considerably more serious and would have caused the discontinuation of the work of the transformer group for a considerable period.

Question No. 8: Does the Commission of Experts know that house-turbine No. 17 at the First Moscow Power Station was not supplied by Metro-Vickers? (Page 53 of the Indictment.)

Answer: The Commission of Experts knows that house turbine No. 17 at the First Moscow Power Station is not one supplied by the Metro-Vickers firm.

Members of the Commission of Experts:

Golubtsov
Brailo
Novikov
Ulatov
Snetkov
Smirnov

The President: Has the Defence any questions?

Defence: No.

The President: Has the Prosecution any questions?

Roginsky: No.

The President: Accused Monkhouse, have you any questions to put to the Commission of Experts?

Monkhouse: I have no questions but I consider that it is not all quite correct; there are certain points which are debatable. I think that there is room for argument with the Commission, but this is not the place for an argument. If cases occurred when we did not carry out the guarantee, if there were such cases, they should have been made known to our firm through the Electro-Import and Arcos. I think that in this decision there is room for argument.

Roginsky: I cannot hear Monkhouse well.

The President: The accused Monkhouse said that there are certain points in the conclusions of the Commission of Experts which are debatable.

Roginsky: I presume that if accused Monkhouse has a basis for refuting any assertion made by the Commission of Experts, it will be necessary to do so immediately at this session; morever, this refutation must relate to the concrete facts of the charges against Monkhouse. We have repeatedly pointed out here, and the Court has borne us out in this, that the questions connected with the supply of equipment by the firm generally are not the subject of the investigation by this Court. We are exclusively investigating the concrete facts of the crimes charged to each one of the accused sitting in the dock. Only from this point of view can the conclusions of the Commission of Experts be considered.

Monkhouse: If the conclusions of the Commission of Experts must be considered from this point of view, I have no more questions, since I think that you will agree that in the majority of cases the answers given by the Commission of Experts point to defects which could not in any way be attributed to the accused.

Roginsky: This is a question of the evaluation of the facts and this evaluation will be made in the argument between the parties in the case.

The President: Has the Prosecution any additional questions?

Roginsky: No.

The President: Applications to the Court?

Roginsky: No.

The President: Has the Defence any questions?

Smirnov: Permit me to ask the accused MacDonald two questions of a purely biographical character.

The President: You may.

Smirnov: I want to ask MacDonald—when, at what age did your leg begin to hurt. You injured it, fractured it? How long were you deprived of the use of this leg without some kind of appliance?

MacDonald: Five years.

Smirnov: You wore an appliance from when you were eleven until you were sixteen?

MacDonald: Yes.

Smirnov: In your family there are also two sisters and a brother. The brother is still quite young, and the sisters are a bit older, or is it that the brother is older and one of the sisters is quite a young girl?

MacDonald: One sister is 26 years old, the other is 21. My brother is also 21.

Smirnov: Are they twins?

MacDonald: Yes.

Smirnov: Your brother and older sister are working?

MacDonald: All three are working.

Smirnov: I have no more questions.

Libson: A question to accused MacDonald. Tell me, please, when you worked in Moscow, or when you worked outside of Moscow at other power stations and came to Moscow, did you usually live where all the Englishmen lived, that is, in the hostel?

MacDonald: Yes.

Libson: Did you sleep and eat there, were you there all the time?

MacDonald: Yes.

Libson: I have a question for the accused Oleinik. Tell me, when you worked at the Moscow Power station where did you live?

Oleinik: In a hotel.

Libson: In what hotel?

Oleinik: Minskoye Podvorye.

Libson: Were you often at the Englishmen's hostel?

Oleinik: I was there once. But I was at the office almost every free day or every other free day—two or three times a month.

Libson: Were you often at the office?

Oleinik: Two or three times a month.

Libson: I have no more questions.

The President: I declare the judicial investigation at an end. After the adjournment we will have the speech of the State Prosecutor, Vyshinsky. I have one question for the Defence. Have you arranged the order in which you will speak?

Libson: Kaznacheyev will speak first, then Schwartz, Pines, Libson, Smirnov, Braude, Dolmatovsky, Lidov, and Kommodov.

The President: The Court will adjourn for half an hour.

*
* *

Commandant: Please rise. The Court is coming.

The President: Please be seated. The proceedings are resumed. Comrade Vyshinsky, the Public Prosecutor.

Vyshinsky: Only a couple of days, perhaps, separate us from the decisive moment when the final summing up of the whole of our work of the past days will be made and when in this summing up the authoritative word of the Supreme Court will be pronounced on this case. Little time separates us from the moment when will be given distinctly, explicitly, clearly, definitely and categorically for the last time in this case the qualification of all the various events that were the subject of examination during our judicial investigation, of the preliminary investigation that preceeded it, the qualification of the sum total of those social and political facts which lie at the base of the present trial.

This summing up should be and will be very important, because, even compared with other cases that have come before the Supreme Court in previous years, the present case has exceptional significance; the present case must be characterized as a case which has exceptional, even world significance, as a case upon which the attention of the whole world, of the toilers of this country, of the toilers of all countries, of all our friends and of all our enemies, is concentrated.

All those enemies who are blinded by their class hatred, who are seized with feelings of class enmity and rage; who on the eve of this trial forgot the bounds set by the sovereignty of our State, went beyond the limits of what is permissible in international relations, and tried to exercise upon the trend of this trial, of this case, moral pressure that revealed that frequently anti-Soviet circles, convulsed in hysterics, lose their necessary and highly extolled coolness and step over the boundaries of what is permissible, and of course receive a proper and deserved rebuff.

I have no doubt that in future, too, they will receive a similarly determined rebuff which will compel them to understand that the land where socialist society is being built, that the land which fifteen years and more ago threw off the yoke of the capitalists and landlords, will ignore every demand that runs counter to the interests of the proletariat, of the proletarian revolution, of the proletarian dictatorship, no matter whence these attempts may come.

The insolent, arrogant demands of certain foreign circles, as I have said, received a deserved rebuff. And they will receive this rebuff in the future if they for a moment forget that they are dealing with the U.S.S.R., the land of great socialist construction, the land that has won for itself emancipation from its own capitalists and landlords who were abolished by the October Revolution, the land which won for itself State independence, which is becoming more and more consolidated with every year of our existence, on the basis of the great social, economic and political gains of our Great October, on the basis of the magnificent successes achieved by our first Five-Year Plan, on the basis of the great and inexhaustible creative forces of the masses of the toilers of our country which under the leadership of our great Communist Party are building a new socialist society.

We never permitted, we do not permit and never shall permit anyone to interfere in our internal affairs, no matter what manoeuvres, hysterics, cries, noise and clamour they may raise. One cannot refrain just now from recalling the cries and hysteria of certain circles in England who lost their balance, who have not properly understood, or who have totally failed as yet to understand the thought expressed three years ago by Comrade Stalin concerning the "rock" that stands in the way of improving our economic ties with bourgeois states.

At the Sixteenth Congress of the Communist Party, Comrade Stalin in delivering the political report of the Central Committee said:

> "It is said, further, that the rock is our Soviet system, collectivization, the fight against the kulaks, anti-religious pro-

> paganda, the fight against wreckers and counter-revolutionaries among the 'men of science' like the banished Besedovskys, Solomons, Dmitrievskys, etc.
>
> "But this is becoming quite diverting," said Comrade Stalin, "it seems that they do not like the Soviet system. But then we do not like the capitalist system, we do not like the fact that tens of millions of unemployed in their countries are compelled to starve and live in want, while a small crowd of capitalists own billions of wealth. But since we have agreed," says Comrade Stalin in this historic political report, "not to interfere in the internal affairs of other countries, is it not clear that it is not worth while reverting to this question?—Collectivization, the fight against the kulaks, the fight against wreckers, anti-religious propaganda, etc., represent the inalienable right of the workers and peasants of the Union of Soviet Socialist Republics, a right fixed in our Constitution. We must and we will carry out the Constitution of the U.S.S.R. with the fullest consistency. It goes without saying, therefore, that those who refuse to have regard for our Constitution can pass on—can go their own way."

These gentlemen, you see, do not like our Constitution, our Soviet system, our Soviet Court and they express their dislike of our Constitution and our Soviet system and our Soviet Court by slander, insinuation, distortions, falsifications—in a word, by the methods they usually employ to bring "moral pressure" to bear upon public opinion in their own countries, to protect their narrow, crude, cruel, inhuman, capitalist class interests. They do not like our Soviet Court because it is a class court, and they try to slander it by saying that since it is a class court, that is, a court that guards the interests of the working class and of the proletarian State, it is not a court, and that in the country where the court consists of toilers, where the court acts in the interests of the toilers, where the court directs its moral and political influence against the exploiters, against the enemies of the toilers—in that country there is no justice.

Mr. Patrick, as we can judge from the debate that took place in the British House of Commons recently, on the Bill empowering the government to place an embargo on Soviet goods, declared:

> "The whole idea of justice" (apparently in the Land of Soviets, because he was speaking about the Soviet Court), "in fact, is on the basis of class. That fact was brought home to me very vividly in the Supreme Court of Moscow a couple of years ago when I sat through one of these State trials, on a very hard chair looking at an enormous red banner hung behind the judge's table, at which the judges were sitting and smoking. (Mr. Hennon: 'Judges smoking?'—Mr. Patrick: 'Yes.') Upon the banner," continued Mr. Patrick, "in large white letters was written, 'This Court is the organ of the Proletariat.' That is one of Lenin's classic remarks; typical of his sayings quoted as text on all occasions. Those words mean precisely what they say. The Court is the organ of the proletariat, and by a simple chain of Communist doctrine . . . the court is the organ of class war, and exists for that main purpose. . . ."
>
> "But," Mr. Patrick continued, "the class war itself has long since ceased to be a reality. It was genuine enough, I have no doubt, in the early days of the Revolution and of the civil war. . . . A long time has passed since then, and the resistance of the bourgeoisie has now been utterly and completely crushed."

By this, Mr. Patrick wanted to say that, since there is no class war, there is nothing left for the court to do from the point of view of the logic of the communist program which regards and recognizes the court to be an organ that protects the interests of the proletariat.

We have never concealed and do not conceal the genuine class nature of our court, the genuine class tasks which confront our judiciary.

We, always and everywhere, through the mouths of our teachers, and by our constant work on the theoretical and practical sectors of socialist construction, have admitted the class nature of our court as well as the whole of our state; we have never isolated a single one of our tasks from the general and fundamental tasks of realizing and protecting the interests of the working class, and we have never isolated from these tasks the tasks of our juridical reality, of our juridical work.

Lenin, right at the very beginning of the revolution pointed precisely to this really great distinguishing feature of our Soviet justice.

> "In place of the old court," he said, concerning our October Revolution, "it has begun to create a new people's court, or to put it more correctly, a Soviet Court, built up on the principle of the participation of the toilers and the exploited classes, and only of these classes, in the administration of the State. The new court was necessary first of all for the struggle against the exploiters who are trying to restore the old domination, or to cling to their privileges, or else secretly, by deception, to get back some particle of these privileges."

The Soviet Court is the court of the Soviet State, the court of the working class; it is the court of the toilers of our country who are carrying out the grand historical tasks of building up socialist society in our country which serves as an example and a model for our class brothers in all other countries who are fighting for their social emancipation.

In contrast to this court, the court in all capitalist countries always was and has remained a court that realizes and protects the interests of the capitalist classes, the classes that exploit and oppress human labour.

> "In capitalist society," says Lenin, "the court was mainly an apparatus of oppression, an apparatus of bourgeois exploitation."

And when we are told that our Soviet Court is a class court and that you who are sitting in this Court are doing your work unjustly because you stand on the basis of a class doctrine, these utterances are nothing more than the usual attacks which bear witness to the methods of falsification and slander which the exploiters usually resort to in order to gloss over the real class and exploiting nature of their own courts, as well as of the whole of their state.

Certain gentlemen in the House of Commons try to contrast our Court with their court and their justice and point out that between our justice and the justice of England, say, there is this difference that in English courts justice is administered, whereas it is useless seeking for justice in the Soviet Court.

For example, Major Hills, speaking in the House of Commons not so long ago in connection with the Metro-Vickers case, openly said:

> "Justice in this country (that is, England) and the procedure in any civilized country, either in America or in any civilized part of Europe, is not comparable with the procedure in Russia."

Replying to Sir Stafford Cripps, he went on to say:

> ". . . He [Sir Stafford Cripps] always assumes, and puts up, as a dialectical smoke screen, that there is a system of justice in Russia. He knows very well that there is none."

Major Hills is a brave major if he dares to say that which I unfortunately was obliged to quote at this session of the Supreme Court at the risk of offending your ears. But this major was not badly answered by his own countrymen, by other members of Parliament.

For example, at this very session of the House of Commons, Sir Stafford Cripps said:

> "The right honourable and learned gentleman, the Lord Advocate, if he were here, would, I am sure, bear me out in what I say with regard to the Scottish Silks case. It was months after the arrest and release on bail of the Scottish Silks defendants before the charges were fully formulated."

Whole months passed before the charge alone was fully formulated!

Or take Mr. Kirkwood, who declared that in 1913 the Member for Dumbarton [Mr. Kirkwood] was arrested at 1:30 a.m., thrown into a cell and deported without a trial. He was kept from his wife and family for sixteen months.

It is not I who say this. This is said by Mr. Kirkwood. This is said by Sir Stafford Cripps. This is said by members of the British Parliament, by Englishmen who have not lost their sense of reality and who are able with uncorrupted eyes to see this reality in capitalist countries which mocks at what there is called justice.

Nor do these capitalist gentlemen like our court procedure

and our trials, which are directed against counter-revolutionaries and wreckers—who always and without fail meet with the warm support, sympathy and protection of definite circles of the bourgeoisie and particularly—I must say this precisely at this trial—of certain definite circles of the British bourgeoisie.

Speaking about this trial, that is, this very case which is the subject of our present deliberations, Mr. Runciman, the President of the Board of Trade, said:

> "The staging of trials such as this on charges of sabotage occurs frequently in Russia. Careful search has been made, and we have been unable to discover a single instance where one of these trials has not resulted in a condemnation."

What can this mean? It can mean only this, that we do not put people in the dock for nothing. The prosecution authorities and organs of preliminary investigation, before putting any citizen, their own or of another country in the dock on the charge of any crime, very carefully weigh all the circumstances and adopt an extremely cautious attitude towards this act.

But if the British President of the Board of Trade intended to say that not in a single one of these trials can we find a case of acquittal, then this already comes within the bounds of direct misrepresentation of facts. And in order not to dwell on this question too long, in order, in passing, as it were, to refute assertions of this kind, I shall turn to an historical fact concerning one of our great trials, and incidentally, one of our great trials of wreckers, that is—to the Shakhty trial, at which Potemkin, Schtelbrink, Otto and Meyer were acquitted.

Four of the accused in one of the greatest wrecking trials, in a trial of counter-revolution in the Donbas, of a counter-revolutionary organization which tried to blow up our All-Union "stokehold," to strike a heavy blow at our fuel industry!

After this, how can one say that all our trials end in a conviction? It is true that the President of the Board of Trade talks about the careful preliminary investigations made in order to draw the conclusion which he conveyed to his fellow citizens in the House of Commons. But is must be said that these careful investigations are as obviously defective as some of the turbines supplied by Metro-Vickers, about which citizen Monkhouse spoke here yesterday.

You know that the bourgeoisie have always tried to hide the true class nature of all their institutions, and of such an institution as the Court in particular. I could quote a number of highly authoritative and valuable facts testifying to precisely this historical and constant attempt on the part of the capitalist and exploiting classes to conceal and gloss over the true exploiting nature of their State institutions, and of their courts in particular.

But, Comrade Judges, long, long ago this was well and exhaustively exposed, particularly in regard to the question as to what the much extolled courts even of the English State represent. Marx, in his *English Constitution* gives an analysis with an exhaustive and withering characterization of the class nature of the courts in capitalist countries. He says that:

> "English trial by jury as the most perfect form, is the consummation of juridical falsehood and injustice."

Indeed, what does any court in capitalist countries represent? Speaking of the English courts Marx says:

> "Those who are too poor . . . receive for preliminary perusal only the indictment and the original evidence given before a Justice of the Peace. Hence, he does not know the details of the evidence brought against him (and for the innocent, this is the most dangerous thing of all): he must reply immediately the prosecution has finished and can speak only once. If he has not exhausted everything, if he cannot get witnesses, he is doomed."

After that we are told that justice reigns precisely in those countries where there is a system which many decades ago called forth the ruthless appraisal given of this institution by the founder of scientific socialism and one of our great teachers, Karl Marx. But many years have passed since then, and every year brings fresh examples which confirm the superb correctness of this appraisal. And today, we could find an incalculable number of such examples.

The sword of class justice is turned against the interests of the toilers and by its nature is not justice. The English weekly, *The New Leader,* characterizes the Meerut trial as the greatest scandal in the sphere of political persecution, the most shameful in the judicial annals of the world.

And who of those who read the press do not know that this monstrous trial has dragged on for four years already during which thirty revolutionaries, Indians and Englishmen, charged with communist activity and with organizing the revolutionary trade union movement, have been literally mocked by class justice? For four years the preliminary investigations dragged on with its examination with the aid of those methods which were also applied in the recent trial in England of the officer Stewart on the charge of espianage, namely, "the third degree," by keeping the prisoners in inhuman conditions, by every method of exerting real physical and moral pressure—all these methods were put in operation by this bourgeois, so-called justice, in the defence of which speak bourgeois Members of Parliament, who, from the floor of Parliament, hurl their charges, as unsupported as they are offensive, against the only genuinely free country in the world, against the Land of the Soviets, against the only real justice in the world, the justice of the Soviet Court, which exercises the will of the proletariat that is creating a new life, that is building up a new socialist society.

Nor do these gentlemen like our court procedure, our method of preliminary investigation, to which much attention was devoted in those debates as well as to the whole of this case and to the general questions of our court procedure, which I cannot refrain from dealing with now. During those debates, special reference was made to the fact that according to our method of preliminary investigation the accused has no legal aid. One of these "witty" Members of Parliament said: "First confession and then legal aid." We have already seen from the remarks of Sir Stafford Cripps and Mr. Kirkwood where it is, indeed, that people who are prosecuted are deprived of all protection. Yes, our Code of Procedure and our laws of procedure do not provide for the participation of defending counsel in the preliminary investigation stage, but that is because our law itself, and I must mention this today, both in Paragraphs 111 and 112 of the Code of Criminal Procedure, impose upon the organs of the State the duty of fully investigating the case from all sides—

the duty of investigating the circumstances that incriminate, as well as those that prove the innocence of prosecuted persons, aggravating as well as mitigating circumstances.

And when our enemies, in an outburst of class rage and blind class hatred, say that under these conditions there can be no guarantees for the establishment of judicial truth and want to refer to other so-called civilized countries, it will not be difficult to parry this thrust by referring, for example, to one of the latest Codes of Criminal Procedure, namely, the German Code of 1924. I speak precisely of that period, and not of the present period connected with the triumph of fascism in Germany. According to Paragraph 147 of the German Code of Criminal Procedure the defence called to take part in the preliminary investigation is permitted to examine the materials of the preliminary investigation only in those cases "when this does not endanger the aims and tasks of the preliminary investigation."

We guarantee the rights of the accused not only in court, but also in the process of the preliminary investigation, and particularly by that very Article 206 of the Code of Criminal Procedure of which we have more than once spoken in the course of this judicial investigation.

I am dealing with this question only because all the general talk that was heard in the House of Commons about our justice and our juridical system, about our method of procedure, was not abstract talk—it took place in connection with the present case, and certain circles of the English bourgeoisie hoped to discredit both the preliminary investigation of this case and the Court itself, which, of course, must also bear in mind the material of the preliminary investigation

More than that, we witnessed here how certain of the accused—I will name Thornton, I will name Monkhouse—at all events, tried to pursue here, before our Court, in the process of this judicial investigation what was properly speaking the line they were ordered to pursue and which found expression in the first part of the so-called *White Paper* about which we have all heard. Thornton's fable about the "moral pressure," on which he came a scandalous cropper, and Monkhouse's fable about his eighteen-hour examination, which was lengthened to nineteen hour examination in the British Parliament (they stuck another hour on), the story—I don't know who set it going—but the story which Monkhouse publicly tried to use here as a method of defence, for which he had to pay by having to apologize to the Supreme Court—all this, Comrade Judges, directly corresponds with a telegram published in the *White Paper,* signed by Sir R. Vansittart, and sent to Sir Esmond Ovey, which I would like to quote here—this is a document bearing the number 27. This telegram raises the curtain upon the incident of Monkhouse's action in this Court. "The Soviet Ambassador," telegraphs Sir R. Vansittart to Sir Esmond Ovey, "came to see me today at my request." This is what he says in document No. 27, published in the *White Paper.*

> "I said that he would be aware, from what had passed yesterday in the House of Commons, of the reason for this interview. Indignation in this country (in England) at the arbitrary arrest and harsh treatment of British subjects in Russia was growing, would grow, and would grow rightly. Feeling was widespread that the allegations against these men were grotesque and hysterical; and that these arrests were a stage performance, and a very bad one at that, mounted simply to disguise, by serving up scapegoats," (it is Thornton and Monkhouse who are the scapegoats) "the ill-success of certain industrial undertakings in Russia. The Soviet Government" (says the document) "might say what they liked; but public opinion here would never look upon this performance in any other light."

And so, on the 16th of March this telegram bearing the number 27, which has become part of the history of this trial and of British diplomacy, was sent, and yesterday, April 15, at the morning session, Monkhouse tried to declare that:"this trial was a frame-up against Metro-Vickers" based on the evidence of terrorized prisoners. But even a "timid" man like Thornton could not quote a single fact to indicate precisely how he was terrorized and the only thing that he could say in this case was the following: "I don't know myself what frightened me."

I have already said that I do not know who is inspiring whom in this case, but there is one thing about which I have no doubt.

and that is, that British public opinion has been misled by a number of cleverly carried out manoeuvres. I think that one of the great services this trial will render will be that it has exposed these distortions, that it has established the truth as it really is, that it has shown public opinion in England and even those circles which are hostile to our State, that they have been cruelly misled. Indeed, we have the declaration of the Secretary of State for Foreign Affairs that Monkhouse, "having had no charge made against him and being carried off to prison in the early hours of the morning, was subjected to a first examination which began at 8 o'clock in the morning. It went on for nineteen consecutive hours without a break."

"I," said the Secretary of State, "have inquired from our Ambassador about the examiners. On the side of the examiners there were three teams of examiners which took one another's place, but on the side of the person examined he was, of course, the same person all the time."

An interesting communication, and one which could, of course, rouse sad thoughts even in the minds of gentlemen who are quite unprejudiced against our method of procedure. Indeed, nineteen hours of uninterrupted questioning of the poor victim of this examination, the gentleman Monkhouse, one against three teams of examiners—all of them, one after another, attacking this unfortunate Monkhouse!

Nineteen hours! Probably the first one to prevaricate, the first one to lie, was Monkhouse himself. It was he who lied, it was he who started the story about the nineteen hours. It was caught up by those to whom it was convenient and advantageous; it was broadcast far and wide; public opinion was mobilized and on this they wanted to base their demands in connection with this trial—demands which we indignantly rejected.

And when yesterday Monkhouse here declared: "I admit my mistake. I apologize," it seemed to me that he apologized, not to you, Comrade Judges, but that he apologized to those whom he had deceived.

But what actually was the position? We discussed this in sufficient detail yesterday, but permit me to touch upon it briefly today. I will continue reading the communication which was made in the House of Commons by the Secretary of State for Foreign Affairs:

"Mr. Monkhouse was taken back to his cell about 3 o'clock in the morning on March 13, where he remained until 7:30 in the morning, when a second examination started and this examination continued for about seventeen hours."

So this makes thirty-six hours during two days—thirty-six hours of almost uninterrupted examination.

Thirty-six hours! But what actually transpired? It transpired that Monkhouse had lied, that nothing of the sort took place; that all that which was said in the House of Commons, that all that which the honourable gentlemen worried over in connection with this declaration represents "sheer loss," and if I were in their place I would certainly bring a civil action against Monkhouse for . . . loss of time.

This is not the first time that we encounter insinuations, falsifications and vilifications against our Court, against our judicial trials. That happened when we investigated the Shakhty case. That happened when we investigated the "Industrial Party" case. It happened when we investigated the case of the so-called Menshevik Central Bureau.

We have no reason to be particularly surprised that this method is resorted to in the struggle which is waged against us, not only by the remnants of the bourgeoisie that were overthrown by October and by all the fifteen years of our epoch of socialist construction, but also by the bourgeoisie which is ruling in various countries and which they wage ideologically, and very often materially, through the medium of their definite circles who are connected with the remnants of the capitalists and exploiting classes in our country who were defeated and crushed by the October Revolution, and who always find support among these most aggressive and reactionary circles of the world bourgeoisie.

However, the special features of the present trial are not the flood of slander and insinuation about which we have just spoken and with which our enemies, as I have just said, usually meet every trial of wrecking, every one of our blows against counter-revolutionary conspiracy, against counter-revolutionary conspirators.

The special features of the present trial are that it reflects the great class battle, in that it is in the literal sense of the word an act in the class struggle, a struggle between two worlds. The special feature of the trial is that the whole of the five days of our judicial investigation represent, in fact, a five-day class battle, in which two worlds of ideas, two worlds of principles, two worlds of concepts, two worlds of social strivings and fundamental antagonisms of class interests, came into conflict. Among all the things that distinguish this trial of wrecking from trials of wrecking of previous years, the distinguishing feature of this trial is precisely that it is a trial of wreckers who have remained in our land in spite of the fact that all the attempts hitherto made against the successes of socialist production have invariably ended in staggering defeat, in spite of the fact that they have not the slightest hope of success in their wrecking work. It is important to note precisely the circumstances, that although wrecking, which, as Comrade Stalin said, was a sort of fashion several years ago, has now ceased to be a fashion, nevertheless, these wrecking acts continue, are nevertheless organized and, what is important to note just now, are organized in such important branches of socialist economy and socialist industry as electrical development, electrification, power supply, which is one of the most important branches of our economic construction.

It is true that today we encounter forms of class resistance that differ from those we encountered several years ago. In connection with the Shakhty case, the April Plenum of the Central Committee of our Party pointed to the peculiar feature of this form of crime as the manifestation of a special, new form of class resistance of the bourgeoisie to the successes of our socialist construction. This must be said, and special emphasis must be laid on it at the present time.

However, it will be necessary to say at the same time that in spite of the novelty of the shades and forms in which the resistance of the overthrown, defeated, wrecked capitalist exploiting classes whose economic and political rule has been abolished, manifest themselves, that behind these new forms there is concealed the old, not abated, but on the contrary, intensified class hatred of our enemies towards the cause of socialist construction.

Comrade Stalin has said:

> "We must bear in mind the circumstance, that our work on the socialist reconstruction of national economy, which is breaking down the economic ties of capitalism, and which is turning upside down all the forces of the old world, cannot but call forth the desperate resistance of these forces. And that is what the position is, as we know. The malicious wrecking by the upper stratum of the bourgeois intelligentsia in all branches of our industry, the ferocious struggle the kulaks are waging against the collective forms of farming in the countryside, the sabotage of the measures of the Soviet Government by the bureaucratic elements of the apparatus who are agents of the class enemy—such for the time being are the principal forms of the resistance of the dying classes of our country. But we must bear in mind," continues Comrade Stalin, "also the circumstance, that the resistance of the dying classes in our country is not isolated from the outside world, but that it meets with the support of the capitalist environment. Capitalist environment is not simply a geographic concept. Capitalist environment means that the U.S.S.R. is surrounded by hostile class forces who are prepared to support our class enemies in the U.S.S.R., morally and materially, by financial blockade, and at a favourable opportunity, by military intervention. It has been proved that the wrecking operations of our specialists, the anti-Soviet actions of the kulaks, the burning and blowing up of our enterprises and constructions, are subsidized and inspired from outside. The imperialist world is not interested in allowing the U.S.S.R. to stand on its feet and obtain the opportunity of overtaking and surpassing the advanced capitalist countries. Hence the assistance it renders to the forces of the old world in the U.S.S.R. . . ."

An illustration, a serious and glaring illustration of this class struggle is afforded by the present trial, which reflects the criminal activity of certain counter-revolutionary groups which still have their lairs here and there in the U.S.S.R., which are striving, not only to disrupt, retard and slow down the work of our enterprises but even to wreck certain of our enterprises, certain sectors of our socialist construction, to damage our socialist construction.

And what we have seen here during the past few days, all that we have heard from the accused themselves, whether it is from Gussev or Lobanov, Sukhoruchkin or Zorin, Thornton or Monkhousé, or Oleinik—one of the most unattractive types among the accused—or Kutuzova, whom we will describe a little later, all this really goes to prove the existence of these class relationships, these peculiar features of the present forms of this class struggle, which manifest themselves in particular in these acts of wrecking.

It would be a great mistake, however, to assume that the trial of these wreckers of power stations is evidence of the same thing that the Shakhty trial evidenced—that at the present time we have to deal with widespread wrecking among the technical intelligentsia. The Shakhty trial was evidence of the fact that wrecking was a sort of fashion—some engaged in wrecking, others concealed these acts, still others assisted. The Shakhty trial reflected what was then a rather widespread phenomenon among the technical intelligentsia, to its shame be it said. Today, the situation is different. It will be a great mistake to draw a parallel in this respect between this trial and the Shakhty trial, between the attitude of our technical intelligentsia towards wrecking at that time and their attitude at the present time.

There is no doubt that during these years, as a consequence of the great processes that have taken place in our country, which has achieved gigantic victories in socialist construction, a change has taken place in the mood and minds of broad circles of the technical intelligentsia. This conclusion cannot be in the least degree shaken by the fact that this group of wreckers was still to be found in 1931-32, that not all the wreckers in our Soviet land have become extinct. There is nothing unexpected or surprising in this. But these are mere insignificant apostates, the dregs of the technical intelligentsia.

When Comrade Stalin in his historic speech on the new conditions and new tasks of economic construction spoke about the change that had taken place among the technical intelligentsia from the time of the Shakhty trial to approximately the time that historic speech was published, he at the same time said that this change did not yet mean that among the technical intelligentsia there would not be any more wrecking at all. In this, as in all things, Comrade Stalin proved to be right. Comrade Stalin said:

> "Wreckers exist and will continue to exist as long as we have classes and as long as we are surrounded by capitalism. But it does mean that, since a large section of the old technical intelligentsia, who sympathized more or less with the former wreckers, have now turned to the side of the Soviet Government, the active wreckers have become very few in number, that they have been isolated and are obliged to go deeply underground."

And the overwhelming majority of those whom we have dragged by the ears out from underground into the light of day, create the impression of being, I would say, "second rate wreckers."

It is true that among them there is the lecturer Zorin; true that among them are fairly important engineers, for example, Sukhoruchkin, but the predominant types among them are the Oleiniks, Gussevs and Lobanovs, people who engage in wrecking not so much because of their convictions but because of their social nature. We must note a certain diminution in calibre among them, which indicates that wrecking is apparently living its last days in our country. Of course, it will continue to flicker up here and there in so far as classes will remain, in so far as class antagonism will not yet have disappeared and have been removed, in so far as we shall still live in a capitalist environment, which inevitably causes relapses into counter-revolutionary wrecking in the U.S.S.R. It is precisely for that reason that we must continue in the future to preserve our class vigilance and not in the slightest degree abate our determination in the struggle against these phenomena, not in the slightest degree abate our ruthlessness in annihilating these shameful counter-revolutionary phenomena.

What is the main content of the crime in which these people in the dock are incriminated?

The State Prosecution in formulating these charges directs its attention principally along three main lines, on three main groups of counter-revolutionary crimes committed by the accused, namely, 1) wilful damage to mechanisms, machines and equipment; 2) military espionage; 3) bribery. These are very severe crimes that the accused have committed against the State of the proletarian dictatorship, against the Land of the Soviets, against their nation!

It is highly characteristic that although among all wrecking counter-revolutionary groups the so-called ideological motive always merges or is interlocked with crude, base, material interest, in this trial this feature is particularly marked.

I will recall here the explanations given by certain of the accused to my question—"What were you guided by?" and even in reply to the question put by their own defending counsel—"Were you guided by material motives or by ideological motives?" —they mumbled, spread out their hands and said that they find it difficult to formulate, that they find it difficult to answer this question—to such an extent was all this interwoven, to such an extent were they proved to be both politically and morally corrupt. This is not an accident. This too is a phenomenon of the times, a phenomenon which is characteristic of the epoch in which, on the one hand, the working class is growing enormously in its creative power, in its creative construction, is growing in all spheres of its construction—cultural, economic and political—while these last remnants, these broken fragments of the capitalist classes are more and more betraying symptoms of cultural, spiritual and moral insignificance, corruption and degeneration.

Why is wrecking, espionage and bribery so wonderfully interwoven in the actions of nearly every one of the accused in the present case? We are trying electrician wreckers who had organized themselves in counter-revolutionary groups for the purpose of striking a blow at Soviet economy which is fighting for new and newer successes. Of course, we were convinced beforehand—and reality eloquently confirms this—that no such attempt would ever lead to the results the wreckers dreamed of, that every one of the wreckers' cards would be beaten, and at most, as this present trial has shown, would lead to a brief stoppage of a turbine, to brief embarrassments which, thanks to the vigilance, the creative energy and the enthusiasm of the masses of the proletariat, are quickly and resolutely removed and repaired, paralysing the action of these wreckers, neutralizing and liquidating their corrupt influence. And indeed, in spite of all the efforts of the wreckers, in spite of all their destructive work, we have achieved astonishing successes in the sphere of electrification. These successes are testified to by the fact that we now have ten power stations of a capacity exceeding 100,000 kw.—Kashira, Shterovka, Shatura, Krassny Oktyabr (Leningrad), Moges (Moscow State Electric Power Station), Zugres (Zuevka Electric Power Station), Dnieprogres (Dnieper Electric Power Station), Nivges (Gorky Electric Power Station), Chelyabinsk Electric Power Station, and Krassnaya Zvesda (Baku). We have achieved enormous successes in the sphere of electrification which, in the historic words of Lenin, is a fundamental element of communism, because Comrade Lenin said, as you remember, "Communism is Soviet power plus electrification."

In 1928, we had only 18 district stations with a capacity of 610,000 kw.; in 1932, we had 44 power stations with a capacity of 2,500,000 kw. At the present time, the capacity of all our power stations amounts to 4,600,000 kw. as against 1,875,000 kw. at the beginning of the Five-Year Plan.

In 1928, the output of electrical energy amounted to 5,000,000,000 kw. hrs. and in 1932, the total output of electrical energy amounted to 13,500,000,000 kw. hrs.

Well now, you wreckers—what have you got to say to that? All your efforts have failed, and they could not but fail, because against you stands the unshakable wall of the proletariat, against you stands the unshakable wall of the honest Soviet intelligentsia who jointly with the working class is building socialist society; against you stands in full armour the proletarian dictatorship and you are merely a miserable group of apostates of the technical intelligentsia, a group branded with the mark of shame.

I have already pointed out that as a result of great effort, great sacrifices, great self-sacrifice, persistence and labour, we now have ten power stations with a capacity exceeding 100,000 kw. Among these are the very stations which, unfortunately, we now have to speak about in dealing with the groups of wreckers, the hotbeds of counter-revolution, who tried to destroy the young organism of this sector of our socialist economy which is just being built up.

As I have already said, at the present time the very method of wrecking has changed to a considerable degree compared with the methods adopted in previous years. In the present case, four methods of wrecking stand out in striking relief: first, wilful, deliberate concealment of defects by State employees in responsible posts, whose primary and direct duty was to remove them.

Second, delaying the work by every artificial means: unnecessary repairs, bad installation, and so forth; prolonging the period before installations are put into operation, postponing the testing period, prolonging these periods as much as possible.

Third, deliberate damage to machinery, as we saw, for example, in the case which Gussev related here as calmly as if he were relating an epic, when he told us about the damage to the 1,400 h.p. motor, or when Kotlyarevsky told us that he inserted a bolt into the air gap between the rotor and the stator and in this way put a turbo-generator out of action.

Fourth, a more subtle, a more artful, a more cunning and a more concealed and masked method of wrecking, of striking a blow at our industry, namely, when the necessary personnel is deliberately selected in such a way as to suit the aims of the wreckers, when persons unfit for the job are deliberately placed in charge of responsible sectors of the work, when the organizers of wrecking deliberately place people in responsible jobs knowing that they are not trained for them, with the deliberate calculation that an untried stoker will go to sleep on his job, that an inexperienced mechanic will not know when anything is wrong, will not open a valve in time or close a valve in time, when that is necessary, and so forth, and so forth. These are the methods now employed, which possess all the qualities necessary for the success of this wrecking, for it enables the wrecker to operate with very little risk, as operating in this way he can count on a considerable amount of impunity, and finally, he can count on his wrecking activities extending over a long period of time. These wrecking activities are dangerous because very often they are small in themselves, but they go on systematically, day after day, affecting every group of machines or numerous individual machines. It is precisely because these things become so common and an everyday matter that they are capable of blunting the sensitiveness and alertness of certain workers towards these happenings.

The characteristic thing here is precisely the form of these wrecking acts; they are very convenient for the purpose of concealing this wrecking by all sorts of "objective causes," "defects," and the fact that it does not seem to be caused by malicious human intent.

This is very characteristically seen in the analysis of a number of breakdowns which we encounter in the present case and which will be the subject of my further, more detailed analysis.

We know that at the present time the class enemy is crushed, is beaten, he cannot, however much he may desire, make frontal attacks against the Soviet Government, against socialist construction, no matter on what sector of this construction he may reveal his presence. We know that the class enemy, having suffered severe defeat, has now passed from direct frontal attacks to other methods; that he is operating by the method known as quiet sapping. It is precisely this that explains the fact that he becomes less detectable, less vulnerable and hence it becomes less possible to isolate him.

But therein precisely is the great danger of these crimes which in themselves, perhaps, may be small, but which in their sum total represent an enormous social danger. The social danger of the crimes representing the content of this case does not lie in that stations are blown up, nor in that large powerful turbines are put out of action, that a whole system of power supply is put out of action.

No, this could not happen, nor can it happen, because in our country the factories are in the hands of the proletariat; because the working class is sufficiently vigilant to prevent such serious consequences as might result if groups of wreckers, or individual wreckers, could carry on their work with impunity. The danger of the crimes with which we are dealing in this case lies in that the criminals try to strike at minor details and thus create an uninterrupted stream of difficulties, a continuous "breakdown condition," as we saw from individual examples, at individual stations like Zuevka, Mosenergo, the Ivanovo Electric Power Station, Zlatoust, Chelyabinskstroy, and so forth, and so forth.

Throughout the whole course of this trial certain of the accused made several attempts to explain their actions by the fact that they found themselves drawn into counter-revolutionary activities by other persons, particularly by the British installation engineers now in the dock. I will deal separately with the guilt of the English installation engineers in this case. I mention it now in order to indicate the main lines of the Prosecution.

I must say at once that our approach to State employees who have violated their duty to the State, who have lost all feeling for their native land, who have forgotten their duty to their socialist fatherland, must be and will be extremely severe, irrespective of whether they were the "victims" of anyone's cunning, or whether they took the path of crime independently, apart from outside influences.

From this lofty tribune of the Special Session of the Supreme Court we must once and for all declare to our whole country that State employees are State employees, and that they will be treated as traitors to the State if they act in the manner the accused who have been criminally prosecuted in this case have acted.

I must call to mind the decree of the Central Executive Committee of the Union of Soviet Socialist Republics of March 14 this year, which, although addressed directly to the O.G.P.U., is of great importance in principle for us; it is a decree which speaks of the particularly strict responsibility to which employees in State institutions and enterprises will be held for acts of wrecking committed by them and for which they will be called to account with particular severity; and it says that this special severity will be applied to all employees of State institutions and enterprises detected in such crime. Every citizen in our country who is employed in a State institution or enterprise, who is placed in charge of a definite section of work, whose duty it is to secure the proper functioning of this or that institution or enterprise which is an element, a constituent part of the whole of our State system, must bear special responsibility to his society, to his nation, and he cannot be relieved of this responsibility in the slightest degree irrespective of whether he voluntarily took the path of crime, whether he was led on to the path of crime, or whether he was accompanied by anybody on this path of crime.

That is why the State Prosecution in maintaining the charges in this case against the persons in the dock, will, in their appraisal and qualification of the degree of responsibility and guilt of the individual accused, be guided precisely by these considerations and have in view that we must retaliate to every attempt on the part of a State employee to betray his trust in the severest possible manner, and I will go even further and say—even irrespective of the degree and scope of the damage caused to the State by these crimes.

In this case, the State Prosecution regards the State employees to be the main and principal offenders, and it is against these, in the first place, that the Prosecution will turn the edge of their evidence, proof and demands for severe judicial repression. Because it is precisely they, the State employees, who had pledged themselves to work honestly for the proletarian State, who betrayed this pledge, betrayed their trust, betrayed their proletarian State. That is why our attitude towards them will be different from our attitude towards the employees of private firms and private offices, both native and foreign. We must specially emphasize the serious responsibility of our State employees compared with the responsibility of foreign specialists, or of foreigners generally, who perhaps are not specialists, or are specialists of a kind different from the kind we thought they were when they came to work for us, to take part in our general State construction. Of course, the crimes committed by the Thorntons, the Monkhouses, the Cushnys and the MacDonalds are repulsive and atrocious crimes. But there are no words with which to express all the feelings of indignation, to formulate the contempt one feels in speaking of the responsibility of State employees in our country who forgot their duty to their country, who betrayed their socialist fatherland. They betrayed and betrayed so systematically, so continuously that, properly speaking, several of them even forgot that they were State employees and behaved as if they were employees, not of State institutions, but employees of those commercial enterprises which themselves bear very high obligations and very great responsibility towards our State with which they have business relations.

I want to take the opportunity of this part of my speech in order resolutely to rebuff every attempt made by Monkhouse to drag the Prosecution on to the path of attacking certain foreign firms and particularly the firm of Metro-Vickers. A number of questions Monkhouse put to the expert witnesses today, properly speaking, cannot be otherwise appraised than as an attempt to provoke us, an attempt to make this case appear as if it were not Monkhouse that was in the dock, but Metro-Vickers. I immediately uttered a warning against such misunderstandings, and I must emphatically warn you against this now. If we had sufficient facts to formulate a charge against the firm of Metro-Vickers, we would not stop half way; but in this case we must say that we have no grounds for this, that we had no intention, and have no intention, in connection with the present case, of bringing criminal or any other proceedings against Metro-Vickers outside of those provided for in the agreements with that firm. We are not in the least inclined to regard the crimes committed by certain officials in the Moscow office of Metro-Vickers, or even the criminal deeds of certain individuals outside of the U.S.S.R. who have relations with that office, as deeds committed by this firm, as deeds for which this firm as such must bear responsibility. We are speaking of individual persons, either of Monkhouse or Richards; we are speaking of individual crimes, like those which we are now examining, as well as of those which we are not examining at the present time, without any reference whatever to the firm, concerning which Monkhouse made the attempt today to make it appear that it was not he, but the firm, that was in the dock. Monkhouse must give up the idea that he is appearing in this case in any other capacity except one, and that is: as an employee of that firm charged with serious State crimes—and nothing more. Similarly, he must give up the idea that he can appear here in the capacity of representative of the Moscow office and take upon himself the duty of protecting all the other employees of this office who have been prosecuted in this case.

I have already said that the Public Prosecution has built its charge against the accused in the present case along three main lines.

First, wilful damage to machines and equipment; second, military espionage; and third, the system of bribery, which we encountered on a wide scale in examining the individual crimes of the individual accused who are prosecuted in the present case.

On the question of military espionage there has been much talk in the course of the present investigation and certain of the accused pretended that, strictly speaking, they did not properly understand the meaning of this term. This is what Thornton very stubbornly and persistently tried to make us believe when he said that in his conception (this version was supported by Monkhouse, and these two were followed by others of the accused among the English citizens, for example, Cushny) espionage differed very much from the conceptions he obtained in the process of the preliminary investigation, from the formulation of the charge against him. All of them pretended that in their conception, according to our laws, the collection of "any" information is spying, and that where they spoke about admitting themselves guilty of collecting spying information they spoke, if you please, both the truth and the untruth. The truth, because they used the words "spying information" and untruth, because by these words they meant something entirely different from what is implied by the corresponding articles of our Criminal Code.

I think we must introduce clarity into this question. We do not play with the word "espionage." We have an absolutely precise and clear conception as to what espionage is as a counter-revolutionary crime, and we have the right to demand that everyone who comes to the territory of our country shall have an equally clear and precise conception of the interpretation which our laws and our State put upon this word, the significance and content of this crime.

In individualizing and characterizing the position in this trial of each of the accused separately, I will deal especially with the question as to whether either Thornton or Monkhouse had any right to pretend that they had their own conception of what espionage means and to reduce this conception not to espionage, but to collecting "common gossip" and rumours. But at present, I want to deal with the theoretical, if you will permit me to say so, exposition of the concept espionage according to our laws, if only very briefly.

I would ask to be permitted, in view of the interest certain parallels would have, to touch upon this question also from the point of view of foreign law, the law of foreign States, including English law, Statutory Law.

I think this will be useful for our case, from the point of view of the characterization, or appraisal, of the individual responsibility of this or that accused in the present case in connection with the charge that is brought against him in this sphere.

We know that certain persons who are now on our territory, and even whole groups of such persons, are engaged in collecting a variety of information on the territory of our country. But we have never accused, and we do not think of accusing them of espionage merely on the ground that somebody, mixing in certain social circles, quite legally, receives certain information about the economic position of our country, about the harvest, about the progress of this or that economic-political campaign, say the sowing campaign, or the grain collecting campaign, or even about the difficulties that are encountered by this or that branch of our industry, or of our national economy, which is steadily growing in the process of the constant and victorious overcoming of difficulties that arise in its path. We never bring an accusation, and we cannot regard as grounds for prosecution, or for a charge of espionage, economic or political, even against those who utilize information about the political moods of this or that circle of our society, even if it is attempted to use this information about the political mood of these circles against our interests. We cannot, say, demand from persons who belong to other classes, who stand for entirely other class interests peculiar to them, who have a definite and complete world outlook and attitude towards their environment, that they should conceive the phenomena of our reality in the same way as we Soviet people conceive them.

We never raise, and we never will raise the question of responsibility under Article 58-6 of the Criminal Code in a matter regarding the receiving or even the collecting of information of the kind I have just described to the Court, that is, information about the economic situation, political moods, the harvest, various economic campaigns, and so forth, and so on.

But it goes without saying that this does not, and should not, give anyone grounds for trying to conceal real espionage work, in the real sense of the word, by arguing that this was "gossip," as Thornton tried to assert here, at the same time referring to the allegedly very broad conception of espionage from the point of view of our Soviet laws. This is exactly what Thornton says: in admitting that he was guilty of espionage, he says, he thought that in this country spying information meant, not information having military State significance, as it is in actual fact, but all information including such information as I have just spoken about. Why did he argue like that? Perhaps because he wanted to take advantage of the really fairly wide definition in this sphere of the law of capitalist countries, according to which, even such actions which are directed against the interests of separate capitalist groups, or even of individual capitalists, may come under the term of espionage?

Our law does not give the slightest grounds for this. We have an absolutely precise conception of espionage. It is defined with the utmost precision in our operating laws, and it is precisely from the point of view of these operating laws that we will strive to build up the charge of espionage that we bring against a number of the accused in this case.

But first of all, a few words about the manner in which various foreign States regard the question of espionage. If we turn to English law we will find a reply to this question in the material provided by the Official Secrets Act of August 22, 1911, and by a similar Act under the same title, of 1920. Clause 2 of the Official Secrets Act of August 22, 1911, which represents an amendment to the Act of 1889, reads as follows:

> "On a prosecution under this section, it shall not be necessary to show that the accused person was guilty of any particular act tending to show a purpose prejudicial to the safety

> or interests of the State, and, notwithstanding that no such act is proved against him, he may be convicted if, from the circumstances of the case, or his conduct, or his known character as proved, it appears that his purpose was a purpose prejudicial to the safety or interests of the State."

That is how the bourgeoisie protects the interests of its State, its class interests, when it raises the question of responsibility in clauses about espionage.

And further on it reads:

> "... if any sketch, plan, model, article, note, document or information relating to or used in any prohibited place within the meaning of this Act, or anything in such a place, is made, obtained, or communicated by any person other than a person acting under lawful authority, it shall be deemed to have been made, obtained or communicated for a purpose prejudicial to the safety or interests of the state unless the contrary is proved."

That is how the bourgeoisie protects its interests in this sphere.

And what from the point of view of the English Act of 1911 are these "prohibited places," that is, places prohibited "within the meaning of this Act"? A very clear answer to this question is given by Clause 3, which consists of a number of sections including a section containing the following list:

> "... any railway, road, way or channel, or other means of communication by land or water (including any works or structures being part thereof or connected therewith), or any place used for gas, water, or electricity works or other works for purposes of a public character . . ." and so forth, and so on.

That is what is stated in this clause which probably is well known to Thornton as an ex-military man and as a present military spy.

We have another English Act devoted to this question which is a supplement to the two clauses of the Act of 1911, which I have just read. This is the Act of December 23, 1920, where also, but still more emphatically, the bourgeoisie in its own interests, I again emphasize and repeat this, protects and guards its vital State interests, with the aid of Espionage Acts.

I have in mind Clause 2 of this Act which expounds an extremely interesting idea.

> "In any proceedings," it says, "against a person for an offense under section one of the principal Act, the fact that he has been in communication with, or attempted to communicate with a foreign agent, whether within or without the United Kingdom, shall be evidence that he has, for a purpose prejudicial to the safety or interests of the State, obtained, or attempted to obtain, information which is calculated to be, or might be, or is intended to be, directly or indirectly useful to an enemy."

And further:

> "For the purpose of this section . . . a person shall, unless he proves the contrary, be deemed to have been in communication with a foreign agent"—and so on.

Such, Citizen Thornton, are the laws that exist in your country, which protect secrets of military State importance, the violation of which entails extremely serious penalties, for the violation of which the culprit is called very seriously to account. And after that, Thornton tried here to pretend that he was a political infant, a naive person who did not know what espionage was, although he pleaded guilty to collecting, as he himself wrote with his own hand in his depositions, spying information. In addition to this, the law of capitalist States knows also the concept economic espionage, in the sense of guarding so-called industrial secrets. I can quote, as an example, the German Act of March 9, 1932. We have no industrial secrets within the meaning of capitalist law, but we have the concept economic espionage by which is meant the collecting and communicating of economic information which is especially guarded by the State and which is enumerated in a list especially indicated in the corresponding legislative acts, in this case, in the decree of the Council of People's Commissars of the U.S.S.R. of April 27, 1926, which contains an exhaustive list of the kind of information which, if communicated, gives ground for accusation of a crime coming under the term economic or military espionage.

Of course, the different measures that are applied, the difference in the approach to these questions of the various States, is to be explained by the difference in the nature of these States. Generally speaking, we must bear in mind that when speaking about the State of the proletarian dictatorship, about the Soviet State, we are speaking of a government of a special kind, which in the words of Vladimir Ilyitch Lenin is, properly speaking, already a semi-State. Indeed, our State fulfils the task of protecting the interests of the working class, the interests of the masses of the toilers; the sole and fundamental object and task of our State is to protect and guard these interests, to fight against all manifestations of exploitation, against the exploiting classes. Of course our State is of a type, of a kind, of a nature that is altogether different from exploiter States. And although we often employ the term State, we must never forget that, unlike the bourgeois States, the very nature of our State obliges us to adopt an approach to the solution of the problems of our State construction that differs from that which is adopted in these bourgeois States.

This is the position particularly in regard to the question of the responsibility of our State employees, to which I previously referred when I emphasized the special significance which we attach to the responsibility for crimes committed against the State by our employees. This is to be explained by the fact that our employees are the servants of the working people, that they are the servants of our State, which is the State of the toiling masses, the State of the workers and peasants who create all values, all wealth, who are the foundation and the source of the very existence of our State. That does not exist in any capitalist State. Hence, the difference in the approach to the solution of this problem in the sphere of criminal policy. While the bourgeoisie, in making laws directed against employees and against the toilers generally, act exclusively in their own class interests, in the interests of the minority, as against the interests of the masses, we, in directing our laws against employees who betray our State, act in the interests of the toilers and in the interests of the toilers' State, which in this way protects itself against traitors, against any attempt on anyone's part to place their interests in opposition to the interests of the State, which is a toilers' State. The same thing must be said with special emphasis in regard to the question with which I am now dealing concerning espionage as a crime directed against the toilers' State, and which, from this point of view, grows in our eyes into a heinous crime against the working class, against the proletariat and against the whole future of human civilization created by the triumphant successes of our proletarian revolution.

Hence, the stern criminal penalties which we impose upon those who attempt to resort to espionage against the interests of the proletarian State.

The third section of the crimes we are examining in the present trial is that which I have put under the head of bribery. Here too we must start out from the principles that are inherent in our Soviet life, our Soviet system, which distinguish it from the principles inherent in the life, customs, morals and system of mutual relationships prevailing in various circles, in various capitalist countries. Monkhouse could not agree with the Prosecution's appraisal of the 3,000 rubles that were given to Dolgov as a bribe, and he asserted that it was not a bribe, but a present. Of course the concept bribery, the concept larceny, like other concepts to which I have already referred, very often differ in our society and in bourgeois society, and this is quite natural.

There is a passage in the works of Lenin which speaks of this difference. Permit me to quote this eloquent example. Lenin said:

> "When a worker steals a loaf of bread in a bourgeois country, he is sent to prison for it; but when a rich man steals a railway, he is appointed to the Senate. . ."

This, indeed, bears witness to the great difference in principle between views of things: in the eyes of the bourgeoisie the theft of a loaf of bread by a poor man is a crime, but the theft of a whole railway by a rich man is regarded as the manifestation of great statesmanship, of great political virtuosity, deserving of promotion to the Senate.

And so also in the sphere of bribery. We speak of bribery as an evil which corrodes our organism, an evil which must be combated in the severest and most ruthless manner, which must be cauterized out of the system of our relationships. And yet we know that in bourgeois circles, in certain circles, of course I do not want to make too broad a generalization on this—in certain bourgeois circles, enterpreneurs, business, banking circles, and so forth, and so on, yes, and even in bourgeois society as a whole, when we speak of this in principle, bribery is not regarded as a crime, because it is on bribery that the prosperity of various upstarts, careerists, politicians and stock exchange brokers, and so forth, and so on, is based.

Citizens Monkhouse and Thornton, all your talk about this being a "present" because it was "a little one," because it was given as a reward for "work done," for this and for that, is not at all convincing. We regard such "presents" as bribes, because the effect of this act diverts attention, energy, strivings, desires and obligations from the interests of the State to private interests, frequently, in definite cases, in opposition to the interests of the State.

Yes, and this applies to your firm—against whom, I repeat, we have no data upon which to take criminal proceedings in this case, but which, according to your own words and evidence, Citizen Monkhouse, which you tried to repudiate after you had sealed them with your own signature, very often carries out its obligations to the Soviet State unconscientiously. You yourself characterized the latter by saying that, if you were the buyer, you would not buy such equipment which you, as a salesman, dared, however, to sell for the hard-earned people's money paid to you by our country for this equipment.

Let this very Monkhouse and let this very Thornton and those others of their fellow citizens whom I will mention individually in the next part of my speech, who gave bribes to our State employees, and by these bribes corrupted these State employees, won them to the side of their interests and put them in opposition to the interests of our proletarian State—let them not dare to pretend that they link their conception of these actions with the conceptions, not of bribery, but of gifts. The laws of their own country do not permit them to think, to speak, or to defend themselves by such arguments.

I want to mention here several Acts in English Statutory Law dealing precisely with this question of bribery. I have here, for example, The Public Bodies (Corrupt Practices) Act of 1889. From this Act it will be seen that the bourgeoisie are able to guard their public bodies, their public organizations much more strictly and strongly than private enterprises when these private enterprises and organizations dare to come into conflict with the interests of the State.

We have the Act of 1906 which bears the characteristic title "An Act for the Better Prevention of Corruption," the very kind of corruption which the accused here systematically engaged in under cover of their firm, and a similar Act of 1916.

According to the Act of 1889, bribery is defined as:

> ". . .soliciting corruptly or receiving, or agreeing to receive, for oneself or for any other person" (that is what it says, Citizen Monkhouse), "any gift, loan, reward, or advantage, as an inducement to any member or servant of a public body to do or forbear to do anything in respect of any matter in which the public body is concerned."

That is how the position is put. If a State official guards the interests of the institution in which he fulfils any function, then any kind of gift, any consideration that can induce him to do, or forbear to do anything, contrary to his duties, is bribery, which according to this Act, is regarded as a crime.

The same thing applies to the Act of 1906 which reads as follows:

> "If any agent corruptly accepts or obtains, or agrees to accept or attempts to obtain, from any person, for himself or for any other person, any gift or consideration as an inducement for doing or forbearing to do". . . etc., he shall be guilty of bribery.

The Act of 1916 says the same thing and, moreover, makes a very interesting assumption:

> ". . .the money, gift, or consideration shall be deemed to have been paid or given and received corruptly as such inducement or reward as is mentioned in such Act unless the contrary is proved."

That is what the laws say, the laws of the country which sent you here, accused Monkhouse, Thornton and others, for definite purposes, in accordance with the agreement existing between our institutions and your firm whose Moscow representative you are, Monkhouse.

Bribery is bribery, no matter what you call it, its nature is not changed either by laws of a bourgeois State or still less by our laws.

A juridical question may be put as to why in our indictment a special clause is not included on bribery, seeing that we charge the accused with bribery. Why is that clause not included? Why, among all the clauses—58-6, 7, 9, and 11, was no place found for a special clause on bribery, namely, Article 118 of the Criminal Code? The reply to this question is very simple, because when the charge—and I hope the conviction on our charge—of counter-revolutionary crimes is sufficiently supported, bribery is merely a peculiar form of the manifestation of this counter-revolutionary crime, because in these conditions, and under these circumstances, bribery is by its very nature a counter-revolutionary crime, is a great and heinous crime against the State.

This is not simply a bribe that is given for this or that "service" that does not and cannot affect the very foundation of the State relationships. When bribery assumes the character of a means by which counter-revolutionaries attempt to strike a blow precisely at these relationships, to affect precisely these foundations of State relationships, then we can no longer regard it as ordinary bribery in its specific form as expressed in Articles 117 and 118 of the Criminal Code of the R.S.F.S.R., that is, as the receipt of a reward by an official for the fulfilment or non-fulfilment of a duty—but we regard it merely as a peculiar manifestation of a counter-revolutionary crime by means of which the same class resistance to the cause of socialist construction is offered as is offered by counter-revolutionary agitation, or by other varied means of wrecking and resistance which the enemies of our country resort to in their fight against our socialist construction.

We have an analogous case in the decree of August 7, in which under certain conditions, theft (larcency) is regarded not simply as theft, but is raised to the degree of an important political act, which grows into an important counter-revolutionary act, qualified by this decree of August 7, as everyone knows, precisely as a great crime against the State, against our sacred and inviolable socialist property, which is the very foundation of the Soviet system.

That is why there need be no surprise at the fact that we do not present a special clause on bribery out of the numerous Articles of our Criminal Code, but include the element of the crime covered by this Article in the general composition of the crime covered by all the Articles enumerated in the Indictment and the edge of which is turned against the accused with all the sharpness of the Articles on counter-revolutionary crimes, namely 58-6, 7, 9 and 11 of the Criminal Code.

The President: It is now 11:45 p.m. I declare the session adjourned until tomorrow morning.

(At 11:45 p.m. the Court adjourns until 11 a.m., April 17, 1933.)

[Signed] V. V. ULRICH
President of the Special Session of the Supreme Court of the U.S.S.R.

A. F. KOSTYUSHKO
Secretary

MORNING SESSION, APRIL 17, 1933, 11:15 a.m.

Commandant: Please rise. The Court is coming.

The President: Please be seated. The proceedings are resumed. Comrade Vyshinsky, the Public Prosecutor.

Vyshinsky: In passing to the characterization of the separate crimes committed by each of the accused, it is necessary to give a characterization of the events that took place in connection with this criminal activity at certain electric power stations, and finally, to qualify these crimes from the point of view of the demands of our Criminal Law.

A number of stations have been spoken about in great detail throughout the whole course of this judicial investigation. The Zlatoust Electric Power Station, the Zuevka Electric Power Station, the Ivanovo Electric Power Station, the Baku Electric Power Station, and a whole group of electric power stations united in this case and in our materials under the general title of Mosenergo.

Permit me, then, briefly to describe the condition of affairs created at each of these power stations in connection with, and partly as a direct result of, criminal wrecking, counter-revolutionary activity of counter-revolutionaries and wreckers, connected with and working at these stations, who are now being prosecuted in the present case.

The Zlatoust Power Station. In the period of 1931 and 1932 we observed at the Zlatoust Electric Power Station a number of breakdowns systematically repeated month after month. We had here a number of breakdowns, with the 1,400 h.p. motor, which, as you will recall from the material of our judicial investigation served the large-shape mill of the rolling mill shop, which directly served a number of works, including munitions shops and munitions works.

We had the breakdown of the 1,400 h.p. motor at the Zlatoust Electric Power Station on April 10, May 12, June 13, and so forth, and so on, in the course of these two years. But this does not mean that there were no breakdowns before that. There were breakdowns before that. We speak of these breakdowns only because these few breakdowns gave us the clue by which we were able to reveal the true and genuine causes of these breakdowns, and second, because reports were drawn up on these breakdowns, notwithstanding the method adopted by the wreckers, which, incidentally, was either not to draw up any reports of the breakdowns at all, or to deliberately draw up such reports as would conceal the real causes of these breakdowns. We have a number of cases of the breakdown of the 1,400 h.p. motor, the direct result of which was an attempt to strike a blow at the branch of production which in its turn was of fundamental importance for the rolling mill and in particular, had fundamental importance for the munitions industry. Five or six times in succession the motor was put out of action owing to the deliberate and wilful wrecking work of several persons—Gussev, Sokolov and MacDonald, who concentrated their attention and exerted all their efforts precisely on this sector in order to strike at what, from the point of view of the normal process of production and, in particular, the production of munitions, was a very important group of machines at this power station.

But their activities were not confined to this. We have the fact of the freezing of boiler No. 8 when the dampers were left open —also quite deliberately—and when this led to a breakdown.

At the end of 1931, at this same electric power station, the coal conveyor was put out of action. There were two coal conveyors, one of which was in reserve and played a very important role as such. Deliberately and again, very subtly, on the pretext of carrying out reconstruction—a sort of "rationalization" that the accused Gussev talked about—the foundation was destroyed and then the repair of the coal conveyor was undertaken which put it out of action and left the station in a state which, in the language of the wreckers, was given a special technical formula— "breakdown condition."

Finally we have the delay in the re-equipment of boilers Nos

1, 2, and 11, which put the station in a state in which it could have, and did have in fact, only a reduced, and a very reduced capacity, approximately one-half of the normal—from 12,000 kw. normal capacity the station could generate a bare 6,000 kw. You will remember, Comrade Judges, how these breakdowns were brought about. It cannot be said that they were brought about by very complicated methods. On the contrary, as Gussev has already shown here, the breakdown of the 1,400 h.p. motor was brought about very easily by dropping an extraneous metal article into the air gap between the stator and the rotor.

In analysing the causes of these breakdowns and particularly, and most important of all, the breakdown of April 10, we discover that a number of other breakdowns which occurred to this motor, to which I have just referred, the breakdowns of May 12 and June 13 and others, were the direct result of the bad and unconscientious work in removing the causes of the first breakdown—the wilfully and deliberately bad repairs after the first breakdown. It is precisely these repairs to the motor, badly done deliberately after the first breakdown occurred, that were the cause of a number of subsequent breakdowns on this 1,400 h.p. motor. In analysing the causes of this breakdown, the Commission of Experts came to the conclusion that the displacement of the stator iron could take place as a result of the dropping of an extraneous metal article into the air gap, that in normal operating conditions extraneous iron could not find its way into the motor, and could be inserted only artificially.

But when the Commission of Experts analysed these facts on the basis of the report of the breakdown, made on the spot, it of course did not have in mind Gussev's evidence which we heard at this trial, in which Gussev told us how indeed this extraneous piece of iron found its way into the motor, how it was inserted deliberately, wilfully, thanks to the wrecking plans on the basis of which the whole of Gussev's activity from that period developed.

In the winter of 1932 another breakdown occurred at the Zlatoust Electric Power Station of boiler No. 8, which was cold in reserve. This breakdown too was caused deliberately and, as it turned out, not by any God knows what complicated methods, but by simply leaving the damper open, and allowing the water to remain in; and when winter came, the boiler froze and a number of tubes burst. According to the conclusions of the Commission of Experts this breakdown, too, occurred either as a result of the negligence of the boiler house staff, or as a result of malicious intent.

The Defence may take up a position on this alternative and say—the Experts' report proved that the breakdown might have occurred either as a result of malicious intent or as a result of negligence. But the Experts could not say anything else, because they investigated the case conscientiously and objectively and did not have in mind the subjective activity of this or that person. The Experts based themselves entirely on the general technical conditions in which these facts, purely objective facts, occurred. It is our business to characterize these facts from the point of view of personal activity. It is our business to show that in this case too, the cause was not negligence, but precisely malicious intent. Of the two possibile causes in the given concrete conditions in which the breakdown of boiler No. 8 occurred, only one cause played a role, and that was malicious wrecking intent, a counter-revolutionary act directed against the normal operation of this electric power station.

At this same power station, in the beginning of 1932, as I have already said, the reserve coal conveyor was dismantled. Under what conditions could the dismantling of this reserve coal conveyor take place? That is the first question which the preliminary enquiry submitted to the Commission of Experts. And the reply was received that

> "the dismantling of the reserve coal conveyor would be permissible only in the event of this coal conveyor being unsatisfactory or inadequate and in the event of it being possible to substitute for it a new one, for the installation of which all the necessary parts were available and all the preparatory work accomplished."

Thus arises the second question that was submitted to the Commission of Experts, namely, did these three conditions exist at the time the coal conveyor was dismantled? The Commission of Experts replied:

"In this case these conditions did not exist, for in order to install such a coal conveyor all the necessary parts had to be available and all the preparatory work had to have been performed."

Neither the first nor the second was done. Hence, on the basis of a strictly objective analysis of the materials in the case, the Experts came to the conclusion that 'the dismantling of the coal conveyor was done with obviously wrecking aims." Here we do not even require the confession of the criminal, here we do not even require the living perpetrator of these wrecking acts. It is sufficient to have the conclusion of the Experts in order to be able to say that there can be no question here of negligence, there can be no question of criminal negligence. The only thing that could have taken place here was direct wrecking activity directed straight at our Soviet economy, and in this particular case, against the electric power system, because what the accused perpetrated is evidence only of one thing and of one thing alone—it is evidence of malicious wrecking intent, of deliberate wrecking work, of deliberate wrecking destruction, of what we call diversion.

Thus we have a number of breakdowns all of which were the result of deliberate counter-revolutionary acts of diversion of people who, placed by the authorities, by the working class, by the proletarian revolution, in positions in which they were entrusted with State property, not only did not guard and protect it, but tried to damage and cripple it, prepared and perpetrated acts of diversion, waged, if in a concealed masked form, a genuine war against the working class by methods of destruction, by methods of destroying our State property.

At this same station we had also cases of boilers being deliberately put out of action. Sterling boilers Nos. 1 and 2, each with a heating surface of 260 square metres, were put out of action in May 1928 and kept out of action to this day on the direct instructions and with the direct co-operation of MacDonald, according to a plan that was drawn up and systematically and methodically carried out on what seemed a perfectly legal basis: repairs, alterations, reconstruction. A nice "reconstruction" indeed!

The burners are altered, and are altered in such a fashion that in spite of the fact that all the imported equipment necessary for the completion of these alterations has been lying in the station yard since 1930, these alterations have been dragging on for over two years.

And then there is the third boiler, U.M.T. boiler No. 11, which is being altered and installed for the last two and a half years.

What are the causes here? The Commission of Experts says: "The presence of malicious intent or, at least, criminal negligence." But even criminal negligence is nothing more nor less than a manifestation of this criminal intent. And the result? The delay in installing boilers Nos. 1, 2, and 11 resulted in the fact that the station generates approximately one-half of the capacity of the turbo-generators.

The Zuevka Electric Power Station. In June and July 1932, at the Zuevka Electric Power Station, a breakdown occurred on generator No. 3. Why did it occur? Kotlyarevsky told us about this here very calmly. I even thought that Kotlyarevsky, as later on I will have to say about several of the others, for example, Sukhoruchkin, probably felt as if he were at a meeting of some scientific and technical society, calmly delivering an academic lecture on his achievements in the sphere of wrecking. It was an astonishing picture, a monstrous picture! It is monstrous to think that an engineer whose mission it really is to create, that an engineer, fed and sustained on Soviet proletarian resources, at the breast of the proletarian revolution, tries like a snake to plunge his sting into the very heart of the revolution! Kotlyarevsky told us here how he placed a bolt in the generator and caused a breakdown. It is a good thing that this breakdown did not have the consequences that it might have had. But was this the only case? And were there not other extraneous bolts in such places where they had no business to be? We established this, here at this Court examination. Bits of plank, stones, a brush, in the insides of our machines!

On this case the Commission of Experts arrived at very categorical conclusions. It says:

> "Cases in which various extraneous articles (bolts, pieces of board, stone, etc.) were found in generator No. 5, cannot be regarded otherwise than as the result of criminal negli-

gence on the part of the staff installing the machines, or deliberate malice on the part of some person."

"No technician," it adds, " could help understanding that if extraneous objects, especially a bolt, were to get into the air gap of the generator, it might lead to serious damage to the stator and the putting of the whole unit out of action."

At the Zuevka Station we also had a number of breakdowns which occurred on turbine No. 1-3, on the oil pumps, concerning which I would also like to refer to the report of the Commission of Experts, which established: "that the state of the oil pump which was observed on this turbine 1-3, at this Zuevka Electric Power Station, directly endangered the reliability of the turbine and could have been brought about only as a result of the obvious lack of conscientiousness on the part of the persons who had installed it."

On the basis of all the materials that have passed before us at this judicial investigation, we can say that this was not only obvious lack of conscientiousness on the part of those who installed the turbine, but what we characterize as deliberate wrecking activities.

I will not deal with the other breakdowns that occurred at the Zuevka Electric Power Station. I will only have to ask the Court to examine the materials of the Commission of Experts and to remember these facts in their consulting room, and also to remember the appraisal that was given of these breakdowns by the expert technicians, which testifies that as a result of their work, to a certain degree and in a certain period of time, this group of Zuevka wreckers succeeded in reducing certain sections of the Zuevka Electric Power Station to a breakdown condition for a certain period of time.

The Ivanovo Electric Power Station, known as Ivgres. In the period from January 1932 until the investigations in the present case were commenced, that is, the beginning of 1933, here, too, a number of various breakdowns occurred as a result of which certain machines were put out of action. These breakdowns were the results of different causes—the unreliable regulation of the turbine, unreliable blade setting on the turbines, the inaccurate work of the controlling and measuring apparatus, and so forth. Moreover, here we had repeated cases of the motors driving the chain grating of the boilers, I will not say breaking down, but put out of action by a very primitive method—by breaking the cable that fed these motors. The motor of the cable was put out of action as a result of being choked with sand.

Frequent cases occurred of the false switching off of the house feeders. The motor of the smoke-stack of boiler No. 5 was deliberately burnt out by the deliberate closing of the ventilator of this motor. The contact box of the motor of the fire-brigade pump, was also wrecked by dropping extraneous articles into it and in addition to this, the systematic disorganization of the telephone station was practised which interrupted communications between the various departments of the power station, and this of course led to the same results: diminution of the output capacity of the station, which was the object of the activities of the wreckers' group operating at the Ivgres.

I would like now briefly to refer to the *Baku State District Power Station* where we also had a number of systematic breakdowns on turbo-generators Nos. 11 and 12, a number of stoppages of machines commencing in 1928 and continuing to 1930—the breakdown of March 11; and to 1931—the breakdown of February 15; and again in 1931—the breakdown of February 21; and again in 1931—the breakdown of March 22. The causes of these breakdowns were discovered only after turbine No. 11 was opened for inspection before the machines were tested in accordance with the contract, although taking into consideration the magnitude of these breakdowns it must be admitted, as the Commission of Experts assert, that these breakdowns must have been accompanied by some outward symptoms—the knocking of the machine, unusual noise and vibration, disturbance of the smoothness of the motion, which could not but have attracted the attention of the station staff if they were careful and conscientious. The motor was installed in this station by the accused Cushny. It is true that the last breakdowns occurred when he was already in Moscow. But the heritage he left, connected with the breakdowns that occurred in 1928, obviously played its part subsequently.

And finally, the last power station, or rather the group of power stations united by what I have already told you is called the Mosenergo, also testifies to systematic breakdowns throughout the whole of the period of the Five-Year Plan. One can say that the wreckers' group at the Mosenergo had their own Five-Year Plan commencing from 1927-28 and, let us hope, utterly disrupted by the arrest of the wreckers now standing trial.

We have a number of breakdowns at the First Moscow State Power Station on turbines Nos. 27 and 28. Permit me to draw your attention to this positively incredible number of breakdowns which systematically occurred one after another on March 9, May 10, June 16, November 28, and so on. The wreckers put out of action the circulation pumps of the turbines. On December 4, 1931, a breakdown occurs at the Shatura Station, which is also controlled by the Mosenergo. On May 22 and November 18, 1931, and May 9, 1932, breakdowns occur at Orekhovo-Zuevo, at the Electro-Thermic Central Station. All this gives us perfect right to ponder over the causes of these breakdowns, to try and discover the secret of the breakdowns at these stations, which, as has been revealed at this judicial investigation as a result of the questions put by Comrade Roginsky, serve very important and responsible sections of Red Moscow—the Hammer and Sickle Works, the Spartacus Works, the Kremlin, the Krutitsky Barracks and the Dzerzhinsky Barracks. The whole of the radio transmission can be put out of action as a result of a single successful wreckers' act, which put out of action the distributing turbine connected to the 6,600 kw. switchboard.

The power stations of the Mosenergo are not only connected with individual enterprises, individual institutions in our Red Capital, but they are also connected with some of the largest industrial centres of the Moscow Region—Kolomna, Yegorovsk, Podolsk, Sergiyevo, Tula, Zaraisk, Ryazan, Noginsk and Kashira—a whole system of large enterprises of military State importance, upon the work of which rests to a certain extent the strength and might of our Soviet economy, of our socialist industry. Huge works like Electrostahl, the Tula Works, the Hammer and Sickle, the AMO, the Trekhgorny Textile Mill and a number of other textile mills, engineering works, chemical works, cement works and factories, quite apart from a whole system of minor enterprises are supplied with electrical power by the First Moscow

Power Station. It is quite understandable, therefore, why the group of wreckers concentrated their attention on the First Moscow Power Station. Naturally, that is why they found it necessary to work here craftily, subtly, determinedly, with the aid of the most skilled agents. And you see, Comrade Judges, that while in the other cases we had before us such persons as Oleinik or Lebedev, comparatively second-rate individuals, who had got caught in the net of the spies, provocateurs and wreckers, at the First Moscow Power Station we have another group, far more skilled, far more experienced, people of a larger calibre, whom it was rather awkward to pay, whom it was not very decent to pay, although they did pay, and it must be said, paid badly. Lecturer Zorin, about whom I will speak later, engineer Sukhoruchkin, you remember his evidence here, engineer Krasheninnikov, you remember him also, three reliable props of the wrecking counter-revolutionary conspirators at the Mosenergo. These are experienced, cool men, who do not lose their courage as some of their accomplices did, who are able to conceal their wrecking operations, their "work," their "activities," are able to understand each other by a mere word, I will say more, by a mere glance. One of the Counsel for the Defence tried to build up his defence of certain of the other accused by the following question: "Well, the first time you conversed for ten minutes, the next time for twenty minutes, the third time for thirty minutes, altogether your meetings lasted two hours; what could you do in two hours of conversation?" This is a naive argument, which also testifies to the failure to appreciate whom and what we are dealing with. These people—Zorin, Sukhoruchkin, Krasheninnikov—are people who understand what is wanted of them by a mere word, these are people who understand what the expression of the eye says, what a pursing of the lips means, who are able to learn these wreckers' "songs without words" of counter-revolution. And I am not a bit surprised that their conversations were very brief; their fleeting conversations are not a bit surprising!

What do we see at the Mosenergo? I have said—breakdowns at the First Moscow State Power Station, at the Shatura Electric Power Station, at the Orekhovo-Zuevo State Electric Power Station. Thus, we have a fairly long list of breakdowns organized by fairly able and experienced hands.

In concluding this list of breakdowns and wrecking acts I must declare with satisfaction that however numerous these breakdowns were they could not cause our socialist enterprises any very serious damage, that all these wrecking acts were shattered against the might and stability of our enterprises. I must place on record the impotence, the miserable insignificance of these people, an impotence of these wrecking acts similar to that displayed by some of their accomplices, particularly by Thornton, and a similar impotence and miserable insignificance in the organization of their own defence.

Permit me now to proceed to characterize the crimes, the role and the responsibility of each separate criminal. We are confronted with the fact that a number of people have confessed. Under other circumstances, this might have relieved us of the necessity of investigating other proof. We know that according to the laws of procedure in every capitalist State, and particularly according to the laws of procedure in England, the mere confession to the Court by an accused is sufficient to give the Court the right to refrain from entering into a judicial investigation. The same norms of procedure exist in our laws, because it is not always found necessary, after an accused has confessed, to go into all the circumstances of the case for the purpose of testing the correctness of this confession. But in bourgeois law this principle is not accidental. In bourgeois countries the old mediaeval conception of the significance and quality of proof still prevails, in which the confession of an accused was regarded as the best, was regarded as the "queen of evidence."

Hence, from the point of view of those who are watching every step of this judicial investigation and who so nervously watched the progress of the preliminary investigation that they at times lost their coolness and fell into hysterics, we could say that the charge can be taken as fully proved even on the basis of the statements of the accused.

But it must be emphasized, Comrade Judges, that in this exceedingly important trial, in addition to the confessions of the accused, we have a whole sum of objective proof which no forces hostile to us can withstand.

We have never had such a wealth of revealing, accusing, objective material proof as is represented by this file of expert evidence based upon the facts of the breakdowns that occurred, on the investigation of the facts of these breakdowns, on a careful analysis of the causes of these breakdowns and on absolutely categorical conclusions which testify to the fact that these breakdowns did take place and that they were deliberately organized. Thus, we have in our hands all this objective material which testifies to facts which, even with the most lively imagination one could not invent, which really did occur, which are recorded and sealed in reports and photographs, and even in the lying defence of those of the accused who try to discredit everything to which we refer, to which only recently they themselves referred as authentic and absolutely established facts which actually took place. I would ask the Special Session of the Supreme Court, when it discusses its verdict, to pay attention precisely to this aspect of the case, and once again to examine—if only for the purpose of appraising the position of the Prosecution on this question from this point of view—the indictment which we have submitted to the Supreme Court, in which we take as a basis the Experts' report, in which we take as a basis of our charges firmly established facts, and in which we take as a basis material from the technical point of view, from the point of view of technical experts, the very facts, the analysis of which leads to the appraisal of subjective evidence and subjective confessions.

At the preliminary investigation, in my presence, Comrade Roginsky and the Investigating Judge on Important Cases questioned MacDonald, and in the very first ten minutes of our conversation with him on the question of the charges made against him in the course of the investigation by the O.G.P.U., MacDonald confirmed the correctness of his depositions and made supplementary depositions—I think, I am sure, that they were sincere conscientious depositions, which cannot be said of the depositions of his fellow citizens who have been prosecuted in this case, particularly the depositions of Thornton.

This civilian, this modest engineer, who moreover, does not

play the same role in this case as Thornton does, and perhaps for this very reason, found sufficient courage in this case to confess after being caught red-handed at the crimes which he really did commit. This civilian engineer acted more courageously than the brave warrior of Mesopotamia. When we asked MacDonald how it was that he made such depositions, he gave two reasons:

> "1. I wanted to make clear the accusations made against me; 2. Because of the facts and proofs that were shown to me . . . ."

That was MacDonald's reply. And that reply is the truth, because the weight of our evidence is very great, the weight of our evidence is based upon the results of an enormous amount of work performed in the process of the preliminary investigations in an unparalleled shortness of time. This work was the technical test of these acts, of the facts on which—I can say this now with satisfaction—the whole edifice of the case of the State Prosecution is built and firmly stands.

Gussev, Vassily Alexeyevich, chief of the Zlatoust Electric Power Station. From 1918 to 1920 he served in the Kolchak army, for which he had volunteered. In various trials of State crimes we meet, here and there, criminals who have been in the White armies, in counter-revolutionary armies; but not often do we meet such as had volunteered for these armies. Volunteer Gussev, who takes part in the campaigns of the Kolchak army against the army of the workers and peasants, who after the defeat of the Kolchak army draws no lessons from this defeat for himself, continues to remain, properly speaking, the Kolchakist that he was when he volunteered to join the ranks of that army, even when he was no longer in that army.

One day he arrives at the Zlatoust works. Rather quickly he passes from one official post to another and finally we meet him in a post in which he has charge of the fate of the Zlatoust Electric Power Station.

He is the chief of the Zlatoust Electric Power Station which serves the enormous group of enterprises of enormous State importance.

I cannot but comment on the conduct of those persons who permitted this thing to come to pass. Once again this testifies to the lack of class vigilance among certain of our business leaders, which often prevents them from properly distributing their forces in their enterprises, from correctly lining up the cadres of the enterprises, particularly in such an important sector as an electric power station, and still more in an electric power station like Zlatoust.

But just now we are discussing Gussev. Gussev himself fairly well characterized himself as a sharply defined, completely formed type of counter-revolutionary spy and wrecker. He himself attributed this to the environment in which he lived and to his friendly relations with the Shalayevs and Bogoslovskys who have been convicted in connection with other wrecking cases. But this does not alter the case; it only explains it. And so, Gussev damages a motor, and when he is caught, he says—I received instructions from MacDonald to damage the motor of the large-shape mill of the rolling shop of the Zlatoust works for the purpose of stopping the output of shells and of shell billets.

These gentlemen were very seriously interested in shells, and one can quite understand why, just as one can understand *for what purpose* and just as one can quite understand *for whom.* They were very seriously interested. I cannot refrain from saying at once that according to Thornton, who at first "presumed" and then confirmed that Gussev was, to use his own expression, Mac Donald's agent at Zlatoust Works, it was Gussev who systematically engaged in collecting information of a military character and communicated it to MacDonald, while MacDonald communicated it to Thornton. Thornton obtained this information, as he himself says, only from one source, namely, from Gussev. Gussev was the only source of the information which Thornton received. We have already seen what kind of information this was—this was information about the munitions shops, information about shells, information about high-grade steel that is required for aeroplane motors, that is required for these same shells, that is required for cold arms, that is required for the equipment of our Red Army. He collects information, damages machinery and rolling mills! How did he do this?

> "During the inspection of this motor I threw a small piece of sheet metal into the ventilation duct of the stator. Subse-

quently this piece of iron served as the cause of the breakdown, because dropping into the air gap, it caused the displacement of a part of the laminated iron packets of the stator iron and rotor; the displaced iron damaged the wrapping containing the winding of the stator, which was the cause of the breakdown."

The displacement of the iron occurred in several places, says Gussev. But as this defect was not repaired, it not only caused a breakdown, not only damaged the winding of the stator, but also caused further breakdowns as the direct result of the first breakdown and this rained a series of blows upon the very motor which drove this large-shape mill of the rolling shop of the metallurgical works, precisely for the purpose of hindering the output of shells and stopping the output of shell billets.

We are not preparing for war; but we are prepared for war. And from this point of view we must appraise these acts of diversion which were intended to weaken our defence; for it is this—I think it opportune to say once again and it is testified by Thornton's depositions of March 13 concerning his network of spies—that greatly interested Thornton when he spoke about the defence and offence possibilities of the Soviet Union.

Good possibilities! Strong possibilities! Try them, Messrs. spies!

I do not want to analyse in such great detail the wrecking activities of this Gussev in connection with the coal conveyor, because all this material has been examined in the course of the judicial investigation, and you will examine it again very carefully and in the greatest detail outside of this battle of parties, in your consulting room, and you will draw the necessary conclusions.

I will not conceal from the Court my conception of Gussev as of one of the principal figures in this counter-revolutionary conspiracy in the electrical engineering industry. For Gussev I must demand a more severe penalty than for any other of the accused, because of the role he played, because of the character of his crimes and also of the general principles that define the content and the direction of our Soviet criminal policy, concerning which I spoke at sufficient length yesterday, so there is no need for me to revert to it today. And in particular I call your attention, Comrade Judges, to the well known decree of the Presidium of the Central Executive Committee of the Soviets of March 14, this year.

Sokolov, Vassily Andreyevich, an electrician, employed at the same station. At first he served as Gussev's assistant at the power station and was later promoted to the post of chief electrician of the power station.

Sokolov pleaded guilty, but for us his confession is not enough.

What is there in proof of Sokolov's guilt in addition to the confessions he made at the preliminary investigation which were corroborated here? These confessions were corroborated by Gussev. Gussev's evidence does not call forth the slightest doubt, because it is based, not only on the evidence of MacDonald and the others, but also on the objective material that served as one of the main pieces of evidence against Sokolov. This material shows that on the instructions of Gussev, and under Gussev's direct guidance, Sokolov co-operated in and personally carried out a number of wrecking acts which resulted in breakdowns. In particular, he carried out Gussev's instruction to damage the 1,400 h.p. motor, which led to a series of breakdowns. He put the turbo-generator out of action, he struck at the boilers. He delayed the repairs and installation of the coal conveyor, and so forth, and so on. Commencing from the middle of July 1932, he collected and communicated information about the six days' rolling of billets on the large-shape roller and, as we have already said, reported how many out of the total number of billets produced were intended for shells. We must bear in mind, Comrade Judges, that the output of this rolling mill—the leading rolling mill, properly speaking, determines the output of the whole of the rolling shop, and consequently, it is sufficient to be in possession of this information to be able to reply to the question which particularly interests military spies who are working in a direction that is hostile to our Soviet State.

Sokolov and Gussev were old friends even in the Kolchak army; both volunteered for the White army. They ceased to serve in that army when, like rats scurrying from a sinking ship, they deserted it when all the cards of Kolchak's generals were beaten, when, at the same time, the cards of certain foreign generals who supported Kolchak were also beaten. Then, these "brave warriors" showed a clean pair of heels and made for the woods. From the woods they came to us, to our enterprises; but having come from the woods they, like wolves, yearned for the woods.

And the third figure in the Zlatoust wreckers' group—MacDonald, an installation engineer. He arrived at the Zlatoust Electric Power Station in 1929. For a number of years he was hospitably treated in our country and has "paid" us very well for this hospitality.

He worked at the Zlatoust Electric Power Station until April 1931, and entered into wrecking counter-revolutionary relations with Gussev and Sokolov, and with Kotlyarevsky at Zuevka; he co-operated in the work which I described in dealing with Gussev and Sokolov, was caught red-handed and was obliged to confess his guilt. He confessed and gave explanations not only regarding himself but also regarding his accomplices, his fellow citizens.

> "In the summer of 1929," says MacDonald, "I was at Thornton's villa and in conversation with me he said that he was interested in information about the political and economic situation of the U.S.S.R. and he asked me to collect and to convey to him this information."

Yesterday I said that, of course, there is a difference between economic and political information and *their* economic and political information. We do not base our charge of espionage on what Thornton here called "gossip." We do not base our charge on this. But I will try to prove that the information which at the moment of his half-confession MacDonald tried to conceal by the inoffensive term—"political and economic information," "required by our firm" is not the "harmless" information that is of course needed by any firm which has business with us on our territory, but that it was information of a very definite character, information that represents a military State secret, the obtaining, collection and communication of which comes under the definition of espionage within the meaning of Article 58-6 of the Criminal Code of the R.S.F.S.R. I will try to show that it was precisely such information and not "harmless gossip" that Thornton received from MacDonald, and MacDonald received from Gussev, and

Gussev received from Sokolov, that is, received along that peculiar chain which at last is linked up in a whole chain of weighty evidence. I will not deal with the relations between these gentlemen and the firm. I do not know them. I do not want to know them. I do not deal with them. I do not want to deal with them. But everyone sees and understands that it was not in the commercial, not in the business interests of the firm that this information was collected, but in the interests of those about whom Thornton told us during his examination on March 13—and then realized that he had blabbed. But to return to MacDonald.

MacDonald says:

> "When I returned to Leningrad I began to collect information and in addition to information about the mood and the living conditions of the workers, I began to collect special information, namely, information about the work of the "Bolshevik" Munition Works, information about the production of aeroplane motors, and also about the production of guns."

And MacDonald pointed out concretely who gave him this information—Khrustchev, Samarin, Redkin, that is, persons who were caught and convicted in another espionage case.

Thornton said here: how could anyone help knowing about these aeroplane motors when the noise they made when tested could be heard all around; when everyone heard the noise made during these tests? How could anyone help knowing about these guns when all the windows in the whole district shook when they were fired? Guns were fired, windows shook, everybody knows about them. But if what Thornton says is true and everybody knows about these things why should he resort to MacDonald's services and pay him money for them? He should have said to him: "What are you talking this nonsense for, everybody knows this, why should I pay you money?"

You, a business man, you, a practical man, paid money for this, paid him for telling you that motors make a noise and that guns are fired! Is it for this that you paid money, and is this the kind of information you got from MacDonald? Nonsense! Child's prattle! Finally, had MacDonald any grounds for denouncing you? MacDonald, with whom you were always on good terms, MacDonald, who never roused distrust against himself, and who in addition, was your subordinate, who was dependent upon you and not you upon him—what grounds had MacDonald for denouncing Thornton and at the same time denouncing himself? It must be said that MacDonald himself realized that it was necessary to give this evidence because Gussev had already talked, because Sokolov had already talked, because Kutuzova had already talked, and finally, because Thornton himself had already talked. And here I must recall the touching scene that was played here when the attempt was made to retreat, in disorder it is true, but nevertheless to retreat from an occupied position. MacDonald said that he talked because he was shown Thornton's depositions, but it transpires that Thornton talked because he was shown MacDonald's depositions, he talked under the influence of MacDonald's depositions! Finally, it was impossible to understand who influenced whom, who spoke under the influence of whose depositions! One blamed the other, and both got mixed up.

Thus, MacDonald speaks about himself and speaks about Thornton. He speaks quite definitely, quite categorically. He does not speak generally and throw suspicion on Thornton and on himself about spying operations, but points *concretely* to persons, *concretely* to things, *concretely* to circumstances. MacDonald obtained information very cautiously. You remember that we established here the methods by which this information was communicated by Gussev. Gussev did not write: so many shells are being produced. He wrote MacDonald friendly love letters: we are producing so many "tins." He did not send his letters in the ordinary way, but used couriers and messengers, a tenth-rate person it is true, but nevertheless a person who is being prosecuted in this case and concerning whom further investigations are being made, namely, Maria Fedorovna Ryabova. MacDonald, through Ryabova, whom he has special reasons to trust, receives letters from Gussev who, seeing the confidence MacDonald places in Ryabova, himself places confidence in this counter-revolutionary letter carrier. Nevertheless, he writes in code: not *shells* but *tins*.

And the people connected with them figure, not under their own names, but under fictitious names. One is called "Derevo" [tree], another is called "Slessar" [fitter], while still others are called by names by which people are usually called—Vassily, Ivan, but which did not belong to the person concerned. And they used fictitious addresses. They sent a parcel with a letter containing secret information in the name of a fictitious person from a fictitious house in a fictitious street. That house does exist, of course, so does the street, but they were picked out at random, picked out in order to throw dust in people's eyes. Gussev does not sign his letters—Gussev. On one occasion he signed himself Utkin, and on another he signed himself Mochalov, that is what he says. But of course, Comrade Judges, we must bear in mind that in these matters we cannot fail to take into account the circumstance that all this is done secretly, is done cautiously, that documents are burned, that documents are destroyed, that as far as possible no documents are written, while those which in other cases were written were sent where Thornton sent his nine secret diaries—to the city on the Thames, to London. They were safer there!

We asked MacDonald: Did you receive letters from Gussev? He replied: yes. How did he sign them? Utkin? Yes. Did you preserve his letters? No, he says, I threw them into the stove, burned them. Burned them? And then MacDonald, nevertheless, tried to play an artful policy here in Court. He admits that he is guilty, but not as frankly as he should have done if he wanted us to believe that he did only that which he said he did. Caught red-handed, faced with irrefutable proof which astonished him, he nevertheless conducted his defence very cleverly and cunningly, tried wherever possible to retreat, and right from the very beginning said and admitted only what was absolutely impossible for him to avoid saying and admitting. Perhaps in regard to the coal conveyor, about which there was some disagreement, he did not give Sokolov direct instructions. We will leave this conveyor to the scrap of conscience which may have been left to MacDonald. This is not a matter of the coal conveyor, but of the fact that MacDonald is an experienced spy, and I would not say that he is less clever than his partners in the dock, on the contrary, I would say very definitely that in several instances he seems to be much cleverer.

When we established the fact here that he had burned Gussev's letters, MacDonald tried to swerve to the side, and what did he say? He said: I usually burn my letters. But I asked him a second time: From whom else did you receive letters besides Gussev? And he said: From no one else. Hence, we can draw the conclusion that we drew, namely, that he always burned the letters that he received from Gussev. Of course, letters are not burned in order that somebody may see them, and notwithstanding all the skill of organs of investigation, it is sometimes found impossible to restore letters that have been burned.

MacDonald, like many others, is able to make use of a gramophone and slight favours. Incidentally, reference should be made to the methods that are resorted to by all the accused, and particularly the British subjects among them. Advantage is taken of every opportunity. Cushny becomes friendly with the fitters, visits them in their homes, arranges parties. Lebedev meets Elliott at the house of a lady who organizes something in the nature of *petites soirées* and it transpires later—I will ask the Court to put this to the account of Cushny—that "incidentally" conversations are carried on about the Red Army, as for example with Yemelyanov, about the equipment of the Red Army, and so forth, and so on. And Elliott carries on conversations with a certain Baldin, while Lebedev cocks his ears and hears that they are talking about the work of the military department of the Ivanovo Mechanical Works, which Elliott has got his eye on, and Thornton says: "I received information from Elliott."

Thus we see that MacDonald, like Thornton (I will deal with him in detail later), carries on definite military spying operations, collects military information.

In 1930, says MacDonald, before my departure for Zlatoust, Thornton had a second conversation with me, when he asked me to collect for him information about the production of military supplies at the Zlatoust works and also about the state of the power supply at those works. In his depositions MacDonald says: In rather a veiled form, *i.e.,* not as a direct order, he gave me the task of organizing breakdowns at Zlatoust in order to interrupt the work at the plant. He told me that if money was wanted it would not present any difficulty, I could get it from him.

These are the three main points: military espionage, the organization of breakdowns, corruption, money, bribes—the three points, the three main links of this chain of guilt which closes around MacDonald and the others about whom I will speak later on.

Did MacDonald carry out the instructions he received from his chief, Thornton, even if they were not given in the form of a direct order? Yes, it must be admitted that he carried them out. He told Gussev that it was necessary to damage equipment, and it was done. Why had this to be done? In order to disrupt operations at the works, to cause stoppages, including stoppages in the factories working for defence, working for our Red Army. He received money, he transferred money, distributed money. He cannot get away from these facts.

> "I have handed Kotlyarevsky, Vassiliev and Fomicheff from Zugres about 2,000 rubles for their spying and damaging activities. Money was given to each of them separately. I gave Kotlyarevsky about 1,000 rubles. Kotlyarevsky had given me information that I have mentioned in my previous testimonies."

These are MacDonald's depositions. I will add the last depositions made by MacDonald in the offices of the Public Prosecutor of the Republic to the effect that in June or July 1932 the breakdown of the third generator was organized.

> "This breakdown took place as a result of the insertion of a bolt in the air gap of the generator. This was done under my instruction by Fomicheff and Kotlyarevsky."

And here is Kotlyarevsky's second deposition. We asked Kotlyarevsky about this and he replied: Yes, I did it, I inserted the bolt and caused a breakdown. The circle of evidence is complete. MacDonald is caught, caught red handed. MacDonald is cleverer than the others, who on being caught tried to pretend that they were innocent and did this mostly for the purpose of rehabilitating themselves in the eyes of their secret chiefs. MacDonald is more sincere and bolder than the others; forced to the wall by our proofs, he admits what is sufficiently clearly and explicitly formulated in the counts of the indictment charged against him.

I must now pass to the Ivanovo Power Station, but before doing so I would like just once more to deal with a relatively small, but a very characteristic feature directly connected with the activities of MacDonald and to a certain degree with the activities of Monkhouse. I have in mind Gussev's visit to Zuevka and his communicating to MacDonald, who was there at the time, that he thought his position was rather dangerous because the O.G.P.U. had got on the track of wrecking operations. He expressed this fear to MacDonald in a rather alarmed manner, but MacDonald calmed his fears by saying that if anything happened he could always get assistance from an address which he gave him. The address was that of Monkhouse. That address was written in the note which MacDonald gave Gussev at Zuevka in case anything happened, in case of discovery, which, Gussev felt at the time, was already threatening him.

And the second episode, that of Gussev's meeting with MacDonald and Thornton at Khartsisk. At this meeting, to which Gussev had been called by MacDonald, an interchange of views took place on wrecking and espionage work. There can be no doubt whatever about this meeting having taken place, for it is established by the evidence of Gussev and the evidence of MacDonald as well as by the evidence of Thornton himself, who, however, in accordance with the tactics of his defence, denied the criminal character of the conversation that took place.

With these two reminders I would like to conclude the analysis of the episodes which directly concern the three persons I have spoken about—Gussev, Sokolov and MacDonald. I come now to the criminal activity of the accused at the Ivanovo Power Station.

I would like to start with Nordwall. What grounds have we for presenting and supporting within the whole scope of the indictment the charge against Nordwall? I think that we have more than enough grounds for this.

In 1931-32 Nordwall worked at the Ivanovo Power Station as Metro-Vickers' installation engineer. There he came into contact with a group of local wreckers, primarily with Lobanov, and carried on wrecking operations, gave instructions to a group of engineers and technicians at the Ivanovo Power Station—Lobanov and others—to commit wrecking and acts of diversion with the aim of damaging equipment, causing breakdowns, which were carried out by these people on his instructions, and also to conceal defects in the equipment, which was done by Lobanov, Lebedev and others. As a reward for this, Nordwall systematically paid through this same Lobanov bribes amounting to the sum of 5,000 rubles.

Against Nordwall we have first of all the depositions of Lobanov, who here and at the preliminary investigation stated that he had frequently talked with Nordwall, had discussed his discontent with the existing Soviet system and his material position, and gave utterance—as Nordwall himself confirmed here—to anti-Soviet views. On the basis of these relations, he became so intimate with Nordwall that the latter selected him as one of his accomplices. Incidentally, and speaking objectively, it is difficult to say who selected whom to be an accomplice—whether it was Nordwall who selected Lobanov, or whether Lobanov selected Nordwall, and this, by the by, is a feature which characterizes some of the difficulties encountered in the present trial in regard to some of the other accused.

Indeed, every one of the accused who was an employee of one of our Soviet State institutions—and every one of them has admitted this here, and the facts we have at our command confirm it—had for a number of years already made themselves acceptable by their anti-Soviet sentiments and anti-Soviet actions. Under these circumstances it would hardly be correct to argue that there was such an interweaving of relationships between Lobanov and Nordwall that Lobanov, this hardened wrecker, became a wrecker under Nordwall's influence. I would not like to support such an absurdity. I do not think that Nordwall offended one of those little ones, Lobanov, because he is by no means a little one. I have every reason to assume, and I will try later on to prove this by a number of facts, that Nordwall was Lobanov's accomplice, that Nordwall utilized the wreckers' group at the Ivanovo Power Station for counter-revolutionary purposes and interests, that they maintained contact with each other and that they carried on these wrecking operations, for which Nordwall paid money that had been assigned for this wrecking work by the people with whom he and Thornton were connected.

Thus, we have first of all the categorical depositions of Lobanov, which are corroborated by Nordwall, referring to the nature of the conversations and talks that took place between Nordwall and Lobanov. And it is really funny to hear Nordwall say here that on hearing Lobanov express anti-Soviet views he did not support these sentiments, but on the contrary tried to convert Lobanov and almost restored him to the path of righteousness, because if Nordwall had really been five minutes short of being a bolshevik, as he was described by Oleinik, who was a man who to a certain degree suffered from the disease of not being able to hold his tongue, from garrulousness, then Nordwall should have reacted altogether differently to the talk, views and opinions he heard from Lobanov.

And yet, Lobanov's anti-Soviet views, which Nordwall himself spoke about here, not only did not prevent him from becoming intimate with Lobanov, but apparently did not cause any reaction on his part, if we leave out of account his own absolutely improbable version of the manner in which he reacted.

More than that, Nordwall takes a definite part, if you will, in relieving Lobanov's financial embarrassment. The episode with the fur coat is not such a simple episode as it may appear to those who are inclined to sensationally proclaim to the world that the whole charge against Nordwall is built up on a fur coat. The fur coat is a clue, but of course not the only one. Lobanov exposes Nordwall as having carried on wrecking operations jointly with him, as having given him definite instructions, as having paid for carrying out these instructions, and as having promised that the wrecker would have no reason to complain.

More than that, Lobanov testified that in doing so, Nordwall warned him to damage equipment that was not supplied by Metro-Vickers, but if they did damage equipment that was supplied by Metro-Vickers, and for which the period of guarantee had expired, then they were to damage it in such a way as to prevent the blame from falling upon Metro-Vickers.

This is fully corroborated by the position adopted by certain of the accused in the present case on a number of questions connected with their, or their firm's, responsibility—by Monkhouse for example, when he himself enumerated in detail a number of defects in these turbines. He wanted to make it appear that he, as the agent of his firm, and the firm itself, bore no responsibility for this. Everything is as it should be. If he sells, or if with his co-operation they install equipment sold by his firm which, in his own words, if he were an employee of the Commissariat for Heavy Industry he would never have bought, then everything is as it should be, because it is the system of equipment, the type of equipment that is at fault. What Lobanov said here fully corresponds to the position the accused took up and which helped to expose these wrecking operations, namely: It is better to strike at equipment supplied by another firm, but if our own equipment is to be affected then we must argue, as Nordwall argued in a certain case: It is not our business, formally, we need not interfere.

That is why Lobanov's version does not contradict the real state of affairs, the general tactics and conduct of the accused when he tries to combine his activity as a representative and employee of Metro-Vickers with his other activities as a wrecker and a spy engaged in military espionage. This version does not contradict, as a matter of fact, it reveals what was natural, namely, that it was not only possible for this talk and these criminal instructions to have come from Nordwall but that they actually did come from him.

Nordwall pays money. He denies that. But what does he admit? He admits that he gave Lobanov a fur coat which it is alleged Lobanov obtained from a friend, a mutual friend of Lobanov and Nordwall—a certain Taylor. But permit me to ask a question: Why did Nordwall undertake to act as intermediary in this transaction? Is it because he had so much time to spare, or because he wanted to help this Lobanov, who was anti-Soviet-minded and who acted against the Soviets? Of course, there may be a third version, namely, that he did not want to help Lobanov, but wanted to do a favour to his fellow countryman Taylor. It was all the same to Nordwall whether Lobanov would be kept warm with this coat or somebody else, but since Taylor wanted to sell the coat he undertook the function of interpreter and organized the sale. Apparently the Defence too will adopt this version.

But it will be necessary to reveal another small fact, namely, that as a matter of fact Lobanov did not receive this coat at once. He received this coat in Moscow, after some time had elapsed, and he received it through a certain Voronin. And who was Voronin?

Voronin was the interpreter at the Ivanovo Power Station. Hence, Taylor was in a position to impose the function of interpreter, not on Nordwall, but on Voronin, who was the official interpreter there and who brought the fur coat to Lobanov when the latter was not at the Ivanovo Power Station but in Moscow.

When Nordwall was first asked why he intervened in this business of the fur coat, he replied: Because Taylor could not speak Russian. But now we know that an interpreter was available who subsequently took part in this transaction. Then why did Nordwall intervene if the thing was so simple? This first question cannot but serve as indirect evidence corroborating Lobanov's version that he received a coat as a present to supplement the 5,000 rubles he received from Nordwall's secret funds that were assigned by the competent organization for criminal activity on the territory of this country. When Nordwall was questioned about this fur coat he gave several explanations, and at the preliminary investigation he tried to destroy the clues, to deceive, to evade facts. At first he said that he himself received 400 rubles from Lobanov and that on the same day, or the next, he handed this money to Taylor. This is entered in the records, and we remember it very well. He firmly, persistently, and without hesitation declared that he very well remembered having received the 400 rubles. And we asked him: Did you count the money, or did you put it in your pocket straight away? He said: Straight away, without counting. And did you hand the money over to Taylor like that? Without counting? Yes, like that. No, sorry, it was different. It was like this: we paid it through our account at the office.

This is the explanation recorded during the examination in the office of the Public Prosecutor of the Republic. It was put through the books of the office; 400 rubles were transferred from Nordwall's account to Taylor's account. First he says he received the money; but if he received it he should have counted it, because he may have been cheated considering the type of man Lobanov is. Nevertheless he does not count the money. He hands it over. But when he is caught he says: "No, I paid it through the office by transferring it from one account to the other, the office books show that."

What happens next? The investigator together with Nordwall go to the office and together they examine the office books and they find that no sum whatever has been transferred from either account, neither from Taylor's nor from Nordwall's. In those documents in which it is stated that the whole of the personal accounts book was examined, there is nothing that could corroborate Nordwall's second version. Then Nordwall gets excited. A telegram appears, which he sends to London: "Please confirm that at the time in question I transferred a sum of money to pay Taylor." And a reply is received to this telegram stating: "Yes, a sum of 500 rubles was transferred." When Nordwall was asked: "How much?" He said 400, and not 500, but now he says 500, that is, makes his explanation fit in with the telegram which does not corroborate his first version. And what is the result? The result is, first the fur coat was bought. Next, the money was received but not handed over, then handed over but not entered, then transmitted to London. Nonsense, Citizen Nordwall! It won't do! And suddenly, the 500 rubles crop up, they are mentioned here for the first time; Nordwall never mentioned them once at the preliminary investigation and in the corresponding documents. The reason why is clear. It was because Nordwall did not expect the action of the investigators which was the reply to his denials and which immediately exposed them completely. That is why we say that Nordwall cannot get out of this fur coat, and he will now have to wear it himself.

Properly speaking, the coat belongs to you or to the organizations on whose behalf and instructions you were acting. We have not the slightest doubt about that.

We may be told that this is very remote, indirect evidence. We may be told that this is an isolated case, that this is even a minor thing, like the pipe which Nordwall very kindly sold, it is true for only five rubles, but nevertheless sold to this very Lobanov, to this very same anti-Soviet-minded man with whom he discusses these anti-Soviet sentiments. A scene for the gods! This "five minutes short of a bolshevik" presents a pipe to an anti-Soviet-minded man who lets him into the secret of his counter-revolutionary thoughts and sentiments! But very often minor things reveal great things. Very often these minor things serve as evidence which puts us on the track and finally leads to the discovery of the crime in its full scope. It is precisely this that marks the significance of indirect evidence which, taken by itself seems to be of secondary importance.

A slight thing—a pipe, a slight thing—a fur coat, a slight thing—400 rubles, a slight thing—four mistakes systematically repeated one after another by Nordwall, which expose his persistent desire at all costs to take this fur coat off his own coat hanger. But he fails. And it is precisely in the light of these everyday things, against this background, that Lobanov's evidence assumes the significance of proof for the Prosecution.

We not only have Lobanov's depositions, we also have the depositions of such an authoritative witness on these questions against Nordwall as the accused Thornton, we have his list of spies in which, among the twelve out of the twenty-seven agents of the Intelligence Service, is the name of Nordwall as an agent who was engaged in economic and political espionage, in collecting information about the defence and offence possibilities of our Red Army, of our State. Nordwall does not stand alone before this evidence, he is supported on the one side by Lobanov and on the other side by Thornton, and of course it must be admitted that there appears to be something supernatural in the coincidence between the circumstance that this hardened spy Thornton blabs, exposes his network of spies, and in this respect is finished as far as the Intelligence Service is concerned, and on the other hand, the exhaustive evidence of Lobanov who, it seems to me and perhaps to many others, is not an altogether clean-handed person. But we must bear in mind that these people could not have carried out their dirty work with the aid of clean-handed persons. They struck up no friendships with clean-handed persons. When they met clean-handed persons, these clean-handed persons repelled them, in the way, for example, that they were repelled by that clean-handed person Dolgov, who took the 3,000 rubles Thornton gave him as a bribe, brought them to the O.G.P.U., revealed this bribe, and came here to the Public Court and hurled this charge in their faces. They dared not cast the slightest aspersion upon him, but they invented a story about Dolgov being in need of an apartment, that they were sorry for him and tried to help him to get an apartment. Later it transpired that they asked no questions about an apartment. It transpired that nobody asked about these 3,000 rubles. It transpired that they had to wait for the arrival of Richards in order to put this sum in order, and in the meantime they entered this sum in the "suspense account."

We will be told that we are relying on the evidence of Lobanov, but that Lobanov is not a clean-handed type. But tell me, what clean-handed people did they have dealings with? Of course, you drew into the sphere of your criminal influence only people who are not clean-handed, only those upon whom you could rely because of their venality, because of their baseness, or because of their counter-revolutionary convictions—it makes no difference to us here. Therefore, the argument that we cannot rely on evidence like that given by Lobanov creates no impression. That argument must be rejected. We have no right from the standpoint of the logic of the judicial proceedings, we have no right from the standpoint of the logic of evidence to cast aside Lobanov's evidence merely because Lobanov's moral instability is repugnant.

Lobanov. I have spoken about him already. Of course he is a corrupt type. This is a second-rate type of wrecker and spy. It seems to me that he is the embodiment of all the peculiar features of the class of which he is a representative, of the class that is already morally corrupt, that has morally exhausted itself. His father was a factory owner, his brother rented a flour mill; that is his genealogy, which defines his moral fulcrum. We know these fulcrums, we know these morals. They are embodied in Lobanov. But precisely because of these traits, Lobanov was particularly suitable material for counter-revolutionary wrecking work, the more so that this completely coincided with his own views and aspirations. Here we have facts that speak for themselves, we have evidence which proves that Lobanov is a spy and a wrecker.

This is what Lobanov relates about himself: "I systematically put out of action the motors of the boiler chain grating by cutting the cable drive of the motor. I did this in conjunction with Lebedev." In this respect Lebedev is a more reliable type, if one may say so, with greater moral qualities than Lobanov. Probably this is due to the fact that Lebedev is a representative of a different social stratum than the son of a factory owner and brother of a flour miller—Lobanov.

Lebedev corroborates this: "The bearings of the feed pump motor were deliberately choked with sand." Further on, he says: "Frequently the house feeder was switched off, on the pretex of switching on the maximal relay."

Lobanov did this in conjunction with Ugrumov. In the depositions we have Ugrumov's testimony in which he corroborates this statement.

In the middle of March the motor of the smoke pump of boiler No. 5 was put out of order. I referred to this at the beginning of my speech. This also was done with Ugrumov's assistance—he himself says that in his depositions. In conjunction with Lobanov, the cover of the contact box of the fire-brigade pump motor was deliberately left unrepaired in order to permit extraneous objects to drop in and so create a short circuit in the coupling. This was done by Lebedev with Lobanov's co-operation, and this is corroborated by the materials of the preliminary investigation; and all this was done completely in accordance with the plan drawn up by Nordwall.

These are the facts which permit us to say that there cannot be the slightest doubt about the part played by the wreckers' group in the fulfilment of these wrecking operations by Lobanov with the co-operation of Lebedev, and with the co-operation of Nordwall who paid money, the first time 3,000 rubles, the second time 2,000 rubles, which Lobanov distributed among all the accomplices. This is also corroborated by Lebedev. In addition to that, these accomplices were wheedled into doing these things by friendly relations, by friendly services and presents in money, a fur coat, and so forth.

That is why we maintain the charge against Lobanov on all counts enumerated in the indictment.

Lebedev. An ex-senior non-commissioned officer. That is an interesting feature. Spies seek their accomplices among ex-officers and ex-non-commissioned officers. Oleinik testified here that Thornton instructed him to select ex-military men who would be useful in the event of war threatening, in the event of the outbreak of war which has been threatening us all the time, from the very first moment of our existence. Thornton corroborates the fact that he did really speak with Oleinik about selecting men, but he alleges that he spoke about this in a different sense, again in a "gossip" sense, in the same way as he spoke about shells in a "gossip" sense, that is to say, to select men to replace the English personnel with a Russian technical personnel. But at the same time this same Thornton is very much interested to know whether Zorin was an officer, because this non-commissioned officer in the Mesopotamian army has a soft spot in his heart for officers.

Lebedev is charged with complicity with Lobanov in performing acts of wrecking. Who played the leading role in relation to Lebedev and Lobanov? Lebedev set himself the same counter-revolutionary aims which were to undermine the power of our Soviet industry and of our Soviet State. Lebedev fulfilled these aims by taking part in the organization of systematic breakdowns, damage to equipment, and as a reward for his wrecking diversional work he received money—bribes. He himself says that he received 900 rubles. We have no other facts, because, of course, they kept no special books. However, we established that in certain cases someone, for example Thornton, did keep books. But Thornton managed in time to take his diaries, about which Kutuzova told us here, to London and so managed to destroy the clue.

Lebedev corroborated all the evidence that was brought against him and explained that the immediate aim of this counter-revolutionary group was to disrupt the work of the Ivanovo State Electric Power Station by deliberately damaging equipment, by putting machinery out of order, by causing breakdowns, by causing interruption at the station for the purpose of reducing the supply of electricity, and if it were found possible, also for the purpose of completely stopping the supply of electricity to the works which depended upon the Ivanovo Electric Power Station for their power.

Here we must speak about Zivert. I do not want to deal with him in special detail, because the crimes in which he is incriminated are very small. He did not protect the machines that he was working on from dust while they were being turned down. He received small sums of money from Thornton. It seems to me that what he told us here apparently did take place, because we have no reason whatever for throwing doubt on his evidence. In the work that he subsequently did he, to a certain extent, atoned for his crime. Of course he is guilty of the crimes that we are talking about but, Comrade Judges, you will have an opportunity in your consulting room of discussing the question as to whether it would not be possible to regard his preliminary confinement as sufficient punishment for his crime, bearing in mind the honest work he has done since then at the Dnieper State Electric Power Station.

About Sukhoruchkin. We examined Sukhoruchkin here in great detail and I will hardly be mistaken in expressing the conviction that Sukhoruchkin is one of the main and most important figures in this trial, among those now in the dock. We cannot apply to Sukhoruchkin the standard that we apply to Zivert, or to Lebedev. His general cultural level, the responsible post he held at the electric power station, namely manager of the electric technical department, chief of the operation department of the First Moscow Electric Power Station, all testify to the fact that we must make the sternest demands upon this member of the counter-revolutionary group which, acting on the instructions of engineer Thornton, put machines out of order.

At the First Moscow Electric Power Station, Sukhoruchkin carried out a number of wrecking measures. He concealed defects in equipment ,supplied by Metro-Vickers, when it was his official duty to reveal these defects and take measures to secure their immediate and urgent repair and to prevent them from having any disastrous consequences. He concealed defects in the installation of this equipment, and it was precisely his conduct that brought this most important electric power station to a state in which systematic breakdowns occur which diminish the working capacity of the station, which increase the cost of operation. This applies particularly and mainly to equipment obtained from abroad, which thus led to the loss of compensation claims. All this must be taken into consideration in appraising Sukhoruchkin's role in this case, and the degree of his responsibility.

Simultaneously, he carries on diversional operations which represent a very serious crime. Sukhoruchkin enumerated here six cases: first, there was the case of the iron rack, when he personally caused a contact between the lead covering of the single-phase cable of generator No. 26-27 and this iron rack. He related here how he deliberately refrained from inspecting the equipment and when tests were made it was found that two of the switch tanks had not been filled, and that this had led to the breakdown.

He mentioned a third case, when he deliberately delayed the installation of a ventilator in the basement of switchboard No. 4, which, according to his plan, was to have led to the overheating of the cable and to its damage.

He spoke here about the deliberate causing of difficulties in the water reserve system at the station, which led to the breakdown and stoppage of turbines Nos. 22 and 24, to the necessity for repairs, which in its turn could not but result in the diminution of the capacity of the station and the disturbance of the proper operation of these turbines.

He related how difficulties were deliberately created in the boiler room in connection with the extension of heat supply to new heat consumers, which took the form of reducing the temperature during the coldest period of the winter and of reducing the supply of water.

In enumerating these cases, Sukhoruchkin did not exhaust the whole list of his wrecking activities, which bore the character of a sort of rehearsal in the event of war, when it was proposed to put the switch system out of order, the very 6,600 volt switchboard to which I have referred and which had special State and military significance. This is the very switch system which Thornton visited twice, although, it is true, he had permission to do so. But it is important to note that Thornton obtained this permission with the help of Sukhoruchkin from the very Ryazanov who subsequently was exposed as a wrecker and convicted.

Big wrecker Sukhoruchkin. Big damager and disrupter of our economy, a convinced and conscious enemy of the Soviet Union—in the verdict of the Supreme Court he must receive a corresponding and deserved appraisal.

Krasheninnikov. Chief of the repair and installation department of this station. He began by concealing defects in equipment. He concealed defects in the rotor blades of turbines No. 26 and No. 27, concealed the defects in the governing valves of the turbines, concealed the defects in the construction of the packing of the circulation pump of turbine No. 27, which led to a stoppage of this turbine on May 10, 1931; he concealed the defects in the thread of the piston rod of the second governing valve which led to the breaking of this piston rod on April 29, 1932, and to the reduction of the load of turbine No. 26 by 5,000 kw.; he concealed the defects in the soldering of the oil piping which led to the breaking of this piping on December 9, and to a stoppage of the turbine, and so forth. At first sight it might seem that these things are not very serious—concealed certain defects. But this same Krasheninnikov was connected with Oleinik and through Oleinik with Thornton. Again the clue leads to Thornton. This same Krasheninnikov receives money through the same Oleinik and from this very same source—Thornton.

Zorin. Between Zorin and Thornton there is direct connection. Zorin here enumerated five meetings that he had had with Thornton, and in regard to these meetings I have already expressed my opinion. These five meetings prove how, gradually, the criminal counter-revolutionary wrecking connections developed between Thornton and Zorin, and how the latter undertook definite obligations paid for by Thornton, in the same way as everything that was done on Thornton's instructions was paid for.

It is interesting to note that as chief engineer of the heat supply group of the Mosenergo, he, as he expressed himself here, did not carry out any operation functions. Strictly speaking, he went to the place when breakdowns occurred. But it is precisely on these occasions that his operation functions commenced in connection with the repair of these breakdowns. The wide field that was left for Zorin's wrecking activities on these occasions is obvious.

Oleinik. An employee of Metro-Vickers. Whether he was a good employee of Metro-Vickers or a bad employee of Metro-Vickers is not a matter that concerns us. He said here that he "did the very best he could," that he served the firm "conscientiously," just as he did wrecking work "conscientiously." He says: Everything I do, I do conscientiously. This "conscientious" man has a very peculiar notion as to what "conscientiousness" means. This man respected Thornton. But it was he who betrayed Thornton, although the latter had promised him the comforts of life and a deposit in an English bank put by for a rainy day. Oleinik says: I bound up my fate with Metro-Vickers. I linked up the whole of my welfare with them. But Oleinik's welfare, in its turn, was bound up with the criminal work he did, about which he spoke here so much and so garrulously, which makes it unnecessary for me to repeat it. It was under the direct guidance of Citizen Monkhouse and Citizen Thornton, these gentlemen who are so much concerned about Oleinik's fate, that Oleinik's wrecking "services" were rendered.

We know the kind of person Oleinik is. He is the scum of our social life, the dregs of our social life. It is all the more characteristic therefore that it is precisely this scum that deserved the confidence of those citizens who operated under the cloak of their firm; it is all the more characteristic therefore that they took types like Oleinik or Lobanov into their secret service.

Cushny. Cushny worked in Baku. I have spoken about the condition of the Baku State District Electric Power Station in the period from 1927 until recently. Cushny commenced his operations in 1928. I have said that Cushny sowed sufficient seeds to produce their poisonous shoots even after he left. Cushny is exposed, firstly, by the depositions of Yemelyanov—we have already mentioned this in the course of the judicial investigation; secondly, Cushny is exposed by Thornton, who included his name in his list of spies; and finally, Cushny is exposed by MacDonald, who in his depositions of March 12, regarding his criminal activity, says literally the following:

> "The leader of the reconnaissance work in the U.S.S.R. disguised under the shield of Metropolitan-Vickers was Mr. Thornton, who worked in Moscow in the representation of the firm as chief erecting engineer. The head of the representation was Mr. Monkhouse who also took part in this illegal work of Mr. Thornton. The assistant of Mr. Thornton

for travelling purposes and his associate in the espionage work was engineer Cushny, officer of the British army, now an engineer of the firm Metropolitan-Vickers. This is the main group of reconnaissance workers which did the espionage work in the U.S.S.R."

That is what MacDonald says. What Thornton says is evident from an examination of his depositions of March 13, where Cushny's name is included in the list of spies. This coincidence is extremely dangerous for Cushny, and Cushny realizes this danger. Cushny behaves like a tried and experienced spy. What does he start out with? He starts out with what he ended with—with the usual methods of the spy—he refuses to give any explanation whatever. Exposed by the depositions already mentioned, obliged to admit that he really engaged in spying operations, he then, at one examination after another, categorically refuses to make any further depositions.

Here are his depositions of March 22: "I refuse to give any further detailed information of my spying operations in the U.S.S.R. I do not desire to give any motive for refusing to give information to the investigating authorities." That is how a good, strong-minded spy replies.

Cushny is examined on March 23:

Q. "Do you plead guilty to the fact that you, in the U.S.S.R., engaged in collecting espionage information of an economic and political character?"

A. "I do not wish to reply."

That is how this "honest erection engineer" "erects" his reply.

Q. "Do you confirm the evidence you gave when confronted with Thornton on March 22 to the effect that you engaged in collecting espionage information of an economic and political character in the U.S.S.R.?"

A. "I confirm the facts deposed by me when confronted with Thornton on March 22 to the effect that I did really arrange to have such information collected."

Q. "Through whom among the Russians did you collect your espionage information?"

A. "I do not wish to reply to that question."

Q. "What are the reasons for refusing to tell about your spying operations in the U.S.S.R.?"

A. "I do not wish to reply to that question."

Q. "Why do you refuse to reply to the questions put to you previously?"

A. "I do not wish to reply to that question."

This is a classic example of the conduct of an exposed spy under examination, but of a spy who is a little worm-eaten for all that. He nevertheless confessed that he was engaged in spying. Did he not write that he corroborated the facts given in his depositions of March 22, to the effect that he really did communicate espionage information? He did—but he refuses to say from whom he received this information. And why he refuses to say—he refuses to say. What is that called? That is called the denials of one who is caught, caught on the spot. But that does not save Cushny, because every step he takes, he takes on a bog of lies. And he is caught and exposed just as Messrs. Thornton, Monkhouse, Nordwall, Gussev, Sukhoruchkin and the others are exposed.

Cushny is confronted with Oleinik. Oleinik is asked: Can you name the Englishmen who were engaged in collecting espionage information, in spying? Reply: Monkhouse, Thornton, MacDonald, Cushny and others.

Oleinik corroborates this. Thornton corroborates this. But this is corroborated not only by the depositions of Thornton and Oleinik, it is corroborated by Cushny's depositions of March 23, when he refused to name the Russian engineers through whom he carried on these operations. Monkhouse also says that Cushny engaged in spying operations and that he received espionage information from Thornton and Cushny. Oleinik corroborates it. Monkhouse corroborates it, Thornton corroborates it, and finally Cushny himself corroborates it, but later he realized what he had done and declared: "I won't say any more."

You won't say any more? Don't! You have said all you could say, and you have said sufficient to enable us to maintain in full our charge against you of committing acts of diversion and of spying.

The chain of evidence against you is complete. You have no

way out. Cushny, you cannot and you will not be able to break this chain of evidence against you, for it testifies with incontrovertible conviction of your guilt, and the verdict should be given accordingly.

Kutuzova. Here the circumstances are simplest of all. Right from the very beginning Kutuzova set out to make a foreign career for herself, so to speak. She says: I learned English because I wished to get a job with an English firm. Of course, there is nothing wrong about that. But this little feature, this attraction that a foreign firm had for her is interesting from the point of view of the sense of dignity of a Soviet citizen. To work, not for one's own people, but for others. Why? Because, with the others it would be possible to earn more, to get more, because perhaps there would be less work to do, because there, perhaps, there would be greater comfort. And who knows—perhaps these very connections will be useful some day—because in the opinion of all these Kutuzovas, the Soviet Government is not firmly established, and so, when 18 wreckers get together, start work . . . a little exertion, and the Soviet Government falls to pieces—then this service with a foreign firm will be very useful. And so Kutuzova gets this job. She says here: I could not help becoming intimate with them, because we Soviet citizens employed by Metro-Vickers were surrounded by a wall of isolation. Nonsense! Lies! There was no isolation! Dances, evening parties, rendezvous, visits, face powder, perfumes, face cream, etc. What has isolation got to do with it? Drop this fable about isolation which you allege induced you to enter into relationships of a secret, military, espionage, wrecking character! Drop it! The logic of events brought you to this path. But the logic of events was created by your own logic.

Well, you found yourself in this group. You, Kutuzova, were in their secret service. You were the guardian of their secrets. You were not merely responsible secretary of their office, but you were also the responsible secretary of the counter-revolutionary, wrecking, secret group. And you guarded their secrets, and together with them you experienced the fears and the excitement of secrecy. But, supported on the one side by Monkhouse and by Thornton on the other, you stepped over all these difficulties and, joy-riding between Perlovka and Moscow in an English automobile, among these comforts of life, you forgot your dignity, lost your conscience, forgot that you were a Soviet citizen. You sold yourself for money, and you must answer for this according to the laws of our State.

But Kutuzova has several good marks, although she obtained these rather late. She gave sincere, candid explanations. She spared neither herself nor her accomplices. Perhaps she did not tell all she knew, certainly she did not tell all she knew, but what she did tell she told, it seems to me, with a fair amount of straightforwardness and frankness; she described her own criminal "work" and the analogous work of her accomplices, and I think that this is sufficient to take into account in finally deciding Kutuzova's fate.

And once again, as at the beginning of this trial, we have to revert, in closing the circle of our charges, to three persons whom, as I have already informed the Court, the Prosecution does not regard as the central figures in this trial, because right from the beginning, as can be seen from the indictment, from the process of the trial and from my last formulations of the charges here, the Prosecution has held that the central figures have been the citizens of the U.S.S.R., the State employees. But of the British subjects who are charged in this case, we single out three persons, namely, Thornton, MacDonald and Monkhouse. I have already spoken about the second of these, permit me now to say a few last words about the first and the third.

Monkhouse. He has lived in Russia for more than twenty years. The Prosecution considers it proved that Monkhouse, through the medium of a number of his subordinate English engineers and also of several Russian engineers, collected secret information of military State significance; that he took part in the wrecking diversional operations of the aforesaid counter-revolutionary group, and that for this spying, diversional, wrecking work, he systematically paid out various sums of money, gave bribes to Russian engineers to induce them to conceal defects in the equipment supplied by Metro-Vickers. In other words, we take it that his guilt is proved of crimes which in the indictment are enumerated under Articles 58-6-7-9 and 11 of the Criminal Code.

I have just spoken about the accused Kutuzova. Her evidence sufficiently exposes Monkhouse and characterizes his role in these wrecking, counter-revolutionary, spying operations. It was she who witnessed Monkhouse and Thornton drawing up plans to damage turbines and equipment and to put machines out of order. Kutuzova's evidence was corroborated by the depositions of a number of other persons. The system of bribery practiced by Thornton with the co-operation of Monkhouse was corroborated by the episode of the attempt to bribe Dolgov, which neither Thornton nor Monkhouse can deny. Why was a bribe given to Dolgov? The bribe was given to Dolgov to induce him to forbear from fulfilling his duties to his proletarian fatherland. They tried to buy Dolgov—but they failed. He would not agree to it. He not only would not agree to it, but like an honest man he exposed this attempt to corrupt him. Monkhouse was obliged to admit this, and his belated repudiation of his own confessions, bare denials, will not save him. Monkhouse thinks that he has only to say, "I deny," "I do not say now what I said before," to convince us of the truth of his assertion. But Monkhouse not only denies, he also lies, as was the case when he lied about the eighteen hours' examination, for which he had to apologize. He was examined in the office of the Public Prosecutor of the Republic and he said that he does not consider himself guilty on three counts, but he admitted guilt on count 4, and count 4 is precisely the count on which he is charged, together with Thornton, of giving a bribe to Dolgov.

But that is not the only episode. Monkhouse said to the investigator: "I knew that Thornton brought various things for the Soviet engineers and technicians, but I presumed that he received money for these things."

Hence, we can draw the conclusion that not only was Monkhouse aware of this bribery which Thornton engaged in, but took a direct part in giving bribes, as was the case with Dolgov, when 3,000 rubles were written off the books with the special permission of Monkhouse and Richards, etc.

However, I am obliged here to say several unpleasant things not only about Monkhouse, but also about several unpleasant traditions of the Metro-Vickers office. I have in mind Monkhouse's depositions, not about himself, it is true, but about a certain predecessor, named Anton Antonovich Simon. This Anton Antonovich Simon, in the period from 1923 to 1928, was director of business between the U.S.S.R. and Metro-Vickers. He is very interestingly described by this very Monkhouse, Simon's successor and, one can say, successor in the fullest sense of the word. How does Monkhouse describe the fruitful activities of Anton Antonovich Simon? This is what he said: "I knew that Simon had a special fund which he used for bribes." What a revelation, like the "Secrets of the Court of Madrid"!

"I firmly believe," continued Monkhouse, "that he was interested in certain counter-revolutionary movements, but I did not enjoy his confidence. He did not trust me for certain personal and political reasons. I cannot give exact information about his activity in this direction. Simon died in 1927 and immediately afterwards I was appointed Metro-Vickers' manager in the U.S.S.R. Right from the beginning of my work to the present day my chief was Mr. Richards whom I knew in our student days, because he graduated at the same time I did."

We will deal for a moment with this fact. And so, Dolgov is given a bribe. An active part in this is taken by Monkhouse and Richards. Later, when this bribe is exposed, Monkhouse first tries to deny it, but forced to the wall by the evidence, and seeing no way out, he confesses. And here he again tries to show that there was not bribery, that the Metro-Vickers office never practised bribery. And then it transpires that a special fund for the payment of bribes existed. . . .Monkhouse knew that his predecessor systematically engaged in bribing the employees of our Soviet institutions. Monkhouse knew that Simon had a special fund which he used for criminal purposes. It was not only Simon who had this fund; Monkhouse had this fund also. And after all this, Monkhouse says that no bribes were given, that he is an honourable man and does not even understand what bribes are being talked about, that at most presents were given.

That is the position with regard to the bribes, or "presents." What were these bribes paid for? What was the information for which these "presents" were given? These bribes were given for information which Monkhouse collected in the same way as it was collected by the rest of the English spies. We have the evidence of Monkhouse himself which throws light on this aspect of the case. You have his depositions in which he says that he really did receive spying information, principally from Cushny, about whom we have just spoken sufficiently, and from Thornton, whose role in this connection has also been sufficiently exhaustively described.

At the preliminary investigation, during the examination in the office of the Public Prosecutor of the Republic, Monkhouse did not dare to deny the depositions he had made to the O.G.P.U. in which he said that he was engaged in collecting spying information. But he pretended that he did not understand what spying was. But immediately he had to give way and say: "I know the meaning of the word 'espionage,' I understand and know that espionage means collecting and communicating information which is a State secret."

Did you say that? Yes, you said it. Thus you were obliged to admit that you understand what is meant by espionage, that you understand that espionage is meant in the sense that it is spoken of in the charge—collecting State secrets. During the investigation Monkhouse tried to make excursions into philology. For example, from research into the meaning of the word "espionage," he passed on to research into the meaning of the word "illegal."

Monkhouse made this excursion into the realm of philology in connection with the case of Richards' illegal crossing of the Finnish frontier, which Monkhouse has told us about. Correcting himself, Monkhouse added: "Not illegally, but secretly." Very well, that is how we will put it: not illegal operations but secret operations. From the point of view of the Prosecution, this suits me admirably; I do not know whether it will suit Monkhouse.

A characteristic touch. When we speak about Monkhouse we must not forget 1917, we must not forget 1918, when Monkhouse served in Archangel, in the British interventionist forces which waged war against our Soviet Government, against the workers and peasants of our country. There he met Richards, who was serving in the notorious Intelligence Service, and afterwards he maintained contact with him in his work at Metro-Vickers. Let me say that Richards' present connection with the former organization does not interest me in the least now. This is not a casual circumstance any more than is the circumstance that Monkhouse told us about when he said that, tired of military feats in the Archangel interventionist forces, he returned to rest to London and was invited to go to Russia again—not to the North this time, but to the South, to Denikin's army. He refused—because he was tired. I am not in the least interested in his weariness, but what is characteristic is his fruitful work in the interventionist forces under Richards' guidance, which gave sufficient grounds for inviting him to continue his career as an interventionist—not in the North this time, but in the South, in the ranks of Denikin's army.

The interventionists knew to whom they were making such a proposal....

And finally—wrecking, breakdowns, instigation, utilizing individual wreckers, taking advantage of the conditions which, unfortunately, have not been entirely eliminated and which are still possible owing to the existence in our country of remnants of the exploiting classes, owing to the fact that we are living in a capitalist environment which in a way fosters the class struggle in our country, by singling out, mobilizing and directing against us hostile, even though quite insignificant forces.

In order not to revert to this subject again, I would like to turn to another point in connection with Monkhouse which cannot but interest us, and which has already attracted our attention. I want to recall the conversations, and the notes of those conversations, that were carried on between our People's Commissar for Foreign Affairs, Comrade Litvinov, and the British Ambassador, Sir Esmond Ovey, on March 16, 19, and 28, concerning that part which refers to the attempt Monkhouse made, a defeated and unsuccessful attempt, but nevertheless an attempt that Monkhouse made at this Court, to discredit our preliminary investigation. I will touch upon a matter concerning the preliminary investigation, particularly in relation to the English citizens, and incidentally in relation to the Soviet citizens, and that is, the really extraordinary rapidity with which the investigations were conducted.

The arrests were made on March 11, and already on April 12 the work, which resulted in the material which took us five days to examine, was finished. Quite naturally, the work had to be done quickly and persistently, we had to work very hard. Comrade Litvinov was quite right when he said that we had worked so quickly because of the insistence of the People's Commissariat for Foreign Affairs, and the People's Commissariat for Foreign Affairs did all it possibly could to meet the wishes of the British Embassy. In Comrade Litvinov's notes we read that under normal conditions the examination of Nordwall and Monkhouse would have taken several weeks, but we managed to get this done in the course of three days. Hence, it must be borne in mind that if an examination took place throughout the whole of March 12, lasting approximately from 7 to 8 hours, or even 10 to 12 hours, and if on March 13, although with three recesses, Monkhouse or Thornton were subjected to examination three times, it was because, properly speaking, our organs of investigation did this under the direct pressure, as Comrade Litvinov says, of the People's Commissariat for Foreign Affairs, who urged us to get this case finished as quickly as possible in the interests of the arrested persons themselves. And, what is most material for us, as can be seen from this note, none other than Sir Esmond Ovey insisted upon the investigation being completed as quickly as possible. And while, in the endeavour to satisfy these demands, the investigation authorities worked 8, 10 and 12 hours a day, instead of extending the examination over several weeks by examining only 2 to 3 hours a day, suddenly, under somewhat different circumstances, Monkhouse gets up, after having been inspired by others, and makes an attempt to declare that he was exhausted by examinations of 18 hours' duration. No examination lasted 18 hours, but they did last 10 hours and some lasted 12 hours, although with intervals for dinner, with intervals lasting hours for rest and for taking food, for travelling back and forth from the place of detention, which, taken as a whole, represent from 20 to 30 per cent of the whole of the time devoted to the examination. It would be useful to establish this fact in order to be able to take into account all the circumstances which apparently induced Monkhouse to take this path of slander, of malicious untruths, which even caused him a certain amount of unpleasantness and for which he had to apologize.

Thornton. Thornton is charged with the following: with organizing through a widespread network of installation engineers and technicians, employed by the Metro-Vickers office, economic and military espionage. Secondly, with having enlisted for espionage work a number of Russian engineers and technicians; with the organization of breakdowns at a number of power stations in the Soviet Union; with giving bribes for the organization of these breakdowns, and for concealing defects in the equipment installed by the installation staff of the Metro-Vickers office in the persons of certain members of this counter-revolutionary group.

What evidence have we got against Thornton? Firstly, we have against him a number of objective facts like the numerous cases of defects in equipment supplied by Metro-Vickers for a number of power stations, serious and minor defects which caused serious and minor breakdowns which gave rise to prolonged or less prolonged stoppages of turbines and hence caused us serious damage. Undoubtedly, the defects existed. Monkhouse himself has spoken about this. Firstly, it may have been necessary at all costs to conceal these defects in order to protect the interests of the firm. Secondly, to use this as an objective cause, as a screen of objective causes behind which to conceal the subjective, active, counter-revolutionary wrecking work. Thirdly, to utilize the defects in such a way as to stimulate wrecking work by organizing breakdowns. Simultaneously with that, the organization of military espionage, bribery and corruption, which, as I have already said, is one of the methods of work commonly employed by this group, by this criminal gang who are caught and are now completely exposed at this Court.

What grounds have we for asserting and insisting upon Thornton's guilt? We have the following material. Firstly, Thornton's own confession. Thornton pleaded guilty to organizing economic and military espionage. Thornton pleaded guilty to collecting information of an espionage character through a widespread network of agents, of several employees of Metro-Vickers and people not employed by Metro-Vickers, but working in contact with them. He confessed to giving bribes for espionage to Russian engineers and technicians, which bribes were paid either by himself or through certain engineers and technicians employed by the firm. He confessed to giving bribes for wilfully concealing defects in equipment. That was at the preliminary investigation. At this judicial investigation, as you remember, Thornton denied what he had confessed at the preliminary examination with the exception of his confession concerning the collection of economic information, which, he argued, was not a criminal act.

It will be necessary to revert briefly to Thornton's conduct at this trial. Let us take as our starting point a position that is most favourable for Thornton—his confession that he collected information; we will leave out for the moment the character of this information. Let us establish incontrovertible facts, for this will make it easier for us to unravel this knot. And so, Thornton collected information through a number of his employees and through other persons not employees of his firm, with whom he had business and non-business relations. This is an incontrovertible fact and this he has admitted himself.

Secondly, he has admitted that in particular he received information from Zlatoust. Thirdly, he has admitted that he received this information from Zlatoust from Gussev and MacDonald. Fourthly, he admitted that he received no information except that which he received through these persons. This too is incontrovertible.

Now we will see what kind of information he really received from Zlatoust. We will ask Gussev and we will get the reply—information of a military espionage character; the number of shells, types of shells, the work of the rolling mill, information about high-grade steel used for military purposes. This is the evidence of Gussev and MacDonald. Here you have the sum total of facts which can leave no doubt whatever that only one sort of information came from Zlatoust and that was military information. Thus, as they were the only persons from whom Thornton received information, that was the only kind of information he actually received. Thornton's bare denials are confronted with his own document in which he admits that he engaged in espionage of a military character.

How shall we proceed? What should we believe of this?

What should we take as authentic? Quite naturally, the only possible reply is: facts alone can be believed. Did you receive information from Zlatoust? You did, you yourself said that you received it only through Gussev. We will accept that version. You yourself said that you received it only with the co-operation of MacDonald. We will accept that version, no other facts are required. Now let us see what kind of information it was. Both MacDonald and Gussev say the same thing as to the kind of information this was.

But Gussev was *not* the only person through whom Thornton obtained military information!

You will remember the statement, which Thornton does not deny, that he received information from the Mitischy Works about the manufacture of military wagons for the Red Army. He also received information from the Putilov Works. Moreover, he stated that strangers were not admitted to certain departments of the Putilov Works because, he alleges, these shops were transferred to military work, and this was particularly in 1931, in the period, explains Thornton, when the U.S.S.R. was confronted with the complications in the Far East.

Gussev—gives information about shells; somebody else—gives information about Mitischy; MacDonald—gives information about the Putilov Works. Thornton himself observes, listens, looks around to see what is going on. We will include the Bolshevik Works, the guns and the motors, in this point. Elliott collects information about the military department of the Ivanovo Works from people he talks to at an evening party at the house of somebody named Volkova. Oleinik had special instructions to watch troop trains going to Irkutsk.

Then there is the special interest he displayed through Cushny in the state of the Red Army. Thus we have a number of facts, the sum total of which sufficiently convincingly characterizes Thorntons's role in this case.

Thus, we have a whole heap of facts which go to show that Thornton was the organizer of this military espionage. Take MacCracken. According to Thornton's own depositions this MacCracken informed him that when he, MacCracken, travelled to Kuznetsk, he saw many trains carrying military supplies to the

East and also that when he was travelling from Kuznetsk he saw many troops there. Do you see how MacCracken is interested in troops and how Thornton discusses the destination of these trains? And here is Thornton's conversation with Clark. "Clark informed me about various counter-revolutionary acts that he knew of." Here fact is mixed up with fable, principally fables of the type of the Riga canards. By the by, excuse me for asking: was it not in your kitchen that the canards were concocted about a whole carload of dynamite being brought to a certain works in order to blow them up? Simultaneously with those slanders and canards "made in Riga" which are prepared with the direct and benign co-operation of the Thorntons, MacCrackens and Clarks, information is collected about the direction in which troops are moving; even the number of trains is counted. Attention is paid to what these trains are carrying, whether aeroplanes or motor trucks or men.

Everything is pried into, everything is asked about, everything is looked into. That is seen from Thornton's depositions made later than March 13, 1933. Thornton said that he did not feel well on March 13; but what about the 15th? Thornton replied: I felt better. And on the 16th? Answer: Still better. And on the 17th?—ditto. So you see, Citizen Thornton, you felt well and yet you said such "explosive" things as might have blown you up!

Or to proceed further, when Thornton was questioned on March 16:

Q. "What concrete facts in your information did you communicate to Richards about the munitions industry?"

A. "I informed Richards that the new turbine shop of the Putilov Works was closed and that our engineers were not permitted to enter. According to what our engineers said, the shop was transferred to the production of military equipment."

What is that—"gossip"?

Another of Thornton's depositions: "In 1931, when there were complications in the Far East, I informed Richards that a number of the shops at the Mitischy Works had been transferred to the production of wagons for the Red Army. I received this information from our mechanic Waters."

That's the position. Take the depositions of March 12. Here we have a list of ex-officers and soldiers, employees of the firm. A very interesting coincidence. Then follow—Nordwall, Pollit, Riddle, Thornton, Monkhouse, and so on.

Well, Citizen Thornton, how do you stand in regard to military espionage? Not very well, I think, not very well. It follows then that information flowed to you from various directions. Oleinik gives information about the munition works near Perm. Lebedev gives information about the military department at Ivanovo. MacDonald gives information about the testing of guns and motors, about the Putilov Works, about its munition shops. Waters—ditto, Oleinik—about military trains going to Irkutsk carrying guns and aeroplanes. Oleinik is instructed while in the Ukraine to try and organize a small but compact group of ex-officers who might be useful in the event of intervention, in the event of war. Did that conversation take place? Thornton cannot deny it, although he tries to wriggle. "Do you confirm this or not?" I asked Thornton. He said: "I deny that part about selecting men for diversions and espionage, but I remember speaking to Oleinik about selecting a Russian technical personnel to replace the Englishmen. . ."

Whom are you telling this to? You select special people. There they are—Gussev, who is sitting behind you, Lobanov, an ex-whiteguard officer—there is your little network, your diversional group!

That is the position with regard to military spying. That is the position with regard to your own evidence, that is the position with regard to the heap of evidence that we have against you—MacDonald, Oleinik, Gussev, Lebedev and finally Thornton himself—we could bring a whole lot of other evidence against you, but this is sufficient to reveal and brand your role as organizer of military espionage operations. Then there is your document of March 13, which you tried so hard to repudiate. Comrade Judges, when we begin to speak about this document, Thornton loses the last shreds of his self-possession. He jumps up, as we have seen more than once, and says: "I absolutely deny it." Out of ten documents he repudiates precisely this one, but not the document of March 12, which was an earlier one, not the examination of

March 14, which came later, or of the 20th, or of April 1. Not one of these records of the examination of those days disturbs Thornton so much as this one does. Of course, we must say that we must leave this document to Thornton's conscience—it is his document. He alone in the present conditions can establish whether what he said in that document is true or not. By this document he not only exposes, reveals his network of fifteen spies who were engaged in economic and political espionage and the twelve spies who were engaged in military espionage; he also reveals the fact that the operations of this spying organization on the territory of the U.S.S.R. were guided by the British spying organization known as the Intelligence Service through its agent, Richards, who occupies the position of a managing director in Metro-Vickers. But we will leave that entirely to Thornton's conscience, that is, if Thornton has a conscience.

Thornton does not like this document, but the document is a document for all that. Thornton tried to discredit this document by talking about "moral pressure." But why did you not tell in detail what this "moral pressure" was? How was that "moral pressure" brought to bear upon you? He said: "I was told that if I gave correct information it would be all right." I will not hesitate to say the same thing now, in this hall, in the hearing of the whole world: it will be better if you give correct information than if you say what is untrue. Do I by that bring "moral pressure" to bear on you? Then he said: "I was told that if I gave other information I would be useless both in England and in the U.S.S.R." Permit me also to bring such "moral pressure" to bear upon you and to say: Citizen Thornton, you are already useless both here and there, because as a spy you have proved your utter bankruptcy, because you, twenty-four hours after your arrest, betrayed your agents and did that because you are a coward and a traitor by nature, so that even your own British spying organization can no longer trust you. And here, in the U.S.S.R., you are useless, because after all that has passed nothing useful can be expected of you.

There, I have brought "moral pressure" to bear upon you! I have shown what you represent from the point of view of the demands which may be put to you by people who have respect for themselves and respect for others, who can protect their interests and fulfil their duty, which you unfortunately have not fulfilled either to our country, because you betrayed our trust, or to the institution which had confided its secrets to you. And what else did you say about "moral pressure"? Nothing. One more remark. You say that your deposition of March 13 contains an untruth. Let us suppose it does. But have you thought about the fact that when you communicated what you did on March 13, you were playing with people's heads, with the heads of your comrades? Did you appreciate that? No, you will not succeed in discrediting this document. Let it remain on your conscience.

Incidentally, in this deposition you mentioned one other person who is now in the dock—that is Gregory. I must say that a denunciation by an accused, or by any other person can have significance in our Courts only when it is accompanied by some objective evidence, when it does not remain a bare denunciation. When Thornton speaks about Cushny, we see Cushny's activities; when Thornton speaks about Monkhouse, we see Monkhouse's activities; when Thornton speaks about Nordwall, we see Nordwall's activities; when Thornton speaks about MacDonald, we see MacDonald's activities. But when Thornton speaks about Gregory, I must say that Thornton's bare statement, unsupported by any other facts, is insufficient to support the charge against Gregory. I think that a verdict of acquittal can be passed on Gregory.

I have exhausted all the arguments, I have exhausted all the facts at my command, if we are to speak of the most important and the most material of them.

The charge has been formulated, and for the last time. The weight of this charge has been distributed among the individual accused. My task at this stage of our trial is already fulfilled. The principal and main group has been indicated: it is Gussev, it is Sukhoruchkin, it is Zorin, it is Lobanov, it is Krasheninnikov, and it is Sokolov. Then follow the minor and second-rate personages among our citizens. Then comes the group of English citizens—Thornton, Monkhouse, MacDonald, Nordwall, Cushny. Gregory I exclude from the list.

The State Prosecution has no doubt about the verdict which you, Comrade Judges, will pass on this case. In appraising the activities of each of the accused, you will no doubt decide a number of questions that we here in the process of the argument will hardly be able to probe to the full. Particularly, there is the question which I have raised and which you also will have to decide, and that is the question as to who among the various groups of accused in their various planes of contact with each other, organized, instigated, enlisted and directed the others. You will have to decide the measure of criminal repression to be applied to each of them. The charges are based on Article 58 of the Criminal Code, which categorically demands the supreme measure of social protection—death by shooting. And the activities of these people deserve that this sentence be pronounced upon them.

But our Court is a Soviet Court in which the formal demands of the law are not the only motives. Our Court weighs up all the circumstances of the case, our Court heeds the voice of its socialist legal conscience, and it will distribute responsibility among the individual accused before convicting them; it will decide this question from the standpoint of a number of circumstances which the Court always takes into consideration no matter how heinous the crime committed.

The most important circumstance in this case which I, as the representative of the State authorities, am in duty bound to remind you of, is that notwithstanding the wrecking activities of these groups of wreckers, the power and the might of our State has not been shaken. Aye, and it could not and cannot be shaken. In spite of the fact that our class enemies frequently try to strike at our State economy, our State economy continues to grow, its might becomes more and more consolidated and these people turn out to be insignificant pygmies. In passing sentence, we are never guided by considerations of cruelty and revenge. But that does not mean that when you finally decide the fate of the accused and if you find it necessary to pronounce the sentence of the supreme measure of social defence upon any one of the accused, that you will hesitate to do so. You, of course, will pronounce it, and your hand will not tremble when you sign it.

But whichever way you decide, it seems to me beyond question that one very important point in this judicial process has already been decided, and that is, the utter hopelessness of any attempt to hold up the victorious progress of our proletarian revolution.

Already the first spring of our second Bolshevik Five-Year Plan has come, and soon our socialist fields will be replete with ripening corn. This corn will soon come pouring into our cities to reinforce our industries and help to erect still higher the great scaffolding of our socialist edifice. And from the lofty height of this scaffolding of our socialist construction, crowning with new and new victories the efforts, the creative labour and the enthusiasm of the proletariat of our Party under the leadership of the Central Committee, and of the leader of our Party, Comrade Stalin, of the proletariat which is marching along the heroic path of victory, the despicable crimes by which these insignificant, venal, corrupt, and treacherous people, who betrayed the socialist fatherland, and tried to hold up the victorious march of the socialist revolution, will appear still more insignificant, more shameful and more repulsive.

The President: I declaire the session adjourned until 7 p.m.

(The Court adjourns until 7 p.m.)

[Signed] V. V. ULRICH
President of the Special Session of the
Supreme Court of the U.S.S.R.

A. F. KOSTYUSHKO
Secretary

EVENING SESSION, APRIL 17, 1933, 7:20 p.m.

The Commandant: Rise, please. The Court is coming.

The President: Please be seated. The session is resumed.

Comrade Kaznacheyev, member of the Moscow Collegium of Defence.

Kaznacheyev: Comrade Judges, it is difficult to detect anything abnormal in the fact that the Court is trying, must try, and punish the grave crimes, the ghastly picture of which has been unfolded before our eyes during the last few days! There is not a country, there is not a State, no matter what its class nature or the structure of that State may be, that would not punish acts of diversion, that would not punish espionage. Nobody ever expresses astonishment at the fact that the laws of various countries lay down severe penalties for such crimes and that the courts are the bodies whose business it is to detect such crimes, investigate and try them. But when in the Soviet Union the citizens seated here in the dock were charged with these heinous crimes, and among them there happened to be subjects of another country who are charged with being the instigators and organizers of acts for which they would certainly not be patted on the heads in their own countries, then the press of that country raises a furious campaign of slander and lies which can only have one definite aim. The aim of this campaign is to discredit the investigation now proceeding, to discredit our judicial institutions and to prove that these honourable gentlemen are victims of Soviet terror! Certain journalists even went so far as to invent the theory that we make a practice of specially staging trials of this kind.

And so while we here in this hall are hearing the case of these citizens, over there in old England, as we know from the newspapers, prayers are being raised to heaven to the accompaniment of Easter chimes for Thornton and Monkhouse who are almost canonized as saints!

I think that after all that has occurred here in this Court, after all the admissions we have heard from Thornton and Monkhouse and MacDonald, we have a right to assert that this campaign has collapsed, and that the aim of the group of journalists who organized this campaign can never under any circumstances be achieved!

I could, of course, refrain from drawing your attention to all the points I have just mentioned, but all of us witnessed the manner in which the accused British subjects tried here in this Court to continue, to some extent, this campaign of slander and calumny, tried to allege that certain special methods of examination were applied to them and tried to say that they gave certain testimonies under coercion. If all the measures of self-defence adopted by these honourable gentlemen were a matter of indifference to my clients, were entirely neutral as far as my clients are concerned, if the question of the truth or falsity of what they said in the Court were a matter of indifference, I would not dwell on the matter; but, after all, it was a palpable attempt to act in such a way as to bring about certain judicial consequences. In such circumstances, of course, I cannot ignore this attempt and I cannot avoid concentrating your attention upon it. It is along these lines that I ask you to permit me to dwell briefly upon the statements that were made by Monkhouse and Thornton concerning my clients and the other accused who are not British subjects. One of the accused, Citizen Cushny, declared here with exceptional brusqueness: "Oleinik is lying!" And now this attempt to prove that my clients came into Court to tell lies compels me to ask: What grounds are there for this assertion? Where is, I will not say proof, but even a hint of evidence that they are victims of the slander of Oleinik, of Gussev and of the others?

Now, we all know what denunciation is, we all know the meaning that is put into this word. We usually describe denunciation as totally unsupported testimony, testimony that is quite isolated, and in such cases we always speak of the possible, or at least of the supposed motives for the denunciation. If all testimony that is unfavourable to an accused were defined as denunciation, it would be utterly impossible for the courts to administer justice. In this case we were in possession of a rare abundance of evidence which is impossible to get away from, and under these circumstances it seems to me that to utter the word "denunciation" is naive and ridiculous. The so-called "lies" of Gussev and the other accused are corroborated by definite material, they are corroborated by a considerable amount of objective proof! Moreover, if we were to suppose, if even for one moment we were to adopt the viewpoint that Mr. Thornton desires, then we would have to ask: And how can Thornton seriously explain his own admissions? How can he explain the depositions made by MacDonald? Neither of them has given a single plausible answer to this question!

Finally, permit me to dwell on the last point: what did you hear in this Court concerning the motives of denunciation, concerning the possible, or, at least, the supposed motives? The position of my clients Sokolov, Gussev and Oleinik is particularly grave, and you will appraise their testimony in various ways, but no sensible person would suppose that they wanted to aggravate their position, which is grave enough as it is, by denouncing others. I think that all this talk about denunciation, all this talk about "lies" has just one single quality—there is not a shred of even the most elementary, the most primitive human logic in it. I think that all that has passed before you and all the material which is lying on your table give me every justification to declare that the question of whether Gussev and Sokolov told the truth cannot be answered in any other way except in the affirmative.

Gussev, Oleinik and Sokolov have committed serious crimes and they do not deny them; but neither Thornton nor Monkhouse will ever be able to prove that Gussev, Oleinik and Sokolov told lies at the preliminary investigation and that they came into this Court as liars! The judicial investigation has examined the various depositions, has compared them with a considerable amount of material evidence, and these depositions have been objectively corroborated!

The crimes committed by Gussev, Oleinik and Sokolov are immeasurably grave. They came here to answer for these crimes. They now appreciate the gravity of their crimes, appreciate it to the full. And Oleinik, in giving evidence here, found the proper words with which to appraise them; he frankly said: "Nothing can be more vile."

I have not the least intention, of course, of attempting in any way to tone down the horrible picture which they themselves have depicted here. I must say that there cannot be any dispute, and I have no dispute with the Prosecution regarding the qualification of the crimes committed, of the facts attending them or of the social-political estimation of these crimes in the present state of affairs when the question of the enhanced responsibility of State employees has been raised and settled in the decree by the supreme authorities.

Under these circumstances, Comrade Judges, the plea that I can make for the mitigation of the punishment of the accused is very limited.

The trials that have taken place in recent years confirm the thesis that in deciding the question of the fate of the accused, in deciding the question which is most important for them—the question of the measures of social defence that should be applied to them—the main, decisive, the fundamental significance attaches to the question as to how you estimate the confessions made by the accused. The indictment treats Gussev's and Sokolov's confessions as if they were made only because they were confronted with obvious and incontrovertible proof of their guilt.

Permit me to say that, when we are discussing the question of the motives for these confessions, we cannot draw conclusions on the basis of any single moment in the life of the accused, particularly that moment when the accused is obliged to confess under the weight of the evidence. These moments cannot be isolated from all the past life of the accused. It is necessary in such cases to examine the personality and to investigate the soil on which the criminal activity, the criminal counter-revolutionary work of the accused matured.

What do we know about Gussev? Gussev comes from a working class family. His father was an engine driver whose earnings were small. The social roots of Gussev make it impossible to consider him as belonging to the enemy class! But by the will of fate and circumstances Gussev associated, received his education, and finally served in the army (I do not deny that he did that voluntarily) with elements who breathed hatred for the Soviet Government.

Permit me to say a few words on the point to which Comrade Vyshinsky drew your particular attention, I mean the fact that Gussev served as a volunteer under Kolchak.

Comrade Judges, when you proceed to examine the motives of his repentance and the sincerity of his confession, remember that, although Gussev was caught at the grave crimes he committed and was obliged to confess because of the weight of evidence against him, he confessed that he had served under Kolchak of his own accord, he confessed that he had volunteered! He told this of his own accord, notwithstanding the fact that he knew that this point would be noted and taken as an aggravating circumstance! Does not this testify to the sincerity of his confession, to the depth of the psychological change that he has undergone?

It seems to me that Gussev is a product of the environment in which he moved, in which he was raised, in which he lived. I would also ask you to note the fact that while he did not attempt to conceal his counter-revolutionary sentiments in this Court, he, for a number of years, until he met Thornton and Monkhouse, kept these sentiments closely to himself and never transformed them into counter-revolutionary deeds. He began to engage in this activity only after he met these honourable gentlemen, and only after he had received instructions—and I will say frankly also after he had received money from them—to engage in it. The decisive role in transforming Gussev's anti-Soviet sentiments into active counter-revolutionary activity was played by these gentlemen.

I am not yet raising the question of the degree of responsibility and of the measure of social defence that ought to be applied to them and to him, but, in order that we may have a proper perspective of the case, it is important to put the chess pieces in their proper places. It is important for us to know who was the agent and who was the instigator, the initiator. And it is undoubtedly Thornton and Monkhouse who were the instigators, the organizers, the initiators. To get a really proper perspective of this case, we must say that these honourable gentlemen received their main instructions from abroad. The threads lead directly to the British Intelligence Service.

During the judicial investigation, the question arose: Did Gussev at any time try to break away from counter-revolutionary activity, did he try to give it up, was he assailed by any doubts on this score, and vacillations?

What do we know? Gussev wanted to break away, but he did not succeed. "We had gone too far," this is what Gussev testifies on this point. He says further that when he first raised the question of stopping his wrecking and spying activity, these honourable gentlemen quite distinctly hinted that if he did try to stop they would get him exposed. Then, for the first time, the spectre of disclosure loomed up before him.

We know from numerous cases of espionage and wrecking that it is usually very difficult for the culprits to break away from this kind of work—that the gripping hand of the agents of the foreign spying organizations never readily release their hold.

When, on the very first day of the judicial investigation, Gussev said that if his life were spared he was prepared to atone for his guilt, the question could not but arise as to the sincerity of this statement. The argument which I presented only a few minutes ago regarding the sincerity of Gussev's confession should, I think, serve as a basis for deciding this question also in Gussev's favour. In the final analysis it is practically impossible to judge the sincerity or insincerity of a person on the basis of judicial material alone.

But if we have no proof of Gussev's sincerity, what proof or even hint is there of his insincerity. In such cases the question is not decided on the basis of direct or indirect judicial evidence.

This, Comrade Judges, is all the information we have concerning Gussev, concerning the change that has taken place in him, and concerning the biographical data that is necessary to enable us to decide his fate.

What kind of person is Sokolov? Let us examine him. Well, perhaps he is a very close link of Gussev's in this chain. Now what does he represent? The same ideology, the same views, more than that, almost the same biography, the same service under Kolchak- everything the same. And at last a common end—together they engaged in counter-revolutionary work, together they sit in the dock, and tomorrow or the day after they will be waiting for your verdict together, waiting for the answer to the question of their further existence, to the question whether they are to continue among the living or not.

In appraising the motives of Sokolov's confession, I ask you, Comrade Judges, to take into account the following. You will find in the case two declarations of sincere repentance written by Sokolov at the O.G.P.U. long before the trial. Moreover, here at the trial, Sokolov even emphasized points which, it seems to me, justify us in answering the question as to whether his repentance is sincere or not, in the affirmative. Sokolov confessed here that his first wrecking acts were committed as far back as 1927, and that these wrecking acts were committed by him without any complicity with MacDonald and the others. This point should be properly weighed. This point should be appreciated. And if Sokolov's repentance is deep, is sincere, does this not testify to the moral regeneration which has begun within him? Does this not testify to the depth of the process which has started within him? It is true that Comrade the Public Prosecutor, in summing up the case for the Prosecution did not mention concretely the measures of social defence which the Prosecution is demanding against the accused. But we, Comrade Judges, know that under the present conditions, in the present circumstances and at the present moment, the charges preferred against Gussev and Sokolov carry the penalty of the supreme measure of social defence.

Permit me to say that even under these conditions, at the present moment, the supreme measure is applied only in exceptional cases, and the application of this supreme measure is expedient and necessary only in those cases where the question of the regeneration of the accused, the question of the possibility of his correction is finally and irrevocably decided in the negative.

Comrade the Public Prosecutor admitted here that both Gussev and Sokolov are second-rate persons even as wreckers. I confess I find it difficult to define their grade but it seems to me that if they can be put into grades, then they ought to be classified as second, third or fourth-rate, but certainly not as the highest or first-rate.

I think, Comrade Judges, that if no doubts assail you concerning their sincerity and the depth of the change which has taken place in their souls, they might hope that in the sentence that will be pronounced here very soon, the sentence of shooting may be commuted to some other measure of social defence.

I come now to the last of my clients—to Oleinik. Comrade Vyshinsky depicted Oleinik in repulsive colours. Oleinik told you nothing good of himself; he also characterized his grave crime pointedly and quite correctly. Oleinik found himself in the dock in the sixth decade of his life. Oleinik had spent many, many years abroad, and here in our Union he worked for a foreign firm. Oleinik became a part of this firm. Oleinik, as he stated here at the trial, said that his relations with his superiors in the firm were such that he found it difficult to deny them anything. When he embarked on his counter-revolutionary work, Oleinik did not at first realize where the borderline was between the legal and permissible and the illegal and impermissible, when he was collecting the kind of information he had a right to collect and when this work passed into the sphere of the illegal. Thus Oleinik, without noticing it himself, began to engage in espionage, began to engage in actions which are liable to serious measures of social defence. Oleinik could not even imagine how he could live without the foreign bosses. Oleinik is a good specialist with much practical experience. He was an obedient employee, an obedient tool in the hands of Citizen Thornton. Mr. Thornton and the people on whose instructions he operated, converted Oleinik into a robot that performed the tasks it was set to do. Even the Prosecution have admitted that in many cases Oleinik tried to carry out the tasks of espionage but did not always succeed. He was not a good robot by any means. You will decide whether or not Oleinik represents that type of incorrigible criminal which it is necessary to destroy. But in deciding this question do not forget, Comrade Judges, that even if we approach the question of the measures of social defence that ought to be applied to Oleinik from the formal point of view, we have to bear in mind that Oleinik was not a State employee, that Oleinik was an employee of Metropolitan-Vickers and that the law of the enhanced responsibility of State employees concerning which so much has been said here cannot be applied to Oleinik.

Comrade Judges, I am drawing the extremely limited, modest, and perhaps insufficiently weighty arguments that can be advanced in defence of my clients, to a close.

I am not inclined in this case to indulge in lyrical interludes, but I should like to ask you that when, in a day or two, you will draw up your verdict, you will draw up that document of world significance, the contents of which will become known throughout the world, in terms that will enable my clients to glean from its words the hope that perhaps, after the lapse of some term, even if it be a long term, they will one day be given the opportunity to join in that great work of constructing socialist society that is going on in our country... That some day, after a long interval of time, they may be able to participate in this construction as useful citizens and to realize to an even greater extent the depth of the abyss into which they have fallen.

The President: Comrade Schwartz, member of the Moscow Collegium of Defence.

Schwartz: Citizen Judges, the present trial is undoubtedly of international importance. The acuteness of its political significance is clear and obvious. Public opinion in the whole of the Soviet Union is unanimous in its feeling of great indignation evoked by the grave crimes which those who sit behind us in the dock have committed. Indeed, we can put the question in this way—is there a country in the world in which technical personnel, specialists could obtain such opportunities for developing their talent, displaying their abilities and working so unhampered and freely as in the Soviet Union? Is there a country where so much care is taken of technical personnel as in this country? That is why it is very regrettable to observe, very regrettable to learn that the wreckers have not yet finally disappeared, that this disgraceful occupation called wrecking has not yet been forgotten and abandoned. Indeed, is there a country where construction is developing at such a pace as it is here? One can take any corner of the Soviet Union, one need only take Dnieprostroy, the envy of Western Europe. And notwithstanding this there are individual specialists who have not forgotten this disgraceful business called wrecking. It cannot but be admitted that the Russian intelligentsia as a whole not only consider it their duty to work for the building up of socialism, but work with great enthusiasm, and in only a few exceptions, a small handful of the intelligentsia, which is lagging behind the masses, has not yet abandoned this disgraceful occupation. Not only the entire Russian intelligentsia, but the great minds of Western Europe also admit the successes of the Soviet Union and together with us strive to work in the interests of socialist construction. I shall not weary you by quoting extracts from many works and books of the intellectuals of Western Europe; permit me only briefly to quote a passage from Romain Rolland's letter to *Izvestia* in which he wrote:

> "Be sure that with all my energy of which I have sufficient reserves, which will last me for many a day to come, I will defend the heroic cause led by the U.S.S.R. After that famous trial which revealed the blight in the heart of the intelligentsia, which took advantage of its privileged position in order to betray the working people from whose midst it has arisen, it is no longer permissible for any honest and right-thinking intellectual to remain neutral. Our place is with the Union of Soviet Socialist Republics of the workers."

This is the voice of a great thinker, of a great intellectual of Western Europe. He is one of the many who, together with the whole Soviet intelligentsia, is fighting for socialist construction.

An important question arose at this trial. It was raised by the Public Prosecutor. It is the question of making a comparison in regard to wrecking, between our State employees and foreign specialists. It is an important question. Of course, you will see from certain arguments advanced at this trial that in particular cases individual foreign specialists were not only accomplices of this wrecking, but even instigators. Of course, it does not follow from this that the gravity of the crimes committed by the Soviet employees is thereby diminished. On the contrary, a Soviet State employee must be of such type that if a foreign specialist makes a proposal to him that is against the interests of the Soviet Union, he must be the first to give such a rebuff as would kill in the foreign specialist all desire to go on instigating wrecking activities.

Only in this way can this question be decided. That is why in my statements, while defending Soviet employees accused of wrecking activities, I will not attempt to argue that they were induced to commit these acts by foreign specialists and therefore they are less responsible. On the contrary, I believe that a Soviet employee must be firm and sound, that he must treat anyone who attempts to induce him to commit such acts in such a manner as to discourage them once and for all.

But you, Comrade Judges, in deciding this question will take into consideration the circumstance which partly speaks in favour of individual accused—you will not forget the role which other specialists, foreign specialists, have played in this.

Sometimes a situation arises when a man is objectively inclined to wrecking activities. Being ideologically an enemy of Soviet construction, he remains passive, let us suppose, for a definite period of time. When, however, to this is added a strong impetus from outside, from a man with a strong will, such a disposition may change into action. I repeat, this does not diminish the responsibility of a State employee, but it explains much and you, Comrade Judges, in your consulting room will also not be able to ignore this question.

Passing to the defence of the individual accused, I must admit, Comrade Judges, one thing, I cannot dispute the evidence. I am defending accused persons whom it is not possible to defend by contesting the evidence against them. Those whom I am defending have admitted their guilt and in this sense my task is somewhat simplified, but in the psychological sense it is very complicated.

The psychological aspect in regard to some of the accused is not the least important thing in this trial. Take a consistent character like that of the accused Sukhoruchkin, the chief of the operating department of the First Moscow Power Station. You heard his evidence. He is undoubtedly a man of strong will. When you, Comrade Judges, will decide the question about him, you will not only estimate the evidence he gave here, but you will also make an estimate of him as a man. And from this point of view permit me to analyse the character of Sukhoruchkin. He committed very grave crimes. He has sincerely admitted them. Remember how he gave his evidence. His inclinations were anti-Soviet. He did not conceal that from you. Step by step, he disclosed all his wrecking activities, hiding nothing from the Supreme Court. All the time I asked myself this question: Does a man of such strong will as Sukhoruchkin, who has disclosed all his crimes from beginning to end here in this Court and previously at the preliminary investigation, deserve to be believed when he says before the Soviet Court that he repents of the crimes committed by him and that he wishes in the future to work honestly in the interests of socialist construction? I think that it is possible to believe such a man.

Parallel to that, of course, I have to put a number of other questions. What was the contributory cause of Sukhoruchkin, who is a great specialist, engaging in these wrecking activities for a number of years? I believe I will be quite right if I say: Yes, he committed very grave crimes against the Soviet Government. Not only did he not justify the trust placed in him, but he crudely and criminally betrayed that trust. This is quite true. But do not forget the environment in which this Sukhoruchkin moved. He did not believe in the successes of the Five-Year Plan. His anti-Soviet inclinations were becoming more and more pronounced. He became a wrecker. But when he became convinced of the successes of the Five-Year Plan, when he began to be convinced that socialist construction is a real thing, that the Soviet Union is making gigantic strides, Sukhoruchkin, as he declared here, definitely and irrevocably broke with the past.

The former chief of the repair and installation department of the First Moscow Power Station, engineer Krasheninnikov, committed great crimes. Now, the interesting thing is to recall how Krasheninnikov, a Soviet engineer, could come to commit such grave crimes against the Soviet Government. It must be admitted that Krasheninnikov did not begin wrecking activities all at once. Gradually, step by step, he, who already had anti-Soviet proclivities, was moved to enter upon this criminal path. Here, of course, other people played a great role. You will recollect that Krasheninnikov formerly worked honestly and sincerely. Then, while at work, he met the British engineer, Jolley. Jolley began to watch engineer Krasheninnikov. Krasheninnikov argues with Jolley, makes him repair the machines more energetically, install them at a more rapid pace, he is insistent, he swears at Jolley and even lodges complaints against him. Remember Krasheninnikov's story. He went to his superior, engineer Ryazanov, to complain about Jolley. Ryazanov, however, poured cold water on his complaints, advised him to treat Jolley with more latitude, and finally it turned out that his superior, engineer Ryazanov, was convicted for wrecking activities. Krasheninnikov succumbed to the influence of his environment, he gradually slipped down on to the path of crime and wrecking activities. Jolley not only got round him, but he even subjected him to his will. And then we saw Krasheninnikov in a counter-revolutionary organization. Hence you see that the influence of the environment, of certain living persons, played no small part in inclining our Soviet engineer towards the criminal career which he later entered. True, the germs were inherent in Krasheninnikov himself before that.

Jolley departed. Krasheninnikov was handed over to his successor. Instead of Jolley, there appeared at the First Moscow Power Station Thornton's representative, Oleinik, bringing with him an envelope with 500 rubles from Thornton, and Krasheninnikov finally became a member of a counter-revolutionary organization. He committed a whole series of crimes. You remember how Krasheninnikov told us, step by step, in detail, about all the wrecking acts he committed at the First Moscow Power Station. They were grave crimes; there can be no doubt about that.

We were interested in learning Krasheninnikov's attitude to all this, his own estimate of his criminal acts against the Soviet Government. He answered that, by the end of 1932, he felt a sharp change coming over him. He understood and realized the great crimes which he had committed against the Soviet Government. He understood and realized that he had betrayed the trust placed in him by the Soviet Government. He repented, and here one detail of his narrative may be recalled. At the end of 1932, when he was torn away from industry, he had the time and the opportunity to think over the criminal path he had traversed in these last years. He himself realized these crimes, he felt a great change coming over him and along with a detailed narrative about the crimes committed by him, he expressed to the Court his sincere and frank repentance.

Permit me to pass on to the last of my clients, lecturer Zorin. He was chief engineer of the thermic group of the rationalization department. With the example of engineer Zorin before us, we can more easily analyse the situation when a Soviet engineer with anti-Soviet inclinations passes on to active wrecking work under the influence of another person.

You will call to mind the history of Zorin's entry into the counter-revolutionary organization. For nine years he worked honestly and conscientiously at the tramway depot. At the same time he was busy in one of the institutes. He worked as a Soviet engineer should work. He worked both scientifically and practically. Everything ran smoothly and well. Of course, he had the germs of a counter-revolutionary in him, undoubtedly, these elements had not been eradicated at that time, but there was no activity of this sort on his part. But when he became chief engineer of the thermic group he met Thornton. You remember from the data of the investigation in this Court how engineer Zorin was gradually, step by step, drawn into the counter-revolutionary organization. There was his first meeting with Thornton. At this meeting Zorin defended the interests of Mosenergo. It was a business meeting. He defended the interests of Mosenergo, and they felt that in Zorin they had a man who might hinder them. They began to take an interest in Zorin. After the meeting there were business conversations in which Zorin was sounded. Talks about contracts not only of the British firm but also of other firms. Zorin gave some information about the competing firms. An experienced man saw at once that Zorin was a suitable person for conversation.

After some time came the next meeting—"the deeper in the wood, the thicker the trees." Talks begin to assume a definite political character. Zorin was being sounded further, but still he continued to defend the interests of Mosenergo. They became still more interested in him. After this came a third meeting. Still Zorin did not yield. He was still being sounded, he was still an object to be prepared and brought round. At the fourth meeting they came closer to business and, finally, only at the fifth meeting, did Thornton succeed in enlisting engineer Zorin into the counter-revolutionary organization.

Citizen Judges, this is a remarkable phenomenon. Here you note a definite position, that Zorin was not to be had immediately for active operations, but that he yielded to the strong will of a stranger. Zorin joined the counter-revolutionary organization. He has admitted that he committed definite wrecking acts. The 1,000 rubles he received from Thornton was an instalment for future wrecking operations. However, his work did not develop, it was cut short by the organs of the government. Approximately, in November, when he received this money, he came to an arrangement with Thornton. In December, Zorin left for his holidays and Thornton left for England. Zorin did not return from his holiday, because he was arrested. That is why the connections with other members of the organization did not have time to mature.

Thus, Citizen Judges, you see that although Zorin's crimes are grave and serious, still, they are not nearly as great as those of other members of the counter-revolutionary organization. True, this is not due to him, since his counter-revolutionary activity was cut short, but objectively they are not nearly as great.

I believe that the fact that my clients admitted their guilt relieves me of the necessity of going into detail as to individual acts of the crimes committed by them, since we have questioned them at great length during the Court proceedings, it is recorded in great detail in their depositions and there is no need to analyse before the Court each particular act of a wrecking nature. But we are faced with a question of great importance, the question as to what we are going to do with them in the future, what can we propose as a concrete measure of social defence in regard to our clients, particularly in regard to Sukhoruchkin, Krasheninnikov and Zorin? Citizen Judges, in this trial the Public Prosecutor raised a very interesting question; not one, but a number of questions in the field of law. It is a well known fact that the Public Prosecutor is a very gifted and learned lawyer, and indeed this excursion into the domain of our law as well as that of foreign countries is both necessary and useful for this question. Permit me to touch only on one question in the domain of criminal law.

Our criminal law knows "measures of social defence." We have discarded the terminology—"crime and punishment." Of course it is not a question of words.

Permit me to remind you that in scientific circles the question was raised many years ago, when the question of terminology was being discussed, as to the meaning of the concept "punishment" and "measures of social defence." Our criminal law adopted the most revolutionary theories in this domain, and it also adopted the concept and the term: measures of social defence.

What does this mean? It means that the idea of vengeance is alien to our Soviet criminal law. The Soviet Court does not wreak vengeance: it protects the dictatorship of the proletariat from enemies, from dangerous acts. That is why the question as to the measure of social defence is connected at the same time with another great question—what may be proposed to the Court when it has before it people who have committed grave crimes, but who are capable of improving in the future? That is why, in these proceedings, the question as to the measure of social defence is one of the great questions. Of course, the measures of social defence must conform to all the requirements set forth in Clause 9 of the Criminal Code.

The Public Prosecutor said in regard to the accused that they are second-rate wreckers. There is no doubt about that. Wrecking has not yet stopped in our country, but with the pace of our construction, with the successes which the Soviet Union registers every day, with the achievements we are witnessing, these crimes are powerless to diminish the growth of Soviet economy. This once again confirms the successes achieved by Soviet economy, the pace at which socialist construction is progressing. For it, no enemies are, or can be, terrifying. When the question is put in this way, Citizen Judges, you can put alongside of it also the other question as to what measure of social defence is to be applied to Krasheninnikov, Sukhoruchkin and Zorin. Is there a guarantee that Krasheninnikov, Sukhoruchkin and Zorin, after they have served a long term in prison, after their sincere repentance, expressed here before the Supreme Court, may continue to work and be useful to the Soviet economic construction? You have heard their evidence, you have seen them for yourselves, Citizen Judges. Remember how they gave their evidence. There may be different kinds of repentance from the point of view of judicial analysis. There is repentance which tends to minimize guilt. You will give no credence to such repentance. But you are studying the accused who are before you and when you are convinced that after repenting they break completely and irrevocably with the past, you will believe that repentance. If you believe them, you will say that they committed grave crimes against the Soviet Government, but that having appreciated their crimes and repented they must bear a severe measure of social defence by being deprived of liberty and, by their work, by intense work rising to the height of fervor and enthusiasm, repair the damage done to Soviet economy.

This is what I ask you, Citizen Judges, and with this permit me to conclude my speech.

The President: Comrade Pines, member of the Moscow Collegium of Defence.

Pines: Comrade Judges, I can quite understand the indignation against the accused in the dock, and the agitation which moved the Public Prosecutor during his speech yesterday and at this morning's session—it is quite natural and follows from the essence and nature of the present trial. Indeed, not only is every lawyer who has taken part in the present proceedings agitated by the circumstances of this case; every honest rank-and-file Soviet citizen finds it difficult to maintain his equanimity in the face of crimes such as those with which the accused are charged; I say difficult, because these crimes were directed against the main branch of Soviet economy, I say more, directed against socialist construction.

However, permit me to assure you that the Defence will exert all its efforts to maintain complete calm and objectivity in the estimation of the activity of each of the accused whose defence has been entrusted to me, because calmness and objectivity are the best concomitants of a correct solution of the problems facing the Defence.

I must say that in my capacity as Counsel for Lobanov, Lebedev and Zivert I was lucky, lucky for the simple reason that all these three accused chose a correct method of self-defence. All of them, at the first examination at the O.G.P.U. as well as at the subsequent examinations and also at the questioning by the Investigating Judge on Important Cases, repented and confessed all they had on their minds. They opened their hearts, kept nothing back, not a single word, not a single incident, but as I said, in their repentance they set out everything they had committed, explained in detail and sincerely how they had arrived at such a pass.

Lobanov, for instance, at his first examination by the O.G.P.U. on March 24 declared: "I decided to confess to the organs of the O.G.P.U. quite frankly and to disclose all the wrecking work carried out by myself and the British expert Nordwall, in deliberately damaging equipment."

It is clear from these very first words of Lobanov's confession that it is useless and superfluous to speak about qualifying the acts with which Lobanov is charged. It comes under Article 58 of the Criminal Code. There can be no dispute with the Prosecution about that.

The accused have admitted that it was deliberate wrecking. Comrade Judges, the task of the Defence is to convince you by practical arguments that where Lobanov says in his evidence that he is a victim of the British expert Nordwall, you must not follow the example of the Public Prosecutor, who for the rest treated Lobanov's evidence with full confidence, but that you must treat this part of Lobanov's evidence also with full confidence.

If there is any divergence of opinion between myself and the representative of the Public Prosecution in relation to Lobanov, it is solely in regard to this circumstance. The Public Prosecutor said: "I do not want to support Lobanov's version that he is Nordwall's victim." But I must frankly say that that is exactly what he is, and from my point of view, there is very weighty and convincing data and material in the case to prove this.

What is Lobanov? Comrade Judges, you always attach considerable importance to the personality, to the social physiognomy of the accused person who is before you in the dock. From this point of view, also, Lobanov has nothing to boast of. He is the son of a manufacturer, the brother of a merchant who rented a flour mill. He was ten years old when he lost his father. His studies at the secondary school and at the university—at Ivanovo Polytechnical Institute—were paid for by his brother. He told you about the environment in which he moved when he was at the secondary school. Who were his companions? They were people who took part in uprisings. They were also children of merchants, children of capitalists. At the Institute too he was in similar surroundings.

And while the Public Prosecutor is quite right in saying that Lobanov came to the Ivanovo Power Station a morally unstable man, I shall add to that, that also in regard to politics he showed himself an equally unstable man politically, or, to put it more correctly, a man without any political views.

Indeed, what convictions can a man have who, while at the Institute, where he studied from 1920-28, not only took no part in social work, but, on his own admission he took no part in political study circles, took no interest in anything outside his technical studies, and, to his shame be it said, he hardly ever read a newspaper.

An anti-Soviet disposition was bred in him and it found expression in his being discontented generally with everything going on around him. He found his salary insufficient, his home not sufficiently comfortable, his conditions of life unfavourable. He came to work at Ivanovo Power Station, let me say, as an ordinary philistine, a petty-bourgeois type . . .

Comrade Judges. You know very well that we have people with anti-Soviet inclinations. However, there is a gulf separating anti-Soviet inclinations and wrecking activity. For wrecking activities, special qualities are required such as fortunately not many possess. It is not sufficient for a man to have anti-Soviet inclinations. It is not sufficient to be dissatisfied with what is going on around and to desire to have something better for oneself. No, a wrecker must be resolute, must have energy, courage and initiative.

I will say that this resolution, this courage coming near to audacity and cynicism, was instilled in Lobanov's mind by none other than the British expert Nordwall.

Comrade Judges, we must admit that the British specialists were not bound down by stereotyped methods of influencing Soviet citizens, State employees. They always made a very careful preliminary study of any Soviet worker before enlisting him for espionage and wrecking work. They carefully studied his past and his psychology, and their method of influencing him was adapted accordingly. Having made the acquaintance of Lobanov and having convinced himself of Lobanov's social origin by private conversations with him during their journeys in the special train from the power station to Ivanovo, he usually carried on conversations with accused Lobanov on these subjects. Comrade Judges, in one of the conversations, and Nordwall himself told us here in the presence of the Court that there were many such conversations, Lobanov began to relate that he was badly provided for, that he lived badly for an engineer. How did the accused Nordwall, who some here have described as almost a bolshevik, react to that? He didn't say to Lobanov—how is it that you are dissatisfied, you, a young Soviet engineer who has just started work at the power station and who, after a short time, were sent to Leningrad to study, to raise your qualifications as an engineer at the expense of the administration of the power station, you, who are a member of the organization of engineering technical workers, who enjoy a number of privileges, advantages and benefits in accordance with your laws, you, a young engineer, who have worked hardly a year at the station and already receive 500 rubles per month, aren't you ashamed of yourself? No, Nordwall didn't say that. Taking into consideration Lobanov's disposition and psychology, Nordwall told him the following: "In England, our engineers live much better than that." And shortly after that, having met Lobanov at the office he tells him plainly: "Well, we have had enough talking, it's time to start work. You will have no reason to complain."

Comrade Judges, it is impossible not to believe Lobanov, to doubt that this is exactly what happened, that none other but Nordwall got him into the counter-revolutionary organization. Lobanov is truthful even when he admits what is to his own disadvantage. Nobody forced him to say that it was he who recruited Lebedev, who was foreman in his department, into the wreckers' organization. This is the best proof that the man has really told everything. We may believe then, that in respect of Nordwall too, Lobanov has told us the actual truth. It is idle for Nordwall to maintain that all this is not true. According to Lebedev, at the social evenings in which the British specialist Elliott took part, the name of Nordwall was very often mentioned in connection with conversations on the subject of wrecking and of his "business" connections with Lobanov.

Thus, Comrade Judges, I consider that the fact that Nordwall influenced and instigated Lobanov is absolutely proved. Lobanov had served altogether about a year at the power station, and it should be noted that it was the very first post he occupied after graduating from the Polytechnic Institute, because in 1928, although he served at the Ivanovo Power Station, it was as a plain draughtsman and afterwards as a constructor. It was only from 1930 that he began to work as an engineer. The meeting with Nordwall took place in 1931. Lobanov is a common-place philistine, not sufficiently experienced as a specialist, had not yet grasped the entire work of all parts of such a colossal enterprise as the Ivanovo Station, and he was incapable of committing wrecking acts independently, on his own initiative. Until the meeting with Nordwall he worked absolutely honestly. This is confirmed by the fact that he was sent to Leningrad. We know that an institution only pays for the studies of those people who have distinguished themselves by their work and by their attitude to their duties.

Now, Comrade Judges, when the question arises—what should be the measure of social defence to be applied to Lobanov, permit me to say that Lobanov is only thirty-five years old, and to ask, should this man, who, although he has committed an exceptionally great crime, was drawn on to that path of crime by another stronger person, should this man, who in this case was inspired by a British specialist, should this man, who was enticed and urged on by others, suffer an exceptionally severe measure of social defence? He is quite a young specialist and if you will mitigate his lot, I do not doubt that in the course of the rest of his life he will be able to prove that he really can and wants to work for the construction of socialism. Comrade Judges, he has assured us of that and allow me to hope that you believe him.

Permit me briefly to draw your attention to the accused, Lebedev and Zivert.

What is their past?

Lebedev is the son of a bookkeeper in Nizhni-Novgorod. He began to work at the age of sixteen. By the time of his arrest he had behind him thirty years' work as a fitter, mechanic and machinist in various State enterprises.

From the first days of the revolution he also worked at his trade. There was not a stain on his character up to that time, and now, in the fifty-third year of his life, this absolutely honest worker takes the path of a wrecker. It is not necessary to adduce surmises, proof or reasons to be firmly convinced that he was put on that path by no other than the British specialist Elliott. Elliott excellently appraised one weakness of Lebedev—his weakness for a drink in company—and he began to get round Lebedev, with the help of Volkova who worked at the Ivanovo Power Station. One evening Elliott appeared with Volkova in Lebedev's apartment and there, after they had a drink and a good meal to the tune of the gramophone, Elliott began his whispering on the subject of wrecking; the intoxicated man gives his consent and after that he acts all the time under the dictates of Lobanov and Elliott.

Lebedev "worked" badly. They were all dissatisfied with Lebedev's work, he felt disgusted with this work, and in 1931, he left the Ivanovo Power Station on his own initiative, having declined all the advantages which the British specialists promised him and he went to work in another institution.

I hope that I may count on Lebedev being given the opportunity of continuing to work in the future.

Now about Zivert. I have still less to say about Zivert, because I am his second Counsel. His first Counsel was the Public Prosecutor himself, who correctly noted that Zivert's crime was a very small one and that he, undoubtedly, was set on the path of wrecking activities by the accused Thornton. Zivert was a man who all his life was taken up with the question of electrification. He said himself that all his life, his aim and object was to study electrification and electrical engineering.

And, when in 1931 at the Ivanovo Power Station he met Thornton, who kindly offered to explain to him all the details of machines and all the technical questions which interested him, he was delighted with this foreign specialist. Here, too, he testified that Thornton was a pleasant and obliging man.

Simple, trustful, old Zivert did not even suspect that the principal subject he was being taught in the study where Thornton helped him in his technical difficulties was the theory and practice of espionage and wrecking; and because of his simplicity and trustfulness Zivert fell a victim to Thornton.

"You shouldn't work so diligently," said Thornton, and at the same time shoves 500 rubles in Zivert's pocket.

Comrade Judges, Zivert very soon discovered what a terrible company he had joined and definitely determined to make his escape.

He left for Dnieprostroy and broke all connections with both Thornton and the other British specialists. Zivert says: "In 1932 I happened to be in Moscow and met Thornton. Thornton offered me work in the Metro-Vickers office. He offered excellent conditions, 1,000 rubles salary, Torgsin cheques and other advantages." Zivert declined this temptation and continued his work at Dnieprostroy.

Comrade Judges, allow me to rely on it that you will take into consideration all the circumstances in which Zivert accidentally became a wrecker, and that you will estimate his crimes in accordance with that and will not deal with him severely.

(At 9:00 p.m. the Court adjourns until 9.20 p.m.)

* * *

Commandant: Rise please. The Court is coming.

The President: Please be seated. The session is resumed. Comrade Smirnov, Member of the Collegium of Defence.

Smirnov: Comrade Judges, the position and the limits of the defence of the accused MacDonald are first of all determined by his admission of those grave State crimes with which he is charged. This admission, to use the terms employed by Comrade the Public Prosecutor, is sincere, honest and courageous, and discloses in all its details the fact of his criminal activities, and not only of his own, but of a number of his accomplices in this case.

Thus, the factual aspect is beyond dispute and, as one of my comrades has already said, there is no basis for contesting evidence. Neither is there any dispute, of course, on the purely juridical question, the question as to how to characterize the criminal activities of MacDonald. They all fit into the framework of those juridical formulae which are contained in the various sub-sections of Article 58 of the Criminal Code. But there is one field, at first glance perhaps a small field, where the manner in which the Public Prosecutor has dealt with the subject seems to me to offer ground for dispute, namely, in regard to the role of MacDonald in the case, the estimate of his personality, his character and his importance.

The Public Prosecutor, in a convincing and talented fashion has given us a general picture of this case of great political and international importance. He has portrayed with unusual lucidity the general background on which the case unfolded. He has given a deep analysis of the case as a whole. But it seems to me that in the allocation given by the Public Prosecutor to the individual figures he was guilty of some, perhaps a considerable, distortion of the perspective. It seems to me that even the small and quite accidental slip which Comrade the Public Prosecutor made in regard to MacDonald (and which he subsequently corrected), to a certain extent shows that the disposition of the figures against this general, huge background was somewhat difficult and therefore—I do not speak and I will not and cannot speak about Monkhouse's and Thornton's guilt—when all these three accused were put together in one group, it seemed to me that the perspective was distorted. In order to explain to you my idea, in order that it should become more convincing, I must, Comrade Judges, unavoidably revert to some biographical traits relating to the civil engineer, MacDonald, as the Public Prosecutor called him.

Who is MacDonald? Let us bring to mind the scanty data which the material in this case offers us. I turn to his questionnaire, I turn to his depositions which are to be found at the end of Volume XII of the dossier of the case. I recall to mind also what he said here at the Court, and there rises before me a picture of a petty-bourgeois British family in which William MacDonald was born in 1903.

According to this questionnaire and his own statements, we know that his father was an engineer. There was a father, mother and the eldest son, this same William. Three years later a girl was born into this family. And six years after that twins were born, a boy and a girl. It is the family of a British engineer, undoubtedly an engineer in a small way, an engineer who moves from one city to another. William was born in London, studied in Sheffield, where, as he deposed, his family now lives.

What is a British engineer? What is an engineer in England? We have heard here and we know, that sometimes, what is called an engineer in England is hardly more than what here we call a mechanic. Obviously, MacDonald's father should be counted among such engineers. I think that I am not mistaken when I say this because we can judge of the hardships of this family, by the same questionnaire.

We know that William MacDonald, at the age of seventeen, without having completed a higher education, went to work at a salary of three pounds a week. From the same questionnaire and the examination of MacDonald, we know that his sister is working in a library and the youngest brother, who is now twenty-one years of age, works somewhere as a bookkeeper. They are all working in the family. All work, with the exception of the already aged mother who keeps house.

Does such a family generally take an interest in politics? Does such a family have any more or less correct idea about the Soviet Union? In MacDonald's biography there is another circumstance which undoubtedly could not but have its reflection in his entire character, psychology and outlook, and finally in his experience of life.

While still a child of ten or eleven years of age he injured his leg and in such a way that the result was a twist of the bone in his hip. He was confined to bed for a couple of months and then for five years he walked with the help of a special appliance. We can see here living evidence of that. He is lame and probably will remain so for the rest of his life. At any rate, ten-year-old William MacDonald was already a cripple, at first confined to his bed and afterwards forced to wear this appliance.

Had his legs been sound, then perhaps they would have taken him into a working class district where he would have met with some other William of a more common type, he would have seen a corner of a life different from his petty-bourgeois, middle-class, intellectual British family, an idea of which I believe you can gain from Dickens' old novels, or from some other novels, which depict this environment.

And now this sixteen-year-old William MacDonald, who had not seen much of life around him and who probably never left the precincts of his garden or courtyard, as soon as he regained strength, and when he had hardly entered high school, was sent to work, obviously by his father. They cannot think of high school, he must go to work and learn to earn money. It is quite clear to me that for this family, personal well-being, personal comfort, formed perhaps the whole limit of all aspirations in life. This fact alone—that William MacDonald who had just turned sixteen, started work at three pounds a week, which is really a miserable pittance and this miserable pittance he was getting for several years—this, to my mind, shows quite definitely what his social position was. It was not only because he was young, not only because he was a cripple that he did not become an officer, but because he was not a representative of that real bourgeois class of British society, of which we can judge likewise by some of the more modern novels. He was not a representative of those families, members of which get their education in Oxford or Cambridge or who sometimes, like Monkhouse, graduate from two faculties of a university and whom the family can allow to complete the highest education in order that they may get on in the world, equipped for that purpose from head to foot.

And now, a few years later, thanks to his father's friends, as William MacDonald deposed, he was offered work in the U.S.S.R. and here they paid him twelve pounds a week. What is Russia? What is Soviet Russia? What was Russia in 1928? How is William MacDonald to know that? Even if we assume that the family did read newspapers, and I suppose they did, they were exclusively

English papers. As for the English papers, I do not remember who it was, I believe one of the accused Englishmen, but someone in Court has told us something about the kind of information printed in English papers about Soviet Russia.

What ideas could he have had about Soviet Russia when he left for the Soviet Union in 1928? What did he know about it and what could he know about it, except that some bolsheviks were ruling the country, that it is a technically backward country which is striving at all costs to overtake and surpass even the most technically and economically advanced capitalist countries, that they need foreign technical equipment and therefore are in need of foreign mechanics, technicians, engineers and that these mechanics, technicians, engineers are being paid good money and that they are valued, that one can live well here, that one can earn so much money that part of it, a considerable part, could be saved and deposited in the bank.

These are the ideas about Russia with which William MacDonald arrived in Moscow in 1928. Citizen Judges, he arrived here absolutely ignorant of the Russian language. He spoke no Russian and there was no place where he could learn Russian. He arrived here without knowing a single word. Perhaps that is why at first he worked close to the Moscow office, in Moscow, in Leningrad, where he met people who knew his native tongue. But, of course, these people are not of working class families.

Then he goes to Zlatoust. When I begin to think of this, Citizen Judges, I feel ashamed, I am pained and horrified at the thought that Russia, of which William MacDonald had properly speaking no idea at all, appeared to him in the terrible and ghastly image of Vassily Alexeyevich Gussev.

He came to the Land of the Soviets. Who met him here? He came to work here. He had heard that a great work was going on here. But the first man he met was one who began to express to him his dissatisfaction with the Soviet system, who before anything else began to tell him that he did not have sufficient pairs of trousers, that he was not dining sufficiently well and according to his tastes, that he lacked this thing and the other, he began talking to him in the exaggerated language of those ideals of philistine well-being to which he had been accustomed in his circle, in his family. And now, Citizen Judges, it appears to me that in order to reveal the substance, the psychological significance of these ideals we would have to have the penetrating, artistic touch of Dostoevsky, it would have to be done with the pen of a great author and not with the pale words of a Counsel for the Defence. And when the accusation is made, not by the representative of the Public Prosecution, but, I regret to say, from the table of the Counsel for the Defence, that MacDonald was the one who corrupted Gussev, I say: It is not true! Whom did MacDonald corrupt? Did he have to corrupt a voluntary henchman of Kolchak who fought in the ranks of the White army against the Bolsheviks, who in 1922 came to the Zlatoust Power Station in the capacity of assistant foreman, and whom these same Bolsheviks gave the opportunity during seven years to rise to the post of chief of that station? Was this Gussev the one whom it was necessary for MacDonald to corrupt? Is it at all possible to corrupt a person who is capable of selling his own country for a few hundred rubles?

The representative of the State Prosecution spoke here about national dignity. I will not use more lofty words, but all my sense of national dignity revolts at the thought that a Soviet engineer, Gussev, who during these seven years made a career for himself which was excellent even from his own point of view, was capable—for 500 rubles—of selling his country to a foreigner.

And when it is said here that MacDonald was the instigator, that MacDonald was the corrupter, that if it were not for MacDonald, Gussev would have been walking the path of righteousness, that Gussev has undergone some sort of a change, then I say: No, there is no change, because we cannot speak of a change in regard to a person who is capable of selling his country for a mess of pottage. And, Citizen Judges, I wish to say in addition, although this has no direct bearing upon MacDonald, that it was even more strange to listen to the argument of my beloved and respected colleague, Pines, who wondered why it was that the "near bolshevik" Nordwall did not teach Lobanov how to behave, that he did not say to him: What are you doing, Lobanov? Is this the way to behave? You ought to work honestly, be an honest Soviet worker! You are living in the land of socialist construction, and, if you do not work with zeal and enthusiasm, you should at least honestly lay your bricks into the foundation of this new edifice. But what does Lobanov's Counsel expect? What do Sukhoruchkin's Counsel and Gussev's Counsel expect? Do they expect an English engineer to come here to teach Russian State employees who, as Pines himself admits, have experienced nothing but fair treatment at the hands of the Soviet Government (even Lobanov had a very good salary) do they expect an English engineer to stop them in their attempts at wrecking?

No, Comrade Judges, I think as does Comrade the Public Prosecutor that this version about the instigation, about the corruption of poor innocent lambs should be cast aside, that this has nothing to do with the case.

I think that these people came here and found themselves on a soil where these poisonous plants, these terrible weeds were growing without being sown.

Now permit me to deal with MacDonald from another angle.

Who was MacDonald? What was the position he occupied in the firm? Was he of any importance in their Moscow office? Was he ever called upon to take part in any conferences? Nobody has ever said that. We are told he was given definite instructions: Go to Zlatoust, go to Zuevka—and he obediently went from place to place when he was told to do so, he did that which he was told to do. At the same time he was assigned tasks and he was told: Remember, you are working for the firm, you are working for a private enterprise, the interests of your employer should be above everything else.

He remembered that, he knew that. In his bourgeois country, in his capitalist England he had acquired from infancy these very ideas, these very conceptions: the interests of the firm above everything else. And when his superior told him that these interests were so-and-so he believed that, particularly, being a disciplined Englishman, it was his business to obey.

Citizen Judges, I think and I believe the representative of the State Prosecution takes a similar view, that there is a tremendous difference between the way in which we must approach the servants of a socialist State, servants who are the masters of their country, on the one hand, and servants of private capital, foreigners, on the other. This is so clear to me that I think that to speak further on this subject would be like spelling out the letters of words which are simple enough as they are.

Yes, he collected information. He was told: "Collect information," and he collected it. When I am told that MacDonald is a cunning and subtle person I say: No, it is not so. But even if he is a cunning person, he is not such in this case, not at this moment, and was not when he appeared before the investigating judges. There this MacDonald did not resort to any cunning, he did not resort to any tricks, and I think that the lines of one of his last depositions are truthful from beginning to end.

Permit me to quote these lines: it is page 58, Volume XII of his depositions of March 17: "I presume that a certain part in my crime was played by the conditions in which I lived, grew up and developed in England." MacDonald himself said this in his deposition on March 17: "These conditions were the usual bourgeois conditions, which did not enable me to understand correctly what is going on in Soviet Russia."

And further: "I did not occupy a big post in the firm. Apparently Thornton and Monkhouse did not think that I was capable of doing important, independent work. I suppose that owing to these personal qualities of mine I was assigned a comparatively small part in the work against the Soviets." I think that there is hardly any ground for questioning the truthfulness of these depositions since the man made them after he had on five or six consecutive days answered in the affirmative to all the questions as to whether he had committed acts of wrecking, whether he had collected espionage information, whether he had organized acts of diversion.

And now, Citizen Judges, from my point of view this should to a large extent be ascribed to the fact that he was a subordinate person, that in the bourgeois—I should say banal sense of the word—he obeyed the orders of his superiors.

I therefore think that it is incorect to put this person in the same light, to put him on the same plane as Monkhouse and Thornton—irrespective of their guilt, but in regard to their possibilities, to their importance, to the opportunities they had of committing the deeds that are ascribed to MacDonald. Such, I think, was MacDonald's role also in Zuevka. The representative of the State Prosecution dealt very cursorily with this episode, and indeed there is no need to repeat what has been said. Even though Kotlyarevsky was not a volunteer under Kolchak, still, he himself speaks of his anti-Soviet sentiments, of his being very dissatisfied with the conditions under which he lived. Kotlyarevsky himself, with rare—I would say even with naive—cynicism, with a complete lack of this sense of national self-esteem, began to tell MacDonald, almost during their very first meeting, about how hard his life was, about how difficult was his material condition, and so on, and accepted 500 rubles from MacDonald. It is true that Kotlyarevsky says he thought that this money was given to him as a loan, but I doubt whether he really thought of returning it; I doubt whether he for a single moment had any intention of returning it. When, during the second meeting, he brought MacDonald the plans, plans which apparently were rather insignificant from the point of view of military espionage, and when he received the second 500 rubles, although he understood that the first sum was not given as a loan, still he did not have manhood enough to decline the offer and, thinking that he was sinking, he decided to sink even more deeply and to take this further sum of 500 rubles.

Accordingly, in this case as well there are no grounds for talking about Kotlyarevsky being corrupted by someone.

Now, Citizen Judges, I therefore think that, in order to put the person of MacDonald in his proper setting and in his proper light, it is necessary to take into account all these circumstances: on the one hand, MacDonald's subordinate position—he was a rank and file engineer, he himself said here—No, something more than a mechanic, but he did not say that he was an engineer; MacDonald who had no diploma—he spent less than a year in the University—MacDonald's position as a rank and file employee of the firm obliged him to submit to his immediate superiors; and, on the other hand, it is necessary to take into account the conditions of his education, of his life, of his work. Add to this the unusually favourable soil on which were growing the most poisonous flowers of espionage and wrecking activity and on which he happened to tread during the very first years of his work at a time when he already could speak a little Russian, could in some way see what was going on around him.

In my opinion there is another very important circumstance which should serve to mitigate MacDonald's fate—that is, his confession. The representative of the State Prosecution himself did not qualify this confession with that commonplace word "sincere." It was a straightforward, conscientious, manly confession.

Indeed the behaviour of MacDonald, of this civil engineer, was unquestionably more manly than the behaviour of the "brave warrior of Mesopotamia," as the representative of the State Prosecutor called Thornton. If you take into account the subordinate position MacDonald held, if you think of the fact that he had to testify not only against Russian engineers, not only against Russian wreckers, but also against his own countrymen, who were his patrons during his stay in Russia, who perhaps will be in a position to decide his career in the future and whom he looked up to as important personages in his own good old England—then you will agree that it took genuine, real courage to make such a confession.

Citizen Judges, when they speak here of change of heart, of an unusually sudden repentance, I seem to detect a false note in that kind of talk, it seems to me that it is psychologically false. But as far as MacDonald is concerned, I think that precisely because of his social roots he is not a class enemy, that perhaps because he comes from a family of workers and it is easier for him to comprehend what is going on in Russia, that therefore, Citizen Judges, his confession is really conscientious and straightforward.

I will not speak of MacDonald undergoing any change of heart. There was talk here regarding Lobanov's youth. And I also in passing want to stress this circumstance which is perhaps not very significant, that the youngest of all the accused in the dock is MacDonald. He is only twenty-nine years old. He is in his thirtieth year. His life is still before him.

I think that perhaps for the first time in his life, MacDonald has now begun to think under the influence of the really enormous events which have taken place in his own life, and under the influence of all these things which he has at last begun to see with his own eyes. When he came here from the peaceful petty-bourgeois environment of England, his teachers were Gussev, Sokolov, Kotlyarevsky. And when he broke away from this school, never mind why, perhaps he indeed for the first time in his life stopped and asked himself: What has happened? Why did it happen? He stopped to think!

Citizen Judges, there is a small circumstance which for some reason no one else has noted. MacDonald left Zuevka in 1932. Afterwards he was in Orekhovo-Zuevo, and so on. I do not think there were any wrecking acts in that period; had there been any, they would have appeared in the indictment. That being the case I would ask: Was it not in September 1932 that MacDonald began to think?

I am led to think so by this small unnoticed circumstance. There was very much talk here about Thornton's notorious deposition on page 26 of his dossier, about "Thornton's list of spies." And you will remember that in this list there are two main groups. One group contains the names of those who belonged to the spying organization, to the wreckers' organization, and twenty-seven names are mentioned with different sub-divisions. Among these names is also that of MacDonald. But then there is a second section where it says: "On March 11, 1933, the following men were members of the organization." And here MacDonald's name is missing. It makes no difference how you view this document, how you view Thornton's depositions—whether you share the viewpoint of the representative of the State Prosecution that in this document the real truth was represented, that, if anything, Thornton was inclined to add names, as he, inadvertantly perhaps, added Gregory's name, rather than drop some, or whether you will share Thornton's viewpoint (I do not know what his Counsel will say regarding this document) and you will say: Yes, there are lying statements in this document. In neither case will there be any grounds to suppose that Thornton forgot about MacDonald. He might have failed to mention Gregory or somebody else, but MacDonald was a sufficiently noticeable figure, he was all the time under Thornton's immediate supervision and influence and I do not think that he could simlpy forget him in this part of his list.

I think that on March 11, 1933, MacDonald no longer belonged to this organization, that they no longer relied upon him. Here we have confirmation of what MacDonald said: "I did not occupy a big post in the firm. Apparently Thornton and Monkhouse did not think that I was capable."

I think, Citizen Judges, that there is of course no need for me and it would be merely wasting time to dwell on the separate episodes, on the separate facts of MacDonald's wrecking or spying activity. I will not speak of that. But I think that the light in which I have presented this activity, the way I understand it, should be taken into account by you. It seems to me that now, as I said, this man has begun to think, that he is at the cross-roads.

There is a document in the case, one that has not been made public, but which I am certain you will examine in your consulting room. It is on page 62 of MacDonald's dossier, where MacDonald says to the Prosecutor of the Republic: Yes, I realize now what I have done, I understand now that I committed a sin against the Soviet Government, that I committed a crime against the Soviet Government, and I give a solemn oath that I will not do it again.

I think that we should give credence to this oath, to this promise. That there is every ground for believing him. I think that you, Citizen Judges, in your sentence will help this man, who has stopped at the cross-roads, to take the honest road of toil and perhaps to become useful in the future to our socialist country.

The President: The Court will adjourn until 10 o'clock tomorrow morning.

(The Court adjourns until 10 a.m. April 17, 1933)

[Signed] V. V. ULRICH
President of the Special Session of the
Supreme Court of the U.S.S.R.
A. F. KOSTYUSHKO
Secretary

MORNING SESSION, APRIL 18, 1933, 10:30 a.m.

Commandant: Please rise. The Court is coming.

The President: Please be seated. The session is resumed. Comrade Braude, member of the Collegium of Defence.

Braude: Citizen Judges. In the course of the judicial investigation, the accused Thornton declared that he was not guilty of anything except collecting economic information, that he denies most of the depositions he made during the inquiries and the preliminary investigation, yet nearly all the accused engineers and Soviet technicians present speak and testify against Thornton. Testimony and evidence are given against Thornton by his subordinates at work, Kutuzova and Oleinik; the depositions and evidence of Thornton's fellow-countryman, his official collaborator and friend, MacDonald, are also against him; against Thornton we have his own personal testimony, written in his own hand and given at the preliminary examination and the enquiries. And I have to admit frankly, Citizen Judges, that from the viewpoint of formal judicial proof, we have against Thornton what is known as an almost complete chain of evidence, which places Thornton's defence in an extremely difficult position. Yet the accused Thornton insists on his categorical denials. From the first moment the judicial investigations commenced to the very last, the accused Thornton declared that he is not guilty; and this circumstance, regardless of the fact that he alone denies this against all the others, without putting at the disposal of the Defence any documents, or facts, beyond his bare denial, imposes upon his Counsel the duty, which is inevitable in the circumstances, namely, to approach the material in the case analytically and to endeavour to build up another version, other suppositions, another hypothesis, different from that which the Prosecution here asserts.

And so, entering upon this task, which is far from simple,

I must note, Comrade Judges, one circumstance: that it is necessary to introduce certain corrections in the situation that has been created in connection with the testimonies of the accused themselves and the speeches of the Defence.

When one listens to the accused in this case, when one listens to all the engineers and technicians who have given testimony against Thornton, one involuntarily comes to the conclusion that all these people have no minds of their own, that all these people lack initiative, will power, that they are people who have nothing of their own, who were held in leading strings by Thornton, who themselves, without Thornton, can do nothing, can not take a single step. Situations of this kind do not occur in actual life. And when one listens to the speeches of the Defence who, in this respect, I hope they will forgive me for saying so, allowed themselves to be led by their clients, a situation is created which, from the viewpoint of ordinary relations, is absolutely absurd; when one of the Counsel for the Defence tries to assert here, perhaps not without humour, but in a somewhat far-fetched manner, that Thornton had his own studio where the theory and practice of espionage were taught, and that Thornton was the director of that studio, I must say to my comrade that this is proof of his great love of theatrical imagery, but that such attempts to embody this imagery in the flesh are hardly plausible.

And when another comrade of the Defence, led three of his clients by the hand as if they were schoolgirls into Thornton's warm embrace, I must say that it was an extremely naive approach towards the clients.

And when a third Counsel tried to argue that Thornton was a seducer, an instigator, without whose influence no one would do anything criminal, I must say again that this was not a sound or normal approach to the case.

Comrade Judges, we in this country are living in an epoch of the sound materialist conception of human relationship. Idealist ravings about a powerful, all-absorbing personality who subjects all who surround him to his own will, who forces all around him to carry out his desires, do not suit us; the mystical images of demons, of evil geniuses who seduce and tempt others, that were depicted in the speeches of the Defence, do not suit us. From the viewpoint of our materialist conception of the world, we know only sound, normal, human mutual relationship and it is on this plane of mutual relationships that I will try to define my assumptions concerning the charges against Thornton.

Turning to the substance of the charges against Thornton, I would draw your attention, Comrade Judges, to the fact that the principal, the most serious and most terrible charge against Thornton is that of wrecking, of organizing acts of diversion, breakdowns; and this charge, which he denies, is indeed a dreadful accusation.

Is it not a dreadful thing when a person is told: you are one of those who concluded with us, with our country, an agreement to help restore our industry, an agreement to render technical assistance; and instead of that, while pretending that you were carrying out this agreement, you destroy our economy, destroy our industry by creating diversions, breakdowns; with one hand you pretend you are building, and with the other hand you are destroying what you are building and are undermining the heroic efforts of the toilers of our country.

I can understand Thornton repudiating these accusations with horror, Thornton instinctively realizing that this is the most dreadful, the most serious of all the charges levelled against him.

But, Comrade Judges, I must say that even in this connection evidence is given against him by all the Soviet engineers and technicians present here in the dock, by his comrade MacDonald, by Kutuzova, by Oleinik, by almost all those in the dock. Yet there is one thing I must emphasize here, and that is that he himself has not testified against himself anywhere. Notwithstanding his numerous testimonies scattered throughout this voluminous file, no matter what state he was in when he made these statements —he says. he was in a state of fatigue but let that lay on his conscience—never, not once, not in a single one of his testimonies, not in a single declaration has he ever admitted that he is guilty of wrecking and acts of diversion. Such an admission you will not find anywhere.

And when, in spite of the fact that he stands alone against all the rest, by bare denials and without giving the Defence any documents or facts which could refute the declarations of the other accused, he continues to assert that he is not guilty, I am compelled to make some analytical attempt of a hypothetical nature in regard to the other accused, namely: perhaps the position is different; perhaps the other accused are trying to throw the whole blame upon him? In this connection I must say a few words.

For us old hands in the sphere of the law, who have had a quarter of a century's experience of court battles, there is one rule that we regard as a fixed rule, and that is, that as a general rule an accused man in Court always deviates from the truth; whether he deliberately tells lies and denies his guilt, or whether he partly admits guilt, or whether he wants to speak the truth or not, he involuntarily always throws in a certain amount of untruth with the truth, which, in the language of legal psychology, is called a reflex protective movement—trying to pretend he is better than he actually is, trying to lessen his guilt. Hence, the practice in our Courts, the practice of our supreme judicial institutions and of our legislative institutions is to approach the testimonies of the accused and so-called denunciations with extreme caution, independently of whether they are false or true. Our supreme judicial institutions give our Courts direct and precise instructions in this matter and they faithfully carry them out. This instruction tells us to be cautious in our attitude to the denunciations of the accomplices of the accused in the Court, having in view that the testimony of the accomplices alone is weak proof; and yesterday our esteemed opponent, Comrade Vyshinsky, who in our country exercises supreme judicial control and supervision over all Court decisions, revealed this viewpoint of our supreme judicial institutions in an extremely definite, precise, and categorical manner. He said: A denunciation is proof only when it is corroborated by other objective data in the case. My esteemed opponent said this in his speech yesterday, and Comrade Vyshinsky remained true to himself to the end in this viewpoint when he withdrew the charge against Gregory because, although Thornton in some testimony or other had denounced Gregory, the Prosecution find that this point in Thornton's testimonies is not corroborated by objective data and for this reason he withdrew the charge against Gregory. The postulate that Comrade Vyshinsky has laid down gives me the right to put the testimonies of the other accused to the test from the viewpoint of available proof.

Comrade Judges, I must say quite frankly that the situation in this case is somewhat different. Here we have not one denunciation, not one testimony, of one of the accused in the case, but we have numerous, collective and even joint testimony from the point of view of the question as to who is giving testimony; for we have testimonies of different categories—from friends and acquaintances, from people who are intimate and from strangers. Outwardly this makes a convincing impression, for here, quantity develops into quality. Nevertheless, Comrade Judges, I must raise the point that even in this context, even in this circumstance, even in this combination of evidence, such a combination of testimony by accomplices may be strong legal proof only if it is impossible to presuppose the presence of a common motive for giving such testimony, of a common psychological reason which, without a preliminary agreement on their part, would dictate their line of behaviour. I have reason for supposing the presence of this motive with more or less conviction. This motive was revealed to me primarily in the speeches of the Defence, in the testimonies of the accused, who, together with the Defence, or rather the Defence with them, tried to prove that they were blind tools, helpless tools in the hands of Thornton. This motive was revealed to me also in the speech of my esteemed opponent, Comrade Vyshinsky, when he uttered the extremely figurative remark that the accused cannot save themselves by hiding behind Thornton's back. I agree that they are trying to do this. But if they are trying to hide behind Thornton's back, then where is the limit to this? And, if they are trying to hide behind Thornton's back, then, perhaps, they are trying to hide not only part of their guilt, but to throw all the blame and all their crimes upon Thornton? I realize that this theory is hypothetical, but I have the right to raise it and the question that inevitably arises on the basis of this formulation is: might they not have committed these crimes, which Thornton denies, without Thornton? Might they not have done it themselves, without his leadership?

Allow me in this connection to say one or two things: In his speech Comrade Vyshinsky explained in a very interesting manner what wrecking is in our country. I would like to be permitted in a few words to touch on this point once more. Wrecking, indeed, is not a new thing for us. From the moment the bourgeois intelligentsia turned away from counter-revolutionary sabotage and found themselves compelled to take up work with the Soviet Government, a section of the bourgeois intelligentsia began to resort to wrecking and, throughout the history of the existence of the Soviet Government, wrecking, as a form of class struggle, has assumed the most varied forms which, finally, merged into one united wrecking organization, with its leading centre in the U.S.S.R.—remember the *bloc* between the "Promparty," the Toiling Peasant's Party, the Mensheviks and the united emigrant centre abroad, known as the "Torgprom," led and subsidized by the most aggressive imperialist circles.

The wrecking organization was smashed by the O.G.P.U. and by our judicial institutions, but remnants of it have without doubt managed to survive in different parts of our Union, in different branches of our national economy. And it is no accident that certain of the accused here were compelled in reply to questions by the Court to admit that they had had some connection with these remnants. It is no accident that certain of the accused were compelled to confess that even before meeting Thornton they had wrecking inclinations, wrecking convictions, the wrecker's psychology. And this is quite comprehensible because the social roots of some of the accused, the bourgeois survivals of others stimulated by the fierce class struggle that is still going on in our Soviet Union, serve them as sufficient stimulus to continue their wrecking and diversional activities against the only workers' state in the world, against their own fatherland.

I will take certain of the accused in this case at random and you will see that my ideas in this respect will be confirmed by the simplest psychological and political analysis.

Gussev, ex-whiteguardist, who fought in the ranks of the White armies against the Red Army, who took part in shedding the blood of the best sons of the toilers. Gussev, as Comrade the Public Prosecutor expressed it, is a hardened counter-revolutionary.

Sokolov, also an ardent whiteguardist who, according to his own confession, had committed acts of wrecking previously.

Zorin, a counter-revolutionary, convinced counter-revolutionary, who here in the Court had to go so far as to say that he even converted his own personal grudges into grudges against society, into resentment against the Soviet Government. Zorin, who represents a hardened type, soaked in old bourgeois prejudices, who has learned nothing during the whole of the creative work of the Soviet Government, a hardened type of a full fledged reactionary pseudo-scientist, tries to convince us that, in order to take up wrecking work, he had to have five conversations, each of a few minutes' duration, with Thornton, and that this fiery Demosthenes—Thornton—was able to convince him and win him over to wrecking acts, and that without Thornton he would not have been able to do it.

And finally, let us take Sukhoruchkin, who in reply to my questions admitted that his counter-revolutionary convictions fully coincided with the committing of wrecking acts, that they were the result of the very essence of his own convictions, of the very essence of his psychology.

Was an urge, a stimulus in the form of Thornton, necessary in these circumstances, when the impulse—the class struggle in our country, when the impulse—bitter hatred toward the Soviet Union and the toilers of our country, already existed?

Involuntarily I have to ask: Can we consider that they needed Thornton? It seems to me (theoretically of course, but it is confirmed also by my psychological considerations) that they could have committed these crimes, without any instigation from outside.

I will ask another question: Has it been proved, in general, that wrecking did take place? Yes, Comrade Judges, I must say frankly that the file of the Commission of Experts to which Comrade the Public Prosecutor refers, convinces me too. So far there has been no objection to it. The honourable names of the members of the Commission of Experts can call forth no doubts as to the correctness of the Commission of Experts' conclusions. So far the accused have been unable to present any documents which might convince us of the incorrectness of the conclusions of the Commission of Experts. Lastly, I have before me persons who of course did not try to slander themselves when they said that they had committed wrecking acts. Of course, I have not the slightest ground for having any doubt that these wrecking acts took place.

But I repeat that it is an extremely great temptation for those who have been proven guilty of committing these wrecking acts, for those who have committed wrecking acts, to try to hide behind the back of the person who represents in this case the most central figure, the person who was the strongest and the most capable of leading, and who was supplied with the funds assigned for the purpose of seducing, for the purpose of using these allegedly timid, miserable and indecisive creatures.

But there remains the testimony of MacDonald, which is also against Thornton. I may be asked: Well, what about MacDonald? What sense was there in his testifying against his comrade, against his friend? I would have to answer this also in the form of the hypotheses which arise from the inter-relation of circumstances, and say that MacDonald is also one of the accused and that all the features, all the strivings, all the reflex protective movements, which are peculiar to the other accused, are peculiar to him also.

And finally, I have to recall to your mind the words that were uttered here by Thornton. Here he is right, logically speaking. MacDonald committed a certain form of crime, he confessed it. Excellent! Then let him answer for it, in so far as he committed it on his own responsibility and has not proved that he did it on the instructions of Thornton.

And, finally, Kutuzova's testimony. A member of the staff. A friend, as was said here at the trial; a great friend, as she emphasized. Where is the solution to the riddle of her testimony? I shall not try to solve riddles, because in reply to Comrade Vyshinsky's question concerning her personal relations with the accused, she herself gave no reply, and I do not consider I have the right to probe into these personal relations, into the subtle shades of feminine character, which might throw light on the nature of these relations. But I will refer to something else. I will refer to her testimony as such. I would like to submit to you the question which you will decide upon in your consulting room. Is her testimony plausible, real? Is it possible, from the viewpoint of the realities of life, that experienced people—Englishmen—calm, cold, serious and sane, would discuss the most dangerous acts, acts of diversion, would draw up the most dangerous plans about breakdowns and wrecking, in the presence of a member of the staff, no matter how friendly her relations with them may have been, if they did not need her in the work, if they had no need to turn to her during the course of the work, and if she were helping them only in their work of gathering information, in the sense of economic espionage; is it likely that they would inform her about this work?

Finally, I would like once more to draw your attention to the last point in this sphere of evidence: to the testimony of Thornton himself. Nowhere, not in one of his depositions, does Thornton confess that he is guilty of wrecking, confess that he is guilty of acts of diversion, confess that he is guilty of doing undermining work. And if the Prosecutor in his extremely interesting speech also dwelt at length upon Thornton's testimony, and if one considers that during the inquiries and the investigation he was speaking the truth in the majority of cases, then it should be logically possible to continue this thought to the end: if he was speaking the truth in the main, in the majority of cases, then he is speaking the truth also when he denies that he is guilty of wrecking.

I turn to the second charge against Thornton, which he denies, a serious charge, the charge of military espionage and espionage in general. And here, Comrade Judges, I must differ from my client. I consider that according to the law of our land I am obliged to do that. We cannot avoid taking into consideration facts which take place in the Court. And if Thornton, in reply to several questions put to him by the Prosecutor and others, had to confess that he collected economic information, then from the point of view of our law, he is guilty, of course, of economic spying. But he denies military spying, and on this point permit me to express some views which, I think, will, to a certain degree, confirm this denial.

First of all, in order to answer the question as to whether Thornton was engaged in military spying or not, I would draw your attention to his testimony which lies in the files. He has there several depositions and in comparing these depositions (I shall not quote them, in order not to burden your attention) only one thing becomes obvious, and that is that his conception of spying is extremely confused, that his conception of espionage information is extremely indefinite and diffused. In one place he speaks about offence and defence possibilities, and in another place about the collection of political information, but gives as examples only economic information, in a third place he speaks about economic information, but gives examples of political information. It is clear that a man, the product of another environment, of another State system, alien to us, alien to the conditions prevailing in our country, cannot quite understand or appreciate what espionage information is.

But, Comrade Judges, if I were asked whether he obtained military information, whether he obtained information which is a State secret, according to the law, then I would have to say: Yes, he undoubtedly did obtain it independently of his subjective intentions, independently of his subjective wishes, and now I will explain why. Owing to the fact that he had already started on the path of illegally collecting economic information, forbidden in our country, and in view of the psychological peculiarities which I have mentioned, he could not determine the boundary between the permissible and the forbidden, between economics and politics, between politics and military secrets. Especially when it was a question of enterprises connected with the production of munitions, it is quite possible that he also accepted military information, although subjectively his desires and intentions were not directed towards military information.

The second factor which convinces me that he obtained military information independently of his subjective desires is the sight of those people who had fallen so low as to betray the interests of their country and, for the sake of a few miserable pence, gave foreigners information, which they accepted for the benefit of a commercial firm, or perhaps to be used in some other manner. People who start on such a business do not care a scrap what kind of information they give, they would sell anything they could get hold of, military and non-military—and bring it to the person who is paying them, even if the latter did not ask for it.

This is why I think it quite possible; but ought he to answer here for subjective intention—this is a question that you must discuss when you retire to consider your verdict. But in discussing the question of economic espionage, which I admit from the viewpoint of the formal qualification contained in Part II of Article 58-6 of the Criminal Code, in discussing the question of the measure of social defence, you will inevitably have to consider another question, as to whom it is you are dealing with, as to the peculiarities of the psychology of the accused Thornton, which definitely requires that you adopt a different attitude towards him than towards our State employees.

Indeed, Comrade Vyshinsky, the Public Prosecutor, informed us yesterday of some extremely interesting points in English law on espionage, but these points refer to "prohibited" places. They refer to State secrets, and what we in our country, in the land of planned economy, in the country of State trade, call economic espionage is, in the capitalist world, with its anarchy of production, its dominating private trade and dominating private property, the ordinary, everyday perfectly usual phenomenon of the competitive struggle within capitalist economy. There, every firm, every commercial enterprise tries to discover the secrets of the other firm, of its customers, of its partners, of its competitors, and of its rivals, and it is a great pity that the accused brought into our land of planned economy the methods of the capitalist world and without the slightest doubt studied our industry not only as its customer, but also as its indisputable rival on the world market in the near future.

And so, from this point of view, from the viewpoint of the difference in psychology, from the viewpoint of the difference in State systems which foster this psychology, you must take into consideration the points which I have just had the honour to raise, when deciding the measure of social defence to be applied to him.

The question of bribes remains. The Public Prosecutor also read out to us here the laws governing bribery in England. They are interesting laws, but they refer to State officials and we, again, are concerned with representatives of capitalist firms and I must say quite frankly that in capitalist society the employer shuts his eyes to the fact that his employee takes money from a customer, from a partner, and so on. The whole trouble is that the accused transferred these methods of capitalist economy to our country, where there is State, planned economy. They look upon their customer, our State, as upon a private owner; here lies their great mistake and misfortune, but psychologically this can well explain their light-minded approach to our State employees.

In that country it is regarded as legitimate, here it is regarded as a serious crime. And it is from the point of view of this difference in mentality, the difference in the State systems, that you will consider this point.

In dealing with various points I must touch upon the question of the bribe. I am inclined to interpret the question of Dolgov rather differently from the way the accused interprets it. No matter whether he gave Dolgov money to be returned or not, the mere fact that he gave a State employee money is a crime. But taking into consideration the psychological position preceding the giving of this money, you will have to admit that he may have been mistaken in this. But did he give a bribe or did he pay money for wrecking activities? Here I must revert to the views that have been expressed here. I do not agree with the statement made by the accused Thornton because I think that the collection of information ought to be paid for; no one will collect economic and political information for nothing. But caught at economic espionage and wrecking, could they not, I put this question to the Court, try to mitigate their guilt by arguing that the money they got for information was given to them as a bribe to commit acts of wrecking?

I would ask you, Comrade Judges, to take all these points into consideration when you consider the question of Thornton.

The President: Comrade Dolmatovsky, member of the Moscow Collegium of Defence.

Dolmatovsky: Comrade Judges, I am defending Gregory and Nordwall. I will not have to speak much about Gregory inasmuch as the evidence presented at the trial proved insufficient, according to the opinion of the Prosecutor, for him to be convicted.

I believe there is no need for me to speak on the subject. I have only one request. I want to ask, whether it will be necessary in order to avoid any misunderstanding later, to translate for Gregory the few words which will be spoken here. I have discussed this matter with Gregory. He knows what was said here yesterday about him and what I will say, and he is quite satisfied that he does not need any translation, but I will ask that the interpreter inform him of my statement.

The President: Very well. Accused Gregory, do you desire that the speech of the Counsel for the Defence in the part dealing with you, should be translated to you sentence by sentence, or will you be satisfied with a subsequent translation from the stenographic records?

Gregory: Yes, it will be satisfactory to read the translation afterwards from the stenographic records.

Dolmatovsky: My task is much more complex with regard to the accused Nordwall. Evidence against Nordwall was given here by a number of persons. Particularly, there is the very important testimony of the accused Lobanov, Oleinik and Thornton, and the circumstances in connection with which the testimony was given.

I will have to analyse these depositions one by one. But before passing to a detailed analysis of the evidence which has been presented here with regard to Nordwall, I must recall what the representative of the Prosecution said here regarding the accused, Lobanov and Oleinik. He used against them sharper expressions than against any of the other accused.

He said of Lobanov that he was a morally depraved type. Lobanov's Counsel wrongly interpreted the words of the representative of the Prosecution to mean that Lobanov was a politically unstable man. There is a great difference between political instability and moral depravity. He spoke of them precisely in this fashion both in the general part of his speech and when he analysed specifically the charges against each one of the accused individually, because he was generally in doubt whether it was possible to believe anything they said. In the general part of his speech he characterized them as wreckers by nature. In characterizing them in this fashion, he said that they would continue the wrecking under all conditions, that is, he considered that they would continue their wrecking, their mischief, even here at the trial, since they were wreckers by nature. In this connection I believe that it is impossible not to dwell on the following points. If we were to assume for a moment that Nordwall is innocent, that he did not participate in the organization which aimed at such grave crimes, if we assume and recall that he was also a foreign specialist who showed himself in a particularly favourable light in the Soviet Union, then the wrecking work these people carried on, their mischief with regard to Nordwall can be understood. If he is really such a person as he appears in the evidence which I presented at the trial; if the attitude shown towards him at Makeyevka is correct, the attitude which was manifested when he was elected to the Presidium at the celebration meeting, when he was introduced to the People's Commissar of Heavy Industry, when he delivered a speech as a member of the Presidium, when he received a premium of 1,000 rubles, when he was written up not only by the local newspapers, but by the newspapers of the capital as well—I presented here a copy of the issue of *Za Industrializatsiu* which described his work and which stated that it was a model of shock work—I repeat, if on the one hand we assume for the moment, temporarily, that he is not guilty, and if on the other hand we remember that the persons who testified against him are of such a kind that they persist even now in their mischief making, we could then understand why they act in this fashion towards Nordwall and why they testified against him. Oleinik sufficiently exposed himself here, and it is characteristic that the Public Prosecutor did not even deem it necessary to place this light weight figure in the scales against the other accused when he weighed the evidence against Nordwall. He did not even think of Oleinik. But I believe that, although it is not worth while recalling Oleinik as one who testified against Nordwall, something of his testimony should be taken into account in favour of Nordwall.

Oleinik characterized Nordwall as a person who was almost a Bolshevik, who might go to the Worker's and Peasant's Inspection and complain, as one who sympathized with the Soviet Government, as a man whom he, Oleinik, regarded with antipathy. He was forced to state why he regarded him with antipathy—because in Makeyevka where his last activities were carried on, Nordwall was very much respected, was very much appreciated for the good work he carried on there. All these points tell in favour of Nordwall and by no means against him. Oleinik was warned by others that because of this, Nordwall was a dangerous man as far as Oleinik was concerned. If he was dangerous to Oleinik, we must, precisely because of this, state that he could not be considered as dangerous.

Oleinik is an insignificant person. Lobanov is much more complex, but this does not mean that Lobanov's testimony at the trial is trustworthy. We must take from his testimony only those parts which harmonize to a certain extent with facts. At any rate it will be necessary to speak in greater detail about Lobanov. I will state why. It seems to me that with regard to Nordwall, Lobanov cannot be believed.

Before passing to details I will deal with the question which took up some part of the speech of the Prosecutor when he accused Nordwall. I have in mind the fur coat which Nordwall gave to Lobanov. In this connection the Prosecutor stated that Nordwall contradicted himself, that he made four wrong statements which exposed him. What are these statements?

The first incorrect statement. He stated that he received 400 rubles from Lobanov for this coat, and not 500 rubles as he later admitted. I nevertheless fail to understand why it is such an important piece of evidence against Nordwall, that he once mentioned 400 rubles and later testified to receiving 500 rubles, and why it is possible to conclude from this that he had tesified falsely. In the first place, he stated in his testimony: "I think 400 rubles." The incident occurred, over a year ago, and later when he began to recall, to check up, he stated that he received 500 rubles. Had he desired to testify falsely, it would have been simpler to name one sum and to stick to it. But if a man begins to dig into his memory and to contradict himself, the contradiction can be explained by the fact that a certain time has elapsed and that he does not remember the facts, and not in the least because he is trying to conceal something. For this reason I fail to see why he had to state 400 rubles instead of 500 rubles, why he qualified it with "I think," and why this constitutes evidence against him.

Another piece of evidence against Nordwall is that he testified that he did not count the money which he received from Lobanov.

In the record there is no evidence of such a statement. Evidently this was not considered of importance, evidently it was considered that the statement was of such a nature that it could not serve as evidence against him. If he would have to deal with Lobanov now, after what has been revealed here at the trial, he would of course have no confidence in him, but at that time, possibly, he did not deem it necessary to count the money because he trusted Lobanov and he therefore simply put the money into his pocket, possibly counting it later when he got home. I do not see in this any serious material which could serve as evidence against Nordwall.

More complex is the question as to how this money was transmitted. Here again Nordwall said that he does not remember how the transaction occurred. Let us see whether this exposes him. He stated at first that he was in need of money and that therefore Taylor was to get the money from his current account—at first he said that Taylor was to get this money in the office of the Metro-Vickers Company, but later when it was verified that there was no record of this in the books, he recalled that apparently this money was transferred through a London bank. This appears in his testimony of March 28 when he stated that he had savings in a British bank amounting to about 300 pounds. Later he recalled that the money was transferred through the bank. On page 253 of the dossier there is a telegram from the bank received by the Court through the Commissariat of Foreign Affairs. Again I cannot understand why this constitutes evidence which could arouse suspicion. If we think the matter over, we can come to a quite different conclusion, that there is nothing in this that could serve as evidence against Nordwall, that it is only forgetfulness. I will say again that if he had simply wanted to testify falsely, then why did he have to contradict himself? He could have simply said that he received 500 rubles and that he gave them to Taylor. Taylor is not here, and this would have settled the matter. And yet he relates everything in detail, how it took place, and it does not at all contradict what he said before, in particular the fact that he has savings of about 300 pounds in a British bank. And we get the telegram which corroborates that the corresponding sum at the corresponding time was paid by his mother in London to Taylor, a sum of 51 pounds which approximately corresponds to 500 rubles. I believe therefore that in this also there is nothing which could be characterized as evidence against Nordwall.

But the Public Prosecutor has pointed out here another circumstance precisely in connection with the incident of the winter coat. The Prosecutor said: Why was Nordwall needed there as an interpreter when the interpreter, Voronin, was on the spot—what need was there of Nordwall? First, we do not know whether there was an interpreter at that moment in the evening when the conversation had to take place with Lobanov. And secondly, even if an interpreter was available at the time, why should we be surprised that Taylor asked his compatriot to speak to Lobanov about the transfer of the fur coat, the more so since Nordwall asked Taylor to leave the money with him here and that Taylor would get this money in the office in London. I believe that in this also there is absolutely nothing that implicates Nordwall.

Of course, he himself has piled up a good many misunderstandings. All of this had to be checked up. But if all of this is carefully weighed it cannot be considered as evidence against Nordwall.

There remains the big and serious question; what was the testimony of Lobanov, the principal accused who implicated Nordwall, and can we trust everything that Lobanov has testified?

Lobanov stated that he frequently met Nordwall. I believe that after the Court proceedings, it should appear that it was rather Nordwall who told the truth when he stated that they did not meet frequently. Lobanov said that he met Nordwall several times during the course of a month in the power station or on the train. Several times a month would mean three or four times, and this was not denied by Lobanov. And yet it was shown that they both worked at the power station, not six months as Lobanov had at first asserted, but only two months. Indeed, Nordwall was at the Ivanovo Electric Power Station only during the first two months of his work in the Union, September and October. It was approximately from the end of September to the middle of November, thus, only two months. They could therefore have met there six times, perhaps eight times, if we believe Lobanov, but not as many times as he said here.

Finally, it surely must be taken into account that these were the first months of Nordwall's work in the Union. Can it be assumed that he could at this time speak Russian so well that he could converse at length with Lobanov and come to an agreement with him, if, of course, there was no other connection between them such as parties, and so forth? But we have learned that Nordwall did not attend these parties. Hence, in this also, he should be believed. Hence, in this also, it is necessary to place under suspicion the testimony of Lobanov, who stated that they had such long detailed conversations that they could come to an agreement to commit grave crimes.

Moreover, he states that in February, namely, when Nordwall had been here four or four and a half months, he used such an expression as "let's stop talking, it's time to get down to work." Again, if this were Lobanov's formulation of Nordwall's thought, well, it could perhaps be considered. But Lobanov has categorically said during the trial: "This is exactly what Nordwall said." I believe that this characteristic, although a small detail, also shows that Lobanov's evidence is absolutely untrustworthy.

Finally, take their conversations. The Public Prosecutor and Lobanov's Counsel allege that in these conversations, Nordwall expressed anti-Soviet opinions. Nordwall did not corroborate this. On the contrary, he denied it, stating that he had expressed opinions of a contrary character. And it is interesting that Lobanov was also forced to admit at the trial (to be sure he said this in a very disparaging way): "Yes, he did say something to the effect that one should carry out one's duty as an employee." In this connection, he spoke, to be sure, very guardedly and evasively, of some objections on the part of Nordwall in this conversation. Hence, again we must rather believe Nordwall, who stated that he had not expressed anti-Soviet opinions, that he had objected to the anti-Soviet arguments of Lobanov. The Public Prosecutor pointed out that if Nordwall was almost a bolshevik, then why had he regarded so lightly these anti-Soviet opinions, why had he not drawn the conclusion which even a near bolshevik should have drawn. But it must be taken into account that their meetings at Ivanovo took place during the first months of Nordwall's work, and then it would also be necessary to know precisely in what form and how sharply Lobanov expressed his anti-Soviet opinions. If they were only expressed in such a form that he was discontented with the attitude towards the engineering and technical personnel, that his living conditions were difficult, and so forth, then, of course, there was no reason to take any action and to report this conversation. They were ordinary conversations which people frequently engage in, and which do not involve such a situation that they should be reported. Consequently, this point also is not correct, not such that it should be placed in the scales as evidence against Nordwall.

If we take other objective facts, we find again that Lobanov always and everywhere testifies falsely. His Counsel said that on March 24, Lobanov stated that he made an honest confession and that he revealed everything. It is sufficient to examine the records of Lobanov's testimony to become convinced that in not one of his depositions did he testify sincerely, that he continually gave false testimony.

Let us take his and Lebedev's testimony. Comrade Vyshinsky, it seems to me, characterizing Lobanov and Lebedev, quite correctly, stated that Lebedev was a much more positive type morally than Lobanov. But up to this moment there are contradictions in the testimony of these two accused and precisely in the question that is very characteristic in general, and for Lebedev in particular, namely, as to how the money was to be distributed. Lobanov testified that he gave money on two occasions, 500 rubles on each occasion, and at the trial he stated that he gave 1,000 rubles—"to impress him." Lebedev, whom one must rather believe, claims that he received 250 rubles of which 30 rubles was taken back as a loan and was not repaid. Who is more trustworthy in this case, Lobanov or Lebedev? Of course, Lebedev. I therefore consider that in the rest of his testimony also we cannot rely on Lobanov. even when he states that he received money, because what interest could he have in saying that this particular person remitted money and not some other person. This is a question which cannot be solved, since Lobanov is capable of anything. Quite correctly, the

Public Prosecutor pointed out that Lobanov was a morally corrupt man and that he is completely untrustworthy.

Of course, least of all could it be said that Lobanov had to be corrupted. It would indeed be ridiculous to say so. Take Ugrumov's testimony: how does he look upon Lobanov? He has always been a disorganizer of production. Indeed his whole personality shows that he needed no impetus from the outside, that he himself was capable of anything, and yet the situation is presented as if Nordwall tempted him and that without Nordwall possibly he would not have taken this terrible path. On the contrary, when his own Counsel asked him at the trial whether he had had a conversation with Nordwall about ceasing his criminal activity, Lobanov contemptuously and scornfully said with regard to Nordwall—I would not have thought of consulting him on this and would have got along without him if need be. But why could he have got along without Nordwall to discontinue the criminal activities, but needed Nordwall's urging to start the criminal activtities? These considerations too can scarcely bear witness against Nordwall. On the contrary, it must be taken into account that it was not Nordwall who could be the initiator of this business.

Then there is another characteristic feature. Lobanov said in the beginning at the confrontation with Lebedev and in his testimony that he did not attend the parties which Elliott arranged in Ivanovo. At the same time it is characteristic that Nordwall did not take part in these parties. The question is, why? If they are one crowd, if they continually meet each other in any case, why should Elliott attend and why not Nordwall? Rather it should be explained by the fact that in reality the people who attended these parties were alien to Nordwall. It is more likely that he was interested in something else—in his work, in his family life. As is known, he married a Soviet citizen, an employee of the State Publishing House, and he was apparently more taken up with these interests than with social evenings and carouses with Lebedev and Lobanov. Why shouldn't he in general meet Lobanov? There was no reason to think that he could not meet him outside of work. Therefore I think that everything that Lobanov said here about Nordwall is more questionable than those things which Nordwall stated here, and I think that it is rather Lobanov who does not tell the truth than Nordwall.

There remains another serious piece of evidence against Nordwall—this is, in the first place, Thornton's list and his depositions concerning Nordwall, particularly in the matter of the 112 rubles, and in general all his depositions about Nordwall. But again, if we take up these depositions in detail we will arrive at the conclusion that there is nothing that can incriminate Nordwall. In the first place, this matter of the 112 rubles was cleared up here during the Court investigation and it was shown that in Makeyevka, where Nordwall directed the installation of the first Soviet blooming mill, he had to incur expenses. Thornton spoke of 112 rubles and Nordwall speaks of 120 rubles. But in the meantime Oleinik, apparently, also mentioned this money when he said that Nordwall allegedly bribed the workers. It is true that neither the Special Session nor the Prosecution even attempted to take up these words of Oleinik's since they saw that there was apparently no reason to trust him in general. But it is evident that this "bribing" of the workers refers to the payment for certain expenses which the firm had to make and of which Thornton speaks in his deposition of March 12, 1933, when he says that this money was entered in the books to Nordwall's credit, that is, that Nordwall presented a bill and was paid for it.

Now what does Thornton have to say essentially about the spying activity of Nordwall? He said this: "Nordwall, Ivanovo and the Tomsk Works." Nordwall's main activity was confined on the one hand to Ivanovo, but not at the Ivanovo Power Station but at the Shuya Station and at the first sub-station where also the certificate was given, which I have submitted here and which was made out by one of his fellow workers—a responsible person, and then most of his activity was also in Makeyevka. Besides this there were short periods—vacation, Minsk, Kuznetskstroy, Balakhno, and so on, but the main work was at Ivanovo and at Makeyevka. Now Thornton says, "Ivanovo and the Tomsk Works." "This man was in Ivanovo for the installation of the sub-station switch and then he directed the installation at the Tomsk Works. Nordwall learned to speak Russian very quickly while he lived in Ivanovo. He was a new person to me and I think that while he was in Ivanovo he gave me no information." He talks about information in Makeyevka, but regarding Ivanovo he says that he thinks he gave no information whatever while he was there.

Of course, the supposition may be made that Thornton says this because it is necessary for him to conceal his criminal work in Ivanovo. But it does not appear from anything, that Thornton had to conceal something in this case. So he says that he was a new man to him.

And further: "When I visited him at the Tomsk Works at the beginning of this year he gave me the following spying information. He confirmed by finding out from someone, I don't know whom, that Metro-Vickers would of course receive an order for the transmission for the planing mill and other equipment. He also gave me general (espionage) information about the living conditions of the workers and so on at Makeyevka."

And further: "We had some difficulty with the induction motors. He fixed this and sent a bill for 112 rubles, which sum I entered in the books to his account.

What was Thornton's further statement about Nordwall?

"In my opinion Nordwall was and is sympathetic towards the Government of this country. He once told me his opinion about the Red Army. I do not remember what it was exactly, but his opinion coincides with mine."

If Nordwall is sympathetic towards the Soviet Government, what he said about the Red Army could only have been something flattering; but what was added by Thornton is irrelevant to the case.

Then further: "Nordwall was for a short time in Kuznetsk with MacDonald. Nordwall considers the Soviet Government stable."

That is what Thornton said about Nordwall. I think that this evidence must be to Nordwall's advantage, and not the reverse.

It is also characteristic that Oleinik, warned by Thornton, says that it was necessary to beware of Nordwall, who was alien to them and almost a bolshevik. This, of course, should be turned to Nordwall's advantage and we must consider that this characterizes him not as a wrecker, but rather as a man who is to be trusted.

Then it is interesting to note that a number of people who gave evidence about other persons to the effect that they took part in acts of wrecking and diversion, for example, MacDonald and Ugrumov, who gave evidence about the group in Ivanovo, never mentioned Nordwall; even Lebedev, when enumerating the members of the group at Ivanovo, sometimes omits Nordwall; he names himself, Lobanov and Elliott but he doesn't name Nordwall, and even when speaking of Nordwall he says only what he heard from Lobanov.

In conclusion, it is characteristic that Lebedev in his evidence says that Nordwall ignored him and speaks of this with resentment. The question suggests itself, if they were accomplices in one group, if they worked in one place—at any rate they worked two months together at the Ivanovo Power Station—why then did Nordwall fail to notice Lebedev? Lebedev, who can be trusted to a greater extent, says that Nordwall had nothing to do with him. More than that, if Nordwall had taken part in the group, he would have come into contact with Lebedev because there would have been no reason or motive for ignoring him.

Thus I think that all the charges which were made here against Nordwall, charges which are of course serious and are based on certain data, must, nevertheless, after the tests to which they were subjected in the Court investigation, be rejected, and I think that if Oleinik considers him to be a dangerous man, we for our part need not consider him dangerous. If Lobanov treats him with contempt, considering that Nordwall is inferior to him, I think he should be placed on a different plane from Lobanov.

I ask the Court to acquit Nordwall.

The President: Comrade Lidov, member of the Moscow Collegium of Defence.

Lidov: The defence of Cushny is a dispute about evidence and a serious dispute about the force and significance of the proof submitted by the Public Prosecutor.

At a trial like the present one, this is a difficult and responsible question. The difficulty of the defence is that the indictment in regard to Cushny is straight and simple. I would say—unusually simple; it is based on three brief statements of the Public Prosecutor. Cushny is mentioned in Thornton's list—consequently he is a spy. Yemelyanov, according to the evidence in one of the volumes of the present case, testified that Cushny, during his stay in Baku, said that it was necessary to damage machinery—consequently he was engaged in acts of diversion. There were conversations at the parties arranged at Medvedev's and at other people's houses—therefore, he was collecting espionage information. Now try and upset these charges. The responsibility falls upon the defence since Cushny himself emphatically denied and continues to deny his guilt. This imposes upon you, as judges, as well as upon myself, as Counsel for the Defence, the duty of verifying the main propositions which the Public Prosecutor submitted for your decision in such a categorical and simple form. We can only verify them by means of a serious analysis, after a serious evaluation of the essence of the proofs.

The main charge against Cushny is the commission of an act of diversion in Baku in 1928. I shall not speak about the fact that this happened in the remote past, five years ago, and we are to examine this event now in 1933. What do we know about this event? If we turn to the source, to the evidence given here in Court by Oleinik who is not well disposed towards Cushny, who has no desire to do anything favourable to Cushny, we see that he told us the following: "The case happened in this way. The stokers changed shifts; instead of experienced stokers in one of the shifts there were inexperienced stokers who joined the shift on their own without the knowledge of the manager. The stokers had no relation whatever to Cushny, they were not in his charge and he was not giving them any orders. The stokers pumped the water, but more than was necessary; the water got into the turbine and caused a stoppage."

This is Oleinik's evidence. This scanty material does not justify us in saying definitely and exactly what happened in Baku in 1928. We have before us neither the report of the investigation of this case, an investigation which undoubtedly took place, nor the Court proceedings which, as Cushny affirms, were instituted against the stokers obviously for negligence, and perhaps against persons who were negligent about this shift. We may or may not believe any particular assertion, but you are unable to do the chief and central thing required of you, as judges, and that is, to verify this proposition, this fact, to estimate and weigh the evidence in the light of all the information that we have at our disposal.

How does my worthy opponent support his conclusions as to Cushny's guilt during his work in Baku? He referred here to Yemelyanov's evidence. We have Yemelyanov's evidence. When examined now in 1933, on being summoned from Baku, he says: "Cushny told me generally, that it was necessary to damage machinery." Two brief lines. When, under what conditions, why—what relation did the fitter Yemelyanov have to these complex installations, did he have any admittance to them, was he asked personally or through somebody else—there is not a word about that in these two lines. The evidence is given in 1933. In the cases of all the other accused, we usually had some confirmation, not only indirect but direct, of the charge of some wrecking activity. We have not a single instance of a case of wrecking that was not prompted by mercenary motives; no wrecking was committed because the man himself wanted to do so. There was always money paid and man was always remunerated.

Can we speak of bribery in the present case? I think I have the right to assert that we cannot.

What does Yemelyanov say about monetary relations? "Sometimes I, like the other workers, borrowed and obtained small sums from Cushny. Sometimes I would return them, but 40 rubles I believe I did not return." That is all that Yemelyanov says—"but 40 rubles I believe I did not return."

Is it conceivable that a Russian worker, who is absolutely uncorrupted, with no anti-Soviet inclinations, and who is not a counter-revolutionary, could be bought for 40 rubles lent to him? Under these conditions can we regard this as proof? Under these conditions, from the point of view of judicial proof, can we consider Yemelyanov's evidence to be reliable judicial proof on this point?

I think that one must really be quite mad, or at any rate a fool, to venture upon such an obviously simple method of action under these conditions. But at any rate we have no grounds for believing that Cushny is a fool. We cannot say that Cushny did not know what he was doing. To say so would mean to admit that Cushny put himself entirely in the hands of Yemelyanov. If Yemelyanov were an honest man, he, after taking the money, would go and denounce him, and he could not do anything else. But if he were a dishonest man, he would, by that, have placed himself in the other's hands and ceased to be master of the situation, he would have become completely dependent upon him, subject to his blackmail, extortions, and so forth.

Does this case resemble the complicated relations which we have in the case of the other accused? I believe that while keeping within the limits of verification of the judicial material, we can and must make the point that Yemelyanov's testimony is not sufficiently categorical; it does not sufficiently set out the circumstances and the motives of the case itself; it is insufficient because of its extreme brevity, because of its indefiniteness and the impossibility of supporting and verifying it by something else; therefore it cannot be taken by us as judicial proof, establishing guilt in the matter of a grave and serious crime against the State.

I have already said that in all the other cases it has always been a question of verifying a particular incident, by testimony or by the examination of one or other of the accused.

Take the accusation against MacDonald. We have continuous verification of the material in the person of, say, Gussev. Take the accused Thornton. Against him there is the evidence of the other accused. But in regard to Yemelyanov I venture to assert that there is no information in the case to the effect that he was suspected of being an accomplice. Until 1933 no proceedings were instituted against him. Just as he was working when Cushny was in Baku, so he continued to work there. During all that time there was no incriminating evidence against him. We must put the question directly and simply— Yemelyanov is an ordinary, simple Russian worker whom, let us assume, Cushny wished to utilize for his wicked aims. And he proposes to him that he should do wrecking work in consideration of an insignificant sum, wrecking work of a most glaring and pernicious character. Is that likely? I believe I am fully justified in submitting to you that this question should be answered in the negative.

But in order to ascertain whether we can deal with this

from the point of view of Cushny's business relations, I think it important briefly to touch upon his life in Baku. The Public Prosecutor has properly stated the question from the point of view of the Prosecution in this matter. The Public Prosecutor has the right to regard every action of the accused with extreme suspicion and caution. The Public Prosecutor raised the point that Cushny was maintaining relations with a number of persons, that he used to visit Yemelyanov and other people, that Cushny made these connections in order to obtain information. But was he getting this information for the purpose of espionage? That is the question. Was he getting this information and was he making these connections in order to obtain data of a definitely criminal nature?

Permit me to draw your attention to the scanty data contained in this thin file called Cushny's dossier, and look at the arguments adduced in connection with this by my worthy opponent.

The Public Prosecutor says that he visited Medvedev. Yes, he did. Medvedev has a wife who speaks English; perhaps it may be possible to find definite clues which point to some sort of relations. Is it possible? Yes, it is possible. But is something else possible? Yes. Perhaps he visited Medvedev simply because his wife spoke English and he as an Englishman took pleasure in being able to speak in his native tongue? Maybe he visited Medvedev because the latter's wife was an interesting person and it was pleasant to speak with her; he is still a young man. Is this also possible?

I understand if the visits paid to Medvedev are looked upon with suspicion, when it is done in order to have them verified. But has anything bad been proved in relation to his acquaintances, his acquaintances of whom he spoke himself in our presence, and of whom we have information in our dossier? No. He attended parties twice at Yemelyanov's, at Bochkarev's, and he was in a restaurant. The Public Prosecutor says that he "used to be" at parties and in restaurants. Let us admit that he was often there. Well, what of it? Was that a counter-revolutionary assembly? Have we in this case a single piece of evidence?

The President: There is evidence in the dossier that Yemelyanov was arrested in connection with the present trial.

Lidov: Quite true—now, in 1933, after the evidence and in connection with the evidence which he gave himself. But I am speaking about data referring to 1928. I shall say a few words about that later on. I do not wish to ignore a single circumstance in the present case or to give you a picture which is exclusively favourable to Cushny. Precisely on the basis of this fact I maintain that Yemelyanov was arrested after he gave this evidence. But who named Yemelyanov and Bochkarev, who spoke about Medvedev? Indeed, we have an absolutely irrefutable document. Did Cushny deny these facts? In the record of March 13 Cushny frankly stated—I visited Yemelyanov, Bochkarev and Medvedev. This is what I spoke about. Of course, these facts must now be verified. It is quite true that Yemelyanov should be suspected. It is quite true that proceedings should be instituted against Yemelyanov. But what kind of meetings were those? We cannot draw the conclusion that because Yemelyanov gave us this evidence now, therefore the persons who visited him in 1928 were of the same definitely suspicious nature. Here again we are in the position that it is impossible to verify this circumstance.

But it is possible to suppose something quite different—that this engineer who came here to work, in the course of his work, meets Yemelyanov and other fitters and mechanics, and that he has not and cannot, by the nature of his work, become part of an intimate circle of specialists, of whom there were not many in Baku in 1928. Can't he sometimes go to the restaurant with his workers, either on his or on their invitation, in order to have a private chat, to learn about the life of the Russian people, to see how they live and to get information? Can we maintain that the information he thus obtained was definitely of a secret nature given for a deliberate purpose by people specially selected, bought or otherwise corrupted? We have no material whatever on this subject.

Permit me also to draw your attention to the fact that such material, if it existed, would certainly have come to light as has happened in relation to the other accused. Such facts were bound to be divulged in one form or another. If the seeds of which the Public Prosecutor spoke were really sown in 1928, you will agree with me that five years is sufficient time in which to verify as to the harvest they yielded in Baku. But we have less data about the Baku Power Station than about the others. Apart from this case, there is no mention of any further acts of a wrecking nature in this region. Therefore, it may be assumed, or presumed, but we cannot, on the basis of these facts, establish it.

The Public Prosecutor maintains that because Cushny sometimes spent his time with the mechanics and fitters, there can be no doubt that he did it in order to get information from them. Granted that this is so, I am ready to adopt the point of view of the Public Prosecutor in order to verify this statement. Let us verify it by Yemelyanov's evidence as to the kind of conversations they carried on, because this is the only source that will help us to throw light on this question. Yemelyanov said, and the Public Prosecutor draws therefrom a very dangerous conclusion, that Cushny took an interest in the moods prevailing in and in the state of supplies for the Red Army. Hence the Public Prosecutor says: here is confirmation of espionage work. But perhaps he took an interest in these moods and in the supply of the Red Army for other purposes, and not for espionage? Perhaps the conversation was only of a general character? We have no indications as to what kind of information was given by any of the company, or what information he received; we only know that he was interested in the moods and in the supply of the Red Army. One may presume that at that time he might have taken an interest in these questions for purposes other than espionage. I think again that nobody can reproach me with being desirous of distorting the perspective of this case.

The year 1928 was the beginning of the Five-Year Plan. A bold challenge was thrown out to the entire world—that in five years we would attempt to do what had taken them many decades to achieve. We invited an Englishman, a specialist, a representative of a powerful country of a high technical standard that he might teach us, as pupils, and give us technical aid. And he knows and understands that. But he knows something else, namely, that this challenge meets with hostility, that at that time, as now, we were confronted with the danger of military action against us so as to stop the progress of the U.S.S.R. Granted that sceptics smiled and said that this was a trifle, but very many people across the frontier understood it and were seriously alarmed. Now do you imagine that any foreigner would not take an interest in what kind of forces we have and whether we could withstand the attacks of some powerful country, say, Great Britain, who considers herself the ruler of the waves? With what forces are you going to meet the attack? What have you exactly, what is your army like, and what is its strength? These are questions which can and must interest a spy, a special Intelligence agent, but they are also questions which interest any foreigner, any traveller, and they are sure to interest him. And if Cushny tells you that he was not interested in such questions, then subjectively it is correct that they didn't enter into the sphere of his special interests, that he did not set himself such tasks, but there may have been and must have been conversations on that topic.

The difference lies in something else. Comrade Judges, the difference lies in what one is interested in, and how one is interested in it. Now about this we have no material in the case. You know a spy is not interested in what the army is like generally. He is interested particularly in what the army has, quantity of ammunition, quantity of armaments, things which we have in all the other cases. But a man who takes a general interest is interested in whether we have something to fight with, whether we have tanks, machine-guns or aeroplanes, or whether we are people who are engaged only in technical studies. And you remember, and I think it is not necessary to remind you, that recently Comrade Voroshilov in the speech delivered to the whole world recalling those years, said that while in those years we had only a few tanks that we had captured from the enemy, now we have excellent armaments. This gives the Public Prosecutor the right to say, as he did say to Thornton in his speech yesterday: "Try them!" Of course, people were bound to be interested in what we had, since they no longer saw these few, isolated tanks. Comrade Smirnov said here that people who came from Great Britain quite wrongly conceived this land as being some fabulous country sometimes as a country in which every person with heterodox ideas is supposed to be roasted in a frying pan, sometimes as some mysterious sort of giant. He was bound to try to understand what kind of sentiments these people had. A man might have come across individuals, here and there, either enthusiastic or dissatisfied, but on the whole the first question must have been—what about your army? Of course, the answers he receives may serve for the purpose of espionage; it may also serve for the purpose of obtaining correct information for Governments and representatives of other countries, which are deciding in different ways the question about our relations. Naturally, Cushny couldn't get away from that, no more than a man can get away from life. But have we solid grounds for asserting that Cushny was collecting certain secret information about particular details of armaments, of the system of armaments, supplies, the quantity of shells, and so on? I repeat that apart from material in a general form, apart from Yemelyanov, we have no material in this case. And from the point of view of judicial proof, this material is not sufficient to support a charge of military espionage.

More than that. I consider, Comrade Judges, that we have some material which forces me as Counsel for the Defence to maintain that there are proofs which not only do not confirm, but which refute the assumptions of the Public Prosecutor on this question, material which is sufficiently convincing, because it emanates from people in respect of whom nobody can say they did not know or knew something but declined to speak. Cushny himself emphatically denied his guilt from the very first moment right up to the end. But there is the list drawn up by Thornton. There, among other names, is also that of Cushny. But is Cushny classed in the list as a military spy? The list is before you. What does it say? He is collecting information of an economic and of a political nature. I am not inclined to think that he could not have collected other information, but in that list Cushny is not described as a man engaged in military espionage. The indictment and the Public Prosecutor put the case in this way: Now MacDonald is a man who gives a direct clue to the case! But MacDonald, in his answer to the question of the Public Prosecutor concerning Cushny said here in the Court: "I presume that Cushny took part in Intelligence work." "I presume." He is very guarded and niggardly in his words.

What does that mean? It means that he cannot say quite definitely. But if he cannot say definitely then, of course, the statement must be verified: what kind of work was it, what was its nature? In this respect we have Kutuzova's evidence. When the question was put to her in Court, she said plainly, Thornton and Monkhouse organized the work of wrecking and were the organizers of the espionage work. If Cushny had played an important role, why didn't she name him, seeing that he worked in the office? This is not accidental. As she herself said, Kutuzova knew everything and it was difficult to hide anything from her. That being so, if the relations were such, if nothing could be concealed from her, she should have known this. I should like to put the question to you from the point of view of judicial proof. Is her evidence to be taken into consideration? It must be.

And now put the categorical, I emphasize the categorical assertion, that definite people were engaged in this activity, alongside of the other points. First, there is no proof against Cushny, except the evidence given by Yemelyanov relating to 1928. Second, we should take into consideration what the President told us here, that proceedings have been taken against Yemelyanov in connection with this case and consequently Yemelyanov has every reason and desire, from motives of self-protection, to say as much as possible about others so as to extricate himself; at any rate, knowing the charges that were brought against other people, he, Yemelyanov, could only utter one general phrase, occupying not more than two lines, in his depositions. Putting all this together, I will say that in the present case there is not sufficient evidence to find Cushny guilty.

But there is one more thing, and this is the main thing. Although my worthy opponent made an extremely attentive approach to the case, nevertheless, in respect of Cushny, he was so brief and sparing of words that he omitted and failed to pay due attention. This is not a reproach. Very often in our work we omit something in our analysis and leave a particular feature not sufficiently explained. In this case it is Oleinik's evidence. Oleinik emphatically maintained in the Court: "I worked until 1929," as he expressed himself, "both in espionage work and in all the other despicable business with Thornton." From 1929 he worked with Monkhouse. It is not my business to go into the question as to whether this is correct or not, but at any rate, this is the evidence as it was given and I am prepared to accept it. Consequently, we must draw the conclusion, that up to 1929 he worked with Thornton. He knew Cushny in 1928, because he worked with him in Baku at that time. Cushny was one of their men, "our man," as they used to say about each other. And now he is not told a single word about Cushny. I understand that in a complicated system of espionage, one spy will never speak about another. This is natural and understandable. It is necessary to check the activity of one man by that of another. But here it is a different matter. They all know each other, and at any rate, a man like Cushny, who is in the centre of the work, could not be kept concealed from Oleinik. Oleinik began to work in the firm earlier, his life, as he himself says, was bound up with the firm, where he acquired a good command of English, where special confidence was shown him and where he was considered as one of their own people. How is it he was never told: "Go to Baku and get in touch with Cushny"? Has Oleinik said anything of the sort? No. In 1932, Thornton reproached him for not doing something properly and said he ought to have taken an example from Cushny, who in 1928 so successfully damaged a turbine in Baku. A strange deposition! It is simply incomprehensible! First of all, Oleinik truly says about himself: "Whatever I did I used to do conscientiously and I also carried out in a most conscientious manner all my work in connection with wrecking and espionage." What he says about himself is true. Then why should Thornton reproach him? What lesson could he give him, and why this conversation in 1932, why set Cushny up as an example to him? On the other hand, in 1928, when it was necessary to tell him about it, nothing was said to him. How is this conversation to be explained? I ask you to consider one incident which made a great impression upon me personally. I cannot draw definite conclusions from it, but in my opinion you, as men who are experienced in testing human relationships in court and in life, cannot ignore this. You remember with what malevolence Oleinik spoke about Nordwall? You could feel the ill will of an old specialist, which he considers himself to be, towards a comparatively young—permit me to use a word which follows from his conception—a young upstart. "These young people come to me and want to teach me; but I know more than they do!" These are his thoughts. Oleinik is to a certain extent ill-disposed to these young British specialists who arrived from England. Perhaps this is understandable.

He is fighting for his existence, for his authority. This man is probably an excellent foreman, and if he had only remained a foreman dealing with turbines and had not engaged in something else, he would have been a valuable worker for us. Hence, we can perhaps understand his somewhat wrong estimation of Cushny. Perhaps the phrase that was uttered by Thornton, we do not know exactly in what form, seemed to be in the nature of a threat. But can the Court arrive at the conclusion that we have here a categorical admission by Thornton made to Oleinik to the effect that in 1928 Cushny carried out that act? Such a conclusion cannot be made.

The conclusion which must be drawn from both the uttered phrase and Thornton's list, as well as from Cushny's statements, is that the collecting of information of an economic and political nature did take place. Yes, but here we approach the question as to how we are to evaluate these actions, and whether they are criminal, and if so to what extent.

I will not repeat what the Public Prosecutor has already said in reference to Article 58-6 of the Criminal Code. That Article of the Criminal Code quite distinctly refers to information that constitutes a State secret and not to the collecting of information in general. There is one exception there—and this is the collecting and communicating of information by the employee of this or that institution which officially prohibits the communication of such information concerning the special work it is engaged in. Cushny does not come under that Article, not being an employee of our State institutions. Consequently the question must be put directly: did Cushny collect information of a secret nature within the meaning of the term—State secret?

It is difficult for me to answer this question. I do not know, it may be presumed, but we have not sufficient data to enable us to state in the verdict that it has been firmly established that Cushny did collect information which falls under the category of State secrets. That being the case, there is some doubt as to whether a verdict of guilty can be passed upon Cushny under Article

58-6. We should not forget to consider certain peculiarities in Cushny's case. If I were to defend a Russian citizen charged with being in such a list, of collecting information of a political or an economic nature for the purpose of communicating it to a foreign State, even if it were information which was not prohibited, I would draw only one conclusion. I would say that this was not only sufficient, but more than sufficient, to charge him with the grave crime and say to him—now please prove that this is not true. This is what the British Act which the Public Prosecutor quoted here has in view. The very fact of such relations, the very fact of communicating information and more so the fact of having obtained monetary remuneration, compels us to put the question as to the public danger of such an act. But it is a different thing when we approach a man like Cushny, who after all is a foreigner, who came to us, and who can and must not only do his work, but cannot help taking an interest in his surroundings, precisely because of the significance, and the great significance of the events going on around him.

I think it would be idle either for the Defence or even for Cushny himself to deny it. Not only he, but all foreigners coming over here are probably instructed to communicate and give information about the life with which they come in contact here.

And we know about it. We read the debates in the House of Commons, not on the situation connected with this trial, debates which reach beyond the study of this or that document and present subjectively a very original opinion, but on the question of relations between different States. We hear them say: according to the reports of our specialists who have been in Russia, such and such phenomena are being observed. And it would be strange if this or that person occupying a responsible position in a commercial enterprise established here would not take an interest in the situation here and would not inform his people about it. And Cushny told us correctly: "When I arrived from any town where I had been working, Thornton or Monkhouse would question me and I would make a report." But can we regard such a report, such information, such a conversation in the same way as we would regard a Russian who would take it into his head to report to

Thornton? I would not dare say a single word, because he is not supposed to go and make special reports even to very esteemed foreigners. But it is a different thing when this is done by Cushny within the limits of his relations. Since we invited him here we have the right to say to him—do not violate the criminal law; do not venture to do what none of our citizens is allowed to do. But a talk with Thornton about the sentiments of the workers, that is your right. You could not help taking an interest in that.

Put yourselves in the position of a man who came to India. Would you not interest yourselves not only in the wonderful flora, and architecture of the country, but, say, also in the sentiments of the toilers, for instance, their attitude towards England? This is quite comprehensible. Cushny would be a liar, and we would not believe it if he had said: "I was a narrow specialist, I worked on turbines, I watched the screws and nuts and blades to see how they were working and then went to bed." Of course he was not like that. Cushny has worked in the U.S.S.R. since 1925. He came over here when he was still a young man. He has been working here for the last eight years. He cannot get away from life. It would have been unnatural. Of course he conversed, of course he took an interest in things. Comrade Judges, you are faced with an extremely complicated task. I understand the Public Proescutor's suspicion. It could not be otherwise, but I repeat that the scanty data before us is not sufficient evidence to convict a man on the charge of collecting information which was a State secret. Sometimes such a conclusion can be drawn because a man buys information and pays for it. With regard to Cushny it is quite different. He paid nobody any money. The petty sums he gave to the workers are not worth talking about.

Let us take the conception of the Prosecution—he gave petty sums. But it cannot be stated with certainty that secret information was obtained; this can only be assumed. I think that he could hardly have expected to obtain secret State information for the 40 rubles he lent to Yemelyanov.

Then, what information could Yemelyanov and other workers supply? This information could only be about the life, about the attitude to what is given to them, and so forth. This is also interesting, this may be injurious to us; but it is not the kind of information which Comrade Vyshinsky spoke about here and the collecting of which is of a criminal nature.

You cannot base a verdict on assumptions. This is an old and simple axiom. You must not draw up such a verdict because an assumption is always the work of our imagination, of the acuteness of our nerve and other sensibilities. One man can make good assumptions, another the reverse. One man formulates his assumptions lucidly and another can hardly put them into shape.

The law is correct. In the practice of law, when it is a question of summing up, assumptions are out of place. There should be only exact conclusions following from proof tested in Court. And we have no proof tested in the Court that would lead us to the irrefutable conclusion that Cushny's guilt has been established on all these three points.

I believe also that the question as to whether Cushny should be convicted or not is not the whole question. That is not the question. This is one of the episodes of this great trial. The verdict will be just as important and just as convincing whether Cushny is convicted or acquitted. But in approaching this question I should like to stress that in my opinion it is necessary to avoid in this verdict everything that might cast a doubt upon its reliability and its force, and when there is any question of doubt at the judicial investigation, then the verdict must not be one of guilty.

The Prosecution itself have shown in the clearest possible fashion that in regard to Cushny we have a case open to great doubt. I refer to the last part of those arguments Comrade Vyshinsky advanced in addressing you when, instead of facts, he gave an estimate of Cushny's behaviour at the preliminary examination. You remember what Vyshinsky said: At the preliminary examination Cushny declined to answer questions. Cushny behaved like a tried and experienced spy. And he contrasted Cushny with Thornton who had immediately told everything. True, the conclusion from this is an unfavourable one; because Thornton told everything, he is an agent, though a bad one, while Cushny, because he told nothing, is also an agent.

Let us not speak of this, however, but of whether it is possible to take this behaviour as evidence against Cushny. Is it possible to offer this to you as judicial proof of guilt? I think that in this respect the Public Prosecutor is wrong and I have the right to raise this question. Did Cushny decline to give evidence at the preliminary investigation? Did he keep silent? Glance at the dossier. Cushny was arrested on the night of March 12. On March 13, he gave detailed testimony in answer to all the questions submitted to him. On March 13, as I said before, he enumerated a number of acquaintances he had in Baku, and told in detail about everything he was asked, about everything which was of interest to the examiners. I consider that an experienced agent would understand at once what it was all about and would at once decline to speak, but here names were given and confirmed, a possibility is offered of verification, of following up the clue. All the connections, all the threads were shown. I have the right to assert that on March 13 Cushny gave evidence.

Two days after that, on March 15, there was a confrontation and an examination. Cushny spoke, gave evidence, confirmed one thing, denied another. On March 22, Cushny said what he has repeated here several times. We, of course, are only going by the records and it is possible that there were intermediate conversations, not of a sufficiently concrete nature, and which were not entered in the records. But up to March 22, Cushny continued to give explanations at the confrontation. He spoke with and contradicted Thornton, declaring that the latter's evidence was correct in one part and wrong in another; he emphatically denied the charge of military espionage, and so forth; he told about the conversations and how they proceeded, and about the kind of information given. Cushny did speak. And only after that, at the second examination on that very day, March 22, when he was asked to name the Russian citizens from whom he had obtained his information and when a number of other questions were put, Cushny replied: "I do not wish to answer or to give any further evidence."

Let us dwell for a moment on this question: Is it, indeed, possible to explain it only in the way the Public Prosecutor has done? I think that if such great importance is attached to this question, it should have been possible to examine Cushny on the subject.

I, for one, as Counsel for the Defence, cannot give evidence on Cushny's behalf. I asked him afterwards but I am not here as a witness.

But if such importance was attached to this point, why was not Cushny asked during the Court investigation: "Why did you not wish to give that evidence," and Cushny would probably have explained why. I do not know whether it would have been convincing for you or not, but we could have verified it and drawn our conclusions. But when the Prosecution leaves this point out, when they do not attach any importance to it, I must say that the accused himself has equally the right not to touch on the question. And why was it possible to attach no importance to it? I have put the question to you whether it is only spies who have a right to be silent. Don't we say in Court to every accused that he has a right to refuse to answer any question he does not wish to answer? And does such a refusal to answer serve as proof of guilt? Never! Does not an Investigating Judge, who, as the Public Prosecutor truly said, in our conditions not only makes charges but also safeguards the interests and the rights of the accused, does not the Investigating Judge say that if you do not wish to answer, it is your right not to do so? Of course, it is much worse if you don't, because you put difficulties in the way of the examination, but generally, you need not answer questions. Isn't this said? And why is it said? Because the law understands that the position of the accused is so difficult and complicated that sometimes he of course has the right not to answer certain questions and there is no need for me to conjecture why this is done, because in this case I shall be speaking onesidely and without data. But you should not overlook even a single line of the evidence.

On March 13, Cushny incidentally answered one question. "Among your acquaintances was there a woman with whom you were in close relations?" He answered: "Yes," and gave the name. Note what happened further. After that, one of the witnesses in this case affirms that the information was given to him by a woman, a close acquaintance. On March 22, the question was put in a different way. Cushny learned that a charge of espionage was being made against him—whether this charge was justified or not, from his point of view, is a different matter—and he said:

"I repudiate it. I think I am not guilty of it." But they continued to accuse him of espionage. He understood that this is a serious crime. He was asked a specific question: "And who gave this information?" He replied: "I do not want to give names." Not give the names—it would be more correct to say, I do not wish to repeat them. This is an essential difference. Precisely: I do not want to repeat them; because they had already been given, but it seems to him that to repeat them in this aspect would cause these people a lot of unpleasantness and embarrassing examination and questioning. This was his right and I cannot say that any other conclusion can be drawn from it except that one may assume that he had serious reasons for not giving evidence. But here in Court, did Cushny utter a single word about wishing to withhold any names? Was there a single question he did not answer? He is not silent here; on the contrary he speaks. Therefore, let us approach this question in the way we ought to approach it. His behaviour when he made his statement does not give us the right to draw conclusions either in his favour, or against him. It was a point which, if we attach any importance to it, ought to be properly elucidated here first.

Now, Comrade Judges, permit me to sum up the whole case as Comrade the Public Prosecutor did. I consider that in consequence of the Court investigation which has taken place before you, in regard to military espionage there is no confirmation of the espionage work in the special sense of the word which calls for punishment, on the contrary it is refuted by the evidence of Kutuzova.

Concerning the wrecking work we must come to the conclusion that we have not sufficient data, because after 1928 there is not a hint as to any acts, either in Baku or in any other place, with which Cushny was concerned.

I must beg your pardon, I made a mistake. Apart from the question of the turbine blades. True, the Public Prosecutor in his speech did not incriminate him in particular, but it follows from the general context, because he, too, had turbines and in his case, too, blades broke. We have the indisputable fact, confirmed by the experts, that the structure of the blades was faulty. Consequently, there were faulty details in the structure of the machine. But Cushny was only installing, only assembling the blades. I do not know whether the machines arrived from England with the blades fixed already or whether they were fixed here, but he was only installing them and not making them. Here various conclusions can be drawn. It may be suspected that someone, somewhere, intentionally built such blades, but Cushny answers here only for himself, and only for failing to adopt measures which he ought to have adopted. And we know in this case that not only did he make declarations about it, but that on the basis of the declarations and statements which he made and which the State institutions made, commissions were appointed and, after long discussions, various measures were drawn up, but these measures were not completely elaborated. This circumstance does not by itself serve as evidence that he was guilty of committing wrecking work, by permitting the turbines to run with such blades. This does not follow from the data which we have.

There remains the collecting of economic and political information, about which I have spoken. Here there may be two points of view. I consider that in so far as it has not been established by the Public Prosecutor that this information was in the nature of a State secret, you, in giving your verdict, will have to take into consideration the arguments of both sides and make a decision accordingly.

I think that with this I can conclude my speech, and I make so bold as to put it to you that you are entitled to draw the conclusion that his guilt has not been proven, because if the verdict in this case wil be of great importance in general, that part of the verdict which will exonerate Cushny of guilt will have an even louder and more convincing echo. If the verdict contains the statement that, in spite of the request of the Public Prosecutor, the Court finds that Cushny has not been clearly proved guilty of wrecking activities and of military espionage, it will be an additional proof that the road from a Soviet Court leads not only to prison, as is the opinion expressed in London, to which the Public Prosecutor referred, but also to freedom. The prison doors must close on those whose guilt has been irrefutably and fully established, because the State must deal thus with every one who tries to damage and undermine its power. But for those whose guilt is in doubt, the path to freedom must be open, however forcibly and authoritatively the Public Prosecutor may plead, because where there is doubt a Soviet Court does not convict.

The President: The Court will now adjourn.

(At 12:40 p.m. the Court adjourns until 1:10 p.m.)

* * *

Commandant: Please rise. The Court is coming.

The President: Please be seated. The session is resumed. Comrade Kommodov, member of the Moscow Collegium of Defence.

Kommodov: Comrade Judges, one may envy the simplicity of those who suppose, and sometimes even assert, that every foreign specialist who comes to the Soviet Union to work does so in one mood—the mood of creative enthusiasm—and consequently cannot be a spy or a counter-revolutionary or a wrecker. I am not so idealistic. Man is man, and as such, his behaviour is guided by impulses. The impulse itself is created by the influence of all kinds of social and psychological factors, upbringing, education, environment, origin, traditions, the conditions of private life, social status and so forth. That is why it is impossible, of course, to assert that all the foreign specialists who come here do so with a single aim. There are doubtless some who come here and bring with them anti-Soviet sentiments, and who, guided by them, perhaps, do more wrecking than good work. I do not for a moment assert, or even assume, that these are the majority. Oh no, I think that the majority, the overwhelming majority of foreign specialists in our country are working honestly and conscientiously. Some of them, perhaps, are conscientious in their work because of professional honesty—as officials; they have taken certain duties upon themselves and they conscientiously fulfil them. In others this degree of professional conscientiousness is probably supplemented by a large measure of curiosity and interest in working under new conditions, in a new and hitherto unknown social system, at new rates of development; and perhaps, when they observe the creative urge of a densely populated country which, with tremendous enthusiasm, sometimes under great hardships, is realizing and embodying ideas which are the finest creations of the human mind, they as honest men, cannot but be stirred. The creative urge of a great people cannot fail to move them. I am convinced that some of them are working with no less enthusiasm than the whole country is working; they are sincere friends of the Soviet Union who understand that the ideal which is the life and soul of the Soviet Union is the ideal of the whole of humanity, that the society which is being built, sooner or later, will be inevitably achieved, that it will become the life of all.

But while holding this conception of the work of foreign specialists, I think, nevertheless, that there may be individual representatives who really come here more for the purpose of wrecking than of working.

This has to be borne in mind in every concrete case. And we find that instances of prosecution of foreign specialists are indeed rare exceptions here. Wrecking, as a means of deliberately destroying the economic life of the nation, as a means of retarding its development, is well known to us in connection with previous trials—the "Industrial Party" case, the Menshevik case, and more especially the Shakhty case. But it is a rare phenomenon—this prosecution of foreign specialists. This is due not only to the carefulness of the authorities, but chiefly to the fact that on the whole, foreign specialists work conscientiously; because in each individual case, when a foreign specialist exceeds the bounds of Soviet law he is criminally prosecuted, and in this respect, his foreign origin and his foreign citizenship affords him no immunity. It is time everybody understood that.

But leaving aside these generalities and turning directly to the personal defence of Monkhouse, the question naturally arises, which of these two categories applies to Monkhouse; does he come under the majority, who honestly and conscientiously carry out the duties undertaken for various motives, or under the wretched minority who forget their duty and, perhaps, under the influence of personal convictions, work unconscientiously and sometimes criminally.

You have heard, Comrade Judges, that the charge against Monkhouse is presented in full scope as given in the indictment.

The charge against Monkhouse embodies the three main lines characterized as espionage, wrecking and bribery.

On the other hand, you have heard Monkhouse's denial of his guilt. In the office of the Public Prosecutor, when he was presented with the indictment, he said: "I don't consider myself guilty of spying; I don't consider myself guilty of wrecking; I can confess myself guilty of being a party to bribery."

Thus, we have two mutually exclusive conceptions.

Our task, as parties to this case, is to present the arguments confirming one or the other version; while from the furnace of the Court's deliberations, on the basis of the material at your disposal, will emerge the truth which will be expressed in your verdict, before which we shall bow our heads in silence.

You understand, Comrade Judges, that in cases of this kind there can be no room for emotional pleading on the part of the Defence. Therefore I shall oppose to the high talent of the other side a careful, detailed, I might even say commonplace analysis of the evidence brought against Monkhouse. I shall conduct this defence, trying as far as possible not to attack anyone at all. To be in the dock is a serious matter for anybody. There is no official standard by which to measure the sufferings of a man when misfortune comes his way, and it is impossible to say whose lot is the hardest. There is no need for me to make anybody's lot harder and I shall try to avoid doing so.

What is the main basis of the charge in the present case? It is not Kutuzova's evidence, of course; neither is it Oleinik's evidence. Even if these were laid aside, the main features of the charge would hold good just the same. The chief basis of the charge is the Zlatoust affair. That is my viewpoint. Gussev's testimony, Sokolov's testimony, MacDonald's testimony, the information given by different people, at different times, and complementing and corroborating each other, sealed by incontestible facts, and the findings of the Commission of Experts—all this forms the basis which, for us of the Defence, is damning in the sense of the conflict of evidence presented.

In the Zlatoust affair especially, all the main lines of the charge—espionage, bribery and wrecking—found precise and strinking expression.

The question of espionage is always a disputable one. English law to which Comrade Vyshinsky referred yesterday contains a very broad interpretation of espionage. And the most important thing to note is that the centre of gravity there is not the objective factors, not the question of what papers and what information were taken, but the subjective factors, namely, what purpose was followed in taking them. Therefore, the width and breadth of interpretation is here very great.

Our law is more just in this respect. Our law, in Article 58-6, takes the objective factors into consideration. This Article, as you know, falls into two parts. The first concerns secrets especially guarded by the law. The second concerns matters which are merely not to be made public.

That is more just. I would say it is more humane. And it leaves no scope for arbitrary personal discretion. But from the standpoint of this more circumscribed law, the espionage which took place at the Zlatoust Power Station leaves no room for doubt in the mind of anyone. It is definitely espionage; for while the character of the information given, whether it is economic or political, may still be open to discussion, it is nevertheless clear to all that when information is given as to the type of shells, or the type of aeroplane engines, or the capacity of munitions production, it is absolutely beyond dispute that this involves a specially guarded State secret.

This is why I say that in this affair, in the Zlatoust affair, all three main lines of the charge assume precise and striking form.

And now I take the liberty of putting a rhetorical question: is it conceivable, is it possible to imagine that one of the most active wreckers who, according to the sense of the indictment, headed the organization, played no part in this work, either directly or indirectly. Let us, in this case, examine the testimony of those who acted as living perpetrators of spying, wrecking and bribery. You heard the testimony given here by Gussev, Sokolov and MacDonald, with exhaustive fullness, with absolute sincerity; and though this sincerity may be the best argument in their defence, be they Englishmen or Russians, the fact remains that they scourged themselves. And, after all, in these testimonies, which were not mere statements, but gave facts, is there a single reference to Monkhouse? Gussev and Sokolov were before you. I put the question emphatically: you said from whom you obtained information, you said to whom you gave information, you said who it was gave you money, but was Monkhouse directly connected with you in any way, or at any time? I got a negative reply. Perhaps you will tell me that this was natural fear on the part of the Russian engineers. I can allow that. But MacDonald is his colleague, MacDonald is his fellow-countryman and I put the question to MacDonald and got the same answer. Comrade Vyshinsky pointed out that one of MacDonald's statements indicates that Monkhouse was the firm's chief and also took part in this illegal activity. That is true, but it should not be forgotten that here in Court, Monkhouse testified to what he thought, what he supposed, and did so not only at the trial. I have the deposition of MacDonald made at the preliminary investigation, page 64, Volume XII, where he says: "I deem it necessary to request to put on record of this interrogation that all directions and instructions on espionage and organization of breakdowns and damaging of machines I received from Mr. Thornton. I deem it necessary also to mention in this protocol that information of spying nature which was passed by me to Mr. Thornton, the latter passed on to the Inteligence Service."

Then another testimony: "I confirmed my guilt in the following . . . that all these crimes against the U.S.S.R. I carried out not only in conjunction with Russian engineers and technicians involved by me but also in conjunction with other employees of the Metropolitan-Vickers Company and whose names were given by me in previous testimonies, directly with Mr. Thornton, supposing the participation in these activities of Messrs. Monkhouse, Cushny and Noel."

This he confirmed also in the Court. But I put the question in another way. There, on the spot, when you were carrying out your wrecking plans, when you were doing spying work, when you received information, when you took money, did you then have any connection with Monkhouse? He answered in the negative. And yet we cannot suspect MacDonald of being biased in favour of his fellow-countrymen, because MacDonald, whose testimony I believe, did mention that he gave to Thornton, his fellow-countryman, information, and so if he remained silent about Monkhouse, it was no accident. I know the objection that will be raised, and which follows logically. It will be said: was Monkhouse necessary when they had Thornton as an intermediary? I shall deal with this question in particular when I analyse the private and business relations between Monkhouse and Thornton. It is the most dangerous point for Monkhouse. I know that. But for the time being, allow me to deal solely with the facts.

These were the circumstances in connection with the Zlatoust Power Station. Take the wrecking activities at other power stations and, Comrade Judges, you will find the same thing. The majority gave testimony that cannot be disbelieved. Some testified with such fervour that their sincerity seemed too overwhelming. Well? Not a single one of these testimonies mention the name of Monkhouse. For me, Comrade Judges, the testimonies of the engineers who worked at the Moscow Power Station are especially important for the following reasons. Oleinik in one of his testimonies said: when Monkhouse sent me to the Moscow Power Station, he said—you will find a group of engineers there who are in sympathy with our firm. And one of them—he mentioned Krasheninnikov—is a "good chap." In the subjective perceptions of Oleinik this has now formed itself into the characterization of a wrecker. For me it is not important how this thought formed itself in the subjective perceptions of Oleinik; I shall take only the facts into consideration.

It would seem, under these circumstances, that it was absolutely essential that there should be direct connection between those who were working and carrying on wrecking at the Moscow Power Station, and Monkhouse. You had before you the accused: Zorin, Krasheninnikov and Sukhoruchkin. Did they say a single word or drop a single hint about Monkhouse? Did they affirm their own direct connection with him? Yet their testimonies were very strong. Take the sincere testimony of Sukhoruchkin, who virtually flayed himself in his contrition—dreadful, convincing testimony. Moreover, is it possible that Sukhoruchkin, in whom a profound spiritual change has taken place, would have spared anyone? For he speaks about Thornton just as simply and with the same sincerity as he speaks about himself. It is your business to believe or disbelieve the testimony he gave in Court about the others; but the important thing for me is that he did not say a single word about Monkhouse, just as Krasheninnikov and Zorin said nothing about him. I will add yet another point. While it could be said that because of the post Monkhouse occupied, he did not go to the provinces frequently, the Moscow Power Station, however, is quite near, and yet you do not see the link, the connection, which should naturally have existed between individual wreckers and Monkhouse. There is none. Is this also an accident?

Thus, it appears that not a single one of the wreckers, who actually perpetrated wrecking in the places where their grave crimes were committed, gave evidence against Monkhouse.

True, one of the accused gave evidence against Monkhouse, and I shall not ignore it. I refer to Oleinik's testimony. I should like to approach the evidence given here with the assumption that a certain amount of confidence can be placed in it. The Public Prosecutor characterized Oleinik as a man who cannot refrain from speaking. He certainly talked, but this is not what is important for me.

Leaving aside all the subjective motives which induced Oleinik to talk so volubly, I will deal only with that part of his evidence in which he points out that Monkhouse was involved. Consequently, I quite correctly put him the question: Tell me, Oleinik, what concrete tasks of a spying and diversional character did Monkhouse give to you? Permit me to make one general remark concerning Oleinik's evidence. Oleinik declared here, and it is indisputably established, that he had dealings with Monkhouse before 1929. After 1929, he ceased to have any direct business dealings with him, but such dealings were established between him and Thornton. I next put the question: Did you commit any wrecking acts before 1929? He answered in the negative, and this is the truth. Thus, in this case also, we come to the conclusion that during the time when Oleinik was in direct touch with Monkhouse, he committed no wrecking acts. In reply to the question of the investigator, Oleinik referred to two cases in which, according to Oleinik, Monkhouse's association is beyond doubt.

Permit me to take Oleinik's evidence without changing a single word; I will say more, Comrade Judges, permit me to take the evidence of Oleinik, believing him.

Question: "What tasks in the nature of espionage and diversion were given you by Monkhouse?"

Oleinik answered: "In 1928, when I went to the Urals, I was instructed to find out about the condition of the works to which I was going, namely, the Nadezhdinsk Works, and, in general, about the state of transport and industry in the Urals."

What was Oleinik's estimate of a job of this kind?

The next question put was: "State in detail how you were drawn into the espionage work?" and he replied: "I worked for the firm for a long time. At first I was given the task of gathering information about the state of industry in connection with the orders, this being connected with the work of the firm. This was in 1928. I considered that I was obliged to do so in the interests of the firm. In 1931, Mr. Thornton told me that it was necessary to obtain information about the state of industry, transport, and electrical energy. And in 1932, Mr. Thornton quite clearly told me that it was necessary to select people for espionage and acts of diversion."

What does this tell us?

In 1928, Monkhouse, while accompanying an employee of his firm, Oleinik, to the Urals, asked him to collect information about the state of industry, and Oleinik regarded it, not as espionage information of a secret nature, but as information necessary in order to get larger orders for his firm. This is how he understood it, and I say that it cannot be understood otherwise.

If you take Oleinik's evidence in this context, just as he said it, without changing anything and believing what he testified, you will find nothing that could fit into the first part of Article 56 of the Criminal Code. But Oleinik said something more important in his evidence.

The investigator not only asked him what instructions were given of a spying nature, but also what instructions were given of a diversional nature. To this Oleinik replied: "I was not given any tasks by Monkhouse in regard to acts of diversion." Here he confirms this. Oleinik points not to one case, but to two.

I will not ignore the second case, and will again take Oleinik's evidence without changing a single word and believing his evidence completely.

"At Shterovka Power Station," said Oleinik, "Monkhouse instructed me to drag out the test periods beyond the guarantee term and to start the turbines without tests being made, because tests were not profitable for the firm."

I submitted to you the letter written by Oleinik to the firm, in which it is stated that chief engineer Vinogradov demanded that the test be postponed, saying that "the apparatus necessary for testing was not yet ready." But even if we draw the worst possible conclusion from what Oleinik said, it will be a question of an act of commercial dishonesty and not of a criminal or counter-revolutionary crime such as those we are now investigating.

This is the only conclusion I can draw from Oleinik's evidence —from evidence which I accept absolutely and completely, without changing a single word.

I will now turn to Kutuzova's evidence. I cannot ignore it inasmuch as, and here I disagree with the Public Prosecutor, it is not a valid argument in law. Here again I would like to approach it with a measure of credence, as I always do with the evidence of witnesses and even with the evidence of accused persons. But I cannot do so; I cannot recognize Kutuzova's evidence as being a sufficiently valid argument in law, for two reasons.

First, Kutuzova gives no concrete facts. Kutuzova says: "I heard," "I know," without giving a single fact to substantiate her evidence. That is the first thing.

The second reason lies in the inherent contradictions in this evidence. For what is the basis of Kutuzova's evidence? In reply to the question: How could you know of the wrecking activities of Monkhouse?—she says: Because of the degree of confidence which both Thornton and Monkhouse felt towards me. I was their employee, had worked for many years, and was their friend. Hence, the degree of extreme confidence, of which she speaks, seems natural. That is true; but in that case, how can one reconcile it with her next statement, which is included in the indictment.

Permit me to read it. Here is the deposition, on page 126, Volume XIX. "As early as 1930 I began to notice that in addition to business connected with the interests and tasks of the firm,

Thornton, Cushny, MacDonald, Monkhouse and other employees in the firm's office were engaged in some kind of illegal work. They had secret conversations with some Soviet citizens, often locked themselves up in their private office, made secret notes, etc."

Can it be said that Kutuzova's testimony bears evidence of the complete confidence of which she speaks? Can it be said that, with the confidence in her which she talks about, it was necessary to lock themselves up in an office to carry on secret conversations? Would it then have been necessary to peer and pry into the nature of the secret conversations, would it have been necessary to guess at them? How can all this be reconciled? But this is not the only evidence. In another place, Citizen Kutuzova says: "I suppose that Thornton and the other workers in the firm's office gave their information to Richards and carried on their espionage under him. I drew this conclusion from the fact that when Richards came over, secret talks were held with him, and besides this, Thornton and Monkhouse mentioned the name Richards in their secret conversations."

Permit me to adduce another piece of evidence: "all this taken together forced me to be more cautious in my attitude towards their behaviour. I did not give up my idea of testing this more exactly and in detail. I chose a convenient moment when Thornton was particularly favourably disposed towards me, having drunk a great deal, and he told me that he not only worked for the firm, but at the same time carried out certain work for the Intelligence Service.

If you take this evidence as a valid legal argument, and believe it, then it is not a question of Monkhouse, but of Thornton. Thus, however I may desire to approach Citizen Kutuzova's evidence with credence, I cannot do so because of the inherent contradictions in it and because of the absence of concrete facts confirming it; neither can I construe from it a legally valid argument that could be made the basis of a verdict. The chain of evidence against Monkhouse is closed by Kutuzova. I shall not have exhausted all the material accusing Monkhouse if I were to leave out Thornton's evidence. When one mentions Thornton's evidence, the question naturally arises: which evidence? You have seen that Thornton frequently changes his evidence.

Comrade Judges, I have always been indulgent in my attitude towards vacillating evidence and moods of the accused. Perhaps this is the natural instinct of Counsel for the Defence, an instinct acquired by years of work as a lawyer. Nevertheless this vacillation forces me, as a lawyer, to be especially cautious in regard to this evidence. Which of Thornton's statements can be accepted in the present case? The Public Prosecutor left this to Thornton's conscience. This is the best attestation to Thornton's evidence, with this we shall close. When we talk about Thornton in connection with Monkhouse's defence, it is as well to raise the question not of Thornton's evidence but of one much deeper and more serious: about the structure of the personal and business relations between these two persons, since this question conceals the greatest danger for Monkhouse.

Let us look into these relations purely on the basis of facts. Between 1911 and 1918 these people were connected by the work they were doing in Russia. In 1918 they both left Russia via Vladivostok. One went to Mesopotamia, and the other to Archangel with the expeditionary force. After that, in 1924 or 1925, they once again enter the service of the same firm—one as an installation engineer, the other as his assistant; then one became the firm's representative, the other an installation engineer. They lived together in one villa.

What is the conclusion to be drawn from these facts? There is only one—here is an atmosphere of true friendship, which gives us the right to say that these two men had no secrets from each other. When Monkhouse is asked, he does not hide his friendly attitude either to Richards or to Thornton. Under these circumstances it is quite logical to ask both Thornton and Monkhouse the question: If you lived so amicably together, if you were linked by so many years of acqaintanceship, fled from Soviet Russia together prompted by the same sentiments, if you have common interests, is it not natural to suppose that in giving information to Monkhouse, you, Thornton, gave all the information you received yourself, and since the information you received, according to Gussev, MacDonald and Sokolov, was doubtless of a spying nature, it follows that you supplied Monkhouse with this information as well?

This is the natural, logical conclusion. And I understand why Comrade Vyshinsky, an experienced court protagonist—for this is not the first time we have met him in the Court and, as he says, crossed swords with him—only asked Monkhouse two questions about espionage work, first: "Did you receive any information?" "Yes, I received information of a political and economic nature." "From whom did you receive it? From Cushny and Thornton?" He replied: "Yes." And there Comrade Vyshinsky stopped.

It would seem that this question should have been followed up by asking what information, since the centre of gravity lay there. But this was not done, and we ask why? Because if Thornton received the information we know of from the evidence of Gussev and MacDonald, and if he was so intimate with Monkhouse that there would be no secrets between them, then the natural, logical conclusion is that the information received from Gussev was given wholly to Monkhouse. Here lies the real danger for Monkhouse.

Comrade Judges, what can be said about this? One of the elementary principles of criminal law and of criminal court procedure in all civilized countries and of law codes is personal responsibility and personal guilt. Those, who in a criminal court invoke group responsibility and in advance vouch for all on the assumption that they are innocent, are gravely mistaken. We shall not defend this position, for it is both wrong in law and shallow from the viewpoint of the State.

But if we recognize personal responsibility and guilt, then in cases of mutual friendship between accused it is always possible to make this psychological mistake, namely, to transpose the impressions received from one of the accused to the other precisely because of these close personal and business relations or sometimes because of the fact that they live together in one place. The records of crime know of such serious mistakes. That is why I consider it my duty to caution you, Comrade Judges, against the possibility of mistakes of this kind. And applying this to the mutual relations which existed between Monkhouse and Thornton, I must say that the position of Thornton in the case is extremely difficult. Difficult because, parallel with his complete denial of his guilt, there is a whole pyramid of evidence, both objective and subjective, which leaves the impression of absolute guilt on the charges levelled against him. Comrade Braude, Thornton's Counsel for the Defence, said here that against his client there is the evidence of Russian engineers, the evidence of his fellow-countryman, MacDonald, the evidence of employees in the firm and, finally, the evidence of Thornton himself. Against Monkhouse there is no such evidence, but there is his close proximity to Thornton against whom there is such damning evidence. This is what makes me apprehend the possibility of a slight mistake in the estimate of the actions of Monkhouse, the possibility of confusing impressions. That would be great injustice, since I can easily allow, Comrade Judges, that while maintaining friendly relations, the feelings of one changed while those of the other remained the same. I can readily conceive of something else happening: that if Thornton is guilty, he may have been acting independently, and even in his own interests. I told you that if Kutuzova's evidence is to be regarded as being valid it must be remembered that Thornton, according to her evidence, was directly connected with certain circles in England. Recall the nine notebooks which, as Thornton himself testifies, were taken by him to England. Recall all the payments made for wrecking, which went on, not here, and not through Monkhouse, but through Thornton. Remember Thornton's own confession in this respect, and then perhaps you will agree with me that I have every right to suppose that Thornton, if he actually did commit crimes, was acting on his own responsibility, independently, in his own personal interests, because Thornton had interests of his own, if you remember his position in pre-revolutionary Russia.

I say that Monkhouse may have changed his attitude. In 1918 Monkhouse was in the expeditionary force in Archangel. This is a point that counts against him. Since then many years have passed. We are living in times when every year counts as a whole epoch, when every year produces a new language of the epoch. And we know that during these years many of those who fought against the Soviet Government, sword in hand, have now come to pay homage and have repented of their old crimes.

Monkhouse has been living in Russia for 20 years, approximately nine or ten years in Soviet Russia, and about ten years in tsarist Russia. Monkhouse, an intelligent man, a man with a broad outlook, cannot have failed to see how the face of our land has changed during these years, how the face of the countryside has changed, how our fields have changed in appearance. He cannot have failed to see all that. He could not, of course, have seen that in 1918. Monkhouse has often travelled in the country on business, to the provinces, and during these years he had opportunities of seeing for himself how the face of the land was changing. He has seen that where formerly there was a tavern, there is now a school or hospital, where the muzhiks used to till the soil with wooden ploughs, tractors and mechanical ploughs are now in operation. Where formerly dugouts in which all those who produced all the wealth once lived like moles, palaces of labour and clubs now rise. Where once only small brick factories were standing, giants of industry are now standing. Monkhouse, an intelligent man with a broad outlook, could not but have observed all this. He is not MacDonald who came over from England only recently and does not know the living conditions and mode of life of the pre-revolutionary village. Who knows but what the contrast between the conditions of tsarist Russia and those of Soviet Russia, the superiority of the latter, has not brought about a certain psychological change?

And if he took part in the expeditionary force in Archangel in 1918, it should not be forgotten that he refused to serve under Denikin. If we are right in regarding the former as a point against him, the latter should be counted as a point in his favour. Let us weigh the evidence advanced by the Prosecution against accused Monkhouse from this point of view, leaving aside all that refers to Thornton, his fellow-countryman and business associate.

I will now turn to the Dolgov bribe. Two versions were given here by Monkhouse. One, which he gave during the preliminary investigation, amounted to an admission that he is guilty also of having given bribes. Now he says that this was money given as a loan. Being confronted with two versions, the question naturally arises as to which of them is truer to life, which the more convincing. If I were to be asked which version is truer to life, I should say, the one that Monkhouse gave during the preliminary investigation, and for the following reason: Giving loans without taking receipts, without the money ever being returned, and to a person for whom you entertain no friendly feelings or family connections—giving loans to a person with whom you have business relations and who receives and decides complaints in connection with the firm's orders, looks very suspicious. I put the question to Monkhouse here: "You yourself said that a receipt should have been taken, but no receipt was taken. You said that the money should have been returned, but it was not returned. In what light would you have viewed this yourself, under these circumstances?" At the preliminary examination it appeared to him in the light of a present. Let it be a present, we shall not quibble about words. But I look upon this present as a bribe. If we admit that this version is possible, the three following facts which establish Monkhouse's attitude towards this bribe must be borne in mind.

The first thing is that the bribe was given when Monkhouse was not in Moscow. Thornton gave it in the absence of Monkhouse. Thus, the latter was faced with an accomplished fact. Second, the money was paid out of Thornton's private account, and third, the money was written off by Monkhouse by order of Richards, his superior.

These facts will enable you, should this version be taken as the correct one, to consider the question of whether this constitutes complicity within the meaning of Article 17 of the Criminal Code, or whether it constitutes failure to report, provided, of course, you do not deem this bribe to have been a counter-revolutionary act. The legal consequences depend upon the legal construction.

In the Court, Monkhouse advanced another version, that of a loan. In support of this he can say but one thing, namely, that the money was put through the books. But when you closely examine these two versions, and when you take into consideration the circumstances under which the money was given, you must be convinced that the more likely version, the one more in harmony with the probabilities of the case, is that which Monkhouse gave during his preliminary examination.

These are the considerations which I wished to put forward in defence of Monkhouse. His case is very complicated; there is strong evidence against him still it is not conclusive. This obliges me, as his counsel, to raise before you the question of the extent to which the actual commission of crime has been proved, and I feel confident that you will answer this question with all the care and circumspection that distinguishes our Court. Your reply will reflect the truth that will come to light as a result of our legal arguments and as a result of an examination of all the evidence submitted in the present case.

The President: Comrade Libson, Member of the Collegium of Defence.

Libson: Comrade Judges. We are coming to the end of the list of the accused who are sitting in the dock. But two of them remain to be considered—engineer Kotlyarevsky and Citizen Kutuzova.

In concluding the round of speeches for the Defense, I should like to preface my plea with a few comments on the general impression produced by the speeches of both the Public Prosecutor and my associates for the Defence.

It now seems as if the entire case and all the arguments advanced by either side fall into two parts. On the one hand we find accused Englishmen, and on the other accused Russians, and it is quite comprehensible and perfectly natural to hear the following idea expressed in the speech of the Public Prosecutor of the Republic. Turning directly to the Defence, he warned us not to imagine that the accused citizens of the U.S.S.R. could hide behind the backs of the English. . .

The Public Prosecutor warned us—members of the Defence—against this facile method of defence. Nevertheless, associate Counsel for the Defence, in discharging the duties entrusted to them, did subsequently make use of this method. Their speeches were permeated with the argument that we have accused Englishmen in the dock and accused Russians in the dock.

I might even say that this tempting method of defence was not discarded even by the comrades who defended the Englishmen.

For instance, we heard it said from the mouth of Comrade Braude that in defending the Russians my associates went to extremes, that we had made it appear that these Englishmen had in some potent, mystical manner brought pressure to bear upon the Russians, in consequence of which they committed crimes. This, of course, is not so. Nor had Comrade Vyshinsky, the Public Prosecutor, also any reason to warn us that the Russians could not hide behind the backs of the English. He was wrong because he himself made that mistake, he himself concealed the English behind the backs of the Russians. Those associates who defended the Russian engineers and did not disregard the material provided by the acts committed by the English were right; Counsel who defended the Englishmen and said that ideas of this sort might lead us astray were, of course, wrong. It is incorrect to term us Counsel for the Defence for the Russians. We Soviet Counsel are quite aware that Richards is not Mephistopheles, that Thornton is not Faust and that the Russian engineers are not Marguerites. While bearing this fully in mind, we must also remember that in analysing the evidence before this Court, upon the basis of which the decision of the Supreme Court of the Soviet Union must be rendered—that in analysing this evidence, we must take everything into consideration and have no right to shut our eyes to anything. It is immaterial to us whether a man is an Englishman or of some other nationality: what is important is whether he is an enemy or not. And we shall consider his actions from this point of view alone; we shall examine the significance of his actions.

There is just one other point, Comrade Judges, which I should like to make.

Some of my associates have already broached this subject, and I am afraid that my utterances may seem somewhat trite. Questions were asked as to what influenced the actions of our clients, what impelled them to commit their crimes, and it seems to me that answers must be given to two questions.

The first is: was the influence of Thornton, Monkhouse, MacDonald and others the sole influence at work or was there, perhaps, a certain subjective predisposition on the part of the accused? Perhaps all the factors necessary for the commission of the crimes were in their minds beforehand, perhaps they really are wreckers in their innermost hearts, in their outlook, in their aims and tendencies; why then bring in the English?

And once we put the question this way we must analyse the past, we must analyse these necessary factors. And if we come to the conclusion that they are in thrall to the past, that these people have not lost their old habits of life and that the irrevocable past is still dear to their hearts, then we can understand this criminal outlook and we say that the English are not at the bottom of the crimes committed by the Russians, and the analysis of the actions of these Thorntons, Monkhouses and others cannot be interpreted in the sense of mitigating their fate, on the plea that they were only their allies in their wrecking activities.

But if we analyse the present and search the hearts of our young Soviet specialists, if we study their lives and see that there are no such prerequisites, then we are compelled to investigate the causes which impelled them to commit these crimes.

And I think, Comrade Judges, that at this point we must consider yet another question of enormous significance and importance.

When we review the past trials of wreckers, and recall the men who were involved in those cases, grey-haired, their faces reflecting deep-rooted convictions, men whose minds had become psychologically congealed, we get a galling and painful picture and one thinks to oneself: this sort of thing must be overcome by other methods. But when we see young men implicated in the present case, it affects us particularly painfully, because these young men, who were brought up under Soviet conditions, are the off-shoot of our Soviet culture; they are especially valuable to us, as is everything that has been created by our new Soviet culture.

That is why in this particular case it is important to analyse all the reasons, all the relevant points, in order to understand how it could come about that these young specialists were implicated in these crimes.

And I think that my client, engineer Kotlyarevsky, will serve as a good illustration for such an analysis. Consider his youth. He is only 29.

He was born in a working-class family. From the documents submitted we know that his father, who is now a chief mechanic at a factory, has been working in industry for 44 years. A working-class atmosphere and a working-class school. And attention should be paid to the fact that the accused did not immediately begin to study in the *Gymnasium* (in 1919-20 there was still a *Gymnasium* there), but first of all studied in a higher elementary school. Accordingly, coming from a poor working-class family, the *Gymnasium* was beyond his means in that little town in the Ukraine, so he attented the *Gymnasium* only after finishing school, only afterwards entering a higher Soviet educational institute.

Thus, we see that there are no social roots, no factors in his family background that could have given rise to anti-Soviet ideas. We see merely working-class, Soviet roots.

He finished the Polytechnical Institute and became a Soviet engineer. Well, perhaps his fate was such that he turned out a failure? Did he find life difficult and become embittered? No, we find nothing like this. He immediately went to work at Shterovka, and judging by the reports of his work, it seems that he immediately won the repute of being a well-trained engincer. Between 1927 and 1931, beginning on the first rung of the ladder he rose to the position of manager of the engine room. Therefore this man was advancing and consequently could not have become embittered or disgruntled with the Soviet Government. He made just a little slip in connection with an inundation. An investigation was begun and he had to sign a pledge not to leave town. The whole affair ended in his complete vindication and he lost nothing. He then takes up work at what for him was the unlucky Zuevka Station, again as a responsible engineer.

Thus, Comrade Judges, we see how even later he progressed in his career as a Soviet specialist and engineer. We see that there is no predisposition, no factors that could turn him against the Soviet Government.

Let us look further. When he arrived at Zuevka the installation work was finished. This point should be noted. Accordingly the whole installation period passed without Kotlyarevsky, as engineer, having had anything whatever to do with the acts of diversion that occurred in connection with the installation work. He arrived in November: until February he worked in peace. When he arrived in Zuevka he found a large group of English engineers already there. You will remember them: they were

MacDonald, Cork, Elliott, Willcott, Hague. Here also Vassiliev and Fomichev were working.

From November to February there is nothing that could cast a slur on him. Then the moment arrived that brought such tragic consequences in its train. You will remember how he related in the preliminary examination and confirmed here that he became acquainted with MacDonald, likewise 29 years old and also a young engineer. The two became closely acquainted. They first came in contact with each other through their work; then a personal friendship developed which became very close; he began to visit MacDonald in his apartment, and MacDonald confirms that Kotlyarevsky is speaking the truth. The noose was tied which subsequently was to ensnare him. He accepted a loan of 500 rubles.

And here, Comrade Judges, we come to the point which, in my opinion, makes it essential to dwell on the question as to whether the steps taken by engineer Kotlyarevsky were really perfectly conscious ones for the purpose of meeting MacDonald, the wrecker, halfway, or whether all this happened because Kotlyarevsky was placed in a helpless psychological position, owing to which he succumbed and committed the crime which he has frankly admitted.

I would draw your attention, Comrade Judges, to the instance in the preliminary examination where he relates that he received the loan of 500 rubles, that it was lent to him in a comradely manner; but that, when the money was already in Kotlyarevsky's pocket, he was approached a few days later with the "innocent" request to obtain a blueprint. He promises to do that. And then, when he brings the blueprints and hands them over, he is given, without his asking for it, a second sum of 500 rubles. What was that? When, as he says, he began to refuse to accept this money, then this good comrade, the pleasant, kind British engineer MacDonald, with whom so many evenings had been spent at Zuevka in listening to the gramophone and drinking tea, became transformed, became cold and harsh, and declared: "You realize the sort of documents you gave me; that is what you were given money for."

Kotlyarevsky already owes 500 rubles, and they begin to blackmail him. He gives way, he takes the money and carries out the foul work which he has described to you in so much detail. The blackmailing tactics, which, irrespective of whether MacDonald was a German, an Englishman, a Russian or a Jew, is an old well-known and well-tried method. Through this kind of blackmail—by which one is given a loan and is put under the obligation to perform what at first sight seems to be some slight service, and then is induced to take more money—one is forced to traverse the whole road and finds himself in the tragic position from which Kotlyarevsky was not strong enough to extricate himself.

Of course, it would have been possible to do a very simple thing; it would have been possible to do in this case as Dolgov did —go to the O.G.P.U. and frankly lay the situation before them. Kotlyarevsky was not strong enough to do that, he was not able to do it, he exhibited weakness. That was the beginning, and the consequences we have in his criminal acts; but do they prove that Kotlyarevsky has fallen so low that it actually cannot be said that there is any hope of his ever returning to the honest family of the working class? I do not think that such is the case.

Let us look into the later dates, the later actions. That was in February, then April, May, June—the period of the breakdowns. What does he admit? He admits, first, that he did not protest actively against the false explanations given as to the causes of the breakdowns and second, that he deliberately threw a bolt into a turbine. That was in April-May-June. In July, Kotlyarevsky ran away from the awful place—he was not dismissed, he ran away. He went on his vacation and did not want to return, did not want to return to the awful mire where he had lost his honour, where he had fallen into such terrible clutches. That was in July 1932, when nothing gave him any reason to suppose that the crimes were already being discovered; everything was quiet. He left the scene of these crimes himself, and went to work at Orgenergo. After that he went to Kazan, where he worked honestly until his arrest.

Comrade Judges, I must anticipate the objections which may be offered to my arguments. Had Kotlyarevsky joined that criminal organization, had Kotlyarevsky lost himself completely, had he considered that he had broken once and for all with our Soviet interests, that he had sold himself to persons engaged in acts of diversion, he, of course, would not have gone to Orgenergo to work, he would not have gone to Kazan, but would have gone where they would have sent him, where they are working. Yet we see that Kotlyarevsky worked where not a single one of these persons, engaged in acts of diversion and now in the dock, was working.

Thus, Comrade Judges, in my opinion we can consider it proved, first, that there is nothing in the past of my client, Kotlyarevsky, which can cause it to be said that this man has carried the poison in him from his past, and that therefore there can be no hope of his being able to correct himself; second, the fact that for a short period of time, under pressure of blackmail, he joined in and committed criminal acts, of which he has sincerely repented, and, third, that he himself quite voluntarily fled from the awful place, because it lay heavy upon his conscience and because he did not want to be one who commits acts of diversion.

I take it, Comrade Judges, that you will bring in the verdict in Kotlyarevsky's case on the basis of these three factors.

Comrades! Our whole life in the Soviet Union is governed by socialist construction. All our architects, all our bricklayers, who are taking part in this work of construction, examine the bricks that are to be used for these new buildings very carefully and see that they are not cracked. If bricks are cracked they do not use them for the foundations, they do not use them for the facades, they put them aside in order to use them in other parts of the building, and this cracked brick, firmly held together with cement, will be useful in our work of construction.

And I am sure that this crack in Kotlyarevsky is only a temporary one, and that you as architects and builders will not fling him aside, but put him carefully aside.

I have still to speak in defence of my second client, Kutuzova. Here too I must commence by replying to my respected comrade, the Public Prosecutor. I cannot in the least understand his description of Kutuzova as a frivolous young lady who takes joy rides in an automobile from Perlovka to the Moscow office; nor can I agree with him when he says that everything that passed in this Court and at the preliminary investigation depicts her as a person who, because of her frivolous tastes, went to work at a place where she could get enough money to clothe herself better, to feed better, where conditions would be more comfortable.

And here, too, Comrade Judges, I ask you to bear in mind certain features in the life of Kutuzova. I think that the material which we have at our disposal depicts an altogether different person. She has been working for her living for twenty years. You know that she comes from a working-class family. She first started work as a teacher, learned French, German and English, continued at work all the time, and we know that her work was highly appreciated. We see that not a single year of her life passed without working. From small beginnings, she achieves big things. Beginning as a typist at Volkhovstroy she becomes secretary to the chief engineer, Graftio, and when the work at Volkhovstroy comes to an end, her reputation as a worker is so well established that when Metro-Vickers requires a secretary for the principal director of the firm, she, evidently on the recommendation of Graftio and other employees, and also on the personal observations made by Monkhouse and Thornton, because they had worked there for a number of years with her, is invited to take the position. It seems to me that it would be wrong to try to make it appear that Kutuzova passed her time as secretary to Metro-Vickers' chief engineers mainly in enjoying the comforts of her job, and in observing acts of diversion. She had an enormous amount of work to do in a big firm, whose employees were scattered over a number of power stations—at Zuevka, at Shterovka, at Chelyabinsk and Baku. She was at general headquarters, which linked up all the threads, which sent out all the orders to hundreds of workers, and, as a matter of fact, she was office manager. She carried on all the correspondence and played a really big part in the office as a Russian employee. But more than that, she lived in the same house with these Englishmen. They had a big house and, of course, as secretary, she managed the house also. That is my impression of Kutuzova. She is a business woman who is really capable of doing important work, and did actually do such work.

And when it is asked here, why was Kutuzova connected with the work of a foreign firm, it seems to me that this is a superfluous question. Since she had worked for a long time at the Treugolnik Factory and she knew French, German and English, since she had come in contact with the Englishmen at Volkhovstroy and, since, on account of her knowledge of languages, she obviously was bound to come in contact with these foreigners, it is therefore quite logical and normal that she should go to work for Metro-Vickers when she was invited to do so.

I think, Comrade Judges, that my client Kutuzova's position as a worker raises no doubt whatever, and now we have only to put two questions in connection with Kutuzova's case and to answer them.

First question: does Anna Sergeyevna Kutuzova speak the truth in her depositions when she tells us, as she put it, what she heard with her ears and saw with her eyes. Quite naturally, my colleagues in the Defence regard Kutuzova's depositions as a denunciation because Kutuzova is one of the accused and not a witness, and, therefore, they strongly object to your believing what she has said.

For example, Counsel for Defence Kommodov, who last spoke, pointed to contradictions in Kutuzova's depositions and drew the conclusion from these contradictions that she is not to be believed. Comrade Kommodov quoted to you parts of her depositions in order to corroborate his views. But he did not finish what he was going to say, either because he forgot, or because it was necessary for him to forget, the other parts of her depositions—about Dolgov's 3,000 rubles, which Kutuzova mentioned, and which is an indisputable fact; about MacDonald, who was always there, and who was the central figure in all these acts of diversion, and, finally, about the parcel that was sent to Gussev, about which also there can be no doubt whatever. These, Comrade Judges, are facts. I deal with this unimportant question only because attempts are being made here to say that Kutuzova is not to be believed, that she is not speaking the truth. But if you are not to believe her, if she is capable of telling lies, then perhaps you will not believe that part of her depositions which is extremely important for me as her Counsel for Defence because it gives rise to the second question, the principal question, namely: why didn't Kutuzova, a Soviet citizen, who, from 1927 to 1932-33 lived with these Englishmen and observed all that about which she afterwards told, speak out before?

We know all the material in this case. We remember very well all that Kutuzova said at the preliminary investigation, all that she stated here about her intimate friendship with Monkhouse and intimate friendship with Thornton having created psychologically complicated relations. After all, this is not a slight matter: she was connected with these people for a number of years; and all this, to a certain degree, psychologically put her under an obligation to them and, consequently, it was very difficult for her to decide to take this step.

Perhaps those comrades who spoke about the specific psychological condition peculiar to her as a woman are right. Perhaps this psychology does play a part in this to some extent. That is so. And you, Comrade Judges, will take all this into consideration. But for me, as Kutuzova's Counsel for Defence, the following is very important: she is telling you the truth and when she was asked about it, she told everything without concealing anything.

And it is also important in regard to Kutuzova that the following facts, concerning which I also beg to differ from the representative of the State Prosecution, are established.

She is charged with being an active accomplice, and the actions to which she confessed must be interpreted as direct and active complicity.

But what are the facts? See how harshly this is formulated in the indictment. Here it says that she systematically sent and handed over money, and so forth. But what facts have we now, after all this has already been gone into in the course of the judicial investigation? The parcel under a fictitious name—Ivanova—was sent to Gussev. It contained a bribe. As we know quite definitely now, the parcel was connected with Gussev's acts of diversion. But we only learned this here! How many parcels passed through her hands?

Of course, she knew that this was an illegal parcel because MacDonald told her to send it under a fictitious name. Of course she knew, but can this fact of her having sent this parcel be regarded as active complicity in wrecking acts? I challenge anyone to bring any facts from which it would be possible to draw the conclusion that she not only knew about, but also facilitated, actively facilitated, a single act of diversion! Did she have any direct connection whatever with persons who played the direct role of diversionists and spies who passed before us? No, Comrade Judges, not a single fact of that kind can be produced.

When my client, Kutuzova, made her depositions, she formulated them in such a way as to say that she was an accomplice, and at the same time she added that she did not report this. But I, as her counsel, cannot agree to the legal formulation she involuntarily gives in expounding the facts. She frankly tells all that she has seen and heard and observed, and says that she could not find the courage to report about this before. She tells of the mental agony she experienced, and how she appealed to Thornton and the others not to drag her into this business. We must give a perfectly precise juridical formulation, because you have to judge according to a definite article of the law, because you will have to decide the measure of social defence to be applied to her.

And I urge, Comrade Judges, that there is no complicity in Kutuzova's actions. There is not that which is referred to in the indictment. All that there is, is failure to report within the meaning of Article 58-12, because there is absolutely not a single fact to prove active participation, to prove her direct complicity. This is typical failure to report, which is also liable to a definite penalty for the crime formulated as: failure to report authentically known, counter-revolutionary crimes.

And my request to you, Comrade Judges, is that when you decide the fate of Kutuzova, when you discuss the question of Article 58-12, and when you, in the light of Article 58-12, discuss the penalty to be inflicted upon her, that you do not forget the tragic position she was in throughout this long period when, as one who had failed to report, and only as such, she carried this fearful secret in her breast, when she was entangled in this psychological net which she was not strong enough to break. You will, of course, understand the terrible agony and punishment that she has already had to bear, and with this in mind, permit her to return to the life of a toiler.

In concluding my defence, Comrade Judges, permit me to express one more thought.

Many of the accused now in the dock have sincerely confessed their deeds. The stories they tell combine to make a picture of fearful crime. But, Comrade Judges, can we forget that this is the year 1933? Monkhouse came to Russia and lived here a long time, right up to 1933, and apparently forgot that the Moscow of 1933 is not the Archangel of 1919 and 1920. But we, in 1933, remember that all these crimes, with which Gussev, Lobanov, Kotlyarevsky and MacDonald are charged, were committed five years ago, in 1928 and 1929. Now that we have achieved such enormous progress, now that we are becoming stronger year after year and, as Comrade the Public Prosecutor has said, we are not frightened by acts of diversion, we have the right and opportunity, severe as the law of March 14 may be in demanding an especially severe approach to the question of the responsibility of State employees, to raise the question of life or death in reply to the actions of these diversionists.

We have the legend in the beginning of Russian history that our forefathers appealed to the Varangians and said: "Great is our land and abundant, come unto us and possess us." Much water has flowed beneath the bridges since then, and the Russian people has passed through many hardships. It has known the yoke of the Tartar, it has known the German rod, it has known other influences with the aid of which the tsars have maintained their throne. But all these collapsed, and today, in 1933, our land is greater and more abundant, but we do not invite anyone to come in and possess us. We do not need Varangians, and the sadly disappointed Varangians stand on our frontiers, the Varangians who today feel unemployed in history and who gaze with envy upon our oil derricks, our belching factory chimneys that spring up every day, our mighty electric power stations which throw new sheaves of electric light upon our developing Soviet construction. And the hearts of the Varangians grow sad as they see the armed Red

Army man on our frontiers. The Varangians look with hatred upon our O.G.P.U., but the latter stands firmly and prevents the enemy from entering, and if anybody does manage to sneak through, he is caught by the ear and dragged into the light. Every act of diversion, every attack, every attempt at attack, is impotent and only causes irritation.

We remain firmly convinced that ours is a great cause. And abroad, the best minds, the purest hearts, like Romain Rolland, Bernard Shaw, and others numbering hundreds and thousands—all the workers—are with us. They believe in our great cause. It is only upon them that we rely; only to them who really understand us do we look; only those who are with us are important for us.

And therefore, Comrade Judges, with the profound conviction that we are engaged in a great cause, with the profound conviction that we will achieve victory in this great cause, that we are strong and indomitable, I ask you, in face of the stern law, to ask yourselves the question—shall it be life or death? And I, as Counsel for Defence, ask that your reply shall not be death.

The President: Does the Prosecution desire to take advantage of its right to reply?

Vyshinsky: No, there is no need for it.

The President: We will now hear the final pleas.

Accused Gussev, do you desire to make a final plea?

Gussev: Yes.

Citizen Judges, I have related to you the crimes I have committed. Here in this Court I once again keenly live through the heinousness of these crimes. I ask the Court to believe the sincerity of my confession and repentance and to enable me, by honest, really honest work in the future, to expiate my crimes and repair the damage I have caused the State.

I give my word that I will devote the rest of my life to honest labour that will be directed towards atoning for the evil that I have caused.

The President: Accused Sokolov?

Sokolov: I have fully admitted the seriousness of all the crimes I have committed. Both at the preliminary examination and at this trial I have again lived through the horror of it. I promise that if I am given the opportunity, I will rectify my mistakes and, by honest labour for the benefit of our socialist fatherland, prove my loyalty to the working class and atone for my crimes for the rest of my life, if my life be spared.

The President: Accused MacDonald?

MacDonald: I plead guilty and I have nothing more to add.

The President: Accused Zivert, do you desire to make a final plea?

Zivert: Citizen Judges. I related to you here how I, a worker, committed crimes against my class. But, as you know, at the time Thornton was at the University in London, I was a shephèrd. I want, by honest labour, to expiate my crime. I feel that I have killed my family and have killed myself, and this is a very bitter experience for me. I hope that the Court will give me the opportunity of atoning for my crime.

The President: Accused Kotlyarevsky, do you desire to make a final plea.

Kotlyarevsky: Citizen Judges. The crimes that I have committed are very severe. I have related all that I have done. I deeply repent my crimes. I ask the Court to give me the opportunity by honest labour to expiate these crimes, and if this opportunity is given me, I promise to devote all my efforts and all my knowledge to this task.

The President: Accused Cushny, do you desire to make a final plea?

Cushny: I want to speak in English.

The President: You may.

Cushny: After hearing the very able defence put up by my Counsel today, there is really very little left for me to say. He has torn to shreds the flimsy fabric put up by the Public Prosecutor. I have said all through that I am not guilty. There has not been a shred of real evidence brought forward against me. And whatever the verdict, I shall leave this court an honest man as I came in.

The President: Accused Lobanov, do you desire to make a final plea?

Lobanov: Citizen Judges, both at the preliminary investigation and here at this trial, I tried in the greatest possible detail to show the severity of all the crimes I have committed and also told you about my life. I do not wish to say any more about that. My only request to the Court is—give me the opportunity to reform and to devote the rest of my life to the great work of construction, to the great aims and tasks of the great proletarian State, and to the cause of building up socialism.

I give my word that if this opportunity is given me, I will devote the rest of my life, as far as my health will permit, to the great tasks which the Soviet State has undertaken. I would ask that you take into consideration the environment which imbued me with certain bad inclinations, and also the fact that I am still young, that I am a criminal who can still be reclaimed.

The President: Be seated. Accused Nordwall?

Nordwall: I wish to speak in English.

The President: You may.

Nordwall: It has been very painful to me to listen to the Public Prosecutor's speech. I am a man that takes interest only in his work and I always do my utmost. I have always supported the interests of the Soviet building plan and have done every possible thing to help them. My private life in Russia has been purely in connection with my own family and living among the Russian people. After the evidence I have heard in this Court against me and after the fairness I received in the G.P.U. after I have been arrested, and as I said before, I have always been a friend of the Soviet Union, and I think this Court has documentary evidence to this effect. I feel sure that after the evidence put before you, the Judge and the jury can only pass one verdict, that is, not guilty. And at this moment I am still a friend of the Soviet Union and I am not afraid to say so even in front of all the press.

The President: Accused Lebedev?

Lebedev: Citizen Judges. I admit my very serious guilt and promise the Supreme Court that if the Court gives me the opportunity, I will atone for my crime.

The President: Accused Thornton?

Thornton: At the beginning of this trial I pleaded not guilty. And I still plead not guilty. I assert that the evidence brought against me are unreliable. That is all I have to say.

The President: Accused Zorin?

Zorin: Citizen Judges, in passing sentence upon me I would ask you to take into consideration the circumstance that at the first examination I fully admitted my guilt, and I would ask you further to take into consideration that if I am given the opportunity, I can still be of service to the Soviet Union in the building of socialism.

The President: Accused Sukhoruchkin?

Sukhoruchkin: I fully admit the gravity of the crimes I have committed. Both at the preliminary examination and here in Court, I sincerely repented and this enables me to ask the Court to give me the opportunity of utilizing my experience and knowledge to atone for my guilt and become an honest Soviet citizen.

The President: Accused Monkhouse?

Monkhouse: In addition to the severe charges which are on the charge sheet against me, in the course of yesterday's summing up by the Public Prosecutor, he added another which I regard as a very serious charge, maybe unofficially, but he added a very serious charge, inasmuch that he accused me of deliberately deceiving the British Government in the communication which I made when I was released from Lubyanka. That is a very unfair statement to me. Because I have made no statements at all which are in adverseness to facts, except the difference in the time, which I can explain, is due to the fact that apparently I was given special consideration when I was in prison. For the conditions I must thank you, but they misled me. Because on the walls of my cell there is a notice about the times meals are served and other regulations observed. That was my only means of judging the time. The Public Prosecutor also accuses me of giving the wrong information as to the number of people who examined me. I stated I was examined by three men. And I still state that. And I can name the men. It is not necessary, I assume. He also stated that time was given me for meals. That those meals were excellent meals brought in from the outside, that is true, but I was not left alone at the meals, and one of the chief men of the Examining Department had his meal with me. And I cannot be persuaded that the conversation which took place was not part of my examination. I only wish to make those remarks because

I very much disliked the insinuation that I deceived the representative of His Majesty's Government.

Now, in reference to the charges which are made against me on the sheet; the first charge is that of spying. And the only serious evidence that I can see against me, accusing me of spying, is a document which has been referred to here as number 26, which was signed by Mr. Thornton. And I would like to say that I have known Mr. Thornton for 22 years and I am perfectly certain that he could not sign a document like that voluntarily. That document contains the names of 27 people all of whom are accused by him of being in a spying organization. One of those men has confessed in this Court that he is associated with Mr. Thornton. Four have not. And I am perfectly certain that the remaining 22 would also not. So that not in any Court of Law, I think I am right in saying it, would it be held as a proof.

Finally, with regard to the charge of spying, I deny having done any spying whatever. I understand spying as a collecting of secret and State information; that I have not done.

The second charge against me is of wrecking. In implicating this charge the Public Prosecutor surprised me very much in taking up the attitude that the interests of my Company and of the Soviet Government are opposed to each other. That is not so and cannot be so. I would ask the Court to remember that the Soviet Government at the present time owes our Company 15,000,000 gold rubles—one and a half million English pounds—and our Company had hoped to get more orders.

The President: This question does not concern the Court. We are not examining a civil action.

Monkhouse: I wish to say, Sir—The conclusion that I wish to make, Sir, is that it would be cutting our own throats to engage in any wrecking activities which would destroy or lessen the capacity to pay of the Soviet Union. I have been very proud in the last eight years to take part in the enormous development which is the electrification of this country. I have been proud and very proud to be associated with such men as the present head of Glavelektro and Glavenergprom and other similar Institutions. And it has always been; and I have done everything I possibly could to help in the work. And in doing so I have taken a natural pride in being associated with it. Therefore, it is to me quite ununderstandable, how it can be brought against me that I am associated with wrecking that work.

Engineers, when they build works of this kind, they look upon them as their own children. And I know of no parents who would put a dagger into the heart of their own child.

The third charge against me is of bribery. I have never given a bribe myself in my life. And I will not give a bribe. The Public Prosecutor yesterday made another reference which I would like to to refer to. He said that the Moscow Bureau of our Company had a bad tradition when I took it over. That is quite incorrect, because there was no Moscow office when I was made manager here. And all my office books have already been to the Public Prosecutor. All of my private diaries for the last nine years have been examined by the O.G.P.U., all my expense accounts, my personal and private expense accounts for the last eight years, have all been in the hands of the G.P.U. And because nothing had been said to me, they have not found one figure that indicates any form of bribery. I was very much shocked by the charge of bribery because it is against my principles.

I have nothing whatever to add except that I stand before you, Sir, absolutely innocent of the charges brought against me.

The President: Accused Krasheninnikov?

Krasheninnikov: I am making this final plea not in order to try and justify myself before the proletarian Court, but in order to ask the Court to take into consideration the fact that I abandoned wrecking operations as early as 1932. That is why at my very first examination by the investigating bodies of the O.G.P.U., I admitted my grave crimes and completely disarmed myself politically there, and I completely disarmed myself politically here.

The President: Accused Oleinik?

Oleinik: On the very first day of my arrest I admitted all the crimes that I committed and I also appreciate my guilt. I repeated this during the investigation and I say it now. I have thought a great deal since that time. I have thought more since my arrest than

I have done for the past fifteen years. Much that was not clear to me before presents itself to me now in a different light. Now, I can see things differently and, for that reason, my attitude towards things has changed.

I have been working for forty years. I commenced work when I was eleven years old and, except for a short interval of time, I can say that I worked honestly; it is only recently that I turned to the path of crime.

To be given the opportunity to work again—that is all I want. I do not dream of anything else. Work—that is all I want. I do not dream of anything else. Work—that is the only aim and consolation of my life.

The President: Accused Gregory?

Gregory: The Public Prosecutor having withdrawn the charges against me, I have nothing to say.

The President: Accused Kutuzova?

Kutuzova: Citizen Judges, I come from a working-class family and from the age of sixteen and a half I have lived exclusively on my own earnings, which were always sufficient, not only to maintain myself but also to assist my numerous relations.

I have been working for twenty years, and of these twenty years I have been in State service for ten years. Among other places, I have worked at Svirstroy and Volkhovstroy, where I was the only woman employee who received a special salary for my honest and conscientious work.

But irrespective of my material position, I never sold myself to anybody. Anna Sergeyevna Kutuzova cannot be bought. Everybody knows this, and nobody has even tried to do this, least of all for perfumes, for face powder, and face cream, a fact which Citizen the Public Prosecutor of the Supreme Court erroneously attributed to me yesterday. Even when I was in State service I had perfumes and powder, and I do not intend in the future to give up these accessories of life.

I will add also that when I worked at Volkhovstroy I also rode on upholstered seats, not in a Buick, but in a Packard.

Citizen the Public Prosecutor also held it against me that I had a special desire to go to work for a British firm. He is right.

I did really have that desire. But this desire arose from the fact that I had become worn out and physically weary as a result of hard, daily, evening and sometimes night work at Volkhovstroy, and I wanted to rest somewhat. And why did I select an English firm? That is quite understandable: because at that time I was acquainted only with representatives of the English firm, and moreover, the German and the French nations were not to my liking.

But in entering the service of the Metro-Vickers agency I continued to work honestly and conscientiously, and no one who knows me would dare to throw up to my face that I did not do my part in fulfilling the first Five-Year Plan. I will be bold enough and even audacious enough to tell the Court and the investigators that perhaps I have done more than many Russian citizens who flaunt the label of State employee.

I never have been and never will be an enemy of the Soviet Government, but I know that my guilt is great and it, too, can be explained. As I have already told the Court, of the six years I have worked for Metro-Vickers, four years I lived almost inseparably and intimately in an English environment and imbibed all their habits and their views about our country. But I had no other way out, as I have already said.Simply because I worked for a foreign firm, many of my former friends turned away from me. And the two or three persons whom I had to meet also feared me and probably did not sleep at night after I left them and perhaps lit candles to Saint Seraphim to guard them from the visits of this sinister Anna Sergeyevna.

Such has been my life. And that is why I did really become very intimate with the Englishmen; as a consequence of this friendship, I committed a great mistake, namely I gave my word never to reveal to anyone the work of the spying, diversional group which has been discussed at this trial and for which I now find myself in the dock.

I do not even take credit for what Citizen the Public Prosecutor gives me credit for, that I at the first examination on the day after my arrest, honestly told what I knew about this case. That is not a very great service. I realize that my guilt still remains very grave, that I crossed the bounds of civic duty. I plead guilty, but I place my hope in the justice of the proletarian Court.

The President: The Court will now retire to consider the verdict.

(At 3.35 p.m. the Court adjourns until 1 a.m., April 19, 1933)

[Signed] V. V. ULRICH
President of the Special Session of the Supreme Court of the U.S.S.R.

A. F. KOSTYUSHKO
Secretary

NIGHT SESSION, APRIL 18-19, 1933, 1 a.m.

Commandant: Please rise.The Court is coming.

The President: The Verdict of the Special Session of the Supreme Court of the U.S.S.R. is to be pronounced.

VERDICT

In the name of the Union of Soviet Socialist Republics.
The Special Session of the Supreme Court of the U.S.S.R. consisting of:
President—*Ulrich, V. V.*
Members of the Court—*Martens, L. K.; Dmitriev, G. A.*
Member of the Court in Reserve—*Zelikov, A. V.*
Secretary—*Kostyushko, A. F.*
For the State Prosecution, the Public Prosecutor of the R.S.F.S.R. *Vyshinsky, A. J.*, and Assistant Public Prosecutor of the R.S.F.S.R., *Roginsky, G. K.*
For the Defense—Members of the Moscow Collegium of Defence: *Braude, I. D.; Smirnov, A. A.; Kommodov, N. V.; Lidov, P. P.; Dolmatovsky, A. M.; Schwartz, L. G.; Pines, I. G.; Kaznacheyev, S. K.; Libson, I. N.;* in open sessions of the Court held on April 12, 13, 14, 15, 16, 17 and 18, in the year 1933, examined the case of:

1. *Gussev, Vassily Alexeyevich;* 35 years of age; born in the city of Penza; single; higher technical education; State employee; not previously convicted; formerly chief of the Zlatoust Power Station; charged with committing crimes coming under Articles 58-6, 58-7, 58-9 and 58-11 of the Criminal Code of the R.S.F.S.R.

2. *Gregory, Albert William;* 52 years of age; born in England; married; higher technical education; British subject; installation engineer employed by the British firm of Metropolitan-Vickers;

charged with committing crimes coming under Articles 58-6 and 58-11 of the Criminal Code of the R.S.F.S.R.

3. *Zivert, Yuri Ivanovich;* 50 years of age; State employee; born in the former Courland Gubernia; a fitter; elementary education; no previous convictions; foreman of installations of transformers and oil switches at the Ivanovo State District Power Station; charged with committing crimes coming under Articles 58-6, 58-7, 58-9 and 58-11 of the Criminal Code of the R.S.F.S.R.

4. *Zorin, Nikolai Grigorievich;* 59 years of age; born in the city of Moscow; higher education; mechanical engineer; married; not previously convicted; State employee; formerly chief engineer of the thermo-dynamic group at the Mosenergo; charged with committing crimes coming under Articles 58-7 and 58-11 of the Criminal Code of the R.S.F.S.R.

5. *Krasheninnikov, Michael Dmitrievich;* 35 years of age; born in the village of Novoye in the former Vladimir Gubernia; higher education; State employee; electrical engineer; married; not previously convicted; formerly chief of the installation and repair department of the First Moscow Power Station; charged with committing crimes coming under Articles 58-7 and 58-11 of the Criminal Code of the R.S.F.S.R.

6. *Kotlyarevsky, Moisei Lvovich;* 29 years of age; born in Bobrinetz, Zinovievsk District; higher education; State employee; mechanical engineer; not previously convicted; married; formerly manager of the turbine department of the Zuevka State Power Station; charged with committing crimes coming under Articles 58-7 and 58-11 of the Criminal Code of the R.S.F.S.R.

7. *Kutuzova, Anna Sergeyevna;* 37 years of age; born in the city of Leningrad; secondary education; not previously convicted; formerly secretary to the representative of the foreign firm of Metropolitan-Vickers in the U.S.S.R.; charged with committing crimes coming under Articles 58-6, 58-7, 58-9 and 58-11 of the Criminal Code of the R.S.F.S.R.

8. *Cushny, John;* 35 years of age; born in Johannesburg, South Africa; shareholder in the British firm Metropolitan-Vickers; Bri-

tish subject; higher education; ex-officer of the British Army; installation engineer employed by the British firm of Metropolitan-Vickers; charged with committing crimes coming under Articles 58-6, 58-7, 58-9 and 58-11 of the Criminal Code of the R.S.F.S.R.

9. *Lebedev, Vyacheslav Petrovich;* 52 years of age; State employee, born in the city of Ivanovo-Voznesensk; secondary education; ex-sergeant-major in the tsarist army; married; formerly foreman at the Ivanovo State District Power Station; charged with committing crimes coming under Articles 58-7, 58-9 and 58-11 of the Criminal Code of the R.S.F.S.R.

10. *Lobanov, Alexander Timofeyevich;* 35 years of age; State employee; born in the former Vladimir Gubernia, in the village of Staropashennaya; son of a factory owner; higher technical education; married; not previously convicted; formerly chief of the operating department of the Ivanovo State District Power Station; charged with committing crimes coming under Articles 58-7, 58-9 and 58-11 of the Criminal Code of the R.S.F.S.R.

11. *MacDonald, William Lionel;* 29 years of age; born in London; son of an engineer; higher technical education; British subject; single; installation engineer; employed by the British firm of Metropolitan-Vickers; charged with committing crimes coming under Articles 58-6, 58-7, 58-9 and 58-11 of the Criminal Code of the R.S.F.S.R.

12. *Monkhouse, Allan;* 46 years of age; born in Stratford, New Zealand; son of a farmer; ex-captain of engineers in the British Army; higher technical education; married; British subject; worked in the U.S.S.R. as representative of the British firm of Metropolitan-Vickers; charged with committing crimes coming under Articles 58-6, 58-7, 58-9 and 58-11 of the Criminal Code of the R.S.F.S.R.

13. *Nordwall, Charles;* 31 years of age; born in Berlin; son of an engineer; higher technical education; married; British subject; installation engineer employed by the British firm of Metropolitan-Vickers; charged with committing crimes coming under Articles 58-7, 58-9, and 58-11 of the Criminal Code of the R.S.F.S.R.

14. *Oleinik, Peter Yeremeyevich;* 52 years of age; born on the Perekrestovschitsa farm, former Poltava Gubernia; secondary education; married; not previously convicted; chief mechanic employed by the firm of Metropolitan-Vickers; charged with committing crimes coming under Articles 58-6, 58-7 and 58-11 of the Criminal Code of the R.S.F.S.R.

15. *Sokolov, Vassily Andreyevich;* 33 years of age; State employee; born in the village of Aksino, Birsk district, Bashkir Autonomous Soviet Socialist Republic; son of a handicraftsman; secondary technical education; electro-technician; married; not previously convicted; formerly assistant chief of the power station of the Zlatoust works; charged with committing crimes coming under Articles 58-6, 58-7, 58-9 and 58-11 of the Criminal Code of the R.S.F.S.R.

16. *Sukhoruchkin, Leonid Alexeyevich;* 39 years of age; State employee; born in the village of Novo Pavloskaya, North Caucasus; son of a merchant; higher education; electrical engineer; married; not previously convicted; chief of the operating department of the First Moscow Power Station; charged with crimes coming under Articles 58-7, 58-9 and 58-11 of the Criminal Code of the R.S.F.S.R.

17. *Thornton, Leslie Charles;* 45 years of age; born in Leningrad; son of a factory owner; British subject; married; higher education; not previously convicted; chief installation engineer employed by the British firm of Metropolitan-Vickers; charged with committing crimes coming under Articles 58-6, 58-7, 58-9 and 58-11 of the Criminal Code of the R.S.F.S.R.

On the basis of the preliminary and the judicial investigations, the Special Session of the Supreme Court of the U.S.S.R. established the following:

For a number of years, systematic breakdowns occurred on boilers, motors, turbines, generators, etc. at large power stations of the U.S.S.R.—at power stations belonging to the Mosenergo, Zlatoust, Chelyabinsk, Ivanovo, Baku and other groups—which put them out of action for more or less prolonged periods and reduced the capacity of the power stations.

A Commission of Technical Experts, set up during the course of the preliminary investigation and called to give evidence before the Court, came to the conclusion on the basis of the materials submitted to it that in all the cases of breakdowns investigated, there was evidence either of criminal negligence or of deliberate wrecking on the part of the technical personnel employed at the above-mentioned power stations.

On the basis of the materials of the judicial investigation that came before the Court, the Court finds that the cause of the aforesaid breakdowns was the wrecking activities of counter-revolutionary groups consisting of State employees employed at these power stations, the majority of them belonging to the senior technical staffs, acting in complicity with certain employees of the British private firm of Metropolitan-Vickers, which is operating in the U.S.S.R. on the basis of a technical aid agreement with the People's Commissariat of Heavy Industry.

I.

1. Chief of the electric power station, State employee *Gussev, V. A.*, ex-volunteer in the Kolchak army, having set himself the aim of causing damage to the State industries and defence capacity of the U.S.S.R., in complicity with his assistant, State employee *Sokolov, V. A.*, and with a number of other persons whose cases are being separately dealt with, committed the following:

a. Systematically, in the period from 1931 to 1932, put out of action the 1,400 h.p. motor which drove the large-shape mill of the rolling shop of the Zlatoust Metallurgical Works, in particular, by inserting a piece of iron in the air gap for the purpose of stopping the output of shells and shell billets. As a result of one of these breakdowns the shell shop was stopped for six weeks;

b. At the end of 1931, he froze boiler No. 8 for the purpose of weakening the boiler system of the power station;

c. At the end of the same year 1931, he put out of action coal conveyor No. 1 by inserting metal objects in the gear drive, as a result of which the gear drive and the foundations were broken. After that, on *Gussev's* orders, the whole coal conveyor was dismantled and was thus put out of action for eighteen months until *Gussev's* arrest;

d. Deliberately and with wrecking intent delayed the installation of boilers Nos. 1, 2 and 11 for long periods.

As a result of the criminal activities of *Gussev,* the capacity of the power station was reduced by half, from 12,000 to 6,000 kw.

2. At the same time, *Gussev* and *Sokolov* prepared a number of breakdowns that were intended to put the power station out of action and to deprive the Zlatoust works of power at the moment of a military attack against the U.S.S.R. which the wreckers expected.

3. The criminal acts of *Gussev* and *Sokolov* were committed in agreement with the employee of the British firm of Metropolitan-Vickers, installation engineer *MacDonald, W. L.,* who took part in drawing up wrecking plans.

4. In addition to the above, on the instructions of the aforesaid *MacDonald, Gussev* and *Sokolov,* directly and through other persons, collected for and communicated to *MacDonald,* to the detriment of the U.S.S.R., secret information of military State importance referring to:

a. the work of the munitions shops of the Zlatoust Works;

b. the production of shells and the type of shells produced;

c. the production of high-grade steel for military purposes, and

d. the mobilization plans of the power station and of the Zlatoust Works.

5. As a reward for committing these criminal acts, *Gussev* and *Sokolov* received bribes from *MacDonald. Gussev* received various sums at various times amounting in all to 2,500 rubles, and *Sokolov* received 1,000 rubles.

6. The criminal acts of *MacDonald* were committed with the knowledge and on the instructions of the British subject and chief installation engineer of the Moscow office of Metropolitan-Vickers, *Thornton, L. C.,* with whom, as well as with *MacDonald, Gussev* personally discussed the wrecking plans at meetings in Zlatoust in 1931 and at Khartsisk Station in 1932. At these meetings, *Gussev* communicated to *Thornton* secret information of military State importance.

The criminal acts of *Gussev, Sokolov* and *MacDonald* come under Articles 58-6, 58-7, 58-9 and 58-11 of the Criminal Code of the R.S.F.S.R. The criminal acts of *Thornton* are qualified below.

II.

The principal wrecker at the Zuevka Power Station was the manager of the turbine department of the station, State employee *Kotlyarevsky, M. L.,* who, with intention of causing damage to the industrial power of the U.S.S.R., caused breakdowns, in June 1932, to turbo-generator No. 3 by inserting a bolt in the generator, and in complicity with *Vassiliev,* subsequently deceased, organized the breakdown of the oil pumps of turbines Nos. 1 and 3, by deliberately causing these pumps to be clogged with dirt.

These wrecking acts were committed by *Kotlyarevsky* in complicity with the aforesaid *MacDonald* from whom, as a reward for these criminal acts, *Kotlyarevsky* received a bribe of 1,000 rubles.

The criminal acts of *Kotlyarevsky* come under Articles 58-7, 58-9 and 58-11 of the Criminal Code of the R.S.F.S.R.

III

At the Ivanovo State District Power Station acts of wrecking were committed by the manager of the operating department, *Lobanov, A. T.,* in complicity with the foreman of the aforesaid power station, *Lebedev, V. P.,* the employee of Metropolitan-Vickers, the British subject *Nordwall, C.,* and with other persons whose cases are being dealt with separately.

1. *Lobanov* organized the following breakdowns:

a. systematically put out of action the motors of the chain gratings by breaking the feeder of these motors;

b. deliberately allowed sand to get into the bearings of the motor of the feed pump of the boilers, as a consequence of which the motor was put out of action;

c. deliberately put out of action the motor of the smoke suction pump of boiler No. 5 by closing the ventilation of the motor;

d. for the purpose of disrupting the work of the power station he often deliberately switched off the house-feeders of the station.

As a result of these wrecking acts, the work of the station was interrupted and the supply of power to the factories and works dependent upon the Ivanovo State District Power Station was reduced.

2. The immediate perpetrator of the breakdowns enumerated in Section 1, paragraphs a and b, was *Lebedev,* acting on the instructions of *Lobanov.*

3. As a reward for the aforesaid wrecking acts, *Lobanov* received from *Nordwall* a bribe of 5,000 rubles, of which he gave about 300 rubles to *Lebedev.*

The crimes committed by *Lobanov, Lebedev* and *Nordwall* come under Articles 58-7, 58-9 and 58-11 of the Criminal Code of the R.S.F.S.R.

4. Independently of the aforesaid persons, but on the direct suggestion of *Thornton,* the foreman at the aforesaid Ivanovo State District Power Station, State employee *Zivert,* in 1931, delayed the installation of the transformer, as a reward for which he received from *Thornton* a bribe in two instalments amounting in all to 800 rubles.

The crimes committed by *Zivert* come under Articles 58-7 and 58-11 of the Criminal Code of the R.S.F.S.R.

IV.

At the Mosenergo Power Stations wrecking was committed by the following persons:

Chief of the operating department of the First Moscow Electric Power Station, State employee *Sukhoruchkin, L. A.;*

Chief engineer of the thermo-dynamic group, turbine department of the Mosenergo, State employee *Zorin, N. G.;*

Chief of the repair and installation department at the First Moscow Electric Power Station, State employee *Krasheninnikov, M. D.*

1. *Sukhoruchkin:*

a. During the period from 1928 to 1932, he conspired with Thornton to conceal serious defects in the equipment supplied by Metropolitan-Vickers, and also concealed defects in the installation of this equipment, which led to a series of breakdowns, to the reduction of the working capacity of the station, and made it impossible to claim from Metropolitan-Vickers the corresponding compensation;

b. At the end of 1931, he personally for the purpose of causing a breakdown at the First Moscow Power Station caused a contact between the lead covering of the single phase cable of generators Nos. 26 and 27 and an iron rack. The breakdown was averted by the vigilance of the workers;

c. In 1930 and 1931, he frequently met Thornton and decided with him the methods to be employed to destroy the power station on the outbreak of war against the U.S.S.R.

2. *Zorin:*

In conspiracy with the aforesaid *Thornton* in 1931 and 1932, with the intention of causing damage to the industries of the U.S.S.R., carried out a number of wrecking measures at the First Moscow Power Station and at the Orekhovo Thermo-Power Station, concealed organic defects in the equipment supplied by Metropolitan-Vickers, which led to systematic breakdowns at these stations, reduced the working capacity of the equipment, increased the cost of operations and led to the loss of compensation claims.

3. *Krasheninnikov:*

During the period from 1928 to 1932, committed a number of wrecking acts at the First Moscow Power Station, concealed defects in equipment supplied by Metropolitan-Vickers, and defects in the installation of this equipment, which led to systematic breakdowns at this station and to the loss of compensation claims.

As a reward for these criminal acts, *Sukhoruchkin, Zorin* and *Krasheninnikov* received from *Thornton* bribes as follows: *Sukhoruchkin*—2,000 rubles and 350 rubles in Torgsin cheques; *Zorin*—1,000 rubles and *Krasheninnikov*—500 rubles.

The crimes committed by *Sukhoruchkin, Zorin* and *Krasheninnikov* come under Article 58-7 and 58-11 of the Criminal Code of the R.S.F.S.R., and other crimes committed by *Sukhoruchkin* come under Article 58-9 of the Criminal Code of the R.S.F.S.R.

V.

As is evident from the above-mentioned facts, the wrecking, counter-revolutionary activities of the aforesaid State employees of power stations were connected with the criminal activity of certain employees of the private British firm of Metropolitan-Vickers.

The Court established the following:

1. The leading role among the employees of Metro-Vickers in the perpetration of counter-revolutionary crimes was played by *Thornton, L. C.,* chief installation engineer of the aforesaid firm, under whose direction acts of wrecking were committed at certain power stations of the U.S.S.R. by the firm's engineers and mechanics, the aforesaid British subjects, *MacDonald* and *Nordwall,* and also by engineer *Cushny,* and citizen of the U.S.S.R., *Oleinik, P. Y.,* a mechanic employed by the firm.

Through the medium of these persons as well as himself personally, *Thornton:*

a. entered into contact with counter-revolutionary groups of Soviet State employees of electric power stations and conspired with them *(Gussev, Sukhoruchkin, Zorin)* to cause breakdowns, to conceal defects in the equipment supplied by Metropolitan-Vickers *(Krasheninnikov, Zivert)* and gave bribes to State employees as a reward for criminal acts they had committed;

b. engaged in military espionage on the territory of the U.S.S.R.; collected through *MacDonald, Cushny* and *Oleinik,* secret information of military importance, and in return for this information, through the aforesaid persons, gave bribes to Soviet State employees *(Gussev, Sokolov* and others).

The crimes committed by *Thornton* come under Articles 58-6, 58-7, 58-9 and 58-11 of the Criminal Code of the R.S.F.S.R.

2. The representative of the Moscow office of Metropolitan-Vickers, *Monkhouse:*

a. was informed of *Thornton's* activities in organizing breakdowns at these stations; in conjunction with counter-revolutionary wrecking groups of Soviet State employees of power stations.

b. was an accomplice in the giving of bribes to State employees of power stations to induce them to conceal defects in the equipment supplied by Metropolitan-Vickers and also to conceal defects in the installation of this equipment, which led to breakdowns.

The crimes committed by Monkhouse come under Articles 58-7, 58-9 and 58-11 of the Criminal Code of the R.S.F.S.R.

3. The executor of *Thornton's* wrecking instructions at the Baku Power Station was the Metro-Vickers installation engineer, *Cushny,* who in 1928 organized at this station the breakdown of turbine No. 11 and who collected secret information of a military nature in order to communicate it to *Thornton.*

The crimes committed by *Cushny* come under Articles 58-6, 58-9 and 58-11 of the Criminal Code of the R.S.F.S.R.

4. The executor of *Thornton's* criminal instructions at a number of power stations (First Moscow Power Stations, *Makeyevka, Motovilikha)* was the employee of the Moscow office of Metro-Vickers, citizen of the U.S.S.R., *Oleinik,* who:

a. systematically concealed defects in the equipment supplied by Metropolitan-Vickers, which led to a series of breakdowns and

b. collected secret military information and recruited agents for *Thornton.*

The crimes committed by *Oleinik* come under Articles 58-6, 58-7 and 58-11 of the Criminal Code of the R.S.F.S.R.

5. *Kutuzova, A. S.:*

While employed as secretary in the Moscow office of Metropolitan-Vickers, knew of the counter-revolutionary work of the aforesaid employees of this firm, systematically handed over and sent monetary rewards to certain of the members of counter-revolutionary groups of State Soviet employees of power stations in return for their espionage and wrecking activities.

The crimes committed by *Kutuzova* come under Articles 58-6 and 58-11 of the Criminal Code of the R.S.F.S.R.

VI.

On the basis of the aforesaid, in view of the circumstances of the cases, the degree of guilt of each of the aforesaid persons as established by the Court, and on the basis of the decree of the Central Executive Committee of the U.S.S.R., of March 14, this year, by which State employees guilty of wrecking are regarded as traitors to their fatherland and must be held more strictly responsible than employees of private enterprises, the Court sentences:

I

1. *Gussev, Vassily Alexeyevich,*

2. *Sukhoruchkin, Leonid Alexeyevich,*

3. *Lobanov, Alexander Timofeyevich,* State employees, citizens of the U.S.S.R., to ten years' deprivation of liberty with loss of rights for five years and confiscation of all their property. In selecting this measure of repression instead of the sentence of shooting, the Court was guided exclusively by the fact that the criminal wrecking activities of the aforesaid convicted persons bore a local character and did not cause serious damage to the industrial power of the U.S.S.R.

II

4. *Sokolov, Vassily Andreyevich,*

5. *Zorin, Nikolai Grigorievich,*

6. *Kotlyarevsky, Moisei Lvovich,* State employees, citizens of the U.S.S.R., for the same reason as above, to eight years' deprivation of liberty with the aforesaid consequences.

III

7. *Krasheninnikov, Michael Dmitrievich,* State employee, citizen of the U.S.S.R., for the same reason as above, to five years deprivation of liberty with loss of rights for five years, without confiscation of property.

IV

8. *Lebedev, Vyacheslav Petrovich,* State employee, citizen of the U.S.S.R., taking into consideration that he was merely a tool in the hands of *Lobanov* and guided by Article 51 of the Criminal Code of the R.S.F.S.R., the Court sentences him to two years' de-

privation of liberty without loss of rights and without confiscation of property.

V

The employees of the Moscow office of Metropolitan-Vickers.

9. British subject, *Thornton, Leslie Charles,* to three years' deprivation of liberty.

10. In the case of British subject, *MacDonald, William Lionel,* in so far as he acted on the direct instigation of his immediate superior, *Thornton,* on the one hand, and in view of his frank confession to his criminal acts at the Court, on the other, and by virtue of Article 51 of the Criminal Code of the R.S.F.S.R., the Court decides to commute the measure of repression demanded by the law to two years' deprivation of liberty.

In the cases of British subjects:

11. *Monkhouse, Allan,*

12. *Nordwall, Charles,* in so far as they did not take a direct part in causing breakdowns at the power stations, and

13. *Cushny, John,* in view of the lapse of time since the crime, of which he is guilty, was committed (1928) and by virtue of Article 51 of the Criminal Code of the R.S.F.S.R., the Court decides to confine itself to ordering their deportation from the territory of the U.S.S.R. and to prohibit their entry into the U.S.S.R. for a period of five years.

The convicted *Monkhouse, Nordwall* and *Cushny* must leave the territory of the U.S.S.R. within three days from the moment of the passing of this sentence.

14. *Oleinik, Peter Yeremeyevich,* citizen of the U.S.S.R., taking into consideration the fact that he was subordinate to Thornton and that he was an employee of a private firm, the Court decides that he be sentenced to three years' deprivation of liberty without loss of rights and without confiscation of property.

15. *Kutuzova, Anna Sergeyevna,* citizen of the U.S.S.R., for the same reasons as above, to be sentenced to eighteen months' deprivation of liberty, without loss of rights and without confiscation of property.

In regard to all the convicted, the period of preliminary confinement shall be counted as part of the period of deprivation of liberty.

VI

16. In the case of *Zivert, Yuri Ivanovich,* State employee, citizen of the U.S.S.R., taking into consideration that by the work he has done since 1931 he has proved that he has sincerely broken off all connections with the wreckers, and by virtue of Article 8 of the Criminal Code of the R.S.F.S.R., the Court decides that no measures of repression be applied to him and that he be released.

17. *Gregory, Albert William,* British subject, in view of the inadequacy of the evidence the Court decides that he be acquitted.

The judgment is final, is not subject to appeal, and goes into effect immediately.

[Signed] V. V. ULRICH
President of the Special Session of the Supreme Court of the U.S.S.R.
L. K. MARTENS
G. A. DMITRIEV
Members of the Court

Moscow
April 19, 1933
1 a.m.

The President: Comrade Commandant, take the accused Thornton in charge and release the accused Zivert. Secretary, take a written guarantee from the accused Nordwall, Monkhouse and Cushny to the effect that they will leave the U.S.S.R. within three days from the time of the reading of the verdict.

I declare the proceedings of the Special Session of the Supreme Court closed.

[Signed] V. V. ULRICH
President of the Special Session of the Supreme Court of the U.S.S.R.
A. F. KOSTYUSHKO
Secretary

THE END

For Product Safety Concerns and Information please contact our EU representative GPSR@taylorandfrancis.com
Taylor & Francis Verlag GmbH, Kaufingerstraße 24, 80331 München, Germany

www.ingramcontent.com/pod-product-compliance
Lightning Source LLC
LaVergne TN
LVHW021001300926
849160LV00007B/210

* 9 7 8 1 0 3 2 4 9 0 4 3 4 *